Resisting Postmodern Architecture

Resisting Postmodern Architecture

Critical regionalism before globalisation

Stylianos Giamarelos

First published in 2022 by
UCL Press
University College London
Gower Street
London WC1E 6BT

Available to download free: www.uclpress.co.uk

A CIP catalogue record for this book is available from The British Library.

ISBN: 978-1-80008-135-2 (Hbk)
ISBN: 978-1-80008-134-5 (Pbk)
ISBN: 978-1-80008-133-8 (PDF)
ISBN: 978-1-80008-136-9 (epub)
ISBN: 978-1-80008-137-6 (mobi)
DOI: https://doi.org/10.14324/111.9781800081338

This book is dedicated to my family, as a small token of my gratitude for their unwavering support over the years. It is my parents' intellectual grandchild.

Contents

List of figures

Every effort has been made to trace copyright holders of images. The author and publisher apologise for any errors and omissions. If notified, we will endeavour to correct these at the earliest available opportunity.

Acknowledgements

No monograph is the fruit of the labour of a single individual. This book would have not been possible without the financial support of the Greek State Scholarships Foundation ('Lifelong Learning' Programme European Social Fund, NSRF 2007–13), the Panayotis & Effie Michelis Foundation, The Bartlett School of Architecture Research Fund and the British Council Venice Fellowship Programme. I am grateful to these institutions. My thanks extend to Professor Georgios Ploumidis and Eleni Galani from the Hellenic Institute of Byzantine and Post-Byzantine studies in Venice, Kalliopi Amygdalou, Elisabetta Carnevale, Penelope Kalafata, Kim Chi Luu and Phuong-Trâm Nguyen, Amy Thomas and Ollie Palmer, Kostas Valaris, and Rafaella Verou for accommodating me during my research trips to Venice, Athens, Rhodes, Rotterdam, Austin, TX and Montréal over the past nine years. I am also grateful to my editor at UCL Press, Chris Penfold, for his patience and for kindly guiding me through the publishing process. The book has indeed benefited from the thorough work and dedication of Jonathan Dore, Ian McDonald and the UCL Press team.

My gratitude extends to Ricardo Agarez, Tom Avermaete, Iain Borden, Petra Brouwer, Elke Couchez, Maarten Delbeke, Davide Deriu, Isabelle Doucet, Zara Ferreira, Murray Fraser, Janina Gosseye, Rajesh Heynickx, Lenore Hietkamp, Christen Jamar, Kristina Jõekalda, Pamela Johnston, Elisavet Kiourtsoglou, Marina Lathouri, Belgin Turan Özkaya, Véronique Patteeuw, Edoardo Piccoli, Dimitris Philippidis, Peg Rawes, Léa-Catherine Szacka, Hans Teerds and the anonymous reviewers of my proposal for their insightful comments and suggestions on earlier iterations of draft chapter manuscripts that informed the writing of this book. Earlier versions of parts of chapters 1, 3, 6, 7, 8 and 9 have been previously published as: 'Building before Theorising Resistance: 118 Benaki Street beyond Critical Regionalism', in *Activism at Home: Architects Dwelling between Politics, Aesthetics and Resistance*, ed. by Isabelle Doucet and Janina Gosseye (Berlin: JOVIS, 2021), pp. 243–55; '"Boomerang Effect": The Repercussions of Critical Regionalism in 1980s Greece', in

Architecture Thinking across Boundaries: Knowledge Transfers since the 1960s, ed. by Rajesh Heynickx, Ricardo Agarez and Elke Couchez (London: Bloomsbury, 2021), pp. 43–59, dx.doi.org/10.5040/97813501 53202.ch-003; 'Greece, the Modern Margin in the Classical Centre: Seven Points for Critical Regionalism as Historiography', *Journal of Architecture*, 25.8 (2020), 1055–88, doi.org/10.1080/13602365.2020.1854328; 'Architecture in the History/Theory Nexus: Building Critical Regionalism in Frampton's Greece', *OASE*, 103 (2019), 79–91; 'Exhibiting the Postmodern: The 1980 Venice Architecture Biennale / Hans Hollein and Postmodernism: Art and Architecture in Austria, 1958–1985', *Journal of Architecture*, 24.1 (2019), 121–30, doi.org/10.1080/13602365.2019.15 69388; 'The Formative Years of Suzana and Dimitris Antonakakis: A Transcultural Genealogy of Critical Regionalism', in *Metamorphosis: The Continuity of Change*, ed. by Ana Tostões and Natasa Koselj (Lisbon; Ljubljana: Docomomo International; Docomomo Slovenia, 2018), pp. 232–40; 'The Anti-Hierarchical Atelier that Could not Last', *San Rocco*, 14 (2018), 122–32; and 'Intersecting Itineraries beyond the Strada Novissima: The Converging Authorship of Critical Regionalism', *Architectural Histories*, 4.1 (2016), art. 11, doi.org/10.5334/ah.192.

Public presentations and invited talks have served as additional sources of feedback at various stages of my research. These included the first and sixth Society of Architectural Historians of Great Britain (SAHGB) Graduate Students Forum/Architectural History Workshop in London (University College London, 3 May 2013; The Gallery, 17 March 2018); the first Architecture Research Moments conference of the ARENA Architectural Research Network in Brussels (KU Leuven, Campus Sint-Lucas, 18 January 2014); The Bartlett PhD Conference (University College London, 15 April 2014); 'The Historiography of Architecture in Greece in the Twentieth and the Twenty First Century' conference in Athens (School of Fine Arts, 23 May 2014); The Bartlett PhD Research Projects 2015 conference (University College London, 24 February 2015); Architecture Research seminar (London South Bank University, 17 March 2015); Atelier 66 Symposium in Athens (Benaki Museum, 17 December 2016); 'Theory's History 196X–199X: Challenges in the Historiography of Architectural Knowledge' conference in Brussels (KU Leuven, 10 February 2017); History & Theory: Contemporary Times lecture series (National Technical University of Athens, 25 May 2017); 'Tools of the Architect' conference in Delft (Delft University of Technology, 24 November 2017); 'Activism at Home: Architects' Own Houses as Sites of Resistance' symposium in Manchester (University of Manchester, 15 January 2018); 'Postmodernism Culturally Reconsidered' symposium (The Bartlett

School of Architecture, UCL, 10 May 2018); Fifth International Meeting of the European Architectural History Network (EAHN) in Tallinn (National Library of Estonia, 14 June 2018); Fifteenth International DoCoMoMo Conference in Ljubljana (Cankarjev Dom, 31 August 2018); Tuesday Lecture series (Aristotle University of Thessaloniki, 28 May 2019); Modern Greek Seminar lecture series (University of Oxford, 31 October 2019); Architecture after Modernism lecture series (University of Manchester, 11 November 2019); Super (Local) Sessions (Aristotle University of Thessaloniki, 20 December 2019); Architecture Talks! (University of the West of England, Bristol, 23 January 2020). I would like to thank the organisers and the audiences of these events for their insightful questions and feedback at key moments of my research.

I am indebted to Suzana and Dimitris Antonakakis. Without their generous response to my multiple requests, a large part of this work would not have been possible. I thank them for agreeing to be interviewed at length on several occasions, for granting me access to their private archive and for permitting me to reproduce the material that illustrates a large part of this book. My thanks extend to Giorgos Antonakakis, Boukie Babalou, Nicholas Boyarsky and Nicola Murphy, Andreas Giacumacatos, Zissis Kotionis, Anastasios M. Kotsiopoulos, Christos-Georgios Kritikos, Åke E:son Lindman, Antonis Noukakis, Dimitris Philippidis, Martin Schmitz, Stavros Stavridis, Panayotis Tournikiotis, Giorgos and Lucy Triantafyllou, Kostas Tsiambaos and Yorgos Tzirtzilakis for granting me access to their private archives or sharing the material that I requested from them. Additional thanks go to Michele Mangione and Elena Cazzaro from the Archivio Storico delle Arti Contemporanee (Fondazione La Biennale di Venezia), Aeron MacHattie, Tim Klähn and Caroline Dagbert from the Canadian Centre for Architecture, Beth J. Dodd and Nancy L. Sparrow from the Alexander Architectural Archives (University of Texas Libraries), Michael Maire Lange from the UC Berkeley Library, Kate Riddle from the Environmental Design Archives (University of California), Eva Lintjes from the Study Centre of Het Nieuwe Instituut, Christina Ioannidou, Iro Kompothanasi and Aphrodite Oikonomou from the National Technical University of Athens School of Architecture Library and Archive, Polina Borisova, Leti Arvaniti Krokou, Natalia Boura and Ioanna Moraiti from the archival collections of the Benaki Museum, Yota Pavlidou from the Constantinos A. Doxiadis Archive, and Konstantinos Thanasakis from the Aikaterini Laskaridis Foundation for their kind assistance. Ricardo Agarez, Anna Ulrike Andersen, Eva Branscome, Vasileios Chanis, Lina Dima, Kim Förster, Platon Issaias, Fanis Kafantaris, Paraskevi Kapoli, Costandis Kizis, Nikos Magouliotis, Vangelis Papandreou and Katerina Tsakmaki, Stephen Parnell, Jacob Paskins, Theodore Sioutis, Léa-Catherine Szacka, Ioanna Theocharopoulou, Kostas Tsiambaos and Richard Woditsch have also been generous in sharing research material of mutual interest.

I am also grateful to all the individuals who agreed to be interviewed for my research: Anthony Alofsin, Spyros Amourgis, Giorgos Antonakakis, Aristide Antonas, Alekos Athanasiadis, Boukie Babalou, Tassos Biris, Savas Condaratos, Elias Constantopoulos, Agnes Couvela, Konstantinos Daskalakis, Eleni Desylla, Pattie Dolka, Steven Farrant, Dimitris Fatouros, Theano Fotiou, Kenneth Frampton, Kostis Gartzos, Kostis Hadjimichalis, Vaso Hadjinikita, Nikos Kalogeras, Kaiti Kamilaki, Tonia Katerini, Dimitris Konstantinidis, Zissis Kotionis, Anastasios M. Kotsiopoulos, Aleka Monemvasitou, Kostas Moraitis, Myrto Nezi, Antonis Noukakis, Dimitris Papalexopoulos, Dimitris Philippidis, Takis Plainis, Annie Platanioti, Yiannis Roussos, Nikos Souzas, Stavros Stavridis, Panayotis Tournikiotis, Panayotis Tsakopoulos, Yorgos Tzirtzilakis, Dina Vaiou, Yiannis Vikelas, Sissy Vovou and the activists who wished to remain anonymous. My research has also profited from my informal conversations and email exchanges with Yannis Aesopos, Nikos Belavilas, Paola Cofano, Vassilis Ganiatsas, Maro Kardamitsi-Adami, Dimitrios N. Karydis, Amalia Kotsaki, Andreas Kourkoulas, Liane Lefaivre, Mary Pepchinski, Carmen Popescu, Tassos Sakellaropoulos, Alexander Tzonis, Stelios Virvidakis and Georgios Xiropaidis.

The intellectual environment of The Bartlett School of Architecture, UCL provided numerous occasions on which to discuss my research with Ben Campkin, Mario Carpo, Megha Chand Inglis, Adrian Forty, Penelope Haralambidou, Jonathan Hill, Barbara Penner, Sophia Psarra, Guang Yu Ren, Tania Sengupta, Nina Vollenbröker and Robin Wilson. The feedback that I received from external audiences and guest speakers – and especially from Matthew Barac, Joseph Bedford, Irina Davidovici, Paul Davies, Tina di Carlo, Mari Hvattum, Ákos Moravánszky, Dimitris Papanikolaou and Emmanuel Petit – was also insightful. Our discussions with Michael Edwards, Andy Merrifield, Louis Moreno, and the Holloway/ Autonomia reading group 2013–14 (Sonia Freire Trigo, Sam Halvorsen, Paddy McDaid, Dan Ozarow, Judith Ryser and Simon Thrope) also found their subtle way into the book. The same goes for our casual exchanges with fellow Bartlett PhD students of the early 2010s: Wesley Aelbrecht, Kalliopi Amygdalou, Marcela Aragüez, Gregorio Astengo, Pavlos Feraios, Judit Ferencz, Claudio Leoni, Carlo Menon, Laura Narvaez, Regner Ramos, Sophie Read, David Roberts, Eva Sopeoglou, Huda Tayob, Amy Thomas, Quyhn Vantu and Freya Wigzell. My thanks extend to the

Bartlett students who followed my Architectural Regionalisms seminar series from 2019 to 2021. My discussions with them have always felt fresh and inspiring.

Finally, I would like to thank friends in London and Athens whose help facilitated a smooth transition to my new life over the past decade: Christina Achtypi, Maria Anagnostopoulou, Georgios Anthitsis, Tilemachos Antonopoulos and Christina Vassilopoulou, Konstantinos Arampatzis, Panos Floros, Orestis Giamarelos and Eleni Diamanti, Giannis Grigoriadis, Lia Hatzidiakou, Anastasia Karandinou, Ioannis Kleftogiannis, Fotis Kotsalidis and Maria Kamilaki, Antonis and Dimitris Koufopoulos, Christos-Georgios Kritikos, Aliki Kylika, Kika Kyriakakou, Sarra Matsa, Anna Mavrogianni, Mica Nava, Yorgis Noukakis, Vasiliki Petsa, Egli Petta, Valia Rassa, Prodromos Sfyriou and Chrissa Trivilou, Anastasia Sylaidi, Fotini Theocharopoulou, Maria Tsemani and Christina Vona. Like an extended family, they were all there for me when I needed them.

Introduction: Four decades

I am writing these lines in 2021, exactly forty years after the first coupling of the words 'critical' and 'regionalism' appeared on a printed page to discuss the work of Greek architects Suzana and Dimitris Antonakakis in Alexander Tzonis and Liane Lefaivre's article 'The Grid and the Pathway' of 1981.[1] Introduced by them then, the architectural theory of critical regionalism was recapitulated by Kenneth Frampton in 1983.[2] It originally aimed to offer an alternative way out of the crisis of 'international style' modern architecture that begged to differ from the postmodern architecture of the 1980s then being propagated as the main solution to the problem. As the large-scale projects of reconstruction that followed the Second World War were changing the face of entire European cities by the 1960s, the sense that these modernist buildings produced an anonymous built environment intensified. Local communities increasingly perceived them as alienating generic technological 'boxes' that neglected their specific cultural identities or needs.[3] Critical regionalism aimed to address these issues by looking at the 'periphery' of the First World to promote architectures that sustained their ties with the specific climatic, topographic, historical, cultural and sociopolitical conditions of their sites. It supported socially engaged practices that addressed the crisis of modern architecture without rejecting its progressive sociopolitical agenda. As such, critical regionalism envisioned an 'architecture of resistance' that could reconcile universal modernisation with the cultural identities of local communities. It promoted civic architectures and practices that retained their ties with specific places to resist both the commodification of the modern built environment and its converse postmodernist transformation into scenography.

Disseminated by the Western European and North American 'centres' of architectural-theory production in the 1980s, critical regionalism enjoyed a positive worldwide reception. The 1990s reinforced its pertinence as an architectural theory which defends the cultural identity of a place that resists the homogenising onslaught of globalisation. In the same decade, it started to be adopted by a wide array of other disciplines, ranging from film theory to philosophy, as a useful framework to explore related questions in these non-architectural fields.[4] Critical regionalism is still popular as an architectural approach today, especially among architects in parts of the world that face resonating challenges as their cities turn into vast metropolises, alienating local communities.[5] Today, its main principles (such as acknowledging the climate, history, materials, culture and topography of a specific place) are integrated into architects' education as hallmarks of good design. This is partly owing to the current teaching practices of architects and academics who were themselves trained by the original theorists and architects of critical regionalism over the past four decades, but also to a younger generation's interest in ecological approaches to architecture and their history.

This book celebrates the fortieth anniversary of critical regionalism as a popular architectural theory of the recent past that can be reappraised for the twenty-first century. It is written in an age of climate emergency at a moment of crisis of globalisation. After Donald Trump's election in the USA and the Brexit vote of 2016 in the UK, the resurgence of insular nationalisms across the globe – from Jair Bolsonaro's Brazil and Viktor Orbán's Hungary to Narendra Mondi's India and Rodrigo Duterte's Philippines – seems to have become the norm of the late-2010s world. This challenge to the incessant globalisation since the 1990s arrives precisely when the alarming signals of the climate emergency demand outward-looking and globally just solutions. In 2020, the Covid-19 pandemic outbreak served as an additional reminder of the fragility of this world system, as closed borders exerted unforeseen pressure on just-in-time global supply chains. As the pandemic instigated soft-power antagonisms, from the crisis-management nationalism of 2020 to the vaccination nationalism of 2021, it also foregrounded the persistently unjust hierarchical structure of the world order. But this was just the most recent symptom of a longer-standing process. It fed into critiques that have, over the past decade, favoured a retreat from globalisation in order to make separate nation states 'great again', as an increasing number of Euro-American citizens feel left out at the losing end of the globalising economy of the last three decades.

In this context, this first study of the overlooked cross-cultural history of critical regionalism, a theory that moved beyond static national identities before globalisation, becomes especially pertinent. The book resituates critical regionalism within the wider framework of debates around postmodern architecture, the Western European and North

American contexts from which it emerged and the cultural media complex that conditioned its reception. In so doing, it explores the intersection of three areas of growing historical and theoretical interest today: postmodernism, critical regionalism and globalisation. Reassessing their intrinsic connections, it goes on to chart significant transformations of regional understandings of architecture in the broader sociopolitical context of the last decade of the Cold War. Based on more than fifty in-depth interviews and previously inaccessible or unpublished archival material from six countries, it transgresses existing barriers to integrate sources in other languages into anglophone architectural scholarship. Accordingly, it also foregrounds overlooked figures whose work has been historically significant for the development of critical regionalism. As such, it demonstrates how, at that time, the 'periphery' was not just a passive recipient but also an active generator of architectural theory and practice. Originally introduced to resist the globalising thrust of postmodernism, critical regionalism was situated within a range of related discourses and practices that were also developed in the course of late twentieth-century globalisation. As such, it is not a theory limited to straightforward rejections of globalisation and postmodern architecture; it is instead part of them, in a cross-cultural circuit that resists master narratives to explore different globalised worlds and outward-facing futures for regional architectures. Through a historically informed critique, the book challenges long-held notions of supposedly 'international' discourses of the recent past, as it offers a rare exposition of the cross-cultural interactions of architectural theory and practice.

The book starts from the original intention of the theorists of critical regionalism to resist the propagated architecture of postmodernism of the 1980s. But as I show in the following chapters, while postmodernism could be resisted as a stylistic preference, critical regionalism could not as easily resist the postmodern condition and the modes of producing architecture in the global context of late twentieth-century capitalism. As such, what these theorists ended up advocating was indeed a variant of resisting postmodern architecture. Similarly, when the narrative of critical regionalism was modified to adapt to the shifting world order of the 1990s, it presented itself as a preferable alternative option: should one have to choose between them, critical regionalism would come before globalisation. But this book argues that there is another, chronological, way in which critical regionalism came before globalisation – as it historically appeared a decade before the globalising 1990s. Returning to this early history of critical regionalism is additionally pertinent at this moment of the twenty-first century, when the globalising thrust of the 1990s seems to be entering another phase of transition. As the recent nationalist isolationist movements are directly related to the processes of globalisation of the past decades, this earlier cross-cultural history of critical regionalism offers a more nuanced response to the current challenges than those suggested by its schematic 'anti-globalisation' iterations after the 1990s.

Globalisations

Focusing on critical regionalism before globalisation does not, of course, imply that disparate areas of the world were not connected before the 1990s. Numerous historians of imperialism and colonialism have traced the emerging capitalist world economy alongside the rise of the modern world further back to 'the long sixteenth century'.[6] But interconnected world economies are not exclusively related with the modern world either, since similar phenomena can be traced in former historical periods stretching back to the expansive empires of antiquity.[7] However, significant differences in terms of scale, investment and growth, intensity, modes of long-distance trade, extraction, migration, outsourced production and the sectors that develop interdependently in each historical period justify the distinction between different phases within this long-standing process of developing world-economic systems. In this long-term perspective, what became known as 'globalisation' in the 1990s and 2000s, when the term was widely circulated and debated as the phenomenon itself intensified, was the latest phase of an ongoing process that developed in different forms and at a slower pace in previous historical periods. The 'global' perspective of the world is increasingly developed after the end of the Second World War and the establishment of international, intergovernmental organisations and initiatives such as the United Nations in 1945 or the Universal Declaration of Human Rights in 1948. The development of cybernetics and systems theory, and the related discussions of the 'problem of the great number' by built-environment professionals in the 1960s, echo the trend to adopt this global vantage and discuss these issues systemically from the perspective of the world as a whole.

When the term 'globalisation' became increasingly current following the implosion of the Second World Soviet Bloc and the triumphant march of First World capitalism in the early 1990s, the theorists of critical regionalism adapted their rhetoric to present their approach as one of resisting globalisation. After 1990, Tzonis and Lefaivre returned to their original term in an attempt to both reinforce its historical depth and define the approach that they had in mind in more detail. But this has also meant that when scholars such as Mark Crinson revisit critical regionalism today, they tend to favour this later approach, outlined in their essay 'Why Critical Regionalism Today?' of 1990.[8] In this text, the couple's emphasis shifted to consolidate critical regionalism in the design techniques of 'defamiliarisation' and 'metastatements'. Appropriately explored by architects who want to avoid literal reproductions of both local and international architectural forms, these stratagems produce architectures that challenge standard conceptions of both globalisation and regionality. As such, Tzonis and Lefaivre's criticality was intended to go both ways; it does not favour the 'local' over the 'global', or vice versa:

> An essential characteristic of critical regionalist buildings is that they are critical in two senses then. In addition to providing contrasting images to the anomic, atopic, misanthropic ways of a large number of current mainstream projects constructed world wide, they raise questions in the mind of the viewer about the legitimacy of the very regionalist tradition to which they belong.[9]

But the distorted reception of the critical regionalist message created a rather schematic opposition of 'the global' with 'the local',[10] at best summarised in mottos such as 'think globally, act locally' and 'glocal' architectures and urbanisms.

Critical regionalism did not originally develop as a response to globalisation after the demise of postmodern architecture and Deconstructivism, as suggested in the early 1990s. Tzonis and Lefaivre's earlier and more historically significant formulation of critical regionalism has remained relatively ignored. Their first essay on the subject, 'The Grid and the Pathway', may have been cited much more than it has actually been read, understood and adopted to affect architectural practice in the anglophone world. This has practically meant that this direction has also been relatively overshadowed in the history of critical regionalism. Returning specifically to the 1980s, this book attempts to retrieve what was lost in this shift of the rhetoric of critical regionalism from the 1990s onwards. In so doing, it also explores the ways in which this earlier cross-cultural history can help one rethink critical regionalism as an unfulfilled project for the twenty-first century on the fronts of architectural theory and practice, history and historiography. I summarise my thoughts on these three fronts in the Epilogue.

Postmodern architectures

For historians of the recent past, postmodern architecture represents the dominant trend of the 1980s following the international impact of the First Biennale of Architecture exhibition in Venice at the start of that decade (Fig. 0.1).[11] Reacting to the large-scale projects of Western European reconstruction, postmodern architects focused instead on the expressive, public face of buildings and the ways in which these communicate with the people on the street to offer them a sense of belonging and identity. The tolerant, pluralist society that emerged after the Second World War needed an inventive architectural language to go with it. This language could profit from the rich architectural past to develop playfully and freely towards the future. In so doing, it would also escape from the austere dictates of the modernist architecture of postwar reconstruction.

The work of practising architects and theorists was already in turmoil before the appearance of the term 'postmodern' in architectural circles, and its subsequent popularisation in the 1980s.[12] Although lacking a name that would unify them at the time, architectural attempts to respond to the crises of modernism after the Second World War flourished. These were historically understood in successively different framings, ranging from the debates on 'monumentality' in the mid-1940s to the 'crisis of meaning' in the early 1970s.[13] In the final instance, however, all these cases addressed a single common enemy that went by many names. The 1960s introduction of systems analysis and cybernetics to debates on the future of the built environment intensified the techno-scientific positivism of architectural production.[14] By the early 1960s, and especially after the publication of Jane Jacobs's influential critique of modernist urban planning in 1961,[15] the main object of architectural criticism was this positivist functionalism: the idea that architectural form follows clearly determined functions that respond to the same universal, scientifically defined, human needs, which can in turn be satisfied by modern technology. Although the reaction to this functionalism was not concerted, architects of the period were at least united in what they opposed. This opposition to rational functionalism was the underlying common ground of all the responses to the diverse crises of modernism after the Second World War (from architects' outward-looking turns to disciplines such as social and structural anthropology, philosophy, linguistics and semiology to inward-looking pursuits of the autonomous language of architecture).[16] Rather tellingly, Peter Eisenman framed his avant-gardist design pursuits of the mid-1970s in terms of

Figure 0.1 Official poster, 'Strada Novissima', First International Architecture Exhibition 'The Presence of the Past', Corderie dell'Arsenale, Venice, 27 July–19 October 1980. B&W photographs by Antonio Martinelli, colour photographs by Mark Smith, artwork by Messina e Montanari

Courtesy of Archivio Storico della Biennale di Venezia, ASAC 'post-functionalism'.[17] As the architectural historian Hanno-Walter Kruft also noted in 1985, '"Post-Modernism" signifies nothing more than a series of heterogeneous attempts to break loose from the functionalist grip'.[18] All these diverging approaches shared the assumption that functionalism was to account for the dual loss of meaning and participation that was collectively attributed to modern architecture.

These diverse developments obviously shared little common ground with the eclectic, playful and ironic, historicist pastiche that came to be associated with postmodern architecture in the decades that followed. As such, what is usually understood by the term 'postmodern architecture' does not cover the diversity of architectural developments of the second half of the twentieth century that critically responded to functionalism. As this book progresses from the first to the last chapters, the 'Postmodern Classicism' of the Biennale becomes only one strand within a more complex field of architectural theory of the time. Whilst several Western architects 'turned postmodern' at the start of the 1980s, by the end of the same decade this debate was already dissipating. The 1980s thus ended up representing the 'postmodern moment' in the history of architecture.[19] What philosopher Jean-François Lyotard had heralded as an epochal shift in the production of knowledge in 1978 was reduced to the dominant stylistic fad of a decade in the architectural circles of the 1980s and the 1990s.[20] Implicit in the recent accounts of the period, this outlook in turn leads to an abbreviated notion of postmodern architecture, which is frequently approached as a momentary lapse of modernist reason. Among others, this book aims to redress this short-sighted stylistic understanding of postmodern architecture by exposing it as a product of a specific historical process.

Revisionist histories

My work is situated within a scholarly field of recent revisits of postmodern architecture. The 2010s witnessed the appearance of new publications on the subject by key figures of this history, such as Charles Jencks and Sir Terry Farrell, who restate their well-known ideas to cement their place in it;[21] by curators, such as Glenn Adamson and Jane Pavitt, who reappraise 'postmodernism' as the reigning style of the 1980s;[22] by historians, such as Geraint Franklin and Elain Harwood, who stress the need to preserve exemplary projects of this architectural style;[23] by theorists, such as Reinhold Martin and K. Michael Hays, who retheorise postmodern projects, practices and discourses in an attempt to emancipate their latent radical potential;[24] and, more recently, by scholars, such as Claire Jamieson and Esra Akcan, who approach key projects and practices of the same period in their specific historical, cultural and sociopolitical terms.[25]

The studies that focus on 'postmodernism' tend to reproduce its historically prevailing, but rather reductive, interpretation as a style, with its established canon of renowned practitioners.[26] It is therefore left to the retheorising and historicising approaches to advance disciplinary knowledge. These scholarly works effectively revise the current understanding of postmodern architecture. The theorists' intention to reactivate the latent implications of postmodern architecture for contemporary critical thinking is certainly commendable. But more theory seems less than apposite to address the question of postmodern architecture today. After all, the original debates of the 1970s and the 1980s historically coincided with the 'gilded age of theory',[27] and such books do not focus on the historical context that rendered the canonical projects of postmodern architecture possible.[28] Studies that share a similar intent to retheorise postmodern architecture but that support their case with solid historical research are less common.[29] As such, I posit that current understandings of the subject suffer not from insufficient theorisation but from inadequate historicisation.[30]

Most of these recent works of postmodern revisionism are still based on debunking and recontextualising what have so far been established as canonical references in Western Europe and North America.[31] As such, they serve as subtle reaffirmations of the same canon. Yet, these well-known references form only the tip of the postmodern iceberg. While these studies have elucidated overlooked characteristics of postmodern architecture, its more contested aspects are practically irretrievable by revisits of the same canon – however critical these may be. Writing the history of minor, silenced or counter-movements within the postmodern framework is a wholly different task, perhaps more apposite for the second wave of studies of postmodern revisionism that has surfaced more recently. A growing number of scholars have recently revisited postmodern architecture not only in wider cultural, sociopolitical and historical terms but also in contexts beyond those of the established canonical references.[32] The proliferation of similar historical studies will enable architects to re-enter the nuanced turmoil of the period and recover more socially and culturally conscious debates in different contexts. Among these, they will be able to retrieve influential feminist, anti-racist, postcolonial, ecological and participatory, as well as early digital, approaches to architecture. Although they were originally muted by the media onslaught of 'postmodernism' after the First Venice Biennale of Architecture exhibition in 1980, such directions seem especially pertinent today. Hence, after a decade of postmodern revisionism, this seems like the end of yet another beginning as these *other* histories of postmodern revisionism await their authors.

Resisting Postmodern Architecture tangentially builds on these studies to reignite the discussion away from its established 'centres'. Since the limited, stylistic understanding of postmodern architecture also prevails in the work of its 'militant' polemicists such as Owen Hatherley,[33] this book focuses on critical regionalism – the first sustained attempt to resist and provincialise these 'central' constructs of postmodern architecture in the 1980s by foregrounding the architecture of 'peripheral' sites and practices within Western architectural historiography. In this context, and especially in the second part of the book, Suzana Antonakaki (1935–2020) and Dimitris Antonakakis (b. 1933), the Greek architectural couple of 'critical regionalism', and their collaborative practice Atelier 66 serve as a fulcrum for the discussion of 'postmodernism' as one strand within a conglomeration of disparate architectural discourses. Underscoring the cross-cultural exchanges between these discourses, the book uniquely highlights their historical interactions, overlaps and dissonances with architectural practice.

Postmodern architecture in Greece

Despite the recent proliferation of revisionist studies of this period, Greece is conspicuously absent from histories of 'international postmodernism'.[34] Perry Anderson's passing reference to Athens as one of the originary loci of postmodernity is the rare, albeit brief, exception to this general rule.[35] As such, the Greek context has not yet significantly contributed to an international discussion of postmodernism.[36] Architecture in Greece in the late 1960s and the 1970s was no exception to this wider cultural trend. It was also absent from the relevant developments in Western Europe and North America, owing to the turbulent history of the country after the Second World War. The civil war of the late 1940s and the ensuing political turmoil that culminated in a seven-year military dictatorship (1967–74) certainly account for this Greek absence. Increased state censorship and oppression, alongside an imposed cultural introversion, meant that Greece practically lost contact with the relevant developments on the Western European front. Rather crucially, the rule of the colonels coincided with the 'global 1968' moment

– one of the most intense periods of critique of the modern project in its entirety.

A history of postmodern architecture in Greece is therefore conditioned by the long shadow of the junta years, since the lost ground was only partially covered after the fall of the colonels by the international news pages of *Architecture in Greece*, the major annual review of architecture in the country.[37] Greek architects were, of course, inclined to understand and discuss recent Western European and North American developments as they emerged from the seven insular years of the junta regime. But in the decade of growing European integration that followed the restoration of democracy and the full accession of the country to the European Community, postmodern practices developed ambivalently in Greece. They encountered resistance at the same time, in that they were adopted by architects who rejected them in theory.

This ambivalence was reflected in the subsequent historiography of postmodern architecture, which registered it as an absence. In his overview of twentieth-century architecture in Greece, for instance, Andreas Giacumacatos referred only to the 'supposed spread of so-called "Greek postmodernism"'.[38] Earlier in the 1980s, Dimitris Philippidis had also noted that '[t]ruly post-modern architecture does not seem to exist in Greece'.[39] At the end of the 1980s, Panayotis Tournikiotis criticised the Greek architectural scene for its theoretical deficiency and its tendency to receive international influences 'as a spectacle, emancipated from its mode of production'. In his opinion, Greek architecture amounted merely to a 'management of established images' of foreign origins that did not constitute a locally defined agenda for the future of the built environment in the country.[40] As such, postmodern architecture in Greece was a contentless endeavour, or a critique without an object, that superficially mimicked Western European and North American developments.

All these accounts by Greek architectural historians share the underlying assumption that the necessary and sufficient conditions for the development of postmodernism were simply absent from the local context; in other words, they are based on an idealised form of modern and postmodern architecture. But as they were constantly measured against this gold standard, most related developments in the Greek architectural milieu were bound to be found lacking almost by definition. Since the Western European model of postmodern architecture did not fully apply to the Greek case, architecture in Greece could not have been 'truly', but only superficially, postmodern. Related attempts could only be regarded as deductive, inauthentic appropriations of the standards set by the Western European and North American 'centres' of architectural production.

But these local developments were not actually lacking a regional version of modern architecture against which to rebel. In the 1980s, Greek architects inexorably developed their own postmodern problematic in intertwined transnational and local contexts. This was even more emphatically so in the case of Suzana and Dimitris Antonakakis, who reacted to the postmodern architecture of the Biennale as active authorial agents of the critical regionalist discourse. Because critical regionalism enjoyed a special relationship with Greece from the outset, the work of Suzana and Dimitris Antonakakis became an ideal case study for this book.

In Greek historiography, the work of the Antonakakis has been only vaguely associated with postmodern architecture. When Elias Constantopoulos, for instance, notes in passing that the two architects historically 'travers[ed] the labyrinthine parts of modern, post-modern and contemporary Greek architecture',[41] he does not clarify exactly how they did so. And while Dimitris Fatouros attempted to steer their 1980s university campus buildings on Crete (Fig. 0.2) away from any association with postmodernism, more recently the same projects were heralded by Dimitris Philippidis as a major exemplar of an otherwise 'hysterically rejected' Greek postmodernism.[42] The Antonakakis' critical regionalism is defined in the interstices of such contested discourses as have been construed around their projects over the past few decades. This book shows how the couple's work both contributed to shaping critical regionalism and was subsequently affected by such theoretical post-rationalisations.

After 'The Grid and the Pathway' was recapitulated by Frampton in 1983, Tzonis and Lefaivre rightfully argued that 'Greek architecture is slowly finding its place in the international scene'.[43] The rhetoric of critical regionalism was clear: it was because these works were regional that they acquired their international significance. This served as a motive for an inward-looking turn of the Greek architectural field. The rationale was simple: if the region could produce work of international significance on its own, then it should remain focused on its existing resources. It should continue to follow its own trajectory, ideally without any distorting contact with foreign developments. Since the local architectural scene had found the answer to the crisis of 'international style' modernism on its own, it was the rest of the world that should be paying attention to Greece and not the other way around. This inward-looking interpretation served the Greek modernists who wanted to resist postmodernism. But at

Figure 0.2 Atelier 66 (Suzana and Dimitris Antonakakis, Aleka Monemvasitou, Boukie Babalou, Antonis Noukakis, Theano Fotiou), Technical University of Crete campus in Akrotiri, Chania, 1982

Suzana and Dimitris Antonakakis' private archive

the same time, it also served the traditionalists who wanted to oppose the modernists. These local architectural audiences were therefore ready to succumb to another round of introversion after the seven years of the military junta. As I show in chapter 7, the obfuscated message of critical regionalism provided the alibi for them both to push their respective progressive and conservative agendas forward by promoting another unproductive inward-looking turn in the local architectural culture.

Forty years of critical regionalism

The empowering effects, alongside the undesired consequences, of critical regionalism were therefore already evident in 1984. Tzonis and Lefaivre regretted this reading of their work that resulted in a reinforcement of traditional borders. The inward-looking, and eventually self-referential, reading of critical regionalism in the Greek milieu short-circuited their original intentions. By the mid-1980s, Frampton had also expressed his dissatisfaction with the 'unfortunate' term 'critical regionalism',[44] as the conservative associations of regionalism with the *Heimatstil* architecture of the Third Reich distorted the critical, progressive dimension of his project.

Meanwhile, the international popularity of critical regionalism was on the rise.[45] This was registered at the first International Working Seminar on Critical Regionalism at Pomona in 1989. Its main organiser, Spyros Amourgis, heralded critical regionalism as 'the most coherent astylistic thesis to emerge in the last twenty years', a genuine alternative to the waning echo of the Biennale's Postmodern Classicism on North American shores.[46] Joined by more than thirty fellow theorists, academics and practising architects, the Seminar offered Frampton, Tzonis and Lefaivre an opportunity to revisit and enrich their discourses.[47] A similar occasion was provided by the seminar 'Context and Modernity' at Delft in 1990. But this was also the last time that the three main theorists of critical regionalism could exchange their views on their shared interests, precisely when their project was gaining momentum on both sides of the Atlantic.

Frampton became increasingly disillusioned with the progressive political front and its potential to withstand the late twentieth century. Especially after Fredric Jameson's devastating critique of critical regionalism as a political project in the Delft seminar of 1990, Frampton practically abandoned the development of his discourse to focus more emphatically on tectonic culture, the other recurring theme in his work in the 1980s.[48] In the following decades, building culture gradually prevailed over the stronger sociopolitical aspirations of his work of the 1970s. In his critique, Jameson noted both the geopolitical impossibility of the project of resistance of regional cultures and the danger of a late-capitalist recuperation of regional authenticity – e.g. as a commodified product of the tourism industry.[49] As such, any attempt at an authentically resistant critical and regional architecture is bound to succumb to the market forces of late capitalism. There is no way that the architectural clusters of resistance to megalopolitan expansion could withstand this recuperation: their refreshing difference to their globally commodified urban surroundings renders them more attractive to capitalist exploitation. In the fourth, revised edition of his critical history of modern architecture of 2007, Frampton concurred that his discussions of the 1980s appeared less relevant at the dawn of the twenty-first century:

> Transnational corporate ascendancy and the decline of the nation state have put into serious question what we can possibly mean by the term 'modern' today, or even the vexed word 'critical', given the ever-expanding value-free domain of digital technology and a Pandora's box of a new nature brought into being by the widespread application of genetic modification.[50]

A few years later, in 2013, he referred to the critical regionalism of the 1980s as his 'naïve proposition of 30 years ago'.[51]

But these developments in Frampton's discourse are not just symptoms of the waning criticality of a time past.[52] The criticality of his regionalist discourse was rather problematic from the outset, as I show especially in the second part of the book. To start with, Frampton's relationship with the 'periphery' was mediated. Effectively an outsider to the locales of his favoured regionalist architects, most of his accounts of the related contexts could only be second-hand – relying on the work of other scholars, such as Tzonis and Lefaivre, or his graduate students in New York, such as Dimitris Varangis. Frampton did not have a way to double-check the validity of his trusted regional mediators. Despite his declared intentions, his analyses of the early 1980s thus glossed over the actual political reality of architectural discourse and production in the locales of critical regionalism. His phenomenological reading of technology and his universalist notion of cultural difference further undermined the generative potential of his discourse. In addition, the structural position of Frampton at the 'centres' of architectural-theory production meant that the local repercussions of his discourse ran against his intended aims. Endowing the 'marginal' figures of remote regions with the aura of the 'internationally famous' architect, critical regionalism ended up reproducing, on the regional level, the effects of the 'star system' that it was originally supposed to resist. Frampton's own accounts of his critical regionalists thus led to an idealised interpretation of their work. As a result, his discourse did not historically fulfil its potential to explore the spaces of debate that it was opening up.

Many of these problems were identified in critiques of critical regionalism that emerged on the architectural, political, postcolonial and globalising fronts across these four decades. Joseph Rykwert expressed his reservations as early as 1983. He questioned the potential viability of the 'dialect regionalism' project of architects such as Álvaro Siza and Gino Valle, since he could foresee the imminent disappearance of the dialect cultures that underpinned it. He therefore concluded, 'that kind of dialect regionalism seems almost as remote as Mr [Quinlan] Terry's classicism'.[53] Since Frampton's approach could easily degenerate to an empty word, it could not serve as a viable alternative to the Postmodern Classicism of the Biennale. Two decades later, Keith Eggener underscored the latent colonialist aspect of Frampton's discourse. He showed how critical regionalism ended up actively marginalising the architectural cultures that it was allegedly vindicating. Rendering regional identity synonymous with the work of an individual architect, critical regionalism 'absorb[ed] culturally and geographically situated activities within an overarching, Euro-American-generated discourse, one bearing relatively little interest in local perspectives on local culture', including the architects' own understandings of their work as 'a response to local circumstances'.[54] More recently, Murray Fraser argued that critical regionalism falls back on the 'homogenisation fallacy' about globalisation. He underscored the need to move away from the binary centre/periphery model of critical regionalist discourse into a study of 'complex trans-cultural networks of exchange'. For Fraser, globalisation is not 'smoothing out everything and creating a single world order'; rather, it is 'constantly creating new kinds of difference and heterogeneity, and in ways that will never be uniform or consistent'.[55] Sharing Eggener's and Fraser's concerns, this book returns to the early history of this discourse to advance a historically grounded critique and reappraise critical regionalism along similar lines, complementing its more recent revisits by other scholars.[56]

Such positive and negative reactions to critical regionalism have led to its development in diverging directions over the last four decades. To cite just two related examples, Vincent Canizaro's comprehensive account of regionalist discourses in architecture reportedly grew out of his 'disaffection for critical regionalism' in the early 2000s. This drove him to consider other regionalisms, including aspects of 'regional planning, bioregionalism, and the lost legacy of regional modernism'.[57] However, as I show in chapter 2, many of these approaches inform the earlier but more overlooked part of the constructive history of regionalism pursued on North American grounds by Anthony Alofsin (b. 1949). Other architects and critics tested Frampton's points of critical regionalism against buildings that seemed to address them, including the Menil Collection project in Houston, Texas, which was analysed in these terms by Richard Ingersoll in 1991.[58] Canizaro has noted that Ingersoll's analysis confirmed the actual possibility of an architecture prescribed by the tenets of critical regionalism.[59] But my historical account of the gradual articulation of this theory begs to differ. In the first part of the book, I show how Frampton's points were related with specific architectural examples from the outset. These buildings as actual possibilities of an architecture of critical regionalism were integral parts of the development of this discourse in the 1980s. More specifically, such projects and the set of relations that developed around them conditioned the development of critical regionalism as an artefact of cross-cultural authorship. In addition, my revisiting of this rare and important intersection of postwar architecture in Greece with the 'international' discourse of critical regionalism in the second part of the book unveils its misalignments with its local origins. Lastly, I show how the distanced theoretical constructs of 'critical regionalism' and 'postmodernism' acquired historical agency, as they had serious and lasting consequences on the Greek architectural culture with which they originally dealt. As such, this book advances a more nuanced and historically contrasted understanding of critical regionalism, as it follows the globalising branches that grew out of its cross-cultural roots.

Globalising branches

The idea that critical regionalism foregrounded a Greek 'architecture of resistance' as a role model for future architectural developments in the 1980s might not be as surprising from the vantage of professional historians. In his 1953 overview of the 130-year history of modern Greece, Nicolas Svoronos had already stressed the people's 'resistant ethos' as the essential characteristic and driving force of the country.[60] Mark Mazower, a British historian whose work has consistently revisited Greece and the Balkans over the past four decades, has also repeatedly suggested that over its 200-year lifecycle, modern Greece found itself at the forefront as either an unexpected pioneer or testbed of large-scale developments in the European continent and beyond.[61] Given that both British historians', Mazower's and Frampton's, outlook was shaped between the 1960s and the 1980s, their shared interest in 'peripheral' sites is a symptom of the historic waning of the British Empire. Interest in the margins historically reflects a crisis of the dominant 'centre', which conversely ignores the 'periphery' in periods of confident growth.

This book has followed a similar approach to more recent works by Greek historians, focusing on the interplay between the details of regional developments in relation to the broader global picture to discuss the early history of critical regionalism. To cite just two related examples, Kostas Kostis has stressed the 'special nation' status that Greece enjoys in the eyes of the Western world and the ways in which this has in turn affected the fate of this 'spoiled' modern nation.[62] But it is Antonis Liakos's account of 'the Greek 20th century' that more clearly situates his national history within wider global trends and transnational shifts in the Western world, the Balkans, the Mediterranean basin and the Middle East.[63]

As a Greek-born architectural historian writing from the distance of a British academic institution, I combine my nuanced insider's view of Greece with an awareness of the 'normalisations' that this view entails. The organisation of my material in two parts reflects my conviction that local architectural developments of interest can only be fully understood from the perspective of the structural position of related sites in the interlocking globalised context of the critical regionalist debates. This context is transnational, if not transcontinental. As such, the two parts of this book recount the process of globalising critical regionalism as a significant intervention in the Western European and North American architectural debates of the 1980s before returning to its cross-cultural roots in Greece. Starting from 'The Presence of the Past' exhibition in Venice, the first part constantly zooms out to expand on the transatlantic development and global dissemination of the discourse of critical regionalism. Conversely, the second part starts from the long-term, zoomed-out perspective of the special place that Classical and modern Greece holds in the European imaginary in the nineteenth and twentieth centuries and constantly zooms in to culminate in a discussion of two specific buildings by Suzana and Dimitris Antonakakis. Serving as two sides of the same coin, both the 'international' and the 'Greek' parts of the book adopt equally cross-cultural or 'global' prespectives. As such, they are both integral to the book's main argument that a geographic opening should apply both to the 'international' and 'regional' sides of any meaningful history of critical regionalism today.

The First Venice Biennale of Architecture exhibition is widely regarded as the show that both established and globalised the canon of postmodern architecture. But in so doing, it also silenced alternative responses to the long-standing impasse of 'international style' modern architecture from the 1960s onwards. The polyphony in theory did not register in practice on the exhibition floor, despite the participation of renowned international critics who represented diverse positions in the debates around postmodern architecture. Chapter 1 sets the scene for the book by focusing on the overshadowed sides of this story. It demonstrates how this original diversity was reduced to a narrowly defined canon of postmodern architecture. It presents the North American architect Robert A.M. Stern (b. 1939) as the crucially overlooked protagonist of the exhibition. Not immediately evident, Stern's agenda of 'traditional post-modernism' nonetheless prevailed to define the main message of the show. In so doing, it also propagated 'postmodernism' as a 'global' phenomenon that could now be allegedly traced from Japan to Western Europe. Chapter 1 resists Stern's 'central' historical construct in order to retrieve the original diversity of debates around postmodern architecture. It revisits the exhibition through the eyes of Greek architects Suzana and Dimitris Antonakakis and their 'peripheral' collaborative practice Atelier 66. Documenting their negative reaction to the show, it aligns the Greek architects' approach with that of Kenneth Frampton, who withdrew from the committee of international critics before the opening of the Biennale. Frampton believed that the unsentimental regionalism of 'provincial' cultures could offer a more constructive response to the enduring crisis of modern architecture. In so doing, it could also resist Stern's 'central' but effectively superficial, nostalgic and scenographic construct of 'traditional post-modernism'.

Frampton was certainly not alone in his critique of Stern's approach to postmodern architecture and the constructive potential of regionalism. From the late 1960s, he had established collegial ties with Tzonis who was also teaching in North American Ivy League institutions around that time. Later, in the 1970s, Tzonis and Lefaivre shared their critical thoughts on 'populist' and 'narcissist' architectural developments with Frampton. It was indeed from their 1981 article 'The Grid and the Pathway' that the British architectural historian borrowed the term 'critical regionalism' in 1982. But Frampton's own theoretical interests have in turn overshadowed the earlier history of regionalism in the architectural debates of the 1980s. Chapter 2 documents Frampton's and Tzonis and Lefaivre's exchanges in the 1960s and the 1970s, and retraces the earlier history and overlooked protagonists of constructive regionalism. Tzonis and Lefaivre wrote their first article on 'critical regionalism' having just finished working on a paper on 'The Question of Regionalism'. This was their response to an invitation by the Swiss sociologist and economist Lucius Burckhardt – an influential figure in architecture, urban planning and landscape design in the German-speaking parts of the world – who was more widely known as the founder of 'strollology' and for his emphasis on the significance of walking in producing knowledge of specific places. But because this first article on 'The Question of Regionalism' was published in German, it has not yet found its proper place in the history of critical regionalism. As a result, its third contributing author, Anthony Alofsin, who was then a graduate student of Tzonis at Harvard University, has also been historiographically overshadowed. The chapter retraces Alofsin's contribution to this article through his earlier paper on 'Constructive Regionalism', focusing on his interest in the work of Lewis Mumford and the possibility for a distinctly North American variant of modern architecture that would not be a direct import of Bauhaus modernism. Hence, the chapter foregrounds the currently overlooked cross-cultural Euro-American roots of regionalist discourses of the 1980s that conditioned the later development of Tzonis and Lefaivre's critical regionalism.

Frampton borrowed the term 'critical regionalism' from Tzonis and Lefaivre's 'The Grid and the Pathway' (1981), their seminal article on the work of the Antonakakis. Chapter 3 shows the ways in which critical regionalism bears the cross-cultural marks of Alofsin's interest in Mumford's modern regionalism; Tzonis and Lefaivre's interest in participatory design; the Antonakakis' appreciation of the architectural work of Team 10; and Frampton's foregrounding of tectonic culture. These cross-cultural roots of critical regionalism also retrieve the socially conscious debates that were muted at the Biennale. Promoting the potential contribution of a regionalism that has not yet emerged else-where to the global future of modern architecture, Frampton also intended to unsettle the transatlantic 'centre/periphery' hierarchy that was reaffirmed in Venice. Through his recapitulation of Tzonis and Lefaivre's theorisations, Greek architects' projects became significant as the buildings that wrote critical regionalism alongside more well-known projects by Alvar Aalto and Jørn Utzon. In the final instance, the cross-cultural authorship of critical regionalism embodied its main theoretical assertion: that the relation of the 'periphery' to the 'centre' is not merely assimilative but also productive and generative. Resisting 'postmodernism' in order to offer a way forward for modern architecture, the 'peripheral' backwaters of architectural historiography reclaimed their precious relevance for the present. They became the marginal but still progressive 'arrière-gardes' of the 1980s that held the solutions to problems instigated by the progressive but equally marginal modernist 'avant-gardes' of the 1920s.

Originally published in an inaccessible annual review of architecture in Greece, it was only after Tzonis and Lefaivre's 'critical regionalism' was recapitulated by Frampton that it had a worldwide impact. But Frampton's own structural position in the international media complex did not serve his goal of turning attention from the 'centres' to the 'periphery' of cultural production. Frampton mainly intended to dissociate critical regionalism from the postmodern architecture of the Biennale. But architectural publishers of the period also sought to establish their standing in the market by investing in opposing aspects of the wider postmodern debates. As diverging agendas of different publishing venues distorted the reception of Frampton's work, his fundamental disagreement with Stern was misconstrued as an inconsequential hair-splitting debate on regionalism. Chapter 4 highlights the inherent media problem of critical regionalism. It shows how the self-perpetuating propaganda of the architectural avant-gardes was reinforced by a vicious circle of risk-averse publishing practices. This would not be broken unless a whole network of related practices was also modified. But this proved difficult even for

Frampton, a scholar with an exceptionally influential position at the Western 'centre' of architectural production. Setting up a publishing strategy of his own, Frampton outlined a series of eighteen monographs on critical architectural practices of 'unsentimental regionality'. By 1985, however, when the series was supposed to have been completed, only two out of his originally proposed eighteen monographs had been published (focusing on the architecture of Tadao Ando, and the Antonakakis). While Frampton was also working on a broader book project on critical regionalism in the same period, he eventually abandoned it.

The retrospective canonisation of the critical regionalist discourse and its eventual summation in three projects and six points does not do justice to Frampton's original aspirations from the 1980s. As I argue in chapter 5, critical regionalism hails from a time when buildings used to write architectural theory. Frampton understood his role as that of an operative critic who could guide and influence the future of architectural practice. His critical regionalism aimed to serve as a useful tool, a unified construct built on diversified architectural practices. Conversely, the way in which Frampton interpreted specific projects enables me to read his critical regionalist project as a whole. To do so, the chapter starts from his 1981 proposal for the series of eighteen books on 'unsentimental regionalist' practices and his later book project on critical regionalism of the late 1980s. While both initiatives were eventually discontinued, parts of them survived or morphed into shorter essays for other projects. Their sporadic and disconnected appearance in an unorganised succession of other publications limited the potential of these projects and architects to contribute to the still developing discourse of critical regionalism in the 1980s. Combining previously unpublished archival material with Frampton's sporadic publications on the architects of critical regionalism from the late 1970s to the mid-1990s, the chapter reconstructs his unfinished book in order to portray critical regionalism as a project of cross-cultural exchange in architecture. But Frampton's rather idealised understanding of this process hinders a more nuanced development of the globalising branches of critical regionalism. This in turn ignites a more focused return to its cross-cultural roots in Greece in the second part of the book.

Cross-cultural roots

Chapter 6 explicates the celebrated reception of critical regionalism in Greece. Until the 1980s, architectural historiography had supported a dual self-image of Greece as the founding Classical centre of modern

Europe and as a marginal site whose architectural endeavours are only validated by their adherence to modern European developments. The history of architecture in Greece had also developed in these dual terms of a modern margin in the Classical centre. Effectively the latest product of the same margin/centre schema, critical regionalism became Greek architects' most celebrated moment in twentieth-century architectural history. It signalled that the marginalised modern architectural production of the country was now restored in the eyes of Western observers. Written between the mid-1960s and the late 1970s, the first histories of architecture in modern Greece emphasised local practitioners' attempts to appropriate regional traditions within their modernist designs. It was in this context that Tzonis and Lefaivre's first article on critical regionalism presented the work of Atelier 66 as a successful combination of the Antonakakis' lessons from Dimitris Pikionis (1887–1968) and Aris Konstantinidis (1913–1993). But with his theoretical ambition to advance a wider critical-design practice across cultures, Frampton generalised Tzonis and Lefaivre's ideas beyond the specific historical context that gave rise to them. Although Frampton's mediated outsider's account of Greek architecture reflected his variegated ties with the region, it effectively short-circuited the original intentions of critical regionalism. Instead of advancing a focused return to the region, it reflected the broader concerns of Western architectural discourses of the 1980s.

Chapter 7 highlights the unforeseen effects of the 'return' of critical regionalism as an 'international' theoretical construct to its originating locus. The competing (local and global) agendas invested in critical regionalism enabled Greek architects to recuperate it either as an unreflective modernist haven from the global sirens of postmodernism or as a plea for nostalgic traditionalism that went against modernism. What aimed to expand the global reach of Greek architecture in theory had the opposite effect of turning the local architectural culture inwards in practice. Since its publication in 1981, Tzonis and Lefaivre's 'grid and pathway' account has also been established as the standard interpretation of the Antonakakis' work for local and global audiences. But this account was intuitive rather than analytical. Although they wrote about Greek architectural culture as informed insiders, Tzonis and Lefaivre also prioritised the dictates of the Western agendas over the specificity of their local material. The chapter shows how the Antonakakis practically used Tzonis and Lefaivre's 'grid' as a means of controlling their allegedly non-hierarchical collaborative practice, Atelier 66. Underlying their building designs, these grids guaranteed the fine-tuned appearance of their architecture. Through the common use of the grid, the presence of the

Antonakakis became so strong that it was difficult for their younger colleagues to rise to co-equal levels of design control. As such, Atelier 66's pursuit of an elusive ethos of non-hierarchical collaborative design in theory became structurally impossible to achieve in practice. Lastly, critical regionalism did not escape a structurally generated media 'star-system' problem of its own. When the Antonakakis became 'internationally renowned' figures of critical regionalism, their personal relations with other Greek architects were negatively affected – culminating in the implosion of Atelier 66 in 1986.

In 1981, Tzonis and Lefaivre traced a local genealogy that combined Konstantinidis's 'rationalist grids' with Pikionis's 'topographically sensitive pathways' in order to inform the work of the Antonakakis. Chapter 8 shows how this account still holds architectural historians' imaginations captive in an inward-looking discussion. But it was in fact an outward-facing cross-cultural genealogy that historically sustained the Antonakakis' critical regionalism. Focusing on their architectural education at the National Technical University of Athens in the late 1950s, this chapter draws out the elements that conditioned the Greek architects' modern understanding of regional traditions. While their strong biographical connection with Pikionis sustained his influence on their work, Konstantinidis's impact was rather limited. In addition to Pikionis's teaching, the factors conducive to their architectural formation lay in their lessons in architectural theory from Panayotis Michelis (1903–1969); the drawing and painting classes of Nikos Hadjikyriakos-Ghika (1906–1994); and the systematic but open-ended modernist teaching of the disciple of Ludwig Mies van der Rohe, A. James Speyer (1913–1986). These cosmopolitan mentors enabled the Antonakakis to rethink the local architectural tradition in a way that rendered their work significant in the critical regionalist framework. This cross-cultural genealogy is aligned both with the original programmatic aims and principles of critical regionalism, and with the two architects' historical formation. But it is also further proof that, in the final instance, critical regionalism represents the 1980s return of the 1960s in global architectural culture.

Chapter 9 focuses on the Antonakakis' apartment building at 118 Benaki Street (1972–5), which was heralded as a flagship project of critical regionalism in the mid-1980s. For its architects, the block embodied a critique of the standard Athenian building typology. But crucially, it also subverted existing design hierarchies, standard modes of production and everyday practices of sharing a collective life within an Athenian apartment building. Revisiting the lived history of this project from the moment of its initial conception to the present, this chapter unveils the multifarious, resilient and dissipating aspects of resistance at 118 Benaki Street. In so doing, it also highlights the tensions that arose between the original resistant intentions and their implementation in practice over four decades. The historically short lifespan of the architects' original intentions also highlights the contradictions involved in attempts to orchestrate unconventional ways of living. Greek developers' reactions, in particular, show how an architecture of resistance can also be received as its exact opposite – a generator of elite circles of the happy few and their indulgent idealisations. Similar problems emerge from residual hierarchies and operative modes that remain unchallenged or resist change. These long-standing tensions unsettle the ways in which this project has been appropriated in order to theorise critical regionalism. As Frampton bypassed the nuanced history of this project, he offered only an idealised image of architectural resistance. But it is only a return to the fullness of the historical image, to the social world as the Antonakakis wanted to see it transformed alongside the contingent fate of their actions, that foregrounds the political core of resistant architectures for the present.

Chapter 10 further exposes critical regionalism as a rigid, idealising discourse that could not follow the transitions of an active architectural practice such as Atelier 66. It focuses on the Antonakakis' Rhodes branch of the Ionian Bank (1983–6), an overlooked project designed and built at the peak of Frampton's advocation of critical regionalism. But at the same time that their ten-year-old Benaki Street project was being celebrated as an exemplar of critical regionalism in 1985, the Antonakakis' most recent reworking of the Athenian modern building typology in the Ionian Bank was not clearly 'resisting postmodernism'. For this reason, the Bank project was omitted from Frampton's monograph. To save the coherence of his critical regionalist discourse around the Antonakakis' work, the British architectural historian could not include a project that verged towards that which his theory was meant to resist. As a result, he glossed over the intricacies of a flourishing practice in full flow at the time of his writing. Beyond the architects' control, the Rhodes branch of the Ionian Bank represented their turn from 'benign' modernist revisionism to 'regressive' postmodernism. In Greece, 'postmodernism' had been resisted to the point that it had effectively become a taboo word – at least, in theory. The ensuing stigma could only be shaken off by returning to the question of relating modernism with the regional tradition. But this cyclical return to the modernity/tradition schema of the 1960s became a vicious circle that undermined the future relevance of the Antonakakis' work for the wider project of critical regionalism.

The book's epilogue uses the historical insights from the preceding chapters to update critical regionalism for the twenty-first century on three fronts: theory, history and historiography. From Frampton's Lifetime Achievement award in Venice in 2018 to more recent *Festschrifts*, critical regionalism is now reappraised as a theory for architectural design. But the 'returns of the 1960s' that remain inherently embedded in this theory, including the fetishisation of concrete as the main building material, can no longer hold in the age of climate emergency. A twenty-first-century update of critical regionalism as a design theory should instead emphasise its close ties with questions of sustainability, towards local futures with a global outlook. If it is indeed to survive as a theory, the study of critical regionalism's forty-year history can also bring to the surface more of its blind spots. As this book shows, the writing of critical regionalism itself was a cross-cultural process that was not limited to the influential texts by Tzonis and Lefaivre, and Frampton. In addition, the positive reception of critical regionalism turned it into a historical agent that affected architects who engaged with it. Hence, critical regionalism's space of authorship is an ever-expanding cross-cultural network that branches out from humans to buildings and texts across decades, and needs to be further explored by historians. As such, even if one accepts that critical regionalism closed its historical circle and failed as theory, it may still survive as history. Through historically informed critique, it can be reinvigorated no longer as a theoretical but as a pertinent historiographical agenda for the twenty-first century. Like Frampton, I have opted to conclude this book with my proposed seven points of critical regionalism as historiography.

Notes

1 Alexander Tzonis and Liane Lefaivre, 'The Grid and the Pathway: An Introduction to the Work of Dimitris and Suzana Antonakakis, with Prolegomena to a History of the Culture of Modern Greek Architecture', *Architecture in Greece*, 15 (1981), 164–78.
2 See Kenneth Frampton, 'Prospects for a Critical Regionalism', *Perspecta*, 20 (1983), 147–62 (p. 162); Kenneth Frampton, 'Towards a Critical Regionalism: Six Points for an Architecture of Resistance', in *The Anti-Aesthetic: Essays on Postmodern Culture*, ed. by Hal Foster (Seattle: Bay Press, 1983), pp. 16–30.
3 See Miles Glendinning, *Mass Housing: Modern Architecture and State Power – A Global History* (London: Bloomsbury, 2021), pp. 81–522.
4 See Martin McLoone, 'National Cinema and Cultural Identity: Ireland and Europe', in *Border Crossing: Film in Ireland, Britain and Europe*, ed. by John Hill, Martin McLoone and Paul Hainsworth (Belfast: Queen's University Belfast, 1994), pp. 146–73; Douglas Powell, *Critical Regionalism: Connecting Politics and Culture in the American Landscape* (Chapel Hill: University of North Carolina Press, 2007); José E. Limón, 'Border Literary Histories, Globalization, and Critical Regionalism', *American Literary History*, 20.1/2 (2008), 160–82; Thorsten

Botz-Bornstein, 'Is Critical Regionalist Philosophy Possible?', *Comparative and Continental Philosophy*, 2.1 (2010), 11–25.

5   See Kenneth Frampton, 'The Predicament of the Place-Form: Notes from New York', in *Contemporary Architecture and City Form: The South Asian Paradigm*, ed. by Farooq Ameen (Mumbai: Marg, 1997), pp. 101–8.

6   See Immanuel Maurice Wallerstein, *The Modern World System: Capitalist Agriculture and the Origins of the European World-Economy in the Sixteenth Century* (New York: Academic Press, 1974).

7   Among others, see Tirthankar Roy, *India in the World Economy: From Antiquity to the Present* (Cambridge: Cambridge University Press, 2012).

8   See Mark Crinson, 'Singapore's Moment: Critical Regionalism, its Colonial Roots and Profound Aftermath', *Journal of Architecture*, 13.5 (2008), 585–605 (pp. 603–4, note 10).

9   Alexander Tzonis and Liane Lefaivre, 'Why Critical Regionalism Today?' (1990), repr. in *Theorizing a New Agenda for Architecture: An Anthology of Architectural Theory 1965–1995*, ed. by Kate Nesbitt (New York: Princeton Architectural Press, 1996), pp. 484–92 (p. 488).

10 Among others, see *Architecture and Identity*, ed. by Peter Herrle and Erik Wegerhoff (Berlin: LIT, 2008).

11 See Léa-Catherine Szacka, *Exhibiting the Postmodern: The 1980 Venice Architecture Biennale* (Venice: Marsilio, 2016).

12 See Charles Jencks, 'The Rise of Post Modern Architecture', *Architectural Association Quarterly*, 7 (1975), 3–14.

13 See Louis I. Kahn, 'On Monumentality', in *New Architecture and City Planning*, ed. by Paul Zucker (New York: Philosophical Library, 1944), pp. 77–88; *Meaning in Architecture*, ed. by Charles Jencks and George Baird (London: Barrie & Jenkins, 1969).

14 See Adam Sharr, 'Leslie Martin and the Science of Architectural Form', in *Quality Out of Control: Standards for Measuring Architecture*, ed. by Allison Dutoit, Juliet Odgers and Adam Sharr (London: Routledge, 2010), pp. 67–78.

15 See Jane Jacobs, *The Death and Life of Great American Cities* (New York: Random House, 1961).

16 See Andreas Kourkoulas, 'Linguistics in Architectural Theory and Criticism after Modernism', unpublished doctoral thesis, University College London, 1986.

17 Peter Eisenman, 'Post-Functionalism', *Oppositions*, 6 (1976), i–iv.

18 Hanno-Walter Kruft, *A History of Architectural Theory from Vitruvius to the Present*, trans. by Ronald Taylor, Elsie Callander and Antony Wood (New York: Princeton Architectural Press, 1994), p. 446.

19 See *The Postmodern Moment: A Handbook of Contemporary Innovation in the Arts*, ed. by Stanley Trachtenberg (Westport, CT: Greenwood Press, 1985).

20 See Jean-François Lyotard, *The Postmodern Condition: A Report on Knowledge*, trans. by Geoff Bennington and Brian Massumi (Minneapolis: University of Minnesota Press, 1984); Jean-François Lyotard, 'Ripetizione, complessità, anamnesi', *Casabella*, 49.517 (1985), 44–5.

21 See Charles Jencks, *The Story of Post-Modernism: Five Decades of the Ironic, Iconic and Critical in Architecture* (Chichester: Wiley, 2011); Terry Farrell and Adam Nathaniel Furman, *Revisiting Postmodernism* (London: RIBA, 2017); *The Return of the Past: Conversations on Postmodernism*, ed. by Owen Hopkins (London: Soane Museum, 2018).

22 See *Postmodernism: Style and Subversion, 1970–1990*, ed. by Glenn Adamson and Jane Pavitt (London: Victoria and Albert Museum, 2011); *La Tendenza: Italian Architectures, 1965–1985*, ed. by Frédéric Migayrou (Paris: Centre Pompidou, 2012).

23 Geraint Franklin and Elain Harwood, *Post-Modern Buildings in Britain* (London: Batsford, 2017).

24 Reinhold Martin, *Utopia's Ghost: Architecture and Postmodernism, Again* (Minneapolis: University of Minnesota Press, 2010); K. Michael Hays, *Architecture's Desire: Reading the Late Avant-Garde* (Cambridge, MA: MIT Press, 2009).

25 Claire Jamieson, *NATØ: Narrative Architecture in Postmodern London* (London: Routledge, 2017); Esra Akcan, *Open Architecture: Migration, Citizenship and the Urban Renewal of Berlin-Kreuzberg by IBA 1984/87* (Basel: Birkhäuser, 2018).

26 Among others, see Owen Hopkins, *Postmodern Architecture: Less is a Bore* (London: Phaidon, 2020); Judith Gura, *Postmodern Design Complete: Design, Furniture, Graphics, Architecture, Interiors* (New York: Thames & Hudson, 2017).

27 Harry-Francis Mallgrave and David J. Goodman, *An Introduction to Architectural Theory: 1968 to the Present* (Chichester: Wiley-Blackwell, 2011), p. 123.

28 Aron Vinegar, *I AM A MONUMENT: On Learning from Las Vegas* (Cambridge, MA: MIT Press, 2008); Emmanuel Petit, *Irony; or, the Self-critical Opacity of Postmodern Architecture* (New Haven, CT: Yale University Press, 2013).

29 See Felicity D. Scott, *Architecture or Techno-utopia: Politics after Modernism* (Cambridge, MA: MIT Press, 2007).

30 For the first historically and sociologically informed study before the current wave of postmodern revisionism, see Magali Sarfatti-Larson, *Behind the Postmodern Façade: Architectural Change in Late Twentieth-Century America* (Berkeley: University of California, 1993).

31 See Eva Branscome, *Hans Hollein and Postmodernism: Art and Architecture in Austria, 1958–1985* (London: Routledge, 2018); Léa-Catherine Szacka, *Exhibiting the Postmodern: The 1980 Venice Architecture Biennale* (Venice: Marsilio, 2016); Jorge Otero-Pailos, *Architecture's Historical Turn: Phenomenology and the Rise of the Postmodern* (Minneapolis: University of Minnesota Press, 2010); *Neo-avant-garde and Postmodern: Postwar Architecture in Britain and Beyond*, ed. by Mark Crinson and Claire Zimmerman (New Haven, CT: Yale University Press, 2010).

32 See Jorge Figueira, *A Periferia Perfeita: Pós-modernidade na arquitectura portuguesa. Anos 1960–1980* (Lisbon: Caleidoscópio, 2014); *Second-World Postmodernisms: Architecture and Society under Late Socialism*, ed. by Vladimir Kulić (London: Bloomsbury, 2019); Florian Urban, *Postmodern Architecture in Socialist Poland: Transformation, Symbolic Form and National Identity* (London: Routledge, 2021).

33 Owen Hatherley, *Militant Modernism* (Winchester: Zero Books, 2009).

34 See *International Postmodernism: Theory and Literary Practice*, ed. by Hans Bertens and Douwe W. Fokkema (Amsterdam: Benjamins, 1997).

35 Perry Anderson, *The Origins of Postmodernity* (London: Verso, 1998), p. 16.

36 See Dimitris Papanikolaou, 'Greece as a Postmodern Example: *Boundary 2* and its Special Issue on Greece', *Κάμπος: Cambridge Papers in Modern Greek*, 13 (2005), 127–45.

37 See *Greece in the 1980s*, ed. by Richard Clogg (London: Macmillan, 1983); *Η Ελλάδα στη δεκαετία του '80: Κοινωνικό, πολιτικό και πολιτισμικό λεξικό*, ed. by Vassilis Vamvakas and Panayis Panagiotopoulos (Athens: Perasma, 2010); *GR80s. Η Ελλάδα του Ογδόντα στην Τεχνόπολη: Συλλογισμός, περιεχόμενο και μεθοδολογία για μια έκθεση*, ed. by Vassilis Vamvakas and Panayis Panagiotopoulos (Athens: Melissa, 2017).

38 Andreas Giacumacatos, *Ιστορία της ελληνικής αρχιτεκτονικής: 20ος αιώνας*, 2nd edn (Athens: Nefeli, 2004), p. 105. Unless otherwise noted, all translations from the original sources in Greek and other European languages are by the author.

39 Dimitris Philippidis, *Νεοελληνική αρχιτεκτονική: Αρχιτεκτονική θεωρία και πράξη (1830–1980) σαν αντανάκλαση των ιδεολογικών επιλογών της νεοελληνικής κουλτούρας* (Athens: Melissa, 1984), p. 44.

40 Panayotis Tournikiotis, 'Κριτική της σύγχρονης ελληνικής αρχιτεκτονικής: Επιμύθιο', *Architecture in Greece*, 24 (1990), 22–4 (p. 23).

41 Elias Constantopoulos, 'On the Architecture of Dimitris and Suzana Antonakakis', *Design + Art in Greece*, 25 (1994), 18–25 (p. 19).

42 See Dimitris Fatouros, 'The Architecture of Dimitris and Suzana Antonakakis: Two Complementary Descriptions', in *Atelier 66: The Architecture of Dimitris and Suzana Antonakakis*, ed. by Panayotis Tournikiotis (Athens: futura, 2007), pp. 46–53 (p. 49); Dimitris Philippidis, 'Η υστερική άρνηση του μεταμοντέρνου στην ελληνική αρχιτεκτονική', in *Η πρόσληψη των μετανεωτερικών ιδεών στην Ελλάδα*, ed. by Ourania Kaiafa (Athens: Moraitis Foundation, 2018), pp. 81–92 (p. 87).

43 Alexander Tzonis and Liane Lefaivre, 'A Critical Introduction to Greek Architecture since the Second World War', in *Post-War Architecture in Greece, 1945–1983*, ed. by Orestis Doumanis (Athens: Doumanis, 1984), 16–23 (pp. 22–3).

44 Kenneth Frampton, 'Μοντέρνο, πολύ μοντέρνο: Μια συνέντευξη του Kenneth Frampton στον Γιώργο Σημαιοφορίδη', *Architecture in Greece*, 20 (1986), 118–21 (p. 120).

45 See Michael Steiner and Clarence Mondale, *Region and Regionalism in the United States: A Source Book for the Humanities and Social Sciences* (New York: Garland, 1988), pp. 9–78.

46 Spyros Amourgis, 'Introduction', in *Critical Regionalism: The Pomona Meeting Proceedings*, ed. by Spyros Amourgis (Pomona: California State Polytechnic University, 1991), pp. vii–xii (p. x).

47 See Liane Lefaivre and Alexander Tzonis, 'Critical Regionalism', in *Critical Regionalism*, ed. by Amourgis, pp. 3–23; Kenneth Frampton, 'Critical Regionalism Revisited', in *Critical Regionalism*, ed. by Amourgis, pp. 34–9.
48 See Kenneth Frampton, *Studies in Tectonic Culture: The Poetics of Construction in Nineteenth and Twentieth Century Architecture* (Cambridge, MA: MIT Press, 1995).
49 Fredric Jameson, *The Seeds of Time* (New York: Columbia University Press, 1994), pp. 189–205.
50 Kenneth Frampton, *Modern Architecture: A Critical History*, 4th edn (London: Thames & Hudson, 2007), p. 7.
51 Kenneth Frampton, 'Towards an Agonistic Architecture', *Domus*, 972 (2013), 1–9 (p. 7).
52 See Ole W. Fischer, 'Architecture, Capitalism and Criticality', in *The SAGE Handbook of Architectural Theory*, ed. by C. Greig Crysler, Stephen Cairns and Hilde Heynen (Los Angeles: SAGE, 2012), pp. 56–69.
53 Joseph Rykwert, 'How Great is the Debate?', *RIBA Transactions*, 4.2:2 (1983), 18–31 (p. 27).
54 Keith L. Eggener, 'Placing Resistance: A Critique of Critical Regionalism', *Journal of Architectural Education*, 55.4 (2002), 228–37 (pp. 230, 233–4).
55 Murray Fraser, 'The Scale of Globalisation', in *Architecture and Globalisation in the Persian Gulf Region*, ed. by Murray Fraser and Nasser Golzari (London: Ashgate, 2013), pp. 383–404 (p. 387).
56 See Thorsten Botz-Bornstein, *Transcultural Architecture: The Limits and Opportunities of Critical Regionalism* (London: Routledge, 2015); 'Critical Regionalism Revisited', ed. by Tom Avermaete et al. Special issue, *OASE*, 103 (2019).
57 Vincent B. Canizaro, 'Preface: The Promise of Regionalism', in *Architectural Regionalism: Collected Writings on Place, Identity, Modernity, and Tradition*, ed. by Vincent B. Canizaro (New York: Princeton Architectural Press, 2007), pp. 10–12 (pp. 11, 10).
58 Richard Ingersoll, 'Critical Regionalism in Houston: A Case for the Menil Collection', in *Critical Regionalism*, ed. by Amourgis, pp. 233–9.
59 See *Architectural Regionalism*, ed. by Canizaro, p. 386.
60 See Nicolas Svoronos, *Histoire de la Grèce moderne* (Paris: Presses Universitaires de France, 1953).
61 For a summative account, see Mark Mazower, 'Democracy's Cradle, Rocking the World', *New York Times*, 30 June 2011, p. A27.
62 Kostas Kostis, *History's Spoiled Children: The Formation of the Modern Greek State*, trans. by Jacob Moe (London: Hurst, 2018).
63 Antonis Liakos, *Ο ελληνικός 20ός αιώνας* (Athens: Polis, 2019).

Part I
Globalising branches

1
Postmodern stage

The First Biennale of Architecture in Venice opened its doors to the general public on 27 July 1980. Since then, it has become established as 'the largest and highest-profile architectural exhibition in the world'.[1] Curated by Paolo Portoghesi (b. 1931) under the general title 'The Presence of the Past', the show arrived at a key moment in the development of postmodern architecture. In her recent book, Léa-Catherine Szacka interpreted this exhibition as a hinge in the history of postmodernism. Serving as 'the end of the beginning', she argued, the show offered a specific way out of the prolonged impasse of modern architecture after the 1960s.[2] In my book, the exhibition sets the scene for what is to follow, since the discourse of critical regionalism originally developed against this background in the 1980s.

Foregrounding an architectural style of historicist eclecticism, the Biennale both established and globalised a canon of postmodern architecture. But in so doing, it also silenced alternative responses to the long-standing crisis of modern architecture. Recent scholarship has already highlighted the plurality of theoretical positions in the postmodern debate before the show. But in this chapter, I focus on some less discussed aspects of the exhibition that proved to be key for the subsequent development of the critical regionalist discourse. In the pages that follow, I highlight crucial moments in the curatorial negotiations behind the production of the exhibition and its content, its subsequent representations and mediations in relevant publications, and its reception by visitors. This enables me to present the US architect Robert A.M. Stern as the show's overlooked protagonist, who has been historically overshadowed by Portoghesi. Not immediately evident, Stern's agenda of 'traditional post-modernism' nonetheless prevailed to define the main message of the show. In so doing, it also propagated 'postmodernism' as a global phenomenon that could now be allegedly traced from Japan to

Western Europe. Retrieving the diversity of debates around postmodern architecture before the show therefore involves resisting Stern's established construct and its narrowly defined canon of Western European and North American architects. While my account is based on the work of specific architects and critics, I am more interested in what these figures represent: a wide-ranging spectrum of sites and approaches to postmodern architecture.

For these reasons, this chapter revisits the major exhibition in Venice through the eyes of Greek architects Suzana and Dimitris Antonakakis and their collaborative practice Atelier 66. Inasmuch as Greece was not on the radar of Western European and North American theorists, it remained a 'provincial' overlooked site of architectural developments. As such, it was conspicuously absent both from the 1980 Venice Biennale and from the first histories and theories of postmodern architecture of the late 1970s. This reflected the cultural insularity of the Greek architectural community at the time. Emerging out of the introversion imposed by the military junta (1967–74), Greek architects were eager to catch up with the prevailing trends in their field. In their eyes, the Biennale offered a comprehensive overview of these recent international developments that had not been widely publicised in Greece before. Hence, several local architects, including Suzana and Dimitris Antonakakis, travelled to Venice to witness the exhibition for themselves.

The two Antonakakis' negative reaction to the exhibition serves as a first step in resisting the show's master narrative and provincialising its content. Before the Biennale, in the late 1970s, the diverse under-standings of postmodernism ranged from stylistic and historicist to phenomenological and political readings of architecture. But while this polyphony in theory was represented by the international critics invited to the show, it did not register in practice on the exhibition floor. While recent scholarship has noted the distorted portrayals of specific architects to fit the agenda of the exhibition,[3] the crucial role that Stern played in defining the show's main message has not been sufficiently highlighted. The archived minutes and handwritten notes from the preliminary committee meetings show how Stern's agenda of 'traditional post-modernism' eventually prevailed. Amid the theoretical polyphony of the critics, it offered a solution to Portoghesi's 'bilingualist' problem of addressing both the Italian and international audiences. In addition, Stern's selected architects dominated the iconic centrepiece of the exhibition, the Strada Novissima. For these two reasons, Stern's agenda served as a platform for the recapitulation of the Italian Neo-Rationalists within the camp of the North American postmodernists. In turn, this offered Charles Jencks (1939–2019) an alibi for the great postmodern synthesis that he had been aiming for in his earlier writings. After the Biennale, Jencks allied with Stern to propagate this agenda further through his theorisations of Postmodern Classicism. His propaganda proved successful, as the exhibition was immediately established as a turning point in the historiographical work of Bruno Zevi, William Curtis and Hanno-Walter Kruft, among others.

Despite the successful propagation of postmodernism by Jencks, Stern and others, the Greek architects were not alone in their appalled reaction to the show. Their critical views were aligned with similar ideas held by numerous Western European peers. For similar reasons, Kenneth Frampton stepped down from his role as an invited international critic at the Biennale a few months before the opening of the exhibition. Opposing the historicist approach that prevailed, Frampton believed that the 'unsentimental regionalism' of 'provincial' cultures could offer a more constructive response to the enduring crisis of modern architecture. In so doing, it could also resist Stern's 'central' but effectively superficial, nostalgic and scenographic construct of 'traditional post-modernism'. Aligned with Frampton's interests, Suzana and Dimitris Antonakakis' work served as a stepping stone to resist and provincialise the show's dominant approach to architecture. In the years that followed, it played its own unique role in the development of the critical regionalist discourse.

Greek architects in Venice

Suzana and Dimitris Antonakakis were among the 36,325 individuals who visited the First Biennale of Architecture.[4] The 10-minute video that I retrieved from their private archive recorded their trip to Venice. During their visit, Dimitris Antonakakis used his Super-8 camera as an architectural notebook. Whenever something attracted his attention, he turned the camera on to record it. As a result, the video is a patchwork of disparate scenes ranging from the streets and lagoons of Venice to the architects' entry to the exhibition. But it also includes public spaces and buildings of note, such as Andrea Palladio's Villa Foscari 'La Malcontenta' in Mira. As a result, the video is partly an architectural pilgrimage and partly a personal exploration of Venice through the lens of Dimitris Antonakakis.

Upon their return to Athens, the two Antonakakis' trip to Venice attracted public interest. Less than a year later, in June 1981, a screening of this video was included in a special event organised by the Association of Greek Architects in Athens. During this event, the couple shared their first-hand impressions of the postmodern architecture that they saw at the Biennale with an Athenian audience of peers and students. But Dimitris Antonakakis's video demonstrates that it was the act of travelling, rather than the celebrated exhibition, that fed in to the two architects' sensibilities. The Antonakakis were as eager to explore the architectural environment in which they found themselves as they were to view the exhibition itself.

In his recording, Dimitris Antonakakis pays little attention to the show that brought him and his wife to Venice in the first place. Apart from random sightings of Aldo Rossi's Teatro del Mondo around the Venetian lagoon and the portal to the Arsenale exhibition, no other Biennale-related material features in the video (Fig. 1.1). As Dimitris Antonakakis's short talk at the 1981 event in Athens suggests, this was not because filming was not allowed in the Arsenale. Although he attempted to 'suspend his judgement' and share 'images and information' on the exhibition 'in the most charitable light possible', Antonakakis was appalled to witness Jencks's lighthearted rejection of the interwar modern movement. He was also disappointed by Jencks's indifference to the contribution of Team 10 – especially in regards to the architects' social role. Even more disheartening was Jencks's favourable presentation of the Classical orders. In the eyes of Antonakakis, they had nothing to do with 'life, human activity, [or] the laws of sun and nature'. Antonakakis thus found himself siding with Gaetano Pesce's intense public reaction to

Figure 1.1   Stills from Dimitris Antonakakis's 1980 Super-8 video: Aldo Rossi's portal to the exhibition and his Teatro del Mondo around the Venetian canals

this 'most reactionary conception of architecture'. The Greek architect concluded that 'it is not the modern movement that is to blame for the poverty of the present city and its architecture; it is our own insufficient understanding and effort to elaborate on its main positions to develop them further'.[5]

This plea for a reconsideration of the legacy of the modern movement aligned Antonakakis with similar critical reactions expressed by Greek architects of his age, who also spoke on the same occasion in Athens. None of them was willing to abandon the modernist project and its still unfulfilled potential.[6] The Greek architects' reaction effectively echoed Aldo van Eyck's (1918–99) plea not to abandon the language of modern architecture but 'to evolve [this] transformed language to express what is being analogously transformed' in civilisation.[7] Approximately three decades later, Van Eyck's critique, at the Sixth International Congress of Modern Architecture (CIAM 6, 1948), of a modernist Rationalism that excluded imagination was still deemed as relevant by this generation of modern Greek architects.

Such a reaction was consistent with Suzana and Dimitris Antonakakis' own formative history. When they visited the 'Presence of the Past' exhibition in Venice, they were already experienced architects. After graduating from the National Technical University of Athens in the late 1950s, both immediately began working together, along with some close friends and colleagues from their student years, as freelance architects.[8] The first projects of their collaborative practice, Atelier 66, bore the mark of their mentor, and former student of Ludwig Mies van der Rohe, A. James Speyer.[9] Speyer had offered the young Greek architects an 'open interpretation' of the modernist tenets.[10] Two decades later, in 1980, his influence was still evident in the work of Suzana and Dimitris Antonakakis. By then, their established ways of working could not easily be challenged by a single architectural exhibition, no matter how major an event 'The Presence of the Past' was heralded to be.

In a recent interview, Dimitris Antonakakis recalled 'rejecting the postmodern' after visiting the Strada Novissima. He added that he and Suzana 'never ascribed to the postmodern eclecticist logic of a "return of forms"'.[11] While the two architects thought that certain critiques of architectural modernism were at least partially legitimate, they did not intend to give up on its fundamental humanist aspirations and aesthetic tenets. Yet, they still thought that modern architects had to address the question of tradition in their practice. As such, the main question raised by the postmodern critics of the Biennale persisted. The question was right, but the historicist response of the exhibition was wrong, because it threatened to render the modern project obsolete. The Antonakakis intended to re-evaluate the past in a way that would not degenerate into formal eclecticism. Without following what was propagated in the show, they grappled with the same postmodern question of re-evaluating the past through their own practice.

Dimitris Antonakakis's footage from Venice in 1980 can therefore be reinterpreted as evidence of this attempt to re-evaluate the architectural past beyond its formal characteristics. Although he never considered this video important (as he mentions in the interview),[12] Dimitris Antonakakis's random record of their travel to Venice demonstrates his personal architectural concerns. Wherever he turns the lens of his camera, from buildings and public spaces to random scenes of everyday life (Fig. 1.2), his architectural gaze is both modern and personal. It is modern because it ignores the superficial characteristics of his subject matter. Whether he is recording Italian vernacular architecture, a Palladian villa, a Renaissance palace, a Baroque or a modern building, his interest lies not in their specific formal features but in their abstract spatial relations. It is these typological observations that in turn reflect Antonakakis's personal architectural concerns. He constantly focuses on details that render architecture as the setting of everyday life. These details allow for varying degrees of privacy from the public urban realm. His interest is especially attracted by minute architectural elements that form inhabited thresholds. He also focuses on the gradual transitions from one material surface to another, and from the public spaces of everyday life to the increased privacy of interior spaces. Staircases, landings, galleries, windows, tight alleys, balconies, semi-enclosed spaces and roofed terraces feature prominently in the video. Their multiple combinations reveal Antonakakis's interest in liminal, transitional surfaces. The inhabitation of these intermediate spaces is usually triggered by subtle design choices. In one instance, a strategically positioned mantel forms a seating space for stopping and resting at the intersection of multiple public trajectories across a building. Antonakakis is also eager to document the qualities of indoor spaces. He appreciates architectural features that serve the cross-ventilation and lighting of these spaces, and their controlled opening to the public, open-air settings that celebrate the mild Mediterranean climate. On a larger scale, he documents buildings that frame and relate to their adjacent public spaces. His recordings portray public space as a playground for both children and adults.

Dimitris Antonakakis's interest in transitions, thresholds and liminal spaces, and the various ways in which people appropriate ambiguous pieces of public furniture, is also reminiscent of Van Eyck's and Herman

Figure 1.2 Stills from Dimitris Antonakakis's 1980 Super-8 video: everyday life, architectural details and spaces of note in Venice and its surroundings, including Andrea Palladio's Villa Foscari 'La Malcontenta' in Mira (bottom)

Suzana and Dimitris Antonakakis' private archive

Hertzberger's (b. 1932) similar approaches. By 1980, Suzana and Dimitris Antonakakis were certainly influenced by the work of these Dutch architects. But such architectural concerns also had their own long history in the two architects' regional architectural formation in late-1950s Greece.[13]

To sum up, Suzana and Dimitris Antonakakis returned to the architectural past as this was expressed and materialised in the present day of the city itself. This past was there in the multiple historical layers of its integration into the urban fabric. From royal palaces to vernacular huts, the Venetian buildings that surrounded the two travellers served as legitimate sources of architectural knowledge – and especially so in the context of the critique of modernism of the period. But if they were to offer a way out of the prolonged impasse of modern architecture, these buildings – and especially, their relations with quotidian public spaces – still needed to be interpreted from a modernist vantage. The past should certainly be revisited, not in the historicist terms of the Biennale but with the modern eyes that could overcome superficial formal characteristics in order to advance typological observations. As such, Suzana and Dimitris Antonakakis aspired to a 'presence of the past' for a modern architecture that could evolve beyond the Strada Novissima. They suggested that architectural qualities of historical precedents missing from the prevailing international style of the time needed to be retained and rephrased accordingly in the language of modernism. As a result, their critical reaction to the Biennale reinforced their conviction in their personal architectural itinerary. They travelled to Venice as 'provincial' architects eager to witness the most recent 'central' trends. But in practice they returned having only reaffirmed what they were already pursuing by themselves: a regionally informed variant of modern architecture. In this pursuit, they were not alone. They effectively shared the concerns of the early Team 10 critiques of modernism – and especially, the anthropological sensibilities of Van Eyck.

Some of Portoghesi's invited critics to the Biennale also favoured this regional and socially conscious response to the prevalent crisis of modernism. But this approach was effectively muted at the exhibition.

Postmodern architecture before the Biennale

From the late 1950s onwards, numerous architects developed their interpretations and responses to the problematic aspects of modernism in different contexts, from Western Europe to Japan.[14] More than a decade later, in the 1970s, architectural historians and critics attempted to attribute retrospective coherence to this variegated set of regional developments. However, no global consensus on a viable alternative to modernism had yet emerged in 1979, when Portoghesi started planning his Biennale in Venice. Seeking to associate the exhibition with the flourishing postmodern discourses of the period, he invited four prominent architectural historians and critics (Vincent Scully, Christian Norberg-Schulz, Charles Jencks and Kenneth Frampton) to participate in two preparatory committee meetings in Venice in November 1979 and February 1980. Their renowned expertise in the variegated architectural developments after modernism could offer a plurality of critical viewpoints on the main theme of the exhibition. In addition, these international critics would afford their established cultural capital to a show that intended to promote positive ways out of the crises of modernism. Still, each of these critics came with a curatorial agenda of his own that coloured his interventions in the related discussions.

At the time, the term 'postmodern' had only recently been introduced into architectural debates. In the mid-1970s, Jencks's and Stern's most systematic accounts of 'postmodern architecture' associated it with the work of North American architects such as Robert Venturi and Denise Scott-Brown, Charles Moore, Aldo Giurgola and Michael Graves,[15] and a series of 'movements' counter to modernism – ranging from the North American 'social realism' of Jane Jacobs to the mid-1970s rise of historical-preservation policies in Western Europe.[16] From the outset, Jencks admitted that this disparate set of 'movements' could not yet coalesce to offer a viable substitute for modernism.[17] Approximately a year later, the editor of *Architectural Design* Haig Beck prompted him to elaborate on his article on Arata Isozaki's 'radical eclecticism' at book length. For Jencks, this served as an occasion to develop his preliminary ideas further and turn postmodernism into his personal historiographical project. *The Language of Post-Modern Architecture* (1977) was the end result.[18]

In the concluding section of this book, Jencks provided specific examples of his aspired, novel architectural paradigm. In addition to the North American architects already celebrated by Stern, Jencks discussed the recent works of Japanese architects Kiyonori Kikutake and Kisho Kurokawa, which attempted to introduce regional features into the language of modernism, and the participatory design pursuits of Ralph Erskine (Fig. 1.3) and Lucien Kroll. Again, he admitted that this inconsistent grouping did 'not yet constitute a single coherent tradition'.[19] However, he did have a clear direction in mind for postmodern architecture. He could see it moving towards a radical variant of

Figure 1.3   Ralph Erskine, Byker Wall estate in Newcastle upon Tyne, 1969–82: Dalton Crescent and exterior view from Dalton Street

eclecticism, already anticipated in the controversial work of Antoni Gaudí (1852–1926), which had been excluded from Sir Nikolaus Pevsner's canonical history of modern architecture due to its idiosyncratic nature (Fig. 1.4).[20] With this project of radical eclecticism in mind, it took Jencks less than a year to revise *The Language of Post-Modern Architecture* after its first celebrated publication in 1977. In the second edition of the book, Jencks offered a more systematic account of postmodern architecture in six discontinuous strands.[21] These now included approximately 100 Western European, North American and Japanese architects. 'Indeed, the

Figure 1.4   Antoni Gaudí, Casa Batlló in Barcelona, 1905–7

seven aspects of Post-Modernism I have out-lined do constitute such an amalgam [of radical eclecticism], even if it isn't yet an interrelated whole … We aren't there yet, but a tradition is growing which dares make this demand for the future.'[22]

Jencks's phrasing of 'the growth of a new tradition' was not incidental. Rather, it was a direct nod to another canonical work in the history of the modern movement – that of Sigfried Giedion.[23] Despite his rhetoric against it, Jencks was still enmeshed in the same, modernist *Zeitgeist* school of architectural historiography. Despite his propagation of pluralism, he shared the underlying assumption of his modernist forebears such as Pevsner. For them, architectural history was written in terms of a succession of 'reigning styles', which coherently expressed the prevailing value systems in each period. For Jencks, these modernist historians also served as role-model propagandists of a new architectural movement. As the self-appointed operative historian of postmodernism, he needed to employ similar tactics. In 1978, he still lacked the coherent value system that Giedion had been able to discern in modernism thirty years earlier. Jencks needed something as wide-ranging as his precursor's modernist 'space-time' concept to hold the plural architectural languages of postmodernism together. To achieve this, he needed to theorise a novel, radical variant of eclecticism. This was Jencks's main hunch at the time. When architects could systematically express these sought-after values through their work, 'the Michelangelo' of postmodernism was bound to arrive. It was only then that postmodernism could supplant modernism as the 'reigning style' of the period. When Portoghesi's invitation arrived in 1979, Jencks's stylistic understanding of postmodernism was one step away from culminating in this radical eclecticism.

Around the same time, Stern had crystallised his alternative theorisation of postmodernism as the novel architectural style. The North American architect has developed a long-standing interest in this subject since his formative years. As a graduate student at Yale University in 1965, he had famously edited an issue of *Perspecta* that featured the first publication of Venturi's text on *Complexity and Contradiction in Architecture*, alongside the work of Moore and Giurgola.[24] In the years that followed, Stern continued to pursue these new directions in North American architecture through his professional and academic practice.[25] In 1975, he described the work of his selected architects as an 'institutionalised counterculture' to the modern movement. This new style relied on a loose attitude of 'cultural and historical inclusiveness', inspired by the work of Venturi and Scott-Brown.[26] By 1980, Stern's account had become more systematic. In his influential article, 'The Doubles of Post-Modern', he explored the 'traditional' and 'schismatic' variants of postmodernism to conclude that 'traditional post-modernism' was the only viable option left for architects of his generation.[27] In his words, 'traditional post-modernism ... argues for a break with modernism and a reintegration with the broader condition of Western humanism, especially with the Romantic tradition ... [It is] characterised by a struggle to use traditional languages without falling into the presumed trap of revivalism'.[28]

Portoghesi's other invited critics (Scully, Norberg-Schulz and Frampton) did not aim to define 'postmodernism' as the 'reigning style' of their time. But they had all developed their own critical outlooks to architectural developments after modernism. In addition, Norberg-Schulz (1926–2000) and Frampton attempted to veer away from the stylistic understandings of Jencks and Stern. As they turned to phenomenology and critical theory to do so, they introduced different perspectives to the postmodern debate of the period.

By 1980, Norberg-Schulz had contributed to the development of postmodernism only obliquely. His studies of intentions and meaning in architecture had informed the early thinking of Jencks and Frampton on these subjects.[29] But Norberg-Schulz did not follow Jencks in his notorious declaration of 'the death of modern architecture'.[30] Although he also opposed functionalism, the Norwegian critic did not equate it with modern architecture in general. Returning to the founding texts of the modern movement, he argued that they aimed at reconstructing human integrity. As he characteristically remarked in his text for the Biennale exhibition catalogue, 'Modern architecture is alive. Its basic aim has always been to heal the split between thought and feeling, which implies the creation of places which allow for human orientation'.[31] Inspired by the phenomenological writings of Martin Heidegger, Norberg-Schulz proposed his own way out of the crisis of modernism. He concluded that architecture needed to return to its authentic roots of place-creation. His phenomenological approach was systematised in the rather essentialist terms of the *genius loci*.[32]

Partly inspired by Heidegger, Frampton was also interested in architecture as a form of place-creation. But he was more influenced by the development of Heidegger's phenomenological teaching in Hannah Arendt's *The Human Condition* (1958).[33] It was her ideas that Frampton adapted to his critical architectural writings of the period, starting from his essay on 'Labour, Work and Architecture' in 1969.[34] Arendt's thought afforded a stronger political twist to Frampton's readings of architecture, which was missing from Norberg-Schulz's similar phenomenological accounts. Like Norberg-Schulz, Frampton disagreed with the wholesale repudiation of modernism. In 1975, he highlighted the polyphonic legacy of Team 10 as a model for responding to the contemporaneous challenges of pluralism in architecture.[35] In the years that followed, the British historian's thinking retained strong affinities with the Team 10 critique of 'tabula rasa' modernism, and their consideration of the existing urban context.[36] By the time he was invited by Portoghesi, Frampton had just finished his decade-long project of writing a critical history of modern architecture. In the concluding section of this book, he advocated 'a balanced critique of the modern tradition' and its 'tabula rasa reductivism' that had been responsible for 'the wholesale destruction of urban culture'. Echoing Team 10, he conceded that 'the emphasis that the "Post-Modernist" critique has placed on respecting the existing urban context can hardly be discredited'. But he was also critical of 'the recent ideologues of Post-Modernism such as the historian Charles Jencks' and the 'aestheticizing intent' of Venturi and Scott-Brown's work. In his eyes, the couple had sacrificed the critical dimension of their projects to the altar of wit and irony. As such, their work could not address the contradictions inherent in the modes of architectural production of the time. It could only 'degenerate into total acquiescence', rendered 'indistinguishable from the environmental consequences of the market economy'.[37]

However, it was precisely 'the Venturi experience' that Portoghesi was 'more interested in' for his exhibition, as he confirmed in a recent interview.[38] Before the Biennale, Portoghesi was well known in Italy as a prominent scholar of Baroque architecture,[39] and an active critic who publicised his views on modern architecture through the pages of popular journals such as *Controspazio*. In the 1970s, he became increasingly interested in critiques of modernism that sought to reaffirm the public face of architecture and its role in shaping a specific urban culture. Italian architects of his generation such as Rossi believed that this could be achieved by establishing relations with the existing urban fabric and the historic architecture of European cities. But North American architects such as Venturi and Scott-Brown had developed an alternative approach that focused more on popular culture and the contemporary spaces of everyday life. Portoghesi wanted his Biennale to highlight both of these strands that seemed to prevail on the two sides of the Atlantic by the late 1970s.

Partly to ensure the participation of Venturi and Scott-Brown, Portoghesi invited Scully (1920–2017), a well-known advocate of the couple's 'inclusivist' contextualist approach to architecture. Twenty-five years earlier, Scully had reinserted the historical regional precedent as a conducive factor in the development of modern architecture. Looking back at the nineteenth-century domestic architecture of North America, he had identified the 'shingle style' and traced its influence in the later residential projects of Frank Lloyd Wright (1867–1959).[40] It was this historically and contextually sensitive approach that enabled Scully to appreciate Venturi's *Complexity and Contradiction in Architecture* (1966) a decade later. In his introduction to the book, Scully heralded Venturi's 'gentle manifesto' as the most important architectural text after Le Corbusier's modernist manifesto *Towards an Architecture* (1923).[41] In 1974, he argued for the relevance of a revival of *The Shingle Style Today*, with the polemical subtitle *The Historian's Revenge*. In this essay-like book, Scully further promoted North American architects such as Venturi and Moore as the true heirs of the Corbusian legacy.[42] By the late 1970s, Scully clearly favoured an 'eclectic' and 'inclusive' turn to history as the way out of the crisis of modernism.

These different agendas formed the background of the critics' discussions in Venice. They ranged from a return to a 'culture of the place' (Norberg-Schulz, Frampton) and 'the rediscovery of history' (Portoghesi, Stern, Scully) to 'the urban form of the street' (Portoghesi) and the 'communicative aspect of architecture' (Jencks). Each agenda represented a different theoretical undercurrent of the exhibition. Taken together, these manifold approaches to modernism and postmodernism could have diversified the content of the show as they were only nominally united in their opposition to functionalism. Each of them suggested a distinctly open-ended trajectory for architecture in the advent of the crisis of the modern movement. Since the Biennale was organised at such a tumultuous moment in architectural discourse, the specific character of the exhibition had to be defined: Would it serve as a publicity stand for a specific interpretation of postmodern architecture, or offer a wider overview of the possible ways out of the crisis of modernism?

The international critics sat around the same table to discuss this question only once, in the second committee meeting of 23 and 24 November 1979. But the groundwork for the exhibition had already been set up by Stern and Portoghesi in the first committee meeting of 14 and 15 September 1979. The decisions of this first meeting had set the exhibition on rails that left little room for manoeuvre to the international critics. Effectively offering no space for negotiations and possible combinations of the different approaches, the Biennale turned out to be a missed opportunity for exploring the diversity of postmodern architectural developments.

Stern's dominance

The two committee meetings of the Architectural Sector of the Biennale of September and November 1979 have left their material traces in the Archivio Storico di Arte Contemporanea (ASAC) in Marghera. These range from the official meeting minutes to handwritten notes, summaries and diagrams related to the discussions. Of particular interest here is a document entitled 'documento Stern', the US architect's detailed proposal for the show. I argue that this document practically formed the backbone of the exhibition from the outset. The ten-page minutes of the first committee meeting reflect Stern's eventual dominance in the curatorial debates.

The first meeting concentrated on the format of the exhibition, its main message and the specific Western European and North American architects and critics to be invited to the show. The exhibition aimed to 'identify the tendencies to abandon the modern movement' in the light of 'the problem of historical memory'.[43] These concerns were also at the core of Stern's approach in his 'Doubles of Post-Modern' essay of 1980. Stern was commissioned to be responsible for the North American architects' part of the exhibition following a recommendation by Philip Johnson (1906–2005),[44] the US architect who became well known as the director of the influential 'Modern Architecture: International Exhibition' at the Museum of Modern Art of 1932.[45] By the late 1970s, however, Johnson had abandoned his earlier modernist work along the lines of Mies van der Rohe's glass houses in order to pursue his interest in historic architectural form. Famously arguing that 'you cannot not know history',[46] he had already started to explore an eclectic approach to architecture – notably, with his AT&T Building and its notorious 'Chippendale top' in New York. When the Biennale opened in 1980, a section of the exhibition served as an homage to Johnson's work, which was by then regarded as an exemplar of North American postmodern architecture – especially after having featured on the cover of *Time* magazine on 8 January 1979.

Aiming to emulate the success of the International Style exhibition that served to promote modernism at a global scale in the 1930s, Portoghesi intended his show to become a similar milestone or transatlantic meeting point of the 1980s. His curatorial vision involved bringing together the new North American tendencies with the contemporaneous work of Italian architects on the grounds of historical memory. However, while the turn to history was understood in terms of a postmodernist rupture with functionalism by the North American architects, their Italian counterparts understood their turn to history in terms of continuity.[47] To meet the demands of both audiences, the exhibition had to adopt a bilingualism. By emphasising rupture, the North American architects favoured an understanding of postmodernism as a novel style. By emphasising continuity, the Italian architects encouraged a processual understanding of postmodernism as a reworking of modern architecture that attempted to forge stronger ties with collective memory by referring to the existing formal types of buildings that comprised the historic city. This unavoidable tension was at the heart of Portoghesi's hesitant association of the exhibition with the 'postmodern' label. It is for this same reason that Stern's agenda of 'traditional post-modernism' eventually dominated the curatorial debate. His emphasis on continuity over rupture with the humanist and Romantic regional tradition of the modern period provided the middle ground needed for the North Americans to meet the Italians, who were also trying to forge links between their modern architecture and the historic city. As such, Stern's approach provided a plausible solution to Portoghesi's problem of bilingualism.

The Strada Novissima was the main carrier of Portoghesi's and Stern's shared message. It is now unanimously heralded as a curatorial masterstroke; without a single exception, all the subsequent curators of the Biennale in Venice from the 1990s onwards felt that their projects had to measure up to it.[48] For this artificial 'street' inside La Corderia of the old Venetian Arsenale, Portoghesi divided the available space into twenty equal allotments – one for each invited architect. The architects were instructed to use their allocated space to mount a small exhibition of their work. They were also encouraged to design the façade of this space as a self-portrait, a public image for their exhibition space and the architects themselves.[49] As they faced one another in succession, forming a 'public street' corridor across the Arsenale, these façades formed the centrepiece of the Biennale. This artificial 'street' had such a communicative power that it singlehandedly set the tone of the exhibition. Stern's prevalence over the selections of the twenty Strada Novissima architects, in turn, rendered the main exhibit a material expression of his agenda of 'traditional post-modernism'. The façades on show resorted to historicism and storytelling to symbolically address architecture's diverse social and political concerns (see Fig. 0.1). This symbolic and predominantly visual approach had already been prescribed by Stern in 1976.[50] It remained constant throughout his subsequent theorisations of 'traditional post-modernism'. In a later interview, Stern defended the decision to invite architects to produce their own façades in the show:

> [This] brought to the public *real* examples of the architects' work as opposed to merely photographs or drawings or models, to the extent that the facades are what they are—finished architectural products with no further aspirations. They are not models for real buildings and are full scale … they are something you can go and see.[51]

The 'documento Stern' shows that the US architect had come to the first committee meeting well prepared. He had already selected the 'seven positions of postmodern architects' to be included in the show.[52] Virtually undisputed throughout the successive committee meetings, his selections were all included in the Strada Novissima. With six of his 'European' counterpart selections also making the final cut, two thirds of the Strada Novissima already bore Stern's stamp by the end of the first meeting. The four new entries after the second committee meeting of November 1979 represent the other critics' comparatively weaker contribution to the Strada Novissima.[53]

The eight-page minutes of this second meeting show that Portoghesi's task was to set the tone amid the theoretical polyphony of his invited critics. In theory, the international critics' section of the exhibition was intended to form an 'intellectual polemic'. But the critics' diverging agendas threatened in practice to obfuscate the main message of the exhibition, as had already been defined and shared by Portoghesi and Stern two months earlier. To avoid this, the exhibition catalogue was eventually proposed as a conciliatory medium. This publication would 'attempt to represent not so much specific postmodern movements, but different positions of architecture after the modern movement'.[54] However, this could only translate into a series of parallel monologues. The understanding promoted by the show was more directly communicated to the general public by the artefacts on show than by the texts in the catalogue.

With the Strada Novissima effectively embodying Stern's 'traditional post-modernism', the last word on the exhibition belonged to him. The discursive disparities of the critics were hardly discernible in a show that promoted postmodernism as a novel style of historicist eclecticism. The exhibition practically distorted an open-ended process of diverse architectural enquiry. Instead of serving as the catalyst that would render the critics' discursive differences manifest, the Biennale offered a one-sided association of postmodern architecture with a variant of eclectic Classicism. Established in the exhibition, this reductive understanding silenced the non-stylistic aspects of the postmodern debate that had formed part of its early histories. To cite just two examples, the rejection of Van Eyck meant that Frampton's favoured promotion of Team 10 as an alternative collaborative model for architectural pluralism was not represented in the show (Fig. 1.5). In addition, the rejection of Ralph Erskine led to an understanding of postmodern architecture that lacked such significant forays into participatory design practices. As a result, the socially conscious aspects in the work of these architects were absent from the understanding of postmodern architecture that was promoted by the Biennale. This impoverished understanding in turn clouded the debates that took place before, during and after the exhibition. Portoghesi's historically sensitive discourse was inexorably associated with Stern's postmodernism. Norberg-Schulz's and Scully's works were also understood in similar terms after the exhibition. Owing to his dominant position, Stern was the only critic who did not compromise his original agenda to argue that the two major statements of the Biennale

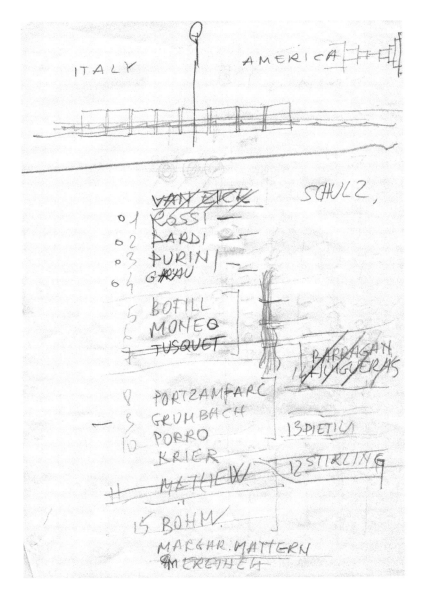

Figure 1.5 Handwritten notes from the first committee meetings of the Architectural Sector of the Biennale in Venice, 14 and 15 September 1979

Courtesy of Archivio Storico della Biennale di Venezia, ASAC

encompassed 'historic preservation' and 'the ability of style to convey meanings that are firmly rooted in all aspects of the culture and not just in some idealized version having to do with technology', as was the case with modernist functionalism.[55] When Jencks sided with Stern's approach after the show, the Biennale was soon established as the canonical reference that marked a turning point in the history of postmodern architecture.

The historiographical mark of the Biennale

The Strada Novissima presented postmodernism as a global phenomenon – pursued by Western European, North American and Japanese architects – when the spotlights of international publicity were falling on Venice.[56] As an operative critic writing 'from the centre of th[e] battlefield', Jencks immediately adapted his postmodernist labels accordingly.[57] Although the Strada Novissima did not cover the full spectrum of his postmodernist agenda of 'heightened communication',[58] Jencks embraced Stern's historicism. He used the show as evidence of the overall synthesis that he had already been pursuing in his earlier writings. After the Biennale, it was already clear that his radical eclecticism was out, and Stern's Postmodern Classicism was in. '[W]e are today undergoing a classical revival of a kind … the classicism is Post-*Modern*, a hybrid style relating more to the free style classicisms of 1900 than the purist approach of 1800 … Post-Modern Classicism [is] the synthesis whose commonalty was confirmed in the 1980 Venice Biennale.'[59] His subsequent promotion of Postmodern Classicism through the pages of *Architectural Design* kept the echo of the Biennale reverberating across the decade.

Less than a year after the Biennale, the editor of *Architectural Design* Andreas Papadakis (1938–2008) organised the first major retrospective exhibition of Stern's work in London in June 1981. In the exhibition catalogue, he republished Stern's defining text of Postmodern Classicism, 'The Doubles of Post-Modern'. The 'alliance between Jencks and Stern' was already obvious for Scully, who noted it in his introduction to the catalogue.[60] This alliance registered in the shifting tone of Jencks's rhetoric. His earlier definition of postmodern architecture as 'one-half Modern and one-half something else' still held. But by 1982 Western Classicism had replaced the regional vernacular as 'one-half of the style toward which Post-Modernists turn'.[61] In the fourth edition of his *Language of Post-Modern Architecture*, he elaborated on this 'new consensus' after the Biennale:[62]

> As you can read in the introduction to th[e] first edition [of *The Language of Post-Modern Architecture*], I said I hope the situation

remains plural and that it doesn't coalesce too quickly into a single approach which it has now done: 'Postmodern Classicism' ... We *do* have a shared language which both the public and profession know about and can enjoy. Soon we may begin creating important distinctions in that language. So the first phase of Post-Modernism is complete.[63]

This intense propagation of the Biennale in subsequent publications rendered the exhibition a noteworthy event in architectural history. It took less than two years for the Biennale to find its place in historical surveys of twentieth-century architecture. In his history of modern architecture of 1982, William J.R. Curtis heralded the exhibition as one of the 'two events in the Western architectural world of 1980' that registered the development of the new eclecticism from North American to Western European grounds.[64] Another three years later, in his comprehensive history of architectural theory of 1985, Hanno-Walter Kruft also noted that '[t]he term "Post-Modern" has since become a catchword ... and is applied indiscriminately to Neo-Rationalists such as Aldo Rossi as well as to others like the "New York Five"'.[65] The almost immediate historiographical reception of the exhibition confirmed the success of Portoghesi's and Stern's curatorial emphasis. Already established by the mid-1980s, their aspired transatlantic convergence of Western European and North American architects still holds well into the twenty-first century when scholars note that 'from a European perspective, [Rossi] is a left intellectual ... and father figure of neo-classical postmodernism'.[66]

The stylistic alliance of Jencks with Stern had also established its historiographical mark by the mid-1980s. In 1986, Manfredo Tafuri unequivocally noted that the Biennale had 'launched a style'.[67] In the revised edition of his critical history of modern architecture in 1985, Frampton also picked out the reliance on formalism and a 'dematerialised' historicism as the distinguishing characteristics of postmodernism. Another measure of the success of the exhibition in defining a new architectural style was the number of 'more recent converts to the Post-Modernist position', who could be already discerned by Frampton only a few years after the show.[68] Again, this impression of the Biennale as a turning point in the history of postmodernism still holds. It is this exhibition that leads Frampton to assert in 2015 that 'in 1980, postmodern architecture would come into its own as the inescapable ethos of the moment' to signal the end of the modern movement in architecture. His '*de facto*' references to the 'inescapable ethos' of the postmodern condition 'both aesthetically and politically' is a subtle reaffirmation of the success of the curatorial and editorial stratagems of Portoghesi, Jencks and Stern.[69]

Since the early 1980s, the stylistic understanding, the formalist historicism and the transatlantic convergence of Italian and North American tendencies have constituted the defining characteristics of postmodernism as a distinct episode in architectural history. This familiar image was established by the Biennale. After this exhibition, what had originally been proposed as a post-hoc label for disparate architectural developments was turned into a single style. This also promoted the establishment of a dividing line between the modernists and the post-modernists. After the Biennale, the manifold non-historicist approaches to the crises of meaning and participation in modernism were no longer considered to form part of the postmodern discussion.[70] The approaches eventually omitted from the Strada Novissima, such as those of Van Eyck and Erskine, were also registered as absences in the subsequent discussions of postmodern architecture. The same was the case for other architects who had been discussed in the meetings, but were not eventually included in the show, such as Luis Barragán, Oriol Bohigas, Mario Botta, Gino Valle, Reima Pietilä and Carlo Scarpa. But all these approaches had historically stemmed from the same problems. As alternative replies to the same questions, they all formed part of the same architectural debate. To cite just one related example, although Van Eyck famously repudiated the Venetian postmodernists, Jencks's key theoretical resort to 'multivalence' also derived from Van Eyck's earlier explorations of 'multi-meaning'.[71] As a result, adopting the Biennale perspective on postmodern architecture means reducing the scope of the historical understanding of a diverse period. Abolishing the artificial boundaries established by these prevailing discourses is the task of architectural historians today. The spectrum of postmodern architecture needs to be opened up again by the complementary discourses that developed around it in the same period, but were eclipsed by the success of this influential exhibition. In this book, I read Frampton's project of critical regionalism as an attempt to resist and provincialise the Biennale approach by reappraising the work of several of these absences from the show floor. But this specific context of postmodernism, as I also argue, obfuscated the main message of critical regionalism and further complicated its implications for architectural historiography.

Some architectural historians had already taken a few steps in this direction at the time. Dating from 1984, Heinrich Klotz's clarification that the '[u]se of the historical vocabulary is not the primary criterion of this new architecture, which we call postmodern' is rather telling.

Moving beyond historicism, his definition opted to foreground fiction and the poetic imagination as the decisive features of postmodern architecture.[72] Yet, the historiographical legacy of the exhibition lingers unquestioned in Klotz's history, as the assimilation of Italian Rationalism and other Western European trends in the history of North American postmodern architecture are still presented as undeniable historical facts. Kruft also kept his distance from the Biennale curators' attempt to 'make the alliance between Post-Modernism and Rationalism a fact, heedless of what is actually built'.[73] His emphasis on the historical facts below the curatorial surface points towards opening up the static understanding of postmodern architecture after the Biennale. This is the historiographical baton that this book picks up. Focusing on critical regionalism, it also attempts to reconsider the settled understanding of postmodern architecture on the historical grounds that enabled the proliferation of discourses around it.

Provincialising postmodern architecture

Frampton, who disagreed with the selection process and wanted to retain his critical agenda, stepped down from the Biennale in April 1980 – approximately four months before the exhibition opening. Demonstrating his personal investment in the project, Stern immediately contacted him to share that he felt 'a bit hurt personally and a bit concerned by [the] innuendo-like tone' of Frampton's resignation letter. In the US architect's view, the crucial difference was between his advocation of 'architecture as an aesthetic task incorporated but not limited to ideology' and Frampton's modernist understanding of architecture as 'some simplistic acting out of a priori ideological beliefs'.[74] Stern did not share Frampton's view that this emphasis on style was a 'populist' and superficial approach of architecture as an exclusively visual symbolic phenomenon. For Stern, this formed part of an attempt to regain architecture's lost ground in expressive capacity, including its ability to communicate with its users and resonate with wider aspects of their cultural formation – even when it did so in playful and ironic ways.

Hence, before the end of 1980, a rupture between Frampton's and Stern's views had also been established. Frampton's critique of the ultimately scenographic architectural approach of the Biennale was published simultaneously with Stern's scathing review of Frampton's critical history of modern architecture.[75] In his critical essay, Frampton noted that in the Biennale the past was 'only *re-presented* as simulation' with 'an indifference to backstage reality'. The emphasis on the visual side of building dissociated it from the non-visual senses and tactile dimensions that anchor works of architecture to the fully corporeal experience of human reality.[76] This critique was 'very understandable' for Norberg-Schulz, who also contacted Frampton to share his concerns about 'the choice of the material for the exhibition'.[77]

Since Stern and Frampton were both teaching at Columbia University then, their heated exchanges continued to unfold in lecture theatres – and have stayed in the memory of those who attended them. As Anthony Alofsin, then a graduate student at Columbia University, recalled in a recent interview:

> It was an exciting moment as Frampton and Robert A. M. Stern were debating in public two fundamental points of view: Stern, the neo-traditionalist champion of post-modernism and Frampton, a proponent of the Frankfurt school. They were both on the same faculty yet opposed each other's world views. Many of us were swept up in the moment, because this is what a university and an architectural community are supposed to do: argue intelligently in a public forum.[78]

The educational impact of exhibitions such as the Biennale and the debates around it was immediately noted by graduate students at the time.[79] For Stern and Frampton, this was clearly a discussion about the future of architectural practice – and they both intended to steer it to their favoured direction, leaving their decisive footprint on a younger generation of architects. Through these public debates, the rupture that was established at the Biennale proved irreconcilable. The heated exchanges between the two colleagues held for decades, as indicated by a humorous student poster of the early 2000s found in Frampton's archive today.[80]

Alienated by the postmodern architecture propagated by the Biennale, Frampton went on to articulate a novel discourse based on his developing interest in architecture's relation to specific regions.[81] Although Frampton did not respond positively to Martin Steinmann's invitation to write about regionalism for a special issue of *archithese* in September 1980,[82] this would become a main preoccupation of his writing immediately after the show. Focusing on regional difference, Frampton's discourse challenged the transatlantic pretensions, the antimodern tone and the superficial historicism promoted by the Biennale. Looking at 'provincial' architectural cultures, he attempted to redirect the architectural public's attention to his favoured responses to the crisis of modern architecture. As Frampton's 'provincial' cultures would be brought into the spotlight, the main message of the Biennale would in turn be provincialised.

This was further reinforced by 'provincial' architects' own negative response to the exhibition, such as that of Suzana and Dimitris Antonakakis. As the vernacular architecture of the Venetian provinces became a more significant experience than the postmodern façades of the Strada Novissima for the two Greek architects, this 'provincial' European couple effectively 'provincialised' what was presented as the 'central' direction of Western architectural practice. 'The Presence of the Past' reinforced the two Greek architects' self-understanding as practitioners whose critical approach to modernism did not degenerate into historical eclecticism. Through their work, they remained committed to their long-standing architectural outlook towards a regional response to the legitimate critiques of modernism that was eventually noted and celebrated by Frampton later in the 1980s. But as was already implied by Steinmann's letter to Frampton of September 1980, this regionalist approach to modern architecture was already developing in other contexts by the late 1970s. Frampton was aware of this, as he was also connected with the Western European and North American theorists that were involved in it – as I discuss in the next chapter.

Notes

1   Stephen Parnell, 'Architecture's Expanding Field: *AD* Magazine and the Post-Modernisation of Architecture', *Architectural Research Quarterly*, 22.1 (2018), 55–68 (p. 61).
2   See Léa-Catherine Szacka, *Exhibiting the Postmodern: The 1980 Venice Architecture Biennale* (Venice: Marsilio, 2016).
3   Among others, see Eva Branscome, *Hans Hollein and Postmodernism: Art and Architecture in Austria, 1958–1985* (London: Routledge, 2018).
4   Margera, Archivio Storico delle Arti Contemporanee (ASAC), Fondo storico La Biennale di Venezia, Architettura, busta n. 787/9.
5   Dimitris Antonakakis, 'Μεταμοντέρνα αρχιτεκτονική: Παρεμβάσεις', *Journal of the Association of Greek Architects*, 8 (September–October 1981), 82–3.
6   See the *Journal of the Association of Greek Architects*, 8 (September–October 1981), 69–83. I return to the modern/postmodern debate in Greece in chapter 10.
7   Aldo van Eyck, cited in Alison Smithson, 'Aldo van Eyck at Bridgwater CIAM 6, 1948', *Architectural Design*, 30.5 (1960), 178.
8   Suzana and Dimitris Antonakakis worked with Kostis Gartzos until 1962. In the early 1960s, they also collaborated with a group of friends and fellow architects (Gabriel Aidonopoulos, Eleni Desylla, Denys Potiris, Antonis Tritsis and Efi Tsarmakli-Vrontisi) in Greek architectural competitions. These architects became the first members of the collaborative practice Atelier 66 in 1965. I return to the inner life of this collaborative practice and its evolution over time in chapter 7.
9   I return to Speyer's formative influence on the two Antonakakis in chapter 8.

10 Suzana and Dimitris Antonakakis, interviewed by Stylianos Giamarelos (Athens: 23 June 2013).

11 Antonakakis, interviewed by Giamarelos.

12 Antonakakis, interviewed by Giamarelos.

13 See chapter 8.

14 See Ernesto Rogers, 'Continuità o Crisi?', *Casabella Continuità*, 215 (1957), 3–4.

15 Robert Stern, 'Post-Modern Architecture' (1975), repr. in *Architecture on the Edge of Postmodernism: Collected Essays, 1964–1988*, ed. by Robert Stern and Cynthia Davidson (New Haven, CT: Yale University Press, 2009), pp. 33–7.

16 See Jane Jacobs, *The Death and Life of Great American Cities* (New York: Random House, 1961).

17 Charles Jencks, 'The Rise of Post Modern Architecture', *Architectural Association Quarterly*, 7 (1975), 3–14 (p. 3). The other six 'counter-movements' were 'Ersatz cities', improvised 'adhocism', advocacy planning, 'radical eclecticism', 'radical traditionalism' and 'political reorganisation'.

18 See Charles Jencks, 'Isozaki and Radical Eclecticism', *Architectural Design*, 47.1 (1977), 42–9; Andrew P. Steen, 'Radical Eclecticism and Post-Modern Architecture', *Fabrications*, 25.1 (2015), 130–45.

19 Charles Jencks, *The Language of Post-Modern Architecture* (London: Academy, 1977), p. 96.

20 Ibid., pp. 87–101; Nikolaus Pevsner, *Pioneers of the Modern Movement from William Morris to Walter Gropius* (London: Faber, 1936).

21 Charles Jencks, *The Language of Post-Modern Architecture*, 2nd edn (London: Academy, 1978), pp. 80–126.

22 Ibid., pp. 128, 132.

23 Sigfried Giedion, *Space, Time and Architecture: The Growth of a New Tradition* (Cambridge, MA: Harvard University Press, 1941).

24 See *Perspecta*, 9/10 (1965).

25 See Robert A.M. Stern, *New Directions in American Architecture* (London: Studio Vista, 1969).

26 Robert Stern, 'Post-Modern Architecture' (1975), repr. in *Architecture on the Edge of Postmodernism: Collected Essays, 1964–1988*, ed. by Robert Stern and Cynthia Davidson (New Haven, CT: Yale University Press, 2009), p. 33.

27 Robert Stern, 'The Doubles of Post-Modern' (1980), repr. in ibid., pp. 128–46 (pp. 136–40).

28 Ibid., pp. 138, 144.

29 See Christian Norberg-Schulz, *Intentions in Architecture* (London: Allen and Unwin, 1963); Christian Norberg-Schulz, *Meaning in Western Architecture* (London: Studio Vista, 1975); Charles Jencks, *Modern Movements in Architecture* (Harmondsworth: Penguin, 1973), pp. 319–20; Kenneth Frampton, Norberg-Schulz's intentions in architecture – notes, 8 handwritten pages, CCA Fonds 197, Kenneth Frampton fonds, 197 – 2017 – 086T, AP197.S1.SS9.001, Norberg-Schulz's intentions in architecture – notes, circa 1975–1990, 197-086-073.

30 Charles Jencks, *The Language of Post-Modern Architecture*, 2nd edn (London: Academy, 1978), pp. 9–10.

31 Christian Norberg-Schulz, 'Towards an Authentic Architecture', in *The Presence of the Past: First International Exhibition of Architecture – Venice Biennale 80*, ed. by Paolo Portoghesi (London: Academy, 1980), pp. 21–9 (p. 29).

32 Christian Norberg-Schulz, *Genius Loci: Towards a Phenomenology of Architecture* (London: Academy, 1980).

33 Hannah Arendt, *The Human Condition* (Chicago: University of Chicago Press, 1958).

34 Kenneth Frampton, 'Labour, Work and Architecture', in *Meaning in Architecture*, ed. by Charles Jencks and George Baird (London: Barrie & Jenkins, 1969), pp. 150–68.

35 Kenneth Frampton, 'Team 10, Plus 20: The Vicissitudes of Ideology', *L'Architecture d'Aujourd'hui*, 177 (1975), 62–5 (p. 65).

36 See Marina Lathouri, 'Reconstructing the Topographies of the Modern City: The Late CIAM Debates', unpublished doctoral thesis, University of Pennsylvania, 2006.

37 Kenneth Frampton, *Modern Architecture: A Critical History* (London: Thames & Hudson, 1980), pp. 288–90.

38 See *Architecture on Display: On the History of the Venice Biennale of Architecture*, ed. by Aaron Levy and William Menking (London: Architectural Association, 2010), p. 38.

39 See Paolo Portoghesi, *Borromini: Architettura come linguaggio* (Milan: Electa, 1967).

40 Vincent Scully, *The Shingle Style: Architectural Theory and Design from Richardson to the Origins of Wright* (New Haven, CT: Yale University Press, 1955).

41 Vincent Scully, 'Introduction', in Robert Venturi, *Complexity and Contradiction in Architecture* (New York: Museum of Modern Art, 1966), pp. 9–11 (p. 9).

42 Vincent Scully, *The Shingle Style Today: Or, The Historian's Revenge* (New York: Braziller, 1974).

43 See 'I. Riunione della Commissione del Settore Architettura – Venezia, 14/15 settembre', 10-page typescript, 1979, ASAC, Fondo storico La Biennale di Venezia, Architettura, busta n. 658, pp. 4, 2.

44 Daralice Donkervoet, 'An Interview with Robert Stern', *Crit.: The Architectural Student Journal*, 11 (Spring 1981), 19–21 (p. 19).

45 See *Modern Architecture: International Exhibition*, ed. by Philip Johnson (New York: Museum of Modern Art, 1932).

46 See Philip Johnson, 'You Cannot not Know History', Robert A.M. Stern Architects Records (MS 1859), Manuscripts and Archives, Yale University Library, New Haven, CT Box 1, file 13.

47 See Antonio de Bonis, 'Paolo Portoghesi and Aldo Rossi', *Architectural Design*, 52.1/2 (1982), 13–17 (pp. 13–14).

48 See *Architecture on Display* ed. by Levy and Menking.

49 Paolo Portoghesi, 'The End of Prohibitionism', in *The Presence of the Past: First International Exhibition of Architecture – Venice Biennale 80*, ed. by Paolo Portoghesi (London: Academy, 1980), pp. 9–14 (p. 12).

50 See Robert Stern, 'Gray Architecture as Postmodernism, or, Up and Down from Orthodoxy' (1976), repr. in *Architecture on the Edge of Postmodernism*, ed. by Stern and Davidson, pp. 38–42 (p. 42).

51 Donkervoet, 'An Interview with Robert Stern', p. 20 (emphasis in the original).

52 These would be represented by Frank Gehry, Michael Graves, Allan Greenberg, Charles Moore, Robert Stern, Stanley Tigerman, and Venturi/Scott-Brown & Rauch.

53 The new entries were Arata Isozaki, Thomas Gordon Smith, Josef Paul Kleihues and Rem Koolhaas (OMA).

54 See 'II. Riunione della Commissione del Settore Architettura – Venezia, 23/24 novembre', 8-page typescript, 1979, ASAC, Fondo storico La Biennale di Venezia, Architettura, busta n. 630, p. 3. Chapter 3 shows that this proposal was meant to address Frampton's objections.

55 Donkervoet, 'An Interview with Robert Stern', p. 20.

56 The exhibition was characteristically covered in architectural journals, such as *Controspazio*, 1.6 (1980); *Architectural Review*, 168.1003 (1980) and *Architectural Record*, 169.4 (1981). But it also featured in daily newspapers and popular press, such as *The Times*, 3 June 1980; *L'Europeo*, 22 July 1980; *La Repubblica*, 30 July 1980; *La Stampa*, 31 July 1980; *Il Tempo*, 1 August 1980; *Wall Street Journal*, 8 August 1980; *L'Espresso*, 17 August 1980; *El Pais*, 20 September 1980; *Herald Tribune*, 4–5 October 1980; *Le Monde*, 9 October 1980; and *Matin de Paris*, 1 November 1980, among others.

57 Charles Jencks, *The Language of Post-Modern Architecture*, 4th edn (New York: Rizzoli, 1984), p. 6.

58 Charles Jencks, 'Counter-Reformation: Reflections on the 1980 Venice Biennale', *Architectural Design*, 52.1/2 (1982), 4–7 (p. 5).

59 Charles Jencks, *The Language of Post-Modern Architecture*, 3rd edn (London: Academy, 1981), p. 5 (emphasis in the original).

60 Vincent Scully, 'The Star in Stern: Sightings and Orientation', in Robert Stern and Vincent Scully, *Robert Stern* (London: Academy, 1981), pp. 8–19 (p. 19).

61 Charles Jencks, *Current Architecture* (London: Academy, 1982), pp. 12–13.

62 Jencks, *The Language of Post-Modern Architecture*, 4th edn (New York: Rizzoli, 1984), pp. 147–54.

63 Charles Jencks, 'Post-Modern Classicism – The Synthesis: An Interview with Charles Jencks', *Architectural Design*, 54.3/4 (1984), 61–3 (pp. 62–3).

64 William J.R. Curtis, *Modern Architecture since 1900* (Oxford: Phaidon, 1982), p. 380.

65 Hanno-Walter Kruft, *A History of Architectural Theory from Vitruvius to the Present*, trans. by Ronald Taylor, Elsie Callander and Antony Wood (New York: Princeton Architectural Press, 1994), p. 443.

66 Ole W. Fischer, 'Architecture, Capitalism and Criticality', in *The SAGE Handbook of Architectural Theory*, ed. by C. Craig Crysler, Stephen Cairns and Hilde Heynen (Los Angeles: SAGE, 2012), pp. 56–69 (p. 63).

67 Manfredo Tafuri, *History of Italian Architecture, 1944–1985*, trans. by Jessica Levine (Cambridge, MA: MIT Press, 1989), p. 189.

68 Kenneth Frampton, *Modern Architecture: A Critical History*, 2nd edn (London: Thames & Hudson, 1985), p. 308.
69 Kenneth Frampton, *A Genealogy of Modern Architecture: A Comparative Critical Analysis of Built Form* (Zurich: Lars Müller, 2015), pp. 9, 17.
70 See Vittorio Gregotti, 'Open Letter to Léon Krier', *Architectural Design*, 52.1/2 (1982), 24.
71 See Aldo van Eyck, 'R.P.P. (Rats, Posts and Other Pests)', *Architectural Design News Supplement*, 51.7 (1981), 15–16; Francis Strauven, *Aldo van Eyck: The Shape of Relativity* (Amsterdam: Architectura & Natura, 1998), p. 473.
72 Heinrich Klotz, *The History of Postmodern Architecture*, trans. by Radka Donnell (Cambridge, MA: MIT Press, 1988), pp. 420–1.
73 Kruft, *A History of Architectural Theory from Vitruvius to the Present*, pp. 445–6.
74 Robert Stern, letter to Kenneth Frampton, 21 May 1980, CCA Fonds 197, Kenneth Frampton fonds, 197 – 2017 – 114T, AP197.S3.001, Personal and professional correspondence 1980, 1980, 197-114-022.
75 See Robert Stern, 'Giedion's Ghost: A Review of Frampton's *Modern Architecture: A Critical History*', *Skyline* (October 1981), 22–5; Kenneth Frampton, 'The Need for Roots: Venice 1980', *GA Forum*, 3 (1981), 13–21.
76 Frampton, 'The Need for Roots: Venice 1980', p. 16 (emphasis in the original).
77 Christian-Norberg Schulz, letter to Kenneth Frampton, 21 May 1980, CCA Fonds 197, Kenneth Frampton fonds, 197 – 2017 – 114T, AP197.S3.001, Personal and professional correspondence 1980, 1980, 197-114-022.
78 Anthony Alofsin, interviewed by Stylianos Giamarelos (Austin, TX: 8 April 2019), edited draft: 3 December 2019, pp. 12–13.
79 Maria Tracy, 'Exhibitions and the Public: Venice Biennale', *Crit.: The Architectural Student Journal*, 11 (Spring 1981), 17–19 (p. 19).
80 See 'GSAPP! Smackdown: Bodies of Theory, Bodies of Work, Bodies of Pure Power' poster, CCA Fonds 197, Kenneth Frampton fonds, 197 – 2017 – 116T, GSAPP ephemera, circa 2000, 197-116-007.
81 See Kenneth Frampton, 'Mario Botta and the School of the Ticino', *Oppositions*, 14 (Fall 1978), 1–25.
82 Martin Steinmann, letter to Kenneth Frampton, 10 September 1980, CCA Fonds 197, Kenneth Frampton fonds, 197 – 2017 – 114T, AP197.S3.001, Personal and professional correspondence 1980, 1980, 197-114-022.

2
Polyglot histories

Kenneth Frampton was not alone in his critique of Robert Stern's approach to postmodern architecture, and in his belief in the constructive potential of regionalism. It was, in fact, from a seminal 1981 article on the architecture of Suzana and Dimitris Antonakakis by Alexander Tzonis and Liane Lefaivre that Frampton recapitulated 'critical regionalism' in late 1982 and further developed his own ideas around it in 1983.[1] While the British historian repeatedly acknowledged that he had 'borrowed' Tzonis and Lefaivre's original term,[2] it was his version of the critical regionalist discourse that historically prevailed. To date, Frampton's most popular article on critical regionalism from 1983 has been cited 4.5 times more often than Tzonis and Lefaivre's most cited book on the same subject from 2003.[3] The positive reception of Frampton's discourse has created the impression that the history of critical regionalism starts in 1983. Approximately four decades later, in 2019, phrases such as 'Kenneth Frampton coined the phrase Critical Regionalism' still appear on the pages of informed magazines such as the *Architectural Review*.[4] Critical or vindicatory anniversary reappraisals of critical regionalism – appearing, for example, in 2013[5] – tend to follow the same chronology, as if critical regionalism was indeed only defined by Frampton in 1983. As a result, a wider range of developing discourses on regionalism in architecture in the late 1970s have also been historically overshadowed. Several factors, including language barriers and the relative structural position of each author in the Western European and North American hierarchies of architectural-theory production, have historically contributed to this. As such, the potential of these earlier, multiple cross-cultural roots of critical regionalism has also remained historically untapped. But even if one was only interested in delving deeper into Frampton's version of critical regionalism, they would still need to revisit this history. The British historian's long-standing ties with these earlier authors of critical regionalism certainly influenced and enriched his own thoughts on the subject. This is the first in a series of chapters that revisit the early history of critical regionalism to reconstruct a fuller picture of this discourse as an artefact of cross-cultural authorship. Forty years later, the multiple and interconnected roots and branches of regionalist thinking in the second half of the twentieth century seem to regain their relevance.

Focusing on the ties between the well-known protagonists prior to the publication of their most influential essays, this chapter explores this earlier but currently overlooked history that links the critical regionalist discourse with architectural sensibilities of the 1960s. From the late 1960s, Frampton had established collegial ties with Tzonis, a Greek scholar who was also teaching in North American Ivy League institutions at the time, which remained strong well into the 1980s. Tzonis and Lefaivre wrote their first article on 'critical regionalism' in 1980, having just finished working on a paper on 'The Question of Regionalism' in response to an invitation by the Swiss sociologist and economist Lucius Burckhardt, whose wide-ranging research touched on architecture, urban planning and landscape design.[6] But because this first article on 'The Question of Regionalism' was published in German, in a publication that mainly featured the work of relatively less well-known German architects, it has not yet found its proper place in the history of critical regionalism.[7] As a result, its third contributing author – Anthony Alofsin, then a graduate student of Tzonis at Harvard University – has also been historiographically overshadowed. This chapter retraces Alofsin's contribution to this article, highlighting his interest in the work of Lewis Mumford and the possibility for a distinctly North American variant of modern architecture.

Shared political outlook

Tzonis and Frampton first met in the USA in the late 1960s. Their close and friendly rapport, evident in their correspondence between 1969 and 1989, was not only owing to their shared experience as expatriate Europeans appointed at US Ivy League institutions. Sharing similar political beliefs, both men seemed eager to apply them in their architectural teaching and research. Frampton arrived as a fellow at Princeton University to pursue his study of the Maison de Verre in 1965, and was eventually appointed to teach there from 1966 to 1971.[8] From 1965 to 1968, Tzonis was appointed as a fellow at Yale University, collaborating with Serge Chermayeff in researching design and planning methodologies.[9] In 1968, he was appointed to teach at Harvard University. By the end of that year, the two men had already met through the established networks of Ivy League institutions.[10] Throughout their decades-long correspondence, their collegiate friendship was reinforced. In addition to following each other's work and research interests, the two men shared concerns, professional aspirations, career opportunities and more personal confessions on their hardships and plans for the future.[11] From the outset, Tzonis and Frampton discussed their work, liaised with each other's professional and editorial networks and explored the possibility of working together on subjects of shared interest, such as a journal issue on the architecture of protest, activism and the ecological movement. Their correspondence reflects Frampton's consistent trust in the work of Tzonis and Lefaivre in the 1970s. When the British historian returned to London with a three-year sabbatical in 1974, he asked whether the couple could assist in teaching his 'Comparative Critical Analysis' course at Columbia University, in his absence, in 1975–6.[12]

Regarding Tzonis as an important member of 'the left-wing critical intelligentsia of the moment',[13] Frampton frequently found his colleague's ideas stimulating for the development of his own thoughts. In his draft typescript for a conference that explored alternatives in US architectural education in 1971, Frampton noted in handwriting on the margins: 'Alex Tzonis: "Socialism means confrontation i.e. bringing the conflict in the society at a conscious level … [C]onformism means burying this conflict"'.[14] A decade later, when he was asked what he means by the word 'critical', Frampton essentially repeated Tzonis's words: 'by critical I mean self-conscious, and self-conscious to a degree that one recognises one lives in a society of contradictions, and that these contradictions permeate architecture'.[15] Frampton's sympathy for his colleague's political analyses of architecture is also evident in his decision to reject Thomas L. Schumacher's (1941–2009) ambivalent review of Tzonis's book *Towards a Non-Oppressive Environment* for publication in *Oppositions* in 1973.[16] Like Tzonis, Frampton believed that the predicament of architectural production in the late twentieth century had deep social roots. As such, it could not be resolved by quick techno-scientific fixes, and Schumacher's irreverence to theory was off the mark.

But it was Tzonis and Lefaivre's first co-authored article 'The Populist Movement in Architecture' that proved more significant for Frampton, as the British historian consistently used the term 'populism' and similar arguments to dismiss Venturi's and Jencks's approach to postmodern architecture in the early 1980s.[17] Resting on the ideals of 'order' and 'expertise', Tzonis and Lefaivre argued in their article, the postwar welfare state's experts scientifically defined the minimum standards that satisfied objectively defined human needs from a living environment. The architect's job was then to ensure that these objectively defined properties were integrated into their design of buildings and public spaces. The bureaucratic mechanism of the welfare state in turn ensured that living environments adhered to these principles, and guaranteed their equal distribution across the general population. Developing as a critique to this approach, the populist movement of the 1960s instead promoted 'freedom' and 'pluralism', which could be implemented through the inclusion of 'conflict and arbitration within the design process'.[18] 'Populist' projects aimed at transforming the institutional role of the designer as the expert who imposes the universal norms of the welfare state to populations with diverse backgrounds, needs and preferences. But by equating liberation with users' equitable right to self-expression, this movement failed to also address their dependence on existing hierarchical structures of supply chains and ownership of the means of production in the rising private-market economy of the period. Even in the most successful examples of grassroots, bottom-up DIY and self-build initiatives, the user was only free as a consumer, but not as a producer, of their own living environment. Challenging the successful welfare-state model of the 1950s without addressing the structural changes beneath the surface of architectural production in the late 1960s, the populist movement 'also limited the prospects in our society for architectural policies beneficial for the general interest, offering nothing in their place but freedom in a design supermarket and an increasingly fragmented and privatised world'.[19]

Joint writing project

By the time Tzonis and Lefaivre wrote their more widely discussed articles on critical regionalism in the 1980s, the couple had crystallised their joint writing style. Their approach was distinguished by its balanced mix of history and conceptual analysis with manifesto-like conclusions. It combined Tzonis's earlier 'systematic analysis' with Lefaivre's informed 'study of historical development'.[20] While each author's individual contribution to these texts is difficult to pin down, Lefaivre's input is certainly reflected in their refined arguments and their increased attention to conceptual subtleties, etymologies and semantics. This in turn rested on her individual background, as Lefaivre's view of architecture was also informed by her formative studies in psychology at

McGill University. As such, it was also inspired by the wider field of the humanities, including literature. The couple's most celebrated texts of the period were indeed those that combined the relative strengths of each author to advance distinctly innovative and nuanced accounts of architectural culture. In these texts, historical inquiry was accompanied by an exploration of crucial shifts in the underlying conceptual system of seemingly contingent theoretical developments, reflecting the two authors' different areas of expertise. Their ongoing conversations 'about architectural history, creativity, theory, cognition, cognitive history, and criticism, and many other things besides' constituted a two-way street.[21] While Tzonis encouraged Lefaivre to focus on architectural history, she mediated his transition from systems thinking and sociology to history and the humanities. Through his collaboration with Lefaivre, Tzonis's work was gradually re-Europeanised – adopting not only the 'French' approach to history but also new, wide-ranging references to cultural anthropologists, sociologists, economists and historians.[22] Lastly, the shift in tone from Tzonis's earlier, manifesto-like writing to a stronger emphasis on analysis and criticality[23] reflects Lefaivre's further contribution to their joint writing project. Tzonis's resulting wide-ranging purview was appreciated by students, such as Anthony Alofsin, who attended his courses in the late 1970s – and who still recall their mentor's lectures forty years later:

> I was most impressed with his concept of legitimisation, of architectural phenomena as a legitimising force for power and control ... Tzonis was really the first theoretician at the GSD [Graduate School of Design] ... among the best lecturers in all of Harvard University ... Tzonis had a broad grasp of theory because he was an intellectual with an open mind ... It's sad that Harvard didn't keep him ... the kind of critique that Tzonis represented [was] like looking from the outside in, and architects being stuck in the interior.[24]

Tzonis and Lefaivre started exploring the subject of regionalism in response to an invitation by Lucius Burckhardt, then professor of the socio-economics of urban systems at the Gesamthochschule Kassel and president of the German Werkbund. Burckhardt stood out in the German-speaking parts of the world for his 'outstanding contribution to shaping public opinion on architecture in Germany in the 1970s and 80s, with quite singular impact'.[25] As an active, civically minded public intellectual, he had a career-long interest in social research. His informed view of this bigger picture enabled his work to move freely between different design scales, from the forces and processes involved in producing industrial and architectural objects to urban and regional planning, landscape and environmental studies. This emphasis on the big picture is what must have attracted Burckhardt to the work of Tzonis and Lefaivre. He appreciated their essay on the populist movement so much that he included it in his list of studies that shaped his Werkbund 'criteria for a new design' of 1977.[26] These addressed design as a social process rather than a set of abstract principles removed from the cycle of production and consumption of concrete objects. Burckhardt's ensuing questions to designers involved the ethical sourcing and manufacturing of raw materials, labour and working conditions, the expected lifecycles of design products and their possible dependence on central supply systems. In addressing such questions, Burckhardt belonged to the lineage of the politically charged writings of the German landscape designer and author of 'the green manifesto' of 1919, Leberecht Migge (1881–1935).[27] He was especially interested in Migge's view that gardening is not about nature but work; 'it is a form of agriculture, but without the edible yield'.[28] As one of the early proponents of ecological and sustainable design, Burckhardt positioned design within the wider framework of the welfare state and market economies. For this reason, he was especially interested in Tzonis and Lefaivre's distinction between 'welfare state' and 'participatory' design practices in the populist movement. His work highlighted similar ways in which values, needs and planning decisions shifted, as they depended on malleable power structures and hierarchies of private and public ownership.

Burckhardt invited Tzonis and Lefaivre to explore the concept of regionalism after an event on the crisis of modern architecture and the legacy of the Werkbund at Harvard University in April 1980.[29] He was then in touch with young architects in German-speaking countries who were interested to work with the specific resources, potential and capacities of their regions. They envisioned a promising alternative, participatory, sustainable and ecological way of building in response to the crisis of modern architecture. Entitled 'Dirt', Burckhardt's lecture at the event summarised his critique of modern urban planning, his similar plea for engaging with the reality of design problems in people's everyday lives and its connection with the question of regionalism:

> A sensible road width is one that can be divided by the number of traffic lanes; any remainder, a half-lane, would not make sense. Admittedly, a half-lane would make cyclists' lives a lot easier. But

cyclists are dirt as far as traffic engineers are concerned: a remainder that somehow refuses to disappear … So we actually never learn how to solve problems in a way that leaves a remainder, which is to say, we never learn how to deal with reality. And that is why the world is full of remainders, of odd ends of lots and the like … Even an individual project planned without a remainder will give rise to a remainder when realized alongside another, likewise perfectly planned project. To plan for reality therefore means to plan projects that cater to the existence of such remainders, and that anticipate human behavior. With a stroke of luck, this type of planning might then also reap the beauty once inherent to the older towns and villages in our traditional cultural landscape.[30]

Constructive regionalism

Tzonis and Lefaivre did not write their first article on regionalism alone. They were joined by Alofsin, who was then following Tzonis's courses as a mature graduate student at Harvard University. Like Burckhardt before him, Alofsin is not frequently mentioned in discussions of critical regionalism. Notably, his students of the mid-1990s at the University of Texas at Austin who were interested in it were 'pleasantly surprised to "discover" [Alofsin's] association with this subject'.[31] Today, Alofsin is mainly known for his rigorous scholarship on Frank Lloyd Wright.[32] But as he claimed in 2005, his 'phrase and concept of Constructive Regionalism', an eight-page typescript of May 1980 that Alofsin delivered to Tzonis and Lefaivre when they were working together on 'The Question of Regionalism', was 'the precursor to [the] term "critical regionalism"'.[33] Although the term 'critical regionalism' was not used throughout this first text of the three authors on this subject, its main theoretical contours were already visible. But the story behind its authorship breaks out into several more different roots and branches.

Alofsin was first introduced to Tzonis as an undergraduate student of Visual and Environmental Studies at Harvard College in the late 1960s.[34] But it was his meeting with John Brinckerhoff Jackson (1909–96), one of the founding scholars of US cultural landscape studies in the mid-twentieth century, that proved more significant for him at that time.[35] After his graduation in 1971, Alofsin worked as a sculptor and restorer of antique eighteenth- and nineteenth-century artefacts in New Mexico, where Jackson was also based, and their casual everyday exchanges stayed with him. In 1977, he also worked for the architectural

Figure 2.1 Top: San Miguel Church, Socorro; bottom: the Capitol Bar of the mining-boom era of the 1870–80s, Socorro

firm of Conron and Lent in Santa Fe, surveying the historic buildings of Socorro, a nineteenth-century town of the mining boom in New Mexico.[36] This served as a formative experience for Alofsin's thinking on regional architecture in the USA. In Socorro, he witnessed the adobe architectures and settlements of 'the earliest Indian Pueblo and Spanish times', but also 'the Anglo influence of the Territorial period' and 'the wild exuberance of the mining boom years to the present' (Fig. 2.1). This made him realise that 'a real multidimensional culture existed here, visible in architecture and unique in America'.[37] In the late 1970s, Alofsin concluded that Socorro's buildings represented centuries-long stylistic adaptations that stimulated his interest in the historic processes that lay beneath them.[38] Still, the lessons from this cross-cultural regional architecture of the past for the present were decidedly modern. The study of Socorro's architecture was intended to 'inspire new vitality and new harmonious construction while not imitating the past'.[39] Alofsin's later move to the San Francisco Bay Area further enriched his first-hand encounter with regional architectures in the USA (Fig. 2.2) that had also attracted the attention of Lewis Mumfrod in the 1940s:

> The Bay Area provided an urban counterpart to New Mexico with its exuberant Victorian houses and beautiful work by Bernard Maybeck as well as some superb Beaux Arts designs by John Galen Howard. In these two locales—the Bay Area and Northern New Mexico—you could experience the diverse expressions of regional architecture that had evolved by accretion over time, spoke to the life [of] its people, and sustained them—all without the stylistic dictates of modern functionalism.[40]

Alofsin returned to Harvard University as a student at the Graduate School of Design in 1978. Based on his experience from his travels across the country, and his work on documenting historic structures, he 'was primed to think about identity and what had been and might be an American architecture that said something about who we are as a nation. Thinking about national identity was, for that moment, a sign of optimism'.[41] Taking Tzonis's courses in 1979 familiarised him with critical theory.[42] Alofsin's notes from these lectures highlight Tzonis's view of the crisis of modern architecture, as the course's structure followed that of his book *Towards a Non-Oppressive Environment* (1972). Surveying design methods from the 'pre-rational' societies of antiquity to the 'rational' societies of modernity, in his book Tzonis argued that oppression cannot be eradicated by technology because it remains embedded in the social norms and practices of hierarchical power structures. Sociology does not help either as it creates another sphere of rationality, prone to developing abstractions that hover above the real social issues on the ground. As such, the route towards non-oppressive environments passes through social change via a designer's direct, active (rather than theoretical) engagement with society in cultivating emancipated social relations.[43] Since social change should go hand in hand with any proposed change in the language of architecture, neither the top-down, techno-scientific approach nor the project of postmodern architects of the late 1970s could achieve the aims that they set for themselves. Such insights stayed with

Figure 2.2 Bernard Maybeck, Chick House, Oakland, California: exterior general view and patio, photographed by Roy Flamm

Roy Flamm collection of California architectural photographs, BANC PIC 1978.059 Ser. 8:1—PIC and BANC PIC 1978.059, Ser. 8:9—PIC, © The Regents of the University of California, The Bancroft Library, University of California, Berkeley

Alofsin, who implemented them in his later text on 'Constructive Regionalism'.

Conversely, Alofsin left a strong impression on Tzonis who described him as 'a very hard working, imaginative, enthusiastic, and very well organized student' with an 'excellent' and 'unique' level of 'understanding of historical problems in architecture' and 'an intuition in searching in the right places'.[44] For these reasons, Tzonis asked his trusted student to assist with the Werkbund event in April 1980 and to join him and Lefaivre in writing the text that Burckhardt requested afterwards.

Within six weeks, Alofsin handed his part of the text to Tzonis, an eight-page typescript entitled 'Constructive Regionalism'. This text investigated the plural meanings of regionalism, inspired by contemporary debates on the multiple versions of modernism. Alofsin's rationale was simple: the regionalism that was discredited in the heroic interwar phase of the modern movement, mainly because it had been associated with the *Heimatstil* architecture of the Third Reich, could be revisited in the 1980s, when modernism had in turn been discredited and a way out of its crisis was sought elsewhere. Alofsin argued that a wider understanding of regionalism was necessary to promote 'general applications', as the twentieth century had witnessed different regional expressions, ranging from the folkish German architecture before the First World War to the English modernism of James Stirling and its Scandinavian and Californian variants. He found this wider understanding in the work of Mumford, who presented Henry Hobson Richardson (1838–86) as the 'first truly American regional architect'.[45] Mumford had noted how Richardson worked with the region not in a provincial, narrow-minded and inward-looking way but in pursuit of 'a universal expression of form in the context of a regional architecture … an open-ended search connected to urban landscape and locale and the traditions of architecture itself'.[46] This pursuit of a universal form rendered his work significant for three different traditions of North American architects – respectively exemplified in the work of Buffington, Sullivan and Root; Wright; and Howard and Maybeck. Still underappreciated at the time, Mumford's reading of the output of the San Francisco Bay architects as 'a modern, regional architecture that provide[s] a critique to the International Style' served as the basis for Alofsin's constructive regionalism.[47]

For Mumford, the variegated works of the Bay Area demonstrated that regional architecture is not a one-way street but an open space of interpretation that can accommodate diverse approaches by different architects (Fig. 2.3). This was an architecture that served the 'reconciliation of the universal and the regional, the mechanical and the human,

Figure 2.3 William W. Wurster, Green Residence: main entrance and exterior porch, photographed by Roger Sturtevant

William W. Wurster Collection, Environmental Design Archives, UC Berkeley

the cosmopolitan and the indigenous', without 'ignor[ing] particular needs, customs, conditions, but translat[ing] them into the common form of civilization'.[48] Following Mumford's interpretation, Alofsin's constructive regionalism also sought to 'respond to local colors, materials, and customs; … embrace traditions and transform them; … be wed to its setting, in either rural or urban landscape; … foster craft and push the limits of technology; … speak to the individual and search for the universal'.[49] Aiming for universal architectural expression would not necessarily turn constructive regionalism into a novel, homogeneous style because it would be based on different social relations between the architect and the community. Alofsin envisioned the architect-artist serving as a co-equal member of a community, not an artificially isolated member of an enlightened elite that shows the way forward to the rest of the population.[50]

The co-authored question of regionalism

For Tzonis and Lefaivre, 'The Question of Regionalism' could only serve as the next instalment in their own series of writings, following the narrative arc from 'the populist movement' of the 1960s to the reactionary 'narcissist phase' of the 1970s. As the oil crises of the 1970s meant reduced commissions and unemployment for architects and the welfare state seemed unable to respond to the ensuing restructuring of the global economy, Tzonis and Lefaivre argued, practitioners renounced the social role of architecture: developing their self-absorbed 'paper architecture' projects, they approached it as a design discipline with relative autonomy from social and economic issues. They studied this autonomous field of building types and their formal variations over time, irrespective of the historical and social formations that gave rise to them. Highlighting the negative aspects of this new phase in architecture, Tzonis and Lefaivre concluded with their plea for the architecture of the 1980s which 'desperately needs a new humanistic involvement and an explicit rational discourse; and above all, it needs a constructive attitude and an open dialogue'.[51] In a lecture in Delft in June 1979, Tzonis further elaborated:

> strengthening the capability of the profession to understand the context within which it operates is a priority of the next phase of modern architecture, the humanistic phase. Which means that, in addition to creating and implementing design, architecture must also generate knowledge about the instruments through which its interventions may be most effective, knowledge about the social impact of design, about the relation between *built form* and *social formations*.
>
> Such research will have to investigate projects in their totality, as mechanical constructions and as containers of activities, as

micro-environments and as complexes of signs, as controls of human relations which channel the flow of power, reinforce or weaken dependencies, dominations and reciprocities ... A basic feature of the new humanistic approach is the introduction of a historical point of view. Only through a study of their complex unfolding in time can the relations between built form and social formation be comprehended.[52]

As such, the concluding lines of Alofsin's typescript that referred to architecture's 'own autonomy and its own cultural life' were not welcome by Tzonis and Lefaivre, who still present this approach as their nemesis to this day. The reference to 'facades that are faces of architectural tradition and local life' also left room for a similarly undesirable interpretation of postmodern façadism, similar to the one promoted through the Strada Novissima in the Biennale.[53] This had already occurred on North American shores in the work of Charles Moore, a representative of the third generation of the regionalist architects of the Bay Region in the 1960s, that served as the cover image for the third edition of Jencks's *The Language of Post-Modern Architecture* in 1981 (Fig. 2.4). For these reasons, this part of Alofsin's manuscript was omitted from their co-authored 'Question of Regionalism'.

Alofsin's typescript summarised a late twentieth-century architect's reflection on principles for devising relevant architectural forms and practices for co-equal members of regional communities. Tzonis and Lefaivre worked on the text following their trademark approach to analysing questions of architecture and design. As a result, the co-authored 'Question of Regionalism' moved away from Alofsin's programmatic discussion of twentieth-century design principles to a historically grounded account of sociopolitical developments that accompanied each reappearance of regionalism across three centuries. Several of Tzonis and Lefaivre's original ideas and insightful associations were added to the text, ranging from the roots of Romantic regionalism in the Picturesque garden to twentieth-century reactions to the universal norms of modernist design.[54] While 'Mumford's Contribution' remained at the heart of the article, both the overall framing of Alofsin's main argument and the discussion of specific architects were radically modified by Tzonis and Lefaivre's major edits and additions.

The couple presented regionalism as an alternative response to the critiques of modernism through 'the conscious application of particular and local design principles as opposed to generally applicable and universal norms'.[55] The first two sections, on the English Picturesque

Figure 2.4 Top: Charles W. Moore, Donlyn Lyndon, William Turnbull and Richard Whitaker (MLTW), Sea Ranch Condominium #1, Sea Ranch, California, 1963–7; bottom: Charles W. Moore, Piazza d'Italia, New Orleans, Los Angeles, 1974–8

garden and nineteenth-century Romanticism, discussed regionalism in terms of colonialism, class difference, power structures, patriarchy and production.[56] This also contextualised Tzonis and Lefaivre's discussion of the impact of the welfare state in promoting universal principles. While its 'reformist' agenda enlisted industrial production in the service of 'collective human needs', it also led to the standardisation of buildings from their individual components to their overall architectural form.[57] Critics of the internationalist modern project who historically promoted the return of a variant of regionalism were not only driven by the conservative and fascist agendas of the Third Reich. There were also progressive critics of the modern project, such as Mumford, who felt that its development after the Second World War had misconstrued its original intentions. Siding again with private, instead of collective, interests and global capital then, modern architecture became synonymous with the 'empty forms' of the international style. 'For these latter reformist critics of modern architecture, regionalism, free of any nationalist or racist connotations, became a manifestation of an architecture that satisfied real—read regional—needs versus manufactured—read international— ones.'[58]

Building on Alofsin's account of Mumford in 'Constructive Regionalism', Tzonis and Lefaivre also looked further back at Mumford's writings of the 1920s. In so doing, they underscored the anti-imperialist and anti-despotic dimensions of his social vision that were not significantly addressed by Alofsin's focus on the regionalist debates of the 1940s. Revisiting these same texts for themselves, Tzonis and Lefaivre provided a more comprehensive presentation of Mumford's thinking and associated it with earlier historic phases of regionalist debates. Emphasising his earlier critique of the nineteenth-century North American aristocracy's 'imperial' Beaux-Arts façades that masked shabby architectural structures,[59] Tzonis and Lefaivre traced the way in which this idea of regional architecture reappeared twenty years later in Mumford's critique of 'semi-strong', 'quixotic', 'conceited dogmatic', 'sterile' and 'abstract' modern architecture.[60] But despite his best efforts to promote the regionalist architecture of the San Francisco Bay Region as adhering to the original aims of the modern movement, the equally 'imperial' façades of the international style continued to march across the USA.[61]

Ignoring Mumford's arguments had wider implications for North American architecture. The eventual 'diminution of the promise of regionalism' meant that the work of architects such as Aalto, Stirling and the Scandinavian New Empiricists of the 1950s could not be theoretically supported in the USA.[62] For this reason, Alofsin's proposed principles for 'constructive regionalism' could not be presented as the conclusion. Omitting them, Tzonis and Lefaivre ended 'The Question of Regionalism' with general directions that built on their earlier work on the 'populist' and 'narcissist' phases of architecture in the 1960s and the 1970s, which had ushered in the new 'imperial façades' of Postmodern architecture in the 1980s. While the promotion of pluralism appeared to favour the singular and the particular like regionalism always did, the universal norms of architecture had also resurfaced – from the Postmodern Classicism of the Biennale to Peter Eisenman's 'deep structures' and Aldo Rossi's 'rationalist' pursuits of architectural typologies. Unlike Mumford, Tzonis and Lefaivre lacked a Bay Region architecture to foreground as a positive example of their own historical moment. As such, they did not offer concrete architectural examples to illustrate this approach in practice. They just reiterated the need for:

> ... an architecture which develops from human needs and resists imposed norms ... but also opposes needs which only appear as real ... and makes us reflect on them and understand them better ... The task of regionalism—to quote Lewis Mumford once more—is to 'look behind the mask'. In this sense, regionalism remains an unfulfilled promise rather than a fact of the past.[63]

Mumford's significance

While Tzonis and Lefaivre developed a project of their own based on their previous work, without following Alofsin's points for a 'constructive regionalism', their subsequent emphasis on Mumford seems to have been triggered by Alofsin's typescript. Despite Tzonis's retrospective accounts of the 2000s,[64] in the early 1970s he referred to Mumford's ideas only in passing.[65] Before 'The Question of Regionalism', Tzonis and Lefaivre had not published anything else on Mumford – and Tzonis's course reading lists of the 1970s do not include references to his work.[66] In their writings on Mumford in the 1990s, the couple acknowledged Alofsin's contribution as 'coauthor in our first article on Mumford and critical regionalism'.[67]

In outlining the critical reactions to Mumford's regionalism of the late 1940s, Alofsin did not do justice to the American historian's ideas, as he discussed them only in the abstract terms of theories and neologisms. In Alofsin's later work, Mumford's agenda seems to be reflected in the intention to seek historically overlooked alternatives to 'international style' modernism in the North American and Central European contexts.[68] But Alofsin did not explicitly develop his work in terms of regionalism – either then, or later. In his short bio to Michael Andritzky, one of the three editors of the German publication, he does not mention regionalism as his main research interest but more specifically 'the arrival of Walter Gropius and the depolitization [sic] of modernism in America'.[69] Alofsin's contribution was eventually marginalised because he refrained from actively pursuing his further involvement with the theoretical development of contemporary variants of regionalism in late twentieth-century architecture in order to pursue and develop his conclusions on 'constructive regionalism' as an agenda of his own. His interest was mainly historiographical, and his related work on Wright and the former Habsburg Empire focused on the late nineteenth and early twentieth centuries. By contrast, Tzonis and Lefaivre built on these critical debates between Mumford and the advocates of the international style in their later work. They further explored how Mumford's thinking could serve as a role model for their own aspired approach to regionalism in architecture.

The fact that Frampton's account of critical regionalism became more influential than Tzonis and Lefaivre's original writings by the mid-1980s was partly owing to its convenient summarisation in a series of points.[70] In general, the couple's engagement with the historical, socio-political and cultural context of the architecture of critical regionalism was stronger than that of Frampton. But Tzonis and Lefaivre's accounts were not as clear and effective in concisely articulating the critical regionalist approach as a prescriptive design theory that could guide architects' practice in the future. In their aversion to providing 'recipes' for the architecture of the future, which was already evident in their omission of Alofsin's points of 'constructive regionalism' from their first co-authored text on the subject, their theory became less clear and effective than that of Frampton. The couple effectively summarised their critical regionalism in five points two decades later than Frampton, when they discussed tropical architecture in the early 2000s. This was the first time that Tzonis and Lefaivre eschewed summarising critical regionalism in vague keywords such as 'defamilarisation' and 'strangemaking' in order to promote their own set of points. These favoured advanced technology over nostalgic craftsmanship, sustainability over the Picturesque aestheticisation of the landscape, a multicultural community over a traditional community and the fusion of local and global.[71] All these points were entirely based on Mumford's approach. As such, Mumford's central positioning in Tzonis and Lefaivre's project cannot be underestimated. This is the subtle but most significant way in which Alofsin's 'Constructive Regionalism' was conducive to the later development of critical regionalism by Tzonis and Lefaivre, who drew from a richer pool of Mumford's works.

The multilingual history of critical regionalism

'The Question of Regionalism' was published as part of Burckhardt's series of inexpensive paperbacks for the Werkbund, which also aimed to promote viable alternatives for the future of architecture at that time. In his introductory remarks, Burckhardt noted the multiple overlaps between the main themes of the book: participatory design and self-building, ecological architecture, and regionalism. As such, he emphasised the significance of 'decentralised, small-scale and self-sufficient' models of architectural production that remained 'open to the reality of everyday life and utopia'. If people were to regain control of their living environments, modern cities could also avoid turning into highways interspersed with office blocks.[72] In this context, self-building was not the endeavour of individualists; it resulted rather from the preservation and development of collective knowledge about constructing and managing houses in relation to specific environmental conditions.[73] Burckhardt was certainly inspired by 'The Question of Regionalism', as more than half of the works he cites in his short essay are directly related with the work of Tzonis, Lefaivre and Alofsin.[74] His other texts in the same volume discuss the 1960s 'artificial village' projects by architects in the UK, Denmark and Switzerland. In these projects, 'continuous motifs … are not always derived from the region in which the "village" is located, or originate in the local style', but they are always transformed to adapt to the needs of the present (Fig. 2.5).[75] As such, they point towards 'a new regionalism – without a direct model – … associatively adapted to the landscape, climate, topography and local building and craft traditions'.[76]

The fact that Burckhardt invited Tzonis to contribute an essay on regionalism in the first place shows that this debate was alive in Western Europe at that time. Reading lists for Tzonis's courses included Bernard Huet's 'Formalism, Realism' article of 1977, which also seems to have informed Tzonis's conception of regionalism.[77] But the subsequent reception of critical regionalism has now overshadowed the related debates that preceded it. Regionalism was not only discussed by Tzonis, Lefaivre, Alofsin, Burckhardt and Frampton. It was very much in the air

Figure 2.5 'Seldwyla' settlement in Zumikon near Zurich (est. 1974), conceptualised by Rolf Keller (architects: Rudolf and Esther Guyer, Rolf Keller, Guhl & Lechner & Philipp, Manuel Pauli, Fritz Schwarz): southeastern view

Adrian Michael, 2019, CC BY-SA 3.0, via Wikimedia Commons

in North American and Western European magazines and institutions of the time, which usually discussed it within the broader framework of the postmodern debate in architecture. To cite just one example, 'regionalism' was one of the five main questions in the open discussion of the *Harvard Architecture Review* conference at the GSD on 8 December 1980, where it was interwoven with issues of referential form, history, contextualism and postmodern space, instigated by the crisis of modern architecture.[78] Burckhardt's argument that regionalism is equally important as a means of architectural self-expression of the people within a regional community is also historiographically significant in terms of the relationship of critical regionalism with postmodern thinking.[79] As Burckhardt crucially notes from the outset, the themes of ecological, regional and self-building are only three out of the four 'postmodern currents' that were originally discussed in the international Darmstadt Werkbund talks. The fourth one was Italian architects' new approaches to 'rationalism', or the nemesis of Tzonis and Lefaivre's agenda.[80] Burckhardt also noted how the 'postmodern' approach to regionalism derives from the integration of regionally inflected elements in 'upscale architecture'. This process in turn 'internationalises' these regional features in the same way that Le Corbusier internationalised his influences from Mediterranean architectures in the early twentieth century.[81] These are the first of several signs that the lines which the proponents of critical regionalism wished to draw between their approach and postmodern theories and practices of architecture were rather thin, if not blurred.

The idea of architecture's autonomy, especially as this was developed by the 1970s proponents of the 'narcissist phase', remains the recurring nemesis in Tzonis and Lefaivre's autobiographical account of 2017. Constantly juxtaposing the projects of autonomy with ecological approaches to architecture, the couple seem eager to build a pertinent ecological narrative for the evolution of critical regionalism in the twenty-first century. Aligning with this narrative, sustainability – one of the crucial 'issues suppressed by postmodernism' – effectively becomes their critical regionalism of the 1990s.[82] In the same context, Burckhardt returns to discuss 'ecological architecture' as part of Tzonis and Lefaivre's attempt to link sustainability with critical regionalism in 1992. But Burckhardt notices a contradiction in terms in this project, as he concludes:

> Ecology's most important problem is that it is invisible. You cannot produce the visual sensation of harmony simply by being ecological any more than the reverse ... The same is the problem with architecture; you cannot see an ecological building. Of course you can build the image of an ecological house ... Or you can calculate how to save energy and how to clean up the environment. The problem with the second is that nobody will take pictures of it and publish it.[83]

Although Burckhardt triggered Tzonis and Lefaivre's original interest in the question of regionalism, his voice has not been included in recent histories and revisits of critical regionalism. This has certainly been a loss for the architectural community. Burckhardt understood the wider socio-economic ecological picture, emphasising the entire lifecycle of production from raw materials to the eventual disposal of the product as questions that had to be addressed by designers in the late 1970s. Compared with the abstract, idealised contrasts between place and technological production that prevailed in Frampton's version of the same discourse, Burckhardt's grounded ideas could have proved more constructive in promoting critical regionalism's development in the direction of ecology and sustainability. Burckhardt's understanding was also more wide-ranging than that of Tzonis and Lefaivre. It encompassed all functions of the environment, including the effects of the design professionals on the landscape and their impact within this wider ecosystem. By contrast, Tzonis and Lefaivre's approach was until then primarily human-centric. It was mainly based on systems theory, as this was translated into architecture and planning in Tzonis's early work with Chermayeff.

In addition, research into Burckhardt's role in the conception of critical regionalism would have also shown why resisting postmodern architecture was more complicated than the authors of critical regionalism originally expected. In his later writings, Burckhardt's stance towards postmodernism was not negative. For him, 'postmodernism' was a necessary term to refer to the contemporary condition. Having said that, Tzonis and Lefaivre's work certainly influenced Burckhardt's thinking on 'the new regionalism' in the 1980s. His account of its development as bottom-up resistance and countermovement to the top-down imposition of the abstract architectural languages of 'academicists' echoes Tzonis and Lefaivre's ideas.[84] But Burckhardt also emphasised how this new regionalism was intertwined with postmodernity, especially through its emphasis on the special case. This in turn meant that a discourse that focused on the specificities of diverse regions could suddenly become globally relevant in the 1980s.[85] Despite its close ties with postmodernism, which was usually associated with a neoconservative stance, Burckhardt argued that the new regionalism was progressive and aligned with the aspirations of the Left. Precisely because it foregrounded the specificities of each region, it could not be conflated with the *Heimatstil* of the Third Reich that attempted to establish the same generic 'folk' architecture across the Alps.[86] As Burckhardt concluded:

> … the new regionalism is not the same as the old regional styles. There was Baroque, which came from Rome, and then there were such delights as Mexican Baroque, which is a provincial style of architecture; for missionaries had brought along engravings from Rome and worked with local artisans and so something emerged that, while not as accomplished as the Roman Baroque, was oriented to it nonetheless, was a provincial variation on it, with folkloric touches. But precisely this regionalism is the one we will find no more. For certain it is dead, for the information is there: every architect now has the complete information. And provided he is at this global level he uses regional elements for works that are not

provincial but that have a global level and are oriented to the global language of architecture.[87]

For these reasons, this overlooked history of the question of regionalism – with all its distinct voices – is significant in discussing critical regionalism today. Burckhardt's comments of 1984 can now serve as a critique of the oversimplified thesis that prevailed in the understanding of Tzonis and Lefaivre's 'peaks and valleys' version of critical regionalism as a form of resistance to the homogenising onslaught of a globalisation that flattens local differences.[88] Transgressing historic language barriers to return to this multilingual early history of critical regionalism retrieves nuanced branches of the new regionalist thinking that are more relevant today. At the turn of the millennium, Frampton did touch on intertwined questions of architectural, urban and landscape design in his manifesto for the twenty-first century.[89] But Burckhardt's wider interests in landscape as the expression of an intertwined relation of nature/culture (Fig. 2.6) and his development of strollology, with its focus on the significance of walking in producing knowledge of specific places, could have also informed the discourses of critical regionalism and refreshed their relevance in the late twentieth century. These remain strands of critical regionalism that can still be meaningfully developed today.

Alofsin was also the only thinker on the question of regionalism to address it directly in terms of national identity. Frampton, Tzonis and Lefaivre tended to avoid the thorny issues that are usually associated with this discussion. By contrast, Alofsin's interest in regionalism was linked with such questions from the outset – especially since his historiographical project was to trace an indigenous American modernism before the arrival of Gropius in the USA. His long-standing interest in the work of Wright is also aligned with this pursuit of the USA's regional version of modernism, as the first distinctly North American style that was not imported from Europe but was developed by local architects (Fig. 2.7). Alofsin specifically aimed to retrieve this overlooked prewar history of 'progressive' American modernism and highlight its crucial differences from the 'radical' European modernism that followed it to alter its course in the postwar period.[90] His later work on the regional architectures of the emerging nation states after the early twentieth-century dissolution of the Austro-Hungarian Habsburg Empire further pursued these questions.[91]

In their early texts on critical regionalism, Frampton, Tzonis and Lefaivre did not talk about regionalism in terms of national identity. They

Figure 2.6 Lucius Burckhardt, '0m [Point Zero] Walk', Wilhelmshöhe landscape park, Kassel, 1985, photographed by Monika Nikolić, in Lucius Burckhardt, *Why is Landscape Beautiful? The Science of Strollology*, ed. by Markus Ritter and Martin Schmitz (Basel: Birkhäuser, 2015), pp. 14–15
© Martin Schmitz Verlag | Berlin

emphasised cultural identity instead, and rejected negative associations of their critical regionalism with nationalism as a misreading of their main thesis. To address this, they repeatedly returned to Mumford's work to present it as the exemplar of their aspired regionalism's difference from

Figure 2.7 Frank Lloyd Wright, Taliesin West in Scottsdale, Arizona, 1937

Andrew Horne, 2010, CC BY 3.0, via Wikimedia Commons

previous regionalist movements in architecture.[92] As Alofsin noted when I interviewed him in 2019:

> An inherent tension exists between nationalism and regionalism. Assuming the possibility of a national identity means that a set of unifying shared themes exists and is put into practice. The historical symbolism of the United States of America operated on that assumption, but from the outset there was ethnic, religious, and social divergence which sought expression outside the norms and problematized a unitary national expression. National identity is often a myth propagated for political reasons. Regionalism proposes the possibilities of a more local identity that resonates with people and place. Bernard Maybeck's architecture could be identified as exemplifying the Bay Regional style, but it could not be extrapolated throughout a large country with immense variety of geography, settlement patterns, and ethnic diversity. In smaller confines, like the nation states that struggled to emerge from the grip of the Austro-Hungarian empire, a regional identity might pass also as a national identity … But the roles of regional styles in portraying national ambitions is problematic.[93]

As such, Alofsin was essentially aiming at a bottom-up approach of regional architectures. *The Struggle for Modernism* (2002) is indeed his pursuit of a bottom-up American modernism that was historically overshadowed by the top-down European variant of modernism. As I show in the following chapters, this is different from Frampton's (and to an extent Tzonis and Lefaivre's) implicit prioritisation of the modern as the overarching ('critical' or 'defamiliarising') language that then accommodates the 'disjunctive episodes' of vernacular architectures. An elaboration of Alofsin's idea in this context might have led to a very different development of regional architecture.

This early but overlooked history of critical regionalism therefore suggests that if this discourse is to be meaningfully reappraised for the twenty-first century, it first needs to open up and embrace its existing cross-cultural and cross-disciplinary ecological roots – as it was doing in the 1970s, in its early days before globalisation. While the discourse of critical regionalism has emerged out of the successive efforts of a series of authors who have been historically overlooked, most accounts or revisits have focused only on one version of this discourse or the work of only one or two authors. This has notably narrowed the scope of a discourse that resurfaces as much more promising when viewed as a collective multifarious cross-cultural and cross-disciplinary effort. It is now more constructive to look at critical regionalism beyond these individual figures. As regionalism was at the core of the debates of the early 1980s, what emerges as the collective work of these figures is more significant today. When no single version of critical regionalism is prioritised over others, they all add up to a significant contribution to related questions that extend to the present. Only when critical regionalism is reconstructed as that which it has historically been, a cross-cultural and cross-disciplinary development, can it also serve as a useful precedent that can be relevant again in the twenty-first century.

The interpretative lens of cross-cultural and cross-disciplinary authorship extends to the canonical articles on critical regionalism by Tzonis and Lefaivre, and Frampton. Focusing on them, the following chapters foreground more overlooked authorial agents. Among others, these include the buildings that 'wrote' critical regionalism, and the architects and thinkers who are still in the shadows. As Alofsin also noted during our interview, because 'The Question of Regionalism' 'was in German and published in an obscure little paperback, it was unknown in America'.[94] The language barrier certainly played a significant role in this outcome and, in this sense, 'The Grid and the Pathway' had better luck historically. Orestis Doumanis, the Greek publisher who commissioned

Tzonis and Lefaivre to write their seminal article on the work of Suzana and Dimitris Antonakakis, always thought of his annual review of *Architecture in Greece* as a bilingual edition in Greek and English. But the establishment of specific texts and figures as influential also involves the structural position of each outlet in the global media complex, as I show in the following chapters.

Notes

1 See Alexander Tzonis and Liane Lefaivre, 'The Grid and the Pathway: An Introduction to the Work of Dimitris and Suzana Antonakakis, with Prolegomena to a History of the Culture of Modern Greek Architecture', *Architecture in Greece*, 15 (1981), 164–78; Kenneth Frampton, 'Prospects for a Critical Regionalism', *Perspecta*, 20 (1983), 147–62; Kenneth Frampton, 'Towards a Critical Regionalism: Six Points for an Architecture of Resistance', in *The Anti-Aesthetic: Essays on Postmodern Culture*, ed. by Hal Foster (Seattle: Bay Press, 1983), pp. 16–30.

2 See Kenneth Frampton, 'Μοντέρνο, πολύ μοντέρνο: Μια συνέντευξη του Kenneth Frampton στον Γιώργο Σημαιοφορίδη', *Architecture in Greece*, 20 (1986), 118–21 (p. 120).

3 Liane Lefaivre and Alexander Tzonis, *Critical Regionalism: Architecture and Identity in a Globalized World* (Munich: Prestel, 2003).

4 See Véronique Patteeuw and Léa-Catherine Szacka, 'Critical Regionalism for our Time', *Architectural Review*, 1466 (November 2019), 92–8 (p. 92).

5 See Catherine Slessor, 'Editorial View: Reframing Critical Regionalism for the Current Age', *Architectural Review*, 25 July 2013. Online. www.architectural-review.com/essays/editorial-view-reframing-critical-regionalism-for-the-current-age/8651301.article (accessed 30 June 2021).

6 See Lucius Burckhardt, *Why is Landscape Beautiful? The Science of Strollology*, ed. by Markus Ritter and Martin Schmitz (Basel: Birkhäuser, 2015), pp. 45–50.

7 See Alexander Tzonis, Liane Lefaivre and Anthony Alofsin, 'Die Frage des Regionalismus', in *Für eine andere Architektur: Bauen mit der Natur und in der Region*, ed. by Michael Andritzky, Lucius Burckhardt and Ot Hoffmann (Frankfurt am Main: Fischer, 1981), pp. 121–34.

8 See Kenneth Frampton, 'Maison de Verre', *Perspecta*, 12 (1969), 77–109, 111–28.

9 See Serge Chermayeff and Alexander Tzonis, *Shape of Community: Realization of Human Potential* (Hammondsworth: Penguin, 1971).

10 See Alexander Tzonis, letter to Kenneth Frampton, 30 January 1969, CCA Fonds 197, Kenneth Frampton fonds, 197 – 2017 – 114T, AP197.S3.001, Personal and professional correspondence 1969, 1969, 197-114-011.

11 Among others, see Alexander Tzonis, two postcards to Kenneth Frampton, 13 January 1971 and 1971, CCA Fonds 197, Kenneth Frampton fonds, 197 – 2017 – 131P, AP197.S4.006.

12 Alexander Tzonis and Liane Lefaivre, postcard to Kenneth Frampton, April 1975, CCA Fonds 197, Kenneth Frampton fonds, 197 – 2017 – 129P, AP197.S4.004.

13 Kenneth Frampton, 'Reflections on *Perspecta*: The End of the Beginning', 10-page typescript, 2001, CCA Fonds 197, Kenneth Frampton fonds, 197 – 2017 – 103T, AP197.S1.SS9.018, Reflections on Perspecta the end of the beginning, 2001, 197-103-032, p. 5.

14 Kenneth Frampton, 'Polemical Notes on Architectural Education', 1971, 19-page draft typescript, CCA Fonds 197, Kenneth Frampton fonds, 197 – 2017 – 002T, AP197.S1.SS1.044, Copy of Architectural Education USA: Issues, Ideas and people, ca. 1976-1980, 197-002-014, p. 6.

15 John McKean, 'Towards the Unknown Region', *Architects' Journal*, 176.50 (15 December 1982), 19–21 (p. 19).

16 See Thomas L. Schumacher, 'Alexander Tzonis, Towards a Non-Oppressive Environment', 3-page book review typescript, CCA IAUS, C1-84 @ C1-120, IAUS files, 57 – 007, B 50 5 04, Schumacher / Review of Tzonis, C1-110, p. 3.

17 See Kenneth Frampton, *Modern Architecture: A Critical History* (London: Thames & Hudson, 1980), pp. 288–90.

18 Alexander Tzonis and Liane Lefaivre, 'In the Name of the People: The Development of the Contemporary Populist Movement in Architecture' (1976), repr. in *What People Want: Populism in Architecture and Design*, ed. by Michael Shamiyeh (Basel: Birkhäuser, 2005), pp. 288–305 (p. 300).

19 Ibid., p. 305.

20 Alexander Tzonis and Liane Lefaivre, *Times of Creative Destruction: Shaping Buildings and Cities in the Late C20th* (London: Routledge, 2017), p. 93.

21 Liane Lefaivre, *Leon Battista Alberti's Hypnerotomachia Poliphili: Re-Cognizing the Architectural Body in the Early Italian Rennaisance* (Cambridge, MA: MIT Press, 1997), p. xi. Cf. Alexander Tzonis and Liane Lefaivre, 'The Anti-Aesthetic: Essays on Postmodern Culture': Μια βιβλιοκρισία', *Design + Art in Greece*, 16 (1985), 64.

22 Tzonis and Lefaivre, *Times of Creative Destruction*, p. 93.

23 See ibid., p. 75.

24 Anthony Alofsin, interviewed by Stylianos Giamarelos (Austin, TX: 8 April 2019), edited draft: 3 December 2019, pp. 3–5, 14, 28. See Anthony Alofsin, *The Struggle for Modernism: Architecture, Landscape Architecture, and City Planning at Harvard* (New York: Norton, 2002), p. 264.

25 Jesko Fezer and Martin Schmitz, 'The Work of Lucius Burckhardt', in *Lucius Burckhardt Writings, Rethinking Man-made Environments: Politics, Landscape and Design*, ed. by Jesko Fezer and Martin Schmitz (Vienna: Springer, 2012), pp. 7–26 (p. 18).

26 See Lucius Burckhardt, 'Criteria for a New Design' (1977), repr. in *Design is Invisible: Planning, Education, and Society*, ed. by Silvan Blumenthal and Martin Schmitz (Basel: Birkhäuser, 2017), pp. 36–9 (p. 38).

27 See Leberecht Migge [Spartakus in Grün], 'Das grüne Manifest', *Die Tat*, 10.2 (1919), 912–19; David H. Haney, *When Modern Was Green: Life and Work of Landscape Architect Leberecht Migge* (London: Routledge, 2010).

28 Lucius Burckhardt, 'Nature is Invisible' (1989), repr. in *Why is Landscape Beautiful?*, ed. by Ritter and Schmitz (Basel: Birkhäuser, 2015), pp. 45–50 (p. 49).

29 See Tzonis and Lefaivre, *Times of Creative Destruction*, pp. 121–2.

30 Lucius Burckhardt, 'Dirt' (1980), repr. in *Lucius Burckhardt Writings*, ed. by Fezer and Schmitz, pp. 166–9 (pp. 168–9).

31 Vinit Mukhija, handwritten note to Anthony Alofsin, Alexander Architectural Archives, The University of Texas at Austin, Anthony Alofsin Archive, ALFSN 00142, ALFSN Box 128, Series E: Personal Papers, Constructive Regionalism with Alex Tzonis, 1980–2006, ALFSN(128.3).

32 See Anthony Alofsin, *Frank Lloyd Wright – The Lost Years, 1910–1922: A Study of Influence* (Chicago: University of Chicago Press, 1993); *Frank Lloyd Wright: Europe and Beyond*, ed. by Anthony Alofsin (Berkeley: University of California Press, 1999); and Anthony Alofsin, *Wright and New York: The Making of America's Architect* (New Haven, CT: Yale University Press, 2019).

33 Anthony Alofsin, 'Constructive Regionalism', 2005, Alexander Architectural Archives, The University of Texas at Austin, Anthony Alofsin Archive, ALFSN 00142, ALFSN Box 128, Series E: Personal Papers, ALFSN(128.4). See Anthony Alofsin, 'Constructive Regionalism', in *Architectural Regionalism: Collected Writings on Place, Identity, Modernity, and Tradition*, ed. by Vincent B. Canizaro (New York: Princeton Architectural Press, 2007), pp. 368–73 (p. 368).

34 Alofsin, interviewed by Giamarelos, p. 2.

35 See Alofsin, *The Struggle for Modernism*, p. 262; John Brinckerhoff Jackson, *Discovering the Vernacular Landscape* (New Haven, CT: Yale University Press, 1984).

36 See Anthony Alofsin, letter to Peter Serenyi, 23 February 1980, Alexander Architectural Archives, The University of Texas at Austin, Anthony Alofsin Archive, ALFSN 00142, ALFSN Box 126, Series E: Personal Papers, ALFSN(126.2).

37 Alofsin, interviewed by Giamarelos, p. 7.

38 John P. Conron, *Socorro: A Historic Survey* (Albuquerque: University of New Mexico Press, 1980), p. 3.

39 Ibid., p. 36.

40 Alofsin, interviewed by Giamarelos, p. 8.

41 Alofsin, interviewed by Giamarelos, p. 8.

42 Alofsin, *The Struggle for Modernism*, p. 7.

43 Alexander Tzonis, *Towards a Non-Oppressive Environment: An Essay* (Boston: I Press, 1972).

44 Alexander Tzonis, recommendation letter for Anthony Alofsin, 26 February 1979, Alexander Architectural Archives, The University of Texas at Austin, Anthony Alofsin Archive, ALFSN 00142, ALFSN Box 123, Series E: Personal Papers, Harvard application, Recommendations, 1978–1986, ALFSN(123.5).

45 Anthony Alofsin, 'Constructive Regionalism', 8-page typescript, 26 May 1980, Alexander Architectural Archives, The University of Texas at Austin, Anthony Alofsin Archive, ALFSN 00142, ALFSN Box 128, Series E: Personal Papers, Constructive Regionalism with Alex Tzonis, 1980–2006, ALFSN(128.3), p. 1.

46 Ibid., p. 2; see Lewis Mumford, *The South in Architecture* (New York: Harcourt, Brace & Co., 1941).

47 See Vincent Scully, 'Doldrums in the Suburbs', *Journal of the Society of Architectural Historians*, 24.1 (March 1965), 36–47; George R. Collins and Adolf K. Placzek, 'MAS 1964: The Decade 1929–1939: Introduction', *Journal of the Society of Architectural Historians*, 24.1 (March 1965), 3–4; Alofsin, 'Constructive Regionalism', 1980, pp. 3–4.

48 Lewis Mumford, 'The Architecture of the Bay Region', in *Domestic Architecture of the San Francisco Bay Region*, ed. by Robert M. Church (San Francisco: Museum of Art, Civic Center, 1949), unpaginated (p. 2).

49 Alofsin, 'Constructive Regionalism', 1980, pp. 5–6.

50 Ibid., p. 6.

51 Alexander Tzonis and Liane Lefaivre, 'The Narcissist Phase in Architecture', *Harvard Architecture Review*, 1 (Spring 1980), 53–61 (p. 61).

52 Alexander Tzonis, 'The Predicaments of Architecture: Narcissism and Humanism in Contemporary Architecture', *Harvard Graduate School of Design Publication Series in Architecture*, A-7906 (1980), 1–17 (p. 17; emphasis in the original). This text was also published in French; see Alexander Tzonis and Liane Lefaivre, 'Narcissisme et humanisme dans l'architecture contemporaine', *Le carré bleu*, 4 (1980), 1–17 (p. 15).

53 Alofsin, 'Constructive Regionalism', 1980, p. 7.

54 See Alexander Tzonis, Introduction to Methodologies of Design in Architecture, Alexander Architectural Archives, The University of Texas at Austin, Anthony Alofsin Archive, ALFSN 00142, ALFSN Box 4, Series B: Research, GSD Alexander Tzonis, 1986, 1998, 2000, ALFSN(4.17); Alexander Tzonis, 'Commentary', *Le carré bleu*, 3 (1970), 3.

55 Tzonis, Lefaivre and Alofsin, 'Die Frage des Regionalismus', p. 121.

56 Ibid., pp. 121–4.

57 Ibid., p. 124.

58 Ibid., p. 125.

59 Ibid., pp. 125–6; Lewis Mumford, *Sticks and Stones: A Study in American Architecture and Civilisation* (New York: Boni and Liveright, 1924).

60 Lewis Mumford, 'The Skyline', *New Yorker*, 11 October 1947, p. 104.

61 Tzonis, Lefaivre and Alofsin, 'Die Frage des Regionalismus', p. 129.

62 Ibid., p. 129.

63 Ibid., p. 133.

64 See Alexander Tzonis, 'Preface', in Lefaivre and Tzonis, *Critical Regionalism*, pp. 6–7 (p. 6); Tzonis and Lefaivre, *Times of Creative Destruction*, p. 38; Lewis Mumford, 'Introduction', in Artur Glikson, *The Ecological Basis of Planning* (The Hague: Nijhoff, 1971), pp. vii–xxi.

65 Tzonis, 'Commentary', p. 3.

66 Alexander Tzonis, Arch. 1-1b Introduction to Theories of Program and Function in Architectural Design, Alexander Architectural Archives, The University of Texas at Austin, Anthony Alofsin Archive, ALFSN 00142, ALFSN Box 123, Series E: Personal Papers, folder ALFSN(123.2).

67 Alexander Tzonis and Liane Lefaivre, 'Lewis Mumford's Regionalism', *Design Book Review*, 19 (Winter 1991), 20–5 (p. 25).

68 See Alofsin, *The Struggle for Modernism*; Anthony Alofsin, *When Buildings Speak: Architecture as Language in the Habsburg Empire and its Aftermath, 1867–1933* (Chicago: University of Chicago Press, 2006).

69 Anthony Alofsin, letter to Michael Andritzky, 21 October 1980, Alexander Architectural Archives, The University of Texas at Austin, Anthony Alofsin Archive, ALFSN 00142, ALFSN Box 128, Series E: Personal Papers, Constructive Regionalism with Alex Tzonis, 1980–2006, ALFSN128.3.

70 See Frampton, 'Towards a Critical Regionalism'; Kenneth Frampton, 'Ten Points on an Architecture of Regionalism: A Provisional Polemic', *Center*, 3 (1987), 20–7.

71   Liane Lefaivre and Alexander Tzonis, 'The Suppression and Rethinking of Regionalism and Tropicalism After 1945', in *Tropical Architecture: Critical Regionalism in the Age of Globalization*, ed. by Alexander Tzonis, Liane Lefaivre and Bruno Stagno (Chichester: Wiley, 2001), pp. 14–58 (pp. 24–9).
72   See Lucius Burckhardt, 'Einführung', in *Für eine andere Architektur*, ed. by Andritzky, Burckhardt and Hoffmann, pp. 119–20 (p. 120); Lucius Burckhardt, 'Selberbauen, ökologisch bauen, regional bauen', in *Für eine andere Architektur*, ed. by Andritzky, Burckhardt and Hoffmann, pp. 9–13 (pp. 9–10).
73   Burckhardt, 'Selberbauen, ökologisch bauen, regional bauen', p. 11.
74   Lucius Burckhardt, '"Künstliche Dörfer"', in *Für eine andere Architektur*, ed. by Andritzky, Burckhardt and Hoffmann, pp. 161–5 (p. 165).
75   Ibid., p. 161.
76   Burckhardt, 'Einführung', p. 120.
77   Tzonis, Arch. 1-1b Introduction to Theories of Program and Function in Architectural Design; Bernard Huet, 'Formalisme/Realisme', *L'Architecture d'Aujourd'hui*, 190 (April 1977), 35–6.
78   Jeffrey Horowitz, December 8th conference questions, 5-page letter to *The Harvard Architecture Review* panel participants, 2 December 1980, Alexander Architectural Archives, The University of Texas at Austin, Anthony Alofsin Archive, ALFSN 00142, ALFSN Box 6, Series B: Research, GSD: Program Documents, 1980–1986, ALFSN(6.8).
79   Burckhardt, 'Selberbauen, ökologisch bauen, regional bauen', p. 12.
80   Ibid., p. 9.
81   Burckhardt, 'Einführung', pp. 119–20.
82   Tzonis and Lefaivre, *Times of Creative Destruction*, pp. 195–6.
83   Lucius Burckhardt, 'On Ecological Architecture: A Memo', in Alexander Tzonis and Liane Lefaivre, *Architecture in Europe since 1968: Memory and Invention* (London: Thames & Hudson, 1992), pp. 42–3 (p. 43).
84   See Lucius Burckhardt, 'Recycled Regionalism' (1984), repr. in *Design is Invisible*, ed. by Blumenthal and Schmitz, pp. 176–82 (pp. 177–8).
85   Ibid., pp. 179–80.
86   Ibid., pp. 181–2.
87   Ibid., p. 182.
88   See Liane Lefaivre and Alexander Tzonis, *Architecture of Regionalism in the Age of Globalization: Peaks and Valleys in the Flat World* (London: Routledge, 2012).
89   See Kenneth Frampton, 'Seven Points for the Millennium: An Untimely Manifesto', *Architectural Review*, 206.1233 (1999), 76–80.
90   Alofsin, *The Struggle for Modernism*, p. 13.
91   See Alofsin, *When Buildings Speak*.
92   Tzonis and Lefaivre, *Times of Creative Destruction*, p. 128.
93   Alofsin, interviewed by Giamarelos, p. 19.
94   Alofsin, interviewed by Giamarelos, p. 9.

3
Authorial agents

Léa-Catherine Szacka has argued that the Biennale marked, among other things, 'the beginning of the end' for postmodernism in architecture. After his disagreement with the selection process, Kenneth Frampton resigned from Paolo Portoghesi's international committee of invited critics. This represented the first schism within a loose group of critics who were only united by their shared interest in architectural developments after modernism.[1] Owing to the different focus of her research, Szacka stops short of following this 'schismatic' trajectory beyond the Biennale. In this chapter, I pick up this discussion to continue to follow the cross-cultural authorship of critical regionalism.

I start by tracing the evolution of Frampton's regionalist discourse after his resignation from the Biennale through a close reading of three key texts: 'From Neo-Productivism to Post-Modernism' (1981), 'The Isms of Contemporary Architecture' (1982), and 'Modern Architecture and Critical Regionalism' (1983).[2] I argue that, in reacting to the Biennale, Frampton attempted to open a novel, discursive space delimited by the opposing extremes of technocratic functionalism and scenographic historicism. His discourse reinserted socially conscious themes, approaches and projects that had formed an important part of postmodern architectural developments in the previous decades but were effectively silenced after the Biennale.

The significance of critical regionalism in the international milieu is a direct result of the cross-cultural process of its writing. For the definitive formulation of his discourse, Frampton borrowed the term 'critical regionalism' from Alexander Tzonis and Liane Lefaivre's 'The Grid and the Pathway' of 1981.[3] Considering this tripartite relationship between the Greek architects, the British historian, and the Greek and Canadian theorists, I present critical regionalism as a historical artefact of cross-cultural authorship. To corroborate this, I trace Frampton's contact with key figures of the Greek architectural circles and the incorporation of 'The Grid and the Pathway' in his regionalist discourse, the development of Tzonis and Lefaivre's own discourse in 'The Grid and the Pathway', the contribution of Suzana and Dimitris Antonakakis to this text through their correspondence with Tzonis and Lefaivre in 1980 and the meetings and exchanges of Frampton with the Antonakakis in Athens and Hydra in the early 1980s. The ensuing discourse of critical regionalism bears the footprints of Tzonis and Lefaivre's interest in participatory design; Alofsin's foregrounding of Mumford's modern regionalism; the Antonakakis' appreciation of the work of Team 10; and Frampton's engagement with phenomenology in order to explore the lived corporeal experience of architecture that involved the full spectrum of human senses beyond sight alone, and tectonics as the expressive poetics of architectural construction and its political implications. Frampton's intention to turn the attention of the global architectural community from the 'centres' to the 'periphery' of cultural production afforded his project a crucial cross-cultural dimension. Foregrounding the potential significance of a 'peripheral' regionalism that has not yet emerged elsewhere for the global future of modern architecture, Frampton effectively 'provincialised' the celebrated postmodern architecture of the Biennale. In the final instance, the cross-cultural authorship of critical regionalism embodied its main theoretical assertion: that the relation of the 'periphery' to the 'centre' is not merely assimilative but also productive and generative, as it offers a way forward for modern architecture.

Frampton's regionalism

Frampton was ambivalent in his relation both to the legacy of a redundant techno-scientific modernism and the historicist scenography of the Biennale. Voicing his opposition to the 'postmodern pluralist' interpretation of the show, he eventually resigned:

> I entertained the illusion that it would be possible for me to keep my distance from the overall ideology of the show by simply writing a critical article and allowing this to go forward in the exhibition catalogue. I have indeed finished this text. But the critical position it adopts is so extremely opposed to all that could be summed under the category 'post-modernism', that I have realised it would be absurd for me to advance the essay in this context ... Indeed it has recently become clear to me that I could only make a public spectacle

of myself, by being the so-called critic from within … It is one thing to mount an international exhibition whose theme is to demonstrate the present reaction against the reduced categories of modern architecture. It is another thing to manifest the triumph of an unstructured pluralism through a curiously partisan approach to the apparent procedure of selection and display.[4]

Reflecting on the Biennale, Charles Jencks also admitted that Frampton's inclusion in the advisory committee was an 'anomaly'.[5] Frampton withdrew in order to retain his own critical position in the discursive field. The possible commodification of his discourse by its association with the Strada Novissima would render its criticality insufficient for the task at hand. The Biennale had inadvertently offered him the occasion to reconsider the critical role of architecture. In his interview with Szacka, Frampton described his resignation in terms that prefigured critical regionalism: 'I withdrew because I felt that this was not so much a postmodern, as an antimodern polemic … I felt [the selected architects'] stance was cynical rather than critical. I also didn't like the transatlantic exclusivity that was being implicitly emphasised'.[6] While Frampton related to aspects of the postmodern critique, he resisted the total opposition to modernism suggested by the Strada Novissima. The exclusively transatlantic character of the exhibition also limited the potential criticality of the show. As he clarified in his letter to Stern, Frampton felt that the role of invited critics as 'commissioners' was decorative, and this was reflected in 'how prejudicially the work had been selected'. The eventual exclusion from the selection process of Ignasi de Sola-Morales, whose work Frampton had witnessed and appreciated after meeting this Spanish architect and theorist at the Institute of Architecture and Urban Studies (IAUS) in New York in the 1970s, was the final straw. Frampton was aware that his decision would 'probably affect [his] future relations with many people', but he felt that 'there are in the last analysis important issues at stake and these have to take precedence over hitherto amiable personal relations'.[7]

After the Biennale, Frampton pursued a discourse to articulate a way out of his ambivalence. He did not deny that there was a problem with modern architecture. On the contrary, he believed in its serious consideration. Addressing this problem would foster a critical understanding of the historical predicament facing the profession. Frampton intended to consider the latent possibilities for future developments that critical understanding might open. For this reason, he refused to succumb to matters of 'personal patronage' in a selection process that underplayed alternative contributions to the theme of the Biennale, such as the work of Gino Valle (1923–2003).[8]

In his writings of the period, Frampton was partly inspired by the Heideggerian notions of place and dwelling.[9] He was also influenced by the political twist afforded on these phenomenological notions by Hannah Arendt – especially through her definition of the space of appearance and the triad of labour, work and action, as this was presented in her book on *The Human Condition* (1958).[10] Leaving the life of the mind aside, Arendt's human condition is defined by action, the *vita activa* within the shared world that humans create for themselves through their work. Focusing on what humans actually do, Arendt argued that human labour is only related with the needs of surviving in a frequently hostile natural environment. But the work and actions of humans are distinguished by the will to escape from this painful natural condition into a human-made world. While Frampton used Arendt's distinction between labour and work as a way to distinguish building (as a process that develops out of necessity) from architecture (as the stable points of reference of the human lifeworld),[11] her ideas can also be related with his enduring suspicion of the dictates of techno-scientific optimisation and their implications for architecture. As Arendt argued, during the process of making a world for themselves, humans tend to ignore their limitations. As such, they end up creating self-made technological prisons that no longer cover their physiological or psychological needs and could eventually lead to their self-destruction.

Substituting 'architecture' for Arendt's 'action' and influenced by Herbert Marcuse's critical discourse,[12] Frampton regards place, technology and dwelling as politically loaded terms. In his case, place-creation inherently implies a political gathering in pursuit of common projects. Architecture as action equals bringing people together in a civic world that they can share. For this reason, Frampton aspired to 'a critical theory of building' concerned with the 'creation of place'.[13] In 1974, he had thematised both the ontological and the political implications of the production of place as that of sustaining an active public sphere.[14] His intention to open a discussion about modes of architectural production differentiated him from his North American peers at that time. For Frampton, this opposition between place and technological production, which involved politics, was key for the architectural predicament of the 1970s. In this light, he argued that '[t]he current architectural debate as to the finer stylistic points of Modernism versus Post-Modernism appears to be somewhat irrelevant'.[15] Before the Biennale, Frampton was looking for the right words to articulate his project, registering the problems of the modern project without giving up on its progressive legacy.[16]

As Frampton put it later, he intended his discourse to encompass architectural practices that addressed the 'total division between the aesthetic and the political avant-gardes'.[17] In an unpublished typescript of 1978 titled 'The Resistance of Architecture', he had already argued against the very idea of this 'l'art pour l'art' division in the field of architecture. '[W]here architecture was restrained by power and the forces of material production from being fully liberating or liberative in its expressions it was at the same time *resistant* to the separation of art and politics suffered by the other arts, for architecture was suffused with power.'[18] In the same text, Frampton discussed the instrumentalisation of architecture as a fixed edifice and a stable, civilising symbol of universal values and imperial power – as opposed to the processual, rooted cultures of building – in the long history of Western humanism from the fifteenth century to the present. He concluded that 'the resistance of architecture can only be realized through the establishment of the monument; that is to say, through the creation of bounded realms and large-scale representative forms and through the realization of micro-urban precincts within which a liberative culture can be nurtured and sustained'.[19] For this reason, he attempted to displace architectural discourse from Jencks's stylistic 'battle of the labels' to the broader existential, cultural and sociopolitical field.[20] Opposing the transatlantic exclusivity of the Biennale, Frampton also intended to recalibrate international architectural interest in the 'provinces' of Western cultural production. Tracing the genealogy of his nascent critical regionalism from 1980 to 1983, I argue that Frampton's reportedly 'finished' text for the Biennale catalogue was his first essay on this matter.[21] As such, I add historical nuance to Szacka's speculation that the famous 1983 text on critical regionalism 'reads as if it were – or had its origins in – the text Frampton had written for the 1980 Venice Architecture's Biennale catalogue'.[22]

As a renowned historian and theorist in the 1980s, Frampton had numerous venues for publishing his work at his disposal. These ranged from the journal of the IAUS *Oppositions* in the USA to *Architectural Design* in the United Kingdom. As such, the possibility of him leaving a reportedly 'finished' text of his in the shadows seems rather slim. For this reason, I argue that Frampton's article 'From Neo-Productivism to Post-Modernism' (published in *L'Architecture d'Aujourd'hui* approximately six months after the Biennale and further reworked to be published as 'The Isms of Contemporary Architecture' in *Architectural Design* in 1982) is the text missing from the 1980 exhibition catalogue. Frampton seems to have been constantly returning to these ideas after he had finished writing his critical history of modern architecture in the late 1970s. A first note on a lecture on 'The Isms of Contemporary Architecture' appears in Frampton's archived agenda on 12 March 1980, very close to the deadline for submitting his text to Portoghesi.[23]

To begin with, 'From Neo-Productivism to Post-Modernism' provides an overview of the most important architectural developments after the 1960s and classifies them into four major trends. This is in line with Frampton's preferred interpretation of the exhibition's theme as a documentation of 'the present reaction against the reduced categories of modern architecture'.[24] The appearance in the title of the word 'post-modernism' is another significant clue. In his other texts of the same period, Frampton tended to avoid using this term.[25] He preferred to refer to architectural work in the vein of Robert Venturi and Denise Scott-Brown under the rubric of 'Populism'. In a text for the catalogue of an exhibition dedicated to postmodern architecture, however, he could not avoid employing the term 'postmodern' as he also aimed to challenge it in order to highlight the difference with his own theoretical position. Lastly, the context in which the article appears is equally significant. Historically, *L'Architecture d'Aujourd'hui* had served as one of the major international beacons of modernism. Frampton's decision to publish his article in those symbolically loaded pages functioned as a statement of his intended dissociation from the postmodernists of the Biennale.

The article marks the first articulation of Frampton's regionalist alternative to the four ideologically defined '-isms' of architectural practice: 'neo-productivism' (with its emphasis on technological optimisation, autarchy and autonomy from its immediate context), 'neo-rationalism' (with its emphasis on typological studies of historic architectural contexts), 'structuralism' (with its emphasis on anthropological studies) and 'participationism/populism' (with its emphasis on contextualism). In the final instance, his taxonomy comes down to the polar dichotomy of universal productivism and kitsch populism as two equally undesirable opposites. Frampton had already developed this idea in 'The Resistance of Architecture', in which he also noted the positive potential of the original Soviet Productivist Group and their Constructivist architecture of the 1920s:

> To a degree Productivism sought to dev[e]lop a new *rooted* culture based on the everyday production of the people themselves and on the fulfillment of their immediate informational needs. Productivism posited a Constructivist-cum-Dadaist culture in a state of perpetual revolution, in which cultural form, as collectively determined, did *not* necessarily presuppose the constant optimization of the highest technical capacity.[26]

But since this potential was not historically fulfilled, the neo-productivism and kitsch populism of late capitalist architectures were united in their incapacity for place-creation.[27] And while the Structuralist approach of Dutch architects and the Neo-Rationalist approach of Italian architects constituted more promising responses to the crisis of modern architecture, they also needed to be further developed in this respect.

Hence, Frampton presented regionalist works as an alternative to universal productivism that also avoids the 'trap of folklorism'. He calls this regionalism both 'realist' and 'neo-constructivist'.[28] Alluding to Oriol Bohigas's Catalan manifesto, 'realism' is a shorthand for the cultural and sociopolitical aspirations of Frampton's discourse. This had become a focal term in architectural debates from the late 1950s onwards. The various discourses that developed around 'realism' attempted to move away from the individual project and towards the collective that conditions its production in areas such as the cantons of Switzerland, Italy and Spain.[29] Frampton had closely engaged with this discourse in the late 1970s, when he distinguished the work of Mario Botta.[30] 'Neo-constructivism', on the other hand, points towards a specific aesthetic sensibility.[31] Rooted in the modernist tradition, this sensibility promotes the industrialisation of a construction that remains 'in direct response to the needs of the society [architects] live in'.[32] To lend credibility to his project, Frampton evokes Pierre Chareau's Maison de Verre.[33] This historical precedent shows that his architectural discourse is not limited to wishful thinking. It reveals an already existing, yet latent, direction that requires further development.[34]

His conclusion offers an unsystematic mix of features that are crucial for his later articulations of critical regionalism. In Frampton's words, these features comprise 'an authentic if restricted regional movement'. To 'reestablish critical precepts', this regional movement 'retranscribes elements of the vernacular without [postmodern architecture's] recourse to pastiche'. Its priorities consist of 'restor[ing] the urban structure in those places where it is still intact'; 'identify[ing] those buildings which give form to the shapeless metropolis'; and 'emphasis[ing] the threshold, [and] making it the most [monumental and] significant element of construction'. As such, Frampton's regionalism promotes a synthesis of '[r]ational modes of construction and traditional artisan forms … in an intelligent syntax' that allows for 'gradients' in expression, a densification of micro-environments and the development of the tactile alongside the visual aspects of buildings. Accepting 'that architecture is of necessity the culture of the arrière-garde', it also resists 'the cult of the star', 'the self-destructing potential of so-called paper architecture', 'the insidious cult of the image' and 'the media themselves' with their 'capacities to undermine' it.[35]

'From Neo-Productivism to Post-Modernism' set the foundations for Frampton's critical regionalism. In the months that followed, the British historian revised this original text to carry his regionalist discourse forward in the dual terms of theory and practice. In 'The Isms of Contemporary Architecture' of 1982, he enriched his anthology of regionalist architects.[36] The major theoretical input came from an essay by Paul Ricoeur that was recommended to him by the architectural phenomenologist Dalibor Vesely after the publication of the critical history of modern architecture.[37] Starting from March 1981, Frampton incorporated this reference to Ricoeur as part of his polemic.[38] He echoed the French philosopher's plea for a hybrid 'world culture' that would reconcile the needs of 'rooted culture' with the demands of 'universal civilisation', a distinction that Frampton had already explored in his earlier discussion of 'The Resistance of Architecture' in 1978 – albeit without referring to Ricoeur. In architecture, this reconciliation could only be carried out by 'deconstruct[ing] universal Modernism' through a procedure of 'synthetic contradiction'. In other words, this regionalism was not another architectural style but a two-way process. In Frampton's 'dialectical synthesis', 'values and images which are quintessentially rooted' in local cultures of building would be employed to 'adulterate' modernism. At the same time, 'these basic references' would be 'adulterated' in return 'with paradigms drawn from alien sources'.[39]

Ricoeur's writing enabled Frampton to stress the cross-cultural dimension of this regionalism. Although the French philosopher's discourse discussed universal civilisation and national cultures as general categories, Frampton insisted on centring his regionalism on individual figures. He argued that these figures 'condense[d] the artistic potential' of their regional culture 'while reinterpreting cultural influences coming from the outside'.[40] A few months later, in his RIBA Annual Discourse on 7 December 1982, Frampton clarified these ideas further. 'Talented individual' figures work simultaneously 'in tune with the emerging thought of the time ... with commitment towards some form of rooted expression'. This distinct way of working allows these individual figures to produce the expression of a regionalism 'not yet emerged elsewhere'. Due to this uniqueness, their regionalist expression bears wider 'significance for the world outside itself'.[41] Unlike the nationalist regionalisms of the recent past, Frampton's aspirations were therefore far from static and introverted. The displacement of interest to 'marginal architectures of resistance' challenged the dominant understanding of cultural transformation. This was no longer a one-way dissemination of ideas from the hegemonic 'centre' to the dependent 'periphery'. This was also why the historicism of the Strada Novissima was additionally problematic: it short-circuited the dialectic nature of this relationship. Furthermore, the transatlantic exclusivity of the Biennale perpetuated a distorted understanding of cultural exchange and development.[42]

The title of Frampton's talk at the RIBA was 'Modern Architecture and Critical Regionalism'. It was the first public presentation of his discourse under the rubric of 'critical regionalism', which was widely disseminated through his celebrated essays of 1983.[43] The term served as a condensed expression of Frampton's ideas. He borrowed it from Tzonis and Lefaivre, who had first used it in their article on the work of the Antonakakis, 'The Grid and the Pathway' (1981). For this reason, the Greek architectural couple found their place in Frampton's list of critical regionalists in late 1982. Their apartment building at 118 Benaki Street in Athens eventually became one of the flagship projects of critical regionalism (Fig. 3.1).

Figure 3.1   Suzana and Dimitris Antonakakis, apartment building at 118 Benaki Street, Athens, 1972–5: main elevation, photographed by Dimitris Antonakakis, 1975

Suzana and Dimitris Antonakakis' private archive

Promoting critical regionalism, Frampton intended to offer a practical opening to a future for modern architecture in contradistinction to the historicism of the Biennale. Five years after the show, the revised edition of his critical history of modern architecture concluded with a chapter that effectively fused his earlier articles of 1983 to summarise the main features of critical regionalism. Frampton's promotion of the place-form resists the modernist expansion of megalopolitan development, as it creates clusters of civic life, while the emphasis on the tactile and the tectonic aspects of architecture resist postmodern scenography.[44] As such, critical regionalism focuses on:

(1) qualifying the 'naïve utopianism' of the modern project to focus on 'the small rather than the big plan', without abandoning its 'emancipatory and progressive aspects';

(2) the capacity of buildings to define a specific place and territory, meaning that they should not be conceived as 'free-standing objects';

(3) rejecting the scenographic in favour of the tectonic approach to architecture;

(4) responding to 'specific conditions imposed by the site, the climate and the light' through a treatment of 'all openings as delicate transitional zones' against the 'optimising thrust' of ubiquitous air conditioning;

(5) re-emphasising tactility in the perception of architecture to resist the hegemony of the visual 'in an age dominated by media to the replacement of experience by information';

(6) assimilating elements from the regional vernacular as 'disjunctive episodes' within the architectural structure, to avoid their treatment as hermetic contentless forms and leading to 'the paradoxical creation of a regionally based "world culture"'; and

(7) unsettling the hierarchy between 'dominant cultural centres' of architectural production and 'dependent dominated satellite' peripheries that passively assimilate it.[45]

The preceding analysis of the projects included in this new final chapter demonstrated practical applications of these theoretical points. As such, the 'provincial' backwaters of architectural historiography reclaimed their precious relevance for the present. They became the marginal but still progressive 'arrière-gardes' of the 1980s that held the solutions to problems instigated by the progressive but equally marginal 'avant-gardes' of the 1920s.

Tzonis and Lefaivre's critical regionalism

Critical regionalism is the discursive footprint of ideas travelling through cultures. A close reading of Frampton's texts on the subject reveals his elective affinities with the work of architectural phenomenologists such as Christian Norberg-Schulz and his conviction that fenestration has 'an innate capacity to inscribe architecture with the character of a region and hence to express the place in which the work is situated',[46] and his long-standing interest in the work of Vittorio Gregotti and the belief that '"in-laying" the building into the site ... has a capacity to embody, in built form, the prehistory of the place, its archaeological past and its subsequent cultivation and transformation across time ... layering into the site the idiosyncracies of place ... without falling into sentimentality'.[47] But more crucial for the definitive enunciation of this discourse was the British historian's link with Tzonis and Lefaivre, and the Antonakakis.

In his introductory text to the 'Modern Architecture and the Critical Present' feature in *Architectural Design* (1982), Frampton surveyed his formative history. He associated his experience from his years of service as a technical editor for *Architectural Design* (1962–5) with his early 1980s appraisals of architects neglected by the contemporaneous star system after the Biennale. By pulling disparate threads of his historical trajectory together, Frampton signalled their synthesis into a novel, discursive whole. Many of his 1982 additions to his list of 'figures ... hidden ... in the interstices' had already featured in *Architectural Design* from 1962 to 1965. The Greek architect Aris Konstantinidis was among them.[48]

The architecture of modern Greece was not a novel discovery for Frampton in the early 1980s. As the technical editor of *Architectural Design*,[49] by the mid-1960s Frampton had already hosted a monographic feature on the work of Aris Konstantinidis (in volume five of *Architectural Design* in 1964).[50] Orestis Doumanis (1929–2013), the soon-to-be publisher of the country's annual review *Architecture in Greece* (1967–2013) was also enlisted as the magazine's Greek correspondent (from the first volume of *Architectural Design* in 1965 and onwards). Thus established in the 1960s, Frampton's link with the region continued to grow thereafter.[51]

In his work as an editor, Frampton was primarily influenced by Alberto Sartoris's *Elements of Functionalist Architecture* (1932). In this early survey of modern architecture, Sartoris had attempted to provide an atlas of the novel architectural developments of the time. Thirty years later, Frampton's generation of British historians intended to undertake a similar task. By the early 1960s, they were additionally inspired by Brutalism's 'attempt to find its way in the pursuit of this "lost" continuity of the pre-war modern movement'.[52] Frampton's 'encyclopaedic' editorial aspiration resulted in thirty-one issues of *Architectural Design* that covered the globe-spanning development of modern architecture. Deliberately moving away from the dominant centres of cultural production, Frampton's edited issues included extensive features on non-European territories (such as Chile, Brazil and Mexico) and architectural practices:

> It seemed very important that at the early 1960s it was possible — for some architects, at least — to have a direct relation with the city-state or ... the region they lived in ... when I looked around me as an editor of an architectural magazine, I noticed that a certain level of activity and authenticity was apparent in the work carried out in several provincial cities ... for the last 20 years already ... I had this probably strange interest for cultural work you couldn't find in the so called Anglo-Saxon centres. I then borrowed this unfortunate expression 'critical regionalism' to refer to this sort of work. The expression comes from the extremely interesting article 'The Grid and the Pathway' by Alexander Tzonis and Liane Lefaivre.[53]

Frampton's long-standing contact with Tzonis and Lefaivre meant that he was one of the first in the anglophone world to read an article 'hiding away' in the 'obscure journal' *Architecture in Greece*.[54] Reading their article when his own variant of regionalism was discursively coalescing, Frampton came across a theoretical analysis that combined some of his own critical and aesthetic concerns. This is also why he immediately adopted the term 'critical regionalism'. In the final instance, it was this article that allowed him to discuss the work of the Antonakakis in the terms that he himself preferred.

Like Frampton, Tzonis and Lefaivre had turned to regionalism to articulate their aspired response to postmodernism. When Doumanis commissioned them to write an article on the work of the Antonakakis in early 1980, he also gave them the opportunity to develop their ideas further. The Greek publisher's request was meant to support Dimitris Antonakakis's candidacy for a chair of architectural design at the National Technical University of Athens.[55] It formed part of an orchestrated effort to support and promote the Antonakakis' work internationally through the related networks of the Greek publisher and figures such as Dimitris Fatouros (1928–2020).[56] The architecture of Suzana and Dimitris Antonakakis provided Tzonis and Lefaivre with a concrete case study for a region with which Tzonis was readily familiar. Their formerly abstract overview of regionalist movements in the history of Western architecture could now become integrated within the familiar sociopolitical and economic developments of modern Greece. Moreover, the work of the Antonakakis itself offered the authors an opportunity to explore the actual possibilities for an architectural expression of their aspired regionalism. This concrete architectural dimension had been left unexplored in their first article on the subject.

The agenda of participatory design from 'The Question of Regionalism' was still discernible in the background of 'The Grid and the Pathway'. It acted as the gold standard against which the Antonakakis' and any future architecture of critical regionalism had to be measured: 'No new architecture can emerge without a new kind of relation between designer and user, without new kinds of programs', read the concluding lines of 'The Grid and the Pathway'.[57] Tzonis and Lefaivre's agenda thus reintroduced some of the original postmodern pleas of the 1960s, which had been relatively silenced after the Biennale, into the debates of the 1980s. As a 'child' of postmodern times, Tzonis and Lefaivre's critical regionalism was no longer opposed to the 'repressive absolutist regimes and their restrictive academic pseudo-universal theories of the past' but to the 'despotic aspects of the Welfare State and the custodial effects of modernism'.[58]

Tzonis and Lefaivre identified two major design patterns in the work of the Antonakakis that they connected with two different historical phases of Greek regionalism: the 'grid' and the 'pathway'. Following a longer historical trail from eighteenth-century German architects such as Karl Friedrich Schinkel to twentieth-century Greek practitioners such as Aris Konstantinidis, the 'grid' was defined as 'the discipline which is imposed on every space element'. Representing a more recent phase of Greek regionalism, dating back to the late nineteenth century and exemplified in the work of Dimitris Pikionis, the 'pathway' was defined as 'the location of place elements in relation to a movement'.[59] More significantly, these two 'major patterns' were not just discussed in formal design terms but also contextualised within the sociopolitical history of modern Greece from the nineteenth to the twentieth century.

Tzonis and Lefaivre asserted that the first phase of regionalism could be traced to eighteenth-century European movements that were rooted outside of Greece. The artistic ideals of these Romantic movements such as 'uniqueness, particularity, distinctiveness, variety … emerge in the eighteenth century in opposition to what is then perceived as the exaggerated uniformity' and alleged universality of Classical architecture.[60] But while the German Romantics such as Johann Wolfgang von Goethe rebelled against the imposition of the rule of Neo-Classicism, Tzonis and Lefaivre argued, in Greece it was the perceived return of Classicism to its native land that informed this first phase of 'historicist regionalism'. Foreign scholars such as Henry-Russell Hitchcock noted the 'somewhat ironical' character of nineteenth-century buildings such as Christian and Theophile Hansen's Neo-Classical trilogy of the National Library, the University and the Academy of Athens because their '[c]onventional … international Greek Revival mode' paled in comparison as it stood in direct 'proximity to the great fifth-century ruins'.[61]

But modern Greeks tended to embrace nineteenth-century Neo-Classicism. It was received not as a foreign imposition but as an appropriate regional architectural expression with emancipatory, democratic connotations. In Tzonis and Lefaivre's words, the Neo-Classical grid was a carrier of 'autochthonous values and aspirations of freedom' for nineteenth-century modern Greeks. In their eyes, the spirit of the place *was* Classicism. In addition, its perceived contrast to the 'Oriental' ruler rendered Neo-Classicism anti-despotic and reinforced its legitimacy for the 'reawakened' modern nation state after four centuries of Ottoman control.[62] This in turn explains the positive reception of the 'grid' pattern in the work of German architects such as Leo von Klenze (1784–1864) and Ernst Ziller (1837–1923), who effectively built modern Neo-Classical Athens in the nineteenth century, and their modernist successors in the twentieth century, including Mies, Konstantinidis and the two Antonakakis. With the conviction that one can still build in a modern way with locally available materials and technological means,[63] Konstantinidis became famous for projects that combined stone-wall structures with concrete slabs to blend in with the Greek landscape, following the vernacular structures that he systematically photographed across the country (Fig. 3.2). But behind these unique buildings lay Konstantinidis's pursuit of the most effective modular span for structural grids in relation to his desired spatial configurations. The modernist ideal of standardising construction was the ultimate aim of his systematic research on grid spans, which concluded that 2.50 m was ideal for his architecture (Fig. 3.3).

In its preoccupation with 'the spirit of the place', Romanticism, this first European thread of historicist regionalism, was adversarial: anti-imperialist, anti-authoritarian and anti-formalist. The Neo-Classical 'grid' and its implications of ideal harmony and democratic order could often express a detached and overly utopian push forward. By contrast, Tzonis and Lefaivre's favoured, second, phase of Greek regionalism, which they

Figure 3.2 Aris Konstantinidis's photographs of vernacular structures in the Greek landscape (from top: Loutsa; and Mesagros, Aegina), in Aris Konstantinidis, *God-Built: Landscapes and Houses of Modern Greece* (Heraklion: Crete University Press, 1994)

designated as *critical* regionalism, was more self-reflective. This was exemplified in Pikionis's landscaping project around the Acropolis (1954–7) and, more generally, by the design principle of 'the pathway' (Fig. 3.4). In Greece, critical regionalism succeeded where the second wave of

Figure 3.3 (from top to bottom) Aris Konstantinidis, Hotel Triton, Andros, 1958; Hotel Xenia, Mykonos, 1959; Motel Xenia, Larissa, 1959; Weekend House in Anavyssos, 1962–4; 'Standardisation in Construction', in Aris Konstantinidis, *Projects + Buildings* (Athens: Agra, 1981), pp. 220–1

Aris Konstantinidis's private archive

Figure 3.4 Dimitris Pikionis, Acropolis-Philopappou, pathway to the Acropolis, 1954–7, photographed by Alexandros Papageorgiou from the Andiron of Philopappou

© 2021 Modern Greek Architecture Archives of the Benaki Museum, ANA_67_55_145

European regionalism of populist historicism failed.[64] Pikionis's work did not always avoid the pitfall of populist historicist nostalgia; in the decades that followed, it was easily recuperated by traditionalist Greek circles. But Pikionis's regionalism retained its critical edge, as it was not similarly absorbed by those vested interests that were against the progressive aspects of the welfare state.

Having first met Pikionis in 1956 – before he embarked on his architectural studies, first in Athens and then in the USA – Tzonis recalled the vision of this 'old sage' for 'a new tradition to be created within the context of an older tradition' and his belief in an ecumenism 'that can be improved through regionalism'.[65] This view enabled Pikionis to trace affinities between Greek and Japanese, but significantly not Chinese, regional architectural cultures and argue that these could coexist within the same ecumenical framework.[66] In his return to the work of earlier thinkers such as Goethe, Tzonis foregrounded regionalism as a project to 'reconstitute' a community, 'repressed' and 'fragmented' in both space and time, through a work of art or another cultural artefact:

And the significance of architecture is that through space and time it can sustain social bonds that are destroyed by politics, on the one hand, and by trade and industry, on the other ... Ruskin goes another step further ... because he identifies the erosion of social bonds with ecological destruction.[67]

Tzonis and Lefaivre argued that despite the nostalgic undertone of some of his projects, in his best work Pikionis enabled the 'tragic' and 'conflicting' aspects of Greek culture, which were previously muted and smoothed out by the ideal order of the Neo-Classical 'grid', to return to the fore. Composed of repurposed *spolia* spanning millennia, his landscaping project around the Classical Acropolis is a self-reflective collage of Post-Classical Greek culture that historically developed around the same grounds. As such, its visitors past and present are encouraged to meet there and converse with each other as they participate in the same contemplative walk that partly reveals the 'cosmic Spirit', the grand collective project of human civilisation whose different aspects are illuminated by individual cultural traditions.[68] This ecumenical vision behind Pikionis's project also renders it 'pioneering' in its dissent from universalising modernism. By adopting Pikionis's 'pathway' approach to public space and introducing it in the settings of everyday life in their private residential projects in the 1970s, Suzana and Dimitris Antonakakis critically contributed to Greek domestic architecture (Fig. 3.5).[69]

Combining the topographical sensibility of Pikionis's 'pathways' with Konstantinidis's Rationalist 'grids' (Fig. 3.6), the two Antonakakis also transgressed their forebears. When employing these patterns as the main design principles of their residential projects, they also emancipated these 'grids' and 'pathways' from their potentially utopian and nostalgic projections (Fig. 3.7). This critical embeddedness of the Antonakakis' design principles within the specific historical and social context of their time rendered their work uniquely significant for the further development of a 'critical' variant of regionalism in Greece. Focusing on the rooted experience of the place, their architecture was a realistic intervention in the sociopolitical condition at the moment of its production.

Tzonis and Lefaivre's main points became significant contributions to the Western European and North American debates of the 1980s. The concluding lines of 'The Grid and the Pathway' rendered critical regionalism the 'bridge over which any humanistic architecture of the future must pass'. The authors acknowledged the 'unique significance' of the Antonakakis' work 'not only to Greek architecture but also to contemporary architecture in general'.[70] These ideas were aligned with Frampton's own

Figure 3.5 Suzana and Dimitris Antonakakis, House at Spata, 1973–5

Suzana and Dimitris Antonakakis' private archive

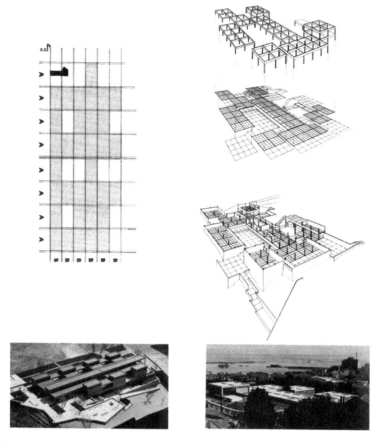

Figure 3.6 Left: Aris Konstantinidis, Archaeological Museum at Ioannina, 1964; right: Suzana and Dimitris Antonakakis and Eleni Gousi-Desylla, Archaeological Museum on Chios, 1965

Aris Konstantinidis's and Suzana and Dimitris Antonakakis' private archives

optimistic aspirations of regionalism as a sort of reformist modernism. In the eyes of Tzonis, Lefaivre and Frampton, the unfinished project of modernity could be saved by the unfulfilled pledge of a regionalism emancipated from its nationalistic connotations.

The Antonakakis' architecture of critical regionalism

Besides Frampton, and Tzonis and Lefaivre, Suzana and Dimitris Antonakakis had themselves also contributed to the theoretical

Figure 3.7 Suzana and Dimitris Antonakakis, apartment building at 118 Benaki Street, Athens, 1972–5
Suzana and Dimitris Antonakakis' private archive

development of critical regionalism. They had done so indirectly through their specific architectural concerns and their exchanges with the three authors of critical regionalism.

Tzonis had first met the architectural couple during his student years at the National Technical University of Athens in the late 1950s. The three of them had remained in contact over the years that followed. Although Tzonis moved to the USA to pursue his graduate studies at Yale University and a subsequent academic career abroad immediately after graduating from Athens in 1961, the three of them retained an occasional correspondence. This is also why Tzonis rose to the occasion when Doumanis prompted him to write a comprehensive article on the architects' work two decades later. In a letter to the couple, written in early January 1980, Tzonis thanked them for having sent him a body of articles to assist him with his writing. By then, the piece was also meant to accompany the exhibition of their work in Delft (set for 27 October to 4 December 1981)[71] following an invitation by Aldo van Eyck.[72] Dimitris Antonakakis had essentially forwarded a copy of the portfolio that he had submitted for his academic candidacy at the National Technical University of Athens. This included a comprehensive list of their projects (with Atelier 66) until 1978, previous publications of the most celebrated among them and a series of articles that Suzana and Dimitris Antonakakis had published in the mainstream and specialised press of the period. The articles covered an array of subjects, ranging from the problems posed by tourist development in Greece, and the points of contact between public and private space, to the unforeseen transformations of residential spaces during their inhabitation and the apartment building in Greece in relation to the role of the architect.[73] This material not only documented Suzana and Dimitris Antonakakis' socially conscious approach to architectural design, it also implicitly developed aspects of the 'pathway' thematic by the time Tzonis and Lefaivre began writing 'The Grid and the Pathway'.

Soon afterwards, draft typescripts of 'The Grid and the Pathway' started circulating between Tzonis and Lefaivre, the Antonakakis and Doumanis. The fifteen-page draft typescript retrieved from Suzana and Dimitris Antonakakis' private archive includes the two architects' handwritten notes. The sporadic corrections, comments and modifications suggested by them added their own touches to Tzonis and Lefaivre's original manuscript. Alongside their suggestions for the typescript, the architects included a list of their proffered projects to illustrate the article. They also used coloured pencils to draw over plans from their selected projects in order to highlight specific spatial qualities and their main architectural intentions (Fig. 3.8).

At first glance, Suzana and Dimitris Antonakakis' notes to the draft typescript are not particularly extensive. Their most crucial contribution to the piece lies in its visual side. The architects provided eloquent figures, drawings and photographs to be used as illustrations for the article. Through these, Suzana and Dimitris Antonakakis implicitly offered their own interpretation of their built projects. In so doing, they also added a layer of historical accuracy to Tzonis and Lefaivre's wider-reaching theorisations. More specifically, the architects clarified the influences that had legitimised some of their key design solutions. For instance, in the draft typescript, Tzonis and Lefaivre had proposed accompanying their discussion of the Antonakakis' Archaeological Museum on Chios (1965) with an image of Konstantinidis's Weekend House in Anavyssos. By doing so, they intended to illustrate the common use of Rationalist 'grids' in the early works of the Antonakakis with Konstantinidis. Although the Weekend House in Anavyssos was indeed an emblem of Konstantinidis's architecture,[74] the Antonakakis disagreed. Instead, they preferred to include images from his Museum in Ioannina, as this project shared more affinities with their Archaeological Museum on Chios in terms of scale, programme and spatial organisation (Fig. 3.6). The museum project was more relevant to the work of the Antonakakis, as the young architects had actually consulted Konstantinidis when designing the Museum on Chios in the early 1960s. They had first met him in the late 1950s as students,

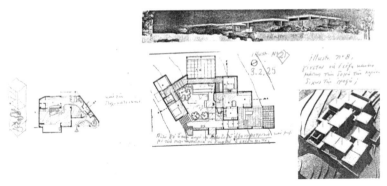

Figure 3.8 A draft typescript of Alexander Tzonis and Liane Lefaivre's 'The Grid and the Pathway', including handwritten notes by Suzana and Dimitris Antonakakis

Suzana and Dimitris Antonakakis' private archive

when they were commissioned to make a model for his Meteora Xenia Motel project.[75]

For another section of the article, the two architects selected images that highlighted key characteristics of their projects (Fig. 3.8). These included the relations between enclosed and outdoor spaces and their usually porous boundaries, as well as their use of thresholds, trajectories and landings as an architectural means of orchestrating movement in the spaces that they designed. To further emphasise the focal points of their design practice, the couple included keywords (such as 'pathway-balcony', 'view-pathway', 'gateway', 'threshold', 'intersection', 'steps', 'widening') in their handwritten notes on the images. Embracing Tzonis and Lefaivre's analysis of the 'grid' and the 'pathway', the Antonakakis intended to reinforce it by turning the article's illustrations into a visual narrative. This is why they noted that the illustrations of their Museum on Chios should emphasise the columns that supported the structure (clearly foregrounding their 'grid' pattern).

In addition, Suzana and Dimitris Antonakakis noted that the constituents of the 'pathway' evident in the photographs of their House at Spata (1973–5) should also be traced in their Benaki Street apartment building (1972–5); in Pikionis's Acropolis landscaping project; and in vernacular architecture. In the two architects' own words, this would 'reveal the structural homologies' between their work. The House at Spata thus becomes the generator of the Antonakakis–Tzonis & Lefaivre correspondence around the 'pathway'.[76] Dimitris Antonakakis used to refer to the internal movement that effectively serves as the backbone for this house in terms of a 'corridor-street'. This term was intended to encompass both the sense of a direct transition from one space to the next and the dynamics of intersecting gazes and chance meetings in an urban street. The illustrations selected by the Antonakakis slightly modified the visual narrative of their architectural patterns and influences. This gave rise to associations and meanings that in turn brought Tzonis and Lefaivre's textual observations into a sharper focus, to align them with the architects' own concerns.

But the Antonakakis' organisation of the visual material also enabled different free associations for a reader's trained eye. The way in which they presented their material on the page, for instance, is reminiscent of Gordon Cullen's discussions of Townscape and the Picturesque in the British postwar context.[77] But in the case of the Antonakakis, this townscape unfolds within a single architectural project. Although Suzana and Dimitris Antonakakis did not refer to Cullen, Tzonis and Lefaivre's article did open with a discussion of the English Picturesque as the 'most prominent' regionalist movement of the early eighteenth century.[78] As such, more subtle associations and references could be generated from the Antonakakis' curation of the visual material.

This architectural concern, which centred on public space in its transitive relationship with other social spaces of increased privacy, had been consciously cultivated over two decades. As a rooted product of

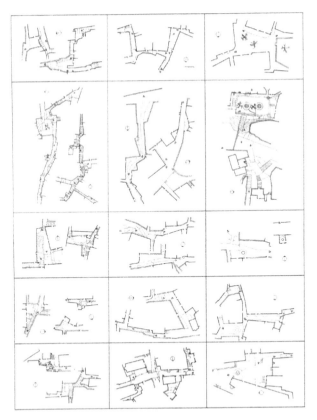

Figure 3.9 Dimitris Antonakakis, Hydra: crossroads, stairways, courts and landings, concluding illustration in Alexander Tzonis and Liane Lefaivre, 'The Grid and the Pathway: An Introduction to the Work of Dimitris and Suzana Antonakakis, with Prolegomena to a History of the Culture of Modern Greek Architecture', *Architecture in Greece*, 15 (1981), 164–78 (p. 177)

Suzana and Dimitris Antonakakis' private archive

Greek culture, it was also key to both Tzonis and Lefaivre's and Frampton's discourses. 'The Grid and the Pathway' closed with a systematic presentation of Dimitris Antonakakis's measured drawings from the island of Hydra (Fig. 3.9). The original drawings, on which the published typological matrix was based, dated back to Antonakakis's student years in the late 1950s. His survey of crossroads, and pedestrian circulation on smooth plateaus and steep slopes, also documented the transitive relations between public and private spaces from streets to courtyards. The observations recorded in this mature student work presaged Suzana and Dimitris Antonakakis' future projects.[79]

A decade later, the two architects (in collaboration with their peers from Atelier 66) surveyed the Cycladic Island settlements following a similar approach, which was theorised by Dimitris Antonakakis in 1973. Because they were published under the Greek military regime, his 'observations on the boundary' that brings public and private space into contact also had undeniable political gravitas: 'The more one area permeates the other, the more its characteristics influence the other and the easier the transition from one to the other ... Semitones are shaped ... The complexity of these mutual permeations variegates the trajectory in Public space and affords Private space an identity of its own.'[80] Antonakakis stressed the architectural need for intermediate spaces that enable the public and private realms to gradually fade into one another. He clarified that this was not a strictly spatial or formal relationship. Abolishing hard boundaries was a matter of social life itself, through the transfer of certain public functions and activities into private spaces, and vice versa (Fig. 3.10). Antonakakis clarified that the processes that shape the boundaries between public and private spaces are 'a result of human behaviour in relation to specific cultural conditions, social structure, political organisation and institutional frameworks determined by the citizens themselves or others that shape their environment'.[81]

From the drawings of the mature student projects to Antonakakis's theorisation of 1973, the sensibilities behind Tzonis and Lefaivre's 'pathway' pattern as a catalyst for social life enjoyed a long history of their own in the architects' work. In Tzonis and Lefaivre's words:

> The pathway is the backbone from which each place grows and to which each place leads. As in the case of the grid, it may control also aspects of the microclimate, the flow of air, the view or the course of service lines; but its primary role is to be a catalyst of social life. Every time its circuit is laid down and every time one passes through it, it can be seen as the reenactment of a ritual, the confirmation of the human community and a criticism of the alienating effects of contemporary life. Together with the grid, the pathway is a commitment to architecture as a cultural object in a social context.[82]

In a case like this, it is difficult to draw a line between the theorists' and the architects' contribution to the development of this discourse. In any case, the published version of 'The Grid and the Pathway' does bear the subtle mark of its reinterpretation by Suzana and Dimitris Antonakakis.

The importance of 'The Grid and the Pathway' as a mediator between the British historian and the Greek architects can hardly be

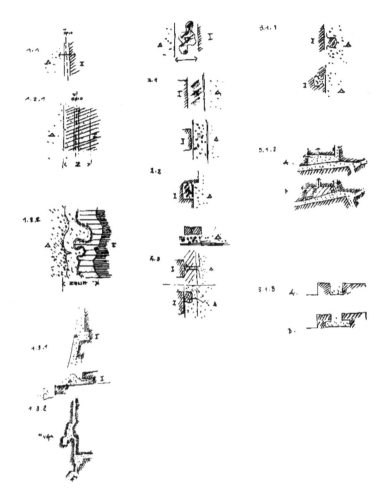

Figure 3.10 Dimitris Antonakakis's illustrations for 'Παρατηρήσεις στο όριο επαφής δημόσιου και ιδιωτικού Χώρου', *Χρονικό* (1973), 169–71
Suzana and Dimitris Antonakakis' private archive

overstated. It offered critical theoretical categories, as well as a broad historical and sociopolitical contextualisation, to Suzana and Dimitris Antonakakis' built work. In other words, the article gave Frampton the tools that he needed to read and understand it as a concrete expression of his own developing regionalist discourse. This is why critical regionalism is a historical artefact of cross-cultural authorship. This mode of production of architectural discourse was also aligned with the main aims behind it. Far from promoting a static cultural insularity, this regionalism was the discursive footprint of architectural concerns travelling through cultures. Thus, the Benaki Street apartment building found its place in the British historian's anthology of critical regionalist projects at the end of 1982.

Frampton's list of critical architectural practices was compiled even earlier. By the end of 1981, the British historian had already formed his vision of 'unsentimental regionality' in the work of selected architects across the globe. Approximately a year after his resignation from the Biennale, his counterattack to the Strada Novissima was clear. The Postmodern Classicism of the Stern–Jencks alliance could not be allowed to dominate the discussion. Attempting to shift international attention away from the Strada Novissima historicists, Frampton outlined a series of eighteen monographs on critical architectural practices. All these monographs were to be published by Rizzoli within two to four years. Predominantly European, Frampton's selections outlined the 'other' side of the Biennale.[83] Not including a single North American architect, Frampton focused on the parts of the same discussion that were not represented at the Strada Novissima. He highlighted architectural practices that developed alternative approaches to the crisis of modernism, ranging from Norman Foster to Suzana and Dimitris Antonakakis. Aware of Tzonis's critical involvement with the work of the architectural couple, in late 1981 Frampton already had him in mind to introduce the Greek architects' work to an international audience.

Since then, Frampton had been in regular contact with the Antonakakis to work on their monograph, and the couple invited him to Greece 'to meet each other and to discuss not only about the publication' but 'also to experience some of [their] built projects'.[84] Frampton finally met them in Greece in July 1983, at the second international architectural symposium organised by Dimitris Fatouros and the Aristotelian University of Thessaloniki (in collaboration with Roy Landau and the Architectural Association) on Hydra. After the symposium, he also spent an afternoon with them in Athens and Filothei, presumably visiting Pikionis's works there and the Antonakakis' own Benaki Street apartment building.[85]

Titled 'A Context for Architectural Culture', the Hydra 1983 symposium aimed to bring together practising architects, educators and critics, and discuss their work in a single common framework. Architectural culture was seen as the combined result of the discourses, beliefs, influences and constraints of those agents that shape architecture as a collective product of this shared context.[86] The symposium marked the first time that Frampton presented the six points of his firmly articulated critical regionalism in Greece. Responding to the symposium's brief, Frampton also clarified that his role was to deliver 'criticism of support ... prejudiced in favour of the effort to build'.[87] In their presentation, which was chaired by Frampton, Suzana and Dimitris Antonakakis in turn focused on key concerns of their projects – including their design through 'construction zoning', 'the significance of movement, the "ambiguity" of architecture (A. van Eyck's "twin phenomena"), the use of colour and their interpretation of traditional Mediterranean case studies'.[88] In the ensuing discussion, members of the audience noted how the two architects 'start from very detailed elaborated elements' in their 'architecture of devotion and detail' that reinterprets 'traditional typologies'. Their work was described as 'liberative micro-place making', as it catered for the human scale and the phenomenological experience of architecture instead of 'naïve functionalism'. But this 'architecture of devotion' demanded the respective 'devotion by the user in order not to create micro-disasters', which demonstrated the high level of 'control of designed space by the architect'. The discussion also touched on the degree to which these elements retain their independence from the specific, small scale of their buildings and their use to become 'patterns at a prototypic level'. These should not be 'very deep to create new architectural forms' whilst avoiding 'produc[ing] surface imitation of vernacular' features. Frampton noted how their 'delicacy of re-interpreting tradition' leads to 'connotations other than those included in the [original] idea'.[89]

In the context of the symposium, Suzana and Dimitris Antonakakis' reflection on their own work through these themes served as a further elaboration and concrete expression of Frampton's theoretical endeavour. Their reference to concerns that they shared with Aldo van Eyck also brought a subtle historical depth to the fore. The Antonakakis were implicitly reconnecting Frampton's regionalism with the original Team 10 critiques of modernism and his appreciation of the Dutch architects of Structuralism. This move was significant in the wider context of the postmodern debates of the period. It brought back another aspect of the diverse responses to the crisis of modern architecture that were relatively silenced after the Biennale. The Antonakakis' reference to Van Eyck insisted on the contemporaneous relevance of Team 10 revisionism in 1983. This was what the Greek architects' own 'regionalism' had always been about, anyway: in broad terms, a sort of critical modernism.

The architects' long-standing concerns fed in to the development of Tzonis and Lefaivre's theoretical discourse on their work, which was in turn assimilated in Frampton's critical regionalism. As such, the discourse of critical regionalism registered the footprint of the mutual exchanges between the architects, historians and critics involved during the early 1980s. For example, it was not long before Frampton also started to discuss the work of Dutch Structuralist architects such as Van Eyck in terms of regionalism.[90] Each of the individual agents participating in this set of relations added a personalised nuance that renders critical regionalism an artefact of cross-cultural authorship. An outcome of a dynamic mode of production of architectural discourse through multifaceted authorship, critical regionalism challenges the artificial boundaries between theory and practice. From the outset, the Antonakakis' built work was at its epicentre. As Tzonis and Lefaivre's discourse was constructed around it, the Greek architects' regional architectural concerns also remained implicit in the background of Frampton's discourse. The same was the case for Tzonis and Lefaivre's socio-economic account of the participatory design movement in architecture. This subtle thread that remained implicit within Frampton's critical regionalism enabled the earlier socially conscious aspects of postmodern architectural developments to re-enter contemporary discussions. The novel discursive space that Frampton explored after the Biennale thus enriched the postmodern debates with a crucial cross-cultural dimension that also hinted at its longer underlying history.

This interplay of the international with the regional dimension was the most important, but also the most easily misinterpreted, characteristic of critical regionalism. The problem was rooted in Frampton's own structural position in the international discursive field, which did not serve the purpose of critical regionalism. As this did not go unnoticed by Frampton's critics over the decades that followed,[91] the next chapter discusses this aspect of the development and dissemination of the critical regionalist discourse, focusing on its inherent media problem.

Notes

1   Léa-Catherine Szacka, *Exhibiting the Postmodern: The 1980 Venice Architecture Biennale* (Venice: Marsilio, 2016), pp. 233–41.
2   See Kenneth Frampton, 'Du Néo-Productivisme au Post-Modernisme', *L'Architecture d'Aujourd'hui*, 213 (1981), 2–7; Kenneth Frampton, 'The Isms of Contemporary Architecture', *Architectural Design*, 52.7/8 (1982), 60–83; Kenneth Frampton, 'Modern Architecture and Critical Regionalism', *RIBA Transactions*, 3.2 (1983), 15–25.
3   Alexander Tzonis and Liane Lefaivre, 'The Grid and the Pathway: An Introduction to the Work of Dimitris and Suzana Antonakakis, with Prolegomena to a History of the Culture of Modern Greek Architecture', *Architecture in Greece*, 15 (1981), 164–78.
4   Kenneth Frampton, 3-page letter to Paolo Portoghesi, 25 April 1980, Fondo storico La Biennale di Venezia, Architettura, b. 658, Mostra internazionale di architettura, "Riunioni commissione architettura: regolamento", 1980–1983, pp. 1–3.
5   Charles Jencks, 'Counter-Reformation: Reflections on the 1980 Venice Biennale', *Architectural Design*, 52.1/2 (1982), 4–7 (p. 4).
6   Kenneth Frampton, interviewed by Léa-Catherine Szacka (via email, 22 April 2009), cited in Léa-Catherine Szacka, 'Exhibiting the Postmodern: Three Narratives for a History of the 1980 Venice Architecture Biennale', doctoral thesis, University College London, 2011, p. 272.
7   Kenneth Frampton, letter to Robert A.M. Stern, 13 May 1980, New Haven, Robert A.M. Stern Architects Records (MS 1859) Manuscripts and Archives, Yale University Library, Box 2, file 13, p. 1.
8   Frampton, letter to Portoghesi, p. 2.

9   See Martin Heidegger, 'Building Dwelling Thinking' (1951), repr. in Martin Heidegger, *Poetry, Language, Thought*, trans. by Albert Hofstadter (New York: Harper Colophon, 1971), pp. 141–60.
10 Hanna Arendt, *The Human Condition* (Chicago: University of Chicago Press, 1958), pp. 198–9.
11 See Tom Avermaete et al., 'A Conversation with Kenneth Frampton: New York, 6 April 2018', *OASE*, 103 (2019), 142–54 (p. 145).
12 See Herbert Marcuse, *Eros and Civilization* (New York: Vintage, 1962); Mary McLeod, 'Kenneth Frampton's Idea of the "Critical"', in *Modern Architecture and the Lifeworld: Essays in Honor of Kenneth Frampton*, ed. by Karla Cavarra Britton and Robert McCarter (London: Thames & Hudson, 2020), pp. 20–42.
13 See Kenneth Frampton, *Modern Architecture: A Critical History* (London: Thames & Hudson, 1980), pp. 280–97.
14 Kenneth Frampton, 'On Reading Heidegger', *Oppositions*, 4 (1974), 1–4.
15 Frampton, *Modern Architecture*, p. 296.
16 See Frampton, 'On Reading Heidegger'.
17 Kenneth Frampton, 'Avant-Garde and Continuity', *Architectural Design*, 52.7/8 (1982), 20–7 (p. 24).
18 Kenneth Frampton, 'The Resistance of Architecture', 34-page typescript, CCA IAUS, C1-36 @ C1-83, IAUS files, 57 – 006, B 50 5 03, C1-42, p. F2 (emphasis in the original).
19 Ibid., p. F28.
20 Charles Jencks, 'The… New… International… Style… e altre etichette', *Domus*, 623 (1981), 41–7.
21 Frampton did not even 'recall having written' this text in the first place, in his email interview with Szacka on 22 April 2009. Frampton cited in Szacka, 'Exhibiting the Postmodern', p. 271 (note 668).
22 Szacka, *Exhibiting the Postmodern*, p. 236.
23 See Kenneth Frampton, 1980 agenda, 4 January 1981, CCA Fonds 197, Kenneth Frampton fonds, 197 – 2017 – 090T, AP197.S6.001, 1980 agenda, 1980, 197-114-011.
24 Frampton, letter to Portoghesi, p. 2.
25 'Post-Modernism' appears only twice in Frampton, *Modern Architecture*, pp. 289, 290. Its first occurrence in inverted commas further emphasises Frampton's reluctance to employ the term in his discourse at that time.
26 Frampton, 'The Resistance of Architecture', p. F17 (emphasis in the original).
27 Frampton elaborated this point in Kenneth Frampton, 'The Status of Man and his Objects: A Reading of *The Human Condition*', *Architectural Design*, 52.7/8 (1982), 6–19 (p. 13); Frampton, 'Avant-Garde and Continuity', p. 21.
28 Frampton, 'Du Néo-Productivisme au Post-Modernisme', pp. 5–6.
29 See 'Realismus in der Architektur', ed. by Bruno Reichlin and Martin Steinmann. Special issue, *Archithese*, 19 (1976); Bernard Huet, 'Formalisme/Realisme', *L'Architecture d'Aujourd'hui*, 190 (April 1977), 35–6.
30 See Kenneth Frampton, 'Mario Botta and the School of the Ticino', *Oppositions*, 14 (1978), 1–25; Irina Davidovici, 'Constructing "the School of the Ticino": The Historiography of a New Swiss Architecture, 1975–1990', *Journal of Architecture*, 25.8 (2020), 1115–40.
31 See Kenneth Frampton, 'Constructivism: The Pursuit of an Elusive Sensibility', *Oppositions*, 6 (1976), 25–44; Jorge Otero-Pailos, *Architecture's Historical Turn: Phenomenology and the Rise of the Postmodern* (Minneapolis: University of Minnesota Press, 2011), pp. 183–249.
32 Frampton, 'Du Néo-Productivisme au Post-Modernisme', p. 6.
33 See Kenneth Frampton, 'Maison de Verre', *Perspecta*, 12 (1969), 77–109, 111–28.
34 Frampton, 'Du Néo-Productivisme au Post-Modernisme', pp. 3, 5.
35 Ibid., pp. xlvi, 5.
36 Frampton's first grouping of regionalist architects comprised Álvaro Siza, Jørn Utzon, Mario Botta, Luis Barragán and Tadao Ando. Rather tellingly, none of them had been invited to participate in the Biennale. His 1982 additions included Oriol Bohigas, José Antonio Coderch, Amancio Williams, Gino Valle, Ernst Gisel, Peter Celsing, Oswald Mathias Ungers, Aris Konstantinidis, Paolo Soleri, Ludwig Leo, Carlo Scarpa, Louis Kahn, Dolf Schnebli, Aurelio Galfetti and Tita Carloni. See Frampton, 'The Isms of Contemporary Architecture'.
37 See Paul Ricoeur, 'Universal Civilisation and National Cultures' (1961), repr. in Paul Ricoeur, *History and Truth*, trans. by Charles A. Kelbley (Evanston, IL: Northwestern University Press, 1965), pp. 271–84; Gevork Hartoonian, 'An Interview with Kenneth Frampton', *Architectural Theory Review*, 7.1 (2002), 59–64 (pp. 59–60).

38   Kenneth Frampton, 'Intimations of Tactility: Excerpts from a Fragmentary Polemic', *Artforum* (March 1981), 52–8.
39   Frampton, 'The Isms of Contemporary Architecture', p. 77.
40   Ibid., p. 82.
41   Frampton, 'Modern Architecture and Critical Regionalism', pp. 20–1.
42   Ibid., p. 18.
43   See Kenneth Frampton, 'Prospects for a Critical Regionalism', *Perspecta*, 20 (1983), 147–62; Kenneth Frampton, 'Towards a Critical Regionalism: Six Points for an Architecture of Resistance', in *The Anti-Aesthetic: Essays on Postmodern Culture*, ed. by Hal Foster (Seattle: Bay Press, 1983), pp. 16–30.
44   Frampton, 'Towards a Critical Regionalism', p. 29.
45   Kenneth Frampton, *Modern Architecture: A Critical History*, 2nd edn (London: Thames & Hudson, 1985), p. 327.
46   Frampton, 'Towards a Critical Regionalism', p. 26. See Christian Norberg-Schulz, *Genius Loci: Towards a Phenomenology of Architecture* (London: Academy, 1980), p. 15.
47   Frampton, 'Towards a Critical Regionalism', p. 26. See Vittorio Gregotti, *Il territorio dell'architettura* (Milan: Feltrinelli, 1966); Lejla Vujicic, 'Architecture of the Longue Durée: Vittorio Gregotti's Reading of the Territory of Architecture', *Architectural Research Quarterly*, 19.2 (2015), 161–74.
48   Frampton, 'The Isms of Contemporary Architecture', p. 82.
49   For Frampton's editorial activity at *Architectural Design* from July 1962 to January 1965, see Stephen Parnell, '*Architectural Design*, 1954–1972: The Architectural Magazine's Contribution to the Writing of Architectural History', unpublished doctoral thesis, University of Sheffield, 2012, pp. 159–87.
50   It was Panos Koulermos (1933–99) who originally brought Frampton in contact with Konstantinidis. A Greek-Cypriot migrant, Koulermos (who additionally served as the magazine's correspondent for Italy) also worked with Frampton at Douglas Stephen and Partners. Frampton considered Douglas Stephen's and Thomas Stevens's influence as crucial for his 'return to the values of the "heroic period"' of the modern movement'. See Kenneth Frampton, 'Μοντέρνο, πολύ μοντέρνο: Μια συνέντευξη του Kenneth Frampton στον Γιώργο Σημαιοφορίδη', *Architecture in Greece*, 20 (1986), 118–21 (pp. 118, 120).
51   This is discussed in more detail in chapter 6.
52   Frampton, 'Μοντέρνο, πολύ μοντέρνο', p. 118.
53   Ibid., p. 120.
54   Vincent B. Canizaro, 'Preface: The Promise of Regionalism', in *Architectural Regionalism: Collected Writings on Place, Identity, Modernity, and Tradition*, ed. by Vincent B. Canizaro (New York: Princeton Architectural Press, 2007), pp. 10–12 (p. 11).
55   Suzana and Dimitris Antonakakis, interviewed by Stylianos Giamarelos (Athens: 23 June 2013).
56   See 'Antonakakis, Dimitris' and 'Antonakakis, Suzana (Maria)', in *Contemporary Architects*, ed. by Muriel Emanuel (Basingstoke: Macmillan, 1980), pp. 36–9; 'Traces of an Itinerary: The Architectural Work of Suzana and Dimitris Antonakakis', exhibition at the Architectural Association, 4–27 February 1982.
57   Tzonis and Lefaivre, 'The Grid and the Pathway', p. 178.
58   Ibid., p. 172.
59   Ibid., p. 164.
60   Ibid., pp. 164–5.
61   Henry-Russell Hitchcock, *Architecture: Nineteenth and Twentieth Centuries*, 3rd edn (Harmondsworth: Penguin, 1968), p. 38.
62   Tzonis and Lefaivre, 'The Grid and the Pathway', p. 166.
63   See Elisabeth Landgraf, 'Interview mit Aris Konstantinidis', *Moebel Interior Design*, 7 (1965), 25.
64   Tzonis and Lefaivre, 'The Grid and the Pathway', pp. 174–6.
65   Alexander Tzonis, 'Πικιώνης-Κωνσταντινίδης: Ασύμπτωτοι: Ηλιού-Τζώνης', transcript of a postgraduate seminar session at the National Technical University of Athens, 1999, Suzana and Dimitris Antonakakis' private archive, pp. 17–27 (pp. 18–19).
66   Ibid., pp. 20–1.
67   Ibid., pp. 26–7.

68 See Dimitris Pikionis, 'Το πρόβλημα της μορφής' (1951), repr. in Δ. Πικιώνης: Κείμενα, ed. by Agni Pikioni and Michalis Parousis (Athens: MIET, 1985), pp. 204–46 (pp. 217–18).

69 Tzonis and Lefaivre, 'The Grid and the Pathway', p. 176.

70 Ibid., p. 178.

71 This explains the almost simultaneous appearance of a translation of 'The Grid and the Pathway' in Dutch. See Alexander Tzonis and Liane Lefaivre, 'Het Raster en het Pad', Wonen-TA/BK, 20–1 (1981), 31–42. I revisit this exhibition in chapter 7.

72 Antonakakis, interviewed by Giamarelos.

73 See Dimitris Antonakakis, Βιογραφικό Υπόμνημα, National Technical University of Athens School of Architecture, 1978, Suzana and Dimitris Antonakakis' private archive; Dimitris Antonakakis, 'Προσεγγίσεις: Προβλήματα τουριστικής ανάπτυξης', Οικονομικός Ταχυδρόμος, 218 (1971), 43–7; Dimitris Antonakakis, 'Παρατηρήσεις στο όριο επαφής δημόσιου και ιδιωτικού Χώρου', Χρονικό (1973), 169–71; Dimitris and Suzana Antonakakis and Costis Hadjimichalis, 'Unforeseen Changes in the Dwelling Space (1)', Design + Art in Greece, 6 (1975), 36–53; Dimitris and Suzana Antonakakis, 'Apartment Houses in Athens: The Architect's Role', Architecture in Greece, 12 (1978), 151–3.

74 See Stylianos Giamarelos, 'The Art of Building Reception: Aris Konstantinidis behind the Global Published Life of his Weekend House in Anavyssos (1962–2014)', Architectural Histories, 2.1 (2014), art. 22. doi.org/10.5334/ah.bx.

75 Antonakakis, interviewed by Giamarelos.

76 This is also why the discussion of the 'pathway' pattern in the final version of 'The Grid and the Pathway' opens with the House at Spata. See Liane Lefaivre and Alexander Tzonis, 'The Grid and the Pathway: An Introduction to the Work of Dimitris and Suzana Antonakakis in the Context of Greek Architectural Culture', in Atelier 66: The Architecture of Dimitris and Suzana Antonakakis, ed. by Kenneth Frampton (New York: Rizzoli, 1985), pp. 14–25.

77 See Gordon Cullen, Townscape (London: Architectural Press, 1961).

78 Tzonis and Lefaivre, 'The Grid and the Pathway', p. 165.

79 I discuss Suzana and Dimitris Antonakakis' mature student projects in chapter 8.

80 Antonakakis, 'Παρατηρήσεις στο όριο επαφής', pp. 169–70.

81 Ibid., p. 171.

82 Tzonis and Lefaivre, 'The Grid and the Pathway', p. 178.

83 See Kenneth Frampton, 4-page letter to Suzana and Dimitris Antonakakis, 21 December 1981, Suzana and Dimitris Antonakakis' private archive. Fourteen out of Frampton's eighteen selected architects were Western European. The non-European group included Barton Meyers (Canada), Kazuo Shinohara and Tadao Ando (Japan) and Balkrishna Doshi (India).

84 See Suzana and Dimitris Antonakakis, 2-page letter to Kenneth Frampton, 5 January 1983, CCA Fonds 197, Kenneth Frampton fonds, 197 – 2017 – 114T, AP197.S3.001, Personal and professional correspondence 1983, 1983, 197-114-025.

85 Suzana and Dimitris Antonakakis, letter to Kenneth Frampton, 6 August 1983, CCA Fonds 197, Kenneth Frampton fonds, 197 – 2017 – 114T, AP197.S3.001, Personal and professional correspondence 1983, 1983, 197-114-025.

86 For the first symposium on Hydra, see Yorgos Simeoforidis, 'Αρχιτεκτονική γλώσσα της δεκαετίας 1980–90: Επιστημονικό συμπόσιο αρχιτεκτονικής στην Ύδρα', Journal of the Association of Greek Architects, 7 (1981), 27.

87 Kenneth Frampton, 'The Case for Regionalism', Hydra, 17 July 1983, 2-page handwritten notes by Anastasios M. Kotsiopoulos, Anastasios M. Kotsiopoulos private archive.

88 Yorgos Simeoforidis, 'ΥΔΡΑ 83 ή Τι συνέβη σε ένα Διεθνές Αρχιτεκτονικό Συνέδριο', Journal of the Association of Greek Architects, 19.5/6 (1983), 13–15 (p. 14); Sibel Dostoglu, 'The Current State of Architecture: A Context for Architectural Culture, Hydra, 1983', AA Files, 5 (1984), 105–6 (p. 106).

89 Suzana and Dimitris Antonakakis, 'Design Presentation', Hydra, 16 July 1983, 2-page handwritten notes by Anastasios M. Kotsiopoulos, Anastasios M. Kotsiopoulos private archive.

90 See Kenneth Frampton, 'Het structurele regionalism van Herman Hertzberger', Archis, 12 (December 1986), 8–13.

91 See Keith L. Eggener, 'Placing Resistance: A Critique of Critical Regionalism', Journal of Architectural Education, 55.4 (2002), 228–37.

4
Media problem

Even if Erdem Erten was right to note in 2004 that critical regionalism 'has received international currency probably more than any other "ism" of the postwar period',[1] this was not a straightforward process of communicating a message through the publicising venues available to architects and critics of the 1980s. This decade signalled a restructuring of the media landscape, including new ways in which architectural publishers started to engage with the public through exhibitions, competitions, symposia and other self-initiated events that went beyond what was simply featured on the printed page. In this constantly shifting landscape of architectural publicity, critical regionalism had to address a media problem of its own in order to get its message across. In this chapter, I read Kenneth Frampton's main texts of the early 1980s in their specific historical context: their respective publication in *L'Architecture d'Aujourd'hui*, *Architectural Design*, the RIBA 1982/1983 lecture series and Hal Foster's anthology of essays on postmodern culture. Frampton originally intended to dissociate his discourse from the camp of the Venetian postmodernists. But less than three decades later, his project was presented as 'the dominant mode of postmodern regional theory'.[2] This chapter will show how this is a symptom of the inherent media problem of critical regionalism in the early 1980s. As diverging agendas of different publishing venues distorted the reception of Frampton's work, his fundamental disagreement with Robert Stern was also misconstrued as an inconsequential, hair-splitting debate on regionalism.

Despite the fact that Alexander Tzonis and Liane Lefaivre's first account of critical regionalism had already been published in English, French, Dutch and Greek by 1982,[3] it was only after 'The Grid and the Pathway' was mentioned in Frampton's best-selling critical history of modern architecture that it made an impact at a worldwide scale. This was owing to language barriers and the comparatively limited outreach of publications such as *Architecture in Greece*, *Wonen-TA/BK* and even the more established *Le carré bleu* in specific continental-European architectural circles. As a result, Tzonis and Lefaivre's subsequent publications in Greek, Dutch and Spanish, in which they continued to develop their ideas on critical regionalism, were rather inconsequential in international debates at the time.[4]

By contrast, it was not long before Frampton's *Modern Architecture: A Critical History* attracted the interest of 'a new generation and a new constituency' of anglophone architects who started to be professionally active after the mid-1960s.[5] Successively republished over the past four decades, this book is now available in more than ten languages, from Spanish to Chinese, and still serves as a textbook in schools of architecture across the globe. Although exact figures are not available, Frampton noted that his publishers Thames & Hudson had already 'sold over 44,000 copies of *Modern Architecture: A Critical History*, in Italy alone' by 1995.[6] Through this extensive global outreach, Frampton's version of critical regionalism took precedence over the earlier account by Tzonis and Lefaivre, who also acknowledged that Frampton's 'writings ... helped raise and spread the issue of critical regionalism more than any other' during the 1980s.[7]

Possibly owing to the unexpected positive Western European and North American reception of critical regionalism, it took Tzonis and Lefaivre two decades to publish their first book-length account of the subject – and another one to usher in their definitive work on critical regionalism, which is still only a decade old at time of writing.[8] Despite the couple's more comprehensive work on the subject, Frampton is still widely regarded as 'the champion of Critical Regionalism' to this day.[9] This fact alone demonstrates how Frampton's specific positioning within the architectural media ecology of the 1980s proved much more impactful and influential for the architectural vision that he intended to promote. The success of critical regionalism as a mainstream architectural discourse is reflected in the list of forty-four architects who have won the Pritzker Architecture Prize to date.[10] More than one out of four of these laureates have either formed part of the critical regionalist canon of the 1980s (from Álvaro Siza to Jørn Utzon), or have been associated with it through Frampton's or Tzonis and Lefaivre's later writings (from Glenn Murcutt to Wang Shu). Other 'critical regionalist' architects were also nominated for this prize earlier in the 1980s – including Aris Konstantinidis, who lost to the 'postmodernist' Hans Hollein in 1985.[11]

As I have already discussed in chapter 2, this does not mean that the increasing interest in questions of regionalism in architecture was

Figure 4.1   Kenneth Frampton lecture at the Faculty of Architecture and the Built Environment, TU Delft, in the 1980s

ARCH284695, Kenneth Frampton fonds, Canadian Centre for Architecture, Gift of Kenneth Frampton

exclusively owing to the 1980s work of Frampton, Tzonis and Lefaivre. Various Western European and North American architectural circles grappled with similar questions at the same time. The 1976 exhibition on the work of Luis Barragán – the Mexican architect who also won the Pritzker prize, in 1980 – at the Museum of Modern Art in New York can be regarded as a culmination of similar developments in architectural thinking at the time.[12] Critical regionalism was historically successful because it built on these existing trends to offer a unifying discourse for such developments across the globe. But it also offered them exposure to wider audiences. In addition to his teaching at Columbia University, which introduced his students to a wide range of architects practising across the world, Frampton publicised his evolving articulations of regionalism at well-attended events in London, New York and other cultural capitals of the Western world (Fig. 4.1). This did not go unnoticed by architects and critics who worked in a similar direction in different contexts. Owing to his earlier publications on the significance of place-making and 'The School of the Ticino' in *Oppositions* in the 1970s, Frampton was soon invited to contribute to their discussions of regionalism in architecture.[13] Even before the addition of the final chapter on critical regionalism in his book in 1985, just after his 1983 publications in *Perspecta* and Foster's anthology, Frampton was regularly invited to lecture about it or contribute with related texts to journals from – in 1984 alone, for example – the USA and the UK to Spain, Mexico, China and Cuba.[14]

While Frampton was interested in 'marginal' practices of the 'periphery', his discourse was still a cultural product of the 'hegemonic centre'. As such, the context and the terminology that Frampton shared with critics such as Charles Jencks rendered his critical regionalism a crucial, yet occasionally indistinguishable, intervention in the postmodern debates of the period. While this was the main media problem of critical regionalism, it is only one of its two sides. For, conversely, Frampton's discourse was also a self-conscious media construct, as I show in the pages that follow.

Postmodern regionalism

The publication of Frampton's 'From Neo-Productivism to Post-Modernism' (1981) in *L'Architecture d'Aujourd'hui* coincided with the agreement between the Biennale and the Festival d'Automne to transfer the 'Presence of the Past' exhibition to Paris.[15] Reaffirming the success of the show in Venice, this agreement signified a growing interest in postmodern developments that also registered in the architectural press of the period. The modified title of the Parisian iteration of the exhibition 'The Presence of History: After Modernism' further reinforced the identification of postmodern architecture with historicist eclecticism.

The February 1981 issue of *L'Architecture d'Aujourd'hui* concentrated on the architectures of the 1970s through the work of twenty-two practitioners, ranging from Norman Foster and Robert Venturi to Herman Hertzberger and Mario Botta. As such, Frampton's article served to classify the general trends represented by most of these architects.[16] But the same issue also featured Vittorio Magnano Lampugnani's proffered classification of the same set of architects in seven directions that partially overlapped with Frampton's five '-isms'.[17] This coexistence of alternative categorisations in the same issue encouraged the conflation of diverging trends. By 1981, critics seemed to be only adding to the proliferation of postmodern taxonomies of architecture. This tendency went back to the publication of Jencks's first 'evolutionary tree' of the six major traditions of modern architecture.[18] The proliferation of alternative groupings reflected not only the pluralist architectural experimentation of this period but also the reception of these diverse developments in different contexts. With 'postmodern' gradually becoming the cultural catchword of the 1980s, however, all these different directions were subsumed into this single umbrella term. From this point onwards, the discussion of architectural developments in different categories seemed only nominal. At best, it was an exercise in the critics' ingenuity in devising new conceptual groupings. But it remained largely irrelevant to the concerns of practising architects of the period. Hence, when the competing narratives of Jencks and Frampton in the early 1980s both included architects such as Botta, the differences between their approaches became harder to discern; their audiences did not necessarily follow the minutiae of their overlapping taxonomies.[19] In this context, Frampton's critical regionalism was only adding to the postmodern turn in architectural discourse.

Yet, this was precisely what Frampton intended to resist. His guest-edited 'Modern Architecture and the Critical Present' issue for *Architectural Design* in 1982 aimed to serve as a counterpoint to Demetri Porphyrios's (b. 1949) and Jencks's earlier issues on Classicism in the same year.[20] But in 'The Isms of Contemporary Architecture', Frampton also admitted the potential overlaps between his own critical categories: 'Regionalism intersects with the other isms of this "taxonomy" so as to remain potentially open to all of them, but only on the condition that they are subordinate to the culture of the region itself'.[21] His discussion of Ricardo Bofill Taller de Arquitectura's Walden 7 project is characteristic here. For Frampton, this was a project that denoted 'that delicate boundary where an initially sound impulse can unexpectedly degenerate into vulgar Populism'.[22] Bofill's reported diversion from Frampton's regionalism equalled selling out to populist scenography and consumerism. But the Catalan architect's original shared concerns with regionalist architects, and their potential 'degeneration' from one category to the other, effectively integrated Frampton's discourse into the postmodern debates of the period.

Frampton's recourse to the same outlets that Jencks and Stern also utilised to promote their agenda – including Andreas Papadakis's *Architectural Design*, which became synonymous with postmodernism across the globe[23] – did not help in rendering the subtleties of his own cause explicit. But in the final instance, Frampton's alternative (tectonic against the Biennale's scenographic) critical route originated from the same concerns. It was the polarisation of the debate between modernists and postmodernists after the Biennale that muddied the waters. Whenever Frampton asserted 'that architects should acknowledge the fundamental importance of the continuing tradition of the Modern Movement', Stern interpreted it as a plea for a purified modernism coming from the opposing camp.[24] Yet, Frampton was clearly in favour of 'a balanced critique of the modern tradition'.[25] His emphasis on the significance of 'the cultural continuity of building', 'maintaining a respect for certain levels of cultural status, rather than ... perpetuating an anachronistic notion of the avant-garde' and 'evoking the memory of a collective, public culture' were additional signs of his critical stance towards international-style modernism.[26] His emphasis on difference and impureness, alongside his critical regionalist terminology, clarified the fact that he was no advocate of purified modernism.[27] Reviewers of Frampton's history, who kept their distance from the Biennale polemics, also regarded his historiographical concerns and tactics as postmodern.[28]

In addition to establishing this debatable dichotomy between a modernist and a postmodernist front, however, the reductive understanding of postmodern architecture after the Biennale also turned the tables of the discussion. This became especially evident in the RIBA lecture series of 1982/1983 devoted to 'The Great Debate' between modernism and postmodernism. It was in this context that Frampton delivered his 'Modern Architecture and Critical Regionalism' talk in 1982. Jencks used his lecture in the same series to launch his counterattack to Frampton. Charging against the polemicists of postmodernism, Jencks argued that they lacked an overarching commitment to a shared goal. Critical regionalism in particular was critiqued for falling short of 'fully social, religious and political goals'.[29] In other words, the Postmodern Classicism of the Biennale had offered Jencks the unifying narrative that he now demanded from his modernist adversaries. The word 'resistance' itself was loaded in this historical context. It is a term that marks the post-Second World War transition of left-wing thinking from global revolution to situated opposition. After 1968, this critique was addressed both to Western capitalism and the Soviet variant of socialism. In this sense, it is also characteristically postmodern. Since 'resistance has occupied the centre of [postwar] regionalist discourse' from Mumford to Frampton,[30] critical regionalism is inevitably a child of postmodern times. Stern's historicist agenda allowed Jencks to present postmodernism in positive terms as a comprehensive proposition for future architectural developments that his fellow polemicists now lacked, since they adopted a weaker, effectively defensive, vision of vague 'resistance'. For the same reasons, Frampton had to systematically present his critical regionalism as a third way out of a dilemma. Again, it was only the reductive, historicist conception of postmodern architecture after the Biennale that enabled

Frampton to assert his difference from Stern, Jencks and Portoghesi. But the terms that they actually used in their discourses were not that different from one another.

This shared terminology made it occasionally difficult to spot differences between the rhetoric of the two self-appointed opposing camps. Frampton's rejection of 'any kind of totalising purity', the insistence on 'the very idea of difference' and 'resistance to a mono-valent propensity' or 'a resistant culture of multiple meaning' are all figures of speech that were also used by Jencks in his polemics against modernism.[31] These terms reflect the two critics' shared cultural ground beyond the field of architecture. Frampton's critical regionalism did not, then, sound that different from Jencks's definition of postmodern architecture as 'one half Modern and one half something else (usually traditional building)'.[32] Although Jencks was more interested in the establishment of a new style, while Frampton discussed building cultures and the historical predicament of a profession that could transform reality, on the surface the terminology of their discourses was the same. This had not escaped Jencks at the time. As he concluded in 1982, 'Frampton is no other character than myself, except in a grey flannel, or black, suit'.[33]

In his concluding lecture in the same RIBA series in 1983, Joseph Rykwert reflected on 'The Great Debate' as a whole, by characteristically wondering how great it had actually been.[34] While the talks of all invited speakers and the occasional comments from the audience were retrospectively published in two issues of the *RIBA Transactions* in 1983, the reception of the series registered in the *Architects' Journal* (*AJ*) within a week after each talk – with respondents of the journal consistently reporting that '[o]nce again the auditorium was full'.[35] The glaring exception seemed to be Rykwert's concluding talk, which was addressed to 'a surprisingly small audience'.[36] While Jencks's lecture of 30 November 1982 had been 'address[ed] to a capacity audience', reaffirming the architectural public's interest in the subject, the *AJ*'s correspondent also noted 'the marked reluctance' of attendants to converse with the speaker. Frampton was reportedly absent at the time, but the prolonged silence 'caused the chairman, Douglas Stephen, to order people to speak from the floor'.[37] This was not the silence of indifference but the silence of underlying tension. The sense of a polemical atmosphere in Jencks's and Frampton's talks was palpable. Jules Lubbock, who spoke in the same series on 1 February 1983, described it as 'far too acrimonious'.[38]

Frampton's talk was also delivered 'to a full hall at the RIBA' on 7 December 1982. In his interview with John McKean, Frampton accepted that the terminology he used sounded similar to that of Jencks, but their significant difference was that his own four '-isms' of architecture 'tried to isolate a set of different ideologies which were structures at a deeper level than mere stylistic idiosyncracy'.[39] In the same interview, McKean also noted how Frampton's selection of architectural examples to demonstrate his theory becomes a mixed bag of well-known and less well-known practices that 'clouds … his position' – especially in the light of the proliferation of taxonomies that circulated in the architectural press at the time, usually recycling the same works in different groupings. For these reasons, Frampton's 'scarcely … fashionable position' remained 'open to attack from both sides'.[40] In his concluding talk, Rykwert was 'more in sympathy with the much-abused Kenneth Frampton' and his regionalism. But shifting the focus from the '12 heroes' of critical regionalism to the work of architects such as Hollein, who had also served as a prominent poster child of the Biennale in 1980, neither Rykwert nor the conclusion of the Great Debate generally helped in differentiating Frampton's cause.[41] By the end of the series in 1983, it rather seemed to have added to the conflation of postmodernism with critical regionalism.

As Peter Blundell Jones noted in his 1986 review of the second edition of Frampton's critical history of modern architecture (1985), the added final chapter on critical regionalism 'reads less like an extension of the old than as a sketch for a whole new history'. Blundell Jones's comment was certainly timely, as Frampton was at that point contemplating devoting a whole book to critical regionalism. This new volume would also serve as an alternative history of modern architecture in the second half of the twentieth century, with the possible inclusion of more 'minor figures' who had remained absent in Frampton's 'comprehensive' work. But while Blundell Jones could tell the difference between Jencks as the 'style man' who is more interested in the image of a building and Frampton as an 'ideas man' who 'looks harder at the buildings than Jencks', he also noted how both authors could not effectively avoid 'perpetuat[ing] the habit of recruiting a building in a single image to support a passing point in the text then dropping it again'.[42] Their intention to affect practice according to a series of points that would serve as major principles for the future direction of architecture led them both to treat buildings as stand-alone images, isolated instances or indexes subsumed to their overarching aspirations.

The association of critical regionalism with the postmodern turn was also encouraged by other cultural discourses that shared affinities with those of Frampton. Hal Foster discerned this when he included the British architectural historian's six points on critical regionalism in his anthology of *Essays on Postmodern Culture*.[43] In doing so, Foster intended to promote a resistant, as opposed to a reactionary, postmodernism that encompassed a wide range of related discourses from feminism to postcolonialism.[44] Foster grouped the selected essays under the umbrella of 'postmodern culture' on the grounds of their shared assumptions and their 'postmodernist strategy'. Because the authors of the essays believed that 'the project of modernity is now deeply problematic', their intention was 'to deconstruct modernism … in order to open it, to rewrite it'.[45]

The criticality that formed the core of this postmodern discourse was the centrepiece of the anthology. This did not go unnoticed by reviewers such as John Roberts, who also emphasised the central significance of Frampton's essay in it by characteristically entitling his review 'Towards an Arriere-Garde, Or, How to Be Modern and Return to Sources'. Siding Frampton with Jürgen Habermas and Edward W. Said, he portrayed them as 'authors who see postmodernism as a continuation and reclamation of modernity (but under very different conditions)', one of the 'two [main] lines of critical postmodern thought'.[46] In their review of Foster's anthology, Tzonis and Lefaivre also noted that the book essentially redefined postmodernism. The couple portrayed the contributing authors as representatives of the new generation of postmodern discourse, which abandoned the pluralist relativism of the previous two decades to adopt a more progressive stance in the 1980s. The couple saluted the authors' historically informed intention to reconnect with emancipatory movements and the wider modern tradition of humanism as a sign of maturity. But they also noted the geographical transition to a transatlantic space, as in the second half of the twentieth century critical social discourses stemmed from North America rather than continental Europe as in the earlier decades of the same century.[47]

Foster's anthologisation of Frampton affirmed the position of his discourse in the postmodern debate. At the same time, it added to the confusion around the exact meaning of the postmodern turn in architecture in the early 1980s. By then, even Frampton's fundamental disagreement with Stern had become obfuscated. In May 1983, Alan Colquhoun referred interchangeably to Frampton's and Stern's approaches as 'calls for a new regionalism in architecture', owing to their shared suspicion of universal technology.[48] In 1986, the Center for the Study of American Architecture at Austin also invited Frampton and Stern to contribute to a symposium on regionalism.[49] Situating his revised ten points on critical regionalism in 'the potential, interstitial middle ground between [the] two irreconcilable "Post-Modern" positions', the

Neo-Historicists and the Neo-Avant-Gardists, Frampton subtly reaffirmed Stern's reading of schismatic/traditional postmodernism.[50] As such, the event did not clearly disentangle Frampton's discourse from Stern's postmodernism.[51] David Kolb, a philosopher who wrote about architecture in the same period, was positive in his evaluation of Frampton's critical regionalism as the most promising approach to architecture at the end of the twentieth century. But he also discussed it as part of the 'postmodern sophistications' of architecture in the 1980s.[52] In the decades that followed, this inexorable relation of critical regionalism with the postmodern condition was also noted by Fredric Jameson and Keith L. Eggener, among others.[53]

In hindsight, there is no doubt that Frampton promoted a sort of critical or regional *modernism*. Yet, the drives behind this were characteristic of his postmodern times. Like other critics of the period, Frampton aimed to reconcile the productive economy of the time with the sociocultural accessibility of civic architecture. Critical regionalism was his way out of the excesses of contemporary architectural culture that spanned from technological reductivism to kitsch populism. Rather tellingly, however, he did not condemn these exigencies per se. It was his different diagnosis of the same crisis that led him to disagree with other postmodern theorists. His discourse revolved around the modernist tenets that needed to be retained and the reductive elements that needed to be eliminated. His formative years at the Architectural Association (AA) in the late 1950s had educated Frampton to regard modernism as superior to the other languages of architecture. He therefore resisted its postmodern treatment as one among other possible design vocabularies.[54] But it was only his refusal to discuss architecture in the stylistic terms of the Biennale that enabled him to regard his critical regionalism as separate from the wider postmodern debates of the period.[55] His recent writing confirms his retrospective understanding of critical regionalism as a child of postmodern times, as an alternative 'ideologically progressive approach to postmodern architectonic form'.[56]

Battle of the publishers

Frampton formed part of the network that promoted the discourse and practice of postmodern architecture, ranging from his involvement with Columbia University, the Institute for Architecture and Urban Studies (IAUS) and its journal *Oppositions* in New York to his enduring ties with *Architectural Design* (*AD*) and the favoured circles of the AA in London.

Despite having stepped down from the Biennale for this reason in 1980, Frampton did not practically escape being the 'critic from within' a transatlantic set of overlapping networks self-appointed to define architectural culture in Western Europe and North America. With one foot in the establishment, he wanted to be able to unsettle it with the other. This ambiguous position proved successful because other media outlets that were left out of these novel, favoured circles, such as the *Architectural Review* (*AR*), embraced the discourse on regionalism. Within the same context of postmodern developments in architecture, publishers of the period sought to establish their standing in the market by investing in opposing aspects of the related debates. This was their way of defending their former establishment position, which had been shaken by their main competitors. Hence, when Papadakis's *AD* adopted the agenda of Postmodern Classicism, the *AR* responded by siding with critical regionalism.

By the 1980s, the *AR* – the 'staidly frivolous prima donna of architectural journalism' of the 1960s[57] – needed to find a new footing to reclaim its central position in related debates, which it had started losing during the 1970s. Although its circulation was consistently greater than that of *AD* until the mid-1970s, as Stephen Parnell has noted, the editors' impression was that it was already losing ground in the late 1960s. As *AD* increasingly became the 'magazine of choice for the young architect and architectural student' with its focus on the broader social role of architecture in the early 1970s, the *AR* also cemented its reputation as 'the magazine of the establishment'.[58] Originating earlier in the 1960s and the 1970s, this sentiment was only exacerbated by Papadakis's business model and publishing strategy. This was effectively the survival tactic developed by an outsider to the field of architecture in order to respond to the established networks around Peter Eisenman's IAUS in New York and Alvin Boyarsky's AA in London. The *AR*, a magazine whose 'high point was the 1930s when it championed modern architecture in the UK', rejected the postmodernism promoted by Papadakis and Jencks through *AD*. While both magazines were sold across the world, the *AR* was particularly concerned with the history of a specific region: England. As such, its campaigns to influence the English authorities and policymakers could only be regarded as 'jingoistic' in other parts of the world.[59] By contrast, *AD* had maintained a consistent future-oriented, global outlook after the end of the Second World War. This was only exacerbated by Papadakis's proactive publishing and transatlantic networking with significant nodes of production of architectural culture in the 1980s.

With postmodernism serving as the period-revival style of the 1980s, the *AR*'s siding with regionalism could be presented as a continuation of its long history, spanning from its neo-Romantic project of reinterpreting the Picturesque as an expression of Englishness in the 1940s to its agenda of sustaining cultural continuity in the development of modern architecture after the Second World War.[60] Frampton regarded the 'pre-war' *AR* as 'exemplary' in its adoption of a clear editorial line. The magazine had then defined both what it was standing against and what it promoted – namely, the interwar modern movement of architecture in Britain.[61] In his eyes, this was a notable editorial feat:

> a gentleman scholar's magazine of exemplary taste and erudition … a critical instrument of exceptional cogency … combined with its use of the large scale, often full page photography to effectively didactic ends … its scholarly appraisal of contemporary historical research and its status as a reliable magazine of record. It was in the pages of the *Review* that the habit of criticizing selected canonical modern works was first put into practice in England.[62]

As such, both the journal and Frampton followed and further developed Sigfried Giedion's historiographical line that distinguished this 'new regionalism' as the most recent strand of modern architecture after the Second World War.[63] In this light, Frampton's emphasis on regionalism is the logical development of Giedion's established canon of modern architecture. Frampton's studies of the oeuvre of Louis Kahn and Alvar Aalto especially seem to be the ones that connect him, the 'Giedion of the 1980s', with the work of his predecessor.

Revisiting regionalism in the 1980s enabled the *AR* to claim that it remained consistent with its long-standing history of supporting 'particular and idiosyncratic local approaches to architecture from its foundations in the Arts and Crafts movement to the present day'.[64] This is also what leads Erten to note that the magazine's renewed focus on regionalism in the 1980s formed part of its attempt 'to recover some of its earlier polemical rigour'. Having joined the *AR* in 1935, its editor James M. Richards set the tone of the magazine's agenda to make its clear stand against period-revival architecture and promote an appropriate modern architecture for Britain. His 'early New Left leaning and his interest in local vernaculars', his opposition to top-down bureaucratic modernism and his support of bottom-up community-led projects that relied on local resources and architectural vocabularies aligned Richards's thinking with Tzonis and Lefaivre's later theorisations of critical regionalism.[65] On the other hand, the magazine's earlier reputation as an establishment voice that stood in the way of the modern developments advocated by the avant-gardes of the 1950s and the 1960s might have also obfuscated the message of critical regionalism as an architecture of resistance. What Frampton, Tzonis and Lefaivre aimed to promote as a moderately progressive voice in the architectural debates of the 1980s was suddenly associated with a magazine known for its reactionary stance in British avant-garde circles of the period. This established reputation of the *AR* in the 1980s could not change overnight. As Frampton characteristically noted, 'despite Peter Davey's best efforts', the 1980s iteration of the magazine was 'but a shadow of its former self'.[66] This might explain why Frampton did not publish in the *AR* when he was originally invited to do so in 1984,[67] before the magazine's new focus and approach to regionalism had been sufficiently clarified and established.[68]

In the 1980s, the *AR* devoted numerous special issues to regionalism and this editorial line continued to be consistently pursued throughout the 1990s to the early 2000s.[69] The magazine was also eager to announce the death of postmodernism as early as in August 1986.[70] While the editorials of this period effectively reiterated the main points of the critical regionalist approach,[71] the *AR* offered a wider perspective by covering different contexts in which modern architecture's links with regional traditions remained stronger, as in Sri Lanka, India and Saudi Arabia.[72] In discussing the architectures of these 'peripheral' contexts, the special issues of the *AR* further promoted the agenda of critical regionalism and extended its globalising branches in unsettling the established hierarchies between the 'centre' that produces the new developments and the 'periphery' that passively assimilates them. As Nabeel Hamdi and Edward Robbins characteristically noted in one of these special issues in 1985: 'To learn how to create better housing in the Third World is to learn how to design for the future in the First'.[73] Ranging from Islamic architecture to 'Brisbane living', Chris Abel's guest-edited special issue on 'Regional Transformations' in 1986 also emphasised the cross-cultural aspect of regionalist architectures, 'suggesting that regional architecture has almost always accepted imported models and that it is in the transformation of model and type that the specific nature of regionalism can be discovered'.[74] It was only in May 1988 that the magazine returned to discussing 'regionalism in the developed world', as in Switzerland and the Scandinavian countries[75] – the regions that remained at the core of Frampton's discussions of critical regionalism. At the end of that decade, Peter Davey summarised why support for modern regionalism, instead of Postmodern Classicism or straightforward traditionalism, was the appropriate path to the civic architecture of the present:

Modernism (and regional interpretations of it) can offer the opportunity of creating cities which are at least as visually rich as the kinds of pastiche flavoured by Prince Charles ... Classicism cannot be made to work at the end of the twentieth century. Its forms were evolved by oligarchic and imperial systems; they cannot be made to clothe contemporary democratic, pluralistic functions with any integrity ... Only developments of Modernism can do this.[76]

Gauging the *AR* readership's response to the adopted critical regionalist agenda is still difficult today. But one can at least ascertain that the magazine and its subsequent editors remained consistent in supporting, revisiting and reappraising similar themes in the decades that followed.[77] Readers' seemingly enduring interest in the subject was recently reaffirmed when Véronique Patteeuw and Léa-Catherine Szacka's 2019 revisit of Frampton's six points on critical regionalism, 'a text which, it seems, never really died in the first place', became the magazine's most read archive story in 2020.[78]

But shaping the architectural culture of the 1980s went beyond the periodically published pages of a journal; critical essays in a magazine no longer seemed sufficient as a communication strategy. If one was to stand a chance against the propagation of postmodernism, they would also have to go against a whole new entrepreneurial strategy, as exemplified by Papadakis in Academy Editions, Eisenman in IAUS or Boyarsky at the AA. This was not limited to the sporadic publications out of which the discourse of critical regionalism seemed to be growing. It also included self-initiated events such as symposia, architectural competitions and exhibitions, and their constant recording in a steady flow of related publications. This multifarious activity further reinforced *AD*'s uniqueness in comparison with its traditional competitors both in the United Kingdom and abroad.[79] Unlike their main competitors, Papadakis's publications did not focus on reviewing and analysing buildings for architects because they were interested in serving not as 'a *reflector*' but as a '*director* of ideas and discourse' in architectural culture, as noted by Parnell.[80] Involving other institutions and media outlets of the establishment, these events also reinforced the ties between various favoured circles whose members appeared interchangeably from the Royal Institute of British Architects (RIBA) to the cover of *Time* magazine. Steadily liaising with these circles himself, Frampton was aware that critical regionalism needed a similar multi-media strategy in order to offer a viable, but also visible, response to postmodernism.

As a result, Frampton set up a publishing strategy of his own through his role from 1979 to 1988 as the Acquisitions/Editorial Consultant for

Rizzoli International Publishers, 'perhaps the most active publisher of books on architecture and design in the U.S.' at that time.[81] As mentioned in chapter 3, by 1981 Frampton had already outlined a series of monographs on critical architectural practices of 'unsentimental regionality' to be published by Rizzoli within two to four years.[82] But rather crucially, Rizzoli was also the house that published Jencks's, Portoghesi's and Papadakis's edited books on postmodern architects in the USA. Predominantly Western European, Frampton's selections outlined the 'other' side of the Biennale: alternative approaches to the crisis of modernism from architects in the same regions. But his plan faced considerable difficulties in practice. By 1985, when the series was supposed to have been completed, only two out of his originally proposed eighteen monographs had been published (Fig. 4.2).[83] By then, Rizzoli was hesitating to undertake the project in its entirety.[84] So, the self-perpetuating propaganda of the architectural 'avant-gardes' was reinforced by a vicious circle of risk-averse publishing practices. If this circle was to be broken, a whole network of related practices also had to be modified. This proved difficult even for someone with an influential position at the Western 'centre' of architectural production like Frampton.

Figure 4.2 Covers of *Tadao Ando: Buildings, Projects, Writings*, ed. by Kenneth Frampton (New York: Rizzoli, 1984); *Atelier 66: The Architecture of Dimitris and Suzana Antonakakis*, ed. by Kenneth Frampton (New York: Rizzoli, 1985)

Rizzoli

Figure 4.3   Poster for the International Design Seminar at the Faculty of Architecture and the Built Environment, TU Delft, 1987

Collection Het Nieuwe Instituut/AFFV, AFFV1308

The fact that Frampton's voice was heard louder than that of Tzonis and Lefaivre, and of other proponents of critical regionalism in the 1980s, owed much to his specific positioning in a powerful node within this networked media structure. But this structure mainly served to promote the new wave of star architects after the Biennale. Since Frampton tapped into the same channels, the critical regionalist architects whom he supported each became another kind of star – however 'alternative' – within the same media ecology (Fig. 4.3). Over the decades that followed, many of them found themselves in similar institutional positions of power, or were commissioned to build large-scale projects across the globe. As such, one of the main victims of this media problem of critical regionalism was the originally intended focus on cultural specificity.

Critical regionalism as a media construct

Despite its adversarial stance towards the star system of architectural media, Frampton's critical regionalism is itself a media construct that reflects his own ambivalent position as 'the critic from within' the avant-gardist network of architectural culture production in the 1980s. His insistence on disseminating his work mainly through *Oppositions*; Boyarsky's AA publications; and, especially, *AD* even after it was clear that Papadakis had sided with Jencks to promote the agenda of Postmodern Classicism may also show that Frampton was steadily interested in the future of architectural culture. Considering his ideas to be relevant for a progressive architectural practice, and not part of the historic establishment of the *AR*, he wanted his work to be publicised through *AD* as a response to the rising neoconservative establishment of Postmodern Classicism that used it as its main venue. The fact that critical regionalism was celebrated to this extent certainly owed much to its dissemination from these specific venues and Frampton's key position in this overarching structure of production of architectural culture. Because he was involved in editorial projects from the outset, Frampton's view of critical regionalism also encompassed the way in which it should be supported by architectural media.

In his retrospective accounts of the years that he served as a technical editor of *AD*, Frampton routinely mentions how this was for him a formative experience for the later formulation of critical regionalism. Under his editorship in the early 1960s, the magazine shifted away from the earlier 'grand polemics' of Team 10 to cover more aspects of continental European architecture. Combined with Monica Pidgeon's personal interest in issues related to South American architecture in Peru and Chile, among others, the magazine 'became even more international'.[85] When interviewed by Parnell in 2009, Frampton noted how his work for the magazine 'made [him] aware of continental Europe in a way which [he] had not been aware of before', of architects and their 'particular connection' to their 'provincial cities of Europe' and of the 'cultural potential' of 'this kind of decentralised relationship between the architect and the city'.[86] As he wrote in 1965, these Western European 'city-states' were significant for the civic architectures designed by their local 'princes'.[87] These included Oswald Mathias Ungers in Cologne, Gino Valle in Udine and Aris Konstantinidis in Athens (Fig. 4.4), among other 'peripheral' architects 'largely ignored by the Anglo-American press' at the time.[88]

Equally important was the production of architectural discourse and periodicals in these overlooked 'city-states' that also documented and promoted specific tendencies. The 'World News' section, introduced in Frampton's last edited *AD* issue in January 1965, included reports and translated excerpts from architectural publications in France, Germany, Switzerland, Italy and Spain. Frampton consistently believed that

Figure 4.4 Covers of *AD* magazine (January, March and May 1964) designed by Kenneth Frampton, demonstrating the more extensive geographic coverage under his editorship between July 1962 and January 1965

ARCH284700–ARCH284702, Kenneth Frampton fonds, Canadian Centre for Architecture, Gift of Kenneth Frampton

so-called 'little' magazines such as *Controspazio* and *Arquitectura Bis* could aim to cover the 'enormous lacunae in the existing publications' in comprehensively documenting less well-known but significant projects.[89] In the early 1990s, he highlighted the well-known *AA Files*, *Assemblage* and *9H* as 'three critical journals of consequence' from the 1980s, 'in addition to two important bilingual magazines; *Daedalus* and *Tefchos*, edited out of Berlin and Athens respectively'.[90] Another decade later, he added more publications to this earlier list, including Luis Fernandez Galleano's *Arquitetura Viva*, 'perhaps the best magazine of record in any language today'; Pier Luigi Nicolin's *Lotus*; and Nancy Levinson's *Harvard Design Magazine*, 'one of the most literate magazines currently in the field'.[91] The inclusion of these 'peripheral' magazines alongside those produced in the Anglo-American 'centres' embodied Frampton's insistence on the co-production of architectural discourse and the critical regionalist abolition of the centre/periphery divide. But what even more significantly unified such diverse publications in Frampton's mind was a specific editorial attitude and his firm belief in the didactic role of the architectural press.

As he later noted, Frampton's role models were editors such as Ernesto Rogers and his 'brilliant *Casabella Continuità*' with its 'graphic flair and the mature cultivation that emanated from its pages'; and Vittorio Gregotti, whose editorials reflected his 'erudition, pertinence and acerbic critical lucidity'.[92] Focusing on specific buildings and its sustained architectural criticism of them, Frampton's 'unilateral' *AD* became more interested than its rivals in outlining the specific contours of an 'authentic' architecture.[93] For Frampton, issues of *AD* were similar to book projects. They aimed to articulate and comprehensively develop a clear main point. Every issue foregrounded a strong voice about architecture and the critical culture that the magazine intended to promote. While Frampton's rather limited 31-month tenure at the helm of *AD* certainly did not alter the course of architectural culture at the time, it had – as Parnell concludes – significantly increased his own cultural capital as an esteemed critic with a distinguished and independent voice and approach to architecture.[94] It was indeed thanks to the connections established through this editorial role that Frampton was commissioned to write his critical history of modern architecture by Robin Middleton, who was then serving as the acquisitions editor for Thames & Hudson.[95] But the British historian clearly intended to remain involved with architectural publications after he stepped down from his role at *AD* in 1965. His archive includes a five-page typescript that outlines *Plan*, a new journal of architecture that he envisioned in 1967.[96]

After moving to the USA and joining Eisenman's initiative at the IAUS in the early 1970s, Frampton could further develop his ideas through his editorial work in *Oppositions*. Retrospectively describing their group as 'a bunch of elitists, self-styled … members of the media establishment' of New York,[97] Frampton notes how Eisenman envisioned him as 'the new Sigfried Giedion' who would set the standards of good taste for architecture after modernism. In keeping with his earlier editorial line of focusing on significant projects rather than promoting a specific movement, however, Frampton continued to feel that 'there wasn't a group that [he] felt [he] could readily become the Sigfried Giedion of'.[98] Besides, it was rather clear that the editors shared diverging views on the exact focus and mission of the journal. For this reason, they soon – after the second issue, in fact – abandoned the idea of writing joint editorials and switched to alternating in penning the opening piece. The IAUS and *Oppositions* became known for establishing the New York–Venice axis of architectural exchanges. This was especially the case after 1974, when the IAUS abandoned its earlier focus on urban studies and ties with local government in order to turn its attention to outward-facing exhibitions, lectures and symposia that attracted distinguished non-American guests from Europe and Japan.[99] This lively hive for the architecturally minded crowds of New York thus turned into 'an international meeting place for architecture and social issues'.[100] By 1978, when the IAUS launched its popular newsletter *Skyline*, it had already been established as a 'hall of power'.[101] But this did not come without the related power games, which took their toll on the journal's capacity to be effectively critical. Frampton recalled how:

> ... various editorial members ... claimed to review these books [by Venetian authors], but never had the courage to do so because that of course would mean as coming out into the open vis-a-vis the powerful Venician [sic] Marxist establishment ... I can tell you editing magazines is sometimes very revealing about the frailty of the species and also the limit of ideological commitments.[102]

Despite such shortcomings, Frampton did not lose his faith in the role of architectural publishing.[103] When he began advancing the cause of critical regionalism in the 1980s, he regarded magazines as a crucial factor in his aspired project. As he argued, including marginal cultures in modern studies of the built environment was significant because 'unevenness of development may apply in any field and perhaps to some extent in every country'. All nations could be considered both as 'developed' in some respects and as 'developing' in others. Foregrounding the USA as a prominent example, Frampton noted how a country 'on the pinnacle of the world's pyramid when it comes to the development of electronics' looks like one of the developing countries when one focuses on its 'means of locomotive transit'. Hence, critical regionalism does not address provincial cultures that are in some sense lacking; it rather demonstrates how the alleged 'centres' of architectural developments are also lacking in some respects when compared with the 'peripheries'. As such, Frampton concluded that '[i]n a world in which there is no longer a fixed center and a periphery magazines have potentially a crucial role to play in the cultivation of high levels of critical local culture'.[104] The same is the case for 'little magazines' of schools of architecture. As these are caught up in a similar 'star system' of mutual competition, Frampton could further elucidate the significance of his critical regionalism:

> an architectural school can certainly be conceived today as a cultural 'region,' and it is precisely the self-cultivation of this region which will enable it to resist, without falling either into reactionary hermeticism on the one hand or into the media juggernaut of universal civilization. As with architectural schools, so (at least potentially) with the editorial boards of little magazines.[105]

It was large-scale and complicated power games that got in the way of the bigger publishing houses such as Rizzoli, where 'it [was] not easy to maintain a clear line'.[106] Frampton believed in establishing a hard editorial position that not only included but also excluded. This was the price that an editor had to pay. Magazines should not aim for liberal, pluralist inclusivity but should clearly define the boundaries of their position and cultivate it as they see fit in order to realise its full potential. Frampton believed that the same should be the case in architectural education.[107] In the long run, architectural culture would only benefit from the patient cultivation of a clearly assumed position.

At the same time, magazines and their editorial policies could be enlisted in the critical regionalist revolt against the dominance of the single photogenic image that turned buildings into impressive scenography, leading to a disembodied perception of architectural space. Designing architecture for it to be photographed 'from a preferred side' led to the creation of buildings that looked like two-dimensional drawings. The greatest loss from this process lay in the tactile side of architectural creation, as the capacity of the architect to turn structural necessity into a poetic work by using specific materials that both act and show how the building resists gravity and withstands the seasons was overlooked. Architectural magazines could redress this by adopting specific representational stratagems. These included:

> ... publishing the one work as completely as possible from many different aspects, that is to say, a full set of design drawings, equally comprehensive initial sketches and interior drawings, together with large size constructional details and large format general views and above all, large format photographs of the specific details. This fragmented record in depth would then give the reader an adequate mental map of the work, without providing him or her with an encapsulated 'image' of the piece.[108]

For the same reason, Frampton remained consistent in his conviction that architectural publications should not be too far removed from practice to enter the realm of exclusively 'metatheoretical issues'.[109]

When it was clear that Rizzoli would not commit to publishing his proposed series in its entirety, Frampton started working on a book project on critical regionalism. Again, it was not long before he abandoned it. But because Frampton frequently had opportunities to revisit, polish and publish his partially completed drafts as short essays on various occasions, traces of this unfinished book can be found in his publications of the 1980s and the early 1990s. Bringing together these texts with previously unpublished archival material, the next chapter reconstructs the cross-cultural aspects of Frampton's lost book of critical regionalism.

Notes

1   Erdem Erten, 'Shaping "The Second Half Century": *The Architectural Review* 1947–1971', unpublished doctoral thesis, MIT, 2004, p. 294.

2   See *Architectural Regionalism: Collected Writings on Place, Identity, Modernity, and Tradition*, ed. by Vincent B. Canizaro (New York: Princeton Architectural Press, 2007), p. 420.

3   See Alexander Tzonis and Liane Lefaivre, 'The Grid and the Pathway: An Introduction to the Work of Dimitris and Suzana Antonakakis, with Prolegomena to a History of the Culture of Modern Greek Architecture', *Architecture in Greece*, 15 (1981), 164–78; Alexander Tzonis and Liane Lefaivre, 'Het Raster en het Pad', *Wonen-TA/BK*, 20–1 (1981), 31–42; Alexander Tzonis and Liane Lefaivre, 'Expression régionale et architecture contemporaine: "de la trame au cheminement": l'œuvre de Dimitri et de Suzanne Antonakakis', *Le carré bleu*, 2 (1982), 1–20.

4   See Alexander Tzonis and Liane Lefaivre, 'De terugkeer van regionalisme', *Bouw*, 9 (April 1983), 9–11; Alexander Tzonis and Liane Lefaivre, 'Lewis Mumford en de gevaren van regressief regionalisme', *Bouw*, 10 (May 1983), 15–18; Alexander Tzonis and Liane Lefaivre, 'Het naoorlogse regionalism en de toekomst van kritisch regionalisme', *Bouw*, 11 (June 1983), 16–18; Alexander Tzonis and Liane Lefaivre, 'A Critical Introduction to Greek Architecture since the Second World War', in *Post-War Architecture in Greece, 1945–1983*, ed. by Orestis Doumanis (Athens: Architecture in Greece Press, 1984), 16–23; Alexander Tzonis and Liane Lefaivre, 'El regionalismo critico y la arquitectura española actual', *Arquitectura y Vivienda*, 3 (1985), 4–19.

5   John McKean, 'Towards the Unknown Region', *Architects' Journal*, 176.50 (15 December 1982), 19–21 (p. 19).

6   Kenneth Frampton, letter to Massimo Zelman, 22 September 1995, CCA Fonds 197, Kenneth Frampton fonds, 197 – 2017 – 120T, AP197.S3.002, Personal and professional correspondence 1995, 1995, 197-120-003.

7   Alexander Tzonis and Liane Lefaivre, 'Why Critical Regionalism Today?' (1990), repr. in *Theorizing a New Agenda for Architecture: An Anthology of Architectural Theory 1965–1995*, ed. by Kate Nesbitt (New York: Princeton Architectural Press, 1996), pp. 484–92 (p. 490).

8   See Alexander Tzonis and Liane Lefaivre, *Architecture of Regionalism in the Age of Globalization: Peaks and Valleys in the Flat World* (London: Routledge, 2012).

9   Stephen Parnell, '*Architectural Design* 1954–1972: The Architectural Magazine's Contribution to the Writing of Architectural History', unpublished doctoral thesis, University of Sheffield, 2012, p. 369.

10 See The Pritzker Architecture Prize, Laureates, www.pritzkerprize.com/laureates (accessed 2 July 2021).

11 See Aris Konstantinidis, Εμπειρίες και περιστατικά: Μια αυτοβιογραφική διήγηση, 3 vols (Athens: Estia, 1992), III, pp. 233–6.

12 See *The Architecture of Luis Barragán*, ed. by Emilio Ambasz (New York: Museum of Modern Art, 1976).

13 *Archithese*, letter to Kenneth Frampton, 9 January 1981, CCA Fonds 197, Kenneth Frampton fonds, 197 – 2017 – 114T, AP197.S3.001, Personal and professional correspondence 1981, 1981, 197-114-023.

14 See Robert Bostwick, letter to Kenneth Frampton, 27 July 1984; Peter Davey, letter to Kenneth Frampton, 24 May 1984; Miguel Angel Roca, letter to Kenneth Frampton, 12 August 1984; Antonio Toca, letter to Kenneth Frampton, 18 September 1984; Zhang Qinnan, letter to Kenneth Frampton, 27 February 1984; Lisa Findley, letter to Kenneth Frampton, 7 November 1984; Roberto Segre, letter to Kenneth Frampton, 20 June 1984, CCA Fonds 197, Kenneth Frampton fonds, 197 – 2017 – 115T, AP197.S3.002, Personal and professional correspondence 1984, 1984, 197-115-001.

15 See *L'Après Modernisme: La Présence de l'Histoire*, ed. by Jean Marie Genet and Bernard Deroy (Paris: L'Equerre, 1981) and Léa-Catherine Szacka, *Exhibiting the Postmodern: The 1980 Venice Architecture Biennale* (Venice: Marsilio, 2016), pp. 220–9.

16 See Kenneth Frampton, 'Du Néo-Productivisme au Post-Modernisme', *L'Architecture d'Aujourd'hui*, 213 (1981), 2–7.

17 See Vittorio Magnano Lampugnani, 'Avant-Gardes Architecturales 1970–1980', *L'Architecture d'Aujourd'hui*, 213 (1981), 8–13.

18 See Charles Jencks, *Modern Movements in Architecture* (Harmondsworth: Penguin, 1973), p. 28.

19 See Kenneth Frampton, 'Mario Botta and the School of the Ticino', *Oppositions*, 14 (1978), 1–25; Charles Jencks, *The Language of Post-Modern Architecture*, 4th edn (New York: Rizzoli, 1984), pp. 151–2.

20 See 'Free-Style Classicism', ed. by Charles Jencks. Special issue, *Architectural Design*, 52.1/2 (1982); 'Classicism is Not a Style', ed. by Demetri Porphyrios. Special issue, *Architectural Design*, 52.5/6 (1982).

21 Kenneth Frampton, 'The Isms of Contemporary Architecture', *Architectural Design*, 52.7/8 (1982), 60–83 (p. 82).

22 Ibid., p. 78.

23 See Stephen Parnell, 'The Birth and Rebirth of a Movement: Charles Jencks's Postmodern Odyssey in *AD*', *Architectural Design*, 91.1 (2021), 48–55.

24 See *Architectural Design*, 52.7/8 (1982), 49; Robert A.M. Stern, 'Giedion's Ghost: A Review of Frampton's *Modern Architecture: A Critical History*', *Skyline* (October 1981), 22–5.

25 Kenneth Frampton, *Modern Architecture: A Critical History* (London: Thames & Hudson, 1980), p. 288.

26 Kenneth Frampton, 'Avant-Garde and Continuity', *Architectural Design*, 52.7/8 (1982), 20–7 (p. 26).

27 Kenneth Frampton, 'The Resistance of Architecture: An Anthological Postscript', *Architectural Design*, 52.7/8 (1982), 84–5 (p. 85).

28 See Alan Colquhoun, 'Modern Architecture and the Liberal Conscience', *Architectural Design*, 52.7/8 (1982), 47–9 (p. 48); David Dunster, 'Maid in USA', *Architectural Design*, 52.7/8 (1982), 50–1 (p. 50); Rafael Moneo, 'The Contradictions of Architecture as History', *Architectural Design*, 52.7/8 (1982), 54.

29 Charles Jencks, 'Post-Modern Architecture: The True Inheritor of Modernism', *RIBA Transactions*, 3.2:1 (1983), 26–41 (p. 29).

30 Vincent B. Canizaro, 'Introduction', in *Architectural Regionalism*, ed. by Canizaro, pp. 16–33 (p. 22).

31 See Frampton, 'The Resistance of Architecture', p. 85; McKean, 'Towards the Unknown Region', p. 19.

32 Jencks, 'Post-Modern Architecture', p. 40.

33 Ibid., p. 30.

34 See Joseph Rykwert, 'How Great is the Debate?', *RIBA Transactions*, 4.2:2 (1983), 18–31.

35 Bob Allies, 'Aalto's Architecture Redefined?', *Architects' Journal*, 177.8 (23 February 1983), 30–1 (p. 30).

36 See 'Rykwert Debunks the Great Debate', *Architects' Journal*, 177.25 (22 June 1983), 35.

37 See 'High Jencks at the RIBM', *Architects' Journal*, 176.49 (8 December 1982), 22.

38 Charlotte Ellis, 'Great Debate off Course', *Architects' Journal*, 177.6 (9 February 1983), 27–8 (p. 27).

39 McKean, 'Towards the Unknown Region', p. 19.

40 Ibid., p. 21.

41 See 'Rykwert Debunks the Great Debate'; Rykwert, 'How Great is the Debate?', p. 27; Eva Branscome, *Hans Hollein and Postmodernism: Art and Architecture in Austria, 1958–1985* (London: Routledge, 2018), pp. 24–76.

42 Peter Blundell Jones, 'History in the Making: *Modern Movements in Architecture*; *Modern Architecture: A Critical History*', *Architects' Journal*, 183.13 (26 March 1986), 80.

43 See Kenneth Frampton, 'Towards a Critical Regionalism: Six Points for an Architecture of Resistance', in *The Anti-Aesthetic: Essays on Postmodern Culture*, ed. by Hal Foster (Washington, DC: Bay Press, 1983), pp. 16–30.

44 See Hal Foster, 'Postmodernism: A Preface', in *The Anti-Aesthetic*, ed. by Foster, pp. ix–xvi (p. xii); Craig Owens, 'The Discourse of Others: Feminists and Postmodernism', in *The Anti-Aesthetic*, ed. by Foster, pp. 57–82; and Edward W. Said, 'Opponents, Audiences, Constituencies and Community', *Critical Inquiry*, 9.1 (1982), 1–26.

45 Foster, 'Postmodernism: A Preface', pp. ix, xi.

46 See John Roberts, 'Towards an Arriere-Garde, Or, How to Be Modern and Return to Sources', *Art Monthly*, 69 (September 1983), 28–30.

47 See Alexander Tzonis and Liane Lefaivre, 'Het onvoltooide project van de moderniteit', *Bouw*, 18 (September 1984), 23–4; Alexander Tzonis and Liane Lefaivre, 'The Anti-Aesthetic: Essays on Postmodern Culture' : Μια βιβλιοκρισία', *Design + Art in Greece*, 16 (1985), 64.

48 Alan Colquhoun, 'Regionalism and Technology' (1983), repr. in Alan Colquhoun, *Modernity and the Classical Tradition: Architectural Essays 1980–1987* (Cambridge, MA: MIT Press, 1989), pp. 207–11 (p. 207).

49 See Malcolm Quantrill, 'Stern Regionalism', *Architectural Review*, 180.1073 (July 1986), 4–5.

50 See Kenneth Frampton, 'Ten Points on an Architecture of Regionalism: A Provisional Polemic', *Center*, 3 (1987), 20–7 (p. 27); Robert A.M. Stern, 'The Doubles of Post-Modern' (1980), repr. in *Architecture on the Edge of Postmodernism: Collected Essays, 1964–1988*, ed. by Robert A.M. Stern and Cynthia Davidson (New Haven, CT: Yale University Press, 2009), pp. 128–46.

51 See Robert A.M. Stern, 'Regionalism and the Continuity of Tradition', *Center*, 3 (1987), 58–63.

52 See David Kolb, *Postmodern Sophistications: Philosophy, Architecture, and Tradition* (Chicago: University of Chicago Press, 1990).

53 See Fredric Jameson, *The Seeds of Time* (New York: Columbia University Press, 1994), pp. 189–205; Keith L. Eggener, 'Placing Resistance: A Critique of Critical Regionalism', *Journal of Architectural Education*, 55.4 (2002), 228–37 (p. 229).

54 See Kenneth Frampton, *Modern Architecture: A Critical History*, 2nd edn (London: Thames & Hudson, 1985), pp. 306–8.

55 See Kenneth Frampton, 'Some Reflections on Postmodernism and Architecture', in *Postmodernism: ICA Documents*, ed. by Lisa Appignanesi (London: Free Association, 1989), pp. 75–87.

56 Kenneth Frampton, *A Genealogy of Modern Architecture: A Comparative Critical Analysis of Built Form* (Zurich: Lars Müller, 2015), p. 17.

57 Jan Christopher Rowan, 'Editorial', *Progressive Architecture* (January 1964), 99.

58 Stephen Parnell, 'AR's and AD's Post-War Editorial Policies: The Making of Modern Architecture in Britain', *Journal of Architecture*, 17.5 (2012), 763–75 (pp. 770–3).

59 Parnell, 'Architectural Design 1954–1972', p. 389.

60 To cite just one example, see J.M. Richards, 'The New Empiricism: Sweden's Latest Style', *Architectural Review*, 101.606 (June 1947), 199–204. For the earlier post-WWII history and agenda of the magazine, see Erten, 'Shaping "The Second Half Century"'.

61 Kenneth Frampton, 'Responses to the Design Book Review Questionnaire', 11-page annotated typescript, CCA Fonds 197, Kenneth Frampton fonds, 197 – 2017 – 098T, AP197.S1.SS9.013, Kenneth Frampton responses to the Design Book review questionnaire, 1985, 197-098-043, p. 4.

62 Kenneth Frampton, 'Reflections on *Perspecta* : The End of the Beginning', 10-page typescript, 2001, CCA Fonds 197, Kenneth Frampton fonds, 197 – 2017 – 103T, AP197.S1.SS9.018, Reflections on Perspecta the end of the beginning, 2001, 197-103-032, p. 7.

63 See Sigfried Giedion, 'The New Regionalism' (1954), repr. in Sigfried Giedion, *Architecture, You and Me: The Diary of a Development* (Cambridge, MA: Harvard University Press, 1958), pp. 138–51.

64 Peter Davey, 'Regional Meaning', *Architectural Review*, 187.1125 (November 1990), 34–5 (p. 35).

65 Erten, 'Shaping "The Second Half Century"', p. 294.

66 Frampton, 'Reflections on *Perspecta*', p. 8.

67 See Peter Davey, letter to Kenneth Frampton, 24 May 1984.

68 See Kenneth Frampton, 'The Usonian Legacy', *Architectural Review*, 182.1090 (December 1987), 26–31; Kenneth Frampton, 'Seven Points for the Millennium: An Untimely Manifesto', *Architectural Review*, 206.1233 (1999), 76–80.

69 See Peter Davey, 'Regionalism: Time to Review and Renew', *Architectural Review*, 210.1257 (November 2001), 34–5.

70 See E.M. Farrelly, 'The New Spirit', *Architectural Review*, 180.1074 (August 1986), 6–12 (p. 7).

71 Peter Buchanan, 'Only Connect', *Architectural Review*, 176.1052 (October 1984), 22–5 (p. 23).

72 See the related editorials by Peter Buchanan, 'With Due Respect: Regionalism', *Architectural Review*, 173.1035 (May 1983), 14–17; Gillian Darley and Peter Davey, 'Sense and Sensibility', *Architectural Review*, 174.1039 (September 1983), 22–5.

73 Nabeel Hamdi and Edward Robbins, '3rd World', *Architectural Review*, 178.1062 (August 1985), 12.

74 Chris Abel, 'Regional Transformations', *Architectural Review*, 180.1077 (November 1986), 36–43 (p. 37).

75 See Juhani Pallasmaa, 'Tradition and Modernity: The Feasibility of Regional Architecture in Post-Modern Society', *Architectural Review*, 183.1095 (May 1988), 26–34.

76 Peter Davey, 'Urban Authenticity', *Architectural Review*, 187.1115 (January 1990), 22–3 (p. 23).

77 See Catherine Slessor, 'Editorial View: Reframing Critical Regionalism for the Current Age', *Architectural Review*, 25 July 2013. Online. www.architectural-review.com/essays/editorial-view-reframing-critical-regionalism-for-the-current-age/8651301.article (accessed 30 June 2021); Catherine Slessor, *Concrete Regionalism* (London: Thames & Hudson, 2000).

78 See AR Editors, 'AR Reading List 040: Most Read Archive Stories', *Architectural Review*, 18 December 2020. Online. www.architectural-review.com/archive/reading-lists/ar-reading-list-040-most-read-archive-stories (accessed 3 July 2021); Véronique Patteeuw and Léa-Catherine Szacka, 'Critical Regionalism for our Time', *Architectural Review*, 1466 (November 2019), 92–8 (p. 93).

79 Stephen Parnell, 'Architecture's Expanding Field: *AD* Magazine and the Post-Modernisation of Architecture', *Architectural Research Quarterly*, 22.1 (2018), 55–68 (pp. 58, 63). See Charles Jencks, 'Notes on an Architectural Culture', in *British Architecture*, ed. by Andreas Papadakis (London: Academy, 1982), p. 12.

80 Parnell, 'Architecture's Expanding Field', p. 56.

81 Kenneth Frampton, cover letter to Richard Ingersoll, 9 September 1985, CCA Fonds 197, Kenneth Frampton fonds, 197 – 2017 – 098T, AP197.S1.SS9.013, Kenneth Frampton responses to the Design Book review questionnaire, 1985, 197-098-043.

82 Kenneth Frampton, 4-page letter to Suzana and Dimitris Antonakakis, 21 December 1981, Suzana and Dimitris Antonakakis' private archive.

83 See *Tadao Ando: Buildings, Projects, Writings*, ed. by Kenneth Frampton (New York: Rizzoli, 1984); *Atelier 66: The Architecture of Dimitris and Suzana Antonakakis*, ed. by Kenneth Frampton (New York: Rizzoli, 1985).

84 Kenneth Frampton, 2-page letter to Suzana and Dimitris Antonakakis, 27 July 1984, Suzana and Dimitris Antonakakis' private archive.

85 Parnell, '*Architectural Design* 1954–1972', p. 169. See Kenneth Frampton, 'Homage à Monica Pidgeon: An AD Memoir', *AA Files*, 60 (2010), 22–5 (p. 24).

86 Kenneth Frampton, interviewed by Stephen Parnell (23 November 2009), quoted in Parnell, '*Architectural Design* 1954–1972', p. 284.

87 Kenneth Frampton, 'The Work of Epaminoda', *Architectural Design*, 35.1 (January 1965), 3.

88 Frampton, 'Homage à Monica Pidgeon', p. 24.

89 Transcript of the ensuing discussion, CCA Fonds 197, Kenneth Frampton fonds, 197 – 2017 – 002T, AP197.S1.SS9.004, Transcript of Little Magazine Conference, including abstracts, circa 1975, 197-002-008, p. 119.

90 Kenneth Frampton, 'Bibliography', 7-page typescript, [1992?], CCA Fonds 197, Kenneth Frampton fonds, 197 – 2017 – 010T, AP197.S1.SS4.023, Draft of the bibliography and introductory note to the third edition of *Modern Architecture: A Critical History*, ca. 1980–1985, 197-010-025, p. 1.

91 Frampton, 'Reflections on *Perspecta*', p. 8.

92 Frampton, 'Homage à Monica Pidgeon', p. 23; Frampton, 'Responses to the Design Book Review Questionnaire', p. 3.

93 Parnell, '*Architectural Design* 1954–1972', pp. 185, 187.

94 Ibid., p. 370.

95 Frampton, 'Homage à Monica Pidgeon', p. 25.

96 See CCA Fonds 197, Kenneth Frampton fonds, 197 – 2017 – 114T, AP197.S3.001, Personal and professional correspondence 1967, 1967, 197-114-001.

97 Kenneth Frampton, 'Oppositions and after', 36-page typescript, 1983, CCA Fonds 197, Kenneth Frampton fonds, 197 – 2017 – 089T, AP197.S1.SS9.004, Oppositions and after, ca. 1970–1985, 197-089-020, p. 6.

98 Frampton, 'Oppositions and after', p. 2.

99 See Suzanne S. Frank, 'The Institute for Architecture and Urban Studies, The First Phase (1967–1974)', 57-page typescript, 1997, CCA Fonds 197, Kenneth Frampton fonds, 197 – 2017 – 002T, AP197.S1.SS3.009, Publications entitled Resurrecting the Avant-Garde The History and Program of Oppositions, 1988, 197-002-009, pp. 43, 46.

100 Frank, 'The Institute for Architecture and Urban Studies', p. 59.

101 Ibid., p. 50.

102 Frampton, 'Oppositions and after', pp. 29–30.

103 Ibid., p. 31.

104 Kenneth Frampton, 'Seven Points for an Ideal Magazine of Architecture', 4-page annotated typescript, CCA Fonds 197, Kenneth Frampton fonds, 197 – 2017 – 089T, AP197.S1.SS9.004, Seven points for an ideal magazine of architecture, circa 1990–2000, 197-089-054, p. 4.

105 Frampton, 'Responses to the Design Book Review Questionnaire', pp. 10–11.

106 Ibid., p. 11.

107 Kenneth Frampton, 'Towards a Critical Understanding: A Discussion with Kenneth Frampton', 7-page typescript, 1985, CCA Fonds 197, Kenneth Frampton fonds, 197 – 2017 – 104T, AP197.S1.SS9.019, Towards a critical analysis: a discussion with Kenneth Frampton, 1985, 197-104-046, pp. 1–2.

108 Frampton, 'Responses to the Design Book Review Questionnaire', pp. 5–6.

109 Frampton, 'Reflections on *Perspecta*', p. 9 (emphasis in the original).

5
Lost books

Unlike other architectural tendencies, critical regionalism became a movement without a book to define it. Throughout the 1980s and the 1990s, it developed only through a series of widely disseminated but not systematically orchestrated journal articles or book chapters. The inclusion of Kenneth Frampton's text in Hal Foster's emblematic anthology of 'resistant' postmodern culture in 1983 certainly marked a high point in this history. But despite the positive reception of Foster's edited volume across different cultural fields, this was not a book on critical regionalism in the same way that Charles Jencks's successive iterations of *The Language of Post-Modern Architecture* attempted to prescribe current architectural developments.[1] While the fundamental ideas that underpin critical regionalism were there in Frampton's best-selling *Modern Architecture: A Critical History*, albeit only as an afterthought in the last chapter, this book could not be regarded as an equivalent to that of Jencks or Philip Johnson and Mark Wigley's influential account of *Deconstructivist Architecture* (1988) later in the same decade.[2] The first book-length account of critical regionalism by Alexander Tzonis and Liane Lefaivre appeared only in 2003, and its more comprehensive history was published in 2012. By then, the whole project had already been reframed in terms of resistance to the homogenising forces of globalisation.[3] As a result, the early history of critical regionalism before globalisation has been historically overshadowed. This chapter attempts to reconstruct this lost framework in order to recalibrate the whole project of critical regionalism in terms of its cross-cultural roots and globalising branches.

While Frampton's work was reportedly 'influential on current practice',[4] his proposed book series on eighteen 'unsentimental regionalist' architects was effectively cancelled by Rizzoli in the mid-1980s and his subsequent book project on critical regionalism later in the same decade also remained unfinished. But some of the related texts were eventually reframed to find their way into his *Studies in Tectonic Culture* (1995). Frampton has repeatedly noted that Fredric Jameson's critique in *The Seeds of Time* (1994) made him lose his faith in critical regionalism as a political project.[5] But this does not sound as convincing when one revisits Frampton's texts from the same period. Despite his best intentions to engage in these discussions, Frampton consistently eschewed the sociopolitical dimension of specific conditions of production and development. From *Modern Architecture: A Critical History* (1980) to *Studies in Tectonic Culture* (1995), the problem was there from the start. Reviewers of his books at the time of their publication noted how his critical history of modern architecture 'does not relate particular developments to specific realities of organisation and production'.[6] In addition, 'the cultural/political dimensions of his argument are confined to a short epilogue' in his *Studies in Tectonic Culture* (1995) when '[t]hey should have been central'.[7] More specifically, Jameson's critique further discouraged Frampton from pursuing the broader political project of critical regionalism. The British historian decided to focus on his studies of architectural tectonics instead, whether or not this was also grounded in a specific regional culture. As this emphasis on tectonic form favoured discussions of structure in relation to landscape and climate,[8] to questions of geography rather than history, it further removed Frampton's critical discourse from the sociopolitical context that conditions regional projects.

Despite having practically abandoned the whole project by the 1990s, Frampton could not omit critical regionalism from the retrospective compilation of his essays on architecture and design *Labour, Work and Architecture* (2002).[9] Looking back at his writings from the temporal distance of two decades, Frampton selected his 1983 essay from Foster's anthology as his most representative text on the subject. In this essay, Frampton approaches critical regionalism from a general theoretical perspective, based on six main points. In passing, he refers to two architectural projects, Alvar Aalto's Säynätsalo Town Hall (1949–52) and Jørn Utzon's Bagsvaerd Church (1973–6). In the republished version of 2002, the British historian added a photograph of Dimitris Pikionis's landscaping project around the Acropolis (1954–7) as a cover image for the essay. This move suggests that his main points can be summarised through these three projects, which form the canonical core of critical regionalism.

Aalto's, Pikionis's and Utzon's projects effectively summarise critical regionalism as an architecture that works on a topographic continuum and opposes technological exhibitionism. It does so by combining standardised and non-standardised construction logics to embody novel cross-cultural meanings for architecture. These cannot be directly associated with Western or Eastern civilisations, as this kind of architecture hybridises cultural references in enigmatic spiritual spaces for secularised modern societies. It is a kind of architecture that cannot be reduced to sight alone, as it has to be experienced by the full sensorial spectrum of the human body.

Tactile surfaces and the interplay of materials with their specific smells, sounds and textures that are tacitly perceived by the moving body are constitutive parts of this architecture; they do not merely complement its visual qualities. Aalto's Säynätsalo Town Hall serves as a good case in point here. It demonstrates the architectural significance of alternating tactile experiences of buildings, as opposed to an exclusively visual perception of their most photogenic aspects. Describing the way in which a visitor advances from the dark entry stairs to the luminous council chamber, Frampton shows how the architectural materials that one sees and feels on their feet, from the solid brick-treaded stairs to the slippery polished wooden parquet, contribute to the claustrophobic atmospheres of these spaces and build up a sense of arrival at the important point (Fig. 5.1). This is then reinforced by the related 'tectonic display' of 'fanlike, wooden trusses that splay upward to support concealed rafters above a boarded ceiling' in the council chamber.[10]

But this retrospective summation of critical regionalism in six points and three projects does not do justice to Frampton's original aspirations. More nuanced aspects of his approach that were discussed as 'prospects' of critical regionalism, based on other architectural projects, have been comparatively overshadowed. This chapter attempts to retrieve them, because critical regionalism hails from a time when buildings used to write architectural theory. From Jencks's postmodernism to Tzonis and Lefaivre's critical regionalism, architectural discourses of the 1980s were customarily constructed around analyses of specific projects. Through this process, buildings became significant authorial agents. Based on Frampton's original proposals for the book series of 1981 and his book project of 1989, this chapter reconstructs the lost book of critical regionalism. Frampton understood his role as that of an operative critic who could guide and influence architectural practice. From the outset, his critical regionalism aimed to serve as an operative tool, a unified construct built on diversified architectural practices. Conversely, the way in which he interpreted specific projects helped him to further elucidate his main theoretical points. Still, dissonances between the architects' intentions and the theorist's aspirations were not entirely avoided. As it revisits specific architectural projects from Frampton's original list of

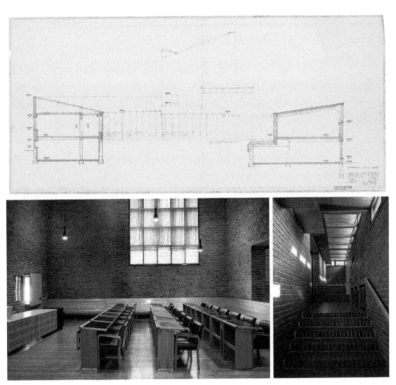

Figure 5.1 Alvar Aalto, Säynätsalo Town Hall, Säynätsalo, Jyväskylä, 1949–52. Top: Section, 3.10.1950; bottom left: Council Hall, photographed by Pinja Eerola, Alvar Aalto Foundation, 2018; bottom right: stairs to the Council Hall, photographed by Maija Holma, Alvar Aalto Foundation, 2014

Alvar Aalto Foundation

'unsentimental regionalist' practices of 1981, this chapter reads these buildings as manifestations of the overarching project of critical regionalism. More than Frampton's own theoretical concerns, it was the specificity of these key projects that wrote the lost book of critical regionalism.

While Frampton effectively stopped developing his critical regionalist discourse after the late 1980s, his outline of the tectonic trajectory in the last chapter of his *Studies in Tectonic Culture* (1995) concludes with a return to Paul Ricoeur's question of 'becoming modern and returning to sources'.[11] In Frampton's mind, discussions of tectonic culture and critical regionalism are therefore closely associated. His later texts of the 1990s continue to inform his critical regionalism, despite the fact that Frampton increasingly shies away from using this term then. In his words:

> ... the presentation and representation of the built as a constructed thing has invariably proved essential to the phenomenological presence of an architectural work and its literal embodiment in form. It is this perhaps more than anything else that grounds architecture in a cultural tradition that is collective rather than individual; that anchors it, so to speak, in a way of building and place-making that is inseparable from our material history ... One may argue that the tectonic resists and has always resisted the fungibility of the world.[12]

What is not freely interchangeable or easily standardised invariably involves the collective engagement of a community. As such, it cannot be easily replicated in order to enter the circuit of commodification. Since tectonic culture remains essentially marginal in emphasising the tactile experience of buildings, it retains a core 'vestigially resistant' to the reduction of architecture to photogenic images or scenography.[13] As such, the critical regionalist undercurrent is still perceptible in Frampton's writings of the 1990s. The key reference that enables this synthesis of critical regionalism with tectonic culture is found in the work of Vittorio Gregotti (1927–2020).

Gregotti's place was indeed central in the discourse of critical regionalism. 'Building the site', the recurring Mario Botta quote in Frampton's writings, springs from Gregotti's book on *The Territory of Architecture* (1966).[14] In his *Studies in Tectonic Culture* (1995), Frampton notes Gregotti's significance in highlighting the 'cosmogenic implications of the earthwork' and connects his thoughts with Pikionis's landscaping project around the Acropolis.[15] For Frampton's generation, Gregotti is additionally significant as the figure that reconnected the thought of the Italian Tendenza from the approach of architecture as an autonomous discourse back to the social relations and cultural values that it entails. His conviction that the 'full tectonic potential of any building stems from its capacity to articulate both the poetic and the cognitive aspects of its substance' and that 'one has to mediate between technology as a productive procedure and craft technique as an anachronistic but renewable capacity to reconcile different productive modes and levels of intentionality' in order to do so is another reason why Gregotti's work is fundamental for Frampton's later thinking on tectonics and its entanglement with the main questions of critical regionalism.[16]

Frampton's book project

As soon as Rizzoli discontinued his proposed series, Frampton embarked on a separate book project on critical regionalism in early 1986. The book would focus on 'a number of "schools" ... together with short essays on a number of different architects'. His underlying motivation remained the same: 'to assemble a body of work and theory which indicates the possibility for something other than the reactionary Post Modernism which has such a deleterious influence today'.[17] Frampton's archive includes two versions of an eighty-seven-page typescript labelled as the draft of that book.[18] Its content suggests that the year of writing is 1990. The finalised text was eventually published as 'Contemporary Architecture 1945–1985' in Encyclopaedia Britannica's *The Great Ideas Today 1990*. But it is practically a selective compilation of Frampton's earlier publications.[19]

More informative about Frampton's intentions is the five-page typescript of his research proposal for 'Modern Architecture and Cultural Identity' written towards the end of the academic year 1988–9. Therein, Frampton noted that the positive reception of critical regionalism put him 'under a certain pressure to elaborate this thesis in the form of a book'. This book was to follow a two-part structure similar to his two most popular articles of 1983, with a first section dedicated to the development of his theory and the second one serving as 'the documentation of current critical architectural practice throughout the world'.[20] Building and expanding on Frampton's earlier work on the subject, the theoretical section aimed to stretch back to encompass nineteenth- and twentieth-century critical thinkers and sociologists such as Ferdinand Tonnies and Herbert Marcuse in order to elaborate on the historical development of the concepts of 'culture' and 'civilisation' and their subsequent roles in Ricoeur's philosophy. The rise and fall of the twentieth-century avant-garde was also to be further elucidated by references to the work of Georg Lukacs and Peter Weiss, among others.[21] Stressing the anti-utopian practices of architects such as Frank Lloyd Wright, Richard Neutra, Alvar Aalto and Jørn Utzon, and their willingness to transform reality one specific bit at a time, Frampton then aimed to stress the 'ecological or bio-regional' tendency of their work by assessing it against related practices of the time and the theories of Henryk Skolimowski and Gregory Bateson, among others.[22] It was proposed that the book next focused on the well-known characteristics of the architecture of critical regionalism, such as the mutual embeddedness of buildings and their sites, which produces place-forms instead of free-standing sculptures in the environment; variegated architectural responses to the local climate over the yearly seasons instead of maximising the efficiency of air conditioning in sealed, technological building envelopes; and the poetics of construction, which could encompass local craftsmanship, materials and modes of production in order to showcase 'the quality of the local light'.[23] It was intended that the second section of the book would open with a comparative reading of the 'schools' of Ticino and Porto followed by a general survey of twenty-two critical architectural practices from eleven countries – with Colombia, Egypt and Uruguay added to the standard, and still mainly Western European, references of critical regionalism (Fig. 5.2).[24]

Since this ambitious book project failed to materialise, Frampton did not elaborate on his theory of critical regionalism based on the

K. Frampton p.3 Research Proposal

of these "schools" of architecture. While these regional cultures remain categorically modern, they have nonetheless been inflected by specific cultural, political, and topographical conditions. The second part will take the form of a general survey of critical practice as this has appeared in different parts of the world during the same period.

Part 1: Comparative Study of Two Regional Schools

(i) The School of Ticino, 1960-1985
Critical Practice in the Ticino area. The work of Rino Tami, Tita Carloni, Aurelio Galfetti, Dolf Schnebli, Livio Vacchini, Luigi Snozzi, and Mario Botta

(ii) The School of Porto, 1960-1985
Critical practice in Northern Portugal. The work of Fernando Tavora, Alvaro Siza, Eduardo Souto di Moura, Adalberto Dias, Jorge Carreira, Jorge Carrilho de Graca, etc.

Part 2: General Survey of Critical Regional Practice

(i) The Theory and Practice of Rogelio Salmona, Bogota, Colombia, South America, 1965-1985
(ii) The Theory and Practice of Tadao Ando, Osaka, Japan, 1975-1985
(iii) The Theory and Practice of Jorn Utzon, Copenhagen, Denmark, 1955-1980
(iv) Topographic Architecture in Greece, 1955-1980 (Pikionis, Konstantinides, Antonakakis)
(v) Topographic Architecture in the Veneto; Venice and Udine, 1955-1980 (Scarpa, Valle)
(vi) Dutch Structuralist Architecture, 1955-1980 (Van Eyck, Hertzberger)
(vii) Spanish Tectonic Form in Barcelona and Madrid, 1965-1985 (Oiza, de la Sota, Moneo, Viaplana and Pinon, Mateo and Bru)
(viii) Critical Form in the Third World: India, Egypt, Uruguay, Mexico, 1958-1985 (Fathy, Reval, Correa, D'Este, Barragan, Legoretta, etc.)

Poscript/Research

Apart from providing a theoretical grounding and a documentation of contemporary critical practice in architecture, one of the primary aims of this project will be to trace the specific ways in which different cultural tropes and techniques are transformed as they pass from one cultural situation or site to another. In addition, an attempt will be made to show how this same critical practice is doubly articulated, firstly by the interaction of universal and aboriginal techniques, and secondly, by the mediation of so-called "high" (modern) technology by "intermediate" (traditional) technology. In all this attention will be paid to the ideological/political implications of the resultant tectonic space.

Figure 5.2   Last page of Kenneth Frampton's research proposal for a book on critical regionalism, 1989

ARCH284708, Kenneth Frampton fonds, Canadian Centre for Architecture, Gift of Kenneth Frampton aforementioned additional philosophical references. Nor did he significantly expand on the work of the non-European architects that featured as new entrants in his list. Yet, what he did write about his favoured architectural practices of critical regionalism on various occasions over two decades builds a sufficient picture of the second part of this lost book. The discontinuation of Frampton's book projects was certainly a blow to the wider impact of his critical regionalist agenda. But judging by the two books of the series that were published, it seems that his contribution would have been limited to short introductory texts. His plan was to ask historians and critics who could serve as informed insiders to write the long introductory texts to the individual books in the series (Fig. 5.3). As this project was eventually shelved by Rizzoli, the texts were not gathered to enrich Frampton's discourse from these multiple regional perspectives. Most of these authors had already written significant texts about Frampton's favoured architects. But their sporadic publication in venues of varying visibility meant that they could not work together as a group effort to further sophisticate and advance the cause of critical regionalism.

The fact that the book series was eventually discontinued did not, however, obstruct Frampton's developing ideas on critical regionalism. Given their short length, his introductory texts would not have offered him the word-space to fully develop any new ideas on the subject. But they would have helped him to consolidate the potentially diverging agendas of selected authors. He would have been able to ensure that some of his main points were consistently presented in each book, effectively bringing all the architects concerned more closely together under the rubric of critical regionalism. It is therefore reasonable to suggest that Frampton's ideas on the work of the architects that appear in his original list can be gleaned from introductory texts that he wrote on the occasion of other, related publications in the same period.[25] Taken together, these texts elucidate his less systematically presented ideas on critical regionalism during the 1980s. As such, they provide a fuller picture of critical regionalism that was not comprehensively gathered into a single book. Focusing on these texts, I aim to retrieve significant but relatively overlooked aspects of Frampton's developing ideas of critical regionalism, especially in relation to cross-cultural exchange and his own stated aim 'to trace the specific ways in which different cultural tropes and techniques are transformed as they pass from one cultural situation or site to the other'.[26] This aspect of critical regionalist discourse was especially significant as a viable alternative to the more playful and superficial approach of postmodern historicist eclecticism that also aimed to produce multivalent architectural form.

LIST OF MONOGRAPHS IN THE PROPOSED SERIES

These volumes are arranged in a suggested order of appearance. It is intended, as will be seen from the section Format below, that each monograph will be introduced by a fairly short critical essay. To this end the list gives (1) name and title, (2) country and (3) proposed author of the cirtical article.

1. G.M. Ungers	Germany	(Heinrich Klotz)
2. K. Shinohara	Japan	(Hajime Yatsuka)
3. Jørn Utzon	Denmark	(C.N. Schulz)
4. Renzo Piano	Italy	(Ludwig Glaser)
5. Mario Botta	Switzerland	(Martin Steinman)
6. Norman Foster	England	(?)
7. A. Siza y Viera	Portugal	(D. Cabral del Mello)
8. Barton Meyers	Canada	(George Baird)
9. H. Hertzberger	Holland	(A. Luchinger)
10. Rafael Moneo	Spain	(Tomas Llorens)
11. J.I. Linazasoro	Spain	(D. Porphyrios)
12. D. Antonakakis	Greece	(A. Tzonis)
13. H. Ciriani	France	(Michel Kagan)
14. B. Dhosi	India	(C. Correa)
15. Tadao Ando	Japan	(Hiroyama Akyoshi)
16. Sverre Fehn	Norway	(see S. Williams)

Other possible titles would address the work of:

17. Gino Valle	Italy	(Joseph Rykwert)
18. Vittorio Gregotti	Italy	(Kenneth Frampton)

Depending on whether a four or six monograph schedule is adopted this program some four or two years to complete.

FORMAT AND CONCEPTION

(1) It is suggested that the Centro Di Format is basically adopted for this series. 8 1/2" wide by 9" high. Around 180 pages. Coated paper. Perfect binding. Stiff, but flexible. San serif type. Setting very similar to Centro Di.

(2) However, the actual conception and breakdown of each book would differ from Centro Di and would consist of the following:

(a) A preface by the editor of the series (1000 words or less)
(b) An interpretative essay from between 3000 and 5000 words, plus footnotes, diagramatic illustrations, etc.
(c) A chronological survey of the work to date, consisting of brief descriptions, black and white photos and line drawings.
(d) A more extensive section with color and black/white photographs and a relatively full set of drawings which documents the most significant work by the architect achieved to date. This documentation should be accompanied by a extensive description, etc. This building may not necessarily be the most recent be the most recent but this might often be the case.

Figure 5.3 Kenneth Frampton's original list of eighteen architectural practices for his proposed book series with Rizzoli, Kenneth Frampton, four-page letter to Suzana and Dimitris Antonakakis, 21 December 1981, p. 3

Suzana and Dimitris Antonakakis' private archive

Regionalisms of cross-cultural exchange

Frampton's favoured architects and projects help him to elucidate key but vague concepts of his theory of critical regionalism, such as Ricoeur's 'mythical nuclei' of humanity's diverse cultures. The cross-cultural references in the work of Pikionis, Utzon and other architects are especially significant from this vantage point, as they demonstrate the diverse ways in which one could design across cultures.

In his landscaping project around the Acropolis, Pikionis incorporates 'idiosyncratic fragments from this fissured continent and island cosmos' that constitute 'a metaphorical, *national* and yet universal narrative, as dispersed in time as in space'.[27] Composed of repurposed *spolia* spanning millennia of Greek culture, from Hellenistic tombstones to balconies and debris from the rapidly demolished Neo-Classical residences of 1950s Athens, Pikionis's project does not impose a pre-determined order on its diverse source material. It forms, rather, a wide-ranging collage of Post-Classical Greek culture. Combined with occasional allusions to Japanese structures (Fig. 5.4), this simultaneous and non-hierarchical coexistence of fragments of Greek culture across the centuries – from Hellenistic antiquity through the Byzantine period to the modern age – invites the visitor's contemplative response. For Frampton, this 'admixture of sympathetic alien cultures' was a way for a regionally inflected architecture to survive in the age of modernism.[28] Following Pikionis's 'pathway', visitors need to sense, meet and discuss the specific contribution of Greek culture to the 'cosmic Spirit' – the grand, collective project of human civilisation, whose different aspects are destined to be illuminated by individual cultural traditions.[29] The central significance of Pikionis's 'simultaneously sensual and tectonic' but also 'cross-cultural' work for Frampton's critical regionalist project lies in its transgression of the West's 'obsession with representation'.[30] This is related to Utzon's similar attempts to combine elements from plural, both Western and Eastern, cultures.

Frampton elaborates on Utzon's oeuvre as an exemplar of multiple cross-cultural references – 'in part Islamic, in part Chinese, in part an antique type of Mediterranean or African origin' – as in his patio house with its integrated atrium and lightweight roof.[31] Frampton is especially attentive to Utzon's attraction to Eastern cultures through details and design strategies that allude to multiple cultural strands. These include the affinity of building materials with the landscape that produces them in Morocco, the experience of different horizons as one stands at the top of a Mayan pyramid, the Chinese ceramic tradition and the method of building timber roof structures through combinations of a limited number of specific parts and the Japanese architectural syntax of walls and partitions – as well as Utzon's emulation of traditional Islamic cities in his urban schemes and his references to Greek agoras, medieval labyrinths, or Middle Eastern bazaars as 'cities-in-miniature'.[32] But Utzon's preference

Figure 5.4   Dimitris Pikionis, entrance to the courtyard of St Dimitrios Loumbardiaris, in the pathway around the Acropolis, Athens, 1954–7, photographed by Kostas Tsiambaos

Kostas Tsiambaos's private archive

for 'organically profiled clear-span structures' also situates his work within 'a particularly Baltic ethos' that connects it with that of architects such as Aalto or Hans Scharoun.[33] Utzon's cross-cultural approach to design is especially significant for his emphasis on lived experience that

Figure 5.5 Jørn Utzon's podium/pagoda sketches and other explorations of his platform/plateau design concepts, in Jørn Utzon, 'Platforms and Plateaus: Ideas of a Danish Architect', *Zodiac*, 10 (1962), 112–40 (pp. 116–17).

© Utzon Archives / Aalborg University & Utzon Center

transgresses mere visual affinity. When he compares Japanese floors with European walls and Mexican plateaus of pre-Columbian pyramids, he understands that the different embodied effects of these elements on the user are culturally conditioned. They signify the extent to which different civilisations have worked with the 'opposition between the culture of the light and the culture of the heavy'. The typical 'heavyweight masonry podium [with] a lightweight timber roof floating over it' in Chinese architecture, summarised in his characteristic podium/pagoda sketches of the early 1960s (Fig. 5.5), becomes a frequently adopted trope in Utzon's work.[34]

For Frampton, Utzon's Bagsvaerd Church is exemplary as a project that lies at the crossroads of Eastern and Western cultures. It has affinities

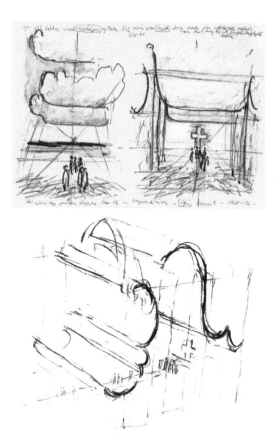

Figure 5.6 Jørn Utzon, sketches for the Bagsvaerd Church, 1973–6

© Utzon Archives / Aalborg University & Utzon Center

with precedents ranging from the Nordic Gothic Revival of Jensen-Klint's Grundtvig Church to the Chinese pagoda form and Wright's Unity Temple of 1904.[35] But while its vaults still allude to the heavens of Christianity, their shell forms, which unfold as a Chinese ('Hanseatic', 'Shaker or even Shinto') pagoda in section, create a different atmosphere (Fig. 5.6). They bring in qualities of light that one does not usually encounter in Christian churches.[36] Bagsvaerd Church's interior roof structure prioritises the symbolic intent of architectural form over its constructional optimisation (Fig. 5.7). This is further reinforced by Utzon's detailing and material transpositions, in which the standardised concrete parts and infills are clearly distinguished from the in situ constructed parts through the imprints of the required formwork.[37] As the structural form supports the intended lived experience, a religious space that does not have an

Figure 5.7   Jørn Utzon, Bagsvaerd Church interior, 1973–6

© Utzon Archives / Aalborg University & Utzon Center

easily identifiable direct precedent in architectural history is created. For these reasons, Utzon's Bagsvaerd Church remains significant as the 'homecoming' of the Danish architect's cross-cultural vision, 'the ideal of an emerging world culture that, while springing from local traditions, transcends them at the same time, thereby reintegrating and revitalizing different traditions through a kind of cultural transmigration'.[38]

Carlo Scarpa's work is also significant for its subtle introduction of cross-cultural references, as in his Fondazione Querini Stampalia project, where water in marble fountains and concrete drains flows from the east 'to evoke the dependency of Venice on the Orient but also Scarpa's own genealogy; his self-characterization as "a man of Byzantium, who came to Venice by way of Greece"'.[39] Frampton also notes how a Chinese influence is especially apparent in the ways in which Scarpa organises the walled gardens of his projects, including their ponds, tiling, and 'artificial

Figure 5.8 Carlo Scarpa, garden of Palazzo Querini Stampalia, Venice, photographed by Paolo Monti: Servizio fotografico (Venezia, 1963)

horizons' (Fig. 5.8).[40] But Scarpa's unique contribution to the cross-cultural side of the evolving discourse of critical regionalism lies in his regular employment of motifs such as the double circle, which could refer to multiple Western, Eastern, mythical and mystical sources – ranging from the yin–yang symbol to Bernini's Sant' Andrea al Quirinale in Rome.[41] Such cross-cultural references enable Scarpa to transcend the limitations of Western traditions and create new kinds of spaces. This is more starkly evident in his Brion Cemetery project, where he also uses the Chinese character for 'double happiness'. Working within the Christian tradition of sin and redemption and the Eastern positive acknowledgement of mortality, Frampton argues, Scarpa produces 'a transcultural, ecumenical expression'. Using motifs hybridised from multiple Western and Eastern sources, he manages to express different, usually Eastern, cultural values in the given Western context of his work.[42]

Figure 5.9 Top: Alvar Aalto, Säynätsalo Town Hall, Säynätsalo, Jyväskylä. 1949–52; bottom: Kenneth Frampton in front of Alvar Aalto's Säynätsalo Town Hall in the 1980s

Tiia Monto, 2018 (top), CC BY-SA 4.0, via Wikimedia Commons; ARCH284698, Kenneth Frampton fonds, Canadian Centre for Architecture (bottom), Gift of Kenneth Frampton

But it was not only exceptional cases of European architects such as Utzon, Scarpa and Pikionis who explicitly worked with multiple cultural strands, from north to south and east to west. Numerous Western European architects of the twentieth century found themselves in a similar position when they attempted to combine the rising interwar language of modernism with their rooted, local architectural traditions. Such examples interested Frampton because he intended to underscore the strong modernist core of his architectural approach. This is why Aalto's position in the critical regionalist discourse is especially significant (Fig. 5.9), despite the fact that his projects did not attempt to connect to architectures beyond Europe. An established modern master who connects Frampton's endeavour with Giedion's historiography of the rise of the modern generation of 'new regionalists', Aalto is equally important for his 'anti-star' attitude that foregrounds architecture as the product of a collective cultural effort rather than the exceptional result of individual genius.[43] In the 1930s, his work was informed by the fading, longer tradition of Finnish National Romanticism and the only recently established architectural language of modernism.[44] Conversely, regional architectures such as that of Sverre Fehn (1924–2009) can also hide a strong, modernist core. Arguing that Fehn's work is practically imbued with Jean Prouvé's 'structural economy', Frampton posits that it 'has its ultimate origin in a pre-war Parisian avant-gardist *poésie de technique*'.[45]

Architects such as Henri Ciriani (b. 1936), whose acclaimed projects were realised in the 1970s and the 1980s, show that cross-cultural exchange can also be understood in terms of working within multiple modernist traditions. For Frampton, Ciriani's oeuvre represents the strongest expression of the work of French Rationalists and their attempt to retain a sense of civic character in their large-scale projects after the Second World War, as in his Noisy II project in Marne-la-Vallée (1980). The front of Ciriani's project defines a civic, public face of architecture against the modernist new-town plan of Marne-la-Vallée. Serving as the entrance portico to a bounded urban realm, this project embodies a critique of modernist urbanisation and the reductive functionalism of the 1950s.[46] Ciriani's debt to the work of Italian Neo-Rationalists such as Aldo Rossi shows that this variant of cross-cultural exchange becomes a way of testing specific theoretical ideas on the ground of architectural practice. When the same concepts are realised in different ways, they can keep their distance from undesirable features of the original sources such as 'the poetic nihilism' of Rossi's built works. In other cases, they reformulate currently overshadowed sociocultural notions of modernist housing projects as urban units or microcosms. To do so, Ciriani hybridises the monumental forms of the Italian Neo-Rationalists such as the 'viaduct form' of the Gallaratese projects with elements drawn from the earlier tradition of French modernism. This 'radical rupture' between the Neo-Rationalist conception of the autonomy of architecture and the modernist conception of the social role of the architect is what mainly interests Frampton in Ciriani's ambivalently 'heroic' work.[47] Ciriani is one of the few architects on Frampton's list to offer concrete examples of addressing 'the incomplete project of modernity' by critically reappraising and further developing earlier iterations of modernist traditions in different contexts.

The same approach of working with multiple modernist traditions is combined with a slightly different interest towards the East in the work of Oswald Mathias Ungers (1926–2007). Frampton highlights Ungers's willingness to engage with Russian Constructivism in his pursuit of avant-gardist architectural form.[48] This shows not only how the East–West divide of the Cold War world limited the cultural traditions at architects' immediate disposal but also the ways in which architects could engage with them in practice, including the recapitulation of the most promising avant-gardist traditions of the Soviet Bloc of the early twentieth century. Frampton is mainly drawn to Ungers's projects for their attempt to both relate and define themselves as perimeter blocks – clearly bounded places against the modern, 'placeless' urban backdrop of Berlin, the exemplary divided city of the Western European world at the time. Ungers understands that such a modern city remains open, fragmentary and incomplete. Any attempt to reclaim its supposedly lost total image would therefore be futile.[49] Precluding nostalgic allusions to an illusory 'lost whole', which would turn the historic city into 'an empty scenography' such as that promoted by the postmodernist architects of the Biennale, Ungers's 'doubly articulated goal of achieving a dialectic between place-form and place-lessness'[50] is crucial within the wider developing discourse of critical regionalism. Frampton's related texts stress architecture's capacity for place-creation through the clearly bounded urban types of the perimeter block, the galleria or the atrium as a means of resistance to the relentless, placeless expansion of the megalopolis.[51] But they do not discuss the kinds of relationships that this bounded, resisting domain of architecture could still constructively establish with its immediate, albeit 'placeless', urban surroundings. The way in which Ungers's work had to engage with the specific context of Cold War Berlin adds more sophisti-cated approaches to a discussion that Frampton's later texts on critical regionalism tended to address in terms of a polar opposition.

Lastly, cross-cultural exchange is an internal process that occurs within the canon of critical regionalist architects themselves. In many cases, Frampton discusses the work of architects of critical regionalism as rearticulations and further developments of his recurring favourites, such as Mario Botta's notion of 'building the site'; Álvaro Siza's idea that architects do not invent anything new, as they only discover and transform what is already there; or Jørn Utzon's cross-cultural references and tectonic articulation. Rafael Moneo's (b. 1937) biographical link with Utzon, and the affinity of his work with that of Aalto, reinforces his connection with the exemplary projects of critical regionalism. It also partly explains how his projects similarly combine his respect for

Figure 5.10 Rafael Moneo, in collaboration with Ramon Bescós, Bankinter Building, Madrid, 1973–7

Luis García (Zagarbal), 2014 (top), CC BY-SA 3.0 ES, via Wikimedia Commons; Triplecaña, 2018 (bottom), CC BY-SA 4.0, via Wikimedia Commons

Mediterranean Rationalism, the organic strand in modern architecture and European Romanticism. This aspect of his work seems to have been additionally informed by the cross-cultural exchange on Brutalism between England and Spain in the late 1950s, with James Stirling's Leicester University Engineering Laboratory (1959–63) emerging as a crucial reference.[52] Frampton reads Moneo's Bankinter Building, designed in collaboration with Ramon Bescós, in Madrid (1973–7), in order to trace a multitude of potential references and possible allusions (Fig. 5.10). These reveal 'the multivalency running through the entire work' via the juxtaposition and inflection of these references and precedents.[53]

Figure 5.11 Carlo Scarpa, interior architectural details of Palazzo Querini Stampalia, Venice, photographed by Paolo Monti: Servizio fotografico (Venezia, 1963)

Fondo Paolo Monti, BEIC, Civico Archivio Fotografico of Milan, SER-s5010-0004886, CC BY-SA 4.0, via Wikimedia Commons

In a similar vein, Scarpa's embrace of his Byzantine heritage draws subtle connections between his work and the related approach of Pikionis, who also sought to work with multiple layers of Greek and other cultural histories. Scarpa's 'use of montage as a strategy for integrating heterogeneous elements' could be associated with Pikionis's work, furthering Frampton's analysis of this aspect of critical regionalism.[54] The Greek and the Venetian architect also worked in similar ways. They combined craftsmanship with draftsmanship, creating feedback loops between their acts of drawing and making as one constantly informed the other.[55] The two architects also seem to follow a similar approach in their handling of the ground. In both cases, the ground is not 'merely a serviceable covering laid over an abstract plane, but … an elevated artificial datum to be read as a tactile palimpsest'.[56] Scarpa goes beyond Pikionis in following the same approach not only in outdoor spaces and gardens but also in the ground floors of buildings such as the Querini Stampalia project (Fig. 5.11). In Scarpa's work, raising the general datum – as in the Brion Cemetery and the Querini garden – also becomes a method of creating the

Figure 5.12 Carlo Scarpa, Museo de Castelvecchio, Verona, 1953–65

Seier + Seier, 2016, CC BY-NC 2.0, www.flickr.com/photos/seier/31986928545/in/photostream

clearly bounded place that is sought by the architecture of critical regionalism. Scarpa's Museo de Castelvecchio in Verona (1956–75) works like an insertion of Pikionis's 'pathway' into a public building (Fig. 5.12).[57] Frampton indeed reads the project as 'a continuously unfolding promenade that would mark its progress through space by the discrete articulation of

Figure 5.13 Carlo Scarpa, Museo de Castelvecchio, Verona, 1953–65

different elements' (Fig. 5.13).[58] Scarpa attentively locates each of the artworks within this promenade not as a fetishised exhibit but as one of these different elements and objects of interest that are subtly articulated to be found along the way. In Greece, Suzana and Dimitris Antonakakis had also applied the 'pathway' principle in buildings – but they did so only in their private residential projects such as the House at Spata (1973–5). Scarpa's employment of the same principle within a public building therefore demonstrates another way in which Pikionis's work on the Athenian landscape could inform building projects in other parts of Europe.

Critical regionalism as collective culture

The fact that Frampton's favoured architects of critical regionalism are also connected is not coincidental. The British historian's unwavering interest in 'schools' such as those of Ticino and Porto demonstrates the central role of the collective aspect in critical regionalist architectural practices. Situating the work of Botta in the context of his Ticinese colleagues (including Aurelio Galfetti, Flora Ruchat-Roncati and Luigi Snozzi, among others) demonstrates how architecture both works as a cultural agent and realises the collective vision of a societal formation. While this thinking could be associated with a variant of rooted cultural development, it also remains close to the main intentions of the modern project in architecture. Modernist buildings were significant as social agents, because they embodied the vision of a modern society for the identity that it aspired to forge for itself through its arts, science and politics. At the same time, Frampton singles Botta out as the catalytic individual figure of this collective. This became a staple feature of his reading of critical regionalist architecture, in which it is usually the work of the talented individual architect that produces the most accurate expression and best moment of a given cultural context.[59] Nonetheless, Frampton acknowledges that Botta's unrealised but important larger-scale projects, which serve to establish 'a new urban situation' by augmenting or reactivating the latent civic potential of a given city fabric, are usually done in collaboration with other prominent Ticinese architects such as Snozzi. Frampton appraises Snozzi as an architect of the Left whose work maintains collective urban culture and the institutions that support it, such as the city-state, the canton and the village. Constructing a political body, these institutions in turn maintain the continuity of a place over time.[60] However, Frampton's 'School of the Ticino' was not consciously functioning as a collective. Among others, the Ticinese architects lacked a shared cause or manifesto before they were grouped together by Martin Steinman for the 'Tendenzen' exhibition of 1975.[61]

Critical regionalism is itself a collective culture that is gradually shared and developed from one generation of 'organic' modern architects such as Wright to the next generation of Aalto, Utzon and Fehn. Gino and Nani Valle's engagement with the work of Aalto and Scarpa in turn leads to the most fertile early period of their career, from the late 1940s to the late 1960s.[62] In the same period, Suzana and Dimitris Antonakakis understand their collaborative practice Atelier 66 as a collective that shares not just a workspace but an everyday life coloured by their interest in architecture, including their frequent trips around Greece. As such, they constantly try to establish and refine their shared approach to architecture. In a similar vein, Frampton positively notes how Herman Hertzberger also 'continued to extend and to refine ... the precepts of his mentor' Aldo van Eyck, finding this continuity 'unique in the annals of twentieth century architecture'.[63] Realising that Structuralism was clearly a Dutch school of architectural thought without any followers outside of

Figure 5.14 Scenes from Atelier 66 architects' visit to Jørn Utzon's Bagsvaerd Church, 1987

Lucy and Giorgos Triantafyllou private archive

the Netherlands proved significant for the development of Frampton's thinking on regionalism.[64]

Even more important than the theorists' conceptual analyses is the establishment of those mutual ties that nourish the architects' specific sensibilities. These range from their shared emphasis on 'distinguishing between supported and supporting elements' through their 'articulation of the load bearing and the load borne' and their material sensibilities (in the case of Scarpa and Fehn) to the ways in which these architects allow for 'the past to speak' through their work (as in the case of Utzon and Fehn).[65] This is what has probably led scholars such as Mary McLeod to note that the architects of critical regionalism seem to have more in common between themselves than with their immediate contexts and local cultures.[66] This was not only owing to their shared interests. Some of these architects started to communicate, visit and study each others' work after being grouped together by Frampton in the 1980s (Fig. 5.14). Through his discourse, the British historian also continued to reinforce

Figure 5.15 Kenneth Frampton's 2016 visit to Glenn Murcutt's Fredericks/White House, Jamberoo, New South Wales, Australia, 1981–2/2001–4

ARCH284697. Kenneth Frampton fonds, Canadian Centre for Architecture, Gift of Kenneth Frampton

the links between them as he consistently highlighted mutual sensibilities with every new entry on his favoured list of critical regionalist architects (Fig. 5.15).

Frampton is aware that the production of an architecture of critical regionalism depends on social structures and values such as those of 'the vestigial "city-state" … as a nexus of identity and political independence' or 'decentralized forms of socio-political autonomy' backed by the prosperity of regions like Ticino in the 1970s or the 'Iberian peninsulas' in the 1980s.[67] More significantly, however, he appreciates the work of groups and architects such as Martorell, Bohigas and Mackay, who worked from a similar 'frontier-ghetto' context but also remained connected to 'the radical, not to say rebellious, cultural traditions of Catalonia'.[68] This strong connection to a progressive political movement was something that Frampton sought but could rarely find in his selected projects of critical regionalism. He frequently notes the 'recurrent paradox' in the work of politically committed architects such as Siza who end up realising their 'finest works in the service of the middle class'. This raises the broader problem of the viability of critical regionalism as a political project that can be successfully sustained in 'a mass-media

Figure 5.16 Herman Hertzberger, the 'social plan' of Centraal Beheer offices, Apeldoorn, 1968–72, photographed by Willem Diepraam (left)

Courtesy of Atelier Herman Hertzberger

consumerist society' that does not allow for 'any kind of return to the collective norms which guaranteed the urban unity and cultural vitality of cities in the past', as it constantly reinforces the desire for the stand-alone petit-bourgeois house in the suburb.[69] Hertzberger's elaborate detailing, which intended to render his architectural structures accessible and open to appropriation by their users, was the best example that Frampton offered to demonstrate a sort of social engagement that is directly linked to the tactile aspects of architecture (Fig. 5.16).[70] While Hertzberger's example could steer the critical regionalist discourse away from a potential fetishisation of the tectonic form and the individually experienced phenomenological qualities of a project at the expense of its collective social aspect, this still falls rather short of Frampton's wider political aspirations. As such, he is especially interested in Martorell and Bohigas's collaboration with other Catalan modernists from the 1950s onwards and their relation to the old nationalism of the late nineteenth century that rendered Barcelona the epicentre of modernist developments, as if anticipating the politics of decentralisation in 1980s Spain.[71]

If Frampton's reconstructed globalised survey suggests that critical regionalism gradually developed as a distinct collective culture, this resulting collective should be further interrogated – especially since critical regionalism was positively received on account of its alleged inclusiveness. Referring steadily to Ricoeur, Frampton consistently stresses this cross-cultural aspect of critical regionalism through a 'process of assimilation and transformation' that remains 'impure by definition', as a rooted culture attempts 'to recreate its own tradition while appropriating foreign influences at the level of both culture and civilization'. He frequently adds that this has also been historically the case, as 'all cultures, both ancient and modern, seem to have depended for their intrinsic development on a certain cross-fertilization with other cultures'. In his understanding, Ricoeur's suggestion is that regional cultures need to be 'ultimately constituted as locally inflected manifestations of "world culture"'.[72] But a closer look at Frampton's accounts of cross-cultural exchanges reveals that most of these are strictly intra-European, as in the cases of Fehn and Ciriani. As such, the overarching purview of critical regionalism gravitates towards Western Europe. From the outset, Frampton was mainly interested in individual European countries that represent 'unknown continents' in the historiography of modern architecture.[73] This is the world that he wants to write about. His use of Louis Althusser's terms here implies that an epistemological shift might be instigated by the 'discovery' of the Spanish and other overlooked 'continents' in modern, but still at its core decisively European, architectural historiography.

The widest-ranging goal of Frampton's emphasis on cross-cultural exchange is to advocate for a combination of Western and Eastern cultural references in architecture, because this is a way for tactile sensibility to find its place in Western architecture. In his critical review of the Biennale, he concludes that 'reinterpret[ing] the tradition of the West in terms of the East' is a way to overcome 'the closure of Humanism', when 'the "dominant" modes of Western architectural thought ... enter their decline':

> We have, in my view, but two choices; either to embrace the profound intuitions that the pre-Humanist Orient has had about the *tactile* significance of place or to face, without any redress, the prospect that neither late Capitalism, nor State Socialism, both subject to the dictates of Taylor, have any need within themselves for the dialectical realization of desire, as this may be embodied within the domains of culture and art.[74]

His discussion of architects such as Utzon shows that his view of this hybridised East/West approach is informed by a rather generic, superficial understanding. Frampton's 'East' and 'West' are not especially open to forming sophisticated hybridised architectural cultures. His view of the East is effectively idealised and essentialising, if not Orientalising. In his later texts, Frampton emphasises an 'equally complex, cross-cultural attitude' in the potentially Islamic references in the work of Luis Barragán that also seem to encompass his 'preoccupation with the indispensable privacy of the courtyard house', or in the 'oriental ... Islamic and Shintoesque ... affinities' with the architecture of the Ottoman Empire and the 'more archaically' Mediterranean, even Cretan, references of Siza's projects.[75] Even when Frampton discusses the work of 'Oriental' architects such as that of Tadao Ando, he tends to analyse it by relating it back to the work of Western architects and thinkers with whom he is readily familiar – such as Adolf Loos and Ludwig Wittgenstein.[76]

As a critic, Frampton seems unsurpassed in drawing connections between qualities of buildings as concrete manifestations of abstract ideas and material realisations of cultural values. He consistently notes how the structural logics employed by his architects of critical regionalism are not only statically sound but also serve as metaphors that underline specific design intentions. Their loadbearing function is coupled with an expressive function that conveys a cultural meaning, closely related to the specific context of their site, in the widest sense of the term. To cite just one example, the forking structure of Fehn's Nordic Pavilion for the Venice Biennale in 1962 mirrors the bifurcated trunk of the tree that grows inside it (Fig. 5.17).[77] Convinced that material selection and articulation matter, Frampton remains attentive to details that signify cultural values. He either discusses the ways in which these details express cultural meaning or highlights the contrasts and inflections that underpin his analysis of them. For Frampton, architecture is inherently imbued with cultural significance as architects work with specific values and ideas to arrive at built forms. These ideas can in turn be traced in their buildings' plan, section and elevation drawings; structural logics; modes of production; or their intended use. As such, architecture is a cultural text that can be read alongside those of philosophers, cultural theorists and sociologists. This approach forms the core of Frampton's thinking about architecture, and this is how it is still remembered by his students of the 1980s.[78] It is the reflection of his conviction that there is no divide between architectural theory and practice, as both of them are integrated in a process that results in meaningful buildings and environments that remain sensitive to the needs of the communities that create them.

Frampton rightly notes that Utzon's interest in the Orient is a way out of the Eurocentrism of his fellow modern architects.[79] But he is less

Figure 5.17 Sverre Fehn, Nordic Pavilion at the Giardini Biennale, Venice, 1962

Åke E:son Lindman, 2010

interested in elucidating how the specific mode of cross-cultural exchange develops in each case. His discussion of the work of Moneo, among others, points more strongly towards potential precedents than actual processes of creative exchange and the ways in which these have informed architectural practices in the late twentieth century. The exact ways in which Moneo 'discerned' and further developed Utzon's 'art of contradictory synthesis of East and West' in his own work is only mentioned as a possibility without being sufficiently explored, let alone demonstrated, by Frampton.[80] As such, cross-cultural exchanges are discussed rather superficially – without a deeper, situated understanding of their historical mechanics. The recurring, dualist framework of the idealised abstractions of East and West leads to an essentially reductive understanding of the cross-cultural dimension of regional architectures. Hence, this is an aspect of critical regionalism that can be further explored and enriched today.

Frampton only sporadically alludes to the historical process of cross-cultural encounter. To cite just one example, he rightly notes that Aalto's reference to Japanese architecture in the mid-1930s was only driven by his attempt to overcome modern functionalism through a return to the Finnish vernacular; it did not spring from his actual contact with Japanese culture.[81] Conversely, cross-cultural references are more difficult to trace in Gregotti's built work, although the Italian architect collaborated with the Japanese architect Hiromichi Matsui from the mid-1960s to the early 1970s.[82] But Frampton's interest is mainly driven towards understanding how Utzon's work, for example, contributes to generating 'non-Eurocentric' architectural form.[83] As such, Frampton also overlooks other significant aspects of the critical regionalist discourse. Discussing Utzon's Sydney Opera House, he rightly notes that this project goes beyond 'building the site' to building 'an image for the nation' through the metaphors embedded in its symbolic shell form, which addresses and mediates between the city and the dynamism of the harbour.[84] But again, such remarks in Frampton's discussions of critical regionalism are few and far between. While connections between regionalism and nationalism were already there in Tzonis and Lefaivre's original grappling with the question of regionalism, they were mostly overlooked in Frampton's texts from the same period.

In the final instance, Frampton seems to be driven more by a persistent, clearly philosophical, quest for 'universality'. This is especially evident in his discussion of Bruno Taut's concept of the 'city crown', the 'universal phenomenon' of the landmark civic project that has allegedly assumed 'different forms in different places and at different times, whether a Greek temple, a Gothic cathedral, an Indian stupa, or a Chinese pagoda'.[85] The inconspicuous exterior form of the Bagsvaerd Church, with its corrugated asbestos and its modular framing and glazing, does not betray its impressive content (Fig. 5.18). The fact that this standardised exterior subtly hints at its sophisticated interior (Fig. 5.19) through the suggestive colouring of grouped modules also demonstrates Frampton's point that cross-cultural references can only be contained as 'disjunctive episodes' within an overarching modernist language of construction that prevails. As I have already noted, in each of the eighteen proposed books of 1981 Frampton intended to include his short foreword to that specific architectural practice followed by a longer introductory text by an invited critic.[86] With these dual introductions to the monographs, he seems to have consciously aimed at combining the views of the mediated outsider (himself) with that of the informed insider (the invited critic) from specific regions and their cultural contexts. The replication of this same structure in each book also sets the tone for the priority of the modernist outsider over the 'disjunctive' local scholar in the discourse of critical regionalism.

Tzonis and Lefaivre's 'The Grid and the Pathway' was only one of the texts by 'home scholars' to be recapitulated in Frampton's accounts of critical regionalist architects. An earlier study by Kiyoshi Takeyama, for

Figure 5.18 Jørn Utzon, Bagsvaerd Church exterior, 1973–6

© Utzon Archives / Aalborg University & Utzon Center

example, helps Frampton to advance his argument about the relevance of Ando's work as a critique of the Japanese context by discussing how he consciously transforms the sixteenth-century Sukiya teahouse style in his modern architectural work.[87] But while Frampton acknowledges that 'Ando's work is at its most subversive in a Japanese context', he still reads him primarily as a cross-cultural critic of both Western and Eastern cultures. He especially highlights the cross-cultural relevance of Ando's discussion of the non-structural but symbolic role of the post in Japanese architecture and the Classical rhythm of the Western colonnade, because they face a shared problem. Both of these long-standing structures have been rendered obsolete by the ubiquitous frame of construction in reinforced concrete that can cover far larger spans with less and more sparsely spaced posts.[88] Frampton does the same when he discusses the architecture of Hiromi Fujii in 1987. He invariably starts from Western references before discussing the 'unequivocally Japanese' features of

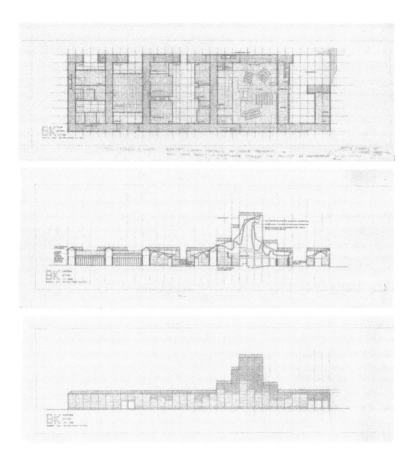

Figure 5.19 Jørn Utzon, Bagsvaerd Church plan, section and elevation drawings, 1973–6

© Utzon Archives / Aalborg University & Utzon Center

Fujii's projects and their role in the collective culture of Japanese architecture through their links with the work of other local architects of his generation. In both instances, the Western framework prevails as Fujii's and Ando's work is discussed with reference to Western thinkers and architects ranging from Jean-Paul Sartre and Martin Heidegger to Clement Greenberg and Sigmund Freud, and from Dutch Constructivism to Peter Eisenman's post-functionalism.[89] But Frampton also does the same in a European context. He keeps reading the work of regional architects, such as that of the Antonakakis, through canonical references from his critical history of modern architecture – like Mies, Le Corbusier, Wright's organicism and triangulated grids, and the Rationalist planning principles of the Dutch Structuralists.[90]

However, this is probably the result of the effort of a single individual who undertakes the contradictory task of globalising a discourse that needs to remain sensitive to the realities of architectural practice on the ground. Despite Frampton's ever-expanding pool of references and his growing familiarity with different sites, his frequently impressive associations of architects' work across different contexts encounter the limits of an individual who can only remain an outsider to the local cultures that he discusses. This is why the same connections with the established architects and thinkers of Western Europe and North America also seem to constantly recur in his discussions of the work of regional architects from Mexico to Japan. As such, the globalising branches of Frampton's critical regionalism increasingly seemed to overlook their specific cross-cultural roots.

Cross-cultural roots and globalising branches

Looking back at the original proposal for the book series of 1981, the book project of 1989 and the ways in which Frampton discussed the work of specific architects in more detail highlights various ways in which the critical regionalist discourse could have been further developed. The proposed theoretical elaboration of critical regionalism's main points through a deeper historical and philosophical understanding of the concepts of 'culture' and 'civilisation' and additional references to the thought of Tonnies, Lukacs, Weiss, Skolimowski and Bateson could also be updated with references to architecture in the age of the Anthropocene today. Developing the practical side of Frampton's project, on the other hand, is not only a matter of accumulating specific buildings that exemplify more ways in which the main points of critical regionalism can be materialised. Perhaps more significantly, one needs to study how these points are interwoven with the associated architectural works. The tectonic form and phenomenological qualities of a building are not significant only in themselves in the context of individual experiences. Equally important are the ways in which these tactile qualities catalyse social life by encouraging users' diverse modes of interaction with the building, and thus promote a specific civic culture. Such examples transgress Frampton's subsequent focus on tectonic form, which drove his discussions away from the wider political, and more nuanced cross-cultural, dimensions of critical regionalism in the 1990s. As these links have tended to be historically overlooked, their reappraisal remains significant today.

While several of the architects on Frampton's list were eventually discussed by him on different occasions as part of other publishing

Figure 5.20 Kenneth Frampton with Yumiko and Tadao Ando in Japan, 1981

ARCH284696, Kenneth Frampton fonds, Canadian Centre for Architecture, Gift of Kenneth Frampton

ventures, others were left in the shadows of mainstream critical regionalist discourse. Kazuo Shinohara (1925–2006), Barton Meyers (b. 1934), José Ignacio Linazasoro (b. 1947) and Balkrishna Vithaldas Doshi (b. 1927) were not discussed in detail by Frampton. The British historian's expertise and the architects whom he eventually discussed covered only specific parts of the continental Western European territory with which he was more readily familiar (Germany, Switzerland, Britain, the Netherlands, Spain and Portugal) and Japan, where he travelled in 1981 (Fig. 5.20).[91] As a result, contexts such as Canada and Norway or figures with cross-cultural trajectories, such as the Peruvian architect Henri Ciriani and his career in France, were left out of the spotlight. But they can still enrich cross-cultural discussions today through the specificity of their contexts, which will move beyond Frampton's generic combinations of Western and Eastern cultures through essentialised architectural forms – such as Utzon's insertion of a reinterpreted pagoda inside a standardised modular structure in Denmark.

Frampton's accounts of critical regionalist architects leave their reader wondering whether it is the architects themselves who draw these inferences to the established Northern European architectural canon. It seems increasingly likely that the formative years of a British architectural critic educated in this northern tradition during the rise of Brutalism of the 1950s and the 1960s have shaped the lens through which he then tends to analyse architectural examples from diverse regions. It is these kinds of problems and questions that this book intends to further highlight and pursue through the more detailed, historically situated analysis of the Greek examples that follow in the second part.

Frampton's 1986 letter and detailed questionnaire to Fernando Tavora demonstrates that the British historian essentially provided second-hand accounts of regional architectural practices. His questions to the Portuguese architect on that occasion range from general information on twentieth-century architects and theorists who have shaped the architectural culture of the 'school' of Porto to requesting a copy of a two-volume book project on the Portuguese vernacular.[92] As an outsider, Frampton could only produce mediated accounts of local practices as he had to rely on the local informed insiders in each cultural context. Focusing on Frampton's relationship with Greece, the next chapter will demonstrate how his analysis is indebted to the 'originary locus' of critical regionalism. This did not just follow Tzonis and Lefaivre's original account, since Frampton also developed his own understanding of the Greek context through his personal ties with and travels to the country. Greece represents an ideal locus from which to return to the roots of critical regionalism before globalisation, and not only because it coincides with the first coining of the term by Tzonis and Lefaivre in 1981. It is also the specific cultural context that has been alternately discussed by all three main theorists of critical regionalism. As such, it enables a clearer elucidation of the historiographical issues that arise from the accounts of both mediated outsiders such as Frampton and 'home scholars' such as Tzonis and Lefaivre. Returning to the cross-cultural roots of critical regionalism in Greece, the second part of the book thus highlights the ways in which the three theorists' accounts have contributed to the historical agency of their discourse – including the multifarious ways in which it has affected architectural practice in this context.

Notes

1 The sixth revised and expanded edition of *The Language of Post-Modern Architecture* was published in 1991, following the previous revised editions of 1978, 1981, 1984 and 1987. The definitive seventh edition was retitled and published in 2002. See Charles Jencks, *The New Paradigm in Architecture: The Language of Post-Modernism* (New Haven, CT: Yale University Press, 2002).
2 See *Deconstructivist Architecture*, ed. by Philip Johnson and Mark Wigley (New York: Museum of Modern Art, 1988).
3 See Liane Lefaivre and Alexander Tzonis, *Critical Regionalism: Architecture and Identity in a Globalized World* (Munich: Prestel, 2003); Liane Lefaivre and Alexander Tzonis, *Architecture of*

Regionalism in the Age of Globalization: Peaks and Valleys in the Flat World (London: Routledge, 2012).

4   Peter Blundell Jones, 'History in the Making: *Modern Movements in Architecture*; *Modern Architecture: A Critical History*', *Architects' Journal*, 183.13 (26 March 1986), 80.

5   Fredric Jameson, *The Seeds of Time* (New York: Columbia University Press, 1994), pp. 189–205; Kenneth Frampton, '2018 Plenary Talk by Kenneth Frampton', Society of Architectural Historians, 21 May 2018. Online. www.sah.org/about-sah/news/sah-news/news-detail/2018/05/21/2018-plenary-talk-by-kenneth-frampton (accessed 6 July 2021).

6   Charlotte Benton, 'The Ideology of Modernism Explained', *Architects' Journal*, 172.40 (1 October 1980), 641.

7   Richard Weston, 'Corrective Studies in the Art of Construction', *Architects' Journal*, 203 (7 March 1996), 54.

8   See Tom Avermaete et al., 'A Conversation with Kenneth Frampton: New York, 6 April 2018', *OASE*, 103 (2019), 142–54 (p. 147).

9   Kenneth Frampton, 'Towards a Critical Regionalism: Six Points for an Architecture of Resistance' (1983), repr. in Kenneth Frampton, *Labour, Work and Architecture: Collected Essays on Architecture and Design* (London: Phaidon, 2002), pp. 76–89.

10 Kenneth Frampton, *Studies in Tectonic Culture: The Poetics of Construction in Nineteenth and Twentieth Century Architecture* (Cambridge, MA: MIT Press, 1995), p. 12.

11 Ibid., p. 376.

12 Ibid., p. 375.

13 Ibid., p. 377.

14 Ibid., p. 26.

15 Ibid., p. 8.

16 Ibid., p. 26.

17 Kenneth Frampton, letter to Fernando Tavora, 5 February 1986, CCA Fonds 197, Kenneth Frampton fonds, 197 – 2017 – 115T, AP197.S3.002, Personal and professional correspondence 1986, 1986, 197-115-003, pp. 1–2.

18 See CCA Fonds 197, Kenneth Frampton fonds, 197 – 2017 – 010T, AP197.S1.SS5.001, Draft of Critical regionalism (1960–1980) by Kenneth Frampton, circa 1980–1983, 87-page typescript, 197-010-038; CCA Fonds 197, Kenneth Frampton fonds, 197 – 2017 – 087T, AP197.S1.SS9.002, Developments in contemporary architecture (1945–1985), circa 1985, 1995, 87-page typescript, 197-087-065.

19 Kenneth Frampton, 'Developments in Contemporary Architecture 1945–1985', in *The Great Ideas Today 1990* (Chicago: Encyclopaedia Britannica, 1990), pp. 2–67. The text includes portions of Frampton's previously published writings in his guest-edited *AD* issue *Modern Architecture and the Critical Present* (1982), his *Modern Architecture: A Critical History* (1985), and his 'Twilight Gloom to Self-Enclosed Modernity: Five Japanese Architects', in *Tokyo, Form and Spirit*, ed. by James R. Brandon and Mildred S. Friedman (Minneapolis, MN: Walker Arts Center, 1986), pp. 221–41.

20 CCA Fonds 197, Kenneth Frampton fonds, 197 – 2017 – 088T, AP197.S1.SS9.003, Modern Architecture and cultural identity – research proposal, circa 1983, 5-page typescript, 197-088-088, p. 1.

21 Ibid., p. 2.

22 Ibid., p. 3.

23 Ibid., pp. 3–4.

24 Ibid., pp. 4–5.

25 See Andrew Leach and Nicole Sully, 'Frampton's Forewords, etc.: An Introduction', *OASE*, 103 (May 2019), 105–13.

26 CCA Fonds 197, Kenneth Frampton fonds, 197 – 2017 – 088T, AP197.S1.SS9.003, Modern Architecture and cultural identity – research proposal, circa 1983, 3-page typescript, 197-088-088, p. 3.

27 Kenneth Frampton, Introduction to Greek edition [of *Modern Architecture: A Critical History*, 2nd edn] by Kenneth Frampton, 9-page handwritten draft, August 1985, Suzana and Dimitris Antonakakis' private archive, p. 6.

28 Kenneth Frampton, 'For Dimitris Pikionis', in *Mega XI, Dimitris Pikionis, Architect 1887–1968: A Sentimental Topography*, ed. by Dennis Crompton (London: Architectural Association, 1989), pp. 6–9 (p. 8).

29 See Dimitris Pikionis, 'Το πρόβλημα της μορφής' (1951), repr. in Δ. *Πικιώνης: Κείμενα*, ed. by Agni Pikioni and Michalis Parousis (Athens: MIET, 1985), pp. 204–46 (pp. 217–18); Savas

Condaratos, 'Dimitris Pikionis 1887–1986: A Sentimental Topography: AA Exhibition Gallery, Members' Room and Bar, 6 June – 4 July 1989', *AA Files*, 20 (Autumn 1990), 55–62.

30   Kenneth Frampton, 'Μοντέρνο, πολύ μοντέρνο: Μια συνέντευξη του Kenneth Frampton στον Γιώργο Σημαιοφορίδη', *Architecture in Greece*, 20 (1986), 118–21 (p. 121).

31   Kenneth Frampton, 'Jørn Utzon: Transcultural Form and Tectonic Metaphor', in *Studies in Tectonic Culture*, pp. 247–98 (p. 248).

32   Frampton, 'Jørn Utzon: Transcultural Form and Tectonic Metaphor', pp. 253–5, 257, 264, 268, 273, 280, 293, 295.

33   Ibid., p. 248.

34   Ibid., pp. 247–8; Jørn Utzon, 'Platforms and Plateaus: Ideas of a Danish Architect', *Zodiac*, 10 (1962), 112–40.

35   Frampton, 'Jørn Utzon: Transcultural Form and Tectonic Metaphor', pp. 284–5.

36   Ibid., pp. 286–8, 290.

37   Ibid., p. 285.

38   Ibid., p. 292.

39   Kenneth Frampton, 'Carlo Scarpa and the Adoration of the Joint', in *Studies in Tectonic Culture*, pp. 299–333 (p. 305).

40   Ibid., pp. 305–6.

41   Ibid., pp. 312–13.

42   Ibid., pp. 318–19.

43   Kenneth Frampton, 'The Legacy of Alvar Aalto' (1998), repr. in *Labour, Work and Architecture*, pp. 234–53 (pp. 235–6).

44   Ibid., p. 236.

45   Kenneth Frampton, 'The Architecture of Sverre Fehn', in Per Olaf Fjeld, *Sverre Fehn: The Thought of Construction* (New York: Rizzoli, 1983), pp. 9–17 (pp. 11–12, 16).

46   Kenneth Frampton, 'Entre héroisme et métier', in *Henri Ciriani*, ed. by François Chaslin (Paris: Electa, 1984), pp. 13–14 (p. 14).

47   Ibid., p. 13.

48   Kenneth Frampton, 'O.M. Ungers and the Architecture of Coincidence', in *O.M. Ungers: Works in Progress, 1976–1980, Catalogue 6*, ed. by Kenneth Frampton and Silvia Kolbowski (New York: Institute of Architecture and Urban Studies, 1981), pp. 1–5 (p. 1).

49   See Oswald Matthias Ungers, 'Planning Criteria', *Lotus*, 11 (1976), 13–41.

50   Frampton, 'O.M. Ungers and the Architecture of Coincidence', p. 2.

51   See Kenneth Frampton, 'Towards a Critical Regionalism: Six Points for an Architecture of Resistance', in *The Anti-Aesthetic: Essays on Postmodern Culture*, ed. by Hal Foster (Washington, DC: Bay Press, 1983), pp. 16–30 (p. 25).

52   Kenneth Frampton, 'Moneo's Paseo: The Bankinter' (1981), in *Labour, Work and Architecture*, pp. 278–87 (pp. 283–4).

53   Ibid., pp. 285–7.

54   Frampton, 'Carlo Scarpa and the Adoration of the Joint', p. 299.

55   Ibid., pp. 307–10.

56   Ibid., p. 320.

57   Ibid., pp. 321–5.

58   Ibid., p. 321.

59   Kenneth Frampton, 'The Will to Build', in Emilio Batisti and Kenneth Frampton, with Italo Rota, *Mario Botta: Architetture e progetti negli anni '70* (Milan: Electa, 1979), pp. 7–13 (pp. 7–8).

60   Kenneth Frampton, 'L'opera di Luigi Snozzi, 1957–1984', in *Luigi Snozzi: Progetti e architetture 1957–1984*, ed. by Kenneth Frampton (Milan: Electa, 1984), pp. 9–29 (pp. 28–9). Frampton did not write an introductory text for another book that appeared as part of his edited series with Rizzoli on Ticinese architects: Werner Seligmann and Jorge Silvetti, *Mario Campi – Franco Pessina Architects* (New York: Rizzoli, 1987).

61   See *Tendenzen: Neuere Architektur im Tessin. Dokumentation zur Ausstellung an der ETH Zürich vom 20. Nov.–13. Dez. 1975*, ed. by Martin Steinmann and Thomas Boga (Zurich: ETHZ Organisationsstelle für Ausstellungen des Institutes gta, 1975); Irina Davidovici, 'Constructing "the School of the Ticino": The Historiography of a New Swiss Architecture, 1975–1990', *Journal of Architecture*, 25.8 (2020), 1115–40.

62   Kenneth Frampton, 'Modern and Site Specific: The Architecture of Gino Valle 1945–2003', *Plan Journal*, 4.1 (2019), 223–6 (pp. 224–5).

63 Kenneth Frampton, 'The Structural Regionalism of Herman Hertzberger' (1986), repr. in *Labour, Work and Architecture*, pp. 288–97 (p. 291).

64 John McKean, 'Towards the Unknown Region', *Architects' Journal*, 176.50 (15 December 1982), 19–21 (p. 20).

65 Frampton, 'The Architecture of Sverre Fehn', pp. 11, 15–17.

66 Mary McLeod, 'Architecture and Politics in the Reagan Era: From Postmodernism to Deconstructivism', *Assemblage*, 8 (1989), 23–59 (p. 36).

67 Frampton, 'Developments in Contemporary Architecture 1945–1985', p. 67.

68 Frampton, 'The Will to Build', p. 8.

69 Kenneth Frampton, 'Poesis and Transformation: The Architecture of Alvaro Siza', in *Alvaro Siza: Poetic Profession*, ed. by Kenneth Frampton (Milan: Electa, 1986), pp. 10–23 (p. 21).

70 Frampton, 'The Structural Regionalism of Herman Hertzberger', p. 289.

71 Kenneth Frampton, 'Entre rationalisme et régionalisme: l'oeuvre de Martorell, Bohigas et Mackay', in *Martorell, Bohigas, Mackay: Trente ans d'architecture, 1954–1984*, ed. by Kenneth Frampton, trans. by Raymond Coudert (Paris: Electa, 1985), pp. 7–25 (p. 7).

72 Frampton, 'Developments in Contemporary Architecture 1945–1985', pp. 33–4.

73 Frampton, 'Moneo's Paseo: The Bankinter', p. 279.

74 Kenneth Frampton, 'The Need for Roots: Venice 1980', *GA Forum*, 3 (1981), 13–21 (p. 21; emphasis in the original).

75 Frampton, 'Developments in Contemporary Architecture 1945–1985', pp. 37–8; Frampton, 'Poesis and Transformation: The Architecture of Alvaro Siza', pp. 11, 15.

76 See Kenneth Frampton, 'Tadao Ando's Critical Modernism', in *Tadao Ando: Buildings, Projects, Writings*, ed. by Kenneth Frampton (New York: Rizzoli, 1984), pp. 6–9 (pp. 7–8).

77 Frampton, 'The Architecture of Sverre Fehn', p. 11.

78 Mary Pepchinski, email exchange with Stylianos Giamarelos, 6 July 2020.

79 Frampton, 'Jørn Utzon: Transcultural Form and Tectonic Metaphor', p. 259.

80 Frampton, 'Moneo's Paseo: The Bankinter', p. 287.

81 Frampton, 'The Legacy of Alvar Aalto', p. 244.

82 Frampton, *Studies in Tectonic Culture*, p. 365.

83 Frampton, 'Jørn Utzon: Transcultural Form and Tectonic Metaphor', p. 294.

84 Ibid., pp. 296–8.

85 Ibid., p. 249.

86 See Frampton, 'Tadao Ando's Critical Modernism'; Koji Taki, 'Minimalism or Monotonality? A Contextual Analysis of Tadao Ando's Method', in *Tadao Ando: Buildings, Projects, Writings*, ed. by Frampton, pp. 11–23; Kenneth Frampton, 'Greek Regionalism and the Modern Project: A Collective Endeavour', in *Atelier 66: The Architecture of Dimitris and Suzana Antonakakis*, ed. by Kenneth Frampton (New York: Rizzoli, 1985), pp. 4–5; Alexander Tzonis and Liane Lefaivre, 'The Grid and the Pathway: An Introduction to the Work of Dimitris and Suzana Antonakakis in the Context of Greek Architectural Culture', in *Atelier 66: The Architecture of Dimitris and Suzana Antonakakis*, ed. by Frampton, pp. 14–25.

87 See Frampton, 'Tadao Ando's Critical Modernism', p. 8; Kiyoshi Takeyama, 'Tadao Ando: Heir to a Tradition', *Perspecta*, 20 (1983), 163–80.

88 See Frampton, 'Tadao Ando's Critical Modernism', pp. 7–8; Tadao Ando, 'From Self-Enclosed Modern Architecture Towards Universality', in *Tadao Ando: Buildings, Projects, Writings*, ed. by Frampton, pp. 138–42.

89 Kenneth Frampton, 'Fujii in Context: An Introduction', in *The Architecture of Hiromi Fujii*, ed. by Kenneth Frampton (New York: Rizzoli, 1987), pp. 8–13 (pp. 8–10).

90 Frampton, 'Greek Regionalism and the Modern Project: A Collective Endeavour'.

91 See Kenneth Frampton, 'Modernism's Diffusion: Japan Diary Summer '81, Part 1', *Skyline* (April 1982), 26–9; 'Part 2', *Skyline* (May 1982), 26–9; 'Part 3', *Skyline* (June 1982), 22–5.

92 Frampton, letter to Fernando Tavora, p. 3.

Part II
Cross-cultural roots

6
Celebrated reception

A visually powerful spread from William J.R. Curtis's *Modern Architecture since 1900* (1982) provides the most memorable juxtaposition of the Villa Savoye and the Parthenon in the canonical historiography of twentieth-century modernism. As the British historian notes in the main body of his text:

> A 'classic' moment of modern architecture, [the Villa Savoye] also has affinities with the great architecture of the past ... In the Villa Savoye one recognises echoes of old Classical themes: repose, proportion, clarity, a simple language of trabeation. Perhaps one may even go so far as to suggest a reminiscence of the Parthenon, which had so obsessed Le Corbusier twenty years before [in his *voyage d'Orient*] ... In its tense mathematical relationships and tight contours, in its radiating power to the setting, the Villa Savoye also invoked qualities Le Corbusier had admired in the great Classical prototype ... Its individual elements – the *piloti*, the strip-window, etc. – were elevated, like the columns and triglyphs of a Greek temple, to the level of timeless solutions: the abstraction of its forms implied a lofty and spiritual role for architecture. Above all, though, the architectural language of the Villa Savoye was the result of a radical quest, a returning to roots, a rethinking of the fundamentals of the art ... an architecture supposedly reflecting natural law.[1]

Serving both as an origin myth and a gold standard, the 2,500-year-old Parthenon of Classical Athens is paradoxically the Greek building that features most prominently in Western European and North American histories of twentieth-century modern architecture, from Reyner Banham to Colin Davies.[2] By contrast, architecture in modern Greece is predominantly absent from these books. This strong presence of the Classical past in the place of a modern present suggests that the history of architecture in Greece has developed in terms of a modern margin in the very centre of Classical civilisation.

In this chapter, I explore the intertwined history of the cultural construction of the Classical centre alongside its modern margin to elucidate the emergence and significance of critical regionalism as the most celebrated moment of Greek architecture in the twentieth-century historiography of modernism. I start from northwestern European countries such as Britain, France and Germany in order to illuminate the deep historical and cultural roots of this margin/centre duality, and explore its repercussions in modern Greek architectural historiography before the emergence of the critical regionalist discourse in 1981. This long-term cross-cultural historiographical overview of a single region introduces a longer historical perspective into recent attempts to revisit critical regionalism.[3] Despite its celebrated global reception as 'one of the most influential academic propositions since the 1980s' because of its alleged inclusiveness,[4] my long-term historiographical perspective enables me to argue that the critical regionalist discourse on Greece proves less contextually sensitive than its authors had suggested. With his theoretical ambition to advance a wider critical design practice across cultures, Frampton generalised Tzonis and Lefaivre's ideas beyond the specific historical context that gave rise to them. As such, his account effectively short-circuited the two theorists' original intentions. Instead of advancing a focused return to the region, Frampton's mediated, outsider's account of critical regionalism reflected the broader concerns of Western architectural discourses of the 1980s. Since the rest of the world became familiar with the work of these Greek architects mainly through Frampton's accounts, the final part of the chapter examines how the British historian's perspective on Greece was historically shaped and conditioned through his variegated ties with local architectural circles.

The geopolitical foundation of the Classical centre

Greece is customarily regarded as the 'Classical centre' or 'the cradle' of Western civilisation. From politics and philosophy to architecture, histories of Western culture start from Greece.[5] They refer to figures of Classical antiquity such as Pericles and Aristotle, and buildings such as the Parthenon as founding figures and exemplars for the subsequent development of Western civilisation. But regarding Greece as the 'Classical centre' of the West is a modern thesis. For more than two millennia, the Athenian democratic polity of the fifth century BCE was not the positive exemplar that the modern world now takes for granted. For feudal Europe, Classical Athens served as a negative example. Successive critics of Athenian democracy from the Roman period onwards portrayed it as irrational, unstable and ineffective.[6] For instance, Plutarch and Cicero argued that the Athenian polity failed to acknowledge the feats of great political figures, because it was often seduced by hyperbolic rhetoric and hedonist pursuits. These authors invariably attributed the eventual fall of the Classical Athenian empire to the failures of democracy as a system of governance.[7]

As a child of the late eighteenth century, the revered conception of Classical Athens is therefore relatively recent. It is no coincidence that two of the three main pillars of the French Revolution, 'liberty' and 'equality', were also foregrounded in Thucydides's encomium of democracy (in his reconstruction of Pericles's funeral oration).[8] It forms part of a wider cultural movement to associate ancient democracies with the seismic repercussions of the North American and French Revolutions of 1776 and 1789 across Europe.[9] Later in the twentieth century, strong supporters of ancient Athenian democracy, such as the French historian Gustave Glotz (1862–1935) and the American-born British Classicist Sir Moses Israel Finley (1912–1986), filled the remaining gaps that reinforced the French Revolution's links with its Classical forerunner. These authors presented the missing third pillar of 'fraternity' as an integral part of the ancient democratic project. Funded by the profits of the Athenian empire, they argued, the public projects of the Classical age were constructed to serve both upper- and lower-class citizens.[10] In so doing, these scholars completed a long historical circle of reappraising Classical Athens as a model for modern democracies.

In her book *Europe through Greece* (2006), historian Nassia Yakovaki has illuminated the spatial and geopolitical registers of this long history.[11] Classical Athens was only 'rediscovered' as part of the process of the historical construction of a distinctly modern 'European consciousness' and territory. As this secular 'Europe' gradually took the place of the older world of 'Christianity', both Athens and democracy became more relevant than earlier references to ancient Jewish and Egyptian cultures. From the late seventeenth to the early nineteenth century, Greece was effectively invoked to redefine the relationship of modernity to antiquity. Roman civilisation, the undisputed cradle of the Classical in the predominantly

Latin-speaking and Italo-centric Renaissance,[12] was gradually demoted to a degenerate copy of the refined Greek original.

Hence, when architectural historians such as Curtis assert that the Parthenon gave Charles-Édouard Jeanneret 'a glimpse of an elusive absolute which continued to haunt him', they do not refer to an exclusively affective personal experience on the part of the young Swiss architect.[13] When European architects travelled to Greece to draw inspiration for their modern buildings in the twentieth century,[14] they also perceived themselves as the latest addition to a longer historical chain. This perception started with a shift in the itinerary of late-seventeenth-century travellers,[15] such as Jacob Spon and George Wheler, to include Athens alongside Rome in the European Grand Tour as the joint 'classic grounds' of modern culture.[16] Starting from Athens, Spon reaffirmed, modified or disproved modern and ancient sources in order to reconstruct the topography of ancient Greece in its entirety. It was within this territory that the remnants of ancient civilisation could be empirically studied in their contemporary state.

Modern Greece became a major political project for Europe in the following decades. With Athens as its capital city, it was geographically established as a distinct European territory, a novel division within the united Ottoman Empire.[17] Greece became an ideal mirror for a European civilisation that aimed to be established as uniquely original and possessed of 'genius' in order to affirm its supremacy over existing and recently colonised cultures of the Old and New Worlds. Greece enabled Europeans to recognise their new, superior face in their major historical precedent as the most advanced state of humanity of their time. In the eighteenth century, the celebrated works of Montesquieu (1689–1755) and Johann Gottfried Herder (1744–1803), among others, promoted geographically determinist 'theories of climate' that tied nations and their respective cultural and political character to their land.[18] Hence, when the emerging modern nation state legitimised its founding on the ancient city-state model, the territory of ancient Greece as the birthplace of democracy became increasingly significant. It was the oldest layer in the long history of the cultural and geographic unity of modern European civilisation that was also first established in the eighteenth century. Conversely, the *Grand Turc*, a figure idolised by sixteenth-century European travellers to the Levant, gradually transformed into an Orientalised despotic ruler who acted as the nemesis of the democratic West. For the philhellenes of the late eighteenth and early nineteenth centuries, the tragedy of the modern European world was that the birthland of democracy was under authoritarian rule.

The Classical centre of art and architecture

Within this broader geopolitical context, the art and architecture of ancient Greece played a significant role of their own. When Johann Joachim Winckelmann (1717–1768) established the aesthetic superiority of the original Greek artworks over their Roman copies in the mid-eighteenth century, he significantly added that their simplicity and grandeur was not only owing to the close ties of Greek civilisation with nature but also to their development within the free *polis*.[19] Polity, art and the land that nourished them were deterministically inseparable. In addition, Winckelmann promoted the Classicist mimesis of the unsurpassed Greek art as a way forward for modern art.[20] At the same time, James Stuart and Nicholas Revett surveyed the antiquities of Athens in order to further legitimise the supremacy of Greek over Roman art through their allegedly superior and scientifically precise measurements (Fig. 6.1).[21] As the cultural significance of the monumental remains of ancient Greece rose for Europeans, the rule of the city of Athens by 'such professed Enemies of the Arts as the Turks are', Stuart argued in 1762, threatened these ancient models of artistic perfection. 'The reason

Figure 6.1   James Stuart surveying the west end of the Erechteion on the Athenian Acropolis, in James Stuart and Nicolas Revett, *The Antiquities of Athens Measured and Delineated*, 3 vols (London, 1762–94), II (1787), chapter II, plate II

Aikaterini Laskaridis Foundation Library

indeed, why those Antiquities have hitherto been thus neglected, is obvious. Greece, since the revival of the Arts, has been in the possession of Barbarians … The ignorance and jealousy of that uncultivated people may, perhaps, render an undertaking of this sort, still somewhat dangerous.'[22] Owing to these authors, by the end of the eighteenth century, Greek Revivalism and Neo-Classicism had become the international styles of modern European architecture. In the early nineteenth century, Western European and North American architects used the eighteenth-century depictions of antique monuments as templates to reproduce parts of the Parthenon (Fig. 6.2). Among others, such buildings include Giovanni Antonio Selva's Mausoleum of Antonio Caneva in Possagno, Italy (1819), Leo von Klenze's Walhalla in Regensburg, Germany (1821–42) and Alexander Jackson Davis and Ithiel Town's United States Custom House in New York (1831–42).[23]

Figure 6.2   Leo von Klenze, Walhalla in Regensburg, Germany, 1821–42

Avda, CC BY-SA 3.0 (top), via Wikimedia Commons; Simon Waldherr, 2018 (bottom), © Simon Waldherr / commons.wikimedia.org/wiki/User:SimonWaldherr / CC BY-SA 4.0

Built between the 1820s and the 1840s, these projects coincided with the rise of the modern Greek state. Established on the ruins of its ancient democratic past, modern Greece was, in the final instance, a grand political project for modern Europe. British, French and Russian imperial powers envisioned the modern state of the Classical cradle of democracy as a 'model kingdom' for nineteenth-century Europe.[24] The Greek Revolution of 1821 was ignited at a crucial moment of the so-called Age of Revolution (1789–1848), rekindling the democratic emancipatory impulse in the Balkans after the oppressive backlash to the French Revolution and the subsequent repression of liberal movements across Europe earlier in the same century.[25] In the decade of the ensuing Greek War of Independence, the realisation of this grand European vision involved large-scale expeditions and campaigns such as that of Guillaume-Abel Blouet. These included architects, historians and archaeologists, escorted by military forces. Orchestrated by the French Government, their mission was to locate, reconstruct and excavate, if necessary, ancient sites of Classical Greece in Attica, the Peloponnese and the Cyclades.[26]

The 'Classical centre' thesis also owes its longevity to successive historical and theoretical reinterpretations that have repeatedly been generated around it. In the nineteenth and twentieth centuries, the same Classical ruins were constantly revisited in order to instigate novel debates about the past and future of architecture in modern Europe. Well-known figures and instances of this long history include Gottfried Semper (1803–1879), who reconstructed the colourful Greek temple to react to Winkelmann's earlier 'white' history of ancient art;[27] Eugène Viollet-le-Duc (1814–1879) and Auguste Choisy (1841–1909), who included reconstructions of the Parthenon as the perfect example of ancient architecture in their influential histories;[28] and Le Corbusier, who, in *Vers une Architecture* (1928), juxtaposed Greek temples with automobiles in order to suggest that modern architecture needed to establish its own refined exemplar of the new machine-age standard.[29] In the same way that ancient architecture went from unrefined Paestum to sophisticated Athens, and just like Citroën went from the early carriage-like models to the streamlined *chassis* of the Delage Grand Sport, Le Corbusier argued, so did architecture need its own modern Parthenon. Since then, modern architects such as Ludwig Mies van der Rohe have either aspired to build the 'Parthenon of the twentieth century', as in the New National Gallery in Berlin (1961–8), or referred to it when they undertook projects in Greece, as in the case of Walter Gropius and the US Embassy building in Athens (1959–61).[30] Greek architects, such as Patroklos Karantinos (1903–1976), whose projects in Athens were also photographed in direct

Figure 6.3 Patroklos Karantinos, School on Kalisperi Street under the Acropolis in Athens, 1931–2, south elevation, unknown photographer

Andreas Giacumacatos's private archive

association with the Parthenon (Fig. 6.3), are no exception to this modernist rule.

The marginalisation of modern architecture

Karantinos's Primary School on Kalisperi Street under the Acropolis in Athens (1931–2) demonstrates how the canonical historiography of modernism continues to construct Greece as the modern margin in the Classical centre. As Sigfried Giedion's photographs from the same project document, in August 1933 delegates of the Fourth International Congress of Modern Architecture (CIAM) visited this and other modernist buildings in Athens, including Karantinos's Primary School on Charokopou Street in Kallithea (1931) and Stamo Papadaki's Villa Fakidis in Glyfada (1932–3). But although they approvingly witnessed Greece's modern architecture (Fig. 6.4), these modernist architects and scholars did not refer to it in subsequent publications. When they published their modern architectural projects in relation to Greece, they only associated them with the country's timeless spirit.[31] They either referred to the Classical Parthenon and other

Figure 6.4 Patroklos Karantinos, School on Kalisperi Street under the Acropolis in Athens, 1931–2, photographed by Sigfried Giedion in August 1933

© gta Archives/ETH Zürich, CIAM

Pre-Classical temples in the proximity of Athens or to the Pre-Classical, anonymous island vernacular that had already achieved an 'unconscious' modernism of 'perfect match between form and function'.[32] The eleven pages on modern Greek architecture in Alberto Sartoris's *Elements of Functionalist Architecture* (1935) that featured only projects by Papadaki (1906–1992), Karantinos, and Ioannis Despotopoulos (Jan Despo, 1903– 1992) are the rare exception to this rule.[33] Whenever canonical histories of the modern movement foreground Greece, it is – again – because of its past. Their consistent reference to the Classical centre legitimises modernism as a timeless aesthetic. This in turn restores a sense of continuity in the history of architecture.[34] At the same time, however, modern architecture in Greece is pushed to the margins as a 'peripheral' satellite of the international avant-garde. It therefore seems that modern Europe is only interested to discuss its own self-image in the mirror of Classical Greece. The rest is out of sight. With the European spotlight on its revered past and its present state in the shadows, Greece finds itself in a dual position – simultaneously at the centre and on the periphery of modern architectural historiography.

From the age of Stuart and Revett, the Western European gaze on architecture in Greece was selective and remained so. It isolated objects

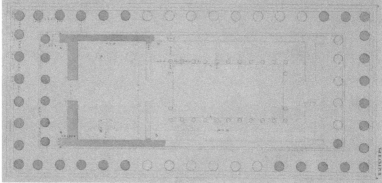

Figure 6.5 Top: View of the eastern portico of the Parthenon, with the mosque built after the 1687 explosion in the interior, in James Stuart and Nicolas Revett, *The Antiquities of Athens Measured and Delineated*, 3 vols (London, 1762–94), II (1787), chapter I, plate I; bottom: Plan of the Parthenon, measured by James Stuart, in ibid., II (1787), chapter I, plate II

Aikaterini Laskaridis Foundation Library

of interest that informed contemporary architectural developments, and marginalised the surroundings of these objects (Fig. 6.5). Treated as the cradle of Western civilisation, Classical Greece continues to overshadow its modern version in the eyes of the Western observer. As Yakovaki has also noted, Athens is gradually 'summarised in the Parthenon', as 'the description of [the city] equals the description of its antiquities'.[35] From the eighteenth to the twentieth century, this centralisation of the Classical at the expense of the modern is consistently reproduced. In historical surveys such as David Watkin's *A History of Western Architecture* (1986), Greece is only relevant as the cradle of the Classical.[36] Even when North American scholars such as Vincent Scully critiqued the reading of ancient Greek temples as 'isolated objects', yet again they did not mean to study them in their modern but rather in their ancient context and landscape. They aimed to understand these temples as 'formal expressions of their deities [and] in relation to their specific sanctuaries and settings'.[37] No modern examples are of interest in twentieth-century Western European and North American studies of architecture in Greece.

National(ist) historiography

Conversely, from the other side of the mirror, Greece looks at the West to see only itself refracted through the European gaze. Because modern Europe defines itself through ancient Greece, modern Greece is in turn defined by this European gaze to its Classical past. Through its glorified past, Greece understands itself as ever-relevant to modern European developments. But Greece can also only reclaim its own Classical legacy through its refraction in modern Europe.

Completed in 1966, François Loyer's (b. 1941) two-volume doctoral thesis stood out as the first comprehensive history of architecture in modern Greece from the early nineteenth century to the mid-1960s.[38] In many ways, the unprecedented and original work of this young French scholar served as a point of reference that paved the way for similarly ambitious studies by Greek historians such as Dimitris Philippidis (b. 1938). But Loyer's work remained untranslated, unpublished and rather inaccessible for five decades.[39] Its potentially wider impact on Greek architectural historiography was curtailed before the publication of Philippidis's history of *Modern Greek Architecture* (1984), which has since been established as a definitive milestone in the historiography of architecture in Greece.[40] Instead, a limited number of short articles and books in the 1960s and the 1970s attempted to offer brief historical surveys of architecture in twentieth-century Greece. Taken together, these texts both reproduce and develop the same dual self-image of Greek architecture as the 'glorified centre' or the 'periphery' lagging behind the Western avant-gardes. Anthony C. Antoniades's history of *Contemporary Greek Architecture* (1979) and Dimitris Fatouros's brief survey of local architecture and art (1967) exemplify these main approaches in the early historiography of modern architecture in Greece, before the first theorisation of critical regionalism in 1981.[41]

Antoniades (b. 1941), a Greek architect with graduate studies in the UK and the USA who has also taught in British and North American universities, represents the 'glorified centre' thesis here. His writing is that of an informed insider who is exposed to the Western European and North American architectural developments of the late 1970s. Antoniades internalises the Western 'Classical centre' conception that European civilisation starts in Greece in order to reproduce it on various occasions throughout his history of *Contemporary Greek Architecture* (1979). In his book, Greek architecture seems always already *avant la lettre*, showing the way forward for Western architecture as a whole. For him, the modern international style had Greek roots owing to the Cubism of the Mediterranean (Cadaqués) and Le Corbusier's lessons from his travels in the country.[42] Antoniades additionally argued that from the mid-1930s the work of Dimitris Pikionis already defied the principles of international style modernism to explore themes of the postmodern problematic – such as the inclusivist concern for the 'user', 'meaning', 'signs and symbols' and 'collages' of traditional and modern elements – three decades before these issues attracted the attention of Brent C. Brolin, Charles Jencks and Peter Blake.[43] 'The post-modern essentially starts with the Greek Pikionis', claims Antoniades.[44] But this 'glorified centre' thesis, I would argue, can also lead to an uncritical nationalist tone.

A decade earlier, Fatouros (1928–2020) presented a more nuanced picture. He also highlighted Greek architects who drew modern design principles from their studies of traditional architecture. In this sense, he worked within a weaker 'glorified centre' thesis that was rooted in the reappraisal of the Cycladic vernacular settlements by the international delegates of the Fourth CIAM of 1933.[45] Finding the modern in the traditional, strongly believing in the legitimising validity of this connection, fuelled the work of this generation of Greek architects. But Fatouros also acknowledged the 'peripheral' side of the story – a 'good number of other artists' whose work is derivative, as they 'merely follow in their own ways the major [Western European and North American] artistic currents of our time, adapting them ... to Greek conditions and the Greek reality'.[46] A dual picture emerges more clearly here: although Greece finds its traditional architectural principles aligned with modernism, it also needs to adapt these international developments to the regional context. Greek architects internalise modern European developments as inseparable parts of their own regional legacy. By becoming modern, they stay Greek.

This is not another case of Greek exceptionalism. As Barry Bergdoll has also noted, in the course of the twentieth century the Mediterranean vernacular 'sustained both discourses of transcendent timelessness and of nationalist specificity, of both rootedness and regionalism and of innocence or freedom from learned and cultured symbolism, of a quest for abstraction and of the search for meaning'. In the final instance, it 'continually oscillated between its role as Modernism's other and its foundation myth'.[47] It is this dual oscillation between 'alternative margin' and 'founding centre' that led to the development of critical regionalism in Greece.

Critical regionalism in history

Antoniades's and Fatouros's studies summarise the late-1970s state of architectural historiography in modern Greece, which is presented as an unjustly marginalised but certainly glorious centre of modern and postmodern architectural developments in Western Europe and North America. This is the context in which Alexander Tzonis and Liane Lefaivre's first theorisation of critical regionalism in 'The Grid and the Pathway' appeared in 1981. Focused on the architecture of Suzana and Dimitris Antonakakis, the article effectively explores the historically established dynamics of the alternative modern periphery to act as a founding centre for the future of architecture. Published at a moment of uncertainty after a prolonged crisis of Western European and North American modernism, it forms part of a wider trend to reconsider the 'centre' from the viewpoint of its 'margins'.

In the decades that followed, critical regionalism was criticised as a colonialist discourse that actively marginalised the regions it addressed. In the early twenty-first century, Keith L. Eggener and Mark Crinson developed this critique by focusing, respectively, on Mexico and Singapore.[48] But in the case of Greece, the dual 'modern margin'/'Classical centre' schema adds further complications. In this context, and owing to modern Greeks' internalisation of the ever-relevant 'glorified centre' thesis, critical regionalism more emphatically restores an already marginalised modern architectural production – at least in the eyes of Western European and North American observers.

Twentieth-century Greek architects received critical regionalism in more or less the same way their nineteenth-century ancestors had received the historicist Neo-Classical regionalism before it: like a homecoming of modernism to its founding roots. But this also shows how local twentieth-century architects had themselves internalised the marginalisation of Greek modernism. As I discussed earlier, this was a long-standing process at work since the founding of the modern Greek state, and certainly long before the advent of critical regionalism. In this light, critical regionalism is especially significant in the Greek context. Its advent signals that the work of modern Greek architects is no longer celebrated as significant, yet peripheral (as in Sartoris's encyclopaedic overview of functionalist architecture in the 1930s). In the 1980s, it becomes globally significant precisely because it is regional.

This was especially strongly emphasised when Kenneth Frampton incorporated Tzonis and Lefaivre's account in the second revised edition of his *Modern Architecture: A Critical History* (1985). In an added final chapter, the British historian posited the idea that the crisis of canonical modern architecture could be resolved from the standpoint of what had until then been excluded from the picture.[49] It is only through Frampton's critical history and its celebrated global reception that the regional modernisms of the margins became suddenly relevant for the centre of the canon. Closing this last chapter, and effectively concluding Frampton's history, the Athenian apartment building at 118 Benaki Street by Suzana and Dimitris Antonakakis offered an alternative way forward and out of the crisis of modernism. This was the first time that regional modern projects in Greece had been deemed at least as significant as their Classical forebears for Western European and North American architects. For, rather significantly, the critical regionalist discourse emerged at the heyday of Postmodern Classicism – another high point for international interest in Classical Greece.[50] In its modern and ancient variants, then, architecture in Greece is at once a source of regional modern alternatives to and one of the focal points of the postmodern Classical centre. Tzonis and Lefaivre advanced a third alternative option to reclaim Classicism from postmodern historicist architects by reappraising it as part of a modern humanist tradition. To do so, they followed the paradigm of Classical tragedy as an art form of collective expression that offered a cathartic resolution of existing social conflict and antagonisms.[51] As a result, in the mid-1980s, both the modern Greek periphery and the Classical Greek centre shared the international spotlight to promote opposing agendas for the future of architecture.

Critical regionalism has now cemented its place as the 'major contribution' of modern Greece to 'global architectural thinking' of the twentieth century.[52] But international scholars who celebrate critical regionalism today tend to take for granted a historical accuracy and contextual sensitivity that was often missing from Tzonis and Lefaivre's account. When they were writing in the 1980s, the two critics put a stronger emphasis on the regional side of their argument. Their main intention was to foreground the 'realist' connection of the architecture of Suzana and Dimitris Antonakakis with its regional context and the most established figures of architecture in modern Greece. This is why the Pikionis–Konstantinidis influence on the work of the architectural couple was stressed. But on closer inspection, their original and insightful analysis proves rather intuitive. It is not based on solid historical evidence. Stressing the regional connection, the two critics disregarded the actual history and the richer cross-cultural genealogy that shaped the Antonakakis' architectural outlook, as I argue in chapter 8. When Frampton incorporated Tzonis and Lefaivre's account in his later writings, he also reproduced and further magnified these discrepancies as he promoted critical regionalism to wider global audiences.[53] Instead of advancing a focused return to the region, his mediated outsider's account of critical regionalism in Greece reflected the broader concerns of Western European and North American architectural discourses of the 1980s: a critical defiance of the international style, top-down, bureaucratic modernism of the welfare state.

An Englishman in Athens

The global outreach of Frampton's best-selling *Modern Architecture: A Critical History* magnified its significance for Greek architects. Before Frampton's publication, internationally established Greek practitioners such as Constantinos A. Doxiadis (1913–1975) and Georges Candilis (1913–1995) were known for their post-Second World War projects beyond Greece's borders – from Islamabad to Toulouse-Le-Mirail. Frampton's book was especially significant because this was the first time in half a century that contemporary Greek architecture had been included in a globally celebrated history of modernism. Its inclusion was additionally significant because the British historian did not merely aspire to update Sartoris's earlier globally inclusive survey of functionalist architecture, adopting the 'neutral' tone of his work. Frampton's stance was clearly polemical. With his last chapter on critical regionalism, he aimed to intervene in the crucial architectural debates of the 1980s. After being included in this book in 1985, architects who had been working in a relatively isolated way, as they had not built projects outside Greece, found themselves at the forefront of international developments in modern architecture.

The good news for Greek architecture meant that the translation of Frampton's book was soon under way. In his preface to the Greek edition, Frampton went further to describe Athens as 'the modern city par excellence'.[54] The British historian suggested that Greece should be proud of a city that was at that time not especially appreciated, and an architecture that was usually ignored, by its residents. At the same time, Frampton edited the Rizzoli monograph on the work of Suzana and Dimitris Antonakakis' Atelier 66, which included a new short introductory text by him and a substantially revised version of Tzonis and Lefaivre's 'The Grid and the Pathway'.[55]

For these reasons, Frampton gradually became the favourite historian of Greek architectural circles. He was regularly invited to contribute with short texts on numerous occasions when Greek architecture was to be presented to a local or international audience through group exhibitions or monographs on individual architects.[56] As such, while Frampton certainly did not intend to be assigned this role, he became the 'international' historian of architecture in Greece. In the eyes of local architects, he was the spokesperson for the country's marginalised modern architecture. For them, it was rather obvious: had Frampton not recapitulated 'critical regionalism', both Greek architecture and Tzonis and Lefaivre's ideas would not have enjoyed this global exposure. It was from Frampton's vantage point, that of the mediated outsider Englishman in Athens, that the Western world became familiar with modern architecture in Greece. The way in which his mediated view of modern architecture in Greece was historically shaped is therefore a key aspect of the cross-cultural roots of critical regionalism.

In his preface to the Greek edition of his critical history of modern architecture, Frampton presented Greece as a locus that shaped him as an architect and critic.[57] His relationship with the country goes further back than the 1980s. Frampton visited Athens in October 1959.[58] This is when he first walked on Pikionis's recently completed pathway around the Acropolis, without knowing anything about its architect then.[59] In the early 1960s, he visited Greek friends on holiday trips with his partner and continued to frequently visit the country on several occasions over the next two decades.[60] Undated archived sketches from his travels to Greece show that specific building details attracted his interest – ranging from balconies to window shutters and the whitewashed, outlined, stone pathways of the Cycladic islands to the sculptures of mythical animals on top of Pikionis's favourite vernacular house of farmer and builder Alexandros Rodakis on Aegina (Fig. 6.6).[61]

Figure 6.6 Kenneth Frampton, notebook sketches from his travels in Greece

ARCH284703–ARCH284705, Kenneth Frampton fonds, Canadian Centre for Architecture, Gift of Kenneth Frampton

In the 1970s, Frampton also visited Cyprus, recording his experience and thoughts on a difficult, divisive moment in the country's modern history.[62] It is the Greek-Cypriot architect Panos Koulermos (1933–1999) who remained Frampton's lifelong link to Greece throughout the twentieth century. Signs of Frampton's appreciation of his friend include his editing of the comprehensive posthumous monograph on the work of Koulermos, after delving into the architect's archive.[63] Frampton was also there to contribute with short introductions or other texts for Koulermos whenever he was invited to do so, even for relatively small and less-significant publications.[64] The two architects met as colleagues at Douglas Stephen and Partners in London in the early 1960s. This period marked Frampton's first steps not only as a professional architect but also as a critic, historian[65] and technical editor of *Architectural Design*. Koulermos had already liaised with Konstantinidis when Frampton edited the monographic feature on the Greek architect's work in *Architectural Design* in May 1964. In the decades that followed, Koulermos and Frampton even retained a small professional practice together and stayed in regular correspondence. Through Koulermos's long letters, Frampton retained a good sense of everyday life in Greece under the rule of the colonels (1967–74).

During this period, Koulermos invited Frampton to participate in an international Workshop on Environmental Design (WEDAG) in 1972 that also included contributions by significant modern Greek architects such as Konstantinidis and Takis Zenetos (1926–1977).[66] During the workshop, Frampton attended a lecture by the Greek sculptor Theodoros (1931–2018). The British historian's handwritten notes testify to his fascination with Theodoros's claim that 'any "technological" form of art is situated at the "arrière-garde" of the technology of today' and the sculptor's discussion of photography and the ensuing 'photogeny' of the work of art as 'indispensable' to its global dissemination, leading to 'a fundamental differentiation of our artistic sensibility'.[67] A decade later, his writings on critical regionalism transposed Theodoros's notions about sculpture to the field of architecture. In his most widely read text on critical regionalism of 1983, Frampton famously insisted on the crucial role of an arrière-garde that could both eschew a mindless technological optimisation and resist the reduction of architecture to a single photogenic image, reclaiming it as a fully embodied space of public life and collective expression.[68]

Through his editorial role at *Architectural Design*, Frampton also established his connection with the Greek publisher Orestis Doumanis who served as the magazine's Greek correspondent since 1965. In 1967, Doumanis started publishing the annual review *Architecture in Greece*. Through a network of Greek architects in London and Athens – such as Aristidis Romanos (1937–2020), Yorgos Simeoforidis (1955–2002) and Savas Condaratos (b. 1933) – Frampton's texts were consistently translated and published in Greece throughout the 1970s and the 1980s.[69] Through Doumanis's annual review, the British historian also expanded his networking with Greek architects.

Frampton read 'The Grid and the Pathway' only a few months after its original publication in Greece because, as discussed in chapter 2, he had also been consistently in direct contact with Tzonis and Lefaivre since the early 1970s. The couple themselves sent their updated manuscript of 'The Grid and the Pathway' to Frampton in October 1982, and they were in regular correspondence as they collaborated for the Rizzoli monograph on Atelier 66.[70] They also consistently followed the British historian's texts on modern Greek architecture throughout the 1980s.[71]

Adopting Tzonis and Lefaivre's views on the work of Greek architects, Frampton adds Pikionis and the two Antonakakis to the canon of regionalist architects he had been compiling on his own since the late 1970s. But his early texts for these architects also document his weaker ties with their work. The last pages of his *Modern Architecture: A Critical History* that became a reason for Greek architects to celebrate are essentially an extensive excerpt from 'The Grid and the Pathway' on the work of Konstantinidis, Pikionis and the Antonakakis. As an outsider to the Greek context, Frampton finds it difficult to trace the cultural nuances in the work of Pikionis and the two Antonakakis. In these cases, he largely follows Tzonis and Lefaivre's 'Grid and Pathway' interpretation. But he still tries to see it in theoretical terms broader than Tzonis and Lefaivre's historically embedded design patterns. Frampton adds that the 'grid' and the 'pathway' could be respectively regarded as an alternative formulation of Ricoeur's distinction between 'civilisation', the technological–scientific framework that is potentially universalised across the globe, and 'culture', which addresses the human sense of belonging developed by different societies and their specific, central, mythical nuclei. In other words, he resorts to theory in order to address an endemic problem of the cross-cultural aspirations of his critical regionalism. As expected, this stratagem is not always successful. To build an architectural discourse on cross-cultural grounds, to be able to adopt a nuanced dual perspective, one ideally needs to be familiar with the specificities of at least two contexts. This is why Frampton's outsider discussion of Pikionis's work is less insightful than the informed insiders' account by Tzonis and Lefaivre. Although Frampton trod Pikionis's pathway around the Acropolis in 1959, he does not add anything related to his lived experience to Tzonis and Lefaivre's account. And although he had also visited the apartment building at 118 Benaki Street by Suzana and Dimitris Antonakakis by 1983, he is limited to describing it in 1985 as 'a layered structure wherein a labyrinthine route drawn from the Greek island vernacular is woven into the regular grid of the supporting concrete frame'.[72] Frampton was less interested in Greek architecture itself than in the ways in which it could be integrated in his overarching project of overcoming the crisis of modernism.

When Frampton worked on the Atelier 66 monograph for Rizzoli, he also contacted other historians of Greek architecture such as Antoniades, then professor at the University of Texas at Arlington. This exchange enabled Antoniades to share his objections to Tzonis and Lefaivre's interpretation. Because the architecture of the Antonakakis is costly and the two architects do not address the related design problems on the larger urban scale despite their Left-sounding rhetoric, Antoniades argued, their work 'represents only one aspect of Greek architecture, one which photographs very well and has ties with part of the Greek past, yet one which has done very little to solve the larger problems of Greek architecture today'.[73] Antoniades's texts on Pikionis were also helpful for Frampton, who later added them to the reading list for his course at Columbia University when articles on modern Greek architecture by local scholars in English were difficult to trace.[74]

The case of Konstantinidis is different, since the British historian had been familiar with his work since the 1960s. In contrast to Pikionis and the Antonakakis, Konstantinidis had already found his place on Frampton's list of regionalist architects before the publication of 'The Grid and the Pathway'. This familiarity also enabled Frampton to go beyond Tzonis and Lefaivre's account. To illustrate his critical regionalism, Frampton opted to discuss the first house by Konstantinidis in Elefsina in 1939 and his designs for a garden exhibition in Kifissia in 1940. Neither of these projects was discussed by Tzonis and Lefaivre. But they were significant for Frampton since they enabled him to differentiate his interpretation of Konstantinidis's work from theirs, and to escape the rather exclusive and austere framework of 'the grid' in his later texts.

But even when he develops these additional insightful aspects, Frampton's understanding is still mediated by the work of his Greek students in New York. As such, it is not entirely clear how he can claim that his contact with Greece shaped him as an architect and critic. While he regularly visited places, buildings and people in Greece, it is the network of his Greek-born colleagues, researchers, students and acquaintances in London, New York and Athens that effectively conditions his understanding (Fig. 6.7). As an outsider to the Greek context, Frampton relies on secondary sources that are available in English to develop his thoughts on the local architectural scene.

In the late 1970s, Aris Konstantinidis's son Dimitris was one of Frampton's graduate students at Columbia University. Not only did this

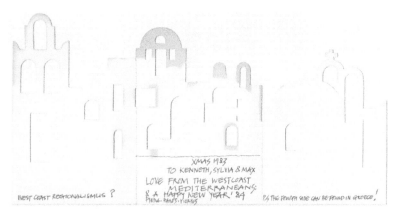

Figure 6.7 Koulermos family and Yorgos Simeoforidis, Christmas card to Kenneth Frampton, 1983

ARCH284706, Kenneth Frampton fonds, Canadian Centre for Architecture, Gift of Kenneth Frampton

Figure 6.8 Photograph of one of Dimitris Konstantinidis's first projects on Patmos, sent as a postcard to Kenneth Frampton on 7 January 2003

ARCH284707, Kenneth Frampton fonds, Canadian Centre for Architecture, Gift of Kenneth Frampton

refresh the British historian's ties with the Greek architect but it also enabled him to obtain a rare copy of Konstantinidis's book *Elements of Self-Knowledge* (1975) in English.[75] Together with the monographic feature that he edited for *Architectural Design* in May 1964, this book remains Frampton's main primary source on the work of this Greek architect from the 1980s onwards. Selected excerpts from Konstantinidis's published diary entries, which were translated from the original Greek by Frampton's doctoral student Ioanna Theocharopoulou later in the 1990s and are now found in the British historian's archive, are not mentioned in Frampton's texts on Konstantinidis.[76] But his contact with Dimitris Konstantinidis holds well into the 2000s – decades after the young Dimitris graduated and started working as a professional architect in Greece (Fig. 6.8).[77]

Frampton's primary sources on Pikionis were even more limited. Alexandra Papageorgiou, who wrote an essay on the work of her grandfather Dimitris Pikionis as a graduate student in the USA, also translated some of his texts into English.[78] These translations and 'Sentimental Topography', a significant essay that was translated on the occasion of the Pikionis exhibition at the Architectural Association in

1989, constitute Frampton's only primary sources on the sophisticated work of this architect. In his successive texts on architecture in Greece from the 1980s onwards, Frampton consistently reproduces the same excerpts from this limited pool of sources. For this reason, he cannot also double-check the validity of his secondary sources. Earlier in the 1980s, for instance, his student Dimitris Varangis discussed the focal role of the courtyard in Pikionis's residential projects. Frampton quoted this part of Varangis's essay in his own text, together with his student's overarching interpretative framework of the development of modern architecture in Greece. It was through such texts that Frampton worked to understand the Greek architectural scene or to select specific projects for architectural monographs, as documented by his extensive handwritten notes on his students' submitted essays.[79]

Frampton's hesitation to write more about architecture in Greece is evident even today in the recent publication of the fifth revised edition of his critical history of modern architecture.[80] The archived notes related to what became an eight-page chapter on Greece are very short. They are also less well-researched than Varangis's essay from the 1980s. Based on the same references across decades, they do not reflect the development of a more nuanced understanding of architecture in Greece (although photographs of more recent works by Nikos Ktenas, Andreas Kourkoulas and Maria Kokkinou, Georgios Makris and Agnes Couvelas are included). Contrary to what Greek architectural circles might have unrealistically expected of him, frequently treating his words as those of an insightful authority on the subject, Frampton did not obviously regard himself as a historian of Greek architecture.

Despite these structural shortcomings, Frampton's contribution to the global history of critical regionalism and its relationship with Greece remains uncontested. This is why I still discuss him as a historian of Greek architecture in this chapter, as this is also how he was frequently received by Greek architects who wore their inclusion in Frampton's texts as a badge of honour. Owing to his mediated relationship with the local architectural scene, Frampton could add new insights only when he saw new works by the same architects in exhibitions and publications in which he was somehow involved. His additional observations were usually based on this novel material, which Frampton consistently tried to associate with other Western European references. This is his rather overlooked, but still significant, contribution to the discourse of critical regionalism that was forged around the interpretation of modern architecture in Greece in the same period. When Frampton recapitulated

Tzonis and Lefaivre's theorisation of critical regionalism, he did not abandon his own earlier concerns. He did not merely expand his list of regionalist architectural practices to include Tzonis and Lefaivre's Greek examples; he also read them in subtly different ways. These readings in turn pushed the historical specificity of the 'grid and pathway' interpretation into the background in order to highlight Frampton's own priorities around a theory of critical regionalism. The British historian's introductory text for the Rizzoli monograph on Atelier 66 is more outward-facing than the inward-looking account of Tzonis and Lefaivre. Furthermore, it is aligned with the Antonakakis' own baffled response to the strictly regional genealogy that was propagated by 'The Grid and the Pathway' and its significance for their 'critical' practice. In addition to Pikionis and Konstantinidis, Frampton explicitly refers to Le Corbusier, Aldo van Eyck and Mies van der Rohe as a second, equivalent thread of influences in the work of the Antonakakis.[81] And while this is another intuitive rather than historically documented analysis, it does foreground the dual face of the Antonakakis' work that had been foreshadowed by the almost exclusively local 'grid and pathway' schema by Tzonis and Lefaivre.

Frampton's interest in the cross-cultural aspects of critical regionalism becomes more apparent in his later texts. In his most comprehensive study of Konstantinidis's work to date, the British historian argues for potential references to Japanese architecture in the garden-exhibition project in Kifissia of 1940, which can be similarly traced in the late work of Pikionis. In the same text, Frampton also discusses the Archaeological Museum of Ioannina. Contrary to Tzonis and Lefaivre, he does not focus on the exemplary use of the grid in this project but on the way in which Konstantinidis situates his building in the existing topography.[82] In other words, Frampton notes the 'topographically sensitive' aspects of the work, implying that Pikionis's 'pathway' can also be traced within Konstantinidis's austere 'grids'. This can therefore be read as another combination of 'the grid and the pathway' instead of being exclusively related with just one of these two design principles, as Tzonis and Lefaivre's account seemed to imply. As such, Frampton's account enriches the 'critical regionalist' interpretation of Konstantinidis's work.

On the other hand, his exclusively phenomenological reading of Pikionis's work emphasises the solitary experience of the moving body through an undulating topography. For this reason, it comes across as less successful than Tzonis and Lefaivre's interpretation – which insisted on the ritualistic, communal, socially engaging dimension that rests at the core of their interpretation of 'the pathway'.

But even when some of Frampton's interpretations for the larger scale diverted from, or simply distorted, the sociopolitical condition in Greece, they proved to be historically useful. His clearly formal reading of Athens was nonetheless the first well-known and unequivocally positive appreciation of 'the modern city par excellence' by an architect.[83] The significance of this statement for subverting the negative predisposition of Athenians, who used to describe it at the time as a monstrous 'city of cement', and leading to the reappraisal of Athens on its own terms from the late 1980s onwards cannot be easily measured.[84]

Above and beyond the individual projects, Frampton's discourse advocates a critical design practice that emerges across cultures. This higher and more broadly applicable end is another reason why his analyses tend to move away from the historical nuances of specific regional contexts. Frampton's regionalism aspires to stay true to the progressive and liberating promises of the modern project. For this reason, his selected regional practices also need to be somehow generalised in order to render them more relevant and operative for diverse architectural practices across the globe. To extrapolate and theorise the general points of this design practice more effectively, Frampton has in turn needed to downplay or bypass some historical specificities of the 'critical regionalist' projects. This is how a regionalism 'that has not yet emerged elsewhere' could acquire 'significance for the world outside itself'.[85] Frampton's ready access to major publishing venues at the Western European and North American 'centres' of architectural theory production, such as *Oppositions* and *Architectural Design*, have further reinforced this sense of global relevance for his selected 'critical regionalist' projects from the 'periphery'. Greek and other regional architects of the period experienced the global dissemination of their projects as empowering. On the other hand, this move away from history effectively short-circuited Tzonis and Lefaivre's original intentions to arrive at an architectural theory that emerges primarily from a focused return to regional specificities. In his effort to render these local practices globally operative and significant, Frampton endangered the very premise of the critical regionalist project. To avoid the paradox of neutralising these architectures through theoretically abstracting and extrapolating his main points, he also needed to tread a fine line around their historical and cultural specificities. His portrayal of Athens, and Greece as a whole, exemplifies this complex entanglement of an outsider's 'critical regionalist' account in the history/theory nexus.

Frampton's Greece

Frampton presented Greece from the vantage point of the 'central' architectural debates of the 1980s. For his North American and Western European audience, Frampton's Greece became a unique locus of modernism in a postmodern world. Because it historically developed following the normative models of nineteenth-century Neo-Classicism and twentieth-century modernism, Frampton argued, Athens is inextricably linked to the modern project.[86] Rather schematically, the British historian attributed the widespread acceptance of modernism in the Greek context to the coincidence of the Purist formal play of white volumes under the sunlight with the regional vernacular of the island settlements. But rather crucially, Frampton continued, modern architecture in Greece did not produce a universally optimised, generic built environment. The variegated topography of the region meant that each project needed to adjust to a specific, and in most cases irregular, site.[87] In other words, modernism was universally applied in Greece only because it was also locally modified. This is how, despite the overarching urban grid of the normative general plan, areas of modern Athens retain a sense of the island settlements. In conjunction with this landscape, the strong natural light intensifies the phenomenological perception and existential qualities of people, places and things in Greece.[88] Whether he refers specifically to Athens or to Greece as a whole, the modern grid and the fragmented urban experience of the island settlements are the main categories through which Frampton understands the architectural production of the country.

Because he follows his strong leaning towards phenomenology, Frampton also tends to essentialise, instead of historicising, architectural production in Greece. This moves him further away from Tzonis and Lefaivre's original theorisation. While their account is unavoidably schematic, as it attempts to cover 150 years of historical development of the modern Greek state in fifteen pages, the couple nonetheless attempted to interpret the design principles of 'the grid and the pathway' situated within this sociopolitical history of Greece. It is precisely the embeddedness of these design principles into specific historical and social contexts that renders the architecture of Greek practitioners uniquely significant for the development of a 'critical' regionalism, after all.

This specific and historically defined context is absent from Frampton's discussion. Despite the declared intentions of their author, the British historian's studies of the early 1980s do not address the sociopolitical contexts of architectural discourse and production in

Greece. It is only in the late 1990s that Frampton gains a fuller understanding of the process behind the modern face of Athens. And again, this is provided by the research of one of his doctoral students, Ioanna Theocharopoulou.[89] It is the specifically Greek modalities of culture and production, the way in which the fragmented ownership of small plots of land and the small-scale Greek construction industry organises the production of the built environment, resulting in the seemingly 'unselfconscious achievement' of Athens as 'the modern city par excellence'. Yet, as I show in chapter 9, Suzana and Dimitris Antonakakis define their 'critical regionalism' through their opposition to this same popular, small-scale, but ultimately private and commodified modality that produces the city that Frampton idealises.

Owing to the above, the discourse of critical regionalism is effectively misaligned with the architectural intentions behind the projects that it discusses. As a theory, Frampton's critical regionalism is not predicated on the projects that supposedly exemplify it. His theoretical points are not directly associated with the historical projects that he discusses; as such, theory does not follow from architectural practice in the same line of reasoning. Frampton's points only partially happen to overlap with the historical features of the selected projects. This is not an incidental mismatch owing to Frampton's necessarily mediated, outsider's accounts of diverse regional contexts. It is, rather, a structural feature of his discourse: in Frampton's critical regionalism, theory consistently comes before history. Located at the heart of his discourse, this tension has formed part of the theoretical development of critical regionalism over time. Frampton's greater interest in the broader principles that he can extrapolate takes precedence over the specificities of the projects that he discusses.

Because he puts theory first, Frampton also tends to ignore other projects by the same Greek architects that do not fit within his aspired 'critical regionalist' framework. For instance, as I show in chapter 10, when he traces a possible 'postmodernist turn' in the two Antonakakis' Rhodes branch of the Ionian Bank (1983–6) he stops discussing their work; his later texts on Greek architecture concentrate only on Pikionis and Konstantinidis.[90] But this in turn obstructs a more nuanced understanding of the development of these regional practices over time. And it is yet another sign that, like the architectures that it addresses, critical regionalism is also implicated in a history/theory nexus, which needs to be foregrounded in order to further the critical development of this discourse in the twenty-first century.

For Frampton, critical regionalism was a theory that aimed to oppose the reduction of architecture to an isolated, scenographic image. But even his own architectural discourse ended up utilising local projects as contextless images, because these seemed to satisfy the general aims of Western European and North American theorists of the time. In the mid-1980s, Western Europe and North America continue to use architecture in Greece as a way to look at themselves in the mirror. Once again, Europe is only interested in discussing its own self-image. The only difference is that this time it looks at the mirror of modern (and not ancient Classical) architecture in Greece. While modern architecture in Greece is finally out of the margins, the context and the conditions that define it are practically absent. This time, it is not modern architecture itself that is missing from the picture, as was the case earlier in the nineteenth and twentieth centuries, but the Greek context that renders it 'critically regional'.

In this sense, critical regionalism canonically 'classicises' Greek modernism in the same way that the eighteenth century had 'classicised' Athens. Despite the sincere efforts of individual authors, some of whom enjoy the insider's 'cultural intimacy'[91] with this specific region, the nuanced specificities of the Greek context are effectively absent from their discourses. From this vantage point, the postcolonial critiques of critical regionalism resurface as valid. But even before Frampton incorporated Tzonis and Lefaivre's discourse into his later writings, Greek historians such as Dimitris Philippidis remained sceptical of the potential generalisation of critical regionalism with its emphasis on establishing connections with specific places and traditions. Philippidis argued that if 'grids' and 'pathways' were to turn into general rules for Greek architectures of place-creation, they would degenerate into superficial platitudes. Devoid of their deeper original philosophical and social gravitas in the writings of Pikionis and Konstantinidis, they would again lead to allegedly place-bound but essentially iconographic, contentless forms.[92] This is probably why the famous points of critical regionalism were not historically adopted as guiding principles for the further development of architectural production in Greece. Because they are only superficially related to the concerns and aspirations of Greek architects on the local ground of their everyday practice, they do not offer them any specific direction for the future.

Critical regionalism and the discourse around it continues to determine to a great extent the way in which architecture in Greece is received to date. But in so doing, it also limits the related discussion to a series of projects from the 1970s. In the particular case of the Antonakakis, this means that a major part of their work, which spans approximately four decades after the first theorisation of critical regionalism, is not included in this big picture. This historical process has almost short-circuited the original aims of critical regionalism regarding the relationship of the 'periphery' with the 'centre'. It is rather clear that the 'periphery' has not become a locus of architectural and discourse production, which is regarded as significant for the 'central' debates. In fact, it is again the 'central' debate that defines the terms of the discussion in the 'periphery' that absorbs it.

For the above reasons, the mission of a historian of critical regionalism today is different to that of its original theorists in the 1980s. From the early 2000s, a succession of studies that seem to spring from Keith Eggener's critique have traced the specific social and historical contexts and the original, local architectural intentions that hide behind the veil of the critical regionalist debate. Today, one can also start shifting one's historical perception of this discourse from such a negative critique to a more positive or charitable interpretation of critical regionalism as an unfinished project. The blind spots and limitations of this discourse invite one to write histories of these architectures that will be more sensitive to their specific historical contexts and conditions than those of Frampton and Tzonis and Lefaivre, by resituating buildings in their original contexts and modes of production. Without the limitations of the pursuits of the 1980s, without necessarily believing that one writes the manifesto for the humanistic architecture of the future, critical regionalism can become a cross-cultural historiographical agenda of the so-called 'periphery' today. And the writing of this cross-cultural history of critical regionalism, which started with an Englishman in Athens, can potentially be under-taken from the reverse vantage point of a Greek-born architectural historian in London.

Notes

1   William J.R. Curtis, *Modern Architecture since 1900* (Oxford: Phaidon, 1982), pp. 193–5.
2   See Reyner Banham, *Theory and Design in the First Machine Age* (London: Architectural Press, 1960), pp. 227–8; Charles Jencks, *Modern Movements in Architecture* (Harmondsworth: Penguin, 1973), pp. 102, 117, 163–4, 192; Colin Davies, *A New History of Modern Architecture* (London: Laurence King, 2017), p. 191.
3   See 'Critical Regionalism Revisited', ed. by Tom Avermaete et al. Special issue, *OASE*, 103 (2019); Véronique Patteeuw and Léa-Catherine Szacka, 'Critical Regionalism for our Time', *Architectural Review*, 1466 (November 2019), 92–8.
4   Duanfang Lu, 'Entangled Modernities in Architecture', in *The SAGE Handbook of Architectural Theory*, ed. by C. Greig Crysler, Stephen Cairns and Hilde Heynen (London: SAGE, 2012), pp. 231–46 (p. 242).

5   See *The Oxford History of Western Philosophy*, ed. by Anthony Kenny (Oxford: Oxford University Press, 2000); Janet Coleman, *A History of Political Thought*, 2 vols (Malden, MA: Blackwell, 2000); David Watkin, *A History of Western Architecture* (London: Barrie & Jenkins, 1986).

6   See Jennifer T. Roberts, *Athens on Trial: The Antidemocratic Tradition in Western Thought* (Princeton: Princeton University Press, 1994); Claude Mossé, *Regards sur la démocracie athénienne* (Paris: Perrin, 2013).

7   See Plutarch, *Lives of the Noble Greeks and Romans*, Loeb Classical Library (Cambridge, MA: Harvard University Press, 1914); Cicero, *De Republica,* Loeb Classical Library (Cambridge, MA: Harvard University Press, 1928), I, 16, 25, 42–3, 45, 69; III, 35, 47.

8   Thucydides, *History of the Peloponnesian War*, Loeb Classical Library (Cambridge, MA: Harvard University Press, 1919), II, 37, 1–2.

9   See Frank M. Turner, *The Greek Heritage in Victorian Britain* (New Haven, CT: Yale University Press, 1981), pp. 187–204.

10 See Gustave Glotz, *La Cité grecque* (Paris: Renaissance du Livre, 1928), p. 140; Moses I. Finley, *Democracy Ancient and Modern* (London: Chatto & Windus, 1973).

11 See Nassia Yakovaki, *Ευρώπη μέσω Ελλάδας: Μια καμπή στην ευρωπαϊκή αυτοσυνείδηση, 17ος–18ος αιώνας* (Athens: Estia, 2006).

12 See *Itinerarium Italicum: The Profile of the Italian Renaissance in the Mirror of its European Transformations*, ed. by Heiko A. Oberman and Thomas A. Brady Jr (Leiden: Brill, 1975).

13 Curtis, *Modern Architecture since 1900*, p. 105.

14 See Konstantinos Xanthopoulos, *Alvar Aalto and Greece: Trailing Ariadne's Thread* (Athens: Melissa, 2019).

15 See John Towner, *An Historical Geography of Recreation and Tourism in the Western World, 1540–1940* (Chichester: Wiley, 1996).

16 Jacob Spon and George Wheler, *Voyage d'Italie, de Dalmatie, de Grèce, et du Levant fait aux années 1675 et 1676* (Lyons, 1678).

17 Yakovaki, *Ευρώπη μέσω Ελλάδας*, pp. 333–70.

18 Montesquieu, *De l'Esprit de Loix; Ou du rapport que les Loix doivent avoir avec la Constitution de chaque Gouvernement, les Moeurs, le Climat, la Religion, le Commerce, &c.; à quoi l'Auteur a ajouté des recherches nouvelles sur les Loix Romaines touchant les Successions, sur les Loix Françoises, & sur les Loix Féodales* (Geneva, 1748); Johann Gottfried Herder, *Ideen zur Philosophie der Geschichte der Menschheit*, 4 vols (Riga and Leipzig, 1784–91).

19 See Johann Joachim Winckelmann, *Geschichte der Kunst des Alterhums*, 2 vols (Dresden, 1764).

20 See Hugh Honour, *Neo-classicism: Style and Civilisation* (Harmondsworth: Penguin, 1968).

21 See James Stuart and Nicolas Revett, *The Antiquities of Athens Measured and Delineated,* 3 vols (London, 1762–94).

22 James Stuart, 'Preface', in ibid., I, pp. i–viii (p. v).

23 See *The Parthenon and its Impact in Modern Times*, ed. by Panayotis Tournikiotis (Athens: Melissa, 1994).

24 See Eleni Skopetea, *Το 'Πρότυπο Βασίλειο' και η Μεγάλη Ιδέα: Όψεις του εθνικού προβλήματος στην Ελλάδα 1830–1880* (Athens: Polytypo, 1988).

25 See *The Greek Revolution: A Critical Dictionary*, ed. by Paschalis M. Kitromilides and Constantinos Tsoukalas (Cambridge, MA: Belknap, 2021); Eric J. Hobsbawm, *The Age of Revolution: Europe, 1789–1848* (London: Weidenfeld & Nicolson, 1962).

26 Abel Blouet et al., *Expédition Scientifique de Morée ordonnée par le Gouvernement Français: Architecture, Sculptures, Inscriptions et Vues du Péloponèse, des Cyclades et de l'Attique, mesurées, dessinées, recueillies et publiées*, 3 vols (Paris: Firmin-Didot, 1831–8).

27 See Gottfried Semper, *Anwendung der Farben in der Architektur und Plastik des Alterhums und des Mittelalters* (Dresden, 1836).

28 See Eugène Viollet-le-Duc, *Entretiens sur l'Architecture* (Paris, 1863), pp. 398–9; Auguste Choisy, *Histoire de l'Architecture* (Paris: Gauthier-Villars, 1899), pp. 307–9, 316, 407.

29 Le Corbusier, *Vers une Architecture*, 3rd edn (Paris: Crés, 1928), pp. 106–7.

30 See Panayotis Tournikiotis, 'Quoting the Parthenon: History and the Building of Ideas', *Perspecta*, 49 (2016), 153–66.

31 See Sigfried Giedion, 'Pallas Athéné ou le visage de la Grèce', *Cahiers d'Art*, 1–4 (1934), 77–80; *L'art en Grèce, des temps préhistoriques aux débuts du XVIIe s.*, ed. by Christian Zervos (Paris: Cahiers d'Art, 1934).

32 Anastasios Orlandos, 'Αι ημέραι του συνεδρίου εν Ελλάδι', *Τεχνικά Χρονικά*, 44–6 (1933), 1002–3.

33 Alberto Sartoris, *Gli Elementi dell'Architettura Funzionale: Sintesi Panoramica dell'Architettura Moderna*, 2nd edn (Milan: Hoepli, 1935), pp. 289–99.

34 Among others, Colin Rowe's and Demetri Porphyrios's 'classicising' analyses of canonical modernist projects argued against an alleged break with the past. As such, they further contributed to restoring this sense of continuity in the history of architecture. See Colin Rowe, *The Mathematics of the Ideal Villa and Other Essays* (Cambridge, MA: MIT Press, 1987); Demetri Porphyrios, *Sources of Modern Eclecticism: Studies on Alvar Aalto* (London: Academy, 1982).

35 Yakovaki, *Ευρώπη μέσω Ελλάδας*, pp. 370, 382.

36 See Watkin, *A History of Western Architecture*.

37 Vincent Scully, *The Earth, the Temple, and the Gods: Greek Sacred Architecture*, 3rd edn (New Haven, CT: Yale University Press, 1979), p. xiv.

38 See François Loyer, 'L'architecture de la Grèce contemporaine', unpublished doctoral thesis, Université de Paris, 1966. In the same year, Kostas Biris's comprehensive urban history of *Athens from the Nineteenth to the Twentieth century* was also completed and published. In this light, 1966 becomes a turning point in the historiography of architecture and urbanism in modern Greece. See Kostas Biris, *Αι Αθήναι: από του 19ου εις τον 20όν αιώνα* (Athens: Urbanism and History of Athens, 1966).

39 A reworked version of the first volume of Loyer's 1966 doctoral thesis was only recently published in French. See François Loyer, *L'architecture de la Grèce au XIXe siècle, 1821–1912* (Athens: École française d'Athènes, 2017).

40 See Dimitris Philippidis, *Νεοελληνική αρχιτεκτονική: Αρχιτεκτονική θεωρία και πράξη (1830–1980) σαν αντανάκλαση των ιδεολογικών επιλογών της νεοελληνικής κουλτούρας* (Athens: Melissa, 1984).

41 See Dimitris Fatouros, 'Greek Art and Architecture 1945–1967: A Brief Survey', *Balkan Studies*, 8.2 (1967), 421–35; Anthony C. Antoniades, *Σύγχρονη ελληνική αρχιτεκτονική* (Athens: Karangounis, 1979).

42 Antoniades, *Σύγχρονη ελληνική αρχιτεκτονική*, p. 47.

43 See Brent C. Brolin, *The Failure of Modern Architecture* (London: Studio Vista, 1976); Charles Jencks, *The Language of Post-Modern Architecture* (London: Academy, 1977); Peter Blake, *Form Follows Fiasco: Why Modern Architecture Hasn't Worked* (Boston: Little, Brown and Co., 1977).

44 Antoniades, *Σύγχρονη ελληνική αρχιτεκτονική*, p. 196.

45 See Chris Blencowe and Judith Levine, *Moholy's Edit: The Avant-Garde at Sea, August 1933* (Zurich: Lars Müller, 2019); Matina Kousidi, 'Through the Lens of Sigfried Giedion: Exploring Modernism and the Greek Vernacular in Situ', *RIHA Journal*, 0136 (2016). Online. journals. ub.uni-heidelberg.de/index.php/rihajournal/article/download/70203/version/60526/63551 (accessed 12 July 2021).

46 Fatouros, 'Greek Art and Architecture 1945–1967', p. 434.

47 Barry Bergdoll, 'Foreword', in *Modern Architecture and the Mediterranean: Vernacular Dialogues and Contested Identities*, ed. by Jean-François Lejeune and Michelangelo Sabatino (New York : Routledge, 2010), pp. xv–ix, xvi, xviii.

48 See Keith L. Eggener, 'Placing Resistance: A Critique of Critical Regionalism', *Journal of Architectural Education*, 55.4 (2002), 228–37; Mark Crinson, 'Singapore's Moment: Critical Regionalism, its Colonial Roots and Profound Aftermath', *Journal of Architecture*, 13.5 (2008), 585–605.

49 See Kenneth Frampton, *Modern Architecture: A Critical History*, 2nd edn (London: Thames & Hudson, 1985), pp. 313–27.

50 See Charles Jencks, *Post-Modernism: The New Classicism in Art and Architecture* (London: Academy, 1987); George Hersey, *The Lost Meaning of Classical Architecture: Speculations on Ornament from Vitruvius to Venturi* (Cambridge, MA: MIT Press, 1988); John Onians, *Bearers of Meaning: The Classical Orders in Antiquity, the Middle Ages and the Renaissance* (Cambridge: Cambridge University Press, 1988).

51 See Alexander Tzonis and Liane Lefaivre, *Classical Architecture: The Poetics of Order* (Cambridge, MA: MIT Press, 1986).

52 Murray Fraser, Alicja Gzowska and Nataša Koselj, 'Eastern Europe, 1900–1970', in *Sir Banister Fletcher's Global History of Architecture*. ed. by Murray Fraser, 2 vols (London: Bloomsbury, 2019), II, pp. 944–81 (pp. 967–8).

53 See Frampton, *Modern Architecture: A Critical History*, 2nd edn, p. 327.

54 Kenneth Frampton, 'Πρόλογος του Kenneth Frampton για την ελληνική έκδοση', in Kenneth Frampton, *Μοντέρνα αρχιτεκτονική: Ιστορία και κριτική*, trans. by Theodoros Androulakis and María Pangalou (Athens: Themelio, 1987), pp. 14–16 (p. 14).

55 See *Atelier 66: The Architecture of Dimitris and Suzana Antonakakis*, ed. by Kenneth Frampton (New York: Rizzoli, 1985).

56 Among others, see Kenneth Frampton, 'Life Begins Tomorrow', in *Europa nach der Flut: Kunst 1945–1965*, ed. by Sílvia Sauquet and Johann Lehner (Vienna: Künstlerhaus Wien; La Caixa, 1995), pp. 539–53 (pp. 552–3).

57 Frampton, 'Πρόλογος του Kenneth Frampton για την ελληνική έκδοση', p. 14.

58 CCA Fonds 197, Kenneth Frampton fonds, 197 – 2017 – 107T, AP197.S1.SS9.022, Kenneth Frampton passport, 1952, 197-107-001.

59 Kenneth Frampton, 'For Dimitris Pikionis', in *Mega XI, Dimitris Pikionis, Architect 1887–1968: A Sentimental Topography*, ed. by Dennis Crompton (London: Architectural Association, 1989), pp. 6–9 (p. 6); Kenneth Frampton, postcard to Mr & Mrs W.H. Frampton, 6 October 1959, CCA Fonds 197, Kenneth Frampton fonds, 197-2017-128P, AP197.S4.003.

60 His archived passport documents show that he entered Greece in 1963, 1964, 1969, 1972, 1974, 1981 and 1983. See CCA Fonds 197, Kenneth Frampton fonds, 197 – 2017 – 107T, AP197.S1.SS9.022, Kenneth Frampton passport, 1962, 197-107-002; CCA Fonds 197, Kenneth Frampton fonds, 197 – 2017 – 107T, AP197.S1.SS9.022, Kenneth Frampton passport, 1973, 197-107-003.

61 CCA Fonds 197, Kenneth Frampton fonds, 197 – 2017 – 107T, AP197.S1.SS9.022, Kenneth Frampton architecture, 1987, 197-107-015. See Klaus Vrieslander and Julio Kaimi, *Το σπίτι του Ροδάκη στην Αίγινα* (Athens: Akritas, 1997).

62 Kenneth Frampton, Cyprus in Transition, 4-page typescript, CCA Fonds 197, Kenneth Frampton fonds, 197 – 2017 – 107T, AP197.S1.SS9.022, Cyprus in transition by Kenneth Frampton, Tel-Aviv, circa 1960–1970, 197-107-026.

63 See Kenneth Frampton, *Panos Koulermos: Opera completa* (Mendrisio: Archivio del Moderno, 2004); CCA Fonds 197, Kenneth Frampton fonds, 197 – 2017 – 100T, AP197.S1.SS9.015, Panos Koulermos book project, 2003–2004, 197-100-025.

64 See CCA Fonds 197, Kenneth Frampton fonds, 197 – 2017 – 088T, AP197.S1.SS9.003, Panos Koulermos, 12 case per gli dei di olimpo circa 2005–2010, 197-088-056.

65 See Douglas Stephen, Kenneth Frampton and Michael Carapetian, *British Buildings 1960–1964* (London: Adam & Charles Black, 1965).

66 See T. David, '"Pratt in Greece": Summer 1972 in collaboration with Workshop of Environmental Design, Athens, Greece (WEDAG)', *Architecture in Greece*, 7 (1973), 236–43; CCA Fonds 197, Kenneth Frampton fonds, 197 – 2017 – 100T, AP197.S1.SS9.015, Panos Koulermos book project, 2003–2004, 197-100-025.

67 Theodoros, 'Instead of a Sculpture', 6-page typescript, September 1971, CCA Fonds 197, Kenneth Frampton fonds, 197 – 2017 – 114T, AP197.S3.001, Personal and professional correspondence 1972, 1972, 197-114-014, pp. 5–6.

68 Kenneth Frampton, 'Towards a Critical Regionalism: Six Points for an Architecture of Resistance', in *The Anti-Aesthetic: Essays on Postmodern Culture*, ed. by Hal Foster (Washington, DC: Bay Press, 1983), pp. 16–30.

69 See *Architecture in Greece*: 8 (1974), 115–19; 10 (1976), 58–64; 11 (1977), 102–10; 17 (1983), 58–69; *Art + Design in Greece*: 7 (1976), 16–31; 10 (1979), 45–55; 14 (1983), 27–32.

70 Alexander Tzonis and Liane Lefaivre, postcard to Kenneth Frampton, 23 October 1982, CCA Fonds 197, Kenneth Frampton fonds, 197-2017-130P, AP197.S4.005; Alexander Tzonis and Liane Lefaivre, 2-page letter to Kenneth Frampton, 22 November 1982, CCA Fonds 197, Kenneth Frampton fonds, 197 – 2017 – 114T, AP197.S3.001, Personal and professional correspondence 1982, 1982, 197-114-024; Alexander Tzonis and Liane Lefaivre, letter to Kenneth Frampton, 28 December 1984, CCA Fonds 197, Kenneth Frampton fonds, 197 – 2017 – 115T, AP197.S3.002, Personal and professional correspondence 1984, 1984, 197-115-001.

71 Liane Lefaivre, postcard to Kenneth Frampton, 14 October 1989, CCA Fonds 197, Kenneth Frampton fonds, 197-2017-129P, AP197.S4.004.

72 Frampton, *Modern Architecture: A Critical History*, 2nd edn, p. 326.

73 Anthony C. Antoniades, 2-page letter to Kenneth Frampton, 23 August 1982, CCA Fonds 197, Kenneth Frampton fonds, 197 – 2017 – 114T, AP197.S3.001, Personal and professional correspondence 1982, 1982, 197-114-024, p. 2.

74 See Anthony C. Antoniades, 'Dimitris Pikionis: His Work Lies Underfoot on Athen's [sic] Hills', *Landscape Architecture* (March 1977), 150–3; CCA Fonds 197, Kenneth Frampton fonds, 197 – 2017 – 008T, AP197.S1.SS2.088, GSAPP handbook and course reader for Modern Architecture seminar, 1988–1989, 197-008-010.

75 Aris Konstantinidis, *Elements for Self-Knowledge*, trans. by Kay Cicellis (Athens: self-published, 1975).

76 CCA Fonds 197, Kenneth Frampton fonds, 197 – 2017 – 010T, AP197.S1.SS5.017, Critical regionalism – Aris Konstantinidis proposal outline, ca. 2010, 197-010-054.

77 Dimitris Konstantinidis, four postcards to Kenneth Frampton, 7 January 2003, CCA Fonds 197, Kenneth Frampton fonds, 197-2017-129P, AP197.S4.004.

78 CCA Fonds 197, Kenneth Frampton fonds, 197-2017-036T, AP197.S2.004, For Dimitris Pikionis by Alexis Papageorgiou (Greek), circa 1970–1990, 197-036-051; The Spirit of Tradition by D. Pikionis (Greek), circa 1970–1990, 197-036-053.

79 See Dimitri Varangis and Robert Condia, A Sensibility to Region, 49-page typescript, CCA Fonds 197, Kenneth Frampton fonds, 197 – 2017 – 010T, AP197.S1.SS5.014, A sensibility to region by Dimitri Varangis and Robert Condia, 1978–1989, 197-010-051.

80 CCA Fonds 197, Kenneth Frampton fonds, 197 – 2017 – 010T, AP197.S1.SS4.028, Drafts of the 5th edition of Modern architecture a critical history, ca 2014–2016, 197-010-030.

81 Kenneth Frampton, 'Greek Regionalism and the Modern Project: A Collective Endeavour', in *Atelier 66: The Architecture of Dimitris and Suzana Antonakakis*, ed. by Frampton, pp. 4–5.

82 See Kenneth Frampton, 'L'opera di Aris Konstantinidis', in Paola Cofano and Dimitris Konstantinidis, *Aris Konstantinidis 1913–1993* (Milan: Electa, 2010), pp. 8–15 (p. 10).

83 Frampton, 'Πρόλογος του Kenneth Frampton για την ελληνική έκδοση', p. 14.

84 For a recent attempt to evaluate Frampton's contribution from this vantage point, see Ioanna Theocharopoulou, *Builders, Housewives and the Construction of Modern Athens* (London: Black Dog, 2017), pp. 15–17.

85 Kenneth Frampton, 'Modern Architecture and Critical Regionalism', *RIBA Transactions*, 3.2 (1983), 15–25 (p. 20).

86 Frampton, 'Πρόλογος του Kenneth Frampton για την ελληνική έκδοση', p. 14.

87 See Frampton, 'Greek Regionalism and the Modern Project: A Collective Endeavour', p. 4.

88 Kenneth Frampton, 'Μοντέρνο, πολύ μοντέρνο: Μια συνέντευξη του Kenneth Frampton στον Γιώργο Σημαιοφορίδη', *Architecture in Greece*, 20 (1986), 118–21 (p. 121).

89 Kenneth Frampton, 'Foreword', in Theocharopoulou, *Builders, Housewives and the Construction of Modern Athens*, pp. 6–7 (p. 6).

90 Kenneth Frampton, 'A Note on Greek Architecture: 1938–1997', in *Landscapes of Modernisation: Greek Architecture 1960s and 1990s*, ed. by Yannis Aesopos and Yorgos Simeoforidis (Athens: Metapolis, 1999), pp. 12–14.

91 See Michael Herzfeld, *Cultural Intimacy: Social Poetics in the Nation-State*, 2nd edn (New York: Routledge, 2005).

92 Philippidis, *Νεοελληνική αρχιτεκτονική*, p. 377.

7
Inadvertent repercussions

The temporal distance of four decades now enables architectural historians to interpret critical regionalism as a situated historical artefact. In this chapter, I focus on the repercussions of this discourse in order to show how the border-crossing theory of critical regionalism acquired historical agency through the specific conditions of its production and dissemination in the context of 1980s Greece. More specifically, I highlight the unexamined 'boomerang effects' of the refracted 'return' of critical regionalism as an international theoretical construct to its originating locus. Based on original archival evidence and oral-history interviews, I explore the historical consequences and implications of critical regionalism for the local architectural milieu.

In the pages that follow, I show not only how an 'international' theoretical construct appropriated a 'regional' design practice in order to embark on its own global course in the 1980s but also how this historical course affected the design practice from which it originated, and the broader field of architecture in Greece, in unforeseen ways. Owing to the competing agendas – both local and global – that were historically invested in it, Greek architects used critical regionalism both as an unreflective modernist haven from the international sirens of postmodernism and as a plea for a national traditionalism that went against modernism. What had theoretically been devised to expand the global outreach of Greek architecture had the opposite effect of turning the regional architectural culture inwards. These inward-looking ramifications of critical regionalism in 1980s Greece practically short-circuited the original theoretical intentions of its authors.

In order to demonstrate this, I use the celebrated reception of critical regionalism in Greece as my starting point. To explain this success, I look more closely back to the first histories of architecture in modern

Greece of the mid-1960s, before the publication of 'The Grid and the Pathway' in 1981. This enables me to foreground the historiographical and theoretical reasons for the positive reception of critical regionalism in the local architectural milieu. More specifically, I argue that Tzonis and Lefaivre's article offered a reconciliation for the deep-seated Pikionis/Konstantinidis divide established by these first histories. In addition, 'The Grid and the Pathway' offered a renewed understanding of the work of Pikionis. The article reappraised his work when its significance for the Greek architectural milieu was at a nadir. But after Frampton's recuperation of 'The Grid and the Pathway', Pikionis's ambivalent relationship with modernism gained increasing relevance in the international postmodern context of the period. As such, Tzonis and Lefaivre's article led to an unexpected posthumous interest in the work of Pikionis. Lastly, the local reception of critical regionalism was associated with modernism. This enabled Greek architects to recuperate the revered project of the generation of the 1960s that had been abruptly brought to a halt by the imposition of the military junta in 1967. Critical regionalism was interpreted through the 1960s lens of relating modernism with the Greek architectural tradition, which was also the shared main line of local architectural historiography.[1]

I then trace the threefold impact of the critical regionalist discourse more specifically on Suzana and Dimitris Antonakakis and their architectural practice. Before the publication of 'The Grid and the Pathway', the two Antonakakis were consistently portrayed as outward-facing modernists. But after this publication, accounts of their work became increasingly inward-looking as they were understood as being literally 'deeply rooted … inside the dialectic of Greek culture'.[2] This almost exclusive association of the work of the Antonakakis with Pikionis and Konstantinidis still holds the imagination of architectural historians captive. But the repercussions of critical regionalism on the Antonakakis were not only theoretical and historiographical; they also affected the architects' personal relations within the Greek architectural milieu, and their legacy. The 'international' celebration of their 'peripheral' work reflexively endowed the couple with the aura of the distinguished architect in Greece. In 2015, Costandis Kizis characteristically referred to Dimitris Antonakakis as 'maybe the only internationally renowned Greek architect of his generation'.[3] But this estranged the architectural couple from their peers – including Konstantinidis himself, who broke his ties with the Antonakakis in the mid-1980s. It also accelerated the implosion of their 20-year-old collaborative practice Atelier 66, in 1986.

Inward-looking repercussions

Although not immediately perceptible to an external observer, 'The Grid and the Pathway' was a significant intervention in the Greek architectural milieu of the early 1980s. It offered a way in which to reconcile the Pikionis/Konstantinidis divide that had haunted the local architectural field since the 1960s. Established by Orestis Doumanis in 1964, this either/or opposition was the defining dilemma for the future of architecture in Greece between modernism and traditionalism.[4] The normative message of Doumanis's analysis was that a 'Greek school' of national architecture should abandon Pikionis in favour of Konstantinidis. Before the publication of 'The Grid and the Pathway', Konstantinidis was associated with the assimilation of architectural qualities of the regional vernacular in his consistently modernist designs. Conversely, owing to the versatile references, replications, mixes and matches of regional architectural forms, Pikionis's work was easily associated with traditionalist approaches. Approximately two decades later, 'The Grid and the Pathway' presented this binary opposition as a false dilemma. After its publication, one no longer had to take sides since the influence of Pikionis and Konstantinidis could be successfully combined and transgressed in the work of a younger architectural generation. Focusing their analysis on the work of Pikionis, Konstantinidis and the two Antonakakis, Tzonis and Lefaivre offered a novel reading of the Greek architectural milieu. As a result, the discourse of critical regionalism corroborated the co-equal institutionalisation of Konstantinidis and Pikionis as 'the two most important figures in the generation of contemporary Greek architecture'.[5] In the 1980s, Greek architects increasingly understood themselves as guardians of this regional variant of modernism in the lineage of Konstantinidis and Pikionis: this was now the defining genealogy of modern architecture in Greece.

In this context, 'The Grid and the Pathway' effectively offered a reappraisal of Pikionis's work. Although his celebrated status in the local architectural field is hardly disputed today, Pikionis's regional reception was not positive from the outset. His now internationally renowned, award-winning landscaping project around the Acropolis (1954–7) was originally denounced in Greek journals of the period as – in the words of Anastasios Salmas, for example – a 'forgery' and an 'assault' on the archaeological sites.[6] By contrast, it was immediately celebrated by non-Greek architects such as Kisho Kurokawa – whose comments went in the exactly opposite, 'sacrilegious' direction: 'The Acropolis, as I had anticipated, had made no impression upon me, but ... this road by Pikionis did have something to say to me ... I thought that while the Parthenon may express the dead form of ancient Greece, Pikionis' road expresses the living space of present-day Greece.'[7] But as Frampton characteristically noted after he unknowingly visited Pikionis's project in 1959 and mentioned it to his 'close Greek friends', he was surprised that they did not customarily refer to this project. 'When questioned, they knew of it and they knew the architect's name but they did not truly understand the significance of the achievement.'[8]

From Doumanis's original article in 1964 to the publication of 'The Grid and the Pathway' in 1981, the Pikionis/Konstantinidis divide was only deepened. In the decade following Pikionis's death in 1968, esteem for his work was steadily on the decline in Greece. This was due to the emergence of a circle of upper-class traditionalists who regarded the ethnographer Angeliki Hadjimichali (1895–1965) as their unofficial leader.[9] As self-proclaimed Pikionists, these individuals posited that they were the rightful heirs to his legacy. In his history of architecture in Greece, Anthony C. Antoniades marked 1976 as the year that this 'irreverence' towards the work of Pikionis reached its highest point: this was the moment that it was derided as 'ruinology'.[10] Konstantinidis himself encouraged this pejorative approach through his critical allusions to the 'scenographic' work of Pikionis and its negative association with postmodernism in his later writings.[11] Traces of such views survive in Greek architectural discourse to this day. They are especially evident in the writings of architects such as Yannis Kizis who recognise Konstantinidis as the genuine role model of the Greek architect and refuse to discuss Pikionis's work as properly architectural. Kizis prefers to refer to Pikionis as 'a philosopher, mentor, painter', implying that his 'artistic approach to architecture' was problematic as a blueprint for future developments as it 'led to neotraditional buildings by his imitators and their complacent nouveaux riches clients across Greece in the late 20th century'.[12]

In this light, 'The Grid and the Pathway' was also an attempt to save Pikionis's work from its association with nostalgic 'ruinology' and conservative traditionalism. In contrast to Salmas and Konstantinidis, Tzonis and Lefaivre described the 'pathway' around the Acropolis as 'a catalyst of social life ... the reenactment of a ritual, the confirmation of the human community and a criticism of the alienating effects of contemporary life'.[13] In so doing, they foregrounded the collective sociocultural and critical aspects of Pikionis's work that were attuned with the pursuits of a younger generation of modern Greek architects of the period.

'The Grid and the Pathway' was also published at the most intense moment of the Western European and North American postmodern debate, in 1981. In this context, Frampton's recapitulation of Tzonis and Lefaivre's critical regionalism afforded Pikionis's 'previously obscure and marginal' work an unexpected posthumous relevance. As Frampton characteristically noted in 1989, '[t]he last thirty years have changed our way of evaluating architecture'.[14] The Greek architect's ambivalent relationship with modernism reinforced the pertinence of his work. Over the course of the 1980s, Pikionis was rather unexpectedly brought into the international spotlight (Fig. 7.1). Within a decade, international exposure of his work ranged from an exhibition of Greek Architecture in Delft (1981) to monographic exhibitions at the Architectural Association in London (1989; Fig. 7.2) and the Fifth Biennale of Architecture in

Figure 7.1 Poster for the Antonakakis–Pikionis exhibition, organised by Aldo van Eyck, Georges Candilis and Agni Pikionis, at the Greek Festival, TU Delft, 27 October–1 December 1981

Collection Het Nieuwe Instituut/AFFV, AFFV153

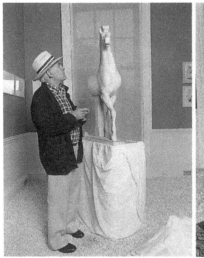

Figure 7.2 Views of 'A Sentimental Topography', exhibition of Dimitris Pikionis's work at the Architectural Association in London, 5 June–7 July 1989

Paul Barnett, 1989

Venice (1991).[15] Frampton's significance in this process cannot be underestimated, especially given the lukewarm reception of Pikionis's work by local architects of the 1960s and the 1970s. Despite the shortcomings that I discussed in chapter 6, outsiders' accounts remain undeniably important in noting figures and works that might have been overlooked by local circles for various reasons that do not necessarily register from a transnational vantage point. Through the globally celebrated reception of critical regionalism, modern Greek architects such as Pikionis found their canonical place in Western European and North American architectural discourse.[16] This is especially evident in William J.R. Curtis's successive editions of *Modern Architecture since 1900*. Sharing Frampton's intention to extend the earlier canon, Curtis contributed to the debates around regionalism and modernism in the 1990s. After having overlooked modern Greek architects in its two first editions, Curtis's revised third edition of 1996 praised Pikionis's 'acute sensitivity to the genius loci'.[17] In the specific case of Pikionis, who was not interested in publicising his work like Konstantinidis was,[18] this was combined with the consistent decades-long efforts of his daughter Agni Pikioni to organise her father's archive and present his work to Greek and international audiences.[19] A xeroxed copy of one of these publications on the landscaping project around the Acropolis found in OMA's archive in

Rotterdam today suggests that Pikionis's 'pathway' served as one of the main references for their award-winning competition entry for two libraries at Jussieu in Paris, conceived as an 'interior boulevard', in 1992.[20]

Nowadays, Pikionis is established as 'one of the leaders of … "Mediterranean Modernism"'.[21] Heralded as 'the country's most talented architect', his award-winning landscaping project around the Acropolis is also celebrated as 'one of the twentieth century's most important architectural achievements, not just in Greece, but globally'.[22] The fact that this project was recently used to illustrate an unrelated discussion between Peter Zumthor and Mari Lending on the Swiss architect's latest work testifies to its current iconic status. Representing an architecture with strong ties to the history of a place, Pikionis's project served as a silent witness of Zumthor's work – subtly encouraging the reader to associate it with two recent projects in Norway.[23] These are all symptoms of the positive reception of critical regionalism, which has in turn rendered Tzonis and Lefaivre's 'grid and pathway' interpretation indispensable to international architects and scholars. Forty years later, their account still holds: recent books on Pikionis's work, such as Alberto Ferlenga's *Le Strade di Pikionis* (2014), concentrate exclusively on the Greek architect's use of the pathway, considered in isolation from other prominent characteristics of his oeuvre.[24]

After 'The Grid and the Pathway' was incorporated into Frampton's work, Tzonis and Lefaivre rightfully argued that 'Greek architecture [was] slowly finding its place in the international scene'.[25] But the wider postmodern context in which this development was situated was essentially absent from the Greek understanding of critical regionalism of the period. Historically serving as a discursive haven, critical regionalism maintained Frampton's and the Greek architects' progressive distance from the reactive historicism of the Venetian postmodernists. According to the rhetoric of critical regionalism, it was because these works were rooted to their specific region that they acquired their international significance. However, this also served as a motive for an inward-looking turn of the Greek architectural field. The rationale was simple: if the region could produce work of international significance on its own, then it should remain focused on its existing resources. It should continue following its own trajectory, ideally without any distorting contact with international architectural developments. The local architectural scene had already found the answer to the crisis of international style modernism on its own. As such, it was the rest of the world that should be paying attention to Greece and not the other way around.

This inward-looking interpretation served the Greek modernists who wanted to resist postmodernism. In the preface to the second edition of his critical history of modern architecture, Frampton explicitly referred to critical regionalism as a 'revisionist' variant of modernism.[26] Greek modernists used critical regionalism as an opportunity to revive the revered project of the generation of the 1960s that had been abruptly brought to a halt by the imposition of the military junta in 1967. They still sought to relate modernism to the Greek architectural tradition. At the same time, critical regionalism also served the traditionalists who wanted to oppose the modernists. Both of these architectural audiences succumbed to another round of introversion after the seven years of the military junta (1967–74). The obfuscated message of critical regionalism provided an alibi for both parties to push their respective progressive and conservative agendas forward. These undesired consequences of the otherwise empowering effects of the critical regionalist discourse were already visible in 1984. In their survey of architectural developments in Greece at the time, Tzonis and Lefaivre regretted this reinforcement of traditional borders.[27] By then, the inward-looking, and eventually self-referential, reading of critical regionalism had reversed the focal intentions of 'The Grid and the Pathway'. Tzonis and Lefaivre's discourse had inadvertently reinforced a cultural insularity. In the mid-1980s, critical regionalism was used as an excuse to look inward and backward rather than outward and forward as its cosmopolitan authors had originally intended.

Boomerang effect

This inward-looking turn was also reflected in the accounts of Suzana and Dimitris Antonakakis' work after the publication of 'The Grid and the Pathway'. The couple's initial steps in the architectural profession coincided with the appearance of the first historical surveys of architecture in modern Greece, and their work found its place in all of them. Their inclusion in these histories situates their architectural concerns in the Greek context of the 1960s. Like their peers, the two Antonakakis address the question of tradition – which serves as the focal point of the cultural debates of the period. From the mid-1960s to the late 1970s, Suzana and Dimitris Antonakakis were consistently portrayed as outward-facing practitioners who referred to the work of Ludwig Mies van der Rohe and Le Corbusier.[28] Following the positive reception of Tzonis and Lefaivre's account in Greece and abroad in the early 1980s, however, the interpretation of their work became increasingly inward-looking. Focusing on their rhetoric, for instance, Dimitris Philippidis highlighted the Antonakakis' work in relation to Konstantinidis's agenda. In his canonical history of architecture in modern Greece, he portrayed the couple as the 'major successors of Konstantinidis's message'.[29] Successive accounts of their work by Greek and international scholars from Jean-Louis Cohen to Costandis Kizis have not seriously challenged this regional genealogy of Pikionis and Konstantinidis.[30] This is further testament to the impact that Tzonis and Lefaivre's account still has on the imagination of architectural historians, who have not escaped from the interpretative grip of 'The Grid and the Pathway' four decades later.[31] However, this account is not historically accurate. It distorts the actual formation of the Antonakakis' architectural outlook in late-1950s Greece.

In historical terms, the Antonakakis' contact with Konstantinidis was rather slight. They had first met him during their student years in the late 1950s. At the start of their career in the early 1960s, Konstantinidis had also agreed to advise them on their winning competition entry for the Archaeological Museum on Chios in 1965.[32] In addition, he had appreciated the work of the young architectural couple on the furniture design of the Theotokos Foundation and had asked for their permission to publish it abroad.[33] However, their correspondence waned over the years – especially after the publication of 'The Grid and the Pathway'. For Suzana and Dimitris Antonakakis, Konstantinidis's influence thus remained almost as distant as that of Mies van der Rohe. Even if they did study his built work for themselves,[34] his influence in the formation of their architectural outlook was not as important as posited by Tzonis and Lefaivre. It was not built upon the deeper ties of a personal biographical connection, as in the case of Pikionis. Suzana Antonakaki references Konstantinidis only four times in the 107 articles that she wrote for her monthly column on architecture in the popular daily newspaper *Ta Néa* between 1998 and 2009. By contrast, her substantial references to Pikionis number more than fifteen. Furthermore, three years before the publication of 'The Grid and the Pathway', Dimitris Antonakakis did not even mention Konstantinidis as an indirect influence in the short memorandum booklet for his academic candidacy at the National Technical University of Athens in 1978.[35] As such, the couple's understanding of tradition through modernism, and thus their critical regionalism, was clearly shaped by an altogether different set of influences that harked back to their student years at the National Technical University of Athens in the late 1950s, as I discuss in the next chapter.[36]

For these reasons, Tzonis and Lefaivre's 'grid-and-pathway' interpretation could only present itself as an open question to Suzana and

Dimitris Antonakakis. The theorists' words challenged the architects to rethink the role of the major influences in the development of their work. However, the architects' own insider perspective on their personal formation also meant that they did not remain passive recipients of others' accounts. In the decades that followed, they both rebelled against the 'grid and pathway' interpretation in order to promote their specific architectural concerns, and tried to reinterpret their projects in that light. To counter a strictly inward-looking reading of their work, they consistently underscored its 'international' sides in global and regional fora, from the early 1980s onwards.[37] When they presented their work at the opening of the exhibition of Greek architecture in Delft in November 1981 as a 'synopsis' of their 'itinerary' – a title that echoed Tzonis and Lefaivre's 'Grid and Pathway', which had just been published in Dutch – they did not refer to Konstantinidis at all. They foregrounded Pikionis as the figure who had made them understand how to connect with the Greek region through the depths of time. At the same time, they presented Aldo van Eyck's Orphanage in Amsterdam, and not Konstantinidis's Museum in Ioannina, as the main reference for their grid in the Archaeological Museum on Chios (Fig. 7.3). As they noted, the only difference was that they had needed to break Van Eyck's 14 × 14 units down to a 7 × 7 grid, for structural, antiseismic reasons.[38] Concluding their presentation, the two Antonakakis summarised the main aims and features of their work in five points: 'non-authoritarian spaces'; 'autonomous cells that belong to a greater unit'; 'dual character of structural loadbearing elements that define spaces'; 'study and elaboration of movement' through the building and its site; and 'elaboration of gradients and boundaries'.[39] In the late 1990s, Dimitris Antonakakis went as far as devoting a master's seminar series to the systematic study of the work of Pikionis and Konstantinidis. As he characteristically remarked in his preliminary notes for the seminar, retrieved from the architects' private archive, Tzonis and Lefaivre had used these two architects 'intuitively rather than analytically … to set up the scene of "critical regionalism" in Greece'.[40] Through this seminar, Antonakakis voiced his frustration with critical regionalism with regard to its actual meaning and the work of Pikionis and Konstantinidis.

However, the ramifications of 'The Grid and the Pathway' were not confined to the discursive plane of architectural history. Critical regionalism also affected the architects' personal relationships with their peers. Unlike Pikionis, Konstantinidis was still alive when 'The Grid and the Pathway' was published in Greece. Recently retired, he was then devoting the last years of his life to constructing the legacy of his work

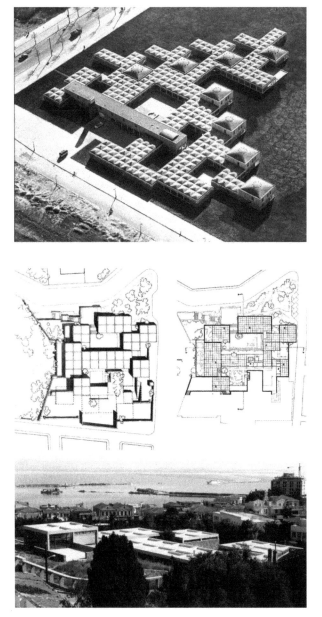

Figure 7.3 Top: Aldo van Eyck's Orphanage in Amsterdam, 1960, photographed by KLM aerocarto; centre and bottom: plan drawings and photograph of Suzana and Dimitris Antonakakis and Eleni Goussi-Dessyla's Archaeological Museum on Chios, 1965

© Aldo van Eyck, from the Aldo van Eyck archive (top); Suzana and Dimitris Antonakakis' private archive (centre and bottom)

– from the systematic organisation of his archive to the recording of his thinking in written form. Dissatisfied with the presentation of his projects and ideas in 'The Grid and the Pathway', he reportedly informed Tzonis that the coupling of his life's work with that of Pikionis and a younger generation of architects was inappropriate and unfounded.[41] In response to his dissatisfied pleas, Tzonis and Lefaivre modified their account to reappraise the work of Konstantinidis in the revised version of 'The Grid and the Pathway' for Frampton's monograph of 1985. They emphasised the superiority of the 'lucid, tectonic, functionalist intention' of Kontantinidis's 'austere, rough, uncompromising structures' over the Greek National Gallery project (1966–75) by the office of Pavlos Mylonas and Dimitris Fatouros (where Dimitris Antonakakis had also worked during Fatouros's absence in the USA in 1966–7). Tzonis and Lefaivre's reappraisal culminated in an unequivocal acknowledgement of Konstantinidis as 'the doyen of contemporary Greek architecture'.[42] But whether Konstantinidis actually read the updated version is not clear. For the same reasons, he did not take part in the Delft exhibition in 1981 as its organiser Aldo van Eyck intended to base it on Tzonis and Lefaivre's 'grid and pathway' interpretation of architecture in Greece. As such, it was originally set to focus on Konstantinidis's work, in addition to the architecture of Dimitris Pikionis and Suzana and Dimitris Antonakakis that made it to the show floor (Fig. 7.4). The two Antonakakis lost contact with Konstantinidis after another failed attempt to organise a monographic exhibition to honour his work – this time, with the Technical Chamber of Greece in 1985. Konstantinidis not only felt insulted by the poor technical support offered by the Chamber but he also questioned the overarching aesthetics, the introductory texts, the overall quality of the ensuing exhibition catalogue and the intentions of the organisers.[43] As the Antonakakis put it in a recent interview, the publication of 'The Grid and the Pathway' and its eventual recapitulation by Frampton also generated hostility around them.[44] The damage to their personal relationship with Konstantinidis was only one of the undesired costs of the critical regionalist story, as the ramifications of the globally celebrated discourse extended to unsettle the non-hierarchical equilibrium of their collaborative practice Atelier 66.

An imploding collective

In his introduction to his 1985 monograph, Frampton highlighted Atelier 66's 'cultivated sense of collectivity'. He saw this shared ethos as an

Figure 7.4 Views of the Pikionis and Antonakakis sections from the exhibition at the Greek Festival, TU Delft, 27 October–1 December 1981

Suzana and Dimitris Antonakakis' private archive

essential characteristic of the practice of critical regionalism, which 'consciously cultivates its own roots … to arrive at its expressive form'.[45] But while Frampton was right to emphasise the collective spirit of Atelier 66, his account idealised the way in which the firm actually operated, some twenty years after its founding. By the time his celebratory monograph was published, Atelier 66 had grown to twelve partners (Fig. 7.5). But less than a year later, its apparently 'stable' structure had already dissipated. Based on interviews with its members,[46] I retrace the inner life of this collaborative architectural practice in order to show how Frampton's critical regionalist discourse accelerated its inevitable implosion.

NAME	UNIVERSITY EDUCATION	SPECIAL ACTIVITIES	Time of participation in Atelier 66	
G.AIDONOPOULOS	Architect N.T.U. 1963		1965-1967	1978-1982
D.ANTOJAKAKIS	Architect N.T.U. 1958 Instructor N.T.U 1959	.Member of the council of the Assoc. of Greek Architects 1961-62 .President of the Assoc of the NTU Teaching Personnel 1975-77 .Vice President of the Central Council of the Panhellenic Assoc.of Academic Teaching Personnel 1976-77	1965-	
E.GOUSSI-DESYLLAS	Architect N.T.U. 1960		1965-1972	1980-1982
S.KOLOAYTHA-ANTONAKAKIS	Architect N.T.U.1959	.Member of the council of the Assoc. of Greek Architects 1971-72 .President of the Department of Architects of the Technical Chamber of Greece 1982-84	1965	
D. POTIRIS	Architect N.T.U. 1959		1965-1967	1980-1982
E.TSARMAKLI-VRONDISSI	Architect N.T.U. 1960		1967-1972	1980-1982
C. HADJIMICHALIS	Architect A.U.T. 1968 MA Urban and Regional Planning UCLA 1976 Ph.D. Regional Planning UCLA 1980 Senior Lecturer A.U.T.1982		1968-1974 1974 - 1980	
G. ANTONAKAKIS	Architect 1970 Universite de Genève		1970	
A.MONEMVASSITOU-ANTONAKAKIS	Architect N.T.U. 1969 Instructor N.T.U.1971		1972	
B.BABALOU-NOUKAKIS	Architect N.T.U. 1970 Instructor N.T.U. 1971		1972	
A. NOUKAKIS	Architect N.T.U. 1970		1972	
E. MORETTIS	Architect N.T.U. 1970		1972-75	
A. POLYCHRONIADIS	Architect A.U.T. 1968 Diplome I.U.P. Institut de Paris 1970		1975	
D.VAIOU-HADJIMICHALIS	Architect N.T.U. 1974 MA Urban Design, UCLA 1977 Instructor N.T.U. 1982		1975	
D. RIZOS	Architect N.T.U. 1971		1978	
TH. FOTIOU	Architect N.T.U. 1969 DEA en Geographie Urbaine Paris X Nanterre 1982 Instructor NTU 1972	.Vice President of the Central Council of the Panhellenic Association of Academic Teaching Personnel 1978 .Member of the Central Council of the Panhellenic Assoc. of Academic Teaching Personnel 1982	1979	
C. DASKALAKIS	Architect N.T.U. 1970		1976	

TIME OF PARTICIPATION . . . . //////////
PART TIME PARTICIPATION ≘ MILITARY SERVICE ||||||||
TIME OF POST GRADUATE STUDIES ⠪⠊⠅⠪⠪

Figure 7.5 Document outlining the structure of Atelier 66 and its evolution over time for Kenneth Frampton's edited monograph with Rizzoli, 1982

Suzana and Dimitris Antonakakis' private archive

Suzana and Dimitris Antonakakis attempted to establish a non-hierarchical structure of design collaboration within their collective practice. But my interviews with the other architects of Atelier 66 constantly highlighted the following issues and concerns: excessive workload, and the members' varying commitment to the shared process; personal lives that were increasingly out of sync due to the widening age and professional-experience gap between the Antonakakis and the younger members; the Antonakakis' strong design signature over the projects; and the Atelier 66 architects' gradually diverging interests in different design scales (urban planning vs architecture). This constellation of factors and tensions accumulated over time to render Suzana and Dimitris Antonakakis the leading authorial figures of their collaborative practice. The two architects' overarching control of the design process became increasingly evident in their practice over the years that followed.

Atelier 66 was formed in 1965 when the two Antonakakis teamed up with Eleni Gousi-Desylla, a friend from their student years at the National Technical University of Athens. Consciously striving for a non-hierarchical office structure, they were soon joined by their close friends and contemporaries Gabriel Aidonopoulos, Denys Potiris and Efi Tsarmakli-Vrontisi. Such collaborative offices were not uncommon in Greece at the time. Partly, this was a local expression of a broader international trend instigated by early critiques of functionalism – and of the authoritarian design practices of modern architects – in seminal texts like Jane Jacobs's *The Death and Life of Great American Cities* (1961). Suzana and Dimitris Antonakakis shared these concerns. They believed that opening up the design process could 'contain and continue a previous conversation' with architects, places, 'the rigours of life, [and] the interventions of the inhabitants'. In turn, this could be an antidote to the anonymous urban environment generated by the vulgar commodification of modernist tenets by the Greek construction industry.[47] On a less ideological and more pragmatic level, however, collaborative practices also enabled young architects to enter competitions for large-scale projects that would have been beyond their reach as sole practitioners according to the legal framework of the period.[48]

The early 1960s were a boom time for construction in Greece. This fact was largely driven by the development of the tourist industry, with its required infrastructural network across the country and the large-scale resorts that started to be erected at the same time, as Greek banks were also keen to invest in them.[49] This boom continued unabated even after the colonels seized power in 1967, with their regime actively seeking to promote economic growth as a means of shoring up popular support – a time-honoured method of dictatorships the world over. In 1968, planning regulations and building codes were substantially modified to allow for larger-scale structures,[50] as the construction sector became especially significant for the colonels' propaganda. Architects were encouraged to consider buildings as stand-alone objects, independent from the confines of specific sites or their wider urban contexts. Effectively, this cleared the way for the construction of Athens' first high-rises (such as the Panormou Tower), among other large-scale projects.

The regime also organised a series of competitions for public buildings, including schools and hospitals.[51] Like any other young practice, Atelier 66 took part in some of these competitions. If Greek architects had reservations about participating in a joint venture with their dictators, these were mostly outweighed by the attraction of being able to work on projects of a larger scale than the standard apartment building. At the same time, such projects offered architects an opportunity to resist the regime's grandiose briefs through modest architectural proposals – especially on sensitive historical sites such as the Akronafplia Fortress in Nafplion, or in public monuments meant to memorialise significant political figures of modern Greece like Eleftherios Venizelos. But such politically loaded projects and commissions could also create ruptures within a group. While Atelier 66's architects were aligned in their left-leaning political beliefs, some of them adopted harder positions than others – refusing to participate in competitions for public buildings even after a democratically elected right-wing government had succeeded the fall of the colonels in 1974. Suzana and Dimitris Antonakakis frequently found themselves in the position of the referee in such debates, as they believed that the group's left-leaning politics could be expressed in its approach to architectural space and its design. They were confident that their specific design sensitivity would enable their work to keep its clear distance from the right-wing drives behind such commissions.

It was in fact a competition win, for the Archaeological Museum on Chios in 1965, which allowed the Antonakakis to rent an office space on Yianni Statha Street and set up Atelier 66. Their chosen name echoed that of the Swiss Atelier 5, whose projects were often published in *L'Architecture d'Aujourd'hui* in the early 1960s, to emphasise collective work instead of singling out individual architects. Competitions also formed the lifeblood of the practice – a stable source of commissions for Suzana and Dimitris Antonakakis, who were not inclined to spend time on public-relations exercises to entrepreneurially promote their work to potential clients. Since the flow of work was erratic, each architect in the office needed to maintain alternative sources of income, working either as freelancers or for a larger firm. The office served as a shared workspace for whoever needed it, whether they were working on their own or with other members of the group. Each contributed proportionally to the running costs. Over the years, this fluctuating cast of architects would also work with a group of trusted craftspeople that had gradually formed around the Atelier's work and was attuned to its specific needs.[52] Any architect of Atelier 66 could therefore tap into this shared resource of reliable craftsmanship, whether they wanted to use it for a collective project or one of their individual works.

This capacity of Atelier 66 to remain flexible as a group, expanding and undergoing constant renewal when necessary, was rather unusual. While other Greek collaborative firms did not seem to grow beyond the three or four original partners, numerous young architects joined Atelier 66 over the years. All of them entered on equal terms to the founding partners. This meant that they were equally paid for their participation in specific projects and winning entries to architectural competitions, even when Suzana and Dimitris Antonakakis' professional experience exceeded theirs by more than a decade. Under these terms, a group of thirteen collaborating architects was gradually formed without the financial support of a steady monthly wage.[53] Many of these fellow architects were often family members, friends or former students of Dimitris Antonakakis at the National Technical University of Athens. In any case, they were not employees in the traditional sense. They listened to the same music or poetry on the radio while working in the office, they shared similar political beliefs, they frequently went on trips together. There were no office 'protocols' and the general mood was relaxed, joyful and friendly (Fig. 7.6). Voicing an opinion was positively encouraged. In

Figure 7.6 Atelier 66 architects and the family of their clients in the House in Oxylithos, Evia, 1973

Suzana and Dimitris Antonakakis' private archive

Figure 7.7 Top: Atelier 66 architects on the road, 1970s; Atelier 66 architects in Olympia, 1980

Suzana and Dimitris Antonakakis' private archive (top); Giorgos Antonakakis's private archive (bottom)

this way, the culture of companionship of the original group of friends in the 1960s was perpetuated through to the 1980s – and so, too, was a sense of youthfulness, with the injection of the new arrivals (Fig. 7.7).

Given the relative autonomy of each architect in the office structure, the decision to work as a large group on a competition submission typically entailed intensive weekend and after-hours charrettes. The tendency of Suzana and Dimitris Antonakakis to dismantle and rethink the original brief, and then to explore multiple possible solutions, only added to the workload. Every competition went right down to the wire. And yet, as stressful as this model was it did ensure a high-quality proposal – giving a sense of satisfaction that compensated to some extent for the demanding workload.

In the mid-1970s, when Suzana and Dimitris Antonakakis finished their apartment building on 118 Benaki Street, Atelier 66 occupied the ground floor. As the office space was now, not coincidentally, within the couple's own apartment building, the boundaries between their home (on the first floor) and working lives (on the ground floor) soon became blurred. Practically working from home, Suzana Antonakaki was rarely absent from the office. The additional responsibilities of childcare after schooltime for Suzana, and Dimitris's weekly teaching duties, meant that the couple frequently resumed their office work or found the time to work together after the end of a normal working day when their two children had been tucked up in bed. Having worked together with her colleagues in the office throughout the day, Suzana gathered up design issues and questions that she still needed to discuss with Dimitris for the projects to proceed. As such, working long into the after-hours until past midnight was not unusual – and the couple ended up spending more time on shared projects than the other Atelier 66 architects did. In theory, the terms of the collaboration within the practice were relaxed and flexible as other members of the group also had to attend to their own teaching and family commitments.

But in practice, the younger members of the team felt compelled to follow the Antonakakis' lead and devote more of their leisure hours to work. More than an office, Atelier 66 was in this sense an entire way of life almost exclusively dedicated to architecture. Suzana and Dimitris Antonakakis consistently prioritised the architectural project beyond fees, friendships, social relations or standard working hours (Fig. 7.8). They were driven by their conviction that a collective could achieve much more significant results than the relatively powerless individual architect. But this sacrificing of free time increasingly became a problem for the younger architects of the group. The lack of shared timetables and

Figure 7.8   Atelier 66 architects' summer workshop in Alikianos, Crete, 1982

Lucy and Giorgos Triantafyllou private archive

commonly agreed schedules effectively meant that there was no boundary between work and leisure time, and this was especially the case the closer one got to a submission deadline. Younger colleagues were then expected to continue to work until late on a Saturday night instead of enjoying it with friends and loved ones, as such abnormal working hours had become normalised in practice. They felt that the work engulfed their personal lives, which were at a different phase and out of sync with those of their senior colleagues whose priorities regarding work/life balance were different.

As they embraced new colleagues to their collective practice, Suzana and Dimitris Antonakakis also strove to be attentive to their needs and aspirations. They consistently foregrounded Atelier 66 before mentioning every collaborating architect involved in the publicised projects. They mentioned Atelier 66 even when they were the sole authors of the work, a practice that was not consistently followed by other architects of Atelier 66 when they published their individual projects. Conversely, members of the group who had studied in Thessaloniki, such as Costis Hadjimichalis and Boukie Babalou, brought with them more recent architectural references – including the thinking of Robert Venturi and Aldo Rossi,[54] and their mentor Fatouros's interest in informal settlements and building practices. This blended well together with the two Antonakakis' interest in small-scale extension projects to existing residential buildings, a good example of the way in which the collective work of the office was shaped around a common ground of interests that could be refreshed by new entries to the group.[55] Hadjimichalis, who was also interested in actively promoting the work of the Atelier to wider audiences, frequently produced the finalised, inked drawings for these publications or laid out the related presentations. As the work of the office fed into Hadjimichalis's own academic interests, he was motivated not only to publicise but also to explore the potential footprint of these projects in architectural education when he taught abroad as a doctoral student in Los Angeles in the late 1970s. For several other architects of the group, the Atelier's projects also served as a solid foundation for teaching and lectureship appointments at Greek academic institutions in the 1970s and the 1980s.

But the influx of fresh blood and novel ideas through the constant intake of young architects was not reflected in either Atelier 66's design practices or its end products. This was a group consciously seeking to transgress authoritarian modernist approaches to architectural design. But the terms of this transgression were only ever set by Suzana and Dimitris Antonakakis, the de facto leaders of the collaborative practice.

Despite the best efforts of the Antonakakis to emphasise co-equal team work, the outward reception was that of a practice of (anonymous) associate architects led by the (eponymous) couple. Their style was the house style: every project that came out of Atelier 66 was, above all, associated with the two Antonakakis. The number of different architects involved in the office was therefore an irrelevance, because they all designed in the same way. This was especially the case for former students of Dimitris Antonakakis, who continued to regard him as a kind of mentor long into their professional lives. What began as a break from the conventional singular and heroic office of modernist architects – such as the ateliers of Le Corbusier, Aalto or Mies van der Rohe – ended up resembling this very model.

Although Dimitris remained the initial prompt for several of his former students to join the Atelier, the main creative force in the office was Suzana. When these young architects arrived at the ground floor of 118 Benaki Street, they met a woman architect as dynamic and charismatic as their mentor. Their shared first impression was that Suzana was the hidden protagonist of Atelier 66 who had been potentially overshadowed by Dimitris's stronger public presence through teaching. In their everyday life in the office, Suzana led the design process and rigorously defended the design ideas that she put on paper. This was an especially empowering feeling for young women who started their professional lives as architects with Suzana Antonakaki as an encouraging role model. On most of their projects, she was the lead architect – and especially so between 1977 and 1981, when Dimitris's attention was diverted by his professorial candidacy at the National Technical University of Athens. Husband and wife developed their own way of working over the years and, in the idealising eyes of their peers, it seemed that they could communicate complex and profound design intentions with the merest glance across a drawing board – as if they were working in direct unison. In the later years of the office, the intimacies of this professional relationship between the couple deepened the divide between the Antonakakis and their younger colleagues, who lacked their experience and, increasingly, did not share the same interests or points of reference. The decade of professional experience that typically divided them from the couple often stopped them from picturing themselves as co-equal partners. They worked more like collaborating architects who were also apprentices. After all, they had just started working for an architectural practice that was already well known for its unique approach in the Greek architectural field. For many of them, their work at Atelier 66 was equivalent to a graduate programme in architectural design and

Figure 7.9 Atelier 66 architects' 1982 visit to their Lyttos Hotel project in Anissara, Crete, 1977

Lucy and Giorgos Triantafyllou private archive

construction, complete with site research and building visits (Fig. 7.9). As such, the professional work of these young peers covered gaps in their architectural education. But this also made them feel that they got out of the experience much more than they contributed to the work of the office.

Yet, the office also benefited from the input of younger members, especially when commissions were not limited on the architectural scale but touched on issues of urban design. For Costis Hadjimichalis, Alekos Polychroniadis, Konstantinos Daskalakis and Dina Vaiou, this focus mirrored the scale of projects that they had worked on individually during their graduate studies in Greece or abroad. At this design scale, the younger colleagues brought with them a confidence that translated into competition success. As such, Atelier 66 built up a collective portfolio of urban-planning projects. But in the process, two different aspects began to emerge within the practice: a line started to be drawn between the (mainly architectural) work of Suzana and Dimitris Antonakakis, and the (mainly urban) work of Atelier 66. These two worlds collided in 1980, leading to what some members of the office described as a 'design crisis'. The couple, it seems, had given in to an almost 'baroque' obsession with adding small-scale detail to already elaborate drawings for complex, large-scale projects. This 'crisis' coincided with the commissioning of such sizeable projects as the university buildings on Crete in the early 1980s. The major difficulties arose when the younger architects wanted to go beyond Dimitris Antonakakis's teachings, in pursuit of an individual expression of their own. By this point, Atelier 66 had become a group of increasingly maturing architects whose collaboration over the years accentuated both their individual differences and their converging approaches to design.

To deal with the emerging differences, which had already been apparent in the 1970s, the office developed a strategy of splitting design teams in two and allowing one proposal to compete against the other. Both proposals were pinned to the walls of the studio in order to instigate a collective discussion on a preferred option. The main issue was whether an alternative approach could be convincingly developed within the same overarching design principles. The egalitarianism of this theoretical intent, however, masked a practical reality that saw the proposal developed by the team led by Suzana and Dimitris Antonakakis advance in nearly every case. In some cases, the couple went the extra mile to themselves design the other architects' proposals – only to more clearly highlight their problems. This was another symptom of their prevailing presence in the office. Atelier 66's architects did not spend the same amount of time in the office as Suzana and Dimitris Antonakakis, who returned to it later in the evenings. As such, a collective project could easily take another direction after the couple had spent another night's work on it in the absence of the others. This often became a point of no return; reverting to an older version of the same project afterwards proved very difficult in practice. Lacking the Antonakakis' design experience, their younger colleagues also found it harder to argue their corner. The usual iterative back-and-forth of the design process notwithstanding, it seems that collaboration in Atelier 66 followed a linear development effectively controlled by Suzana and Dimitris Antonakakis.

Even within this uneven process, consensus was not always possible. For example, in the competition for the Tavros City Hall (1972) Atelier 66 submitted two entries – one of which won, while the other received a commendation (Fig. 7.10). But the two proposals were drastically different. Whereas the winning entry gathered the programme into a single self-enclosed volume, the alternative proposal worked with shorter building blocks that connected to the surrounding public spaces on various levels. In other words, the same practice had produced opposing architectural solutions to the same brief.

Atelier 66 was further fractured when working on commissions. The masterplan and general design principles of a large-scale project were devised collectively, but once these had been agreed the office members

Figure 7.10   Atelier 66, two entries to the architectural competition for the City Hall in Tavros, Athens, 1972

Suzana and Dimitris Antonakakis' private archive

split into smaller groups of two or three – each taking on responsibility for specific sections of the plan or the design of individual buildings. The idea was to introduce a measure of variety into the work. Several group discussions that preceded these decisions also presented opportunities to theorise the work of Atelier 66. During these discussions, however, serious ruptures did not materialise because in the final instance the collaborating architects always fell back on the common design principles that stemmed from the practice of Suzana and Dimitris Antonakakis. In retrospect, this seems like the coping mechanism of a group that understood its internal tensions but preferred not to address them at length.

Atelier 66 architects generally regarded the EKTENEPOL housing project in Komotini (1981) as the best example of their collective practice in action. For this competition entry, they defied the original development plan in order to create a building complex with labyrinthine open-air routes of varying degrees of privacy and openness. As such, 220

Figure 7.11 Atelier 66, housing project for the personnel of a mining company, Distomo, 1969, photographed by Dimitris Antonakakis, 1970
Suzana and Dimitris Antonakakis' private archive

apartments were configured around a series of open spaces and outdoor routes of differing widths that served as piazzas, playgrounds and streets. This was the project that Dimitris Antonakakis cited in 1988 as the cornerstone of Atelier 66's residential work during the 1980s: 'the single-family houses that we realised in the 1970s were apparently and consciously influenced by our Distomo housing project of the late 1960s; similarly, the houses that we designed in the 1980s refer more or less directly to the logic or the elaboration of the EKTENEPOL housing project' (Figs 7.11 and 7.12).[56] However, it was not the collective aspects of this project that interested him the most but the specific housing typology that they had explored there, and that he and Suzana Antonakaki would continue to develop in residential projects later in the same decade.

Unsurprisingly, the architects' recollections of the important design debates in the office during the 1980s differ. These mismatches in turn indicate the widening divergence of interests within the group. Suzana and Dimitris Antonakakis, for instance, remember these discussions revolving around their own main concerns: the implementation of the grid and the exact metric relations between the various design elements. Which module – 90 cm, 86 cm or 83 cm – would they choose to control every aspect of the design through their grids, from the overall dimensions

Figure 7.12 Atelier 66, model of EKTENEPOL housing project competition entry, Komotini, 1981

Suzana and Dimitris Antonakakis' private archive

of a room to the door and window openings? Once this decision was made, a series of new questions arose. Does this grid refer to the top or the bottom of the window opening? Does one start from the floor – and if so, from which point exactly (the slab, or the final covered or tiled surface)? For Suzana and Dimitris Antonakakis, such questions were of the utmost importance. Their private archive includes countless sketches on tracing paper with metric variations on the single theme of a specific design detail before arriving at a final decision (Fig. 7.13). The three-dimensional grid was an instrument of design control that defined the basic 'horizons' of a building, the individual details of which could then be safely elaborated by one of their collaborators. This was the other side of the celebrated use of the grid by the two Antonakakis. In the context of collaborative design in Atelier 66, the grid was also an instrument of control of an allegedly non-hierarchical practice. As such, the pursuit of an elusive ethos like non-hierarchical collaboration was not only implemented but also conditioned by the specific tools and structures that underlay its design practices.

But this obsessive concern with the micro-scale of architectural details was not necessarily shared by all their Atelier 66 peers. Others were much more interested in discussing problems on the larger, urban

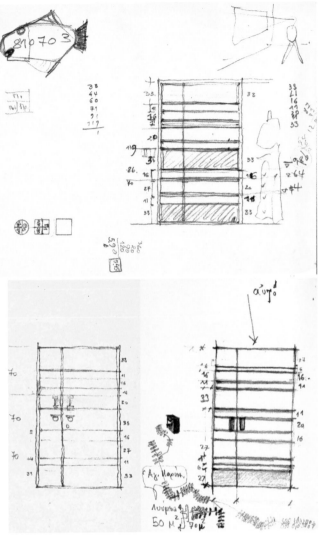

Figure 7.13 Suzana and Dimitris Antonakakis, sketches exploring modular and metric variations to design a door for their apartment building at 118 Benaki Street, Athens, 1974

Suzana and Dimitris Antonakakis' private archive

scale – what, for example, was an acceptable level of repetition of modular architectural units, and how could these be organised in functional urban zones? They were less interested in the design details of a window frame or a staircase railing, over which Suzana and Dimitris Antonakakis could conversely obsess.

It was around this point in time that the work of Suzana and Dimitris Antonakakis attracted Kenneth Frampton's attention. Although in print he celebrated Atelier 66's 'cultivated sense of collectivity', the British historian had originally intended to focus on the husband-and-wife team alone. From their correspondence, one can see that it was the Greek couple who insisted on including Atelier 66 in the title of the monograph, as they consistently did on other, similar occasions.[57] But title aside, the content of the book makes it clear that Frampton is directing his praise specifically at Suzana and Dimitris Antonakakis. Following this international recognition, the couple thought that it was time to re-set their relations with their partners – and this was also understood by their colleagues. Rather than maintaining the pretence of equality, the couple needed to assert their leadership – something facilitated by the fact that the last of the original partners from the 1960s had gone their own way in 1983, and the rest of their co-workers were now much younger than the two Antonakakis. In 1986, only a year after the publication of Frampton's monograph, the couple assumed overall control of the office as the collective practice officially imploded on friendly terms.

Stressing continuity over rupture, the Antonakakis now refer to 1986 as a significant moment in the evolution of Atelier 66.[58] In practical terms, however, 1986 marked the end of the non-hierarchical experiment of their collaborative practice. Suzana and Dimitris Antonakakis were joined by a new group of even more fresh-faced architects, who now worked as employees (Fig. 7.14) – including their son Aristide Antonas, who was by then old enough to join them. In an interview only a few years after the implosion of Atelier 66, both Suzana and Dimitris Antonakakis referred to its original collaborative terms as 'utopian'.[59] Their young collaborators had not been able to define their own creative route independent from the Antonakakis' distinctive architectural idiom and way of working. And that is why Atelier 66 could not effectively last. The Antonakakis' multifarious cultural references and their obsession with the minutest design details set a limit as to how far their architectural practice could go. The scale of projects that they could undertake, and their subsequent legacy, was limited by the design route that they had opted to follow. In this context, the final word belonged to Suzana and Dimitris Antonakakis. The design presence of the Antonakakis became so strong that rising to partner status was almost impossible for any of their younger colleagues. For this reason, a novel prospect for the future development of Atelier 66 could not emerge from within. Since this was only nominally a partnership of equals, the collaborative practice lacked

Figure 7.14 Atelier 66 architects (from top: Efi Koumarianou, Elena Papageorgiou, Lucy Triantafyllou, Xenia Tsioni, Matina Kalogerakou, Suzana Antonakaki) at the ground floor of 118 Benaki Street, 1994

Lucy and Giorgos Triantafyllou private archive

a structure that would enable it to carry on and develop further into the future. Contrary to the architects' original intentions, Atelier 66 was, in the final instance, always Suzana and Dimitris Antonakakis. By 1986, the non-hierarchical, collaborative practice that the two Greek architects had envisioned in 1965 could no longer last to survive its inadvertent idealisation by Frampton. Instead of rejuvenating and propelling it into the future, its international celebration thus signalled its eventual implosion.

In this sense, critical regionalism ended up reproducing on the regional level the effects of the star system that it was originally supposed to resist. Although Suzana and Dimitris Antonakakis did not become 'stars' of critical regionalism with commissions to build across the globe, as was the case for Mario Botta and Tadao Ando from the 1990s onwards, their international recognition nonetheless accelerated the dissolution of 'the cultivated sense of collectivity' of Atelier 66. Frampton's dissemination of critical regionalism from his own structural position at the 'centre' of Western European and North American theory production resulted in this boomerang effect of critical regionalism on the local architectural practices that he had selected to foreground. Three decades later, Dimitris Antonakakis wrote in the disappointed tone of the Greek architectural milieu's internalised inferiority complex and its short-sighted politics of resentment:

> We underestimate architecture in Greece and revere only whatever is presented in the international scene, because we cannot, or do not want to, see it from a distance and evaluate it in the global context … we regard this [international] work as something alien and inaccessible. Owing to the great technological and economic factors involved, it bears no relation to the everyday reality of Greek architectural production … The French, the British, the Germans … believe that their architecture is not only naturally situated in the global context, but it also shapes it … [As a result,] if a Greek work happens to transgress the borders of our country … to be discussed in the supranational global context, the Greek architectural community regards it as 'hyperbole'. Instead of instigating a renewal and a reevaluation of the Greek architects' endeavours, such an occurrence produces a short-lived turmoil that is followed by a constant 'conspiracy of silence' that attempts to reduce, to annul the significance and the contribution of this work to any relevant developments.[60]

As such, the international recognition of Suzana and Dimitris Antonakakis' work did not historically fulfil its empowering creative potential for the Greek architectural field as a whole. On the contrary, it practically reinforced the regional inferiority complex that I outlined in the previous chapter. This also seemed to be at the source of the hostility towards the Antonakakis generated by critical regionalism. By this point, the original intentions of Tzonis, Lefaivre and Frampton had been historically short-circuited by this refracted 'return' of the international discourse of critical regionalism to its originating context. The same was the case for other loci across the world, where the theoretical construct of critical regionalism had comparable effects in architectural practice. Their study in detail as situated historical artefacts will further elucidate similar unexamined 'boomerang effects' of knowledge transfers and border-crossing architectural theories in the late twentieth century.[61]

Notes

1   See Orestis Doumanis, 'Εισαγωγή στην ελληνική μεταπολεμική αρχιτεκτονική', *Αρχιτεκτονική*, 48 (1964), 1–11 (p. 1); Dimitris Fatouros, 'Greek Art and Architecture 1945–1967: A Brief Survey', *Balkan Studies*, 8.2 (1967), 421–35 (p. 422).

2   Alexander Tzonis and Liane Lefaivre, 'The Grid and the Pathway: An Introduction to the Work of Dimitris and Suzana Antonakakis, with Prolegomena to a History of the Culture of Modern Greek Architecture', *Architecture in Greece*, 15 (1981), 164–78 (p. 178).

3   Costandis Kizis, 'Modern Greek Myths: National Stereotypes and Modernity in Postwar Greece', unpublished doctoral thesis, Architectural Association, 2015, p. 19.

4   Doumanis, 'Εισαγωγή στην ελληνική μεταπολεμική αρχιτεκτονική'.

5   Panayotis Tournikiotis, 'The Rationale of the Modern and Locus: A View of Greek Architecture from the Seventies to the Nineties', in *20th Century Architecture: Greece*, ed. by Savvas Condaratos and Wilfried Wang (Munich: Prestel, 2000), pp. 53–62 (p. 55).

6   Anastasios A. Salmas, 'Παραποίηση και προσβολή του αρχιτεκτονικού χώρου', *Αρχιτεκτονική*, 9 (1958), 7–9.

7   Kisho Kurokawa, 'Architecture of the Road', trans. by H. Oribe and Y. Sasaki with Constantinos A. Doxiadis, *Ekistics*, 16.96 (1963), 288–93 (p. 288).

8   Kenneth Frampton, 'For Dimitris Pikionis', in *Mega XI, Dimitris Pikionis, Architect 1887–1968: A Sentimental Topography*, ed. by Dennis Crompton (London: Architectural Association, 1989), pp. 6–9 (p. 6).

9   Angeliki Hadjimichali was more interested in the study and preservation of Greek folk culture than in the country's architecture. Beginning in the 1920s, her work ranged from studies on the folk art of Skyros, and Greek ornament and garments, to the nomadic population of the Sarakatsani in the 1950s. See Angeliki Hadjimichali, *Η ελληνική λαϊκή φορεσιά*, 2 vols (Athens: Melissa, 1983); Angeliki Hadjimichali, *Σαρακατσάνοι*, 2 vols (Athens: Angeliki Hadjimichali Foundation, 2010).

10 Anthony C. Antoniades, *Σύγχρονη ελληνική αρχιτεκτονική* (Athens: Karangounis, 1979), p. 49.

11 Aris Konstantinidis, *Εμπειρίες και περιστατικά: Μια αυτοβιογραφική διήγηση*, 3 vols (Athens: Estia, 1992), III, pp. 241–7.

12 Yannis Kizis, 'Πικιώνης, Κωνσταντινίδης και νεοελληνική αρχιτεκτονική παράδοση', *Επίλογος*, 27 (2018), 329–42 (pp. 330, 338).

13 Tzonis and Lefaivre, 'The Grid and the Pathway', p. 178.

14 Frampton, 'For Dimitris Pikionis', p. 6.

15 See the special feature in the Dutch review *Wonen-TA/BK*, 20–1 (1981); Yorgos Simeoforidis, 'Σύγχρονη ελληνική αρχιτεκτονική στην Ολλανδία', *Journal of the Association of Greek Architects*, 9 (1981), 24–6; *Mega XI, Dimitris Pikionis, Architect 1887–1968: A Sentimental Topography*, ed. by Crompton.

16 Among others, see Marja-Riita Norri, 'Six Journeys into Architectural Reality: Directions for the Next Millenium', *Architectural Review*, 199.1190 (1996), 68–74; *Pikionis, 1887–1968*, ed. by Alberto Ferlenga (Florence: Electa, 1999); *Die Architektur, die Tradition und der Ort: Regionalismen in der europäischen Stadt*, ed. by Vittorio Magnago Lampugnani (Stuttgart: Deutsche Verlags-Anstalt, 2000); Juhani Pallasmaa, 'Hapticity and Time: Notes on Fragile Architecture', *Architectural Review*, 207.1239 (2000), 68–74; Zhang Yingle, 'Pikionis, Lewerentz, Venezia and Siza: The Narrative Experience in Eight Itineraries', unpublished doctoral thesis, Escuela Técnica Superior de Arquitectura de Madrid, 2019.

17 William J.R. Curtis, *Modern Architecture since 1900*, 3rd edn (London: Phaidon, 1996), p. 482.

18 See Stylianos Giamarelos, 'The Art of Building Reception: Aris Konstantinidis behind the Global Published Life of his Weekend House in Anavyssos (1962–2014)', *Architectural Histories*, 2.1 (2014), art. 22. doi.org/10.5334/ah.bx; Stylianos Giamarelos, 'Ο Άρης Κωνσταντινίδης εκτός', in *Άρης Κωνσταντινίδης*, ed. by Dina Vaiou (Athens: Greek Parliament Foundation, 2019), pp. 101–36.

19 Among others, see *Quaderns*, 190 (July–September 1991), 76–104; 'L'opera di Dimitris Pikionis', ed. by Marcello Fabbri. Special issue, *Controspazio*, 5 (September–October 1991); *Dimitris Pikionis, 1887–1968: Kreikkalainen arkkitehti*, ed. by Maria-Riita Norri (Helsinki: Suomen Rakennustaiteen Museo, 1993).

20 See: Yanna Economaki-Brunner, 'Keys to a Manipulated Landscape', *Quaderns*, 190 (July–September 1991), 84–98 (pp. 95–6); Rotterdam, Het Nieuwe Instituut, Archief Office for Metropolitan Architecture, OMAR0482, 2903.

21 Jean-François Lejeune and Michelangelo Sabatino, 'North versus South: Introduction', in *Modern Architecture and the Mediterranean: Vernacular Dialogues and Contested Identities*, ed. by Jean-François Lejeune and Michelangelo Sabatino (New York: Routledge, 2010), pp. 1–12 (p. 4).

22 Murray Fraser, Alicja Gzowska and Nataša Koselj, 'Eastern Europe, 1900–1970', in *Sir Banister Fletcher's Global History of Architecture*, ed. by Murray Fraser, 2 vols (London: Bloomsbury, 2019), II, pp. 944–81 (pp. 966, 976).

23 Peter Zumthor and Mari Lending, *A Feeling of History* (Zurich: Scheidegger & Spiess, 2018).

24 Alberto Ferlenga, *Le Strade di Pikionis* (Syracuse: Lettera Ventidue, 2014).

25 Alexander Tzonis and Liane Lefaivre, 'A Critical Introduction to Greek Architecture since the Second World War', in *Post-War Architecture in Greece, 1945–1983*, ed. by Orestis Doumanis (Athens: Architecture in Greece Press, 1984), pp. 16–23 (p. 23).

26 Kenneth Frampton, *Modern Architecture: A Critical History*, 2nd edn (London: Thames & Hudson, 1985), p. 7.

27 Tzonis and Lefaivre, 'A Critical Introduction to Greek Architecture since the Second World War', pp. 22–3.

28 Doumanis, 'Εισαγωγή στην ελληνική μεταπολεμική αρχιτεκτονική', p. 10; François Loyer, 'L'architecture de la Grèce contemporaine', unpublished doctoral thesis, Université de Paris, 1966, pp. 913, 1193; Fatouros, 'Greek Art and Architecture 1945–1967', p. 433; Antoniades, *Σύγχρονη ελληνική αρχιτεκτονική*, pp. 122–7.

29 Dimitris Philippidis, *Νεοελληνική αρχιτεκτονική: Αρχιτεκτονική θεωρία και πράξη (1830–1980) σαν αντανάκλαση των ιδεολογικών επιλογών της νεοελληνικής κουλτούρας* (Athens: Melissa, 1984), pp. 374, 376 (note 566).

30 Jean-Louis Cohen, 'The Mediterranean Brutalism of Dimitris and Suzana Antonakakis' (1994), in *Atelier 66: The Architecture of Dimitris and Suzana Antonakakis*, ed. by Panayotis Tournikiotis (Athens: futura, 2007), pp. 32–45; Kizis, 'Modern Greek Myths'.

31 For the international architects and critics, this was to be expected. They trusted the opinion of Tzonis as an insider in the Greek architectural field.

32 Suzana and Dimitris Antonakakis, interviewed by Stylianos Giamarelos (Athens: 23 June 2013).

33 Aris Konstantinidis, 'Schulmöbel für zurückgebliebene Kinder', *Moebel Interior Design*, 6 (1967), 72–4.

34 See, for example, Suzana Antonakaki, 'Ποίηση και λόγος: Γεωμετρία και ποιητικός λόγος. Όριο και κενό. Δεσμεύσεις και ελευθερία. Προσεγγίσεις στο αρχιτεκτονικό σύμπαν του Άρη Κωνσταντινίδη', in *Άρης Κωνσταντινίδης*, ed. by Vaiou, pp. 69–100.

35 Dimitris Antonakakis, Βιογραφικό Υπόμνημα, National Technical University of Athens School of Architecture, 1978, Suzana and Dimitris Antonakakis' private archive, pp. 7, 66–7.

36 Suzana Antonakaki, 'Αρχιτεκτονική: Επάγγελμα. Επαγγέλομαι — Υπόσχομαι', in *Ίχνη αρχιτεκτονικής διαδρομής: Σουζάνα Αντωνακάκη και Δημήτρης Αντωνακάκης*, ed. by Dimitris Polychronopoulos, 2 vols (Athens: futura, 2018), I, pp. 15–19 (pp. 17–18).

37 Suzana Antonakaki, 'Outdoor "Houses" and Indoor Streets', in *INDESEM '87: International Design Seminar*, ed. by Marc Labadie and Bert Tjhie (Delft: Delft University Press, 1988), pp. 132–49 (p. 132).

38 Suzana and Dimitris Antonakakis, 'Συνοπτική παρουσίαση μιας πορείας', 14-page typed and handwritten notes for the exhibition in Delft, November 1981, Suzana and Dimitris Antonakakis' private archive, pp. 2–3, 6.

39 Ibid., p. 14.

40 Dimitris Antonakakis, 'Πικιώνης / Κωνσταντινίδης: Ασύμπτωτοι', National Technical University of Athens School of Architecture Graduate Seminar Notes, 15 February 2000, Suzana and Dimitris Antonakakis' private archive.

41 Antonakakis, interviewed by Giamarelos.

42 Liane Lefaivre and Alexander Tzonis, 'The Grid and the Pathway: An Introduction to the Work of Dimitris and Suzana Antonakakis in the Context of Greek Architectural Culture', in *Atelier 66: The Architecture of Dimitris and Suzana Antonakakis*, ed. by Kenneth Frampton (New York: Rizzoli, 1985), pp. 14–25 (pp. 17–18).

43 Dimitris Antonakakis, interviewed by Stylianos Giamarelos (Athens: 4 September 2020); Aris Konstantinidis, Εμπειρίες και περιστατικά, II (1992), 200–6; Suzana Antonakaki, 'Στον Άρη Κωνσταντινίδη: Ένα γράμμα που δεν έστειλα', handwritten draft, Suzana and Dimitris Antonakakis' private archive.

44 Suzana and Dimitris Antonakakis, interviewed by Giamarelos.

45 Kenneth Frampton, 'Greek Regionalism and the Modern Project: A Collective Endeavour', in *Atelier 66*, ed. by Frampton, pp. 4–5 (p. 5).

46 My account of the inner life of Atelier 66 is based on a series of interviews that I conducted in 2014: Suzana and Dimitris Antonakakis, interviewed by Stylianos Giamarelos (Athens: 27 May 2014); Giorgos Antonakakis and Aleka Monemvasitou, interviewed by Stylianos Giamarelos (Athens: 12 June 2014); Aristide Antonas, interviewed by Stylianos Giamarelos (Athens: 2 July 2014); Boukie Babalou, interviewed by Stylianos Giamarelos (Athens: 30 May 2014); Konstantinos Daskalakis, interviewed by Stylianos Giamarelos (Athens: 26 June 2014); Theano Fotiou, interviewed by Stylianos Giamarelos (Athens: 25 June 2014); Eleni Goussi-Desylla, interviewed by Stylianos Giamarelos (Athens: 3 July 2014); Costis Hadjimichalis, interviewed by Stylianos Giamarelos (Athens: 3 July 2014); Antonis Noukakis, interviewed by Stylianos Giamarelos (Athens: 27 June 2014); Annie Platanioti, interviewed by Stylianos Giamarelos (Athens: 13 June 2014); and Dina Vaiou, interviewed by Stylianos Giamarelos (Athens: 19 June 2014).

47 Dimitris and Suzana Antonakakis, 'Introduction', in *Atelier 66*, ed. by Frampton, pp. 6–8 (p. 7).

48 This was noted first by Loyer as introducing a 'novel conception of the profession', and later by Antoniades. See Loyer, 'L'architecture de la Grèce contemporaine', p. 1194; Antoniades, Σύγχρονη ελληνική αρχιτεκτονική, pp. 119–20.

49 See Stavros Alifragkis and Emilia Athanassiou, 'Educating Greece in Modernity: Post-War Tourism and Western Politics', *Journal of Architecture*, 23.4 (2018), 595–616.

50 Law 395/1968 allowed the extension of existing or future buildings by one floor. Permissible heights, plot coverage and building volume were practically increased by 30 per cent.

51 These were documented in the architectural-competition pages of the annual review *Architecture in Greece* from 1967 to 1974.

52 This informal group of craftspeople included Charalambos Tzanakakis (furniture), Yannis Tsalapatis (ironwork), Michalis Patelaros (carpentry), Stelios Kostoulakis (concrete), Stavros Panou (wall decorator), Stelios Lasithiotakis (fireplaces) and Yannis Nikoloudakis (wall plasterer). Suzana and Dimitris Antonakakis had also designed extensions and other architectural interventions to some of these individuals' houses.

53 Annie Platanioti, who worked mostly with Suzana Antonakaki and stayed in the office for approximately twenty-five years, was the only exception to this rule.

54 See Boukie Babalou-Noukaki, *8+1 κείμενα για την αρχιτεκτονική και την πόλη*, ed. by Michalis Paparounis (Athens: Doma, 2020). In 1977, Costis Hadjimichalis bought a copy of *De l'ambiguité en Architecture* (Paris: Dunod, 1976), the French translation of Robert Venturi's *Complexity and Contradiction in Architecture* (1966), as a gift for Suzana Antonakaki.

55 See Nikolaos Magouliotis, 'Learning from "Panosikoma": Atelier 66's Additions to Ordinary Houses', *Architectural Histories*, 6.1 (2018), art. 21. doi.org/10.5334/ah.299.

56 Dimitris Antonakakis, Υπόμνημα, National Technical University of Athens School of Architecture, 1988, Suzana and Dimitris Antonakakis' private archive, p. 31.

57 Suzana and Dimitris Antonakakis, 2-page letter to Silvia Kolbowski at Rizzoli, 30 March 1985, Suzana and Dimitris Antonakakis' private archive, p. 2.

58 Theodore Sioutis, 'Ο δάσκαλος, Δημήτρης Αντωνακάκης', unpublished undergraduate essay, National Technical University of Athens, 2017, p. 16 (note 6).

59 Aris Stylianou, 'Το Εργαστήρι-66', *Αρχιτέκτων: Ενημερωτικό Δελτίο Συλλόγου Αρχιτεκτόνων Κύπρου*, 10 (1990), 62–9 (pp. 64, 66).

60 Dimitris Antonakakis, 'Αρχιτεκτονική εκπαίδευση και πράξη: Μία αμφίδρομη εκπαιδευτική διαδικασία', in *Τάσος Μπίρης – Δημήτρης Μπίρης: Το αμφίδρομο πέρασμα ανάμεσα στην αρχιτεκτονική και τη διδασκαλία*, ed. by Lena Kalaitzi (Athens: Papasotiriou/Benaki Museum, 2011), pp. 13–19 (pp. 16–17).

61 To cite just one example, see Ricardo Agarez, *Algarve Building: Modernism, Regionalism and Architecture in the South of Portugal, 1925–1965* (New York: Routledge, 2016).

8
Cross-cultural genealogy

In 1981, Alexander Tzonis and Liane Lefaivre traced a local genealogy that combined Aris Konstantinidis's 'rationalist grids' with Dimitris Pikionis's 'topographically sensitive pathways' to inform the work of Suzana and Dimitris Antonakakis. As I discussed in the previous chapter, this account still holds architectural historians' imaginations captive in an inward-looking discussion. While Tzonis and Lefaivre's article did mention the Miesian influence on the Antonakakis through the teaching of A. James Speyer at the National Technical University of Athens in the late 1950s, it took them only one sentence to transform Ludwig Mies van der Rohe to Aris Konstantinidis, and follow their own interpretative intentions.[1] As such, the historically accurate information included in the article was effectively clouded by the force of the main argument, which focused on the regional context. For four decades, the impact of 'The Grid and the Pathway' centred the discussion on the possible influence of the two older Greek regionalist architects in the work of the Antonakakis. But this inward-looking genealogy of Pikionis and Konstantinidis not only distorts the actual formation of the Antonakakis' architectural outlook; it also obstructs the crucial cross-cultural aspects of critical regionalism as an architectural approach that consistently rests on the combination of ideas and practices that transgress national borders. Returning to the formative years of Suzana and Dimitris Antonakakis at the School of Architecture of the National Technical University of Athens in the late 1950s, this chapter recovers the cross-cultural genealogy that historically sustained their critical regionalism.

On various occasions, the couple mentioned other architects and mentors that they consider influential for their work.[2] At the same time, architectural historians focused on formal affinities between their work and that of an ever-expanding group of architects (including Le Corbusier, Adolf Loos, Alvar Aalto, Mies, Pikionis, Konstantinidis, Aldo van Eyck and

Team 10) whilst neglecting the actual biographical details of the architects' formative years. In this chapter, I attempt to redress this imbalance. Based on original interviews with the architects and unpublished archival material, I draw out the elements that conditioned their modern understanding of regional traditions, as this in turn underpins the significance of their work in the critical regionalist framework. In addition to Pikionis's teaching, the factors conducive to their architectural formation lay in their lessons in architectural theory from Panayotis Michelis, the drawing and painting classes of Nikos Hadjikyriakos-Ghika ('Ghika') and the systematic but open-ended modernist teaching of Mies's disciple A. James Speyer. It was these cosmopolitan mentors that enabled the Antonakakis to rethink the local architectural tradition in modern terms. The poet and painter Nikos Engonopoulos (1903–1985) also introduced the architects to the nuances of the world of colour. Suzana Antonakaki was especially influenced by his drawing classes, while Dimitris Antonakakis appreciated his poetry.

Suzana and Dimitris Antonakakis' introductory text to Frampton's monograph celebrated their opening up to the international scene in the mid-1980s. By 1985, the two Greek architects clearly wrote as representatives of critical regionalism, as they focused on the interplay of international and local features in their work. Looking back on their student years, they discerned two related trends in their architectural education: the international direction that 'assumed the general Western problematic of the period' through the teaching of Michelis, Dimitris Fatouros and Speyer; and the regional direction that 'maintained a creative liaison with contemporary trends, but was primarily interested in uncovering the essence of Greek cultural heritage' (Pikionis and Konstantinidis). As such, the Antonakakis remained 'aware of inter-national practice'; but that was not enough. They believed that this international practice 'must be adapted to the particularities of [their] country, to [be] enrich[ed] with what George Seferis calls "humanisation," when he refers to corresponding tendencies in Greek literature'.[3] The evocation of Seferis and Pikionis was not coincidental. These two major Greek figures were regarded as members of the modernist Generation of the 1930s who acted as a role model for the architects' own generation. Seferis (1900–1971) was the first Greek poet to win the Nobel Prize in Literature, in 1963. His acceptance speech was characteristically devoted to the centuries-long 'struggle for Greek expression' in 'a living language' representative of 'the continuity of our tradition as well as of the need for a critical spirit'. Thinking that 'tradition holds us by the ability to break habits, and thus proves its vitality', Seferis understood Greece as 'a crossroads' that 'has never been closed to foreign currents, especially in its best moments'.[4] Seferis's 'humanisation', a word that had also been employed by Tzonis and Lefaivre to relate critical regionalism with Lewis Mumford, enabled the Antonakakis to discuss critical regionalism in their own terms. However, the architectural couple were also clearly under the grip of the 'grid and pathway' interpretation of their work at that time. This was evident in their reference to the work of Konstantinidis alongside that of Pikionis. But their evocation of their student years is more significant here, as it highlights their importance for the formation of the two architects' outlook.[5]

In one of my interviews with the couple, Dimitris Antonakakis opined that, in the late 1950s, the School lacked a consistent architectural vision of its own.[6] The curriculum of their studies was Corbusian. Design studios followed the thematic manifestos of the Ville Radieuse, focusing on the design of a series of apartment buildings, schools and universities, transport hubs and cultural centres.[7] The critical texts and international publications that they studied at the time were limited. The texts published in Greek periodicals of the late 1950s (Ζυγός and Αρχιτεκτονική) rarely associated the local architectural field with Western developments of modern architecture, as was the norm for other arts and their related publications.[8] The Antonakakis understood that their tutors attempted to follow the trends of the period without assimilating them in an original discourse of their own.[9] In other words, they were passively reacting to external stimuli rather than proactively developing a distinct, positive contribution to contemporary architectural debates. The exceptions to this rule were cosmopolitan mentors such as Pikionis, Hadjikyriakos-Ghika and Michelis.

Pikionis's grid under the pathway

In the short memorandum for his professorial candidacy at the School of Architecture in 1978, Dimitris Antonakakis referred to his lessons from Pikionis and Speyer as the defining moments of his formative years.[10] Pikionis had already emerged as the most significant figure in François Loyer's 1966 history of the turbulent establishment of modernism in Greece. The stochastic approach of Pikionis's teaching offered a dispassionate account of the major cultural, social and political 'querelles' of the interwar and early postwar years. Loyer situated these debates in the additional context of the Kitsikis/Pikionis divide that lay at the heart of the School in the early 1950s. Schematically, this divide revolved around the artistic understanding of the architect as a poet by Pikionis and the market-oriented, commercial conception of the profession by Kostas Kitsikis (1893–1969).[11] Suzana and Dimitris Antonakakis sided with Pikionis in pursuing a poetic approach to architecture against its commodification. Far from being understood as a romantic remnant of a bygone era, as suggested by Doumanis in 1964, Pikionis's wisdom proved inspiring for the younger generations of Greek modernists in diverse ways.[12]

Tzonis and Lefaivre were therefore right to stress the significance of Pikionis's work, and especially his landscaping project around the Acropolis in Athens, for Suzana and Dimitris Antonakakis. The couple cherished their memories from the last years of Pikionis's teaching at the School in the late 1950s. When their old mentor guided his students on a site visit in 1958, Suzana Antonakaki witnessed the poetic world that an architect could build. She understood how this can be done through 'selected viewpoints, crucial spots in the trajectory, ... visual radii, peripheries of circles, ... proportions ... the golden section'.[13] Pikionis showed her how the poetic qualities of her work could be enhanced through harmonic geometric relations. As a student, Dimitris Antonakakis had additionally worked at the project's construction site. He therefore retained a living memory of the 'topographically sensitive' ways in which his mentor organised 'the pathway' that became central in Tzonis and Lefaivre's account. The space around the Acropolis is structured as 'a succession of "critical" points where extended views are possible'. The overall design is based on 'the particularities of each of the locations ... combined with [Pikionis's] geometrical ordering preference'.[14] This ordering preference in turn rested on Constantinos A. Doxiadis's 1937 theory of viewing segments, which posited that the spatial arrangement of buildings in the complexes of ancient Greece followed a plan that centred on the movement of a visitor observing the sites.[15] This spatial arrangement was geometrically determined in relation to a series of crucial fixed points. These were the vantage points for observing the entirety of the complex as a harmonious whole. The total visual field was divided by optical radii (in angles of 30° or 36°) and exact distances (of 100, 150 or 200 feet), which determined the spatial distribution and their placement from one vantage point to the next (Fig. 8.1). In short, this geometric process organised space as a series of vistas that incorporated buildings and their surrounding landscape.[16]

Following Doxiadis, Pikionis used similar circular segments to configure his landscaping project. These segments are 'gridded up' in golden-section divisions (3:5 and 8:13) and the points of their intersection

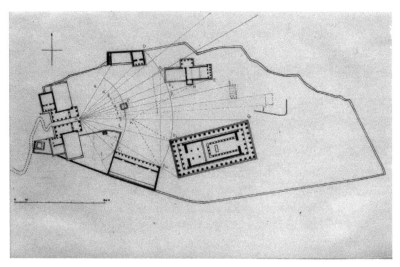

Figure 8.1 Constantinos A. Doxiadis, plan drawing of the Athenian Acropolis and its optical symmetry according to his theory of viewing segments, in Constantinos A. Doxiadis, 'Die Raumgestaltung im griechischen Städtebau', doctoral thesis, Berlin Charlottenburg Technical University, 1936, Fig. 10, Ref. Code 18552

are denoted by the placement of significant objects, ranging from trees to fragments of antique structures (Fig. 8.2). Dimitris Antonakakis therefore concludes that 'the entire route is derived from a series of overlaid grids offering the various possibilities and combinations eventually selected on the spot by Pikionis himself'.[17] In other words, Pikionis's 'pathway' is also underpinned by the 'grid'. Even if 'this type of grid on the ground was a totally different class of grid [to that] being used at the time', both the grid and the pathway can be found in Pikionis. It is only because 'Pikionis never talked about the grid' that Konstantinidis has to play a part in Tzonis and Lefaivre's interpretation of the Antonakakis' work.[18] In his few publications, Pikionis rarely referred to the underlying geometric stratum of his design thinking based on golden-section relations (1:1, 1:φ, 1: $\sqrt{\varphi}$, 1: $\sqrt{2}$) as an underlying organising principle of his work.[19] But one just has to scratch the 'decorative' surface of Pikionis's architecture to see it defined as an art of precise proportions (Fig. 8.3). As Dimitris Antonakakis asserted when interviewed by Maria Dolka in 2002, in their early work Suzana and he 'used the geometrical proportions of the rectangle with the proportions of the numbers to the square root of 3, 5 and of φ. This work with these proportions was a requirement of Pikionis's courses'.[20]

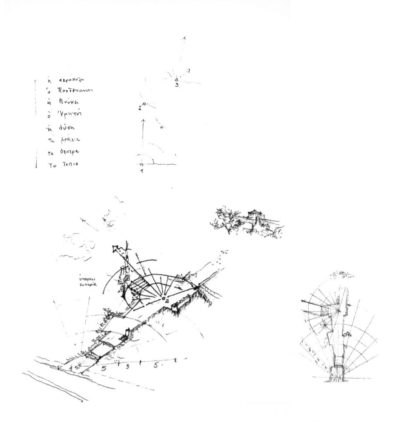

Figure 8.2 Dimitris Antonakakis, sketches outlining the geometric relations that underpin Dimitris Pikionis's Acropolis 'pathway' project, in Dimitris Antonakakis, 'Landscaping the Athens Acropolis', in *Mega XI, Dimitris Pikionis, Architect 1887–1968: A Sentimental Topography*, ed. by Dennis Crompton (London: Architectural Association, 1989), p. 90

Suzana and Dimitris Antonakakis' private archive

Pikionis's recourse to harmonic proportions connects his teaching with prevailing modernist strands in art and architecture at the time. But his intention of addressing the passing of time with architectural means enabled his work to transgress standardised modernist tenets. His remark that there was 'no need to worry about [a specific design element], as it will eventually contract' with the others around it stayed with Dimitris Antonakakis. Pikionis here used the Greek word *syneresis* (literally, the contraction of two vowels into a single vowel or diphthong) to imply that any human artefact will eventually fuse with nature, the ultimate

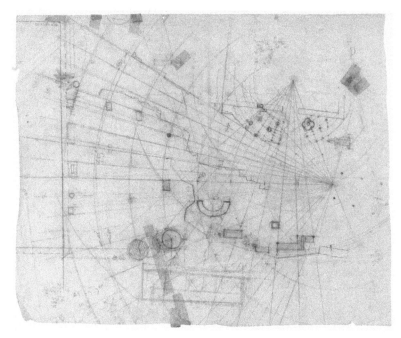

Figure 8.3 Dimitris Pikionis, gridded viewing segments underpinning his design of the pathway around the Acropolis, Athens, 1954–7

© 2021 Modern Greek Architecture Archives of the Benaki Museum, ANA_67_55_37

receiving end of architecture. Acknowledging the passing of time, he intended to work with the patina of decay. But this opened the door to the modernist criticism of his work as a fabrication of 'contemporary ruins' around the Acropolis.[21] For similar reasons of 'eventual contraction' over time, Pikionis allowed a creative space to accommodate the spontaneous, proactive contribution of his craftspeople within his overarching scheme. To do so, he adopted 'the attitude of the craftsman … always explain[ing] what he wanted to do and not how'.[22] He only acted correctively when necessary. In the Acropolis project, 'he would search for the principles by which he could incorporate the mistake into a system of exceptions, thus activating the predetermined geometry'.[23] This way of working through a transgression of rules that in turn emphasised their presence stayed with Suzana and Dimitris Antonakakis, who adopted it as a practice of organising their aspired non-hierarchical design process of Atelier 66 – as discussed in the previous chapter. Like Pikionis's circular gridded segments, the grids that the two Antonakakis agreed to use with the other architects in large-scale projects enabled them to elaborate or control their transgression in the smaller architectural scales of design. This is what their son Aristide Antonas memorably described as the Antonakakis' 'error and rectification' approach, which in turn harks back to Pikionis's earlier 'elaboration and improvisation' around the Acropolis.[24] In addition, Suzana Antonakaki perceptively noted Pikionis's claim that it is where 'the feeling of folk tradition comes into a creative contrast with the contemporary living conditions that novel, genuine, popular forms are born'.[25] Ranging from modernism to folk culture and the regional vernacular structures of anonymous builders and craftspeople, Pikionis's teaching offered Suzana and Dimitris Antonakakis a way in which to integrate multiple traditions into their work.

In my first interview with the architects, Dimitris Antonakakis highlighted the 'notable consistency' of Pikionis's teaching – including 'the defiance of modernism, without being postmodern'.[26] Despite its idiosyncratic appearance, Antonakakis claimed, Pikionis's work had not essentially strayed away from modernism. Because his architecture 'could not be tagged by convenient labels',[27] Suzana and Dimitris Antonakakis never failed to attend or actively participate in and contribute to any public event that intended to save Pikionis's memory from the circle of conservative traditionalists who claimed to act in his name. For the same reason, they set out to defend the work of their mentor from the unfair modernist criticism levelled at him from 1964 onwards. To do so, Dimitris Antonakakis returned to Pikionis's famous declaration of his 'rejection' of the modern movement: 'The Lycabettus School was built in 1933, but as soon as it was completed, I found it did not satisfy me. It occurred to me then that the universal spirit had to be coupled with the spirit of nationhood'.[28] Signalling this turn in his work, his design for the Experimental School in Thessaloniki (1935) mixed modernist principles of spatial configuration with pitched roofs and other formal elements from the vernacular architecture of northern Greece (Figs 8.4 and 8.5). But Antonakakis's reading of Pikionis's 'rejection' statement stressed his old mentor's dissatisfaction with the outcome of a specific project (underlining the 'as soon as it was completed' caveat) and not with the modern movement in general.[29] This has probably less to do with Pikionis's own stance[30] than with the Antonakakis' own self-understanding. Because they understand and present themselves as aporetic, critical modernists, they also want their mentor fighting alongside them in the same camp. When Suzana Antonakaki discussed Pikionis's school on Mount Lycabettus, for instance, she also did so in the critical regionalist terms that had by then been identified with their own work. As such, she extolled Pikionis's intention to 'revise the *type* [of

Figure 8.4 Dimitris Pikionis, School at Pefkakia, Lycabettus, Athens, 1933

© 2021 Modern Greek Architecture Archives of the Benaki Museum, ANA_67_13_22

the building] through its adaptation to the *place* in the wide sense of the term' (emphasis in the original). She portrayed the school as 'a living organism that touches tenderly upon the earth, interprets the mountain and the trees with architectural means, elaborates the movement and completes the landscape'.[31]

Pikionis's contribution to the formation of Suzana and Dimitris Antonakakis' architectural outlook has historically been so significant that the couple can certainly be regarded as his greatest disciples. But it was the additional modernist teachings of their other mentors that conditioned the way in which the two architects developed these insights in their practice.

Regional modernist teachings

Pikionis's reference to harmonic proportions enabled the Antonakakis to associate his teaching with that of their other modernist mentors such as Ghika. Like the 'old sage' Pikionis, Ghika formed part of the revered Generation of the 1930s: a renowned circle of writers, poets and artists who had been the first to attempt to reconcile modernism with regional traditions in order to foreground a cosmopolitan 'Greekness'. To do so, they revisited Greek mythology, the landscape of the Aegean and folk

Figure 8.5 Dimitris Pikionis, Experimental School in Thessaloniki, 1935

© 2021 Modern Greek Architecture Archives of the Benaki Museum, ANA_67_14_176

culture in an attempt to reinforce their ties with existing strands of European modernism.[32] While Pikionis's ambivalent relationship with the modern movement in architecture could not be unanimously appreciated in this context, Ghika's involvement in the organisation of the Fourth International Congress of Modern Architecture (CIAM) in Greece in 1933 left no shadow of a doubt about his artistic leanings (Fig. 8.6). For this reason, he was a living modernist legend in the eyes of young students of the late 1950s.

Ghika's drawing classes delved deep into the use of harmonic proportions in modern art. They started from an analysis of the key elements in a drawing. Ghika then showed how these elements found their place in a specific system of proportions (based on the diagonals of a rectangle and their perpendiculars) and harmonic relations (especially √5 and the golden section, among others). Ghika claimed that these relationships could be extrapolated from works of art of diverse origins. In his inaugural professorial lecture of 1942, he had characteristically concluded that these 'laws' of proportions, axes, framing, balance and symmetry essentially 'condition all the arts, including music, dance, and

Figure 8.6 Nikos Hadjikyriakos-Ghika, *Port at Sunset*, 1957–60, oil on canvas, 66 × 93 cm, Benaki Museum / Ghika Gallery, Athens

poetry. It is these laws of harmony that are occasionally called music or architecture'.[33] To illustrate his theory in class, he selected examples from modern European and traditional Japanese art, claiming that the universal occurrence of the same 'laws' validated their inner 'truth'.[34] Ghika asked his fourth-year students to prove his theory for themselves by uncovering the same underlying proportions in Japanese artworks. He also claimed that the artist's sensibility works towards these relations in an intuitive, unconscious way.[35] This reinforced his argument about the universal validity of the same harmonic proportions. It also implied that the best examples of traditional architecture may well adhere to the same rules.

Ghika's modernist teaching was complemented by that of Michelis, the most internationally accomplished academic of the Athens School of Architecture in the late 1950s.[36] Michelis actively collaborated with an international network of architects, artists and philosophers working in the broader field of aesthetics.[37] His long-standing theoretical work from the late 1930s onwards and his attempt to establish a solid institutional ground for the study of aesthetics in Greece afforded their gravitas to his teaching.[38] Suzana Antonakaki was especially inspired by his work on Byzantine art and architecture.[39] His teaching explored the effect of 'infinite space' in Byzantine churches. Considering their plan and section drawings, Michelis highlighted the successive 'thresholds' within these churches. Filtered by light, both horizontally and vertically, these 'thresholds' implicated an intended move of the soul towards the divine 'infinity' of the sky. Michelis's understanding of the *non finito* as that which constantly opens up to something else also stayed with Suzana Antonakaki. Drawing from these precedents, her later studies of traditional architecture focused on these qualities. In her architecture, she was especially interested in ways of opening the interior to successive permeations from its surroundings.

But Michelis's teaching was not limited to Byzantine architecture. His lectures on reinforced concrete were also memorable for his young students. Starting from technical details, Michelis praised the distinct aesthetic and architectural qualities of this novel building material.[40] In so doing, he also revealed his interest in modern architecture. Originally trained as an engineer, Michelis attempted to convey an overall sense of structural logic and static behaviours of different materials as these could be perceived in the everyday-life experiences of his students, from the way in which tucks and pleats structurally reinforced women's light clothes to architecture.[41]

As such, Michelis's comprehensive theoretical approach addressed modernism and tradition in equal measure.[42] Led by his conviction that architects should also meet academic standards when expressing their thoughts in writing, Michelis initiated the student thesis course in the early 1950s.[43] For Dimitris Antonakakis, this course highlighted the significance of analysing architecture in typological terms.[44] This is more evident in Suzana Antonakaki's thesis of 1959. To present the conclusions from her study of the architecture of Makrinitsa, she devised a typological matrix. Her analysis of houses extended from plan to section, and from the interior to the courtyard (Fig. 8.7). This multifaceted three-dimensional approach made her work stand out as distinctly architectural at the time. Similar outputs by scholars of folk studies, such as those of Georgios Megas (1893–1976), were solely based on plan drawings. As such, the crucial third spatial dimension was missing from these typological surveys of 'the Greek house'.[45] Suzana Antonakaki was also especially attentive to architectural details at various scales – ranging from general layouts to staircases, and from the emerging relationships between the different levels of a house to the interior skylights that lit a space when its windows had to remain shut.[46] In the final instance, Michelis's teaching offered the two Antonakakis a way in which to understand traditional architecture through a modern lens.

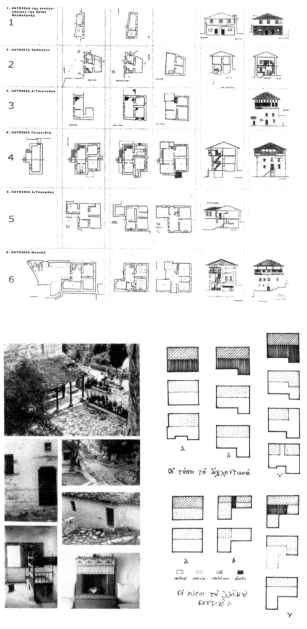

Figure 8.7 Suzana Antonakaki, typological matrix of traditional architecture in Makrinitsa, Greece, thesis at the National Technical University of Athens supervised by Panayotis Michelis, 1959

Suzana and Dimitris Antonakakis' private archive

A year earlier, in his thesis on the island of Hydra, Dimitris Antonakakis had specifically focused on the relationship of the private houses to their immediate public space. For him, this was crucial for understanding the urban layout of a traditional settlement:

> ... the street and the house are inseparably tied together through a courtyard or a terrace that both isolates the house from the street in terms of circulation and acts as a vestibule. In terms of spatial perception, it is the semitone between the house and the street, and in terms of form it blends with the street and the volumes of the houses in such a way that it moves freely, creating alcoves and overhangs, while its paddock remains free and independent from any standardisation. The courtyard is an extension of the street in the house and a cordial opening of the house to the street.[47]

It was the intended association of the public with the private realm that gave rise to such elaborate architectural details. These ranged from decorated doorways that acted as the public faces of inviting houses and their courtyards to landings that mediated the transition from the street to a courtyard (which in turn served as a vestibule).[48] Discussing the most important public spaces of the settlement, Antonakakis also observed the 'automatically created' landings when a street bifurcates, and the '[s]tairs that belong to the street and [the] stairs that belong to the houses ... often built together ... to such an extent that one is led to believe they were made to highlight the house'.[49]

Studying in Greece in the late 1950s, Suzana and Dimitris Antonakakis belonged to an architectural generation that aspired to update their role models' cultural contribution, in pursuit of a modern Greekness. They aimed to combine their lessons from the native tradition with the tenets of international modernism for the Greek world that emerged traumatised from the Second World War and the ensuing civil war (1946–9). This pursuit was intended to bring architects back to focus on the 'real needs' of the region. As such, it was less cosmopolitan than the approach of the previous Generation of the 1930s, who had tried to open 'Greekness' out to the world. The Antonakakis and the generation of the 1960s followed the opposite direction of emphasising their return from the rest of the world back to the specific region that formed the ground of their architectural practice. They explored modernism as a means of returning to the region, not vice versa. Michelis's teaching helped them to do this systematically, with his established methodology of typological analysis. In their individual studies of Greek island settlements, Suzana and Dimitris Antonakakis combined Michelis's lens with Ghika's thesis on the 'unconscious' prevalence of harmonic proportions in human artefacts.

Corbu and Mies in Greece

Through their surveys of traditional settlements in their travels across Greece, the young architects tried to extrapolate the proportions of popular wisdom prevalent in vernacular architecture. But more specifically, through these studies of Cycladic buildings and artefacts, they aspired to confirm Le Corbusier's Modulor.[50] Finding that the height of a pew in St Constantinos Chapel on Paros conformed to the Modulor was a cause for celebration. Le Corbusier had devised the Modulor as a single system of proportions that could cover both practical and aesthetic aspects of modern design. It aimed to address a tripartite challenge of defining: (a) harmonious design relations, (b) directly associated with the human body, with the capacity to (c) meet the coordinating dimensioning demands of standardised industrial production. The resulting system was meant to serve as an ideal toolbox for a new generation of modern designers. Cycladic settlements, on the other hand, were built by anonymous workers whose main concern was to fulfil their immediate practical needs. Uncovering harmonic relationships behind their manual work would therefore mean that both Ghika and Le Corbusier were right. The vernacular tradition of Greece would then be demonstrably connected with the major tenets of modernism. And this would in turn legitimise the 'unconscious' wisdom of the regional builder as a source for enriching modern architecture. Greek architectural discourse of the same period encouraged this association. Fatouros's account of the 'quite natural' influence of Le Corbusier on the Greek field, 'since at some points it coincides with certain of the traditional features of anonymous architecture', is rather telling in this context.[51]

Corbusian tenets remained deeply ingrained in Suzana and Dimitris Antonakakis' architectural approach. In the 107 newspaper articles that she wrote for her monthly column on architecture from 1998 to 2009, Suzana Antonakaki referred to Le Corbusier's work and ideas more frequently than those of anybody else. More recently, in 2016, Dimitris Antonakakis was also critical of the current generation of young Greek architects who seemed intent to 'bury' him rather too quickly.[52] The couple appreciated the Modulor as a method of organising design and maintaining architectural qualities in direct association with the human body. As Suzana Antonakaki characteristically wrote, agreeing word for word with the modernist master:

> In his book *Le Modulor* [Le Corbusier] methodically researches the proportions of the human body, its relation with movement and rest in space, to propose a design tool that will refer to geometric analogies and harmonic proportions ... The conjunction of technique with consciousness, and of exactitude with poetry, characterises the whole of Le Corbusier's textual and architectural production ... The return to archetypes characterises his life, work and death.[53]

Through their studies of the traditional built environment, Suzana and Dimitris Antonakakis similarly pursued archetypes of dwelling in Greece. These archetypes were in turn expected to lead to a poetic architectural expression of their modern times. The fact that many of Suzana Antonakaki's references to Le Corbusier are followed by, and associated with, similar ideas from Pikionis is not coincidental.[54] For the Antonakakis, the questions of modernism and tradition are intertwined. Although 'The Grid and the Pathway' offers a historically misleading account of the Antonakakis' main influences, the major intuition of Tzonis and Lefaivre is accurate. Through their work, the Antonakakis do attempt to associate Pikionis's poetic teaching with modernist tenets.

This is why Speyer's appreciation of the Potamianos House in Filothei (1953–5), the project that Doumanis had mentioned to launch his modernist critique of Pikionis's work in 1964 (Fig. 8.8), was especially

Figure 8.8 Dimitris Pikionis, Potamianos House in Filothei, Athens, 1953–5

significant for the young architectural couple.[55] Coming from a former student of Mies van der Rohe, it confirmed that Pikionis's inspiring teaching was not incompatible with a modernist outlook. Such affinities enabled Suzana and Dimitris Antonakakis to relate Speyer's open approach to modernism with their lessons from other mentors.

Speyer was the only visiting professor in the School at the end of the 1950s (1957–60).[56] In hindsight, he summarised his teaching in Athens as offering students 'some sort of fundamental approach to architecture … show[ing] them what principles meant'. However, he struggled in his task:

> I think it was their first exposure to Miesian architecture. I think they had a superficial knowledge of the International School. They certainly had a superficial idea of Corbusier's architecture … Their understanding of the International Style was as superficial as their understanding of anything else … The architectural school was really of a very low order. It was the flimsiest kind of superficial formalism. They had no idea how to build; they had no idea of the relationship of structure to formal expression.[57]

For students like Suzana and Dimitris Antonakakis – who were attracted by erudite, cosmopolitan professors – his international outlook felt like a breath of fresh air in a rather introverted school. His enduring influence on the young Greek architects cannot be overstated. Speyer offered his Greek students an effective way of organising their diverse, and occasionally divergent, influences into a coherent body of thinking and a systematic method of designing. His unequivocal admiration for the work of Mies, 'the greatest living architect', coupled with his intention to move it further forward was attuned with the Antonakakis' own concerns to do the same with modernism. They were not interested in a static replication of their lessons from the great 'masters' in Greece.[58]

Supervised by Speyer, Suzana Antonakaki's final-year project at the School of Architecture (1959) documents his teaching method. This was based on exploring alternative approaches to the same brief. The method implied that there are no single correct solutions to inherently multifarious architectural problems. Speyer encouraged his students to account for their design decisions with arguments, sketches, and 'working models … for five or six alternative propositions' for the same brief before finalising their design (Figs 8.9 and 8.10). His method enabled Suzana Antonakaki to keep 'a critical distance from [her] own work'. This in turn meant accepting 'the "stochastic adaptations" – that so often arise from real conditions and specificities – with sobriety'. This 'exercise' was valuable

Figure 8.9 Suzana Antonakaki, School of Fine Arts Workshop on Skyros, Greece, final-year project at the National Technical University of Athens supervised by A. James Speyer, photographs of working model, 1959

Suzana and Dimitris Antonakakis' private archive

for the architects' subsequent work. Speyer's method stayed with the couple as a stable point of reference, discipline and control of their design and thinking. In the final instance, Speyer provided them with 'this disciplined decision that allows [them] to control what [they] do'.[59]

It is owing to Speyer's teaching that the Antonakakis used the grid as the main organising mechanism of their design process in Atelier 66. Mies's disciple helped them to understand it not as a rigid straitjacket but

Figure 8.10 Suzana Antonakaki, School of Fine Arts Workshop on Skyros, Greece, final-year project at the National Technical University of Athens supervised by A. James Speyer, main elevations and interior-courtyard perspective drawing, 1959

Suzana and Dimitris Antonakakis' private archive

as an open-ended design principle. As such, the grid could be constantly affirmed and occasionally subverted. This also facilitated the Antonakakis' incorporation of the 'controlled transgression of given rules', originating from their lessons from Pikionis, into their non-hierarchical structure of collective design with their peers in Atelier 66.[60]

Speyer developed a reciprocal learning relationship with his students (Fig. 8.11). Field trips with them to vernacular Greek settlements were so stimulating for him that he also guided Mies in a short tour across Greece in 1959.[61] In addition, Speyer was intrigued by Michelis's strong

Figure 8.11 Scenes from Suzana and Dimitris Antonakakis' student years at the National Technical University of Athens, 1956–60

Suzana and Dimitris Antonakakis' private archive

interest in Byzantine architecture.[62] Spending three years in the country, the US architect cultivated his own appreciation for Byzantine art – which found its place, alongside Miesian furniture, in his personal architectural spaces when he returned to the USA. His own houses on Hydra further document this reciprocity. In the eyes of Suzana and Dimitris Antonakakis, these dwellings served as additional proof that modernism could be combined with Greek tradition. If this could be done by a 'standard-bearer of modernism' such as Speyer,[63] then Pikionis's resorting to tradition could also be counted as a move within the modernist camp. In his own reading of Speyer's houses on Hydra, Dimitris Antonakakis did exactly that; he interpreted them in Pikionis's terms. His descriptions of a 'foundation [transforming] into a bench, a staircase into rows of seats, a flat roof into a garden, … a window with iron work and shutters [into] a bench open to the view' echo Pikionis's transformative use of found objects in the Acropolis project.[64] Besides, modernism and tradition could both speak the same language of 'plainness and austerity'. They were therefore reconcilable, and not in opposition. The key seemed to lie in practising architecture 'without dogmatising the principles of the modern movement' and 'standing free before' the trends of their time like Pikionis had done before them.[65]

Cross-cultural regionalism

The diverse lessons from their student years conditioned Suzana and Dimitris Antonakakis' personal understanding of tradition. However, their relationship with it was complicated. It took Dimitris Antonakakis approximately three decades of professional practice to be able to clarify what tradition meant for him. In 1989, he asserted that it was:

> ... the living quotidian reality of what we build today. This will in turn constitute the tradition of tomorrow; this quotidian reality, with its ruptures, conflicts ... continuities and discontinuities ... that usually express the presence of novel forces who challenge the existing equilibrium.
>
> The struggles of these novel forces that push things forward with their stance and their resistance to the status quo, constitute a tradition we must reclaim, document, expand and enrich, proving its necessity ... I believe that Tradition is a dynamic phenomenon that evolves concurrently with [social] life itself. And it evolves when the inventions of one are validated, adopted and developed by the others ... Hence, tradition should be subjugated by every one of us. It constitutes a challenge to redefine ourselves in the context of a Greek reality we attempt to assimilate. Assimilating the social reality of today through its actual history might eventually enable us to express and transgress it, i.e. carry its tradition forward ... I obviously do not wish to 'reanimate the conditions' of the everyday life of those who built those [traditional] settlements. Neither do I wish to idealise the social relations of the groups that developed within them.[66]

This approach was clearly removed from parochial nostalgia and ossified historicisms. Like Seferis, the Antonakakis understood tradition in terms of the actual everyday life of modern Greeks; it served as an open question for the present that moves towards an uncertain future. Tzonis and Lefaivre were right to note that the work of the Antonakakis moves away from escapist understandings of tradition.[67] It is their insistence on the living and evolving aspect of tradition as an actual part of modern life that makes the crucial difference here. Their apartment building at 118 Benaki Street exemplifies the way in which these beliefs could become integral parts of modern architectural practice, as I discuss in the next chapter.

In the work of Suzana and Dimitris Antonakakis, modernism became a critical tool with which to study regional traditions. This is how the two architects kept their clear distance from the conservative traditionalists of the period. But, despite their admiration for the work of the modernist 'masters', they were also critical of the placeless architecture of Mies and Le Corbusier.[68] In the Antonakakis' work, regional culture also serves to critique modernism. The architects' inquiry moves both ways: modernism is utilised to critique regional culture, and local culture provides a critical view of modernism. As such, the questions of modernism and tradition are intertwined. It is this specific regional aspect of their work that enables the Greek architects to address the prolonged impasse of modern architecture. For Suzana and Dimitris Antonakakis, the study of tradition is meant to confirm the connection of the international (critical) modernist orientation of their work with the Greek (regional) vernacular. This dual, conciliatory relationship of the local with the international aspect affords their work the qualities that sustained the critical regionalist discourses. For the Antonakakis, the question of regional tradition becomes a question of continuity. They pursued the ways in which architectural lessons from the past and bold visions for the future can be appropriately reconciled and responsibly adjusted to the needs of a changing world. Owing to the nuanced genealogy of their architectural formation, their critical regionalism is therefore primarily cross-cultural. And this cross-cultural genealogy is aligned both with the original, programmatic aims and principles of critical regionalism and with the two architects' historical formation. On the other hand, as their architectural outlook was crucially shaped during their formative years at the School this genealogy is also further proof that, in the final analysis, critical regionalism represents the 1980s return of the 1960s in global architectural culture.

Notes

1   Alexander Tzonis and Liane Lefaivre, 'The Grid and the Pathway: An Introduction to the Work of Dimitris and Suzana Antonakakis, with Prolegomena to a History of the Culture of Modern Greek Architecture', *Architecture in Greece*, 15 (1981), 164–78 (p. 166).
2   See Suzana and Dimitris Antonakakis, 'Acknowledgements', in *Atelier 66: The Architecture of Dimitris and Suzana Antonakakis*, ed. by Panayotis Tournikiotis (Athens: futura, 2007), pp. 10–19 (p. 15).
3   Dimitris and Suzana Antonakakis, 'Introduction', in *Atelier 66: The Architecture of Dimitris and Suzana Antonakakis*, ed. by Kenneth Frampton (New York: Rizzoli, 1985), pp. 6–8 (p. 7).
4   Giorgos Seferis, 'Some Notes on Modern Greek Tradition', Nobel Lecture, 11 December 1963. Online. NobelPrize.org. Nobel Media, www.nobelprize.org/prizes/literature/1963/seferis/lecture (accessed 15 July 2021).
5   See Suzana Antonakaki, 'Αρχιτεκτονική: Επάγγελμα. Επαγγέλομαι = Υπόσχομαι', in *Ἴχνη αρχιτεκτονικής διαδρομής: Σουζάνα Αντωνακάκη και Δημήτρης Αντωνακάκης*, ed. by Dimitris Polychronopoulos, 2 vols (Athens: futura, 2018), I, pp. 15–19 (pp. 17–18).
6   Suzana and Dimitris Antonakakis, interviewed by Stylianos Giamarelos (Athens: 27 May 2014).
7   See Dimitris Antonakakis, 'Θουκυδίδης Βαλεντής: Ο δάσκαλος, σημειώσεις από μία δεκαετία', in *Ο αρχιτέκτονας Θουκυδίδης Π. Βαλεντής*, ed. by Chrysa Sachana et al. (Athens: Nisos, 2007), pp. 33–8 (p. 36); Le Corbusier, *La Ville Radieuse: Eléments d'une doctrine d'urbanisme pour l'équipement de la civilisation machiniste* (Bologne [Seine]: Éditions de L'Architecture d'Aujourd'hui, 1933).

8   Dimitris Antonakakis, 'Dimitris Pikionis: Elaboration and Improvisation', in *Mega XI, Dimitris Pikionis, Architect 1887–1968: A Sentimental Topography*, ed. by Dennis Crompton (London: Architectural Association, 1989), pp. 10–15 (pp. 10–11).

9   Antonakakis, interviewed by Giamarelos.

10 Dimitris Antonakakis, Βιογραφικό Υπόμνημα, National Technical University of Athens School of Architecture, 1978, Suzana and Dimitris Antonakakis' private archive, pp. 7, 66–7.

11 François Loyer, 'L'architecture de la Grèce contemporaine', unpublished doctoral thesis, Université de Paris, 1966, p. 1184.

12 See Orestis Doumanis, 'Εισαγωγή στην ελληνική μεταπολεμική αρχιτεκτονική', *Αρχιτεκτονική*, 48 (1964), 1–11; *Συν-ηχήσεις με τον Δημήτρη Πικιώνη*, ed. by Nikos Skoutelis (Athens: Plethron, 2018).

13 Suzana Antonakaki, *Κατώφλια: 100 + 7 Χωρογραφήματα* (Athens: futura, 2010), p. 33.

14 Dimitris Antonakakis, 'Landscaping the Athens Acropolis', in *Mega XI, Dimitris Pikionis, Architect 1887–1968: A Sentimental Topography*, ed. by Crompton, p. 90.

15 See Constantinos A. Doxiadis, *Architectural Space in Ancient Greece*, trans. by Jaqueline Tyrwhitt (Cambridge, MA: MIT Press, 1972). While Doxiadis completed his doctoral study in 1936, similar ideas were explored in Le Corbusier's interwar *promenades architecturales*; Auguste Choisy's earlier, 'Picturesque' reading of the Acropolis by the peripatetic viewer in 1899; and Sergei Eisenstein's reconstruction of the ensemble in terms of a montage sequence in 1937. See August Choisy, *Histoire de l'Architecture*, 2 vols (Paris: Gauthier-Villars, 1899), I, p. 413; Sergei Eisenstein, Yves-Allen Bois and Michael Glenny, 'Montage and Architecture', *Assemblage*, 10 (December 1989), 110–31.

16 See Kostas Tsiambaos, *From Doxiadis' Theory to Pikionis' Work: Reflections of Antiquity in Modern Architecture* (London: Routledge, 2017).

17 Antonakakis, 'Landscaping the Athens Acropolis'.

18 Dimitris Antonakakis cited in Maria Dolka, 'The Grid in Pefkakia Elementary School by Pikionis and the Grid in the Rethimno Faculty of Humanities: Are They so Related as They Appear?', unpublished IB thesis, I.M. Panagiotopoulos School, 2002, p. 5.

19 See Dimitris Pikionis, 'Οικιστικός κανονισμός Αιξωνής: Μορφολόγηση των επί μέρους στοιχείων' (1952), repr. in *Δ. Πικιώνης: Κείμενα*, ed. by Agni Pikioni and Michalis Parousis (Athens: MIET, 1986), pp. 259–65 (p. 259).

20 Antonakakis cited in Dolka, 'The Grid in Pefkakia Elementary School by Pikionis', p. 2.

21 Antonakakis, interviewed by Giamarelos.

22 Antonakakis, 'Dimitris Pikionis: Elaboration and Improvisation', p. 12.

23 Ibid., p. 14.

24 Aristide Antonas, 'The Error and the Rectification' (1994), repr. in *Atelier 66*, ed. by Tournikiotis, pp. 62–71.

25 Antonakaki, *Κατώφλια: 100 + 7 Χωρογραφήματα*, p. 62.

26 Suzana and Dimitris Antonakakis, interviewed by Stylianos Giamarelos (Athens: 23 June 2013).

27 Antonakakis, 'Dimitris Pikionis: Elaboration and Improvisation', p. 11.

28 Dimitris Pikionis, 'Autobiographical Notes' (1958), in *Mega XI, Dimitris Pikionis, Architect 1887–1968: A Sentimental Topography*, ed. by Crompton, pp. 34–7 (p. 37).

29 Dimitris Antonakakis, 'Dimitris Pikionis: Besieging the School at Pefkakia', in Dimitris Antonakakis, *Dimitris Pikionis: Two Lectures* (Athens: Domes, 2013), pp. 154–65 (p. 154).

30 See Yorgos Tzirtzilakis, 'Αρχιτεκτονική και μελαγχολία: Πολιτιστικές πρακτικές στο έργο του Δημήτρη Πικιώνη', *Εν Βόλω*, 31 (2008), 26–35 (pp. 29–32).

31 Antonakaki, *Κατώφλια: 100 + 7 Χωρογραφήματα*, p. 46.

32 See Nikos Hadjikyriakos-Ghika, *Ανίχνευση της ελληνικότητος* (Athens: Efthini, 1994); Dimitris Tziovas, *Ο μύθος της Γενιάς του Τριάντα: Νεωτερικότητα, ελληνικότητα και πολιτισμική ιδεολογία* (Athens: Polis, 2011).

33 See Nikos Hadjikyriakos-Ghika, 'Εναρκτήριο μάθημα στους σπουδαστές του Ε.Μ.Π.' (1942), repr. in *Νίκος Χατζηκυριάκος-Γκίκας: Δάσκαλος ζωγραφικής*, ed. by Sotiris Sorongas (Athens: National Technical University of Athens Press, 1997), pp. 16–31 (p. 28).

34 Antonakakis, interviewed by Giamarelos (2014).

35 Ibid.

36 Michelis's books were eventually translated into English (1955), French (1959), Italian (1968), Serbian (1973), Romanian (1982), Japanese (1982) and Korean (2007).

37 More than half of the fifty-three texts included in the Michelis 'in memoriam' volume were written by non-Greek authors. See *In Memoriam: Panayotis A. Michelis*, ed. by Takis Papatsonis (Athens: Hellenic Society for Aesthetics, 1972).

38 See Panayotis Michelis, *Η αρχιτεκτονική ως τέχνη* (Athens: self-published, 1940).

39 See Panayotis Michelis, *An Aesthetic Approach to Byzantine Art* (London: Batsford, 1955).

40 See Panayotis Michelis, *L'ésthétique de l'architecture du béton armé*, trans. by P. Jean Darrouzès (Paris: Dunod, 1963).

41 Antonakakis, interviewed by Giamarelos (2014).

42 See Panayotis Michelis, *Aesthetikos: Essays in Art, Architecture and Aesthetics* (Detroit: Wayne State University Press, 1977).

43 See Panayotis Michelis, *Το ελληνικό λαϊκό σπίτι, Α': Φροντιστηριακαί Εργασίαι* (Athens: National Technical University of Athens, Chair of Architectural Morphology and Rhythmology, 1960).

44 Antonakakis, interviewed by Giamarelos (2014).

45 See Georgios Megas, *The Greek House, its Evolution and its Relation to the Houses of the Other Balkan States* (Athens: Ministry of Reconstruction, 1951).

46 Suzana Antonakaki, 'Η αρχιτεκτονική της Μακρινίτσας', unpublished undergraduate thesis, National Technical University of Athens, 1959, p. 15.

47 Dimitris Antonakakis, 'Ύδρα', unpublished undergraduate thesis, National Technical University of Athens, 1958, p. 12.

48 Ibid., pp. 12–13.

49 Ibid., pp. 19–20.

50 Kostis Gartzos, interviewed by Stylianos Giamarelos (Athens: 2 July 2014).

51 Dimitris Fatouros, 'Greek Art and Architecture 1945–1967: A Brief Survey', *Balkan Studies*, 8.2 (1967), 421–35 (p. 431).

52 Dimitris Antonakakis, 'Τώρα που ο χρόνος αλλάζει', 29 January 2016. Online. triantafylloug. blogspot.co.uk/2016/01/2-95.html (accessed 15 July 2021).

53 Antonakaki, *Κατώφλια: 100 + 7 Χωρογραφήματα*, p. 214.

54 See ibid., pp. 149–50.

55 Antonakakis, interviewed by Giamarelos (2013).

56 See Vasileios I. Chanis, 'Mies Comes to Greece: A. James Speyer at NTUA', *Prometheus*, 2 (2019), pp. 52–5.

57 A. James Speyer, 'Oral History of A. James Speyer', in *The Chicago Architects Oral History Project*, ed. by Pauline Saliga (Chicago: Department of Architecture, the Art Institute of Chicago, 2001), pp. 1–135 (pp. 99–100). Online. https://artic.contentdm.oclc.org/digital/collection/caohp/id/10267/rec/1 (accessed 15 July 2021).

58 See A. James Speyer, 'Mies van der Rohe', *Architecture in Greece*, 4 (1970), 95–9 (p. 95); A. James Speyer, 'Όταν οι δάσκαλοι γερνούν', *Ζυγός*, 36–7 (1958), 33–6; *Mies van der Rohe*, ed. by A. James Speyer (Chicago: Art Institute of Chicago, 1968); *Mies van der Rohe: Drawings from the Collection of A. James Speyer* (New York: Max Protetch Gallery, 1986).

59 Antonakakis, interviewed by Giamarelos (2013).

60 Antonakakis, 'Acknowledgements', p. 17.

61 See A. James Speyer, 'Ludwig Mies van der Rohe: Εντυπώσεις του κορυφαίου αμερικανού αρχιτέκτονος απο το ταξίδι του στην Ελλάδα', *Αρχιτεκτονική*, 15–16 (1959), 42.

62 Speyer, 'Oral History of A. James Speyer', pp. 100–1; Antonakakis, interviewed by Giamarelos (2013).

63 Pauline Saliga and Robert V. Sharp, 'From the Hand of Mies: Architectural Sketches from the Collection of A. James Speyer', *Art Institute of Chicago Museum Studies*, 21.1 (1995), 56–69, 77–8 (p. 58).

64 Dimitris Antonakakis, 'The Speyer Houses on Hydra', in *A. James Speyer: Architect, Curator, Exhibition Designer*, ed. by John Vinci (Chicago: University of Chicago Press, 1997), pp. 58–71 (p. 66).

65 Ibid., pp. 63, 70.

66 Dimitris Antonakakis, 'Προβληματισμοί σχεδιασμού', *Journal of the Association of Greek Architects*, 21–2 (1989), 65–6, 77 (p. 65).

67 Tzonis and Lefaivre, 'The Grid and the Pathway', p. 178.

68 Dimitris Antonakakis, 'Το μοντέρνο και ο τόπος', *Architecture in Greece*, 30 (1996), 134.

9
Athenian resistance

The camera pans to capture, in 1978, the modern city of Athens as it covers the undulating landscape between the Philopappou and the Acropolis hills. It then zooms in to register specific moments in this seemingly endless urban mass, as four-, five- and six-storey apartment buildings (a typology known as the Athenian *polykatoikia*) succeed one another in invariable repetition. But as the camera moves closer to the foot of Strefi Hill, it is suddenly attracted by a four-storey apartment building that differs from the rest (Fig. 9.1). The viewpoint immediately shifts to the level of the street in order to inspect the main elevation of this unique piece of Athenian architecture at 118 Benaki Street. It then follows a young man, who enters the building to visit the apartment on the first floor. He is the son of Suzana and Dimitris Antonakakis, the architectural couple who designed the building and have lived and worked there since 1974. Tracing his visit to the apartment, the camera highlights its exceptional architectural features. The eye behind it belongs to Alekos Polychroniadis – one of the Antonakakis' peers in Atelier 66, which occupies the ground floor of the same building.

In this chapter, I focus on the Benaki Street apartment building (1972–5), which developed as a critique of the Athenian *polykatoikia*. Suzana and Dimitris Antonakakis detested the simplistic applications of modernist tenets in the production of the built environment of Athens. To satisfy Athenians' 'real needs', the couple argued, architecture needed to 'resist the established patterns of the market'.[1] Opening up the design and production process to the parties involved and affected by building was the only way to restore a relationship based on specific shared values instead of abstract common problems.[2] This was in turn expected to ease the move away from the anonymity of the built environment back to the sense of a community with a shared social life. Spanning across four decades, my historical research behind this chapter enables me to highlight the qualities and limits of this exemplary 'architecture of resistance'.

Thanks to Frampton's attention in the 1980s, this is the Antonakakis' most celebrated project to date; it has enjoyed 'a career of its own'.[3] Subsequent critics have repeatedly assumed that it condenses the meaning of the Antonakakis' oeuvre. For Jean-Louis Cohen, it exemplifies the 'Brutalist vein' in the work of the couple;[4] for Dimitris Fatouros, it serves as 'an excellent example' of 'their organising principles at work';[5] for Alexander Tzonis and Alcestis Rodi, it is 'a shared symbolic act of defiance' that 'opposed the mainstream architecture of the junta and the dogmas of the junta itself';[6] for Yorgos Tzirtzilakis, it 'constitutes something like the last act, the premature farewell of [a direction] for the evolution of a type of building which never managed to reach an exact typological definition'.[7] Despite their differing pessimistic, enthusiastic or dispassionate tones, all these different interpretations acknowledge the significance of this project for the oeuvre of Suzana and Dimitris Antonakakis or within the history of the Athenian apartment-building typology. But the sheer number of these diverse interpretations also

Figure 9.1 Suzana and Dimitris Antonakakis, apartment building at 118 Benaki Street, Athens, 1972–5, main elevation photographed by Dimitris Antonakakis, Athens, 1975

Suzana and Dimitris Antonakakis' private archive

shows that the architects' original intentions and the actual life of the project have been overshadowed, since the building acted almost as an empty signifier waiting to be loaded with a different meaning by each critic in turn.

Based on unpublished archival material and interviews with the architects, residents, engineers and craftspeople involved with the Benaki Street project, I show how the Antonakakis worked within the existing legal framework and beyond the established modes of production to realise their most articulate critique of the Athenian modern building typology. The project thus emerges as the product of a household economy, founded on strong familial and friendly bonds. I trace the evolution of the residents' shared practices of everyday life over time, the way in which the building worked as a four-storey 'single family house', and the specific qualities of regional vernacular traditions that the architects attempted to adapt to the metropolitan built environment.

Resistant architecture

The typical apartment building of Athens was effectively shaped by the building code that aimed to regulate the city's flourishing housing market in 1955. The code covered aspects of the built environment that ranged from the specified contours of new constructions (including the overall height, number of individual floors, window heights, setbacks and penthouses) to architectural details such as the width of balconies.[8] These in turn gave rise to the defining elements of the Athenian apartment building, including the size of the site and the typological characteristics of the host building block; the width of the adjoining streets and their role in the wider urban network; and prescriptions regarding the number of floors and the fraction of the site that could be covered by the building. In addition, the building code prescribed a gradual retreat of the last two or three floors by 2.50 m and the introduction of arcades on the ground floor. These additional measures addressed problems of ventilation, lighting and pedestrian circulation at street level. The typical floor of the Athenian apartment building had to assimilate and adapt to all these requirements and prescriptions.

Contractors added their own layer of requirements to this typology. These varied in accordance with their desired clientele. To maximise profit, they aimed for standardised floors with impressive façades, luxurious lobbies and unsophisticated layouts that allowed for the maximum possible number of rooms. To suit the needs of projected but unknown clients, their architects in turn had to ensure that their designs were sufficiently flexible. They needed to accommodate the variegated needs of the unknown buyers and future tenants of the apartments without subverting the fundamental elements of the overall structure – including staircases, lifts, columns, central heating and plumbing. Architects' room for intervention was further restricted and delineated by the projected desires of the developers' clientele. To cite just one example, they were not allowed to modify the façade of the building as it was the main elevation drawing that 'sold' the project to its future residents. As such, contractors and developers prioritised impressive main façades and luxurious entrance halls over the other sides of the building, which formed the everyday visual setting for all the neighbouring structures in the block.[9]

The standard apartment-building typology of booming postwar Athens was effectively prescribed by these practices and the new building code. Developers and contractors had adapted the modernist tenets of minimalism, standardisation and rational construction to their own speculative ends. Depending on the building regulations for each area of the city, the typical Athenian apartment building was organised over four to six floors. Symmetrical, horizontal balconies were usually the prevalent feature of the building's façade. They reflected an attempt to maximise the number of apartments facing the front of the plot. But the indiscriminate repetition of this same building type across the Athenian basin created an urban environment that was deemed faceless by the 1970s. The immense popularity of this model rightly led Suzana and Dimitris Antonakakis to regard the apartment building as a focal problem of architecture in Greece, as they constantly returned to it on numerous occasions.[10]

Owing to the above situation, the Athenian apartment building was the main typology of a booming construction sector in Greece from the 1950s to the 1980s (Fig. 9.2). As such, its design challenges had also been addressed by Greek modernist architects of Suzana and Dimitris Antonakakis' generation – and the couple had followed their work in the 1950s. The apartment building at 5 Semitelou Street by Nikos Valsamakis (1951) was regarded as a defining exemplar of high-quality apartment-building architecture. In this project, the horizontal, symmetrical balconies of the typical apartment floor were treated as integral parts of the building mass. Organised within a cantilevered gridded structure, they appeared as a porous, semi-enclosed, volumetric extension of the main body of the building. This cantilever also highlighted the entrance hall on the ground floor as different from the apartment floors above it.[11]

Figure 9.2 Inner-city refugee squatter settlement by the banks of the River Ilissos in Athens, photographed by Dimitris Philippidis, 1966

Dimitris Philippidis's private archive

Valsamakis's project thus introduced the main design motifs that were further explored by other celebrated architects of the period. The space defined by the cantilevered end of the balconies and the main building mass became an exercise in architectural elaboration. It seemed as if architects of the period tried out different articulations of this porous, volumetric filter for the Athenian apartment building. Among other devices, their projects experimented with: a playful organisation of the façade within the overarching symmetry of the structure (109 Patission Avenue by Dimitris Fatouros, 1957); an emphasis on the horizontality and flexibility of moving glass panels (Amalias Avenue and Daidalou Street by Takis Zenetos, 1959); and its volumetric division into two separate blocks (Deinokratous and Loukianou Street by Konstantinos Dekavallas and Thalis Argyropoulos, 1960). Such projects formed an inexorable horizon for young architects in the early 1960s.[12] By the early 1970s, after a decade of professional experience, Suzana and Dimitris Antonakakis made their own contribution to this ongoing architectural development.

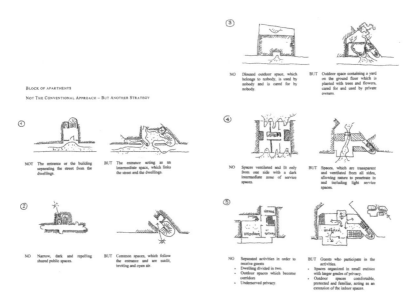

Figure 9.3 Suzana and Dimitris Antonakakis, apartment building at 118 Benaki Street as a critique of the Athenian apartment-building typology in five points

Suzana and Dimitris Antonakakis' private archive

Summarising their ideas in a series of five thematic sketches in the manner of Le Corbusier's five points for a new architecture, Suzana and Dimitris Antonakakis contrast the 'conventional'[13] with 'another strategy' for the *polykatoikia* that focused on: (1) using the entrance 'as an intermediate space, which links the street and the dwellings'; (2) 'sunlit, inviting and open air common spaces'; (3) a living outdoor space with a yard on the ground floor; (4) transparent and cross-ventilated spaces; and (5) 'spaces organised in small clusters with increased grades of privacy' (Fig. 9.3).[14] These crucial design features were clearly highlighted in 1978, when the architects decided to record their Benaki Street project on film. Directed by Atelier 66 architect Alekos Polychroniadis on Super-8 film cassette, the 10-minute colour video records a visit to Suzana and Dimitris Antonakakis' apartment on the first floor.

Framing the visit to the building in juxtaposition to the city around it, the 1978 video records the two Antonakakis' critique of the standard Athenian apartment-building typology and the development of the Greek capital after the Second World War. The camera inspects the main elevation in order to allude to the unique spatial arrangement behind it. It clearly shows that this is not the façade of a standard Athenian apartment building – with the wet spaces and the stairwells at its dark core; the living rooms extending to the horizontal, symmetrical balconies at the front; and the bedrooms at the rear. There is no typical floor plan at 118 Benaki Street. Apparently sculpted rather than stacked on top of one another, most of the apartments span two floors (Fig. 9.4). They can be clearly identified within the overall structure even from the street level, as each of them has its own architectural identity. The camera returns to the aforementioned young male visitor, who enters the building (Fig. 9.5). As he opens the door, he finds himself not in a luxurious lobby but in a stone-paved courtyard. In the architects' own words, the entrance to the building is 'a roofed court' and the staircase serves as 'a continuation of this court, being at the same time open-air and in direct contact with the street'.[15] To get from the urban public space to the private sphere of the apartment on the first floor, the visitor does not disappear into the building's interior but traverses a series of successive open-air and semi-enclosed thresholds. These also serve as occasions for seeing and meeting with the other residents, as they circulate in and out of their apartments, open their windows or enjoy the fresh air on their balconies.

As the visitor enters the apartment, the camera moves to demonstrate the architects' concern for cross-ventilation and natural light, and the gradient interplay of private, semi-public and public spaces on different levels. When the visitor arrives at the heart of it, the apartment presents itself as a city within four walls, with similarly interlocking degrees of privacy and publicness. The double-height living room turns the apartment inside out. When Suzana Antonakaki leans out of her bedroom window, an internal window that gives on to the living room, this interior space echoes the outdoor piazza of a Greek island settlement within the four walls of a metropolitan apartment. The ensuing theatricality also forms part of the architects' original intentions. It creates an atmosphere of a public open space within their personal living environment in a modern urban context. Other qualities of the regional vernacular were also brought in to be adapted to the urban environment. As Suzana Antonakaki wrote in 1981, '[t]he dual orientation (cross-ventilation) that ensures a controlled climate for the interior, corners of life for different times of the day can, with the appropriate spatial arrangement, provide some possibilities-memories of an outdoor life in the narrow limits of the apartment'.[16] This recourse to tradition forms the resistant core of the Antonakakis' architecture, which does not rely on mere formal replication but carries over the memory of spatial qualities of life in the open-air environment of the vernacular settlement. It is from this context that most Athenians originated anyway, following

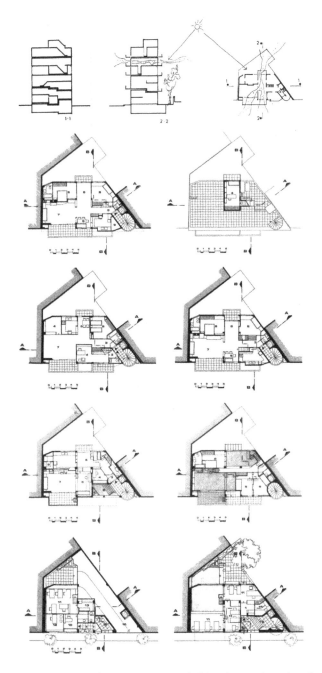

Figure 9.4 Suzana and Dimitris Antonakakis, plan and section drawings for apartment building at 118 Benaki Street

Suzana and Dimitris Antonakakis' private archive

Figure 9.5 Suzana and Dimitris Antonakakis, apartment building at 118 Benaki Street, stills from video by Alekos Polychroniadis, 1978

Suzana and Dimitris Antonakakis' private archive

Figure 9.6 Suzana and Dimitris Antonakakis, sketch of the entry court to the apartment building at 118 Benaki Street, 1975

Suzana and Dimitris Antonakakis' private archive

the unprecedented growth of the urban population in the 1950s and the 1960s after the end of the civil war in 1949.[17]

These ideas were already emphasised in several of the architects' preliminary sketches, which showed how the public street penetrated through the site to form a transitional entry space to the building (Fig. 9.6). Combined with the staged scenes in the video, they reaffirm the coherence of the Antonakakis' intentions from the design phase to the final built result. These intentions were materially accentuated by the pavement in front of the building. Following Pikionis, the Antonakakis also activated the ground as an additional expression of their main architectural intentions. Covered with the same Sifnos stone used throughout the building floors, the public pavement was materially extended to enter the private realm of the Benaki Street apartment building. In other words, the street was part of the building and vice versa; the Sifnos stonework was extended from the building outwards to the public street. This is how the Antonakakis addressed the relationship of their architecture with the public realm. In their view, the public and the private realms did not develop in the isolation of their binary opposition; they were partially interdependent. Hence, architecture for a private project should not hesitate to affect its public contours.

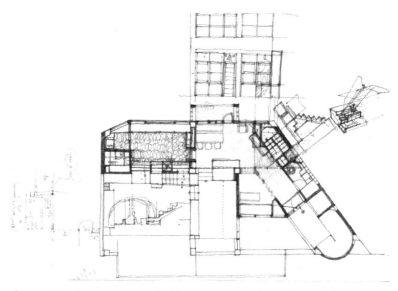

Figure 9.7   Suzana Antonakaki, working sketch for the first floor of the apartment building at 118 Benaki Street, 1973

Suzana and Dimitris Antonakakis' private archive

This holistic approach to architectural design, which challenged conventional boundaries, was also reflected in the architects' drawing practice. A working sketch from Suzana and Dimitris Antonakakis' private archive (Fig. 9.7) serves as a good case in point here. Starting as a plan drawing of the first-floor apartment of 118 Benaki Street, the sketch also includes exploratory approaches to the elevation at the rear, interior views of the main living room and the unfolding of a staircase in space. In other words, the couple considered design objects in their totality. Even when they worked on a single aspect of them, as in a plan drawing, they did not treat it in isolation from its implications for the other drawing planes (section, elevation, axonometric).

Working on 118 Benaki Street enabled Suzana and Dimitris Antonakakis to crystallise their five-point critique of the Athenian apartment-building typology in both still and moving images in the 1970s. Through their architecture, the couple aimed to respect and assimilate the qualities of the natural environment in their building's interior spaces, since cross-ventilation and natural lighting emerged as focal concerns in their designs. Their buildings adapted to the orientation of the site to ensure that both sunlight and fresh air could enter their designed spaces at different times of the day. The architects were also attentive to the evolution of human activity over time, and tried to organise it rationally in the thoughtfully designed spaces of their buildings. Their architecture also valued the blending of public and private realms through successive thresholds between areas of different character, as their designs sought to enrich the quality of users' movement in space. Lastly, all these architectural qualities had to be achieved through simple and honest constructional means.[18]

But such a narrowly defined architectural critique overlooks equally crucial ways in which 118 Benaki Street also resisted and subverted existing design conventions, standard modes of production and quotidian practices of sharing an everyday life within the same Athenian apartment building. It is the lived history of 118 Benaki Street, from the moment of its initial conception to the present, that foregrounds its agency as a resistant experiment of communal living in Athens. Revisiting this history unveils the multifarious, resilient and dissipating aspects of resistance at 118 Benaki Street – from the dominant development model of the *polykatoikia* to communal life and its aesthetics. As such, it also highlights the tensions that gradually arose between the originally resistant intentions and their long-term implementation in practice over four decades.

Resistant mode of production

Postwar Athens was an essentially provincial capital that struggled to address the massive influx of population from the rest of the country without the state funds to satisfy the rising demand for housing. In Greece, public housing represents less than 3 per cent of the total surface area of residential space.[19] As such, the production of new housing projects seemed virtually impossible without the participation of the country's small-scale private sector – from landowners to contractors. To incentivise such partnerships, the Greek state eventually institutionalised the informal practice of the *antiparochi*, a quid-pro-quo agreement between landowners with limited budgets and contractors who could undertake construction but did not own plots of land. Big capital thus played practically no role in shaping modern Athens. Through *antiparochi*, landowners got the best apartments, which they would not have been able to build for themselves, while the contractors who covered the construction cost profited from selling the remaining apartments to third parties. This 'win–win' mechanism proved especially effective for Greece's small-scale housing market, serving as the engine of the nation's construction boom from the 1950s onwards. Its popularity as a mode of production of the Athenian built environment is, in hindsight, not surprising.

It was this commodifying mode of production of the small-scale construction sector that Suzana and Dimitris Antonakakis opposed. They aimed to save the benign, socially conscious aspects of the modern movement from the speculative hands of Greek contractors and developers. To do so, they not only promoted the qualitative aspects of their architecture but they also attempted to give a wider meaning to the notion of state-supported 'participation' of the small-scale private sector in the 1950s that went beyond its exclusive interpretation in economic terms. Their apartment block at 118 Benaki Street served as the occasion to bring together and put in practice ideas that had matured from the two architects' experience with other contractors and developers over the previous decade.[20] In addition, the formation of a cooperative with the other residents, who were also friends of the couple, enabled the two architects to move away from the dictates of the building industry of the period. The Antonakakis aimed to nurture unmediated and personified relations with the future residents of their project. These ties spanned from the preliminary design to the construction process and the subsequent sharing of a communal life within the building. In so doing, the two architects also explored the alternative possibilities for agreements between interested parties that remained latent in the legal mechanism of the *antiparochi*.

The block at 118 Benaki Street is indeed the product of a collaborative process that subverted the established hierarchies in the design, construction and use of space in the standard Athenian apartment. Each of the four families involved contributed what was necessary for the realisation of the communal project: land, labour and capital. The land was offered by the Dolkas and Kannas families, who owned it and wanted to demolish the old Neo-Classical house of Pattie Dolka's parents that still stood there in order to erect a new building in its place. This would enable them to profit from the recently implemented building code that allowed for more square footage on the site. The labour was shared in accordance with each party's professional expertise (the two architects Suzana and Dimitris Antonakakis designed the building; the lawyer Pattie Dolka established the residents' unmediated partnership, exploring the room for manoeuvre in the existing legal framework; the mechanical engineer Lampis Dolkas devised the central ventilation and heating system). The remaining capital to kick-start construction was offered by the Nezis family, another friendly couple who were about to sell a piece of land that they owned in Elefsina in order to get an apartment in Athens. The original plan of these four families was to sell the ground floor of the new building to a third party, as the regulations allowed for it to be used for commercial enterprise. But the wider Antonakakis family (Dimitris Antonakakis's brother Giorgos and his wife Aleka Monemvasitou, and their cousin Costis Hadjimichalis and his wife Dina Vaiou who were also fellow architects in Atelier 66) stepped in to cover the remaining expenses at a later stage in exchange for the ground floor, which became the main office space of Atelier 66.[21] As such, the project developed without interference from other intermediaries. It involved only the parties who were interested in sharing their lives as neighbours in the same building. Starting their own one-off partnership with the other families to erect this building maintained a safe distance from the dictates of the Greek construction sector of the period. It was this move that enabled the Antonakakis to prioritise the architectural qualities that they valued and put them into practice in their sophisticated building design.

The evolution of the Antonakakis' critical design process is evident in their preliminary plans for the building. In the early design stages, for instance, the staircase is not yet the open, public and luminous space of the final drawings (Fig. 9.8). And even when it does come out in the front in a later version of the same drawings, it is more conventionally incorporated into the building mass (Fig. 9.9). As Suzana and Dimitris Antonakakis wrote a decade later, the position of the staircase is 'the most crucial choice in the design of the apartment building' in general. This element not only defines vertical and horizontal movement across the building but it also conditions the distribution of the apartments and their possible flexibility for future conversions. Practical considerations aside, the Antonakakis also regarded the staircase as 'a symbol of the earth–sky relation' in Heideggerian terms. As such, it was deemed worthy of occupying a more significant place than the usual dark recesses of the typical Athenian apartment building.[22]

Suzana and Dimitris Antonakakis' design explored how far it could push the limits of the existing building code in order to produce the desired architectural qualities. The relationship between the design and the regulations was reciprocal. For instance, the two architects labelled the living room of their own apartment a sculptor's atelier to take advantage of the clause that allowed for double heights for workshops. This enabled them to create the signature double-height living-room space and the 'bridge' that runs across their apartment from one end to the other (Fig. 9.10). As Platon Issaias has argued, projects such as the Benaki Street apartment building also constituted a precedent that

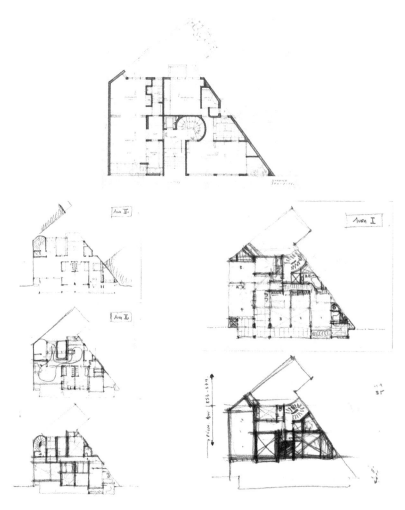

Figure 9.8 Suzana and Dimitris Antonakakis, working sketches of the main staircase in the apartment building at 118 Benaki Street, 1973

Suzana and Dimitris Antonakakis' private archive

'anticipated the modifications of existing regulations'.[23] One of these was the provision for semi-enclosed spaces in the building code of 1985, a cause that Suzana and Dimitris Antonakakis had embraced with their design philosophy of gradual transitions between cross-ventilated naturally lit spaces. Lastly, the modification of the building code midway through the design process in June 1973 effectively led to a second version of the Benaki Street project (Fig. 9.11). The new code no longer

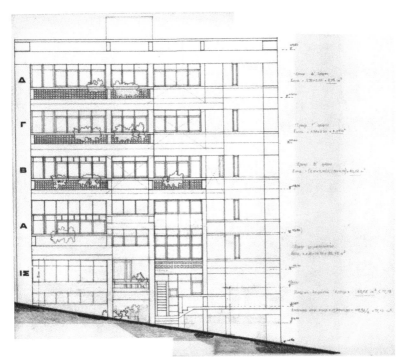

Figure 9.9 Suzana and Dimitris Antonakakis, working drawing of main elevation for the apartment building at 118 Benaki Street, 1973

Suzana and Dimitris Antonakakis' private archive

Figure 9.10 Views of the 'bridge' in Suzana and Dimitris Antonakakis' apartment on the first floor of 118 Benaki Street

Suzana and Dimitris Antonakakis' private archive

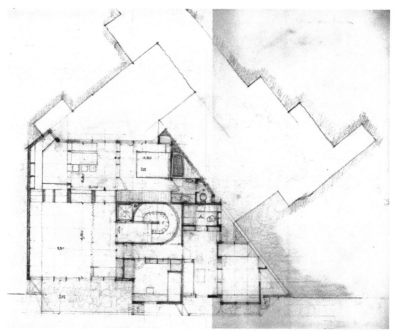

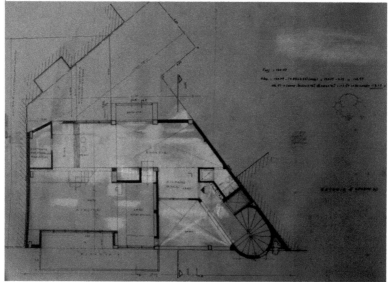

Figure 9.11 Suzana and Dimitris Antonakakis, working plan drawings of apartment building at 118 Benaki Street, before (top) and after (bottom) June 1973

Suzana and Dimitris Antonakakis' private archive

allowed a 10 m deep coverage of the site, irrespective of its configuration. As the building shrank in size, a shared backyard was created – reinforcing the perception of the project by its residents as 'a four-storey single-family house'.[24]

Most of Suzana and Dimitris Antonakakis' preliminary drawings carry the traces of relentless modifications and corrections, the surviving material signs of their elaborate design process (Fig. 9.11). From the phase of the first sketches, the architects established a feedback loop with the future residents. The Antonakakis shared their initial architectural proposals, the future users of these spaces suggested modifications that led to a revised proposal by the architects and so on – for about a year. Suzana Antonakaki worked closely with the other three families who were to inhabit the building. She drew, erased and modified these drawings several times in order to ensure that each apartment met the future residents' needs. Instead of settling for a typical plan to be replicated on all floors of the building, each apartment of 118 Benaki Street is a bespoke piece of architecture. Rather surprisingly, this crucial aspect of their design was not included in the Antonakakis' five critical points regarding the Athenian apartment building. The two architects worked hard to integrate these diverse apartments into a coherent whole. Most of them were configured across two storeys, and the family units were individualised within the overall structure. But this versatile design process was consistently underpinned by the rule of the grid (Fig. 9.11). In a later interview, Dimitris Antonakakis confirmed that their use of the grid came from Pikionis. Their mentor 'used this technique for the ground plan of a building but not for the vertical measurements of the building, i.e. the height. That happens all the time. We use this grid only for the ground floor plan, but not for the individual levels of the building'.[25] This tool enabled the Antonakakis to keep their complicated, holistic approach under control.

When I interviewed them in 2014, the other residents of the building emphasised its conception as an experiment in collaborative living. Children from different families described 'growing up like sisters' in the building.[26] Others described collective cooking sessions with their neighbours in kitchens on different floors; sharing meals with the other families (Fig. 9.12); how the doors of their apartments usually remained unlocked, enabling their children to go up and down the stairs at will. These and other instances of their shared life across the building's four storeys further reinforced the resistant aspects of communal living at 118 Benaki Street, as they also resonated with the architects' original intentions and the residents' shared political beliefs.[27] The experience of communal life in the building was far removed from the metropolitan anonymity of the rest of the Athenian built environment. As 118 Benaki

Figure 9.12 New Year's dinner in Suzana and Dimitris Antonakakis'
apartment with Atelier 66 architects and residents of the apartment
building at 118 Benaki Street, 1991

Lucy and Giorgos Triantafyllou private archive

Street strengthened the social bonds between these families, the
Antonakakis' reinterpretation of tradition in the modern urban context
also steered away from mere nostalgia to become a practice integrated
into everyday life.

Knowing the future residents well enough to design domestic spaces
that would fit their specific needs was the two Antonakakis' personified
response to the anonymous, generic approach of Greek contractors. These
social bonds were crucial for the completion of the project. It was
only through the connective tissue of social relations that this more
'traditionally' collective way of life could be retained and developed in the
transition from the agrarian to the metropolitan condition of atomised
anonymity. In a recent presentation of the project, Dimitris Antonakakis
started from the changing dynamics of Greek domestic space after the
late 1940s. He was mainly concerned with the transition from the single-
family house to the apartment. For Antonakakis, the single-family houses
of the prewar years were cellular social units that integrated extended
family bonds, spanning from the three familial generations (from
grandparents to grandchildren) to aunts, uncles and cousins. As the main
place of reference, the house was the spatial setting that strengthened
these social bonds as it effectively 'glued' the extended family together.
With the move to the big cities and their apartments, these social relations
changed. Domestic space became the locus of meeting of only two

generations (with the grandparents usually moving to an apartment of their own or a private institution). As the cellular social unit decreased in size, the social relations that it used to sustain also atrophied. In Antonakakis's eyes, this in turn led to an impoverished understanding of tradition. It was only through social bonds that tradition could be maintained and further developed.[28] In this light, 118 Benaki Street was also a defence of these traditional domestic values. More specifically, it was an attempt to transform them, to reflect contemporary needs in the metropolitan apartment building.

As such, embedded social relations were also transposed to the mode of production of the building. This formed the second significant layer in the Antonakakis' holistic conception of 'tradition' as a route to an architecture of resistance. The first comprised the spatial typologies that condense the insights of a long-standing relationship of dwelling in the region, which I discussed in the previous section. But there was also a third significant layer in the Antonakakis' understanding of 'tradition': a specific aesthetic language that accompanied it. It is only when one considers these three registers together that the resistant core of the Antonakakis' architecture is fully revealed.

Resistant aesthetics

If the recourse to tradition in the anonymous context of a modern metropolis was to be fully realised, the residents would also have to ascribe to the architects' modernised 'traditional' aesthetic language. If the users of the building did not share this mentality, an architectural project like this could not work. The residents of 118 Benaki Street were conscious of their decisions. They knew that they were living in an unconventional apartment building. They therefore felt that they also had to follow the architects' taste in the interior spaces, to avoid an aesthetic dissonance with their overarching vision.[29] In their eyes, the final word on the overall aesthetics could only belong to the expert architect.

In 2000, in a retrospective account of their relationship with the users of their buildings, Suzana and Dimitris Antonakakis noted that they had been lucky enough to work with 'ideal' residents over the years. They had got to know and mutually trust each other – cultivating strong, friendly bonds with many of them. However, they could not hide their disappointment at several alterations during the construction process or later in the life of the buildings. As they characteristically noted, in the decades that followed and 'despite their old friendships', the owners of their buildings made design 'decisions irrelevant to the intentions that were once regarded as preconditions'.[30] In other words, Suzana and Dimitris Antonakakis could not afford to lose control of their projects even after they had been completed. In this sense, their understanding of architectural authorship was still deeply modernist.

It was not long before the architects noted discrepancies between their aesthetic preferences and those of their neighbours at 118 Benaki Street. The other residents did not want their apartments to be as simple and austere as Suzana and Dimitris Antonakakis had originally designed them with their limited collective budget of the early 1970s. Aesthetic considerations aside, all of them had to settle for the most economical options then available: roughcast plaster for the walls and Sifnos stone for the floors. Despite their initial fascination with these materials as reminiscent of Greek island life, in the late 1990s and early 2000s the

Figure 9.13 Suzana and Dimitris Antonakakis, living rooms of Nezis and Dolkas families' apartments in apartment building at 118 Benaki Street – photographed by Dimitris Antonakakis, 1975 (left); and the same rooms after their refurbishment, photographed by Stylianos Giamarelos, 2014 (right)

Suzana and Dimitris Antonakakis' private archive (left); Stylianos Giamarelos's private archive (right)

residents of 118 Benaki Street replaced the Sifnos stone on the floor of their apartments with marble or timber. For their informed taste, the interior of their apartment could not remain frozen in the 1960s. At some point, they felt the need to change it to follow the new style of the times (Fig. 9.13).[31]

Constructed in the early 1970s, the interiors of 118 Benaki Street were aesthetically aligned with the wider turn to Greek folk art of the time. The carpets, rugs and other small objects that originally covered the floors or decorated the apartments were meant as a cultural expression of this return to folk culture (Fig. 9.14). They represented an authenticity that resisted the superficial recuperation and kitsch abuse of Greek 'tradition' by the dictators of this period (1967–74). This was especially the case for Suzana and Dimitris Antonakakis and their collaborative architectural practice Atelier 66. From their non-hierarchical collaboration methods to the ways in which they designed architectural interiors or dressed themselves, their holistic revisiting of tradition aimed to regain it as an active cultural agent in the present. In so doing, it also signalled a political act of resistance to the junta.[32] The nationalistic overtones of the colonels' regime dictated a cultural introversion that was accompanied by a forced folklore aesthetic. This was further complicated by the regime's simultaneous reliance on the modernised construction industry and recourse to the mythical glory of the past as the main pillars of its propaganda. Several Greek architects unambiguously embraced modernism as a form of resistance to the folklore aesthetic dictates of the regime in order to return to the 'real needs' of the region. Rephrased in a modern idiom, these 'real needs' in turn allowed them to transgress both the imposed aesthetic of the colonels and the straight revivalism of the traditionalists. In this sense, the Antonakakis' work was also a child of its time. Their turn to the regional tradition was inseparable from the prevailing cultural trends of the 1960s from which it emerged.

Residual hierarchies

The residents of 118 Benaki Street shared the impression that the building offered them lessons in architectural quality. In their own words, it taught them how to dwell and feel at home in a house. Their long-term friendship with Suzana and Dimitris Antonakakis also encouraged them to develop an eye for the minute design decisions that affected their everyday life in buildings. The architects were also happy to see their ideas about cross-ventilation and natural lighting, thresholds, openings and communication across the building being actively used and appreciated by the residents.

Figure 9.14 Top: Suzana and Dimitris Antonakakis, first-floor apartment, living room, apartment building at 118 Benaki Street, photographed by Dimitris Antonakakis, 1975; bottom: Atelier 66 architects, 1975

Suzana and Dimitris Antonakakis' private archive

Figure 9.15   (from left to right) Suzana and Dimitris Antonakakis, rear and front elevations of the apartment building at 118 Benaki Street
Suzana and Dimitris Antonakakis' private archive

These aspects of their design depended heavily on the agreement of the parties involved. However, the architect–user hierarchy proved very hard to dissipate, despite the architects' best efforts in this direction.

In addition, the actual life of the residents in the building rendered the architects' original intentions short-lived. These increasingly sounded like the dying echo of a provincial tradition that could not survive the advance of the Athenian metropolis and the individualist urban lifestyle. As such, the unconventional aspects of the residents' shared life gradually faded. When the four families started locking their doors, and central heating was autonomously managed by each individual apartment because of their differing needs during the day, life at 118 Benaki Street increasingly resembled that of the typical Athenian apartment building in the early 1990s. The previous phase in the life of the building has certainly left its mark and the residents still feel connected, but today, each storey effectively functions in isolation from the others. It is therefore only the formal design features that still render the Benaki Street apartment building distinct from the standard Athenian typology (Fig. 9.15). But all the interiors of the other apartments have also been modified now. Suzana and Dimitris Antonakakis' reluctance to lose control of their work after its completion meant that the superior position of the architects in the design hierarchy was not practically subverted.

This was also the case for their collaboration with other professionals in the construction industry. In their texts, Suzana and Dimitris Antonakakis regularly admitted their struggle 'to separate [the] creative work' of their builders and craftspeople from their own 'and to distinguish their contribution to the unique character of the work of Atelier 66'.[33] They strongly believed that the craftspeople significantly contributed to sustaining a tradition rooted in a community.[34] But still, in their actual practice, it was the architects who constantly remained at the helm of the design process. For them, collaboration practically meant getting the craftspeople to understand the architectural intentions and the overarching rationale of their designs. Since these went beyond the standardised solutions of generic apartment buildings, they also challenged their craftspeople. The design philosophy of the Antonakakis posited that this inability to standardise the design details of their work preserved a crucial architectural quality that would otherwise be lost.[35] In an era of industrial standardisation, it harked back to the subtle qualities of 'traditional' human craft and manual work, although custom-made furniture and bespoke set pieces meant that construction costs also rose with them. The architects had developed their own good sense of the use, qualities and properties of various materials. They prepared drawings and models specifically to instruct their craftspeople, laying out the full details needed for the construction of specific parts of their projects.[36]

The work of the architects was so tightly put together that other professionals, like the engineers who collaborated with them, had to be in constant contact with them. Sometimes, the simple dimensional modification of a detail could lead to an extensive reconsideration of the original design. Suzana and Dimitris Antonakakis used the grid so extensively that the measurements of key design elements were proportionally correlated. For the structural design of their buildings, the engineers also had to retain the Antonakakis' intentions intact. As a result, they engaged with the brief in order to solve the problems that arose from these intentions. The spatial plasticity of the Antonakakis' designs – with their successive, slight level changes – were not conducive to the anti-seismic behaviour of their buildings. This was usually solved by reinforcing some key columns in the structural grid. Again, the engineers started working on these details from a preliminary version of the structural grid provided by the architects, who used to divide the building into different construction zones. This draft structural framework was already aligned with key design elements and architectural intentions.[37] Despite the Antonakakis' repeated rhetoric of the creative contribution of the parties involved, the architects' superior role in the design hierarchy was not practically challenged on this front either.

Lastly, Suzana and Dimitris Antonakakis' non-standard approach to the apartment building did not go unobserved by the Greek contractors

Figure 9.16 Suzana Antonakaki, apartment building on 44 Doxapatri Street, Athens, 1978–82, photographed by Dimitris Antonakakis and Sarra Matsa, 2021

Suzana and Dimitris Antonakakis' private archive

of the period. Some of them charged the Antonakakis with elitism.[38] Their critique focused on a question pertinent to the architects' approach: could the design model of 118 Benaki Street and the 'household economy' that underpinned its construction be generalised in order to be applied on a larger scale? When Suzana Antonakaki reused and further developed some of the Benaki project features in the subsequent apartment building at 44 Doxapatri Street in 1978 (Fig. 9.16), the future residents of this building also formed a similar partnership. But they found it more difficult to cooperate as they did not share the friendly ties of the families involved in the Benaki Street cooperative. Generalising a design process that rested on personified interaction with the involved parties proved inherently difficult.

This was another symptom of the Antonakakis' unwillingness to think of their practice in a business sense. For the two architects, this distance from market practices saved their work from degenerating into a commodifiable fad. Nonetheless, their projects were influential for a new generation of Greek architects who followed their approach to materials and individualised apartments across more than one storey. Still, in promoting a practice that did not follow the dictates of the market, the couple were not as successful in debunking the mode of production that they opposed. In the eyes of the Antonakakis, the commodified approach led to a built environment 'bereft of symbols [and] points of reference'. Its fading quality expressed the 'destitution, shallowness, ... bureaucracy, and consumer mania' that characterised a 'commercialised everyday life'.[39] It was this anonymity and the resulting dissolution of social relations that Suzana and Dimitris Antonakakis wanted to address. Their work was also distinct from that of other celebrated architects of the period since the couple did not build exclusively for the upper classes. The lack of a steady circle of clients meant that their clientele opened up to the middle- or even low-income category. In these projects, their major architectural challenge was to maintain the desired quality within a restricted budget.

But as professional architects, the Antonakakis also had to rely on contractors with the business sense that they themselves lacked. The most perceptive of these contractors in turn appropriated some of the two architects' design experimentations, to turn them into a profitable enterprise. This was the case with the idea of incorporating prefabricated balconies in the design of their early 1960s apartment building projects with contractor Nikos Konstantinidis.[40] Konstantinidis found out that the Antonakakis' approach offered a distinct architectural identity at a low cost. His appreciation for their work in turn led him to entrust them with his large-scale tourist projects, such as the Hydra Beach complex and Porto Hydra in the 1970s. In other words, the contractors and developers whom the couple opposed in theory were also required as clients in practice. Some of them enabled the two architects to produce some of their large-scale projects of the highest calibre. While the Antonakakis would not easily admit it, in all aspects of their work during the decade in question they implicitly sided with what they explicitly opposed. Such tensions generated ambiguities and dualities, which were entrenched in the architects' work.

During the 1980s, these contradictions were only further amplified. Faced with sometimes irreconcilable demands, Suzana and Dimitris Antonakakis still had to carry their architectural design practices forward. Ioanna Theocharopoulou's recent work on the construction of modern Athens adds nuance to this bigger picture. From builders to housewives, her historical account of the postwar apartment building traces the rise of an aberrant way of making that is specifically Athenian.[41] This not only contextualises the Antonakakis' work but also suggests the substitution of their agrarian-inspired conception of 'tradition' with its urban equivalent by the 1980s. And this might in turn be another reason why the architects' original resistant intentions proved short-lived, as many of the 'traditional' aspects of their work soon dissipated.

Today's architectures of resistance might therefore need to follow different genealogies of their own that address this concrete Athenian condition and its gradual formation in the late twentieth century. It is only through this sort of nuanced historical engagement that politics can be significantly retained at the heart of architectures and discourses of resistance today.

Retheorising resistance

Tensions and ambiguities that are only revealed when one turns to the lived history of the building over four decades challenge the standard ways in which this project has been appropriated to theorise architectural resistance by critical regionalism and other related discourses.[42] At the end of this chapter, Frampton's mid-1980s idealisation of Athens rings rather hollow:

> At one level, one may look to Athens, if not Greece as a whole, as the paradoxical place of modernity in the midst of the so-called Postmodern era, for perhaps in no other world capital can one find such a widespread acceptance of modern architecture, both as a programme and as a formal language. Athens is surely the modern city par excellence in the sense that the normative Neoclassical city of the nineteenth century was progressively replaced and extended after the early 1950s by an equally normative modern typology … Endlessly repeated with sufficiently subtle variations, … these undemonstrative blocks amount to a remarkably civilised level of urban building, unequalled anywhere in the modern world. This unselfconscious achievement – the autonomous manifestation of a culture rather than the work of a single architect – is all the more successful for having nurtured a richly articulated city.[43]

As I showed earlier in this chapter, the Benaki Street project that Frampton also presents as an exemplar of critical regionalism at the conclusion of his book was opposed to the mode of production that had 'unselfconsciously' produced this 'modern city par excellence'. Bypassing the nuanced history of this resistant project, theoretical appropriations like Frampton's thus offer only a frozen, idealised image of architectural resistance. As this account glosses over the intricacies of a design process conditioned by the Athenian context of the 1970s and its aftermath, it cannot be informative for resistant practices today. It is only a return to the fullness of the original historical image, to the social world as the architects wanted to see it transformed alongside the contingent fate of their actions, that helps to foreground the political core of these resistant architectures and discourses for the present.

The history of an exemplary signifier of critical regionalism like 118 Benaki Street shows how the resistant aspects of the project have also been interpreted differently from its historically variable audiences. These are not limited to the frequently idealising critics; they also include unconvinced residents and derisive contractors. The architects' original intentions foreground the centrality of challenging specific modes of production in order to establish novel forms of collaborative living. But the short lifespan of these intentions in their practical implementation in everyday life also highlights the contradictions involved in architectural pursuits that attempt to orchestrate unconventional ways of living. Their historical fate is more emphatically informative if one wishes to go the extra mile in order to envision these changes on a broader scale. Greek developers' reaction to the architects' intentions, in particular, shows how an architecture of resistance can also be received as its exact opposite, a generator of elite circles of the happy few and their indulgent idealisations. In other cases, problems might also emerge from residual hierarchies and operative modes that remain unchallenged or that simply resist change.

Whenever an apartment building like 118 Benaki Street is posited as a microcosm of an envisioned social change at a larger scale, the temptation to enter into another circle of idealised discourse also grows. In significant respects, the concrete experiment of 118 Benaki Street echoes Gerald A. Cohen's thought experiment of the camping trip that explores how desirable, feasible and difficult it would prove to expand the principles of equity and community from a group of friends to a wider societal scale.[44] Since projects like 118 Benaki Street still form part of legacies and genealogies of more recent attempts to rethink the city of Athens as an urban common,[45] the challenge lies in resisting turning these exemplars into supposedly self-evident images and instead engaging with the full spectrum of their historical contingency.

Suzana and Dimitris Antonakakis' work developed in an increasingly personalised manner. By the mid-1980s, however, the two architects sensed that their practice was constrained by the established mannerisms of their own architectural idiom. Rather ironically, when the Benaki Street apartment building was globally heralded as a flagship of critical regionalism in the mid-1980s,[46] Suzana and Dimitris Antonakakis were designing projects such as the Rhodes branch of the Ionian Bank (1983–6). This building bore the formalist marks of a postmodernism that the architects had witnessed, and allegedly rejected, at the Biennale.

As such, it serves as an ideal case study for the closing chapter of this book.

Notes

1 Dimitris and Suzana Antonakakis, 'Introduction', in *Atelier 66: The Architecture of Dimitris and Suzana Antonakakis*, ed. by Kenneth Frampton (New York: Rizzoli, 1985), pp. 6–8 (p. 6).

2 Dimitris Antonakakis, 'Το μοντέρνο και ο τόπος', *Architecture in Greece*, 30 (1996), 134.

3 Suzana and Dimitris Antonakakis, interviewed by Stylianos Giamarelos (Athens: 27 May 2014).

4 Jean-Louis Cohen, 'The Mediterranean Brutalism of Dimitris and Suzana Antonakakis' (1994), in *Atelier 66: The Architecture of Dimitris and Suzana Antonakakis*, ed. by Panayotis Tournikiotis (Athens: futura, 2007), 32–45 (p. 43).

5 Dimitris Fatouros, 'The Architecture of Dimitris and Suzana Antonakakis: Two Complementary Descriptions' (1994), in *Atelier 66*, ed. by Tournikiotis, pp. 46–53 (p. 47).

6 Alexander Tzonis and Alcestis Rodi, *Greece: Modern Architectures in History* (London: Reaktion, 2013), pp. 210–11, 208.

7 Yorgos Tzirtzilakis, 'Toward a Point Marked X: Some Thoughts about Post-War Architecture in Greece and Some Hypotheses about its Near Future', *Tefchos*, 1 (1989), 21–31 (p. 27).

8 See *The Public Private House: Modern Athens and its Polykatoikia*, ed. by Richard Woditsch (Zurich: Park Books, 2018); Christoforos Sakellaropoulos, *Μοντέρνα αρχιτεκτονική και πολιτική της αστικής ανοικοδόμησης: Αθήνα 1945–1960* (Athens: Papazisis, 2003), pp. 259–379; and Anastasia Paschou, *Gebäudetypologie der Grossstadt: Eine Analyse der griechischen Metropole Athen* (Zurich: ETH, 2001). Online. doi.org/10.3929/ethz-a-004485758 (accessed 20 July 2021).

9 Dimitris Antonakakis, 'Προβλήματα κατοίκησης. Πολυκατοικία: Τυπολογική πολυπλοκότητα ή σύνθετη τυπολογία;', in *Έξι διαλέξεις για την κατοίκηση: Κατοικία, αστική πολυκατοικία, συλλογική κατοικία*, ed. by Nelly Marda, Mattheos Papavasiliou and Sofia Tsiraki (Athens: NTUA School of Architecture, 2014), pp. 55–99 (pp. 63–5).

10 See Dimitris Antonakakis, Βιογραφικό Υπόμνημα, National Technical University of Athens School of Architecture, 1978, Suzana and Dimitris Antonakakis' private archive, pp. 63–4. The *polykatoikia* is also the central theme of most of their texts. See Dimitris and Suzana Antonakakis, 'Three Athenian Apartment Houses', *Design + Art in Greece*, 8 (1977), 58–73; Dimitris and Suzana Antonakakis, 'Apartment Houses in Athens: The Architect's Role', *Architecture in Greece*, 12 (1978), 151–3; Dimitris Antonakakis, 'Πολυκατοικία: Όνειρο ή εφιάλτης;', *Journal of the Association of Greek Architects*, 6 (1981), 68–78; Suzana Antonakaki, 'Κατοικία και ποιότητα ζωής: Η διάσταση του χρόνου στο σχεδιασμό', *Journal of the Association of Greek Architects*, 9 (1981), 50–9; Soula Alexandropoulou, 'Σ' αναζήτηση ενός χώρου γι' ανθρώπινο τρόπο ζωής', *Καθημερινή*, 27 February 1977, 5; and Thanasis Lalas, 'Dimitris & Suzana Antonakakis Interview', *Περιοδικό*, 20 (1985).

11 This feature was obviously welcomed by the Greek contractors and developers of the period. It was in line with their intention to single out the entrance hall as the most luxurious space of the building. In Valsamakis's work, quality architectural design was thus aligned with the local building market and construction industry.

12 Antonakakis, 'Προβλήματα κατοίκησης'.

13 See Suzana and Dimitris Antonakakis, 'Η μεταπολεμική πολυκατοικία ως γενέτειρα του δημόσιου χώρου: Μια πρώτη προσέγγιση', in *Η Αθήνα στον 20ό αιώνα: Η Αθήνα όπως (δεν) φαίνεται, 1940–1985* (Athens: Ministry of Culture; Association of Greek Architects, 1985), pp. 129–35 (p. 130).

14 See *Atelier 66: The Architecture of Dimitris and Suzana Antonakakis*, ed. by Tournikiotis, p. 152.

15 Ibid., p. 151.

16 Antonakaki, 'Κατοικία και ποιότητα ζωής', p. 55.

17 See Richard Clogg, *A Concise History of Modern Greece* (Cambridge: Cambridge University Press, 1992), pp. 148–9; Paraskevi Kapoli, 'Εσωτερική μετανάστευση στην Αθήνα (1950–1970)', unpublished doctoral thesis, National and Kapodistrian University of Athens, 2014.

18 Antonakakis, 'Προβλήματα κατοίκησης', p. 78.
19 See Dimitris Emmanouil, *Η κοινωνική πολιτική κατοικίας στην Ελλάδα: Οι διαστάσεις μιας απουσίας* (Athens: National Centre for Social Research, 2006).
20 Antonakakis, 'Προβλήματα κατοίκησης', p. 86.
21 Pattie Dolka, interviewed by Stylianos Giamarelos (Athens: 9 June 2014).
22 Antonakakis, 'Η μεταπολεμική πολυκατοικία ως γενέτειρα του δημόσιου χώρου', p. 133.
23 Platon Issaias, 'Beyond the Informal City: Athens and the Possibility of an Urban Common', unpublished doctoral thesis, Technische Universiteit Delft, 2014, p. 114.
24 Myrto Nezi, interviewed by Stylianos Giamarelos (Athens: 9 June 2014).
25 Dimitris Antonakakis cited in Maria Dolka, 'The Grid in Pefkakia Elementary School by Pikionis and the Grid in the Rethimno Faculty of Humanities: Are They so Related as They Appear?', unpublished IB thesis, I.M. Panagiotopoulos School, 2002, p. 5.
26 Nezi, interviewed by Giamarelos.
27 See Lampis Dolkas, 'Η Ιθάκη σ' έδωσε τ' ωραίο ταξίδι', in Nikos Diakoulakis et al., *Διαδρομές* (Athens: Epikentro, 2021), pp. 153–86 (p. 174).
28 Antonakakis, 'Προβλήματα κατοίκησης', p. 61.
29 Nezi, interviewed by Giamarelos.
30 Dimitris and Suzana Antonakakis, 'Το ιδανικό σπίτι', *Το Βήμα*, 25 June 2000, 11.
31 Dolka, interviewed by Giamarelos.
32 See Panayotis Tournikiotis, 'Barriers and Jumps in Greek Urban Culture of the 70s', in *Great Unrest: 5 Utopias in the 1970s, a bit before–a bit after*, ed. by Thanasis Moutsopoulos (Athens: Voreiodytiko Sima, 2006), pp. 288–93, 367–8.
33 Dimitris and Suzana Antonakakis, 'Acknowledgements', in *Atelier 66*, ed. by Frampton, p. 11.
34 See Antonakakis, 'Το μοντέρνο και ο τόπος'.
35 See Antonakakis, 'Προβλήματα κατοίκησης', p. 98.
36 Yannis Roussos, interviewed by Stylianos Giamarelos (Athens: 6 July 2014).
37 Alekos Athanassiadis, interviewed by Stylianos Giamarelos (Athens: 8 July 2014).
38 See Antonakakis, 'Προβλήματα κατοίκησης', p. 83; Lalas, 'Dimitris & Suzana Antonakakis Interview'.
39 Antonakakis, 'Introduction', p. 6.
40 Antonakakis, 'Προβλήματα κατοίκησης', p. 82.
41 Ioanna Theocharopoulou, *Builders, Housewives and the Construction of Modern Athens* (London: Black Dog, 2017), pp. 111–45.
42 Among others, see: Hillary French, *Key Urban Housing of the Twentieth Century: Plans, Sections and Elevations* (London: Laurence King, 2008), pp. 150–1; Tzonis and Rodi, *Greece: Modern Architectures in History*, pp. 208–9; Kenneth Frampton, *Modern Architecture: A Critical History*, 2nd edn (London: Thames & Hudson, 1985), pp. 313–27.
43 Kenneth Frampton, 'Πρόλογος του Kenneth Frampton για την ελληνική έκδοση', in Kenneth Frampton, *Μοντέρνα αρχιτεκτονική: Ιστορία και κριτική*, trans. by Theodoros Androulakis and María Pangalou (Athens: Themelio, 1987), pp. 14–16 (p. 14).
44 Gerald A. Cohen, *Why Not Socialism?* (Princeton: Princeton University Press, 2009).
45 Issaias, 'Beyond the Informal City'.
46 Frampton, *Modern Architecture: A Critical History*, 2nd edn, p. 326.

10
Postmodern stigma

The implosion of Atelier 66 coincided with a period of inward-looking formal experimentation for Suzana and Dimitris Antonakakis. Hardly receiving any external input, their work continued to become more personal as the couple dwelled on the repository of references that they had been assimilating over two decades. When critical regionalism celebrated their work in the early 1980s, the two architects were already moving away from practices that had originally attracted international interest in their architecture. Suzana and Dimitris Antonakakis understood that modernism had decisively shaped their work. But after two decades of creative experimentation with its main tenets, they could feel that their architectural creativity was reaching a dead-end. For this reason, returning to their own 'critical regionalist' work of the 1970s and the modernist tenets of their architectural education of the late 1950s were not viable options when they clearly intended to drive their practice forward by the early 1980s. But the only other major source of external references at this point was the postmodernism that they had witnessed at the Biennale. Although they never admitted fully succumbing to it, their architectural practices moved in that direction in the early 1980s. As a matter of fact, their introductory text to Frampton's monograph in 1985, which included invocations of 'journeys in time, … the intermingling of eras, and the poetic freedom of dreams … Cretan palaces, the archaic Kouroi and sanctuaries, the Hellenic house, the Classical and Hellenistic agoras, the Byzantine churches and monasteries, [and] the seventeenth-century settlements' that certainly echo the teachings of their mentor Pikionis, would not sound out of place in the exhibition catalogue of 'The Presence of the Past'. All these precedents required 'identification and interpretation' by the architects, who aimed to retrieve 'the meaning [and] the poetry lost in [the] eroded and oversimplified architectural vocabulary' of vulgar Athenian modernism.[1] By this point, Suzana and

Figure 10.1 Postcard from Rhodes in the 1980s, featuring Suzana and Dimitris Antonakakis' Rhodes branch of the Ionian Bank, 1983–6, on the right

Suzana and Dimitris Antonakakis' private archive

Dimitris Antonakakis clearly understood architectural design in linguistic terms. The change that they felt their practice needed became a question of enriching their formal vocabulary beyond modernism.

In the early 1980s, Suzana and Dimitris Antonakakis were commissioned to turn an existing building within the multilayered historic environment of Rhodes[2] into a branch of the Ionian Bank (Fig. 10.1). Designed and built between 1983 and 1986, this now overlooked project coincided with the peak of Frampton's advocation of critical regionalism. Focusing on this building, in this chapter I read the refurbishment project as an exemplar of the two architects' different approach to the modern Athenian apartment-building typology after a decade of postmodern developments. Precisely when Frampton presented their 10-year-old Benaki Street project as an exemplar of critical regionalism, the Antonakakis were designing the Rhodes branch of the Ionian Bank along postmodernist lines (Fig. 10.2). Based on unpublished drawings, sketches and models retrieved from the architects' private archive and my interviews with the two Antonakakis and their collaborating architects and engineers, I show how this building was effectively turned inside out. The couple focused on its interior function

Figure 10.2 Sotiris Koukis, office building in the Athenian apartment building typology, Rhodes, 1968 (top), transformed into the local branch of the Ionian Bank by Suzana and Dimitris Antonakakis, 1986 (bottom)

Suzana and Dimitris Antonakakis' private archive

as a public space and its exterior form as an inward-looking fortress, whose 'grid' pattern was consciously enriched with 'pathway' elements.

As such, this chapter enables me to further expose critical regionalism as a rigid, idealising discourse that could not follow the transitions of an actively evolving architectural practice such as that of Atelier 66. The Antonakakis' design for the project was completed when Frampton's monograph on Atelier 66 was entering the production stage. Enthused with it, the Greek couple wanted to include their most recent work in the monograph. But Frampton preferred to ignore it in order to save the coherence of his critical regionalist discourse around their oeuvre. As such, he glossed over the intricacies of an architectural design practice that was evolving at the time of his writing. Beyond the architects' control, the Rhodes branch of the Ionian Bank was depicted as representing their turn from 'benign' modernist revisionism to 'regressive' postmodernism.

The project instigated debate about a possible postmodernist turn in the architects' work at a time when this equalled stigmatisation. I argue that this was a symptom of their increasingly personalised architectural idiom, which became self-enclosed and self-referential to the extent that it lost its actual contact with the place. My argument is situated within the development of related debates in Greece, where postmodern architecture had been resisted to the point that it had effectively become a taboo word – at least, in theory. The ensuing stigma associated with the 'postmodern' label could only be shaken off by returning to the question of relating modernism with the regional tradition. But this return to the region was still carried out in the essentialist terms of the 1960s. What had begun as a potential enrichment of the Antonakakis' design practice effectively culminated in a formal exercise. By the mid-1980s, Suzana and Dimitris Antonakakis had almost exhausted the expressive capacities of their modernist architectural idiom. Peer pressure to constantly return to the modernity/tradition schema of the 1960s became a vicious circle that undermined the potential relevance of their work for the wider project of critical regionalism.

Directing the grid

Dimitris Antonakakis has claimed that the façades of the Benaki Street apartment building were the direct result of the interior organisation of space in plan and section.[3] At its core, this is a modernist thesis that echoes similar remarks by Aris Konstantinidis. But as any architect who has ever designed a building could attest, there is no single way in which plan and section drawings can unequivocally produce an elevation drawing. While this is already clear in the Benaki Street apartment building of the mid-1970s, it becomes even more evident in the Ionian Bank project of the mid-1980s. This increasing elaboration of the façade as a relatively autonomous entity of the project characterises the work of Suzana and Dimitris Antonakakis in the early 1980s. It is a symptom of their attempt to reflexively renew their design work.

The two architects ventured in this direction when it became clear that their previous attempts to open up the design process to the parties involved and their peers in Atelier 66 had reached their limits. The modernist urge to control the final design product had effectively brought the non-hierarchical, collaborative practices of Atelier 66 to a halt. This in turn reduced the external stimuli that could refresh Suzana and Dimitris Antonakakis' work. As such, the two architects held more tightly to their own references and their increasingly personal architectural idiom. Unable to challenge their basic modernist tenets further, they had only their repressed lessons from the Strada Novissima to turn to. Focusing on their personal architectural idiom, they embarked on introverted formal exploration. But while they intended to continue to assimilate their interpretations of regional tradition into their modernist design vocabulary, this obsessive return to the same sources also became a burden for their architecture.

In 1988, Dimitris Antonakakis summarised the previous decade of the couple's personal architectural development. He acknowledged that the postmodern debate of the 1980s had encouraged them to 'condense the last two decades of [their] experience, and move with greater courage and freedom'.[4] The Benaki Street block was an original project that embodied the two architects' critical response to the standard Athenian apartment-building typology of the mid-1970s. A decade later, the Rhodes branch of the Ionian Bank offered them the opportunity to work with this generic typology more directly through a design intervention on an existing building. What remained constant in their work throughout this decade was the use of the grid as an ordering device of their diverse architectural gestures. Elias Constantopoulos was the first to highlight this in 1994: 'Reexamining the work of D. and S. Antonakakis, from the apartment building in Argolidos str. (1960) to the Rhodes branch of the Ionian Bank (1983), we observe that the grid is retained, albeit in different form, as the constant field in which the acts of composition take place'.[5] Although the grid remained a stable anchor for their design work, its implementation was not uniform over the years; it also evolved following their design work in the 1980s. In 1987, Suzana Antonakaki noted this when she referred to the grid not only as an organising principle but also as an element of directionality in their later projects:

> There is a dominant aspect that the grid is a neutral and directionless network within which flexibility or not, the permanent or not-permanent partitions of the building are moving. There is also another view that the grid may be capable of defining the directions, in which the bearing elements have a dual function. This is the view that we have chosen and tried to support throughout our work. Trying to have different degrees of privacy in the different places of the building we searched within the interior of the building for memories of the street. In our early work we have used the grid as a neutral (weft-warp) network with columns usually square and equidistant. Later we aimed at solutions, where the grid was defining a direction and an internal passage at the same time. This idea has been implemented on an existing building in Rhodes island. It was the case of a typical office building that has been finally used as a Branch Office of the Ionian Bank of Greece. We created there a public space by proposing an internal street which unfolds from the ground floor up to the terrace ... Starting from the need that the grid has direction-orientation, we were led to the elaboration of the limits and we concluded in creating construction zones, organically bound to the building and capable of using the space between the columns and the opportunity for a dual function of the bearing elements.[6]

In the aftermath of the celebrated interpretations of their work by Tzonis, Lefaivre and Frampton, the two architects consciously attempted to enrich their grid with 'pathway' elements. In liminal cases, the grid coincided with an indoor passage through the building. This is yet another way in which 'The Grid and the Pathway' influenced Suzana and Dimitris Antonakakis' work in the 1980s. The theorists had brought forth a clear conceptual schema that had been unconsciously developed in the architects' work before the 1980s. After seeing their buildings through Tzonis and Lefaivre's lens, the Antonakakis deliberately developed these ideas further in their later projects. If the grid had been the stable modernist aspect of their architecture, it was now consciously enriched with 'pathway' elements. The Rhodes branch of the Ionian Bank exemplified this renewed approach to the grid. Zissis Kotionis, a student of Dimitris Antonakakis who worked in Atelier 66 in the late 1980s, has also noted how the couple's use of the grid differs from that of

Konstantinidis. The Antonakakis' grid is not static like a chessboard but afforded with an 'elastic directionality' that becomes evident in the elements that fill it by sliding into their places.[7]

Transforming Athenian modernism

The commission for the Rhodes project came through Dimitris Andriolas, an acquaintance of Dimitris Antonakakis from his years of leading the Teaching Fellows Union at the National Technical University of Athens in the late 1970s. After the fall of the colonels in 1974, Andriolas became the director of the Ionian Bank. Appreciating the work of the Antonakakis, he contacted the two architects to discuss an edifice that the bank had acquired in 1983. Originally constructed in 1968, the building had profited from the extra height allowed by the modified code under the military junta. By 1983, demolishing the building to erect a new structure in its place was not a viable option, as it would practically mean losing one storey. The new project would have to be shorter in order to conform with building regulations in an area of Rhodes that was designated as a preservation zone following the standards established in the European Charter of Cultural Heritage of 1975. For this reason, Andriolas asked the Antonakakis to work with the existing building. The edifice was then still in use as a commercial-cum-office space. Its architect Sotiris Koukis was a prolific engineer of the period, who had started his professional practice in 1951. Because most of his projects were conventional modernist buildings that followed the typology of the Athenian *polykatoikia*, he rarely published his work. His early-1980s collaboration with Iason Rizos on the Athenaeum Intercontinental Hotel in Athens remains his best-known project to date.

Suzana and Dimitris Antonakakis aimed to 'transform' the banal, modernist apartment-cum-office block both internally and externally.[8] They intended to render it contextually legible as another part of the same whole – i.e. the designated preserved zone of the city. The fact that the building was the tallest around the old fortress called for its integration with its surroundings. By 1983, Suzana and Dimitris Antonakakis had rarely worked in such historic environments. Their most relevant experience was their restaurant, bar and nightclub projects at Akronafplia (1969–70), designed to be 'hidden' within the fortress walls to leave the existing skyline unobstructed. In the process of familiarising themselves with this context, the Antonakakis revisited Pikionis's early-1950s work on Rhodes.[9] The approach of their former mentor served as

Figure 10.3 Left: Old 'tower-house' on Rhodes, photographed by Dimitris Antonakakis, 1983; right: Suzana and Dimitris Antonakakis, Rhodes branch of the Ionian Bank, photographed by Dimitris Antonakakis, 1986

Suzana and Dimitris Antonakakis' private archive

an additional source of inspiration for them. The two architects' own first-hand observations led them to the conclusion that the old houses on Rhodes functioned like small towers. Rarely were their interior spaces and their inner lives extended to the outside world of the city and its public spaces (Fig. 10.3). By contrast, the building that they had to refurbish was a generic construction of the Athenian apartment-building typology.[10] Indiscriminate glass surfaces and balconies enveloped its three floors. Suzana and Dimitris Antonakakis aimed to reverse that.

Tearing the balconies down, their intervention effectively turned the building inside out. The edifice was transformed into an inward-looking volume, whose open ground floor could be permeated by the public life of the city. The wide-open space of the ground floor was intended to form a seamless part of the surrounding outdoor public space. This architectural intention was materially expressed through individual design elements, like large glass surfaces, paving and unconventional door and window frames. In such details, Suzana Antonakaki aimed for

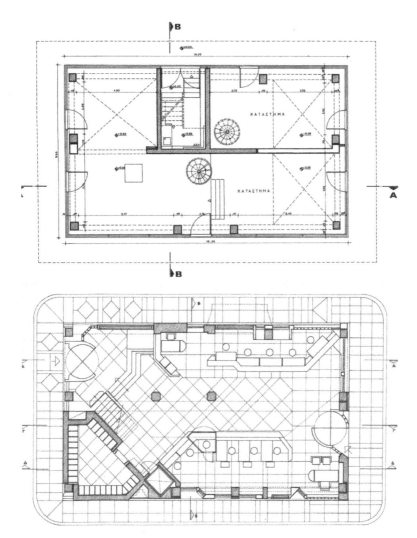

Figure 10.4 Sotiris Koukis, ground-floor plan drawing for office building on Rhodes, 1968 (top), transformed into the local branch of the Ionian Bank by Suzana and Dimitris Antonakakis, 1986 (bottom)

Suzana and Dimitris Antonakakis' private archive

an interplay of the large with the small scale. She worked on the building's interior with the scale of a public space in mind. The two doors on the opposite sides of the building were also intended to encourage a transversal movement through it. As such, they further afforded the interior the aura of a public space (Fig. 10.4). But the existing staircase of

Figure 10.5 Staircase of the Ionian Bank by Suzana and Dimitris Antonakakis, 1986

Suzana and Dimitris Antonakakis' private archive

the building, and its conventional placement at the centre of the ground floor area, was obtrusive for the realisation of this idea. Suzana and Dimitris Antonakakis freed up this space by placing the lift and the money bin on one corner and removing the existing staircase to replace it with a more elaborate structure (Fig. 10.5). This led many observers to believe that they had preserved an imaginary, authentic old staircase of the building. During the opening reception of the bank, the architects were congratulated for retaining the original staircase. They were also asked whether the building was formerly a tower of the Italians. Other attendants of the opening reception felt that this was an edifice that had always been there. Nobody recalled its previous state.[11]

With the configuration of the interior space finalised (and the related structural issues resolved by the collaborating engineers Vasilis and Panagiotis Plainis), Suzana and Dimitris Antonakakis focused on the exterior form of the building. Their elaborate work on the façades attracted the almost immediate association of this project with the postmodernist fads of the period (Fig. 10.6). But this was not the first time that the Antonakakis had elaborated on a building's façade. In the unanimously celebrated Benaki Street apartment building, the two architects had also approached the main elevation as a drawing of special significance. A similar working model that they produced on that occasion focused on the sculptural qualities and the volumetric variations across the main façade of the building (Fig. 10.7). Hence, the practice of elaborate façades enjoyed its own long history in the work of Suzana and Dimitris Antonakakis. In this light, the Rhodes Bank project does not represent an inconsistent 'postmodernist turn'. It is, rather, an evolutionary step within this longer-standing practice of paying special attention to the main elevation of a building. From the façade of 118

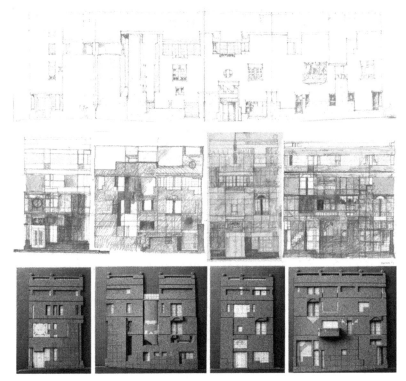

Figure 10.6 Suzana and Dimitris Antonakakis, Ionian Bank, working drawings and models of the four façades, 1983

Suzana and Dimitris Antonakakis' private archive

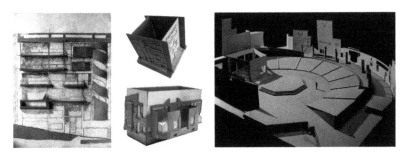

Figure 10.7 Left: Suzana and Dimitris Antonakakis, apartment building at 118 Benaki Street, Athens, working drawing/model of the main elevation, 1973; middle and right: working models for projects of the early 1980s, including the Technical University of Crete campus in Akrotiri, Chania, 1982; and the Rhodes branch of the Ionian Bank, 1983–6

Suzana and Dimitris Antonakakis' private archive

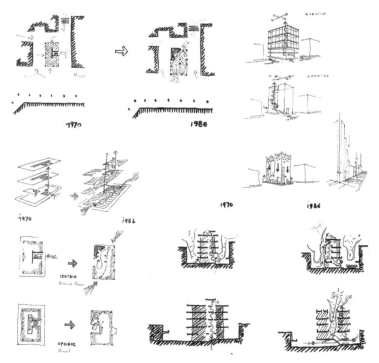

Figure 10.8   Suzana and Dimitris Antonakakis, diagrammatic outline of the main design intentions underpinning the Ionian Bank, 1986

Suzana and Dimitris Antonakakis' private archive

Benaki Street in the 1970s, a thin plane interspersed with volumetric bodies such as the balconies and the staircase, the Antonakakis proceeded to work on the façade as a thick, multilayered surface with its own potential for sculptural expressivity – as can be seen in the Rhodes Bank project. Similar study models from the same period in the two architects' archive further document this direction in their work of the 1980s (Fig. 10.7).

For the new face of the Rhodes Bank project, the Antonakakis drew from their understanding of local buildings as inward-looking fortresses. They effectively sculpted the monolithic volume of the Ionian Bank to create the effect of two interconnected towers (Fig. 10.8). This was not just meant to redress the formal and typological dissonance of the existing building with its immediate context. It was also the architects' deliberate attempt to tone down the relatively large scale of the edifice. Slicing the building in half also reflected its interior organisation around the elaborate novel staircase (Figs 10.9–10.10).

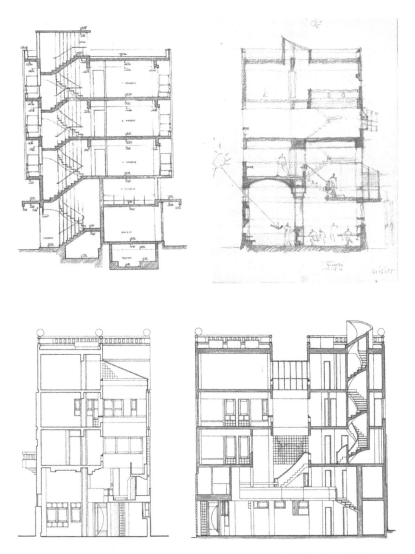

Figure 10.9 Sotiris Koukis, section drawing for office building on Rhodes, 1968, transformed into the Ionian Bank, section drawings and sketches by Suzana and Dimitris Antonakakis, 1986

Suzana and Dimitris Antonakakis' private archive

Once this decision was made, the architects focused on details. With the project located away from the Atelier 66 headquarters in Athens, and the budget not allowing for travel expenses for their trusted craftspeople, they had to work with a local construction crew whom they did not know. This did not keep Suzana Antonakaki from trying out new

Figure 10.10   Suzana and Dimitris Antonakakis, Ionian Bank, exterior
and interior views photographed by Dimitris Antonakakis, 1986
Suzana and Dimitris Antonakakis' private archive

ideas for the first time, however. With the local construction crew, she
experimented with inserting colour into the roughcast plaster – following
an original formula by Nikos Hadjimichalis. But some of the two architects'
ideas did not turn out as expected. For instance, the Antonakakis
originally intended to use dark marble on the lower part of the façade.
They wanted to create the impression that the material used for the public
pavement was also turning upwards to 'climb' the exterior walls of the
bank. This subtle design detail was meant to reinforce the sense of the
building as part of the public domain. The overarching principle was a
logical development from the Benaki Street project, where the Sifnos
stonework extended from the interior floors of the building to the
sidewalk on the exterior. On Rhodes, this idea was lost when the
construction crew used conventional pavement tiles for the surrounding
public space. Other details, like Eleni Vernardaki's ceramics on the façade,
became trademark features of the building. Partly owing to the
Antonakakis' inability to be present on site during construction, it was
this exquisite attention to detail that resulted in an elaborate work of
architecture. Not knowing the local construction crew motivated the two
architects to produce some of their most detailed project drawings to
date, to ensure that the quality of the built result would be as close to their
original intentions as possible.

Figure 10.11 Suzana and Dimitris Antonakakis, Ionian Bank, photographed by Dimitris Antonakakis, 1986

Suzana and Dimitris Antonakakis' private archive

Turning postmodern

The Antonakakis' decision to slice the volume in half to produce the twin-tower effect was not favourably received in the architectural circles of the period. The criticism levelled at the building focused on its external appearance (Fig. 10.11). Owing to its facile association with the postmodern historicist trends of the period, the question lingered: were Suzana and Dimitris Antonakakis 'turning postmodern'? By the end of the decade, Constantopoulos noted that postmodernism in Greece had become a 'non-revolutionary' intention of skin-deep 'aesthetic differentiation'.[12] In most cases, it was limited to an extra ornamental layer to conventional (modernist) structures, as repeatedly noted by critics of postmodernism such as Reyner Banham. This description was broadly in line with the Antonakakis' approach to the Rhodes branch of the Ionian Bank project.

A juxtaposition of projects that the two architects had produced over two decades suffices to document this transition (Fig. 10.12). The austere, and more clearly modernist, projects of their youth in the 1960s were succeeded by the elaborately detailed works of their maturity in the 1980s. But this did not mean that the Antonakakis had abandoned the

Figure 10.12 (from top to bottom) Suzana and Dimitris Antonakakis, apartment building on Argolidos Street, Athens, 1962; Philippas Residence in Glyfada, Athens, 1969; Atelier 66 (Suzana and Dimitris Antonakakis, Boukie Babalou, Antonis Noukakis, Theano Fotiou), Crete University School of the Humanities, Rethymnon, 1981; Atelier 66 (Suzana and Dimitris Antonakakis, Aleka Monemvasitou, Boukie Babalou, Antonis Noukakis, Theano Fotiou), Technical University of Crete campus in Akrotiri, Chania, 1982

Suzana and Dimitris Antonakakis' private archive

defining characteristics of their design practice. In the words of Greek architectural historian Andreas Giacumacatos, the Rhodes branch of the Ionian Bank was still '[h]ighly emblematic' of the architects' trademark design principles. But 'the morphological elaboration' of the project also 'offer[ed] various innovational aspects compared to their previous works'.[13] In a recent interview, Dimitris Antonakakis claimed that their work of the 1980s reflected their feeling that they had already mastered the tenets of modernist design in all their intricacy. They were therefore ready to move beyond them. The Rhodes branch of the Ionian Bank was a project with a strong personal character, and this rendered it significant within their oeuvre. As he characteristically noted, he regarded this building as their own 'comment on postmodernism'. However, he also admitted that this reference to postmodernism was not their deliberate intention at the time. It was, rather, a conclusion that they reached after witnessing the 'awkward' reception of the building. Both Greek architectural circles and their close international peers, such as Aldo van Eyck and Herman Hertzberger, remained unconvinced by this 'highly loaded' project when compared with the clearer lines of their earlier work.[14]

Other international critics reacted more enthusiastically. In a letter to Dimitris Antonakakis in 1987, Carleton Knight III described the Rhodes Bank as 'post-modernism inspired by Le Corbusier'.[15] Working as a contributing editor of the journal of the American Institute of Architects, *Architecture*, Knight intended to publish the project in its pages. But his premature death only a month later meant that his article on the building did not materialise. His positive reaction was nonetheless encouraging for Suzana and Dimitris Antonakakis. Regarding this project as characteristic of their personal work of this period, they intended to publicise it more widely. As such, it featured prominently as the poster child of their exhibition at the ETH in Zurich in 1988 (Fig 10.13). It was also included in the exhibition of their work at the Greek Pavilion in the Fifth Biennale of Architecture in Venice (1991), and their first monographic exhibition at the Institut Français de Grèce in Athens (1994).

The architectural couple were so enthused with the project that they had started promoting it as soon as they had finalised their design. In a letter to Frampton in February 1984, Suzana and Dimitris Antonakakis included material on 'one of [their] last buildings'. Although they did not call it by its name, they referred to it as 'a very challenging project' due to 'the problems of [its] incorporation … within a pre-existing settlement'.[16] Given the fact that the Antonakakis rarely worked in historic environments, and that their university projects of the same period on Crete were at

Figure 10.13 Poster of Suzana and Dimitris Antonakakis' 'Wander through a Greek Architectural Reality' exhibition at ETH in Zurich, 28 October–24 November 1988

© gta Archives/ETH Zürich

the outskirts of major cities, I contend that they referred here to the Rhodes branch of the Ionian Bank. The couple clearly wanted this project to be included in Frampton's monograph. The British historian's reply to the two architects confirms that he received the related material. But despite his positive note that the 'new work is very interesting',[17] the Rhodes branch of the Ionian Bank did not make it to the published monograph – which covers their work from 1963 to 1982. Its exclusion was not a matter of following a specific chronological framework of two decades. Approximately fifteen years later, Frampton noted a 'regrettable regression into historicising, stylistic Post Modernism in the 80s, detectable ... even occasionally in the architecture of Atelier 66, most particularly perhaps in their rather decorative Ionian Bank, built in Rhodes'.[18]

The Frampton–Antonakakis correspondence of 1984 shows that the British historian was aware of the existence of this project at the time that he was promoting the work of the architectural couple as an exemplar of critical regionalism. It is rather clear that by then he could not include a project that leaned towards that which his approach was meant to resist. To save the coherence of his discourse around the work of the Greek architectural couple, Frampton preferred to omit the 'regrettable' Rhodes Bank from the monograph. But in so doing, he also glossed over the intricacies of an architectural design practice that was clearly evolving at the time of his writing. This is an additional aspect of the distorting effect of critical regionalism on the architectural practices that it was allegedly appraising. Panos Koulermos's letter to Frampton of 1986, with three 'promised' photographs of the Rhodes project attached, documents how this building by 'Antonakakis-Scarpakis (?)'[19] could still be interpreted within the critical regionalist framework through its association with the work of their Venetian peer. By then, however, only a year after Suzana and Dimitris Antonakakis' celebrated entry in Frampton's history of modern architecture and the publication of the monograph by Rizzoli, things were already different.

Beyond Suzana and Dimitris Antonakakis' control, the Rhodes branch of the Ionian Bank started to represent their turn to postmodernism. In their accounts at the time, both Constantopoulos and Giacumacatos treated the building as a liminal case.[20] Dubbed 'revelatory' by Giacumacatos, the 'sculptural treatment' of the bank and the 'ambiguous iconographic references possibly introduce[d] a novel phase in their design research'.[21] By the mid-1980s, the work of the Antonakakis was clearly in transition. Atelier 66 imploded at the same time that the two architects were criticised for succumbing to postmodernism. Writing in the left-wing journal *Anti* in 1986, Alexandros Xydis presented their Hartokollis House project on Sifnos (1984) as a 'post-modernist invasion' to the island. The two architects were held to account for lacking a 'lived' experience of the place, and experimenting with 'the "postmodern" style'. They also did so in a landscape that had so far evaded 'exoticisms' and had 'neither the functional nor the aesthetic need for neoclassical eclecticisms'; Sifnos was clearly 'not a place for architectural experiments'.[22]

Fifteen years later, Greek architectural historian Dimitris Philippidis also contended that Suzana and Dimitris Antonakakis had managed to 'assimilate' their experimentations with these 'postmodern' liberties in the spirit of their previous work.[23] In other words, the couple did not suddenly 'turn' postmodern. Rather, the two architects explored these tendencies in the context of their own work. But in the eyes of the architectural audiences of the period, the Rhodes branch of the Ionian Bank looked like an escapee from the Strada Novissima. Its elaborate façades harked back to memories of the postmodernist Biennale; indeed, it was not difficult to imagine the building navigating the Venetian lagoons alongside Aldo Rossi's Teatro del Mondo, which had featured in Dimitris Antonakakis's recording of their trip there in 1980. However, the bank also reflected the architects' conscious attempt to develop their work along the lines of the critical regionalist 'grid and pathway' interpretation. Their attempt to build on the critical regionalist account had led their project to be received as a variant of Strada Novissima postmodernism. Hence, it was not only the shared terminology within the same media ecology that rendered critical regionalism an integral part of the postmodern developments in architecture, as I argued in chapter 4. The Rhodes Bank by Suzana and Dimitris Antonakakis is a symptom of the same phenomenon in architectural design. This was largely owing to the architects' understanding of their creative freedom to move away from the modernist tenets – what they called the 'controlled transgression of given rules'.[24] After all, it was their constant desire for control of the design process that led to their personal, albeit increasingly stale, architectural idiom.

As a result, the two architects found themselves caught up in a postmodern debate that they could hardly follow when it was historically produced.[25] As architectural historian Panayotis Tournikiotis has noted, it was not only Suzana and Dimitris Antonakakis but a whole generation of Greek architects that found themselves in this awkward position, since this 'transitional phase' of architecture was not locally generated but imported from abroad.[26] As such, the assimilation of the foreign 'postmodern' influences lacked a clear theoretical and historical understanding that could offer a meaningful direction to these developments in Greece. For the same reason, the Antonakakis defended the autonomy of their personal design method beyond labels, movements and tendencies that cloud understanding.[27] 'Critical regionalism' was a term devised around their own work at the moment of their frustration with the 'postmodernism' that they had witnessed at the Biennale. While the two architects did intend to move their lessons from modernism forward, it was unclear whether terms like 'critical regionalism' and 'postmodernism' were useful in their pursuit. Both terms proved rather inadequate. Not only were they unhelpful overdeterminations of diverse architectural expressions but they also had serious ramifications on practices of the period, as I have shown in previous chapters. Similarly, the association of the Antonakakis with 'postmodernism' was obfuscating in theory and detrimental to advancing a better understanding of their work in practice.

Short-circuited discourses

In 1980s Greece, as elsewhere, the postmodern debate was conducted in the moralistic vocabulary of modernist discourse. Although the term was rarely defined in the local architectural milieu, 'postmodernism' denoted the external 'Other' that threatened the regional modernist community. As in the 'Great Debate' lecture series at the RIBA in London in 1982–3, the relevant architectural debates in mid-1980s Greece were also conducted in the Manichean terms of modernism versus postmodernism.[28] One side of the debate generated the impression that conservative postmodern architecture had prevailed. Having displaced progressive modern architecture, it argued, postmodernism was a menace that had to be subverted. Aris Konstantinidis's passionate critique of postmodern developments set the intense tone for this side of the debate in Greece.[29] For these architects, 'postmodernism' thus served as the term that cemented the imagined community of 'us', the Greek modernists of the generation of the 1960s, against 'them', the Venetian postmodernists and their unnamed Greek followers.

But this debate did not historically unfold within a single, homogeneous and coherent public sphere. While Orestis Doumanis's established review *Architecture in Greece* followed the publisher's 'modernising' agenda, at least in theory, less well-known publications such as 'Άνθρωπος + Χώρος [*Human + Space*] were quicker to accommodate early discussions of postmodern architecture in Greece and abroad.[30] Each institution and agent of production of architectural discourse and practice thus addressed a different constituency. The other, 'postmodernist', side of the debate created the impression that the conservative establishment of modern architects was excluding a new generation from exploratory practice. The modernists' critique of alternative approaches practically hindered the development of an architecture that aspired to transcend the impersonal grey boxes of postwar apartment buildings.

The debate unfolded within the spectrum of these two extreme positions, in public spheres that historically accommodated their clashes and partial overlaps. In this context, postmodern design practices also developed almost schizophrenically in Greece. They encountered resistance at the same time that they were adopted by architects who rejected them in theory. The 'covert' publication of postmodernist-looking projects in the 'modernist' *Architecture in Greece* is characteristic here. Reminiscent of the emperor's new clothes, aberrant architectural practices were published in plain view – as if they were invisible. When renowned modernists of the 1960s resorted to postmodernist architectural forms in the 1980s, as Nikos Valsamakis (b. 1924) did in his Hotel Amalia project in Nafplio (1980–3), Greek historians and critics employed a series of euphemisms to avoid calling them by this name. Their convoluted, obfuscating qualifications include phrases such as 'an expanded field of new modernism', 'an approach to regional architectural idioms ... that avoids any emotional or scenographic semblance ... in the spirit of a realistic empiricism based on liberal typological solutions and use of materials' or 'a critical attitude to modernist puritanism that repulses its "prohibitions" and is driven to a sort of late modern eclecticism, simultaneously discovering the creative function of memory' without 'challenging rationalism and the syntactic logic of the modern tradition of the twentieth century'.[31] The projects are published, but their accompanying texts read like their customarily deplorable postmodern aspects are not seen.

In this overarching framework, the association of the Antonakakis' work with postmodernism put them almost reflexively on the defensive. As some of the most prominent representatives of their generation of progressive modernists of the 1960s, they could not be suddenly portrayed as siding with the 'regressing' postmodernism of the 1980s. In a 1990 interview, Dimitris Antonakakis asserted that 'the postmodern had not provided [them] with any helpful theoretical structure'. It had only served as a critique of commodified modernism that fed in to the architects' own critical practice. This allowed them to work more freely, insofar as the disciplined decisions that underlay their work were still sturdily defined by their modernist grids. In the same interview, Suzana Antonakaki was also adamant in distinguishing the 'critical regionalist' from the 'postmodernist' stance. She described the regional as the place in which 'Architecture meets history ... not historicism. The "critical" stance towards the past excludes quaint and superficial imitations'.[32] In other words, reconsidering modernism could only be intertwined with a reconsideration of regional architecture. In theory, this enabled the Antonakakis to develop their specific approach of working within a traditional settlement. According to Dimitris Antonakakis, a new building in a historic setting should still 'address the conditions of contemporary life'. It could well be the result of a 'synthesis of particular elements of the traditional cluster' that would nonetheless set its own terms of 'articulation' and 'organisation of space'.[33] As such, it would not merely replicate existing forms of the settlement.

The intense moralism and the architects' anxiety at being stigmatised as postmodernists, especially evident in those who formed part of the generation of the 1960s, short-circuited the postmodern debate in 1980s Greece. Local architects who were interested in the postmodern developments of the period first had to defend them against the scathing critiques of their modernist peers.[34] Throughout the decade, the arguments of both sides effectively remained the same. The emancipatory dimensions and the subversive potential of postmodern approaches to architecture were customarily foregrounded by younger architects – from Antouanetta Angelidi and Dimitra Hondrogianni, who openly expressed their interest in the new developments during the first open debate of the Association of Greek Architects in 1981, to Kostas Moraitis who responded to Konstantinidis's libels in 1988.[35] Having to speak from the defensive against the established guard of their modernist peers, these architects frequently adopted a more dispassionate, conciliatory tone.[36] As early as 1982, Manolis Papadolampakis was appalled by the 'sterility' of a debate based on a series of 'misunderstandings'.[37] Although the term 'postmodern' enjoyed a wider circulation in Greece only after the mid-1980s,[38] Papadolampakis's insight was accurate. In 1985, Yorgos Simeoforidis characteristically noted the mythologisation of the term 'postmodern' and the irreconcilable polemical debates that it instigated in the local context – especially after 'the massive arrival' of Greek graduates who had studied architecture abroad.[39] But this did not practically affect the postmodern debate in Greece. By the end of the decade, Savas Condaratos still bemoaned the local 'absence of theoretical ferment and critical debate'.[40] This superficial engagement with the postmodern problematic could only result in a merely iconographic Greek 'transplant' of forms and collages borrowed from Western European and North American architects.

Despite the occasionally heated rhetoric, the supposed debate was a stale repetition of virtually unchanged arguments and counterarguments. Hardly advancing a nuanced understanding, the debate was also unsuccessful in alleviating the stigma that came with the term 'postmodern' in mainstream Greek architectural discourse. Architects and critics of the period were still hesitant to ascribe the label to the work of their Greek peers. Even when the referents were obvious,[41] implicit allusions remained the 'politically correct' order of the day for referring to the work of a third party.

After this tumultuous but practically ineffective postmodern debate of the 1980s, Greek architectural discourse returned to the familiar grounds of relating modernism with the Greek *topos*.[42] By the end of the decade, Constantopoulos had already noted the incipient 'danger of postmodernism'. According to his account, the Greek turn to the postmodern could cause a 'rupture ... from the recent tradition of fertile concerns around the modern and the autochthonous'.[43] By the 1990s, the related discussions concentrated again on 'the Greek version of the modern'.[44] This turn reflected the culmination of a discourse that had unfolded in parallel with the postmodern debate of the 1980s, instigated by the positive reception of critical regionalism in the mid-1980s. Simeoforidis's proffered return to the 'paradox dilemma' of 'the regional shade of modernism' triggered yet another return to the intertwined questions of modernism and regional cultures.[45] In the meantime, architectural historians had already idealised the 1960s as the 'short-lived spring' of Greek modernism after the end of the civil war in 1949 and before the imposition of the military junta in 1967.[46] Andreas Kourkoulas's concerns about a 'frivolous' postmodern 'rupture with the post-war architectural tradition' of Pikionis, Konstantinidis, Zenetos and Valsamakis represent the prevailing attitude in the early 1990s.[47] By then, the discussion was ready to return to familiar ground for Suzana and Dimitris Antonakakis and the revered generation of the 1960s. Acting as further proof of the inconclusive postmodern debates of the 1980s, however, this discursive turn also obfuscates the work of current historians of the recent past. Even the most recent histories of architecture in Greece after the Second World War avoid addressing the great debate between modernists and postmodernists as the central event that decisively marked the 1980s.[48] As a result, postmodern architecture in Greece remains obscure – if not practically invisible – to this day.

After the mid-1990s, Suzana and Dimitris Antonakakis omitted the Rhodes Bank from their subsequent monographic exhibition catalogues – just like Frampton had done a decade earlier for the Rizzoli monograph. Internalising the negative reaction to their work of the 1980s, they also started to focus more closely on their work of the 1970s in their presentations to international audiences from the 1990s onwards.[49] However, the association of their later work with postmodernism left its deep historiographical stigma. In their recent account, Alexander Tzonis and Alcestis Rodi referred to the work of the Antonakakis from the 1980s onwards as '"collages" of themes that make allusions to a Greek "past", especially a rural past, and a Greek "place", but without any grounding to their site; thus [Suzana and Dimitris Antonakakis] lost the crucial critical dimension that was so effective for the success of their earlier work'.[50] Architectural historians continue to return to the earlier projects of the Antonakakis, as if their later and more personal work is less interesting. As a result, an architectural practice that remained creatively prolific for approximately six decades is today historiographically confined to projects that span only the first two decades of its career, just like Frampton's monograph of 1985. To sustain the coherent myth of critical regionalism, the Benaki Street apartment building remained the poster child of the Antonakakis' oeuvre. Hidden in the shadows for almost three decades now, the Rhodes branch of the Ionian Bank is the other side of this story. This fact highlights the complex and ambiguous relationship between a programmatic discourse and an architectural practice whose independent evolution refuses to be limited by existing theoretical categories.

The Antonakakis were not the only architects to lose Frampton's favour in the 1980s. The same is the case for other formerly 'heroic' group practices such as that of Martorell, Bohigas and Mackay, and old Frampton favourites such as Gino and Nani Valle whose outstanding work of the 1960s 'came to an unexpected still inexplicable conclusion'.[51] Like the Antonakakis, these architects also remained equally productive in the decades that followed. Such cases make it seem as if Frampton acknowledged that he was fighting a losing battle. As the early-1980s projects of these formerly critical practices increasingly surrendered to 'the exigencies of production and an ersatz schematic iconography', the perennial nemesis of his critical regionalism, the end of a heroic period was certainly nigh.[52] But excluding buildings such as the Ionian Bank from the history of critical regionalist architectural practices does not enable one to understand how the intertwined reconsideration of modernism and regional traditions ended up developing in vicious circles by the mid-1980s. This outcome also short-circuited the potential contribution of such work to the wider project of critical regionalism, which aspired to develop beyond a feedback loop of constantly falling back from modernism to regional culture and vice versa.

Frampton is today aware of the unavoidable overlaps of his discourse with larger-scale postmodern developments, as he characteristically admits that 'Critical Regionalism is a postmodern manifestation in itself, both as a theory and a practice'; as such, it 'may be seen as a postmodern attempt to indicate a way of continuing with a relevant modern culture while simultaneously resisting the reduction of architecture to spectacular images'.[53] By contrast, Greek architects continue to reject their labelling as 'postmodern' today. Having internalised the 'neo-modern' design principles that historically prevailed after the 1980s, they avoid publicising their most 'glaring' postmodern works from that period.[54] Devalued by their own architects, postmodern architectures remain hidden and have hitherto gone unpublished. Because they fail to satisfy the historically prevalent modernist criteria of the present, they have been excluded from recent monographic publications.[55] As long as the label of 'postmodernism' persists as a stigma in architects' minds, the writing of this history will remain obfuscated. A new generation of architectural historians is now called upon to transgress the taboo of their predecessors. The closer one looks at the recent past, as I have tried to do here, the more the 'modernist' and 'postmodernist' labels appear as mutually interchangeable taboo words. As one could easily take the place of the other, they both functioned as empty status symbols in practice. The specific positive or negative value that would be attributed to them was determined by the geography and the constituencies that participated in each discussion. The 'us and them' division that constantly shaped the 'modern/postmodern' taboo also reinforced the grouping of imaginary communities around these terms.[56]

But for architectural historians of the 2020s, the important question is not whether the work of an architectural practice should be labelled as 'modernist' or 'postmodernist'. This debate clearly belongs to the 1980s; it is not as constructive in the twenty-first century. Much more interesting is the cross-cultural relationship behind the stylistic 'label', the evolution of architectural theory and practice through this complex interaction within and beyond national borders from the 1980s onwards. The stigmatisation of 'postmodernism' as a taboo subject is not only disorienting but also obfuscates the discussion that proves more relevant for architects today. This is why this taboo needs to be transgressed. Taken together, recent culturally specific studies of postmodern architecture have already started to show how previously overlooked 'peripheral' histories have played their own invisible role in 'international' developments of the 1980s.[57] And this is just the tip of the postmodern iceberg. The proliferation of similar historical studies that will leave the sterile controversy of stylistic labelling behind will also allow for the more socially and culturally conscious architectural debates of the time to be recovered precisely when they seem increasingly relevant. I explore the potential implications of such an approach for critical regionalism in the epilogue.

Notes

1   Dimitris and Suzana Antonakakis, 'Introduction', in *Atelier 66: The Architecture of Dimitris and Suzana Antonakakis*, ed. by Kenneth Frampton (New York: Rizzoli, 1985), pp. 6–8 (pp. 6, 8).
2   See Vasilis Colonas, *Ιταλική αρχιτεκτονική στα Δωδεκάνησα* (Athens: Olkos, 2002).
3   Dimitris Antonakakis, 'Προβλήματα κατοίκησης. Πολυκατοικία: Τυπολογική πολυπλοκότητα ή σύνθετη τυπολογία;', in *Έξι διαλέξεις για την κατοίκηση: Κατοικία, αστική πολυκατοικία, συλλογική κατοικία*, ed. by Nelly Marda, Mattheos Papavasiliou and Sofia Tsiraki (Athens: NTUA School of Architecture, 2014), pp. 55–99 (p. 86).

4 Dimitris Antonakakis, Υπόμνημα, National Technical University of Athens School of Architecture, 1988, Suzana and Dimitris Antonakakis' private archive, p. 29.

5 Elias Constantopoulos, 'On the Architecture of Dimitris and Suzana Antonakakis', *Design + Art in Greece*, 25 (1994), 18–25 (p. 24).

6 Suzana Antonakaki, 'Outdoor "Houses" and Indoor Streets', in *INDESEM '87: International Design Seminar*, ed. by Marc Labadie and Bert Tjhie (Delft: Delft University Press, 1988), pp. 132–49 (p. 144).

7 Zissis Kotionis, 'Ιδιώματα της ελληνικής αρχιτεκτονικής: Δ. Πικιώνης, Α. Κωνσταντινίδης, Τ. Ζενέτος, Δ. και Σ. Αντωνακάκη', in Zissis Kotionis, *Η τρέλα του τόπου: Αρχιτεκτονική στο ελληνικό τοπίο* (Athens: Ekkremes, 2004), pp. 61–95 (p. 83).

8 Dimitris and Suzana Antonakakis, 'Ionian Bank Branch Office in Rhodes', *Architecture in Greece*, 22 (1988), 154–9.

9 Dimitris Pikionis, 'Το πρόβλημα της μορφής' (1951), repr. in Δ. Πικιώνης: *Κείμενα*, ed. by Agni Pikioni and Michalis Parousis (Athens: MIET, 1985), pp. 204–46.

10 For the proliferation of the Athenian apartment-building typology in the periphery of Greece, see Nikos Magouliotis, 'Το Νεο-ελληνικό Maison Dom-ino, σαν ένα ιδίωμα σύγχρονης ανώνυμης αρχιτεκτονικής', unpublished master's thesis, National Technical University of Athens, 2016, pp. 77–125.

11 Suzana and Dimitris Antonakakis, interviewed by Stylianos Giamarelos (Athens: 31 May 2014).

12 Elias Constantopoulos, 'Το τέλος των στυλ ή η αιώνια επιστροφή τους;', *Architecture in Greece*, 24 (1990), 21–2 (p. 21).

13 Andreas Giacumacatos, 'The Rhodes Branch of the Ionian Bank', *l'Arca*, 54 (1991), 70–7 (p. 74).

14 Suzana and Dimitris Antonakakis, interviewed by Stylianos Giamarelos (Athens: 27 May 2014).

15 Carleton Knight III, letter to Dimitris Antonakakis, 23 January 1987, Suzana and Dimitris Antonakakis' private archive.

16 Dimitris and Suzana Antonakakis, letter to Kenneth Frampton, 16 February 1984, Suzana and Dimitris Antonakakis' private archive.

17 Kenneth Frampton, letter to Dimitris and Suzana Antonakakis, 12 March 1984, Suzana and Dimitris Antonakakis' private archive.

18 Kenneth Frampton, 'A Note on Greek Architecture: 1938–1997', in *Landscapes of Modernisation: Greek Architecture 1960s and 1990s*, ed. by Yannis Aesopos and Yorgos Simeoforidis (Athens: Metapolis, 1999), pp. 12–14 (p. 14).

19 Panos Koulermos, letter to Kenneth Frampton, 15 October 1986, CCA Fonds 197, Kenneth Frampton fonds, 197 – 2017 – 115T, AP197.S3.002, Personal and professional correspondence 1986, 1986, 197-115-003.

20 Constantopoulos, 'On the Architecture of Dimitris and Suzana Antonakakis', p. 24; Giacumacatos, 'The Rhodes Branch of the Ionian Bank', p. 74.

21 Andreas Giacumacatos, 'New Rationalism and Critical Empiricism', *Architecture in Greece*, 23 (1989), 53–9 (p. 58).

22 Alexandros Xydis, 'Ο Μετα-μοντερνισμός εισβάλλει στη Σίφνο', *Αντί*, 328 (1986), 50.

23 Dimitris Philippidis, *Μοντέρνα αρχιτεκτονική στην Ελλάδα* (Athens: Melissa, 2001), pp. 155–6.

24 See *Atelier 66: The Architecture of Dimitris and Suzana Antonakakis*, ed. by Panayotis Tournikiotis (Athens: futura, 2007), p. 17.

25 See Elias Constantopoulos, 'Greek Architecture in the Eighties', *Architecture in Greece*, 23 (1989), 63–9; Giacumacatos, 'New Rationalism and Critical Empiricism'.

26 See Panayotis Tournikiotis, 'Greek Architecture at the Unclear Confines Between Theory and Tradition', *Architecture in Greece*, 23 (1989), 70–7.

27 Dimitris and Suzana Antonakakis, 'Τάσεις στη σύγχρονη ελληνική αρχιτεκτονική', *Architecture in Greece*, 23 (1989), 83.

28 Savas Condaratos, 'Ο αρχιτεκτονικός μεταμοντερνισμός ως απελευθέρωση και ως παραίτηση', in *Μοντέρνο-Μεταμοντέρνο*, ed. by Georgios Aristinos et al. (Athens: Smili, 1988), pp. 77–85 (p. 85, note 1).

29 Aris Konstantinidis, *Αμαρτωλοί και κλέφτες, ή η απογείωση της αρχιτεκτονικής* (Athens: Agra, 1987).

30 See Anthony C. Antoniades, 'Μετα-Μοντέρνα Αρχιτεκτονική. Δύο περιπτώσεις: Renato Bofill και Piano-Rogers', *Άνθρωπος + Χώρος*, 6 (1977), 7–16.

31 Andreas Giacumacatos, *Ιστορία της ελληνικής αρχιτεκτονικής: 20ος αιώνας*, 2nd edn (Athens: Nefeli, 2004), pp. 121, 133.

32 Aris Stylianou, 'Το Εργαστήρι-66', *Αρχιτέκτων: Ενημερωτικό Δελτίο Συλλόγου Αρχιτεκτόνων Κύπρου*, 10 (March–April 1990), 62–9 (pp. 68–9).

33 Dimitris Antonakakis, 'Προβληματισμοί σχεδιασμού', *Journal of the Association of Greek Architects*, 21–2 (1989), 65–6, 77 (p. 66).

34 See Georgios Korovesis, 'Αρχιτεκτονική Post-Modern: Μόδα ή νέος προσανατολισμός;', *Άνθρωπος + Χώρος*, 19 (1982), 17–26.

35 See the *Journal of the Association of Greek Architects*, 8 (1981), 80–2; Kostas Moraitis, 'Η Σφίγγα και οι γρίφοι: Εισήγηση για την Αρχιτεκτονική, τα Τέρατα και τα εκφραστικά Πάθη', in *Μοντέρνο-Μεταμοντέρνο*, ed. by Aristinos et al., pp. 161–72 (p. 162).

36 See Condaratos, 'Ο αρχιτεκτονικός μεταμοντερνισμός ως απελευθέρωση και ως παραίτηση'.

37 Manolis Papadolampakis, 'Μεταμοντέρνα πρόθεση', *Άνθρωπος + Χώρος*, 17 (1982), 17–24 (p. 17).

38 See *Design + Art in Greece*, 16 (1985); *Architecture in Greece*, 23 (1989); and *Architecture in Greece*, 24 (1990).

39 Yorgos Simeoforidis, 'Foreword', *Design + Art in Greece*, 16 (1985), 14–15 (p. 15).

40 Savas Condaratos, 'Το γράμμα του Σάββα Κονταράτου', *Architecture in Greece*, 23 (1989), 82–3 (p. 82).

41 See Andreas Giacumacatos, 'Η μέθοδος και το πρόβλημα', *Architecture in Greece*, 24 (1990), 18–19 (p. 19).

42 See Dimitris Antonakakis, 'Το μοντέρνο και ο τόπος', *Architecture in Greece*, 30 (1996), 134.

43 Constantopoulos, 'Το τέλος των στυλ ή η αιώνια επιστροφή τους', p. 21.

44 Among others, see *Metamorphoses of the Modern: The Greek Experience*, ed. by Anna Kafetsi (Athens: Ministry of Culture; National Gallery, 1992); Savas Condaratos, 'Η ελληνική εκδοχή του μοντέρνου', *Architecture in Greece*, 30 (1996), 135–6; Panayotis Tournikiotis, 'The Rationale of the Modern and Locus: A View of Greek Architecture from the Seventies to the Nineties', in *20th Century Architecture: Greece*, ed. by Savvas Condaratos and Wilfried Wang (Munich: Prestel, 2000), pp. 53–62.

45 Yorgos Simeoforidis, 'Foreword', *Design + Art in Greece*, 14 (1983), 16–18 (p. 18).

46 See Helen Fessas-Emmanouil, 'Prestige Architecture in Post-War Greece: 1945–1975', *Design + Art in Greece*, 15 (1984), 34–73 (pp. 45–8).

47 Andreas Kourkoulas, 'Iconology, the Post-Modern Appeal to Memory', *Architecture in Greece*, 23 (1989), 60–2 (pp. 61–2).

48 See Alexander Tzonis and Alcestis Rodi, *Greece: Modern Architectures in History* (London: Reaktion, 2013); Panos Tsakopoulos, *Reflections on Greek Postwar Architecture* (Athens: Kaleidoscopio, 2014).

49 See Dimitris Antonakakis, 'Lecture', in *Technology, Place and Production: The Jerusalem Seminar in Architecture*, ed. by Kenneth Frampton with Arthur Spector and Lynne Reed Rosman (New York: Rizzoli, 1998), pp. 204–7.

50 Tzonis and Rodi, *Greece: Modern Architectures in History*, p. 232.

51 Kenneth Frampton, 'Modern and Site Specific: The Architecture of Gino Valle 1945–2003', *Plan Journal*, 4.1 (2019), 223–6 (p. 225).

52 Kenneth Frampton, 'Entre rationalisme et régionalisme: l'oeuvre de Martorell, Bohigas et Mackay', in Kenneth Frampton, *Martorell, Bohigas, Mackay: Trente ans d'architecture, 1954–1984*, trans. by Raymond Coudert (Paris: Electa, 1985), pp. 7–25 (p. 25).

53 Tom Avermaete et al., 'A Conversation with Kenneth Frampton: New York, 6 April 2018', *OASE*, 103 (2019), 142–54 (p. 147).

54 Savas Condaratos, interviewed by Stylianos Giamarelos (Athens: 25 June 2013).

55 See Maro Kardamitsi-Adami, *Ανδρέας Συμεών: Από τη ζωή και το έργο του* (Athens: Benaki Museum, 2013).

56 See Maria Kamilaki, Georgia Katsouda and Maria Vrachionidou, *Πιπέρι στο στόμα! Όψεις των λέξεων-ταμπού στη νέα ελληνική* (Athens: Kalligrafos, 2015).

57 See *Second World Postmodernisms: Architecture and Society under Late Socialism*, ed. by Vladimir Kulić (London: Bloomsbury, 2019); Florian Urban, *Postmodern Architecture in Socialist Poland: Transformation, Symbolic Form and National Identity* (London: Routledge, 2021).

Epilogue: Three fronts

As the fall of the Berlin Wall accelerated the implosion of the Soviet Bloc and the process of globalisation after the end of the 1980s, critiques of critical regionalism started to multiply, questioning its scope and viability as a project for the future of architectural practice. By then, Alexander Tzonis and Liane Lefaivre had become ambivalent about Kenneth Frampton's recapitulation of critical regionalism. Although they enjoyed the worldwide exposure for the term that they had coined, they were also frustrated by its development as a set of rules for architectural design. Maintaining their distance from the morphotypological approach of Italian Rationalists such as Aldo Rossi, they noted that '[a]n optimum would be located somewhere between the Italian historicism and the "rules" of Frampton', because '[f]ormal rule systems ... are probably less applicable' in the case of critical regionalism.[1] This is what they argued during the 'Context and Modernity' seminar, the last historically significant meeting of the three main authors of critical regionalism, in Delft from 12 to 15 June 1990.[2] Tzonis and Lefaivre also noted how the fall of the Soviet Bloc and the apparent exhaustion of alternative options signalled an age in which architecture would become more amenable to market forces; even 'Critical Regionalism may very well become commercial'.[3] In his talk at the same seminar, Fredric Jameson added that this process would become more visible in the European Community after the signing of the Maastricht Treaty in 1992, which would enable multinational corporations to enter more forcefully into European cultural production.[4] Frampton shared this scepticism towards the market forces to be unleashed by the ensuing policies of the European Community and its member states that had, by that time, already started to destabilise the architectural profession through deregulation.[5] Under such conditions, by the early 1990s it was rather clear that 'Critical Regionalism has served its purpose, as an idea it emerged when the need for such a notion was there ... The need for Frampton's rules has ceased to exist'.[6] By then, Frampton had also noted his dissatisfaction with 'this very awkward term Critical Regionalism' and the numerous misunderstandings that it had already entailed. For this reason, he reportedly avoided using it – effectively leaving Tzonis and Lefaivre as the sole spokespersons for it in the decades that followed.[7]

Frampton was instead driven back to the question of architecture's autonomy, which he found in tectonic culture: the capacity of architectural structure for poetic expressivity.[8] But this focus on construction did not mean that the political horizon was entirely absent from his later work. Rather, his study of tectonic culture enabled Frampton to articulate the way in which the poetics also led to the politics of construction as the autonomy of architecture can be defined by a series of limits:

> limit number 1 would be the limit of the boundary of the work at any one time, a kind of topographic limit. Limit number 2 would be the tectonic constructional limit of the autonomy of construction as tectonic. Limit number 3 would be professional limit, to recognise that this profession has its limits. And also limits vis-à-vis the reciprocity between profession and client ... And the last one is ecological limit, the fact that since this is all related to modernisation and development, then there is this last limit.
>
> Now I think that as you go from the smallest or let us say the nearest limit, the micro-limit, the limit of the boundary, the limit of the actual professional work itself, the tectonic limit, and you go out towards professional limit and ecological limit, you pass from a discourse that is professional qua professional, to a discourse that has to do with citizen qua citizen.[9]

The 1990 conference in Delft was attended by more than 150 participants, including Frampton; Tzonis and Lefaivre; Suzana and Dimitris Antonakakis; Álvaro Siza; and other architects, theorists and critics of critical regionalism.[10] Fredric Jameson, Marshall Berman and Harry Kunneman launched their critiques from the vantage point of the postmodern condition, as this seemed to be reshaped after the fall of the Berlin Wall and Francis Fukuyama's then recent declaration of the end of history.[11] But as the multifarious critiques of critical regionalism came from several sides, they also demonstrated prevailing misunderstandings of the theory by external observers. Hedy d'Ancona – then Dutch Minister of Welfare, Health and Cultural Affairs – spoke for numerous members of her and her parents' generation when she noted the negative connotations of the term 'regionalism' and its ties with the Third Reich. Her comments also registered then developing notions of a transnational European identity that would have to cross regional borders and therefore potentially clash with some of the relatively 'claustrophobic' main tenets of critical regionalism.[12] In his talk, Frampton also mentioned the mid-1980s response of Spanish architects José Luis Mateo and Eduard Bru, who noted that critical regionalism is a short-lived stratagem that soon becomes 'useless' as it only serves to get architects going in a certain direction. As soon as the two practitioners realised that they 'need[ed] to take hold of the modernisation' of Spanish architecture, the critical regionalist approach resurfaced as rather 'sentimental'.[13] Berman also focused his critique on Frampton's reliance on Heidegger's exclusively negative presentation of modernity and universal values, which had nonetheless been disproved by the fall of the Berlin Wall in 1989. In addition, he criticised Tzonis and Lefaivre's approach, because it did not sufficiently foreground regionalism's link with modern nationalist projects.[14]

Given this residual 'chauvinism', including the potential return of 'ancestral hatreds' in Eastern Europe after the fall of the Berlin Wall, Berman did not regard critical regionalism as a viable political project within the condition of postmodernity.[15] This critique was exacerbated by Jameson, who started from a different point to reach the same conclusion. The US philosopher stressed the need to resituate critical regionalism within the field of architectural developments that had given rise to it – including the postmodernism of the Biennale, Neo-Rationalism and Deconstructivism. Despite the resistant rhetoric of critical regionalism, Jameson argued, several of its constantly recurring features – including 'the ideologies of difference rather than identity, the end of utopia, the failure of socialism, the end of the modernist project' – show that all speakers 'are buying [into] the ideology of the market above all', against which they are supposedly rebelling.[16] In other words, critical regionalism was so inextricably linked with the postmodern condition that its alleged resistance to it was only wishful thinking, if not futile. This was not a project that could bring about the sort of change that it evangelised. Kunneman concurred, as even thinkers of the postmodern condition with agendas as diverse as those of Jean-François Lyotard, Francis Fukuyama and Jürgen Habermas agreed 'at least in … that they do not reckon in any way with the possibility of fundamental changes in the basic structure of modern society'.[17]

Tzonis and Lefaivre tried to defend critical regionalism by pointing out the prevailing misinterpretations. They concluded that 'the word region should be seen metaphorically and the word Regionalism could be shortened [to] Realism' in what was heralded as 'a moment of almost historical significance' by the Dutch critic Hans van Dijk.[18] Sharing similar concerns about the problematic term 'regionalism', Frampton also responded approvingly, 'too spontaneously ... with great relief'.[19] In the aftermath of earlier discussions of 'realism' in architecture, the term retained the aspired associations with the project of socialist realism to transform reality through architecture towards creating a 'new humanism'.[20] Nonetheless, students of Frampton in New York when they graduated found themselves in a position similar to that described by Jameson. Although they appreciated the sensitive but small-scale projects highlighted by Frampton, the idea of producing similar works in their professional practice clashed with the reality of working for large firms to detail 40- or 80-storey buildings.[21]

Thirty years later – at the start of this second, tumultuous decade of the twenty-first century – the complex realities of the world seem to call for a rethink of this approach. It is, after all, forty years since the term 'critical regionalism' was first introduced in 1981 and the world was certainly different then. But this is only one part of the story. The other part is that the discourses of critical regionalism were themselves further developed within the process of late twentieth-century globalisation. This was also the time during which the globalising process itself became the object of fierce debates, culminating in the anti-globalisation movement that started to rise at the turn of the millennium. But even that was the tip of an iceberg that had gradually developed in the decades that preceded it. As this book has foregrounded, from the 1980s onwards the global picture was already more complex than implied by its schematic presentation by the three main authors of critical regionalism.

In a way, even critical regionalism ended up inadvertently promoting what it was fighting against. In what follows, I will show how this was historically the case by skimming through three decades to revisit three worlds, three returns, three globalisations, three colonisations and three challenges of critical regionalism for the 2020s.

Three Worlds of the 1980s

One is used to looking at the past in the knowledge of what followed it. Based on this posterior knowledge, one tends to evaluate all one's yesterdays retrospectively today. But the historical subjects of the 1980s did not necessarily imagine that the Berlin Wall would fall in 1989 or that the Soviet Bloc itself would have imploded by 1991. They did not know that the twentieth century would prove to be rather 'short', as the world 'landslided' into an as-yet-unknown new order in its last decade.[22] They did not know that the bipolarity of the Cold War world was about to come to an end. None of that was yet visible at the start of the 1980s, when the influential texts of critical regionalism were first written. The Soviet Bloc, which was also known as the Second World, was still in the game then. And while it had already entered deep into an exhaustive arms race with the USA, it did not seem to blink. The prolonged Cold War period was already four decades old. As such, nothing seemed capable of unsettling the well-established structure of the Three Worlds. The historic agents of the 1980s found it impossible to even imagine the collapse of this world order. And that was the case globally – whether one lived in the First World of the 'free' (Western Europe, North America, Australia and New Zealand) or the Second World of the Soviet Bloc (including the communist states of Eastern Europe, from East Germany to China and Vietnam in Northern and Northeast Asia) or the Third World of the rising postcolonial nations (in Africa and Southeast Asia) and their older counterparts in Central and South America. Sci-fi films of the early 1980s, such as *Blade Runner* (1982), which imagined the world well into the future, included the Soviet Bloc still going strong many decades after its historic implosion in 1991 – in the case of Ridley Scott's iconic dystopia, in a fictitious 2019. Such works of fiction further attest to the incapacity of the imaginaries of the 1980s to envision a different world order.

The First World wanted to constantly demonstrate its superiority over the Second World on all fronts – ranging from the space race to economic and political structures of governance, and from individual liberties to architecture.[23] The arms race and the threat of nuclear disaster were also constantly present for about four decades. But the USA did not overplay its sheer firepower. Rather, it intended to show that its empire was different from the colonial empires of the past. The power of its post-Second World War empire rested not on its guns but on its total economic, political and social superiority.

It is this alleged superiority that structures the hierarchy of the Three Worlds. According to this narrative, all the significant developments take place in the First World and only afterwards are they desirable in the Second and Third Worlds. This is a one-way street, as things circulate in one direction only: from the First to the Second to the Third World – not the other way around.[24] In such a hierarchical structure, Third World 'peripheries' are expected to follow in the footsteps of First World 'centres'. This same idea lies behind the concept of the homogenisation of the world in a single direction, as globalisation unfolds rapidly following the fall of the Berlin Wall in the late 1980s. Believing that this is actually the case, as Lefaivre and Tzonis do in their most systematic account of critical regionalism to date,[25] equals adopting the hierarchy of the Three Worlds – including the idea that the advanced developments of the First World outline the trajectory that the rest of the globe will follow.

Written in the early 1980s, the theories of critical regionalism are the children of this age of bipolarity. As Frampton clearly states in his most widely read text on critical regionalism, it is precisely this Cold War context that makes the position of an avant-garde culture untenable for left-wing thinkers of the period:

> … as long as the struggle between socialism and capitalism persists (with the manipulative mass-culture politics that this conflict necessarily entails), the modern world cannot continue to entertain the prospect of evolving a marginal, liberative, avant-gardist culture which would break (or speak of the break) with the history of bourgeois repression.[26]

Critical regionalism belongs to a special moment of this longer history, since the more certainly this Cold War bipolarity was established as the status quo, the more attempts to transcend bipolar thinking emerged. From the end of the 1960s, several forms of thinking took up this task. They covered a spectrum spanning from Jacques Derrida's 'deconstruction' to the revolutions of the 1970s in the Middle East and the pursuit of *The Third Way* by sociologists such as Anthony Giddens.[27] The ambiguous term 'critical regionalism' was another footprint of this phase of thinking in triads in an age of bipolarity, as it also presented itself as an alternative to the two architectural extremes of modern techno-scientific optimisation and postmodernist scenographic populism. It was the product of an intellectual horizon that was totally dominated by two equally problematic options. This horizon of bipolarity seemed impossible to transgress, then; but it could still be subverted or cracked. The third alternative, to which all these types of thinking aspired, was expected to emerge from the reactivation of tension between two poles. Whether one follows Derrida's ensuing 'undecidability' between the tension of two unsettled poles of meaning, the rejection of First and Second World ideologies in favour of a return to Islamic values during the Iranian revolt in 1979 or Giddens's attempt to envision the 'future of radical politics beyond Left and Right', the underlying structure of this thinking in triads that attempts to transgress the dilemmas of bipolar thinking remains constant.

At the same time, the dependency theory developed by Neo-Marxist scholars such as Andre Gunder Frank argued that 'peripheral' countries should aim to retain their independence from both the First World capitalist and the Second World socialist 'centres' and join the Third World countries in their struggle against imperialism. The capitalist structure of the world economy meant that the 'peripheral' countries of the First and Second Worlds were destined to remain underdeveloped and exploited if their economies were to be guided by the 'central' states. The 'centres' would favour a one-sided development of the 'peripheral' economies towards resource extraction. As such, they would completely ignore all other sectors of the economy that were significant for the local populations.[28] This seems to be the case with the theories of critical regionalism whose rhetoric also favoured the 'peripheries' over the 'centres'. Originally intended to unsettle the rigid understanding of one-way cultural transfers from the 'centres' to the 'peripheries', Frampton advocated for 'peripheries' to become 'centrally' significant for the development of modern architecture. But this does not render regionalist architectures significant on their own terms or in their own right. They are significant only because they can contribute to the debates around the prolonged impasse of modern architecture and suggest a way forward for it. It is still the 'central' direction that is exclusively informed by the 'peripheral' contribution – in the same hierarchical order. The 'peripheries' are asked to adapt to the 'central' conceptions of modernity and processes of modernisation, while the 'centres' simply assimilate some of the most relevant regional insights as processes with which they could work. The hierarchy is still there in Frampton's militant terms of choice. The dominant narrative of the Cold War age suggested that the avant-garde, the marginal progressive culture that could lead the revolution of the interwar years, could no longer hold in the 1980s. In this context, revolution can only be envisioned as resistance and the former avant-garde can only survive as an arrière-garde. As such, 'peripheries' are significant because they share the cultural marginality that the progressive avant-garde seemed to enjoy in the 1920s and the 1930s. The 'peripheral arrière-garde' of the 1980s is the only hope for at least holding the dream of the – initially marginal, but eventually 'centralised' – avant-garde of the 1930s alive. But again, the hierarchy inherent in the terms avant- and arrière-garde is implicitly associated with the forward-looking 'centre' and the backward-looking 'periphery'.

The theories of critical regionalism are written in this context, from a transatlantic space. Their authors are predominantly European immigrants to the USA. Politically, they call themselves socialists or Marxists. But they keep their distance from the actually existing socialism of the Second World. Frampton does so mainly through the critical thinking of Hannah Arendt and the Frankfurt School.[29] Tzonis and Lefaivre write more specifically against state bureaucracies of the First World and the Soviet Union.[30] The 'peripheral' works that they discuss in order to develop their theory of critical regionalism – whether these are located in Athens, Säynätsalo or Bagsværd – are mainly Western European; they belong to the First World. As such, while the theorists of critical regionalism intend to establish a different cultural circuit from the 'margins' to the 'centre', they do not strike at the hard core of the Cold War hierarchy of the Three Worlds. They just encourage the creation of a cultural circuit *within* the First World – from its own 'peripheries' to its own 'centre'.[31] In other words, critical regionalism reinforces the cultural production of the First World from the inside. It does not question its primacy over the other two Worlds. It only suggests that the lessons from the 'periphery' (Greece, Finland, Denmark, Switzerland, Italy, Japan and Spain) are also desirable in the 'centre' of the First World in the USA. But countries such as Finland and Denmark were already significant as role models for a third-way option of 'capitalism with a human face' in the Cold War period. As such, Frampton's rally against the 'transatlantic exclusivity' of Stern's 'central' Italy–USA map of the Biennale only goes as far as the 'peripheries' of the same First World 'centres', such as the Italian-speaking 'peripheries' of Veneto and Ticino. But whether one promotes 'postmodernism' or 'critical regionalism', the underlying assumption remains the same: as First World developments, they will also become attractive for the other two Worlds.

When Frampton argues for 'place-form' enclaves of resistance to the expansion of the megalopolis, he resorts again to the same First World model. He presents its own development as the inevitable future of the other two Worlds. He takes an urban geographer's study of a specific, limited area of the northeastern seaboard of the USA and turns it into a universal model that is destined to spread around the globe.[32] These are ideas about the globe that the First World actively cultivates. And in Frampton's thinking they are non-negotiable. The same goes for his belief that resistance as a solution will come from the First World again.

In the mid-1980s, critical regionalism aimed to unsettle the transatlantic exclusivity of the architectural establishment. It intended to subvert the model of one-way cultural transfer from the producing 'centre' to the absorbing 'periphery'. But the extent of its application was much more limited than its theorists' implications. The theory was all about the First World; the Second World was of course almost entirely absent from the architectural studies of First World theorists at the time. Even Catherine Cooke (1942–2004), the best-known scholar of Russian Constructivism in anglophone architectural circles in the 1980s, was limited to discussing architectural developments of the 1920s and the 1930s – not contemporary architectures of the Second World.[33] At the same time, the First World was definitely more interested in the Third World than in the architectural developments in the Second World. While the Second Biennale of Architecture exhibition in Venice has been historically overshadowed by its more successful predecessor and has not been as extensively discussed, it characteristically focused on the 'Architecture of the Islamic Countries' in 1982 (Fig. 11.1). In such 'underdeveloped' contexts, the cultural product of critical regionalism becomes more attractive and relatable. In other words, through critical regionalism, the First World seems to offer the Third 'intermediate' or 'alternative' steps of 'ascendance' to a version of the First World.

To sum up, in its early years, critical regionalism was geographically limited. Hardly moving beyond the First World, it was more closely aligned with the cross-cultural vision of the rising European Union than with anything else. It was certainly not a project that covered the globe at that time.

Three globalisations of the 1990s

Neoliberal globalisation

The unexpected fall of the Berlin Wall and the Soviet Bloc in the late 1980s offered critical regionalism a new role and a better-defined opponent. The waning of architectural postmodernism at the same time was also conducive to the same direction. In the 1990s, critical regionalism redefined itself. This time, it did so in the context of the emerging globalising process as the debate moved to the model that this process should follow. As the fall of one wall was expected to lead to the fall of all walls and the threat of nuclear catastrophe seemed to be neutralised, the American Empire would also become the uncontested leader – fully emancipated to dictate the path of growth and development across the globe. Renowned political commentators and critics predicted at the time that the world would become 'flat', or that the end of history had now arrived, as the North American model would be the only desirable option across the globe.[34] According to this narrative, former Second and

Figure 11.1 Official poster, Second International Architecture Exhibition: 'Architecture of Islamic Countries', Giardini della Biennale, Venice, 20 November 1982–20 January 1983

Archivio Storico della Biennale di Venezia, ASAC

Third World countries would jostle to become free-market liberal democracies.

Marxist mondialisation

The triumphalist discourses of the First World, the prevalence of neoliberal capitalism and the disappearance of the Soviet Bloc from the world map obliged socialists and Marxists to reconsider their priorities.[35] By then, they had already given up demanding anything that would look like the previous utopias or revolutions of the early twentieth century. At the end of the century, 'resistance' – the term that was most usually associated with 'critical regionalism' – was the postmodern word for 'revolution'. While the theorists of critical regionalism kept using 'resistance' as their main term in the 1990s, their chief opponent was by then clearly the neoliberal version of globalisation. The 'peaks and valleys' that critical regionalists advocated resisted the onslaught of the flat world. At the same time, left-wing thinkers critiqued an undesirable globalisation that was mainly motivated by agents of the capitalist economy who promoted the deregulation of the market, the privatisation of key sectors of the former welfare state and the disappearance of 'class' as an analytical category.[36] They contrasted globalisation with an alternative 'mondialisation' of a clearer ethical, social, cultural and ecological orientation.[37] Recent historical studies by Łukasz Stanek and other scholars have also suggested that the overlooked Second World visions of worldmaking hold the potential to diversify current discussions of plural processes of globalisation.[38] While regions such as the Eastern European bloc of Second World modernisms and postmodernisms were also implicated in related developments in the Third World, they have until recently been overshadowed by the focus of anglophone scholarship on 'the Global South' – or what used to be called the 'Third World' in previous decades.

World architecture

But in his texts, Frampton does not use the terms 'global' and 'globalisation'. To refer to works that he wants to promote, he prefers to use the term 'world architecture'.[39] This alludes to the slightly unclear concept of *Weltliteratur* introduced by Johann Wolfgang von Goethe in the early nineteenth century. By extension, Frampton seems to adopt Goethe's thoughts on 'world literature':

I see more and more … that Literature is a common good of humanity and that it occurs everywhere and at all times in hundreds and hundreds of people. One does it a bit better than the other and swims on top a little longer than the other, but that is all … I therefore like to look into other nations and advise everyone to do the same. National literatures no longer mean much these days, we are entering the era of *Weltliteratur*—world literature—and it is up to each of us to hasten this development.[40]

For Milan Kundera, Gothe's *Weltliteratur* signalled that a cultural product is not necessarily better understood in its own national context: Rabelais, who wrote in French, was best understood by the Russian Mikhail Bakhtin; the Norwegian Henrik Ibsen by the Irishman George Bernard Shaw; and the Dubliner James Joyce by the Austrian Hermann Broch.[41] As such, *Weltliteratur* presupposes a free cultural exchange between co-equals on the same transnational platform. This level playing field is what Frampton implicitly has in mind for his 'world architecture'.

But since then, theories of world literature have also discussed how national canons are constructed in terms of local works that are celebrated by the outsider, anglophone 'centres' of literary production. Like Frampton's anthology of critical regionalist architects, Goethe's *Weltliteratur* library would ideally include one book that would stand for the essence of a specific national culture. Through these book-exemplars of a national culture, a large-scale, pluralist, cross-cultural dialogue could be instigated on co-equal terms. As a result, all national literatures participating in this dialogue would eventually be enriched.[42] It was in this context that the Second World, and especially the European states of the former Soviet Bloc, entered the field of architectural history in the 1990s. At this point, historiography was called upon and funded to take up the new task of building a common European identity that remains multivocal in its unity. Anthony Alofsin's book on Central European architecture is the fruit of 'Tense Alliance', a long-standing collaborative research project with distinguished European colleagues that was partly funded in the 1990s not only by the Getty Museum, the Getty Research Institute for Architecture and the Canadian Centre for Architecture but also by the International Centre for Cultural Research in Vienna.[43]

At the same time, Tzonis and Lefaivre stress the universal skills of architects as the foundation of the design principles of critical regionalism.[44] Clearly stating that one does not need to be Catalan to design a critical regionalist building in Barcelona, they thus respond to one of the most frequent misunderstandings of their theory as a

Figure 11.2 Undergraduate architecture students from the Zurich University of Applied Sciences (ZHAW) on a guided tour of Suzana and Dimitris Antonakakis' House at Perdika, Aegina, 1981, organised by Big Olive, photographed by Christos-Georgios Kritikos, 2019

Christos-Georgios Kritikos's private archive

primarily regionalist, instead of critical, endeavour. But at the same time, this move paves the way for the rise of an alternative globalised star system of critical regionalism. Since the 1980s, renowned projects of critical regionalism have been effectively canonised to form part of architectural pilgrimages (Fig. 11.2) while their architects, such as Dimitris Antonakakis, were invited to teach at Ivy League institutions, such as the MIT, in the 1990s. The fact that Tadao Ando and Renzo Piano are two out of only seven architects who have won all three major architectural prizes of the Western world (the Pritzker Prize, the Royal Institute of British Architects Gold Medal and the American Institute of Architects Gold Medal) is rather telling. Today, several critical regionalist architects of the 1980s are increasingly commissioned to build away from the 'peripheries' from which they originated. For Ando, this international recognition came almost immediately as he was also invited to teach a graduate studio at Yale University, an institution that reportedly relished 'star names', before the end of the 1980s. Since then, an alternative star system of critical regionalist architects has effectively worked under the same terms of neoliberal globalisation – its alleged chief opponent. The problem was already visible in 1989, when Richard Weston concluded his review of Ando's Yale Studio book with Rizzoli on the following note: 'Ando is one of the most interesting architects at work today, but he is in danger of over-exposure. He might do well to apply some of the celebrated "critical resistance" of his work to the solicitations of the media and well-endowed American academies'.[45] Again, the theorists of critical regionalism partially reproduced what they were fighting against.

In the following decade, Tzonis and Lefaivre's theorisations extended to include similar works by architects in other geographical areas. And these almost exclusively came from architects of formerly colonised countries.

Three colonisations of the 2000s

Colonial discourse

It was not long before theorists of world literature noted that the discussion of *Weltliteratur* based on Goethe's idealist conception did not correspond to historical experience. Postcolonial thinkers such as Pascale Casanova stressed how authors that represent national cultures do not actually compete on a level playing field. Rather, they circulate within existing power structures and historically established hierarchies between dominant 'centres' and marginalised 'peripheries'. In practice, what might be called 'world literature' is not Goethe's idealised construct but a reflection of these unequal terms.[46] For a 'peripheral' work of 'minor' literature, the road to international recognition passes through its translation into English. This also serves as a ticket for its host national culture to enter the global arena. The first postcolonial critiques of critical regionalism appeared at the same time as the aforementioned postcolonial critiques of Goethe's conception of 'world literature' in the early 2000s. In 2002, Keith Eggener argued that critical regionalism was an inherently colonial discourse as it actively pushed to the margin the areas that it discussed. These areas had not necessarily understood themselves and their cultural production as marginal before the theorists of critical regionalism started to discuss them in terms of a global picture that was out of the scope of their regional architectural developments and the concerns that underpinned them.[47]

Colonial practice

In addition, Frampton's texts present his favoured architectures of critical regionalism in terms of abstract dichotomies, such as that between technology and placemaking, and idealised, second-hand impressions of local cultures. His texts frequently distort the original thinking and architectural intentions that drove these works, as they ignore the historic and cultural context of their production in a specific place. While the theorists of critical regionalism regarded themselves

Figure 11.3   William S. Lim, Kenneth Frampton and Charles Correa in Chandigarh, India, 1999

ARCH284699, Kenneth Frampton fonds, Canadian Centre for Architecture, Gift of Kenneth Frampton

as socialists or Marxists, they did not effectively address the political context that produced the architectures that they promoted. When Tzonis and Lefaivre expanded the scope of their work in the early 2000s to discuss architectures of critical regionalism in the Tropics, they based their analysis on five points derived from Lewis Mumford, a First World architect who discussed *The South in* [North American] *Architecture* and engaged with tropical regions through his 'Report on Honolulu'.[48] For every Sri Lankan Minnette da Silva (1918–1998), Nigerian Oluwole Olumuyiwa (1929–2000), Zimbabwean Mick Pearce (b. 1938) or the Singaporean Design Partnership of Tay Kheng Soon (b. 1940) and William Lim (b. 1932) that Tzonis and Lefaivre put forward, however, there is also a Jane Drew (1911–1996) and Maxwell Fry (1899–1987) – who educated several of these architects at the Architectural Association – or Richard Neutra (1892–1970), Paul Rudolph (1918–1997) and well-known Brazilian architects, such as Oscar Niemeyer (1907–2012) and Lúcio Costa (1902–1998), with their established links with the First World network of modernist architects, including Le Corbusier.[49] As such, in the attempt to geographically expand critical regionalism, the discourse still seems to develop as a globalising agent of the First World (Fig. 11.3). And when Frampton relies on Paul Ricoeur's text from 1961 to re-address the question of 'how to become modern and to return to sources' at the same time, he omits the postcolonial context and the struggles of rising nations that lead to the rise of this paradox in the first place, as Mark Crinson also noted later in the same decade.[50]

Postcolonial split

The roots of critical regionalism lie at the postcolonial moment of the 1960s when the United Kingdom itself became a 'peripheral' power in the wake of the implosion of the British Empire and the global dominance, after the Second World War, of the USA – the single country that represented an unprecedented 50 per cent of the world's GDP until the mid-1960s. As Frampton, Tzonis and Lefaivre operated from the First World from the outset, however, critical regionalism does not directly address the question of colonialism; it effectively omits it. Historically, critical regionalism developed alongside the rise of postcolonial studies, whose potential as a distinct discipline was increasingly gaining ground in the decades that followed the publication of Edward Said's *Orientalism* in 1978.[51] But as critical regionalism does not cross paths with postcolonial studies, the two discourses developed in parallel. This is why Gayatri Chakravorty Spivak's concept of 'critical regionalism' in her postcolonial scholarship in the same decade, which has also inspired numerous scholars in the humanities from comparative literature to political philosophy, is not based on the discourse of Frampton, Tzonis and Lefaivre.[52] The writing of the history of critical regionalism, the project that Tzonis and Lefaivre clearly took up from 2000 onwards,[53] remains rooted in the 'global' Western European/First World colonial tradition. As such, it does not offer nuanced analyses of cross-cultural exchange since the hierarchical networks of power that condition these exchanges are also kept out of the picture. Frampton's interest in cross-cultural exchange remains focused on an idealised version of 'East meets West' based on the fixed typologies of pagoda roof structures or other static cultural elements such as the 'gravitation' of the Japanese body and its architecture towards the floor, as opposed to the Western 'gravitation' towards the wall.

This is the case not only because the interests of critical regionalism started from, and stayed with, the West but also because from the outset the discourse of critical regionalism was not looking at the present or the future. It was, rather, constantly motivated by the past. In the final instance, critical regionalism is the 1980s return of the 1960s.

Three returns of the 1960s

Aesthetics

As I look again at Frampton's texts alongside the works of critical regionalism from the distance of four decades, I wonder whether his theory is systematic or consistent after all. I have developed the impression that what is really at stake here is the theoretical legitimisation of a specific aesthetic preference. Mary McLeod shared similar concerns in her critique of critical regionalism of 1989 when she noted that Frampton's exemplar buildings 'often share more with each other than with their respective locales', and that this 'raises the question of whether "region" or some more universal criteria of artistic quality – craftsmanship, detail, quality of materials – are the source of their "resistant" qualities'.[54] A mid-1980s interview with Frampton also seems to confirm this suspicion. In the final instance, these are the texts of a British historian whose formative years in architecture coincided with the 1960s generation of the 'New Brutalists'.[55] Frampton's editorial work at *Architectural Design* from 1962 to 1965 summarises his preferences, fifteen years before he has written a single line on critical regionalism. The context of his thinking, from his Marxist leanings to the sensitive architectural language of quiet modernism that he seems to prefer, comes entirely from the 1960s. The theory of critical regionalism is what stays as nostalgia after the revolution of 1968 is cancelled, and the revolutionary prospects seem increasingly slim afterwards. First World capitalism emerges triumphant and the actually existing socialism of the Second World War era degenerates into a bureaucratic state apparatus with authoritarian tendencies.

Politics

Frampton's generation wrestles with the inconclusive revolt of 1968 and a nostalgia for the revolutionary interwar period. In this sense, critical regionalism is also the 1980s return of the 1960s, as Frampton endeavours to provincialise the scenographic postmodern architecture of the 1980s. His alternative remains an arrière-garde, which is as marginal as the aesthetic and social avant-garde of the 1930s. If such an avant-garde is no longer possible in the 1980s, however, it can still be an object of nostalgia – at least, as long as the last role models of the 1960s can hold in the late twentieth century. Suzana and Dimitris Antonakakis were not the only architects whose critical regionalist phase 'came to an unexpected still inexplicable conclusion' after the 1970s: the same was the case with Gino and Nani Valle in the late 1960s, when the scale of their commissions increased and their clientele changed to include bureaucratic institutions, international banks and corporations.[56] Frampton's consistent focus on these early projects reinforces the impression that critical regionalism indeed constitutes the 1980s return of the 1960s.

Concepts

In 1975, Frampton wanted to respond to the challenge of pluralism that was forcefully put forward by the rising postmodern thinking in the First World. He proposed the 1960s pluralism of Team 10 as an alternative.[57] Tzonis and Lefaivre, for their part, stressed the need to transform the relationships between designers and users, echoing the pleas of participatory design practices of the 1960s. At the same time, the social democratic model of the Western European welfare state was presented as the only desirable option within the boundaries set by variants of 'capitalism with a human face'. Tzonis and Lefaivre's insistence on the 'humanistic' dimension of the critical regionalist project,[58] Frampton's hierarchical primacy of the modern language of architecture and Ricoeur's Christian mindset: these were all footprints of 1960s thinking in the critical regionalist theories of the 1980s. As Jameson also noted in Delft in 1990, citing David Harvey, even the 'think globally and act locally' cliché that served as a motto for critical regionalism as a resistant force to globalisation was a slogan that came from the 1960s.[59] Lastly, as I have shown in the second part of this book, critical regionalism served as an excuse to return to the 1960s for architects who yearned for the 'lost spring' of Greek modernism.[60] The intense cultural life of that decade, including student marches and the rise of new political causes and forces in the local scene, was brought to a violent halt by the imposition of the colonels' rule in 1967. This implicit return to the 1960s was an additional reason for the celebrated reception of critical regionalism in this context.

Three challenges of the 2010s

In the opening decades of the twenty-first century, the 1990s triumphalism of First World capitalism and its characteristic motto that 'there is no alternative' has been challenged by the exigencies of the climate emergency. Discussing critical regionalism in this context thus becomes a different story. There is no doubt that the unprecedented rise of China on the scene of the world economy, especially over the last two decades, challenges the established hegemony of the 'First World' West on all fronts. Driven by China, the cumulative rise of the Asian economy has geographically 'rebalanced' economic activity in the Eurasian continent at pre-Industrial Revolution levels.[61] While the early-2020s experience of the locked-down world of the pandemic might eventually lead to a reduced dependency on Chinese-centred supply chains, a Sino–American cold war could be avoided in the twenty-first century simply because the two economies are (on some estimates) almost 365 times more interconnected than the US economy ever was with the Soviet Union in the twentieth.[62] In Branko Milanovic's words, this is the century of 'capitalism, alone' – whether that refers to the US model of liberal meritocracy or the Chinese model of political authoritarianism. The impressive recent performance of this authoritarian variant of capitalism has rendered it increasingly attractive for neighbouring economies, subverting Fukuyama's triumphalist claims of the 1990s that the future of the capitalist economy is intrinsically tied up with liberal democracy. Recent developments have also shown that, contrary to the claims of the Neo-Marxist theory of dependency, a modern country's route to growth today passes through its integration into the global supply chains of the Western world by developing the related infrastructure, institutions and legislation. The rapid development of outsourcing has rendered these chains indispensable parts of the 'central' modes of production for foreign investors.[63] The economic rise of Asia in the age of globalisation means that Asians' opinion on globalisation today is almost twice as positive as that of Europeans. As global inequality is expected to continue to drop in the northern hemisphere over the next few decades, the case of sub-Saharan Africa and the way in which this might be affected by Chinese, US and European projects on the continent is the unknown factor for the future of global inequality, migration flows and the world economy.[64] As China leads the current rise of Asia on the global economic map, its modern recourse to long-standing cultural resources could also lead to a different, Chinese universalist world view and a vision for the future development of the globe 'under the same sky'.[65]

Based on the above analysis, I would therefore like to close this book by wondering if it is still possible to attempt a historically informed update of critical regionalism for the twenty-first century on three fronts: theory, history and historiography.

Owing, among other things, to his work on critical regionalism, Frampton received the Golden Lion for Lifetime Achievement at the Sixteenth Biennale of Architecture in Venice in 2018. Coming from the institution from which he had resigned as an invited critic in 1980, after disagreeing with its promotion of postmodern architecture, his recognition as 'a leader in the influencing of architects to re-value context, place and culture' almost four decades later seemed to open a new historical cycle.[66] Since then, a series of related articles and *Festschrifts* have attempted to reappraise critical regionalism as a theory for architectural design.[67] Indeed, many of the main principles of critical regionalism now form part of architectural education. The emphasis on place, landscape, climatic conditions, orientations of buildings and sites, locally sourced materials and regional building cultures – all of these sensibilities of critical regionalism survive in architects' education across the globe today. In addition, the discourse of critical regionalism enables architects not only to reflectively respond to specific places but also to ask more ambitious questions about the potential of architecture in the modern world, including its capacity to address climate change; it is, after all, an approach that anticipated the principles of sustainable development. This is why practitioners from widely differing backgrounds, ranging from Grafton Architects (est. 1978) in Ireland to Marina Tabassum (b. 1968) in Bangladesh, still cite Frampton's texts on critical regionalism as an inspiration for their work. While several historians have critiqued critical regionalism by now, this has not been the case for practising architects – who are more positively predisposed towards it.

That critical regionalism resonated 'throughout Latin America and to some extent in the Mediterranean, above all in Catalonia ... Greece and to some extent in India'[68] and exerted a lasting influence on architects' practice is an achievement that has become increasingly rare for theoretical discourses in the twenty-first century. Such architectural scholarship today seems to be addressed more to critics and historians than to practising architects. By contrast, critical regionalism is a mainstream concept with which both practising architects and scholars are readily familiar. This legacy of critical regionalism as a working architect's theory is therefore worth maintaining, instead of abandoning the concept altogether. Its wide-ranging endorsement by several architects, but also theorists and historians, across the past four decades calls for building on the existing popularity of this discourse to recalibrate it for the present instead of expecting that a new framework will become instantly as popular and well received across the globe. To do so, one should start from the underlying 'returns of the 1960s' that form part of the critical regionalist vocabulary. Many of them – such as the use of concrete as a main building material in the West, which is almost fetishised by the discourse of critical regionalism – simply do not hold in the age of climate emergency.

Despite these problematic residues from the 1960s, critical regionalism retains an inherent relationship with the question of sustainability in architecture that has its roots in the same period. It is therefore theoretically possible for it to be further updated from the standpoint of climate change as a design theory for the twenty-first century. In so doing, it can capitalise on its original theorists' insistence that this discourse is more directly associated with a specific stance towards design than a specific architectural style. In previous decades, discussions around green, sustainable and resilient architecture have stressed the need to transform an ecological–technological imperative into a new architectural language.[69] But as Lucius Burckhardt already noted in the early 1990s, ecological architecture is not necessarily visible, photogenic or amenable to the creation of its own distinct aesthetics.[70] As a design theory appropriate for the twenty-first century, critical regionalism needs to further encourage reflection on architecture as a critical project that generates an ethical outlook and consciousness in order to live differently at the level of the whole human species in the age of the Anthropocene.[71] Since the impact of human activity on the planet is now registered at a geological scale, externalising the impact of it to an 'exterior' nature – whether that is the atmosphere or the oceans – is no longer an option. In this age of the Anthropocene, nature no longer absorbs; it backfires. Realising this would entail abandoning approaches of regionalism that exclusively associate it with locality in order to think about architecture in terms of its structural place in specific modes of production and global supply chains of materials, including their whole-life cycles and footprints. Recent scholarship has also stressed the need to focus on the locally diversified effects of global climate change on specific parts of the planet, as such global phenomena are experienced differently on the local level: as one region is threatened by flooding, another faces imminent desertification. The world needs architectures that can address these local futures informed by an awareness of the global dimensions of the climate crisis, irrespective of the degree to which architects are ready to adopt the alternative economic and social systems brought forward by the proponents of such ecological movements of localisation.[72]

These are not architectures that just need to be appropriate for new climatic conditions. They also need to be able to respond to the possible emergence of needs for landscapes of retreat, where residents of coastal areas can move after irrevocable sea-level change. Increased migration flows that are expected to be instigated by the effects of climate change in the following decades also need to find their appropriate architectural response. In this way, Frampton's favourite, Hannah Arendt, can once again become relevant for critical regionalism – this time, not for her thoughts on the civic function of architecture and the provision of public spaces of appearance but for her related pleas in texts such as 'We, Refugees'.[73] In any case, it is clear that phenomenological concepts such as Heidegger's 'placelessness' and the postmodern discourses that relied on them are not sufficiently historical to support this sort of analysis of architectural practice. Given the above, there is in any case no 'authentic' place or 'nature' to return to now. As a result, any aspired sense of place can also no longer be discussed as inherent to its material qualities but must be addressed in relation to the cultural practices of the different groups that produce and live in it. In modern global cities, these practices are also conditioned by legal frameworks and economics-of-opportunity areas for developers, including the use of architecture as an economic asset that enables capital to keep circulating in increasingly globalised property markets.[74] Postmodern discussions of architectural styles as representative of the culture of a community do not seem to hold their relevance in a context that is so deeply embedded in policy and economics. Working with this bigger picture of architectural production and its systematic embeddedness within this global economic, political and ecological system – even in speculative terms – could well become the new critical regionalist design stance of this century.[75]

History

Having just turned forty years old, critical regionalism has a history of its own now. And if it is to survive as a theory, its study as history can and should bring to the surface more of its blind spots. While this book has shown that the writing of critical regionalism was a cross-cultural process, further grey areas of its history remain to be explored as its roots go deeper back into not only the twentieth but also earlier centuries.[76] In their later, more comprehensive, histories of regionalism in architecture, Tzonis and Lefaivre discussed such tendencies within the circles of the International Congress of Modern Architecture (CIAM) – with their interest in the Mediterranean in the fourth meeting of 1933 and the CIAM

Figure 11.4 Suzana and Dimitris Antonakakis visit the House at Spata, 1973–5, photographed by Stylianos Giamarelos, 2017

Stylianos Giamarelos's private archive

grid of 1948, or the work of modern architects such as Fry and Drew in the tropical regions of West Africa and India in the 1950s.

But even if one concentrated exclusively on the architects who were celebrated as critical regionalists by Frampton, Tzonis and Lefaivre, there is still ample room for related historical studies – as this book has also demonstrated by focusing, in its second part, on one related architectural practice in depth (Fig. 11.4). The writing of critical regionalism itself was a cross-cultural process that is not historically limited to the texts by Tzonis, Lefaivre and Frampton. It also includes buildings, original texts by the architects who were presented as critical regionalists and wider concerns about the regional in modernism (and after it). It is thanks to these existing debates that architectural and theoretical interest in the question of the local peaked in the 1980s, and for that reason they form part of this history. This book has also shown how the discourse of critical regionalism proved so successful and influential that it became itself a historical agent. As such, it affected architects who engaged with its network or the national contexts in which they practised.[77] The extent to which critical regionalism became a global architectural discourse itself was directly linked with its position within the globalised architectural culture promoted by First World, globalised schools and institutions of architecture that encouraged this process. These aspects are another important part of its history today.

Critical regionalism's space of authorship is therefore rhizomatic. It has no clear boundaries, no end and no beginning. It still is an ever-expanding cross-cultural network that branches out from humans to buildings and texts across decades. The authors who are mainly associated with critical regionalism wrote their related texts of the 1980s aiming to affect the practice of contemporary architects. As such, they paid less attention to the rich historical grounds upon which they had started to tread as they focused more extensively on design features and principles. But Anthony Alofsin, a figure who is still overlooked in contemporary accounts of critical regionalism, can be regarded as an author who developed more clearly the approach of the historian to these questions. His long-standing engagement with Frank Lloyd Wright and his attempt to retrace the history of an indigenous North American modernism that was overshadowed by the Western European architects who taught in the USA after the Second World War demonstrate one way in which the questions of critical regionalism can still be addressed in terms of history.[78] Ricardo Agarez's recent book offers another example, as it discusses the anonymous architecture of 'peripheral' Algarve and the ways in which it can be associated with 'central' twentieth-century debates around modernism and regionalism.[79]

In addition, if buildings are – along with texts – equally important authorial agents of critical regionalism, as I have argued in this book, then their preservation today becomes additionally significant. The fourth decade is a crucial stage in the lifetime of a modern building, which has usually outgrown its original function by then. As such, this key moment determines whether and how it will survive in the future. If, for example, Herman Hertzberger's Centraal Beheer continues to be left abandoned to slowly deteriorate in its current state (Fig. 11.5), the world will not only lose a project that holds a special place in the architectural history of the twentieth century; it will also lose a rare built example of some of the most nuanced political aspects of critical regionalism. As I argued in chapter 5, this is one of the very few projects that show how the tactile materiality of the building and intricate detailing of interior thresholds and surfaces is directly associated with the proactive use of these spaces by its occupants and the ensuing civic character of the architecture of critical regionalism. Conversely, initiatives to promote new uses for such projects – including housing or educational facilities, which could be readily accommodated in Centraal Beheer's modular structure – would not only further demonstrate the validity of Frampton's 'critical regionalist' reading of them; they would also breathe new life into projects that deserve to be saved from both dereliction and oblivion. This is equally important today, because the discourse of critical regionalism tended to emphasise the formal, material and tactile qualities of architectural projects over their long-term inhabitation, as I argued

Figure 11.5 Herman Hertzberger, Centraal Beheer offices, Apeldoorn, 1968–72, photographed by Willem Diepraam (left); Jaap Veldhoen (top right); Patrick Minks (bottom right)

Atelier Herman Hertzberger

in chapter 9. This led to a static perception of these projects as idealised images of architectural 'resistance' frozen in time instead of accommodating their transformations as they aged, their users changed and some of the original design intentions dissipated.

But even if one stayed within a more conventional conception of authorship, there is still significant historical work that can be undertaken – especially in relation to the contribution of women architects and theorists to critical regionalism. Although I have highlighted Suzana Antonakaki's important role in Atelier 66 on several occasions in this book, I have not been able to distinguish Lefaivre's original inputs into her joint writings with Tzonis to the same extent. Access to material from Tzonis and Lefaivre's private archive would help future historians to further highlight how her non-architectural background added nuance, new meanings and subtle metaphors to the critical regionalist discourse. Flora Ruchat-Roncati (1937–2012) in Ticino and Elissa Mäkiniemi Aalto (1922–1994) in Finland are only two of several other women architects whose integral role in the development of the theory and practice of critical regionalism has either been overshadowed by the comparative overexposure of their male partners or needs to be retraced in projects of joint authorship with their regional peers.

Historiography

Standing at the threshold of yet another crucial decade, the start of which was marked by the global Covid-19 crisis, one might be ready to accept that critical regionalism has closed its historic cycle. But even if one supposes that critical regionalism has now exceeded its 'sell-by date' as a theory for architectural design,[80] it can still survive as an unfulfilled historiographical project. To do so, however, it needs to be adapted and updated. The recent fifth revised edition of Frampton's critical history that bears the mark of his graduate courses at Columbia University in the 2010s, also demonstrates the limits of his 'world architecture' approach of architectural historiography.[81] The same is the case with Tzonis and Lefaivre's recent update of their comprehensive history of regionalist architecture with the addition of recent examples from Asia and Africa, among others, in the added closing chapter.[82] Because the three authors essentially still follow the same critical regionalist framework, past shortcomings are still in place in their recent, however ambitiously revised, accounts. As their approaches have by now clearly shown their strengths alongside their limits, it is up to a new generation of scholars to step in and write the more historically aware and contextually sensitive accounts that Tzonis, Lefaivre and Frampton did not deliver. While one could argue that critical regionalism has already created its own school of architectural historiography, as demonstrated by recent scholarship such as Antigoni Katsakou's *Rethinking Modernity: Between the Local and the International* (2020),[83] there is ample room for further development.

No longer limited by the concerns of the 1980s or viewed as a manifesto for a humanistic architecture of the future, critical regionalism can now become a cross-cultural historiographical agenda. Through a historically informed critique, it can be reinvigorated – no longer as a theoretical but as a pertinent historiographical agenda of architecture for the twenty-first century. This agenda can promote the multiple and interconnected modern margins that still exist to a contemporary historiography without a clearly defined centre. The general outlook of critical regionalism that partially critiqued the modern project without regressing into chauvinist nationalisms also seems to be especially pertinent. Adopting such an agenda is even more urgent in the still unsettled process of globalisation after the shock of the pandemic and the recent rise of alt-right, nationalist isolationisms and new walls across the globe. Contrary to the triumphalist predictions of the 1990s, a total of seventy more walls had been established by the mid-2000s.[84] If the 2010s showed that global crises instigate nationalist resurgences, the 2020s also unveiled the structural vulnerability of this world of globally interconnected supply chains. When local accidents can rapidly escalate to become pressing global problems, they can no longer be experienced as spectacular isolated instances from the safe distance of the rest of the world. This decade has already suggested that there is no easy way back to a walled, secured space outside of this conundrum, as such global crises can be resolved only by transnational collaboration and coordination. But this path is still hampered by established inequities and soft-power antagonisms. At the time of writing, these are expressed through Covid-19 vaccination nationalisms, which distract from approaching the vaccines as global public goods in order to address the problem on an appropriate planetary scale.

Following Frampton, Tzonis and Lefaivre, and appropriately revising their best-known points to address the critiques of the recent past, I propose that critical regionalism can now turn from an architectural theory of the 1980s into a manifesto for architectural historiography in the twenty-first century along the following lines:

(1) Critical regionalism invariably foregrounded the work of the 'talented individual' who produced the best moment, and exemplified the essence, of a collective culture.[85] This effectively meant that individual figures became tokens for entire countries such as Greece, whose national territory is home to multifarious cultural expressions. Today, stronger emphasis on a 'small-plan' historiography enables a nuanced focus on the specificities of interlocking contexts that produce regional architectures.

(2) Critical regionalism suggested equations of architectural regions with modern countries. But the world witnessed the historical emergence of a large number of decolonised or postcolonial nation states after the Second World War. These did not register in the discourse of critical regionalism.[86] For Tzonis, Lefaivre and Frampton, context invariably coincided with the confines of free-standing national histories – effectively leading to an understanding

of the world of architecture through existing, and often artificially imposed, national borders. Even the Mediterranean, a constant favourite reference of modern architects, is rarely treated as a region in Frampton's writings on critical regionalism. This was already insufficient in a world increasingly studied in terms of interactions, intersections and overlaps during the parallel rise of postcolonial scholarship in the 1980s. Philosophers such as Peter Sloterdijk, who has argued that the same colonial history can also be traced behind the creation of globalised spaces, can be helpful in this respect. The now planetary air-conditioned interior environment originally enabled the displacement of plants to places where they are not made to grow. Sloterdijk argues that this was essentially a colonial operation that aimed to collapse the differences between the climatic regions of the Earth.[87] As such, subtle interconnections and cross-cultural exchanges that critical regionalism tended to gloss over now demand further scrutiny by architectural historians, as they can lead to more sophisticated understandings of both 'globalised' and 'regionalist' spaces today.

(3) Discarding earlier, idealised essentialisms (such as critical regionalism's favoured juxtaposition of place and production) would also promote the study of more historically complex modalities. These produce not pure but hybrid regional architectures. In the final instance, the nineteenth-century static idea of identity is itself the trademark and footprint of European imperialist history on colonised cultures. The fact that the multiple postcolonial identities of the twentieth century are never pure, but hybrid, is partly owing to the earlier history of imperialism. In these contexts, the forging of identity was primarily led by the economic and political process of postcolonial sovereignty. Looking at regional contexts from this more global comparative perspective challenges these schematic idealisations of critical regionalist phenomenology. To cite just one example, Konstantina Kalfa has recently done so by situating the case of Greek reconstruction after the Second World War and the ensuing civil war in the Cold War context of the late 1940s and early 1950s.[88]

(4) In the 1980s, critical regionalism was one of the first mainstream architectural discourses to promote design principles of environmental sustainability. Working with the site and the specificities of its context, climate and topography also meant favouring architectures of natural light, and cross-ventilated spaces built from locally sourced materials. As a historiographical agenda for the

twenty-first century, critical regionalism remains sensitive to the exigencies of the current climate emergency.[89] Its critical distance from the idealised essentialisms of the 1980s also enables it to address the fluid material and cultural conditions of sites as part of the climatic shifts on a planetary scale – when the very concept of the 'region' is destabilised and can no longer serve as a fixed, static foundation for architecture.

(5)   Focusing on the two Antonakakis, Tzonis and Lefaivre's first theorisation of critical regionalism developed in the 'home scholar'[90] terms of the informed insiders' view of Greek culture from the vantage of powerful Euro-American institutions. But the two critics also extended their theorisation beyond the standard circle of architectural developments, forging links with modern painting and poetry in Greece and with longer-standing European currents. Today, such briefly highlighted links can lead to fully fledged 'interdisciplinary' understandings of transversal cultural develop-ments in specific regions, spanning from the arts to critical archaeologies.[91] Historians' intention to acknowledge and historicise the degree to which they themselves consciously comply with and resist the established cultural luggage or colonial assumptions that they bring to the analysis of diverse regions is also key here. Critical regionalism was historically developed by scholars who worked from a transatlantic First World space affiliated with powerful Euro-American institutions, and this structural hierarchy was taken as a given without being practically addressed or theoretically examined at the time.

(6)   As an architectural theory, critical regionalism historically favoured the Western European and North American conceptions of modernity. Originally envisaged as a '"revisionist" variant of Modernism',[92] it established its own hierarchies in the use of specific architectural languages. The more closely architectural examples followed modernist abstractions (as opposed to regionalist figurations and their then undesirable associations with postmodernism), the more deserving they were to be added to the critical regionalist canon. This was the hard 'imperialist' and 'colonialist' core of critical regionalism, as this discourse did not fundamentally challenge the superiority of Western modernism despite its authors' critical and revisionist aspirations. Other architectures and design cultures were only allowed to be inserted into the overarching modernist design language as 'disjunctive episodes' or 'regional adaptations'.[93] Adopting non-hierarchical

conceptions of architectural cultures in the historiography of the twenty-first century also means moving beyond studies of Western-educated architects in non-Western contexts, if one is to arrive at a decolonised perspective on them.[94]

(7) Colonial approaches to architecture and its history need to be further uprooted, but they are often subtle and hard to identify.[95] Elucidating them calls for further research into the deeper links between nationalism, imperialism, colonialism and racism in architecture.[96] This includes challenging established concepts, starting from the 'non-West' itself, and narrative structures that stem from the Western liberal view of global history and the established Three-World hierarchies of the twentieth-century Cold War.[97] Readdressing questions of provinciality and exploring narrative structures that do not follow Western ideals of resolution and closure, but remain open to ambiguity and contradiction, form possible steps in this direction.[98] Leading to the slow emergence of not-readily-familiar modernities and regionalisms, such studies can break the 'different' as a mirror of the First World West.

Notes

1   Alexander Tzonis and Liane Lefaivre, 'Human Life Remains the Central Issue', in *Context and Modernity: A Post-Seminar Reading*, ed. by Gerard Bergers (Delft: Stylos, 1991), pp. 110–11 (p. 110).
2   Nelson Mota, 'From Critical Regionalism to Critical Realism: Challenging the Commodification of Tradition', *DASH*, 6 (2012), 46–55.
3   Tzonis and Lefaivre, 'Human Life Remains the Central Issue', p. 111.
4   Fredric Jameson, 'Not Avoiding Post-Modernity Would Have Complicated But Also Articulated Things', in *Context and Modernity*, ed. by Bergers, pp. 42–8 (p. 46).
5   Kenneth Frampton, 'The Owl of Minerva: An Epilogue', in *Studies in Tectonic Culture: The Poetics of Construction in Nineteenth and Twentieth Century Architecture* (Cambridge, MA: MIT Press, 1995), pp. 377–87 (p. 377).
6   Maarten Bredero, 'The Necessity of Rules Remains', in *Context and Modernity*, ed. by Bergers, pp. 112–13 (p. 112).
7   Hans van Dijk, 'The Banner Critical Regionalism Hauled Down', in *Context and Modernity*, ed. by Bergers, pp. 16–20 (p. 20). See *The Oxford Companion to Architecture*, ed. by Patrick Goode (Oxford: Oxford University Press, 2009), p. 228; Liane Lefaivre and Alexander Tzonis, *Architecture of Regionalism in the Age of Globalization: Peaks and Valleys in the Flat World* (London: Routledge, 2012).
8   Kenneth Frampton, 'If It is Reduced to an Aesthetic Package Architecture Looses [sic] the Game from the Modernising Force of the Megatrend', in *Context and Modernity*, ed. by Bergers, pp. 28–34 (pp. 29, 32).
9   Ibid., pp. 32–3.
10 *Context and Modernity*, ed. by Bergers, pp. 7, 126–32.
11 Francis Fukuyama, 'The End of History?', *The National Interest*, 16 (1989), 3–18.
12 Hedy d'Ancona, 'A Provocative Note at the Beginning', in *Context and Modernity*, ed. by Bergers, pp. 10–14 (p. 13).
13 Frampton, 'If It is Reduced to an Aesthetic Package', pp. 31–2.

14 Marshall Berman, 'How World Cities Get More World Space', in *Context and Modernity*, ed. by Bergers, pp. 58–64 (pp. 59, 62–3).

15 Marshall Berman, 'The Dream of Perfect Roots and Embeddedness is Something Distinctly Modern', in *Context and Modernity*, ed. by Bergers, pp. 36–40 (pp. 36–7).

16 Jameson, 'Not Avoiding Post-Modernity', pp. 43, 46.

17 Harry Kunneman, 'The End of Modern History', in *Context and Modernity*, ed. by Bergers, pp. 54–7 (p. 56).

18 Van Dijk, 'The Banner Critical Regionalism Hauled Down', pp. 18–19.

19 Frampton, 'If It is Reduced to an Aesthetic Package', p. 29.

20 Bernard Huet, 'Formalisme/Realisme', *L'Architecture d'Aujourd'hui*, 190 (April 1977), 35–6.

21 Mary Pepchinski, email to Stylianos Giamarelos, 25 June 2018.

22 See Eric Hobsbawm, *Age of Extremes: The Short Twentieth Century, 1914–1991* (London: Abacus, 1995).

23 See Frances Stonor Saunders, *The Cultural Cold War: The CIA and the World of Arts and Letters* (New York: New Press, 1999).

24 Reinhold Martin, 'Postscript: A Postmodernist International?', in *Second World Postmodernisms: Architecture and Society under Late Socialism*, ed. by Vladimir Kulić (London: Bloomsbury, 2019), pp. 226–35.

25 See Lefaivre and Tzonis, *Architecture of Regionalism in the Age of Globalization*.

26 Kenneth Frampton, 'Towards a Critical Regionalism: Six Points for an Architecture of Resistance', in *The Anti-Aesthetic: Essays on Postmodern Culture*, ed. by Hal Foster (Seattle: Bay Press, 1983), pp. 16–30 (p. 19).

27 See Jacques Derrida, *Of Grammatology*, trans. by Gayatri Chakravorty Spivak (Baltimore, MD: Johns Hopkins University Press, 1976); Azadeh Mashayekhi, 'The Politics of Building in Post-Revolution Tehran', in *Routledge Handbook on Middle East Cities*, ed. by Haim Yacobi and Mansour Nasasra (London: Routledge, 2020), pp. 196–216; Anthony Giddens, *The Consequences of Modernity* (Cambridge: Polity, 1991); Anthony Giddens, *Beyond Left and Right: The Future of Radical Politics* (Cambridge: Polity, 1994); Anthony Giddens, *The Third Way: The Renewal of Social Democracy* (Cambridge: Polity, 1998).

28 Andre Gunder Frank, *Dependent Accumulation and Underdevelopment* (London: Macmillan, 1978).

29 See Mary McLeod, 'Kenneth Frampton's Idea of the "Critical"', in *Modern Architecture and the Lifeworld: Essays in Honor of Kenneth Frampton*, ed. by Karla Cavarra Britton and Robert McCarter (London: Thames & Hudson, 2020), pp. 20–42; Hannah Arendt, *The Human Condition* (Chicago: University of Chicago Press, 1958); Herbert Marcuse, *Eros and Civilization* (New York: Vintage, 1962).

30 See Cornelius Castoriadis, *La société bureaucratique* (Paris: Union général d'éditions, 1973). Castoriadis's analysis of Soviet bureaucratic states dates back to his texts for *Socialisme ou Barbarie* in the 1940s.

31 Petra Brouwer and Kristina Jõekalda, 'Introduction: Architectural Identities of European Peripheries', *Journal of Architecture*, 25.8 (2020), 963–77.

32 See Frampton, 'Towards a Critical Regionalism', pp. 24–5; Jean Gottmann, *Megalopolis: The Urbanized Northeastern Seaboard a of the United States* (New York: Twentieth Century Fund, 1961).

33 See Catherine Cooke, *Russian Avant-Garde: Theories of Art, Architecture and the City* (London: Academy, 1995).

34 See Thomas L. Friedman, *The World is Flat: A Brief History of the Globalized World in the Twenty-First Century* (London: Allen Lane, 2005); Francis Fukuyama, *The End of History and the Last Man* (London: Hamilton, 1992).

35 See Stuart Hall, *The Hard Road to Renewal: Thatcherism and the Crisis of the Left* (London: Verso, 1988); Pierre Rosanvallon, *Notre histoire intellectuelle et politique 1968–2018* (Paris: Seuil, 2018).

36 See Frédéric Lebaron, *Le savant, la politique et la mondialisation* (Bellecombe-en-Bauge: Le Croquant, 2003).

37 See Jacques Derrida, 'Globalization, Peace and Cosmopolitics', in *The Future of Values: 21st-Century Talks*, ed. by Jérôme Bindé, trans. by John Corbett (United Nations Educational, Scientific and Cultural Organization, 2004), pp. 110–22. For a more recent study of twentieth-century internationalisation and globalisation in architecture, see Mark Crinson, *Rebuilding Babel: Modern Architecture and Internationalism* (London: I.B.Tauris, 2017).

38 See Łukasz Stanek, *Architecture in Global Socialism: Eastern Europe, West Africa, and the Middle East in the Cold War* (Princeton: Princeton University Press, 2020); Christina Schwenkel, *Building Socialism: The Afterlife of East German Architecture in Urban Vietnam* (Durham, NC: Duke University Press, 2020); Vladimir Kulić, 'New Belgrade and Socialist Yugoslavia's Three Globalisations', *International Journal for History, Culture and Modernity*, 2.2 (2014), 125–53.

39 See *World Architecture: A Critical Mosaic 1900–2000*, ed. by Kenneth Frampton, 10 vols (New York: Springer, 1999–2002).

40 Johann Wolfgang von Goethe, 'Frankfurter Ausgabe', in *Sämtliche Werke: Briefe, Tagebücher und Gespräche*, ed. by Friedmar Apel and Hendrik Birus, 12 vols (Frankfurt am Main: Deutscher Klassiker, 1986–99), vol. 12 (1999), pp. 224–5.

41 See Milan Kundera, *The Curtain: An Essay in Seven Parts*, trans. by Linda Asher (New York: Harper Collins, 2007).

42 See David Damrosch, *What is World Literature?* (Princeton: Princeton University Press, 2003).

43 Anthony Alofsin, *When Buildings Speak: Architecture as Language in the Habsburg Empire and its Aftermath, 1867–1933* (Chicago: University of Chicago Press, 2006).

44 Alexander Tzonis and Liane Lefaivre, 'Critical Regionalism', in *Critical Regionalism: The Pomona Meeting Proceedings*, ed. by Spyros Amourgis (Pomona: California State Polytechnic University, 1991), pp. 3–23 (p. 23).

45 Richard Weston, 'Oriental Star: Tadao Ando: The Yale Studio and Current Works', *Architects' Journal*, 190.12 (20 September 1989), 91.

46 See Pascale Casanova, *The World Republic of Letters*, trans. by Malcolm DeBevoise (Cambridge, MA: Harvard University Press, 2004).

47 Keith L. Eggener, 'Placing Resistance: A Critique of Critical Regionalism', *Journal of Architectural Education*, 55.4 (2002), 228–37.

48 Lewis Mumford, *The South in Architecture* (New York: Harcourt, Brace & Co., 1941); Lewis Mumford, 'Report on Honolulu', in Lewis Mumford, *City Development* (New York: Harcourt, Brace & Co., 1945), pp. 84–154.

49 Liane Lefaivre and Alexander Tzonis, 'The Suppression and Rethinking of Regionalism and Tropicalism after 1945', in *Tropical Architecture: Critical Regionalism in the Age of Globalisation*, ed. by Alexander Tzonis, Liane Lefaivre and Bruno Stagno (Chichester: Wiley, 2001), pp. 14–58.

50 Paul Ricoeur, 'Universal Civilisation and National Cultures' (1961), repr. in Paul Ricoeur, *History and Truth*, trans. by Charles A. Kelbley (Evanston, IL: Northwestern University Press, 1965), pp. 271–84 (p. 277); Mark Crinson, 'Singapore's Moment: Critical Regionalism, its Colonial Roots and Profound Aftermath', *Journal of Architecture*, 13.5 (2008), 585–605.

51 See Edward Said, *Orientalism* (London: Routledge; Kegan Paul, 1978); Dipesh Chakrabarty, *Provincializing Europe: Postcolonial Thought and Historical Difference* (Princeton: Princeton University Press, 2000).

52 Gayatri Chakravorty Spivak, *Other Asias* (Malden, MA: Blackwell, 2008); Krista Comer, 'Exceptionalism, Other Wests, Critical Regionalism', *American Literary History*, 23.1 (2011), 159–73.

53 See Liane Lefaivre and Alexander Tzonis, *Critical Regionalism: Architecture and Identity in a Globalized World* (Munich: Prestel, 2003); Lefaivre and Tzonis, *Architecture of Regionalism in the Age of Globalization*.

54 Mary McLeod, 'Architecture and Politics in the Reagan Era: From Postmodernism to Deconstructivism', *Assemblage*, 8 (1989), 23–59 (p. 36).

55 Kenneth Frampton, 'Μοντέρνο, πολύ μοντέρνο: Μια συνέντευξη του Kenneth Frampton στον Γιώργο Σημαιοφορίδη', *Architecture in Greece*, 20 (1986), 118–21.

56 Kenneth Frampton, 'Modern and Site Specific: The Architecture of Gino Valle 1945–2003', *The Plan Journal*, 4.1 (2019), 223–6 (p. 225).

57 Kenneth Frampton, 'Team 10, Plus 20: The Vicissitudes of Ideology', *L'Architecture d'Aujourd'hui*, 177 (1975), 62–5 (p. 65).

58 Alexander Tzonis and Liane Lefaivre, 'The Grid and the Pathway: An Introduction to the Work of Dimitris and Suzana Antonakakis, with Prolegomena to a History of the Culture of Modern Greek Architecture', *Architecture in Greece*, 15 (1981), 164–78 (p. 178).

59 Jameson, 'Not Avoiding Post-Modernity', p. 48.

60 See Stratis Tsirkas, *Η χαμένη άνοιξη* (Athens: Kedros, 1976).

61   See Branko Milanovic, *Capitalism Alone: The Future of the System that Rules the World* (Cambridge, MA: Harvard University Press, 2019).

62   See Fareed Zakaria, *Ten Lessons for a Post-Pandemic World* (New York: Norton, 2020).

63   See Richard Baldwin, *The Great Convergence: Information Technology and the New Globalization* (Cambridge, MA: Belknap, 2016).

64   Milanovic, *Capitalism Alone*.

65   Francesco Sisci, 'Under the Same Sky: A New World-view from China', *Diogenes*, 221 (2009), 74–82.

66   See 'Kenneth Frampton Golden Lion for Lifetime Achievement', *La Biennale di Venezia*, 26 May 2018. Online. www.labiennale.org/en/news/kenneth-frampton-golden-lion-lifetime-achievement (accessed 19 July 2021).

67   See *Critical Regionalism Revisited*, ed. by Tom Avermaete et al. Special issue, *OASE*, 103 (2019); Véronique Patteeuw and Léa-Catherine Szacka, 'Critical Regionalism for our Time', *Architectural Review*, 1466 (November 2019), 92–8; *Modern Architecture and the Lifeworld*, ed. by Cavarra Britton and McCarter.

68   Tom Avermaete et al., 'A Conversation with Kenneth Frampton: New York, 6 April 2018', *OASE*, 103 (2019), 142–54 (p. 150).

69   See Philip James Tabb and A. Senem Deviren, *The Greening of Architecture: A Critical History and Survey of Contemporary Sustainable Architecture and Urban Design* (London: Routledge, 2014).

70   Lucius Burckhardt, 'On Ecological Architecture: A Memo', in Alexander Tzonis and Liane Lefaivre, *Architecture in Europe since 1968: Memory and Invention* (London: Thames & Hudson, 1992), pp. 42–3.

71   Peter Sloterdijk, 'The Anthropocene: A Stage in the Process on the Margins of the Earth's History', in Peter Sloterdijk, *What Happened in the Twentieth Century? Towards a Critique of Extremist Reason*, trans. by Christopher Turner (Cambridge: Polity, 2018), pp. 14–15.

72   See Helena Norberg-Hodge, *Local is our Future: Steps to an Economics of Happiness* (Totnes: Local Futures, 2019).

73   Hannah Arendt, 'We Refugees' (1943), repr. in *Hannah Arendt: The Jewish Writings*, ed. by Jerome Kohn and Ron H. Feldman (New York: Schoken, 2007), pp. 264–74.

74   See Oliver Wainwright, 'Revealed: How Developers Exploit Flawed Planning System to Minimise Affordable Housing', *The Guardian*, 25 June 2015. Online. www.theguardian.com/cities/2015/jun/25/london-developers-viability-planning-affordable-social-housing-regeneration-oliver-wainwright (accessed 19 July 2021).

75   See Neyran Turan, *Architecture as Measure* (Barcelona: Actar, 2020); *Architecture in the Anthropocene: Encounters among Design, Deep Time, Science and Philosophy*, ed. by Etienne Turpin (London: Open Humanities, 2013).

76   Carmen Popescu, 'Flattening History: A Prequel to the Invention of Critical Regionalism', *OASE*, 103 (2019), 49–57; Carmen Popescu, 'Space, Time: Identity', *National Identities*, 8.3 (2006), 189–206.

77   Among others, see Irina Davidovici, 'Constructing "the School of the Ticino": The Historiography of a New Swiss Architecture, 1975–1990', *Journal of Architecture*, 25.8 (2020), 1115–40.

78   See Anthony Alofsin, *Frank Lloyd Wright – The Lost Years, 1910–1922: A Study of Influence* (Chicago: University of Chicago Press, 1993); *Frank Lloyd Wright: Europe and Beyond*, ed. by Anthony Alofsin (Berkeley: University of California Press, 1999); and Anthony Alofsin, *Wright and New York: The Making of America's Architect* (New Haven, CT: Yale University Press, 2019).

79   Ricardo Agarez, *Algarve Building: Modernism, Regionalism and Architecture in the South of Portugal, 1925–1965* (New York: Routledge, 2016).

80   Maria Smith, 'Ethics have a Sell-by Date', *RIBA Journal* (September 2018), 75.

81   See Kenneth Frampton, *Modern Architecture: A Critical History*, 5th edn (London: Thames & Hudson, 2020); Kenneth Frampton, Draft of course outline for A-4616 world architecture and critical regionalism, 2015, CCA Fonds 197, Kenneth Frampton fonds, 197 – 2017 – 029T, AP197.S1.SS2.154, 2015, 197-029-003.

82   Liane Lefaivre and Alexander Tzonis, *Architecture of Regionalism in the Age of Globalization: Peaks and Valleys in the Flat World*, 2nd edn (London: Routledge, 2021).

83   Antigoni Katsakou, *Rethinking Modernity: Between the Local and the International* (London: RIBA, 2020).

84   See Theo Deutinger, 'Walled World', *Vrij Nederland*, 47 (2006). Online. the-department.eu/projects/show/walled-world (accessed 20 July 2021).

85 Kenneth Frampton, 'Modern Architecture and Critical Regionalism', *RIBA Transactions*, 3.2 (1983), 15–25 (p. 21).

86 See Harry Magdoff, *Imperialism: From the Colonial Age to the Present* (New York: Monthly Review, 1978).

87 See Peter Sloterdijk, *In the World Interior of Capital: Towards a Philosophical Theory of Globalization*, trans. by Wieland Hoban (Cambridge: Polity, 2013).

88 Konstantina Kalfa, *Αυτοστέγαση τώρα! Η αθέατη πλευρά της αμερικανικής βοήθειας στην Ελλάδα* (Athens: futura, 2019), pp. 75–89.

89 See Bruno Latour, *Down to Earth: Politics in the New Climatic Regime*, trans. by Catherine Porter (Cambridge: Polity, 2018).

90 Jiat-Hwee Chang and Imran bin Tajudeen, 'Historiographical Questions in Southeast Asia's Modern Architecture', in *Southeast Asia's Modern Architecture: Questions of Translation, Epistemology and Power*, ed. by Jiat-Hwee Chang and Imran bin Tajudeen (Singapore: NUS Press, 2019), pp. 1–21.

91 See Yannis Hamilakis, *The Nation and its Ruins: Antiquity, Archaeology, and National Imagination in Greece* (Oxford: Oxford University Press, 2007).

92 Frampton, *Modern Architecture: A Critical History*, 2nd edn (London: Thames & Hudson, 1985), p. 7.

93 Ibid., p. 327.

94 See Edward Denison and Guang Yu Ren, *Luke Him Sau, Architect: China's Missing Modern* (Chichester: Wiley, 2014).

95 Michael Herzfeld, 'The Absent Presence: Discourses of Crypto-Colonialism', *South Atlantic Quarterly*, 101.4 (2002), 899–926.

96 See *Race and Modern Architecture: A Critical History from the Enlightenment to the Present*, ed. by Irene Cheng, Charles L. Davis II and Mabel O. Wilson (Pittsburgh: University of Pittsburgh Press, 2020); *White Papers, Black Marks: Architecture, Race, Culture*, ed. by Lesley Naa Norle Lokko (London: Athlone, 2000).

97 See Pankaj Mishra, *Bland Fanatics: Liberals, Race and Empire* (London: Verso, 2020).

98 Dana Arnold, 'Beyond a Boundary: Towards an Architectural History of the Non-East', in *Rethinking Architectural Historiography*, ed. by Dana Arnold, Elvan A. Orgut and Belgin T. Özkaya (New York: Routledge, 2006), pp. 229–45.

References

Abel, Chris, 'Regional Transformations', *Architectural Review*, 180.1077 (November 1986), 36–43.

Adamson, Glenn and Jane Pavitt, eds, *Postmodernism: Style and Subversion, 1970–1990* (London: Victoria and Albert Museum, 2011).

Agarez, Ricardo, *Algarve Building: Modernism, Regionalism and Architecture in the South of Portugal, 1925–1965* (New York: Routledge, 2016).

Akcan, Esra, *Open Architecture: Migration, Citizenship and the Urban Renewal of Berlin-Kreuzberg by IBA 1984/87* (Basel: Birkhäuser, 2018).

Alexander, Christopher, *A Pattern Language: Towns, Buildings, Construction* (New York: Oxford University Press, 1977).

Alexandropoulou, Soula, 'Σ' αναζήτηση ενός χώρου γι' ανθρώπινο τρόπο ζωής', *Καθημερινή*, 27 February 1977, 5.

Alifragkis, Stavros and Emilia Athanassiou, 'Educating Greece in Modernity: Post-War Tourism and Western Politics', *Journal of Architecture*, 23.4 (2018), 595–616.

Allen, Barbara L., 'On Performative Regionalism', in *Architectural Regionalism: Collected Writings on Place, Identity, Modernity, and Tradition*, ed. by Vincent B. Canizaro (New York: Princeton Architectural Press, 2007), pp. 421–6.

Allies, Bob, 'Aalto's Architecture Redefined?', *Architects' Journal*, 177.8 (23 February 1983), 30–1.

Alofsin, Anthony, 'Constructive Regionalism' (1980), in *Architectural Regionalism: Collected Writings on Place, Identity, Modernity, and Tradition*, ed. by Vincent B. Canizaro (New York: Princeton Architectural Press, 2007), pp. 368–73.

Alofsin, Anthony, *Frank Lloyd Wright – The Lost Years, 1910–1922: A Study of Influence* (Chicago: University of Chicago Press, 1993).

Alofsin, Anthony, ed., *Frank Lloyd Wright: Europe and Beyond* (Berkeley: University of California Press, 1999).

Alofsin, Anthony, *The Struggle for Modernism: Architecture, Landscape Architecture, and City Planning at Harvard* (New York: Norton, 2002).

Alofsin, Anthony, *When Buildings Speak: Architecture as Language in the Habsburg Empire and its Aftermath, 1867–1933* (Chicago: University of Chicago Press, 2006).

Alofsin, Anthony, *Wright and New York: The Making of America's Architect* (New Haven, CT: Yale University Press, 2019).

Ambasz, Emilio, ed., *The Architecture of Luis Barragán* (New York: Museum of Modern Art, 1976).

Amourgis, Spyros, ed., *Critical Regionalism: The Pomona Meeting Proceedings* (Pomona: California State Polytechnic University, 1991).

Anderson, Perry, *The Origins of Postmodernity* (London: Verso, 1998).

Ando, Tadao, 'From Self-Enclosed Modern Architecture Towards Universality', in *Tadao Ando: Buildings, Projects, Writings*, ed. by Kenneth Frampton (New York: Rizzoli, 1984), pp. 138–42.

Andritzky, Michael, Lucius Burckhardt and Ot Hoffmann, eds, *Für eine andere Architektur: Bauen mit der Natur und in der Region* (Frankfurt am Main: Fischer, 1981).

Antonakaki, Suzana, 'Η αρχιτεκτονική της Μακρινίτσας'. Unpublished undergraduate thesis, National Technical University of Athens, 1959.

Antonakaki, Suzana, 'Κατοικία και ποιότητα ζωής: Η διάσταση του χρόνου στο σχεδιασμό', *Journal of the Association of Greek Architects*, 9 (1981), 50–9.

Antonakaki, Suzana, 'Outdoor "Houses" and Indoor Streets', in *INDESEM '87: International Design Seminar*, ed. by Marc Labadie and Bert Tjhie (Delft: Delft University Press, 1988), pp. 132–49.

Antonakaki, Suzana, 'Teacher and Friend', in *A. James Speyer: Architect, Curator, Exhibition Designer*, ed. by John Vinci (Chicago: University of Chicago Press, 1997), pp. 72–6.

Antonakaki, Suzana, *Κατώφλια: 100 + 7 Χωρογραφήματα* (Athens: futura, 2010).

Antonakaki, Suzana, 'Αρχιτεκτονική: Επάγγελμα. Επαγγέλομαι = Υπόσχομαι', in *Ίχνη αρχιτεκτονικής διαδρομής: Σουζάνα Αντωνακάκη και Δημήτρης Αντωνακάκης*, ed. by Dimitris Polychronopoulos, 2 vols (Athens: futura, 2018), I, pp. 15–19.

Antonakaki, Suzana, 'Ποίηση και λόγος: Γεωμετρία και ποιητικός λόγος. Όριο και κενό. Δεσμεύσεις και ελευθερία. Προσεγγίσεις στο αρχιτεκτονικό σύμπαν του Άρη Κωνσταντινίδη', in *Άρης Κωνσταντινίδης*, ed. by Dina Vaiou (Athens: Greek Parliament Foundation, 2019), pp. 69–100.

Antonakakis, Dimitris, 'Ύδρα'. Unpublished undergraduate thesis, National Technical University of Athens, 1958.

Antonakakis, Dimitris, 'Προσεγγίσεις: Προβλήματα τουριστικής ανάπτυξης', *Οικονομικός Ταχυδρόμος*, 218 (1971), 43–7.

Antonakakis, Dimitris, 'Παρατηρήσεις στο όριο επαφής δημόσιου και ιδιωτικού χώρου', *Χρονικό* (1973), 169–71.

Antonakakis, Dimitris, 'Μεταμοντέρνα αρχιτεκτονική: Παρεμβάσεις', *Journal of the Association of Greek Architects*, 8 (September–October 1981), 82–3.

Antonakakis, Dimitris, 'Πολυκατοικία: Όνειρο ή εφιάλτης;', *Journal of the Association of Greek Architects*, 6 (1981), 68–78.

Antonakakis, Dimitris, 'Η διδασκαλία της αρχιτεκτονικής: Συμβολή στον επαναπροσδιορισμό των στόχων και του περιεχομένου σπουδών στα τμήματα Αρχιτεκτονικής των ΑΕΙ', *Journal of the Association of Greek Architects*, 16 (1983), 39–42.

Antonakakis, Dimitris, 'Dimitris Pikionis: Elaboration and Improvisation', in *Mega XI, Dimitris Pikionis, Architect 1887–1968: A Sentimental Topography*, ed. by Dennis Crompton (London: Architectural Association, 1989), pp. 10–15.

Antonakakis, Dimitris, 'Landscaping the Athens Acropolis', in *Mega XI, Dimitris Pikionis, Architect 1887–1968: A Sentimental Topography*, ed. by Dennis Crompton (London: Architectural Association, 1989), p. 90.

Antonakakis, Dimitris, 'Προβληματισμοί σχεδιασμού', *Journal of the Association of Greek Architects*, 21–2 (1989), 65–6, 77.

Antonakakis, Dimitris, 'Το μοντέρνο και ο τόπος', *Architecture in Greece*, 30 (1996), 134.

Antonakakis, Dimitris, 'The Speyer Houses on Hydra', in *A. James Speyer: Architect, Curator, Exhibition Designer*, ed. by John Vinci (Chicago: University of Chicago Press, 1997), pp. 58–71.

Antonakakis, Dimitris, 'Lecture', in *Technology, Place and Production: The Jerusalem Seminar in Architecture*, ed. by Kenneth Frampton with Arthur Spector and Lynne Reed Rosman (New York: Rizzoli, 1998), pp. 204–7.

Antonakakis, Dimitris, 'Θουκυδίδης Βαλεντής: Ο δάσκαλος, σημειώσεις από μία δεκαετία', in *Ο αρχιτέκτονας Θουκυδίδης Π. Βαλεντής*, ed. by Chrysa Sachana, Aimilia Stefanidou, Sofia Tsitiridou and Aliki Samouilidou (Athens: Nisos, 2007), pp. 33–8.

Antonakakis, Dimitris, 'Θ. Βαλεντής: Πειθαρχία και τρυφερότητα', *Πολίτης*, 162 (2008), 35–8.

Antonakakis, Dimitris, 'Αρχιτεκτονική εκπαίδευση και πράξη: Μία αμφίδρομη εκπαιδευτική διαδικασία', in *Τάσος Μπίρης – Δημήτρης Μπίρης: Το αμφίδρομο πέρασμα ανάμεσα στην αρχιτεκτονική και τη διδασκαλία*, ed. by Lena Kalaitzi (Athens: Papasotiriou/Benaki Museum, 2011), pp. 13–19.

Antonakakis, Dimitris, 'Dimitris Pikionis: Besieging the School at Pefkakia', in Dimitris Antonakakis, *Dimitris Pikionis: Two Lectures* (Athens: Domes, 2013), pp. 154–65.

Antonakakis, Dimitris, 'Προβλήματα κατοίκησης. Πολυκατοικία: Τυπολογική πολυπλοκότητα ή σύνθετη τυπολογία;', in *Έξι διαλέξεις για την κατοίκηση: Κατοικία, αστική πολυκατοικία, συλλογική κατοικία*, ed. by Nelly Marda, Mattheos Papavasiliou and Sofia Tsiraki (Athens: NTUA School of Architecture, 2014), pp. 55–99.

Antonakakis, Dimitris, 'Τώρα που ο χρόνος αλλάζει', 29 January 2016. Online. triantafylloug. blogspot.co.uk/2016/01/2-95.html (accessed 26 February 2021).

Antonakakis, Dimitris and Suzana Antonakaki, 'Three Athenian Apartment Houses', *Design + Art in Greece*, 8 (1977), 58–73.

Antonakakis, Dimitris and Suzana Antonakaki, 'Apartment Houses in Athens: The Architect's Role', *Architecture in Greece*, 12 (1978), 151–3.

Antonakakis, Dimitris and Suzana Antonakaki, 'Η μεταπολεμική πολυκατοικία ως γενέτειρα του δημόσιου χώρου: Μια πρώτη προσέγγιση', in *Η Αθήνα στον 20ό αιώνα: Η Αθήνα όπως (δεν) φαίνεται, 1940–1985* (Athens: Ministry of Culture; Association of Greek Architects, 1985), pp. 129–35.

Antonakakis, Dimitris and Suzana Antonakaki, 'Introduction', in *Atelier 66: The Architecture of Dimitris and Suzana Antonakakis*, ed. by Kenneth Frampton (New York: Rizzoli, 1985), pp. 6–8.

Antonakakis, Dimitris, and Suzana Antonakaki, 'Ionian Bank Branch Office in Rhodes', *Architecture in Greece*, 22 (1988), 154–9.

Antonakakis, Dimitris and Suzana Antonakaki, 'Τάσεις στη σύγχρονη ελληνική αρχιτεκτονική', *Architecture in Greece*, 23 (1989), 83.

Antonakakis, Dimitris and Suzana Antonakaki, 'Το ιδανικό σπίτι', *Το Βήμα*, 25 June 2000, 11.

Antonakakis, Dimitris and Suzana Antonakaki, 'Acknowledgements', in *Atelier 66: The Architecture of Dimitris and Suzana Antonakakis*, ed. by Panayotis Tournikiotis (Athens: futura, 2007), pp. 10–19.

Antonakakis, Dimitris, Suzana Antonakaki and Costis Hadjimichalis, 'Unforeseen Changes in the Dwelling Space (1)', *Design + Art in Greece*, 6 (1975), 36–53.

Antonas, Aristide, 'The Error and the Rectification', in *Atelier 66: The Architecture of Dimitris and Suzana Antonakakis*, ed. by Panayotis Tournikiotis (Athens: futura, 2007), pp. 62–71.

Antoniades, Anthony C., 'Dimitris Pikionis: His Work Lies Underfoot on Athen's [sic] Hills', *Landscape Architecture* (March 1977), 150–3.

Antoniades, Anthony C., 'Μετα-Μοντέρνα Αρχιτεκτονική. Δύο περιπτώσεις: Renato Bofill και Piano-Rogers', *Άνθρωπος + Χώρος*, 6 (1977), 7–16.

Antoniades, Anthony C., *Σύγχρονη ελληνική αρχιτεκτονική* (Athens: Karangounis, 1979).

Archer, B.J., 'First Architecture Biennale in Venice', *Herald Tribune*, 4–5 October 1980.

Architects' Journal, 'High Jencks at the RIBM', 176.49 (8 December 1982), 22.

Architects' Journal, 'Rykwert Debunks the Great Debate', 177.25 (22 June 1983), 35.

Arendt, Hannah, 'We Refugees' (1943), repr. in *Hannah Arendt: The Jewish Writings*, ed. by Jerome Kohn and Ron H. Feldman (New York: Schocken, 2007), pp. 264–74.

Arendt, Hannah, *The Human Condition* (Chicago: University of Chicago Press, 1958).

Aristinos, Georgios, Anna Kafetsi, Andreas Mpelezinis and Sotiris Sorongas, eds, *Μοντέρνο-Μεταμοντέρνο* (Athens: Smili, 1988).

Arnold, Dana, 'Beyond a Boundary: Towards an Architectural History of the Non-East', in *Rethinking Architectural Historiography*, ed. by Dana Arnold, Elvan A. Orgut and Belgin T. Özkaya (New York: Routledge, 2006), pp. 229–45.

Avermaete, Tom, Véronique Patteeuw, Léa-Catherine Szacka and Hans Teerds, 'A Conversation with Kenneth Frampton: New York, 6 April 2018', *OASE*, 103 (2019), 142–54.

Avermaete, Tom, Véronique Patteeuw, Hans Teerds and Léa-Catherine Szacka, eds, 'Critical Regionalism Revisited'. Special issue, *OASE*, 103 (2019).

Avgeridis, Manos, Efi Gazi and Kostis Kornetis, eds, *Μεταπολίτευση: Η Ελλάδα στο μεταίχμιο δύο αιώνων* (Athens: Themelio, 2015).

Babalou-Noukaki, Boukie, *8+1 κείμενα για την αρχιτεκτονική και την πόλη*, ed. by Michalis Paparounis (Athens: Doma, 2020).

Baird, George, *The Space of Appearance* (Cambridge, MA: MIT Press, 1995).

Baldwin, Richard, *The Great Convergence: Information Technology and the New Globalization* (Cambridge, MA: Belknap, 2016).

Banham, Reyner, *Theory and Design in the First Machine Age* (London: Architectural Press, 1960).

Banham, Reyner, *The New Brutalism: Ethic or Aesthetic?* (London: Architectural Press, 1966).

Barbaro, Paolo, 'Biennale: Memoria e provocazione', *La Stampa*, 31 July 1980, 3.

Bell, Daniel, *The Coming of Post-Industrial Society: A Venture in Social Forecasting* (New York: Basic Books, 1973).

Benton, Charlotte, 'The Ideology of Modernism Explained', *Architects' Journal*, 172.40 (1 October 1980), 641.

Bergers, Gerard, ed., *Context and Modernity: A Post-Seminar Reading* (Delft: Stylos, 1991).

Berman, Marshall, 'The Dream of Perfect Roots and Embeddedness is Something Distinctly Modern', in *Context and Modernity: A Post-Seminar Reading*, ed. by Gerard Bergers (Delft: Stylos, 1991), pp. 36–40.

Berman, Marshall, 'How World Cities Get More World Space', in *Context and Modernity: A Post-Seminar Reading*, ed. by Gerard Bergers (Delft: Stylos, 1991), pp. 58–64.

Bernitsa, Petra, *Paolo Portoghesi: The Architecture of Listening* (Rome: Gangemi, 2012).

Bertens, Hans, *The Idea of the Postmodern: A History* (London: Routledge, 1995).

Bertens, Hans and Douwe W. Fokkema, eds, *International Postmodernism: Theory and Literary Practice* (Amsterdam: Benjamins, 1997).

Bhabha, Homi K., *The Location of Culture* (London: Routledge, 1994).

Biris, Kostas, *Αι Αθήναι: από του 19ου εις τον 20ον αιώνα* (Athens: Urbanism and History of Athens, 1966).

Biris, Tasos and Dimitris, 'Τάσεις στη σύγχρονη ελληνική αρχιτεκτονική', *Architecture in Greece*, 23 (1989), 126.

Blake, Peter, *Form Follows Fiasco: Why Modern Architecture Hasn't Worked* (Boston: Little, Brown and Co., 1977).

Blencowe, Chris and Judith Levine, *Moholy's Edit: The Avant-Garde at Sea, August 1933* (Zurich: Lars Müller, 2019).

Blistène, Bernard, '*Les Immatériaux*: A Conversation with Jean-François Lyotard', *Flash Art*, 121 (March 1985), 32–9.

Blouet, Abel, Amable Ravoisié, Achille Poirot, Félix Trézel and Frédéric de Gournay, *Expédition Scientifique de Morée ordonnée par le Gouvernement Français: Architecture, Sculptures, Inscriptions et Vues du Péloponèse, des Cyclades et de l'Attique, mesurées, dessinées, recueillies et publiées*, 3 vols (Paris: Firmin-Didot, 1831–8).

Blundell Jones, Peter, 'History in the Making: *Modern Movements in Architecture*; *Modern Architecture: A Critical History*', *Architects' Journal*, 183.13 (26 March 1986), 80.

Botz-Bornstein, Thorsten, 'Is Critical Regionalist Philosophy Possible?', *Comparative and Continental Philosophy*, 2.1 (2010), 11–25.

Botz-Bornstein, Thorsten, *Transcultural Architecture: The Limits and Opportunities of Critical Regionalism* (London: Routledge, 2015).

Branscome, Eva, *Hans Hollein and Postmodernism: Art and Architecture in Austria, 1958–1985* (London: Routledge, 2018).

Bredero, Maarten, 'The Necessity of Rules Remains', in *Context and Modernity: A Post-Seminar Reading*, ed. by Gerard Bergers (Delft: Stylos, 1991), pp. 112–13.

Brinckerhoff Jackson, John, *Discovering the Vernacular Landscape* (New Haven, CT: Yale University Press, 1984).

Brolin, Brent C., *The Failure of Modern Architecture* (London: Studio Vista, 1976).

Brouwer, Petra and Kristina Jõekalda, 'Introduction: Architectural Identities of European Peripheries', *Journal of Architecture*, 25.8 (2020), 963–77.

Buchanan, Peter, 'With Due Respect: Regionalism', *Architectural Review*, 173.1035 (May 1983), 14–17.

Buchanan, Peter, 'Only Connect', *Architectural Review*, 176.1052 (October 1984), 22–5.

Burckhardt, Lucius, 'Criteria for a New Design' (1977), repr. in *Design is Invisible: Planning, Education, and Society*, ed. by Silvan Blumenthal and Martin Schmitz (Basel: Birkhäuser, 2017), pp. 36–9.

Burckhardt, Lucius, 'Dirt' (1980), repr. in *Lucius Burckhardt Writings, Rethinking Man-made Environments: Politics, Landscape and Design*, ed. by Jesko Fezer and Martin Schmitz (Vienna: Springer, 2012), pp. 166–9.

Burckhardt, Lucius, 'Einführung', in *Für eine andere Architektur: Bauen mit der Natur und in der Region*, ed. by Michael Andritzky, Lucius Burckhardt and Ot Hoffmann (Frankfurt am Main: Fischer, 1981), pp. 119–20.

Burckhardt, Lucius, '"Künstliche Dörfer"', in *Für eine andere Architektur: Bauen mit der Natur und in der Region*, ed. by Michael Andritzky, Lucius Burckhardt and Ot Hoffmann (Frankfurt am Main: Fischer, 1981), pp. 161–5.

Burckhardt, Lucius, 'Selberbauen, ökologisch bauen, regional bauen', in *Für eine andere Architektur: Bauen mit der Natur und in der Region*, ed. by Michael Andritzky, Lucius Burckhardt and Ot Hoffmann (Frankfurt am Main: Fischer, 1981), pp. 9–13.

Burckhardt, Lucius, 'Recycled Regionalism' (1984), repr. in *Design is Invisible: Planning, Education, and Society*, ed. by Silvan Blumenthal and Martin Schmitz (Basel: Birkhäuser, 2017), pp. 176–82.

Burckhardt, Lucius, 'Nature is Invisible' (1989), repr. in *Why is Landscape Beautiful? The Science of Strollology*, ed. by Markus Ritter and Martin Schmitz (Basel: Birkhäuser, 2015), pp. 45–50.

Burckhardt, Lucius, 'On Ecological Architecture: A Memo', in Alexander Tzonis and Liane Lefaivre, *Architecture in Europe since 1968: Memory and Invention* (London: Thames & Hudson, 1992), pp. 42–3.

Canizaro, Vincent B., ed., *Architectural Regionalism: Collected Writings on Place, Identity, Modernity, and Tradition* (New York: Princeton Architectural Press, 2007).

Casanova, Pascale, *The World Republic of Letters*, trans. by Malcolm DeBevoise (Cambridge, MA: Harvard University Press, 2004).

Cassidy, Timothy, 'Becoming Regional over Time: Toward a Reflexive Regionalism', in *Architectural Regionalism: Collected Writings on Place, Identity, Modernity, and Tradition*, ed. by Vincent B. Canizaro (New York: Princeton Architectural Press, 2007), pp. 411–19.

Castoriadis, Cornelius, *La société bureaucratique* (Paris: Union général d'éditions, 1973).

Cavarra Britton, Karla and Robert McCarter, eds, *Modern Architecture and the Lifeworld: Essays in Honor of Kenneth Frampton* (London: Thames & Hudson, 2020).

Chakrabarty, Dipesh, *Provincializing Europe: Postcolonial Thought and Historical Difference* (Princeton: Princeton University Press, 2000).

Chang, Jiat-Hwee and Imran bin Tajudeen, 'Historiographical Questions in Southeast Asia's Modern Architecture', in *Southeast Asia's Modern Architecture: Questions of Translation, Epistemology and Power*, ed. by Jiat-Hwee Chang and Imran bin Tajudeen (Singapore: NUS Press, 2019), pp. 1–21.

Chanis, Vasileios I., 'Mies Comes to Greece: A. James Speyer at NTUA', *Prometheus*, 2 (2019), 52–5.

Cheng, Irene, Charles L. Davis II and Mabel O. Wilson, eds, *Race and Modern Architecture: A Critical History from the Enlightenment to the Present* (Pittsburgh: University of Pittsburgh Press, 2020).

Chermayeff, Serge and Alexander Tzonis, *Shape of Community: Realization of Human Potential* (Hammondsworth: Penguin, 1971).

Chessa, Pasquale, 'Colloquio con Paolo Portoghesi: A Venezia in via del postmodernismo', *L'Europeo*, 22 July 1980, 73–6.

Choisy, Auguste, *Histoire de l'Architecture*, 2 vols (Paris: Gauthier-Villars, 1899).

Christofellis, Alexandros, 'Περιγραφή στίγματος', *Design + Art in Greece*, 16 (1985), 53–4.

Cicero, *De Republica*, Loeb Classical Library (Cambridge, MA: Harvard University Press, 1928).

Clogg, Richard, ed., *Greece in the 1980s* (London: Macmillan, 1983).

Clogg, Richard, *A Concise History of Modern Greece* (Cambridge: Cambridge University Press, 1992).

Cohen, Gerald, A., *Why Not Socialism?* (Princeton: Princeton University Press, 2009).

Cohen, Jean-Louis, 'The Mediterranean Brutalism of Dimitris and Suzana Antonakakis', in *Atelier 66: The Architecture of Dimitris and Suzana Antonakakis*, ed. by Panayotis Tournikiotis (Athens: futura, 2007), pp. 32–45.

Coleman, Janet, *A History of Political Thought*, 2 vols (Malden, MA: Blackwell, 2000).

Collins, George R. and Adolf K. Placzek, 'MAS 1964: The Decade 1929–1939: Introduction', *Journal of the Society of Architectural Historians*, 24.1 (March 1965), 3–4.

Colonas, Vasilis, *Ιταλική αρχιτεκτονική στα Δωδεκάνησα* (Athens: Olkos, 2002).

Colquhoun, Alan, 'Modern Architecture and the Liberal Conscience', *Architectural Design*, 52.7/8 (1982), 47–9.

Colquhoun, Alan, 'Regionalism and Technology' (1983), repr. in Alan Colquhoun, *Modernity and the Classical Tradition: Architectural Essays 1980–1987* (Cambridge, MA: MIT Press, 1989), pp. 207–11.

Colquhoun, Alan, 'The Concept of Regionalism', *Casabella*, 592 (1992), 52–5.

Colquhoun, Alan, 'Critique of Regionalism', *Casabella*, 630–1 (1992), 50–5.

Comer, Krista, 'Exceptionalism, Other Wests, Critical Regionalism', *American Literary History*, 23.1 (2011), 159–73.

Condaratos, Savas, 'Ο αρχιτεκτονικός μεταμοντερνισμός ως απελευθέρωση και ως παραίτηση', in *Μοντέρνο-Μεταμοντέρνο*, ed. by Georgios Aristinos, Anna Kafetsi, Andreas Mpelezinis and Sotiris Sorongas (Athens: Smili, 1988), pp. 77–85.

Condaratos, Savas, 'Το γράμμα του Σάββα Κονταράτου', *Architecture in Greece*, 23 (1989), 82–3.

Condaratos, Savas, 'Dimitris Pikionis 1887–1986: A Sentimental Topography: AA Exhibition Gallery, Members' Room and Bar, 6 June–4 July 1989', *AA Files*, 20 (Autumn 1990), 55–62.

Condaratos, Savas, 'Τάσεις στη σύγχρονη ελληνική αρχιτεκτονική: Έξι σχόλια', *Architecture in Greece*, 24 (1990), 19–20.

Condaratos, Savas, 'Η ελληνική εκδοχή του μοντέρνου', *Architecture in Greece*, 30 (1996), 135–6.

Conron, John P., *Socorro: A Historic Survey* (Albuquerque: University of New Mexico Press, 1980).

Constantopoulos, Elias, 'Greek Architecture in the Eighties', *Architecture in Greece*, 23 (1989), 63–9.

Constantopoulos, Elias, 'Το τέλος των στυλ ή η αιώνια επιστροφή τους;', *Architecture in Greece*, 24 (1990), 21–2.

Constantopoulos, Elias, 'On the Architecture of Dimitris and Suzana Antonakakis', *Design + Art in Greece*, 25 (1994), 18–25.

Cooke, Catherine, *Russian Avant-Garde: Theories of Art, Architecture and the City* (London: Academy, 1995).

Corbusier, Le, *Vers une Architecture*, 3rd edn (Paris: Crés, 1928).

Corbusier, Le, *La Ville Radieuse: Eléments d'une doctrine d'urbanisme pour l'équipement de la civilisation machiniste* (Bologne [Seine]: Éditions de L'Architecture d'Aujourd'hui, 1933).

Corbusier, Le, *The Modulor: A Harmonious Measure to the Human Scale Universally Applicable to Architecture and Mechanics*, trans. by Peter de Francia and Anna Bostock (London: Faber & Faber, 1954).

Costa, L., 'Ma quanto è vecchia la "Strada Novissima"', *L'architetto* (1981), 10–11.

Crimp, Douglas, 'On the Museum's Ruins', *October*, 13 (1980), 41–57.

Crinson, Mark, 'Singapore's Moment: Critical Regionalism, its Colonial Roots and Profound Aftermath', *Journal of Architecture*, 13.5 (2008), 585–605.

Crinson, Mark, *Rebuilding Babel: Modern Architecture and Internationalism* (London: I.B.Tauris, 2017).

Crinson, Mark and Claire Zimmerman, eds, *Neo-avant-garde and Postmodern: Postwar Architecture in Britain and Beyond* (New Haven, CT: Yale University Press, 2010).

Crompton, Dennis, ed., *Mega XI, Dimitris Pikionis, Architect 1887–1968: A Sentimental Topography* (London: Architectural Association, 1989).

Cullen, Gordon, *Townscape* (London: Architectural Press, 1961).

Curtis, William J.R., *Modern Architecture since 1900* (Oxford: Phaidon, 1982).

Curtis, William J.R., *Modern Architecture since 1900*, 3rd edn (London: Phaidon, 1996).

Damrosch, David, *What is World Literature?* (Princeton: Princeton University Press, 2003).

D'Ancona, Hedy, 'A Provocative Note at the Beginning', in *Context and Modernity: A Post-Seminar Reading*, ed. by Gerard Bergers (Delft: Stylos, 1991), pp. 10–14.

Darley, Gillian and Peter Davey, 'Sense and Sensibility', *Architectural Review*, 174.1039 (September 1983), 22–5.

Davey, Peter, 'Post Modern in Venice', *Architectural Review*, 168.1003 (1980), 132–4.

Davey, Peter, 'Urban Authenticity', *Architectural Review*, 187.1115 (January 1990), 22–3.

Davey, Peter, 'Regional Meaning', *Architectural Review*, 187.1125 (November 1990), 34–5.

Davey, Peter, 'Regionalism: Time to Review and Renew', *Architectural Review*, 210.1257 (November 2001), 34–5.

David, T., '"Pratt in Greece": Summer 1972 in collaboration with Workshop of Environmental Design, Athens, Greece (WEDAG)', *Architecture in Greece*, 7 (1973), 236–43.

Davidovici, Irina, 'Constructing "the School of the Ticino": The Historiography of a New Swiss Architecture, 1975–1990', *Journal of Architecture*, 25.8 (2020), 1115–40.

Davies, Colin, *A New History of Modern Architecture* (London: Laurence King, 2017).

De Bonis, Antonio, 'Paolo Portoghesi and Aldo Rossi', *Architectural Design*, 52.1/2 (1982), 13–17.

Denison, Edward and Guang Yu Ren, *Luke Him Sau, Architect: China's Missing Modern* (Chichester: Wiley, 2014).

Derrida, Jacques, *Of Grammatology*, trans. by Gayatri Chakravorty Spivak (Baltimore, MD: Johns Hopkins University Press, 1976).

Derrida, Jacques, 'Globalization, Peace and Cosmopolitics', in *The Future of Values: 21st-Century Talks*, ed. by Jérôme Bindé, trans. by John Corbett (United Nations Educational, Scientific and Cultural Organization, 2004), pp. 110–22.

Deutinger, Theo, 'Walled World', *Vrij Nederland*, 47 (2006). Online. the-department.eu/projects/show/walled-world (accessed 20 July 2021).

Dolka, Maria, 'The Grid in Pefkakia Elementary School by Pikionis and the Grid in the Rethimno Faculty of Humanities: Are They so Related as They Appear?'. Unpublished IB thesis, I.M. Panagiotopoulos School, 2002.

Dolkas, Lampis, 'Η Ιθάκη σ' έδωσε τ' ωραίο ταξίδι', in Nikos Diakoulakis, Spyros Kavounidis, Nikos Koutretsis, Giannis Maroukis, Giannis Meimaroglou, Lampis Dolkas, Vasilis Stefanis and Dimitris Psychogios, *Διαδρομές* (Athens: Epikentro, 2021), pp. 153–86.

Donat, John, ed., *World Architecture* (London: Studio Vista, 1964).

Donkervoet, Daralice, 'An Interview with Robert Stern', *Crit.: The Architectural Student Journal*, 11 (Spring 1981), 19–21.

Dostoglu, Sibel, 'The Current State of Architecture: A Context for Architectural Culture, Hydra, 1983', *AA Files*, 5 (1984), 105–6.

Doumanis, Orestis, 'Εισαγωγή στην ελληνική μεταπολεμική αρχιτεκτονική', *Αρχιτεκτονική*, 48 (1964), 1–11.

Doxiadis, Constantinos A., 'Die Raumgestaltung im griechischen Städtebau'. Doctoral thesis, Berlin Charlottenburg Technical University, 1936.

Doxiadis, Constantinos A., *Architectural Space in Ancient Greece*, trans. by Jaqueline Tyrwhitt (Cambridge, MA: MIT Press, 1972).

Dunster, David, 'Maid in USA', *Architectural Design*, 52.7/8 (1982), 50–1.

Economaki-Brunner, Yanna, 'Keys to a Manipulated Landscape', *Quaderns*, 190 (July–September 1991), 84–98.

Edelmann, F., 'Rue de l'avenir: Les Biennales d'architecture à Venise et à Paris', *Le Monde*, 9 October 1980, 17.

Eggener, Keith L., 'Placing Resistance: A Critique of Critical Regionalism', *Journal of Architectural Education*, 55.4 (2002), 228–37.

Eisenman, Peter, 'Post-Functionalism', *Oppositions*, 6 (1976), i–iv.

Eisenman, Peter and Conference of Architects for the Study of the Environment, *Five Architects: Eisenman, Graves, Gwathmey, Hejduk, Meier* (New York: Wittenborn, 1972).

Eisenstadt, Shmuel N., ed., *Multiple Modernities* (New Brunswick, NJ: Transaction, 2002).

Eisenstein, Sergei, Yves-Allen Bois and Michael Glenny, 'Montage and Architecture' (1937), repr. in *Assemblage*, 10 (December 1989), 110–31.

Ellis, Charlotte, 'Great Debate off Course', *Architects' Journal*, 177.6 (9 February 1983), 27–8.

Emanuel, Muriel, ed., *Contemporary Architects* (Basingstoke: Macmillan, 1980).

Emmanouil, Dimitris, *Η κοινωνική πολιτική κατοικίας στην Ελλάδα: Οι διαστάσεις μιας απουσίας* (Athens: National Centre for Social Research, 2006).

Erten, Erdem, 'Shaping "The Second Half Century": *The Architectural Review* 1947–1971'. Unpublished doctoral thesis, MIT, 2004.

Fabbri, Marcello, ed., 'L'opera di Dimitris Pikionis'. Special issue, *Controspazio*, 5 (September–October 1991).

Farrell, Terry and Adam Nathaniel Furman, *Revisiting Postmodernism* (London: RIBA, 2017).

Farrelly, E.M., 'The New Spirit', *Architectural Review*, 180.1074 (August 1986), 6–12.

Fatouros, Dimitris, 'Greek Art and Architecture 1945–1967: A Brief Survey', *Balkan Studies*, 8.2 (1967), 421–35.

Fatouros, Dimitris, 'Antonakakis' Architecture: The Smooth Logic of Public Places', *9H*, 3 (1982), 43.

Fatouros, Dimitris, 'The Architecture of Dimitris and Suzana Antonakakis: Two Complementary Descriptions', in *Atelier 66: The Architecture of Dimitris and Suzana Antonakakis*, ed. by Panayotis Tournikiotis (Athens: futura, 2007), pp. 46–53.

Faubion, James D., *Modern Greek Lessons: A Primer in Historical Constructivism* (Princeton: Princeton University Press, 1993).

Ferlenga, Alberto, ed., *Pikionis, 1887–1968* (Florence: Electa, 1999).

Ferlenga, Alberto, *Le Strade di Pikionis* (Syracuse: Lettera Ventidue, 2014).

Fessas-Emmanouil, Helen, 'Prestige Architecture in Post-War Greece: 1945–1975', *Design + Art in Greece*, 15 (1984), 34–73.

Fessas-Emmanouil, Helen, *Essays on Neohellenic Architecture: Theory–History–Criticism* (Athens: National University, 2001).

Fezer, Jesko and Martin Schmitz, 'The Work of Lucius Burckhardt', in *Lucius Burckhardt Writings, Rethinking Man-made Environments: Politics, Landscape and Design*, ed. by Jesko Fezer and Martin Schmitz (Vienna: Springer, 2012), pp. 7–26.

Figueira, Jorge, *A Periferia Perfeita: Pós-modernidade na arquitectura portuguesa. Anos 1960–1980* (Lisbon: Caleidoscópio, 2014).

Finley, Moses I., *Democracy Ancient and Modern* (London: Chatto & Windus, 1973).

Fischer, Ole W., 'Architecture, Capitalism and Criticality', in *The SAGE Handbook of Architectural Theory*, ed. by C. Greig Crysler, Stephen Cairns and Hilde Heynen (Los Angeles: SAGE, 2012), pp. 56–69.

Foster, Hal, ed., *The Anti-Aesthetic: Essays on Postmodern Culture* (Washington, DC: Bay Press, 1983).

Frampton, Kenneth, 'The Work of Epaminoda', *Architectural Design*, 35.1 (January 1965), 3.

Frampton, Kenneth, 'Labour, Work and Architecture', in *Meaning in Architecture*, ed. by Charles Jencks and George Baird (London: Barrie & Jenkins, 1969), pp. 150–68.

Frampton, Kenneth, 'Maison de Verre', *Perspecta*, 12 (1969), 77–109, 111–28.

Frampton, Kenneth, 'On Reading Heidegger', *Oppositions*, 4 (1974), 1–4.

Frampton, Kenneth, 'Team 10, Plus 20: The Vicissitudes of Ideology', *L'Architecture d'Aujourd'hui*, 177 (1975), 62–5.

Frampton, Kenneth, 'Constructivism: The Pursuit of an Elusive Sensibility', *Oppositions*, 6 (1976), 25–44.

Frampton, Kenneth, 'Mario Botta and the School of the Ticino', *Oppositions*, 14 (Fall 1978), 1–25.

Frampton, Kenneth, 'The Will to Build', in Emilio Batisti and Kenneth Frampton with Italo Rota, *Mario Botta: Architetture e progetti negli anni '70* (Milan: Electa, 1979), pp. 7–13.

Frampton, Kenneth, *Modern Architecture: A Critical History* (London: Thames & Hudson, 1980).

Frampton, Kenneth, 'Du Néo-Productivisme au Post-Modernisme', *L'Architecture d'Aujourd'hui*, 213 (1981), 2–7.

Frampton, Kenneth, 'Intimations of Tactility: Excerpts from a Fragmentary Polemic', *Artforum* (March 1981), 52–8.

Frampton, Kenneth, 'The Need for Roots: Venice 1980', *GA Forum*, 3 (1981), 13–21.

Frampton, Kenneth, 'O.M. Ungers and the Architecture of Coincidence', in *O.M. Ungers: Works in Progress, 1976–1980, Catalogue 6*, ed. by Kenneth Frampton and Silvia Kolbowski (New York: Institute of Architecture and Urban Studies, 1981), pp. 1–5.

Frampton, Kenneth, 'Avant-Garde and Continuity', *Architectural Design*, 52.7/8 (1982), 20–7.

Frampton, Kenneth, 'The Isms of Contemporary Architecture', *Architectural Design*, 52.7/8 (1982), 60–83.

Frampton, Kenneth, 'Modernism's Diffusion: Japan Diary Summer '81, Part 1', *Skyline* (April 1982), 26–9; 'Part 2', *Skyline* (May 1982), 26–9; 'Part 3', *Skyline* (June 1982), 22–5.

Frampton, Kenneth, 'The Resistance of Architecture: An Anthological Postscript', *Architectural Design*, 52.7/8 (1982), 84–5.

Frampton, Kenneth, 'The Status of Man and his Objects: A Reading of *The Human Condition*', *Architectural Design*, 52.7/8 (1982), 6–19.

Frampton, Kenneth, 'The Architecture of Sverre Fehn', in Per Olaf Fjeld, *Sverre Fehn: The Thought of Construction* (New York: Rizzoli, 1983), pp. 9–17.

Frampton, Kenneth, 'Modern Architecture and Critical Regionalism', *RIBA Transactions*, 3.2 (1983), 15–25.

Frampton, Kenneth, 'Prospects for a Critical Regionalism', *Perspecta*, 20 (1983), 147–62.

Frampton, Kenneth, 'Towards a Critical Regionalism: Six Points for an Architecture of Resistance', in *The Anti-Aesthetic: Essays on Postmodern Culture*, ed. by Hal Foster (Seattle: Bay Press, 1983), pp. 16–30.

Frampton, Kenneth, 'Entre héroisme et métier', in *Henri Ciriani*, ed. by François Chaslin (Paris: Electa, 1984), pp. 13–14.

Frampton, Kenneth, 'L'opera di Luigi Snozzi, 1957–1984', in *Luigi Snozzi: Progetti e architetture 1957–1984*, ed. by Kenneth Frampton (Milan: Electa, 1984), pp. 9–29.

Frampton, Kenneth, ed., *Tadao Ando: Buildings, Projects, Writings* (New York: Rizzoli, 1984).

Frampton, Kenneth, ed., *Atelier 66: The Architecture of Dimitris and Suzana Antonakakis* (New York: Rizzoli, 1985).

Frampton, Kenneth, 'Entre rationalisme et régionalisme: l'oeuvre de Martorell, Bohigas et Mackay', in *Martorell, Bohigas, Mackay: Trente ans d'architecture, 1954–1984*, ed. by Kenneth Frampton, trans. by Raymond Coudert (Paris: Electa, 1985), pp. 7–25.

Frampton, Kenneth, *Modern Architecture: A Critical History*, 2nd edn (London: Thames & Hudson, 1985).

Frampton, Kenneth, 'Het structurele regionalism van Herman Hertzberger', *Archis*, 12 (December 1986), 8–13.

Frampton, Kenneth, 'Μοντέρνο, πολύ μοντέρνο: Μια συνέντευξη του Kenneth Frampton στον Γιώργο Σημαιοφορίδη', *Architecture in Greece*, 20 (1986), 118–21.

Frampton, Kenneth, 'Poesis and Transformation: The Architecture of Alvaro Siza', in *Alvaro Siza: Poetic Profession*, ed. by Kenneth Frampton (Milan: Electa, 1986), pp. 10–23.

Frampton, Kenneth, 'Twilight Gloom to Self-Enclosed Modernity: Five Japanese Architects', in *Tokyo, Form and Spirit*, ed. by James R. Brandon and Mildred S. Friedman (Minneapolis, MN: Walker Arts Center, 1986), pp. 221–41.

Frampton, Kenneth, 'Fujii in Context: An Introduction', in *The Architecture of Hiromi Fujii*, ed. by Kenneth Frampton (New York: Rizzoli, 1987), pp. 8–13.

Frampton, Kenneth, 'Πρόλογος του Kenneth Frampton για την ελληνική έκδοση', in Kenneth Frampton, *Μοντέρνα αρχιτεκτονική: Ιστορία και κριτική*, trans. by Theodoros Androulakis and María Pangalou (Athens: Themelio, 1987), pp. 14–16.

Frampton, Kenneth, 'Ten Points on an Architecture of Regionalism: A Provisional Polemic', *Center*, 3 (1987), 20–7.

Frampton, Kenneth, 'The Usonian Legacy', *Architectural Review*, 182.1090 (December 1987), 26–31.

Frampton, Kenneth, 'For Dimitris Pikionis', in *Mega XI, Dimitris Pikionis, Architect 1887–1968: A Sentimental Topography*, ed. by Dennis Crompton (London: Architectural Association, 1989), pp. 6–9.

Frampton, Kenneth, 'Some Reflections on Postmodernism and Architecture', in *Postmodernism: ICA Documents*, ed. by Lisa Appignanesi (London: Free Association, 1989), pp. 75–87.

Frampton, Kenneth, 'Developments in Contemporary Architecture 1945–1985', in *The Great Ideas Today 1990* (Chicago: Encyclopaedia Britannica, 1990), pp. 2–67.

Frampton, Kenneth, 'Critical Regionalism Revisited', in *Critical Regionalism: The Pomona Meeting Proceedings*, ed. by Spyros Amourgis (Pomona: California State Polytechnic University, 1991), pp. 34–9.

Frampton, Kenneth, 'If It is Reduced to an Aesthetic Package Architecture Looses [sic] the Game from the Modernising Force of the Megatrend', in *Context and Modernity: A Post-Seminar Reading*, ed. by Gerard Bergers (Delft: Stylos, 1991), pp. 28–34.

Frampton, Kenneth, 'Life Begins Tomorrow', in *Europa nach der Flut: Kunst 1945–1965*, ed. by Sílvia Sauquet and Johann Lehner (Vienna: Künstlerhaus Wien; La Caixa, 1995), pp. 539–53.

Frampton, Kenneth, *Studies in Tectonic Culture: The Poetics of Construction in Nineteenth and Twentieth Century Architecture* (Cambridge, MA: MIT Press, 1995).

Frampton, Kenneth, 'The Predicament of the Place-Form: Notes from New York', in *Contemporary Architecture and City Form: The South Asian Paradigm*, ed. by Farooq Ameen (Mumbai: Marg, 1997), pp. 101–8.

Frampton, Kenneth, 'A Note on Greek Architecture: 1938–1997', in *Landscapes of Modernisation: Greek Architecture 1960s and 1990s*, ed. by Yannis Aesopos and Yorgos Simeoforidis (Athens: Metapolis, 1999), pp. 12–14.

Frampton, Kenneth, 'Seven Points for the Millennium: An Untimely Manifesto', *Architectural Review*, 206.1233 (1999), 76–80.

Frampton, Kenneth, *Labour, Work and Architecture: Collected Essays on Architecture and Design* (London: Phaidon, 2002).

Frampton, Kenneth, *Panos Koulermos: Opera completa* (Mendrisio: Archivio del Moderno, 2004).

Frampton, Kenneth, *Modern Architecture: A Critical History*, 4th edn (London: Thames & Hudson, 2007).

Frampton, Kenneth, 'Homage à Monica Pidgeon: An AD Memoir', *AA Files*, 60 (2010), 22–5.

Frampton, Kenneth, 'L'opera di Aris Konstantinidis', in Paola Cofano and Dimitris Konstantinidis, *Aris Konstantinidis 1913–1993* (Milan: Electa, 2010), pp. 8–15.

Frampton, Kenneth, ed., *World Architecture: A Critical Mosaic 1900–2000*, 10 vols (New York: Springer, 1999–2002).

Frampton, Kenneth, 'Towards an Agonistic Architecture', *Domus*, 972 (2013), 1–9.

Frampton, Kenneth, *A Genealogy of Modern Architecture: A Comparative Critical Analysis of Built Form* (Zurich: Lars Müller, 2015).

Frampton, Kenneth, '2018 Plenary Talk by Kenneth Frampton', Society of Architectural Historians, 21 May 2018. Online. www.sah.org/about-sah/news/sah-news/news-detail/2018/05/21/2018-plenary-talk-by-kenneth-frampton (accessed 6 July 2021).

Frampton, Kenneth, 'Modern and Site Specific: The Architecture of Gino Valle 1945–2003', *Plan Journal*, 4.1 (2019), 223–6.

Frampton, Kenneth, *Modern Architecture: A Critical History*, 5th edn (London: Thames & Hudson, 2020).

Frank, Andre Gunder, *Dependent Accumulation and Underdevelopment* (London: Macmillan, 1978).

Franklin, Geraint and Elain Harwood, *Post-Modern Buildings in Britain* (London: Batsford, 2017).

Fraser, Murray, 'The Scale of Globalisation', in *Architecture and Globalisation in the Persian Gulf Region*, ed. by Murray Fraser and Nasser Golzari (London: Ashgate, 2013), pp. 383–404.

Fraser, Murray, Alicja Gzowska and Nataša Koselj, 'Eastern Europe, 1900–1970', in *Sir Banister Fletcher's Global History of Architecture*. ed. by Murray Fraser, 2 vols (London: Bloomsbury, 2019), II, pp. 944–81.

French, Hillary, *Key Urban Housing of the Twentieth Century: Plans, Sections and Elevations* (London: Laurence King, 2008).

Friedman, Thomas L., *The World is Flat: A Brief History of the Globalized World in the Twenty-First Century* (London: Allen Lane, 2005).

Fukuyama, Francis, 'The End of History?', *The National Interest*, 16 (1989), 3–18.

Fukuyama, Francis, *The End of History and the Last Man* (London: Hamilton, 1992).

Gandee, Charles K., 'Behind the Facades: A Conversation with Robert A.M. Stern', *Architectural Record*, 169.4 (1981), 108–15.

Genet, Jean Marie and Bernard Deroy, eds, *L'Après Modernisme: La Présence de l'Histoire* (Paris: L'Equerre, 1981).

Ghirardo, Diane, 'The Deceit of Postmodern Architecture', in *After the Future: Postmodern Times and Places*, ed. by Gary Shapiro (Albany: State University of New York Press, 1990), pp. 231–52.

Giacumacatos, Andreas, 'New Rationalism and Critical Empiricism', *Architecture in Greece*, 23 (1989), 53–9.

Giacumacatos, Andreas, Ή μέθοδος και το πρόβλημα', *Architecture in Greece*, 24 (1990), 18–19.

Giacumacatos, Andreas, 'The Rhodes Branch of the Ionian Bank', *l'Arca*, 54 (1991), 70–7.

Giacumacatos, Andreas, Ιστορία της ελληνικής αρχιτεκτονικής: 20ος αιώνας, 2nd edn (Athens: Nefeli, 2004).

Giamarelos, Stylianos, 'The Art of Building Reception: Aris Konstantinidis behind the Global Published Life of his Weekend House in Anavyssos (1962–2014)', *Architectural Histories*, 2.1 (2014), art. 22. doi.org/10.5334/ah.bx.

Giamarelos, Stylianos, 'Ὁ Ἄρης Κωνσταντινίδης εκτός', in Ἄρης Κωνσταντινίδης, ed. by Dina Vaiou (Athens: Greek Parliament Foundation, 2019), pp. 101–36.

Giddens, Anthony, *The Consequences of Modernity* (Cambridge: Polity, 1991).

Giddens, Anthony, *Beyond Left and Right: The Future of Radical Politics* (Cambridge: Polity, 1994).

Giddens, Anthony, *The Third Way: The Renewal of Social Democracy* (Cambridge: Polity, 1998).

Giedion, Sigfried, 'Pallas Athéné ou le visage de la Grèce', *Cahiers d'Art*, 1–4 (1934), 77–80.

Giedion, Sigfried, *Space, Time and Architecture: The Growth of a New Tradition* (Cambridge, MA: Harvard University Press, 1941).

Giedion, Sigfried, 'The New Regionalism' (1954), repr. in Sigfried Giedion, *Architecture, You and Me: The Diary of a Development* (Cambridge, MA: Harvard University Press, 1958), pp. 138–51.

Glendinning, Miles, *Mass Housing: Modern Architecture and State Power – A Global History* (London: Bloomsbury, 2021).

Glotz, Gustave, *La Cité grecque* (Paris: Renaissance du Livre, 1928).

Goethe, Johann Wolfgang von, 'Frankfurter Ausgabe', in *Sämtliche Werke: Briefe, Tagebücher und Gespräche*, ed. by Friedmar Apel and Hendrik Birus, 12 vols (Frankfurt am Main: Deutscher Klassiker, 1986–99), vol. 12 (1999), pp. 224–5.

Gold, John R., 'The Power of Narrative: The Early Writings of Charles Jencks and the Historiography of Architectural Modernism', in *Twentieth-Century Architecture and its Histories*, ed. by Louise Campbell (Otley: Society of Architectural Historians of Great Britain, 2000), pp. 207–21.

Goode, Patrick, ed., *The Oxford Companion to Architecture* (Oxford: Oxford University Press, 2009).

Gottmann, Jean, *Megalopolis: The Urbanized Northeastern Seaboard of the United States* (New York: Twentieth Century Fund, 1961).

Greenberg, Clement, 'Che cos'è e che cosa non è "Postmoderno": Una sigla retrograda per i filisei degli anni '80?', *Bolaffi Arte*, 104 (1981), 54–61.

Gregotti, Vittorio, *Il territorio dell'architettura* (Milan: Feltrinelli, 1966).

Gregotti, Vittorio, 'I vecchietti delle colonne', *La Repubblica*, 30 July 1980, 15.

Gregotti, Vittorio, 'Open Letter to Léon Krier', *Architectural Design*, 52.1/2 (1982), 24.

Gura, Judith, *Postmodern Design Complete: Design, Furniture, Graphics, Architecture, Interiors* (New York: Thames & Hudson, 2017).

Habermas, Jürgen, 'Modernity versus Postmodernity', *New German Critique*, 22 (1981), 3–14.

Haddad, Elie, 'Charles Jencks and the Historiography of Post-Modernism', *Journal of Architecture*, 14.4 (2009), 493–510.

Hadjikyriakos-Ghika, Nikos, *Ανίχνευση της ελληνικότητος* (Athens: Efthini, 1994).

Hadjikyriakos-Ghika, Nikos, 'Ἐναρκτήριο μάθημα στους σπουδαστές του Ε.Μ.Π.' (1942), repr. in *Νίκος Χατζηκυριάκος-Γκίκας: Δάσκαλος ζωγραφικής*, ed. by Sotiris Sorongas (Athens: National Technical University of Athens Press, 1997) pp. 16–31.

Hadjimichali, Angeliki, *Η ελληνική λαϊκή φορεσιά*, 2 vols (Athens: Melissa, 1983).

Hadjimichali, Angeliki, *Σαρακατσάνοι*, 2 vols (Athens: Angeliki Hadjimichali Foundation, 2010).

Hall, Stuart, *The Hard Road to Renewal: Thatcherism and the Crisis of the Left* (London: Verso, 1988).

Hamdi, Nabeel and Edward Robbins, '3rd World', *Architectural Review*, 178.1062 (August 1985), 12.

Hamilakis, Yannis, *The Nation and its Ruins: Antiquity, Archaeology, and National Imagination in Greece* (Oxford: Oxford University Press, 2007).

Haney, David H., *When Modern Was Green: Life and Work of Landscape Architect Leberecht Migge* (London: Routledge, 2010).

Hartoonian, Gevork, 'An Interview with Kenneth Frampton', *Architectural Theory Review*, 7.1 (2002), 59–64.

Hartoonian, Gevork, 'Critical Regionalism: Whatever Happened to Autonomy', *Fusion*, 4 (2014). Online. www.fusion-journal.com/issue/004-fusion-the-town-and-the-city/critical-regionalism-whatever-happened-to-autonomy (accessed 20 July 2021).

Harvey, David, *The Condition of Postmodernity: An Enquiry into the Origins of Cultural Change* (Oxford: Blackwell, 1989).

Hatherley, Owen, *Militant Modernism* (Winchester: Zero Books, 2009).

Hays, K. Michael, *Architecture Theory since 1968* (Cambridge, MA: MIT Press, 1998).

Hays, K. Michael, *Architecture's Desire: Reading the Late Avant-Garde* (Cambridge, MA: MIT Press, 2009).

Heidegger, Martin, 'Building Dwelling Thinking' (1951), repr. in Martin Heidegger, *Poetry, Language, Thought*, trans. by Albert Hofstadter (New York: Harper Colophon, 1971), pp. 141–60.

Herder, Johann Gottfried, *Ideen zur Philosophie der Geschichte der Menschheit*, 4 vols (Riga and Leipzig, 1784–91).

Herrle, Peter and Erik Wegerhoff, eds, *Architecture and Identity* (Berlin: LIT, 2008).

Hersey, George, *The Lost Meaning of Classical Architecture: Speculations on Ornament from Vitruvius to Venturi* (Cambridge, MA: MIT Press, 1988).

Herzfeld, Michael, 'The Absent Presence: Discourses of Crypto-Colonialism', *South Atlantic Quarterly*, 101.4 (2002), 899–926.

Herzfeld, Michael, *Cultural Intimacy: Social Poetics in the Nation-State*, 2nd edn (New York: Routledge, 2005).

Hitchcock, Henry-Russell, *Architecture: Nineteenth and Twentieth Centuries*, 3rd edn (Harmondsworth: Penguin, 1968).

Hobsbawm, Eric J., *The Age of Revolution: Europe, 1789–1848* (London: Weidenfeld & Nicolson, 1962).

Hobsbawm, Eric J., *The Age of Capital, 1848–1875* (London: Weidenfeld & Nicolson, 1975).

Hobsbawm, Eric J., *Age of Extremes: The Short Twentieth Century, 1914–1991* (London: Abacus, 1995).

Hobsbawm, Eric J. and Terence Ranger, eds, *The Invention of Tradition* (Cambridge: Cambridge University Press, 1983).

Hoelterhoff, Manuela, 'Old Venice Displays Architecture's Future', *Wall Street Journal*, 8 August 1980.

Honour, Hugh, *Neo-classicism: Style and Civilisation* (Harmondsworth: Penguin, 1968).

Hopkins, Owen, ed., *The Return of the Past: Conversations on Postmodernism* (London: Soane Museum, 2018).

Hopkins, Owen, *Postmodern Architecture: Less is a Bore* (London: Phaidon, 2020).

Huet, Bernard, 'Formalisme/Realisme', *L'Architecture d'Aujourd'hui*, 190 (April 1977), 35–6.

Huyssen, Andreas, *After the Great Divide: Modernism, Mass Culture, Postmodernism* (Bloomington: Indiana University Press, 1986).

Ibelings, Hans, *Supermodernism: Architecture in the Age of Globalisation* (Rotterdam: NAi, 1998).

Ingersoll, Richard, 'Context and Modernity', *Journal of Architectural Education*, 44.2 (1991), 124–5.

Ingersoll, Richard, 'Critical Regionalism in Houston: A Case for the Menil Collection', in *Critical Regionalism: The Pomona Meeting Proceedings*, ed. by Spyros Amourgis (Pomona: California State Polytechnic University, 1991), pp. 233–9.

Issaias, Platon, 'Beyond the Informal City: Athens and the Possibility of an Urban Common'. Unpublished doctoral thesis, Technische Universiteit Delft, 2014.

Jacobs, Jane, *The Death and Life of Great American Cities* (New York: Random House, 1961).

Jameson, Fredric, 'Not Avoiding Post-Modernity Would Have Complicated But Also Articulated Things', in *Context and Modernity: A Post-Seminar Reading*, ed. by Gerard Bergers (Delft: Stylos, 1991), pp. 42–8.

Jameson, Fredric, *Postmodernism, or, the Cultural Logic of Late Capitalism* (Durham, NC: Duke University Press, 1991).

Jameson, Fredric, *The Seeds of Time* (New York: Columbia University Press, 1994).

Jamieson, Claire, *NATØ: Narrative Architecture in Postmodern London* (London: Routledge, 2017).

Jencks, Charles, *Modern Movements in Architecture* (Harmondsworth: Penguin, 1973).

Jencks, Charles, 'The Rise of Post Modern Architecture', *Architectural Association Quarterly*, 7 (1975), 3–14.

Jencks, Charles, 'Isozaki and Radical Eclecticism', *Architectural Design*, 47.1 (1977), 42–9.

Jencks, Charles, *The Language of Post-Modern Architecture* (London: Academy, 1977).

Jencks, Charles, *The Language of Post-Modern Architecture*, 2nd edn (London: Academy, 1978).

Jencks, Charles, *Late Modern Architecture* (London: Academy, 1980).

Jencks, Charles, 'Towards Radical Eclecticism', in *The Presence of the Past: First International Exhibition of Architecture – Venice Biennale 80*, ed. by Paolo Portoghesi (London: Academy, 1980), pp. 30–7.

Jencks, Charles, *The Language of Post-Modern Architecture*, 3rd edn (London: Academy, 1981).

Jencks, Charles, 'The… New… International… Style… e altre etichette', *Domus*, 623 (1981), 41–7.

Jencks, Charles, 'Counter-Reformation: Reflections on the 1980 Venice Biennale', *Architectural Design*, 52.1/2 (1982), 4–7.

Jencks, Charles, *Current Architecture* (London: Academy, 1982).

Jencks, Charles, ed., 'Free-Style Classicism'. Special issue, *Architectural Design*, 52.1/2 (1982).

Jencks, Charles, 'Notes on an Architectural Culture', in *British Architecture*, ed. by Andreas Papadakis (London: Academy, 1982), p. 12.

Jencks, Charles, 'Post-Modern Architecture: The True Inheritor of Modernism', *RIBA Transactions*, 3.2 (1983), 26–41.

Jencks, Charles, *The Language of Post-Modern Architecture*, 4th edn (New York: Rizzoli, 1984).

Jencks, Charles, 'Post-Modern Classicism – The Synthesis: An Interview with Charles Jencks', *Architectural Design*, 54.3/4 (1984), 61–3.

Jencks, Charles, *Post-Modernism: The New Classicism in Art and Architecture* (London: Academy, 1987).

Jencks, Charles, *The New Paradigm in Architecture: The Language of Post-Modernism* (New Haven, CT: Yale University Press, 2002).

Jencks, Charles, *The Story of Post-Modernism: Five Decades of the Ironic, Iconic and Critical in Architecture* (Chichester: Wiley, 2011).

Jencks, Charles and George Baird, eds, *Meaning in Architecture* (London: Barrie & Jenkins, 1969).

Jencks, Charles, Paolo Portoghesi, Michael Graves, Eugene Kupper, Fernando Montes and Andreas Papadakis, 'Venice Biennale: Discussion', *Architectural Design*, 52.1/2 (1982), 8–9.

Jencks, Charles and Nathan Silver, *Adhocism: The Case for Improvisation* (London: Doubleday & Company, 1972).

Johnson, Philip, ed., *Modern Architecture: International Exhibition* (New York: Museum of Modern Art, 1932).

Johnson, Philip and Mark Wigley, eds, *Deconstructivist Architecture* (New York: Museum of Modern Art, 1988).

Kafetsi, Anna, ed., *Metamorphoses of the Modern: The Greek Experience* (Athens: Ministry of Culture; National Gallery, 1992).

Kahn, Louis I., 'On Monumentality', in *New Architecture and City Planning*, ed. by Paul Zucker (New York: Philosophical Library, 1944), pp. 77–88.

Kalfa, Konstantina, *Αυτοστέγαση τώρα! Η αθέατη πλευρά της αμερικανικής βοήθειας στην Ελλάδα* (Athens: futura, 2019).

Kalyvas, Stathis, *Καταστροφές και θρίαμβοι: Οι 7 κύκλοι της σύγχρονης ελληνικής ιστορίας* (Athens: Papadopoulos, 2015).

Kamilaki, Maria, Georgia Katsouda and Maria Vrachionidou, *Πιπέρι στο στόμα! Όψεις των λέξεων-ταμπού στη νέα ελληνική* (Athens: Kalligrafos, 2015).

Kapoli, Paraskevi, 'Εσωτερική μετανάστευση στην Αθήνα (1950–1970)'. Unpublished doctoral thesis, National and Kapodistrian University of Athens, 2014.

Kardamitsi-Adami, Maro, ed., *Οι αρχιτεκτονικές σπουδές στο ΕΜΠ 1917–1974* (Athens: National Technical University of Athens Press, 2002).

Kardamitsi-Adami, Maro, *Ανδρέας Συμεών: Από τη ζωή και το έργο του* (Athens: Benaki Museum, 2013).

Katsakou, Antigoni, *Rethinking Modernity: Between the Local and the International* (London: RIBA, 2020).

'Kenneth Frampton Golden Lion for Lifetime Achievement', *La Biennale di Venezia*, 26 May 2018. Online. www.labiennale.org/en/news/kenneth-frampton-golden-lion-lifetime-achievement (accessed 19 July 2021).

Kenny, Anthony, ed., *The Oxford History of Western Philosophy* (Oxford: Oxford University Press, 2000).

Keucheyan, Razmig, *The Left Hemisphere: Mapping Critical Theory Today*, trans. by Gregory Elliott (London: Verso, 2013).

Kitromilides, Paschalis M. and Constantinos Tsoukalas, eds, *The Greek Revolution: A Critical Dictionary* (Cambridge, MA: Belknap, 2021).

Kizis, Costandis, 'Modern Greek Myths: National Stereotypes and Modernity in Postwar Greece'. Unpublished doctoral thesis, Architectural Association, 2015.

Kizis, Yannis, 'Πικιώνης, Κωνσταντινίδης και νεοελληνική αρχιτεκτονική παράδοση', *Επίλογος*, 27 (2018), 329–42.

Klotz, Heinrich, *The History of Postmodern Architecture*, trans. by Radka Donnell (Cambridge, MA: MIT Press, 1988).

Kolb, David, *Postmodern Sophistications: Philosophy, Architecture, and Tradition* (Chicago: University of Chicago Press, 1990).

Konstantinidis, Aris, 'Schulmöbel für zurückgebliebene Kinder', *Moebel Interior Design*, 6 (1967), 72–4.

Konstantinidis, Aris, *Elements for Self-Knowledge*, trans. by Kay Cicellis (Athens: self-published, 1975).

Konstantinidis, Aris, *Αμαρτωλοί και κλέφτες, ή η απογείωση της αρχιτεκτονικής* (Athens: Agra, 1987).

Konstantinidis, Aris, *Η άθλια επικαιρότητα: Η χρυσή Ολυμπιάδα – το Μουσείο της Ακρόπολης* (Athens: Agra, 1991).

Konstantinidis, Aris, *Εμπειρίες και περιστατικά: Μια αυτοβιογραφική διήγηση*, 3 vols (Athens: Estia, 1992).

Korovesis, Georgios, 'Αρχιτεκτονική Post-Modern: Μόδα ή νέος προσανατολισμός;', *Άνθρωπος + Χώρος*, 19 (1982), 17–26.

Kostis, Kostas, *History's Spoiled Children: The Formation of the Modern Greek State*, trans. by Jacob Moe (London: Hurst, 2018).

Kotionis, Zissis, 'Ιδιώματα της ελληνικής αρχιτεκτονικής: Δ. Πικιώνης, Α. Κωνσταντινίδης, Τ. Ζενέτος, Δ. και Σ. Αντωνακάκη', in Zissis Kotionis, *Η τρέλα του τόπου: Αρχιτεκτονική στο ελληνικό τοπίο* (Athens: Ekkremes, 2004), pp. 61–95.

Kourkoulas, Andreas, 'Linguistics in Architectural Theory and Criticism after Modernism'. Unpublished doctoral thesis, University College London, 1986.

Kourkoulas, Andreas, 'Iconology, the Post-Modern Appeal to Memory', *Architecture in Greece*, 23 (1989), 60–2.

Kousidi, Matina, 'Through the Lens of Sigfried Giedion: Exploring Modernism and the Greek Vernacular in situ', *RIHA Journal*, 0136 (2016). Online. journals.ub.uni-heidelberg.de/index.php/rihajournal/article/download/70203/version/60526/63551 (accessed 12 July 2021).

Krauss, Rosalind, 'Sculpture in the Expanded Field', *October*, 8 (1979), 31–44.

Kruft, Hanno-Walter, *A History of Architectural Theory from Vitruvius to the Present*, trans. by Ronald Taylor, Elsie Callander and Antony Wood (New York: Princeton Architectural Press, 1994).

Kulić, Vladimir, 'New Belgrade and Socialist Yugoslavia's Three Globalisations', *International Journal for History, Culture and Modernity*, 2.2 (2014), 125–53.

Kulić, Vladimir, ed., *Second World Postmodernisms: Architecture and Society under Late Socialism* (London: Bloomsbury, 2019).

Kulterman, Udo, 'Space, Time and the New Architecture: About the 1980 Architecture Biennale', *Architecture and Urbanism A+U* (1981), 13–15.

Kundera, Milan, *The Curtain: An Essay in Seven Parts*, trans. by Linda Asher (New York: Harper Collins, 2007).

Kunneman, Harry, 'The End of Modern History', in *Context and Modernity: A Post-Seminar Reading*, ed. by Gerard Bergers (Delft: Stylos, 1991), pp. 54–7.

Kurokawa, Kisho, 'Architecture of the Road', trans. by H. Oribe and Y. Sasaki with Constantinos A. Doxiadis, *Ekistics*, 16.96 (1963), 288–93.

Lalas, Thanasis, 'Dimitris and Suzana Antonakakis Interview', Περιοδικό, 20 (1985).

Lampugnani, Vittorio Magnano, 'Avant-Gardes Architecturales 1970–1980', *L'Architecture d'Aujourd'hui*, 213 (1981), 8–13.

Lampugnani, Vittorio Magnago, ed., *Die Architektur, die Tradition und der Ort: Regionalismen in der europäischen Stadt* (Stuttgart: Deutsche Verlags-Anstalt, 2000).

Landgraf, Elisabeth, 'Interview mit Aris Konstantinidis', *Moebel Interior Design*, 7 (1965), 25.

Lathouri, Marina, 'Reconstructing the Topographies of the Modern City: The Late CIAM Debates'. Upublished doctoral thesis, University of Pennsylvania, 2006.

Latour, Bruno, *Down to Earth: Politics in the New Climatic Regime*, trans. by Catherine Porter (Cambridge: Polity, 2018).

Leach, Andrew and Nicole Sully, 'Frampton's Forewords, etc.: An Introduction', *OASE*, 103 (May 2019), 105–13.

Lebaron, Frédéric, *Le savant, la politique et la mondialisation* (Bellecombe-en-Bague: Le Croquant, 2003).

Lefaivre, Liane, *Leon Battista Alberti's Hypnerotomachia Poliphili: Re-Cognizing the Architectural Body in the Early Italian Rennaisance* (Cambridge, MA: MIT Press, 1997).

Lefaivre, Liane and Alexander Tzonis, 'The Grid and the Pathway: An Introduction to the Work of Dimitris and Suzana Antonakakis in the Context of Greek Architectural Culture', in *Atelier 66: The Architecture of Dimitris and Suzana Antonakakis*, ed. by Kenneth Frampton (New York: Rizzoli, 1985), pp. 14–25.

Lefaivre, Liane and Alexander Tzonis, 'Critical Regionalism', in *Critical Regionalism: The Pomona Meeting Proceedings*, ed. by Spyros Amourgis (Pomona: California State Polytechnic University, 1991), pp. 3–23.

Lefaivre, Liane and Alexander Tzonis, 'The Suppression and Rethinking of Regionalism and Tropicalism After 1945', in *Tropical Architecture: Critical Regionalism in the Age of Globalization*, ed. by Alexander Tzonis, Liane Lefaivre and Bruno Stagno (Chichester: Wiley, 2001), pp. 14–58.

Lefaivre, Liane and Alexander Tzonis, *Critical Regionalism: Architecture and Identity in a Globalized World* (Munich: Prestel, 2003).

Lefaivre, Liane and Alexander Tzonis, *Architecture of Regionalism in the Age of Globalization: Peaks and Valleys in the Flat World* (London: Routledge, 2012).

Lefaivre, Liane and Alexander Tzonis, *Architecture of Regionalism in the Age of Globalization: Peaks and Valleys in the Flat World*, 2nd edn (London: Routledge, 2021).

Lejeune, Jean-François and Michelangelo Sabatino, eds, *Modern Architecture and the Mediterranean: Vernacular Dialogues and Contested Identities* (New York: Routledge, 2010).

Levine, Neil, 'Vincent Scully: A Biographical Sketch', in Vincent Scully, *Modern Architecture and Other Essays* (Princeton: Princeton University Press, 2003), pp. 12–33.

Levy, Aaron and William Menking, eds, *Architecture on Display: On the History of the Venice Biennale of Architecture* (London: Architectural Association, 2010).

Liakos, Antonis *Ο ελληνικός 20ός αιώνας* (Athens: Polis, 2019).

Limón, José E., 'Border Literary Histories, Globalization, and Critical Regionalism', *American Literary History*, 20.1/2 (2008), 160–82.

Lokko, Lesley Naa Norle, ed., *White Papers, Black Marks: Architecture, Race, Culture* (London: Athlone, 2000).

Loyer, François, 'L'architecture de la Grèce contemporaine', 2 vols. Unpublished doctoral thesis, Université de Paris, 1966.

Loyer, François, *L'architecture de la Grèce au XIXe siècle, 1821–1912* (Athens: École française d'Athènes, 2017).

Lu, Duanfang, 'Entangled Modernities in Architecture', in *The SAGE Handbook of Architectural Theory*, ed. by C. Greig Crysler, Stephen Cairns and Hilde Heynen (London: SAGE, 2012), pp. 231–46.

Lyotard, Jean-François, *The Postmodern Condition: A Report on Knowledge*, trans. by Geoff Bennington and Brian Massumi (Minneapolis: University of Minnesota Press, 1984).

Lyotard, Jean-François, 'Ripetizione, complessità, anamnesi', *Casabella*, 49.517 (1985), 44–5.

Magdoff, Harry, *Imperialism: From the Colonial Age to the Present* (New York: Monthly Review, 1978).

Magouliotis, Nikos, 'Το Νεο-ελληνικό Maison Dom-ino, σαν ένα ιδίωμα σύγχρονης ανώνυμης αρχιτεκτονικής'. Unpublished master's thesis, National Technical University of Athens, 2016.

Magouliotis, Nikolaos, 'Learning from "Panosikoma": Atelier 66's Additions to Ordinary Houses', *Architectural Histories*, 6.1 (2018), art. 21. doi.org/10.5334/ah.299.

Mallgrave, Harry-Francis and David J. Goodman, *An Introduction to Architectural Theory: 1968 to the Present* (Chichester: Wiley-Blackwell, 2011).

Marcuse, Herbert, *Eros and Civilization* (New York: Vintage, 1962).

Martin, Reinhold, *Utopia's Ghost: Architecture and Postmodernism, Again* (Minneapolis: University of Minnesota Press, 2010).

Martin, Reinhold, 'Postscript: A Postmodernist International?', in *Second World Postmodernisms: Architecture and Society under Late Socialism*, ed. by Vladimir Kulić (London: Bloomsbury, 2019), pp. 226–35.

Mashayekhi, Azadeh, 'The Politics of Building in Post-Revolution Tehran', in *Routledge Handbook on Middle East Cities*, ed. by Haim Yacobi and Mansour Nasasra (London: Routledge, 2020), pp. 196–216.

Mazower, Mark, 'Democracy's Cradle, Rocking the World', *New York Times*, 30 June 2011, p. A27.

Mazzolini, Andrée, 'Des architectes "réparateurs de ville"', *Matin de Paris*, 1 November 1980.

McKean, John, 'Towards the Unknown Region', *Architects' Journal*, 176.50 (15 December 1982), 19–21.

McLeod, Mary, 'Architecture', in *The Postmodern Moment: A Handbook of Contemporary Innovation in the Arts*, ed. by Stanley Trachtenberg (Westport, CT: Greenwood Press, 1985), pp. 19–52.

McLeod, Mary, 'Architecture and Politics in the Reagan Era: From Postmodernism to Deconstructivism', *Assemblage*, 8 (1989), 23–59.

McLeod, Mary, 'Modernism', in *Forty Ways to Think about Architecture: Architectural History and Theory Today*, ed. by Iain Borden, Murray Fraser and Barbara Penner (Hoboken, NJ: Wiley, 2014), pp. 185–92.

McLeod, Mary, 'Kenneth Frampton's Idea of the "Critical"', in *Modern Architecture and the Lifeworld: Essays in Honor of Kenneth Frampton*, ed. by Karla Cavarra Britton and Robert McCarter (London: Thames & Hudson, 2020), pp. 20–42.

McLoone, Martin, 'National Cinema and Cultural Identity: Ireland and Europe', in *Border Crossing: Film in Ireland, Britain and Europe*, ed. by John Hill, Martin McLoone and Paul Hainsworth (Belfast: Queen's University Belfast, 1994), pp. 146–73.

McMorrough, John, 'Signifying Practices: The Pre-Texts of Post-Modern Architecture'. Unpublished doctoral thesis, Harvard University, 2007.

Megas, Georgios, *The Greek House, its Evolution and its Relation to the Houses of the Other Balkan States* (Athens: Ministry of Reconstruction, 1951).

Michelis, Panayotis, *Η αρχιτεκτονική ως τέχνη* (Athens: self-published, 1940).

Michelis, Panayotis, *An Aesthetic Approach to Byzantine Art* (London: Batsford, 1955).

Michelis, Panayotis, *Το ελληνικό λαϊκό σπίτι, Α': Φροντιστηριακαί Εργασίαι* (Athens: National Technical University of Athens, Chair of Architectural Morphology and Rhythmology, 1960).

Michelis, Panayotis, *L'esthétique de l'architecture du béton armé*, trans. by P. Jean Darrouzès (Paris: Dunod, 1963).

Michelis, Panayotis, *Aesthetikos: Essays in Art, Architecture and Aesthetics* (Detroit: Wayne State University Press, 1977).

Mies van der Rohe: Drawings from the Collection of A. James Speyer (New York: Max Protetch Gallery, 1986).

Migayrou, Frédéric, ed., *La Tendenza: Italian Architectures, 1965–1985* (Paris: Centre Pompidou, 2012).

Migge, Leberecht [Spartakus in Grün], 'Das grüne Manifest', *Die Tat*, 10.2 (1919), 912–19.

Milanovic, Branko, *Capitalism Alone: The Future of the System that Rules the World* (Cambridge, MA: Harvard University Press, 2019).

Mishra, Pankaj, *Bland Fanatics: Liberals, Race and Empire* (London: Verso, 2020).

Mitscherlich, Alexander, *Die Unwirtlichkeit unserer Städte: Anstiftung zum Unfrieden* (Frankfurt am Main: Suhrkamp, 1965).

Moneo, Rafael, 'On Typology', *Oppositions*, 13 (1978), 22–45.

Moneo, Rafael, 'The Contradictions of Architecture as History', *Architectural Design*, 52.7/8 (1982), 54.

Montesquieu, *De l'Esprit de Loix; Ou du rapport que les Loix doivent avoir avec la Constitution de chaque Gouvernement, les Moeurs, le Climat, la Religion, le Commerce, &c.; à quoi l'Auteur a ajouté des recherches nouvelles sur les Loix Romaines touchant les Successions, sur les Loix Françoises, & sur les Loix Féodales* (Geneva, 1748).

Moore, Steven A., 'Technology, Place, and Nonmodern Regionalism', in *Architectural Regionalism: Collected Writings on Place, Identity, Modernity, and Tradition*, ed. by Vincent B. Canizaro (New York: Princeton Architectural Press, 2007), pp. 433–42.

Moraitis, Kostas, 'Η Σφίγγα και οι γρίφοι: Εισήγηση για την Αρχιτεκτονική, τα Τέρατα και τα εκφραστικά Πάθη', in *Μοντέρνο-Μεταμοντέρνο*, ed. by Georgios Aristinos, Anna Kafetsi, Andreas Mpelezinis and Sotiris Sorongas (Athens: Smili, 1988), 161–72.

Moraitis, Kostas, 'Το μέλλον του νεωτερικού αιτήματος: Οφείλουμε να είμαστε διαρκώς μοντέρνοι;', *Architecture in Greece*, 30 (1996), 137–8.

Moschini, Francesco, ed., *Paolo Portoghesi: Projects and Drawings, 1949–1979* (London: Academy, 1980).

Mossé, Claude, *Regards sur la démocratie athénienne* (Paris: Perrin, 2013).

Mota, Nelson, 'From Critical Regionalism to Critical Realism: Challenging the Commodification of Tradition', *DASH*, 6 (2012), 46–55.

Mumford, Eric P., *The CIAM Discourse on Urbanism, 1928–1960* (Cambridge, MA: MIT Press, 2002).

Mumford, Lewis, *Sticks and Stones: A Study in American Architecture and Civilisation* (New York: Boni and Liveright, 1924).

Mumford, Lewis, *The South in Architecture* (New York: Harcourt, Brace & Co., 1941).

Mumford, Lewis, 'Report on Honolulu', in Lewis Mumford, *City Development* (New York: Harcourt, Brace & Co., 1945), pp. 84–154.

Mumford, Lewis, 'The Skyline', *New Yorker*, 11 October 1947, p. 104.

Mumford, Lewis, 'The Architecture of the Bay Region', in *Domestic Architecture of the San Francisco Bay Region*, ed. by Robert M. Church (San Francisco: Museum of Art, Civic Center, 1949), unpaginated.

Mumford, Lewis, 'Introduction', in Artur Glikson, *The Ecological Basis of Planning* (The Hague: Nijhoff, 1971), pp. vii–xxi.

Norberg-Hodge, Helena, *Local is our Future: Steps to an Economics of Happiness* (Totnes: Local Futures, 2019).

Norberg-Schulz, Christian, *Intentions in Architecture* (London: Allen and Unwin, 1963).

Norberg-Schulz, Christian, *Meaning in Western Architecture* (London: Studio Vista, 1975).

Norberg-Schulz, Christian, *Genius Loci: Towards a Phenomenology of Architecture* (London: Academy, 1980).

Norberg-Schulz, Christian, 'Towards an Authentic Architecture', in *The Presence of the Past: First International Exhibition of Architecture – Venice Biennale 80*, ed. by Paolo Portoghesi (London: Academy, 1980), pp. 21–9.

Norri, Maria-Riitta, ed., *Dimitris Pikionis, 1887–1968: Kreikkalainen arkkitehti* (Helsinki: Suomen Rakennustaiteen Museo, 1993).

Norri, Marja-Riita, 'Six Journeys into Architectural Reality: Directions for the Next Millenium', *Architectural Review*, 199.1190 (1996), 68–74.

Oberman, Heiko A. and Thomas A. Brady Jr, eds, *Itinerarium Italicum: The Profile of the Italian Renaissance in the Mirror of its European Transformations* (Leiden: Brill, 1975).

Onians, John, *Bearers of Meaning: The Classical Orders in Antiquity, the Middle Ages and the Renaissance* (Cambridge: Cambridge University Press, 1988).

Orlandos, Anastasios, 'Αι ημέραι του συνεδρίου εν Ελλάδι', *Τεχνικά Χρονικά*, 44–6 (1933), pp. 1002–3.

Otero-Pailos, Jorge, *Architecture's Historical Turn: Phenomenology and the Rise of the Postmodern* (Minneapolis: University of Minnesota Press, 2010).

Owens, Craig, 'The Discourse of Others: Feminists and Postmodernism', in *The Anti-Aesthetic: Essays on Postmodern Culture*, ed. by Hal Foster (Washington, DC: Bay Press, 1983), pp. 57–82.

Pallasmaa, Juhani, 'Tradition and Modernity: The Feasibility of a Regional Architecture in a Postmodern World', *Architectural Review*, 183.1095 (May 1988), 26–34.

Pallasmaa, Juhani, 'Hapticity and Time: Notes on Fragile Architecture', *Architectural Review*, 207.1239 (2000), 68–74.

Papadolampakis, Manolis, 'Μεταμοντέρνα πρόθεση', Άνθρωπος + Χώρος, 17 (1982), 17–24.

Papandreou, Vangelis and Katerina Tsakmaki, 'Πολυαισθητηριακή αρχιτεκτονική για εργάτες εξόρυξης βωξίτη: Ο οικισμός στο Δίστομο των Σ. & Δ. Αντωνακάκη. Επισκέψεις I-VII'. Unpublished undergraduate thesis, University of Thessaly, 2015.

Papanikolaou, Dimitris, 'Greece as a Postmodern Example: *Boundary 2* and its Special Issue on Greece', *Κάμπος: Cambridge Papers in Modern Greek*, 13 (2005), 127–45.

Papatsonis, Takis, ed., *In Memoriam: Panayotis A. Michelis* (Athens: Hellenic Society for Aesthetics, 1972).

Parnell, Stephen, '*Architectural Design*, 1954–1972: The Architectural Magazine's Contribution to the Writing of Architectural History'. Unpublished doctoral thesis, University of Sheffield, 2012.

Parnell, Stephen, '*AR*'s and *AD*'s Post-War Editorial Policies: The Making of Modern Architecture in Britain', *Journal of Architecture*, 17.5 (2012), 763–75.

Parnell, Stephen, 'Architecture's Expanding Field: *AD* Magazine and the Post-Modernisation of Architecture', *Architectural Research Quarterly*, 22.1 (2018), 55–68.

Parnell, Stephen, 'The Birth and Rebirth of a Movement: Charles Jencks's Postmodern Odyssey in *AD*', *Architectural Design*, 91.1 (2021), 48–55.

Paschou, Anastasia, *Gebäudetypologie der Grossstadt: Eine Analyse der griechischen Metropole Athen* (Zurich: ETH, 2001). Online. doi.org/10.3929/ethz-a-004485758 (accessed 20 July 2021).

Pasti, D., 'Facciatisti e facciatosti: Dibattito fra Paolo Portoghesi e Bruno Zevi', *L'Espresso*, 17 August 1980, p. 135.

Patteeuw, Véronique and Léa-Catherine Szacka, 'Critical Regionalism for our Time', *Architectural Review*, 1466 (November 2019), 92–8.

Petit, Emmanuel, *Irony; or, the Self-critical Opacity of Postmodern Architecture* (New Haven, CT: Yale University Press, 2013).

Petrakis, Marina, *The Metaxas Myth: Dictatorship and Propaganda in Greece* (London: I.B.Tauris, 2006).

Petridou, Vasiliki, Panayotis Pangalos and Nefeli Kyrkitsou, eds, *Εργάζομαι άρα κατοικώ: Η περίπτωση του συγκροτήματος κατοικιών των μεταλλείων Μπάρλου στο Δίστομο Βοιωτίας, των Δ. & Σ. Αντωνακάκη* (Patras: University of Patras School of Architecture, 2012).

Pevsner, Nikolaus, *Pioneers of the Modern Movement from William Morris to Walter Gropius* (London: Faber, 1936).

Pikionis, Dimitris, 'Η λαϊκή μας τέχνη κι εμείς' (1925), repr. in *Δ. Πικιώνης: Κείμενα*, ed. by Agni Pikioni and Michalis Parousis (Athens: MIET, 1985), pp. 53–69.

Pikionis, Dimitris, 'Η θεωρία του αρχιτέκτονος Κ. Α. Δοξιάδη για τη διαμόρφωση του χώρου εις την αρχαία Αρχιτεκτονική' (1937), repr. in *Δ. Πικιώνης: Κείμενα*, ed. by Agni Pikioni and Michalis Parousis (Athens: MIET, 1985), pp. 181–96.

Pikionis, Dimitris, 'Το πρόβλημα της μορφής' (1951), repr. in *Δ. Πικιώνης: Κείμενα*, ed. by Agni Pikioni and Michalis Parousis (Athens: MIET, 1985), pp. 204–46.

Pikionis, Dimitris, 'Οικιστικός κανονισμός Αιξωνής: Μορφολόγηση των επί μέρους στοιχείων' (1952), repr. in *Δ. Πικιώνης: Κείμενα*, ed. by Agni Pikioni and Michalis Parousis (Athens: MIET, 1986), pp. 259–65.

Pikionis, Dimitris, 'Autobiographical Notes' (1958), repr. in *Mega XI, Dimitris Pikionis, Architect 1887–1968: A Sentimental Topography*, ed. by Dennis Crompton (London: Architectural Association, 1989), pp. 34–7.

Philippidis, Dimitris, *Νεοελληνική αρχιτεκτονική: Αρχιτεκτονική θεωρία και πράξη (1830–1980) σαν αντανάκλαση των ιδεολογικών επιλογών της νεοελληνικής κουλτούρας* (Athens: Melissa, 1984).

Philippidis, Dimitris, 'Το πρόσωπο και το είδωλο: Η αριστερή αρχιτεκτονική στην Ελλάδα', *Διαλεκτική*, 4 (1990), 15–30.

Philippidis, Dimitris, 'Αλληγορία του μοντέρνου στην ελληνική αρχιτεκτονική', *Architecture in Greece*, 30 (1996), 138–40.

Philippidis, Dimitris, *Μοντέρνα αρχιτεκτονική στην Ελλάδα* (Athens: Melissa, 2001).

Philippidis, Dimitris, 'Η υστερική άρνηση του μεταμοντέρνου στην ελληνική αρχιτεκτονική', in *Η πρόσληψη των μετανεωτερικών ιδεών στην Ελλάδα*, ed. by Ourania Kaiafa (Athens: Moraitis Foundation, 2018), pp. 81–92.

Plutarch, *Lives of the Noble Greeks and Romans*, Loeb Classical Library (Cambridge, MA: Harvard University Press, 1914).

Popescu, Carmen, 'Space, Time: Identity', *National Identities*, 8.3 (2006), 189–206.

Popescu, Carmen, 'Flattening History: A Prequel to the Invention of Critical Regionalism', *OASE*, 103 (2019), 49–57.

Porphyrios, Demetri, 'Sketch of a Post-Functionalist Architecture', *Architecture in Greece*, 12 (1978), 68–85.

Porphyrios, Demetri, *Sources of Modern Eclecticism: Studies on Alvar Aalto* (London: Academy, 1982).

Porphyrios, Demetri, ed., 'Classicism is Not a Style'. Special issue, *Architectural Design*, 52.5/6 (1982).

Portoghesi, Paolo, *Borromini: Architettura come linguaggio* (Milan: Electa, 1967).

Portoghesi, Paolo, 'The End of Prohibitionism', in *The Presence of the Past: First International Exhibition of Architecture – Venice Biennale 80*, ed. by Paolo Portoghesi (London: Academy, 1980), pp. 9–14.

Portoghesi, Paolo, *Postmodern, the Architecture of the Post-Industrial Society* (New York: Rizzoli, 1983).

Portoghesi, Paolo and Bruno Zevi, 'Is Post-Modern Architecture Serious?', *Architectural Design*, 52.1/2 (1982), 20–1.

Poulantzas, Nikos, *The Crisis of the Dictatorships: Portugal, Greece, Spain* (London: NLB Humanities Press, 1976).

Powell, Douglas, *Critical Regionalism: Connecting Politics and Culture in the American Landscape* (Chapel Hill: University of North Carolina Press, 2007).

Quantrill, Malcolm, 'Stern Regionalism', *Architectural Review*, 180.1073 (July 1986), 4–5.

Reichlin, Bruno and Martin Steinmann, eds, 'Realismus in der Architektur'. Special issue, *Archithese*, 19 (1976).

Richards, J.M., 'The New Empiricism: Sweden's Latest Style', *Architectural Review*, 101.606 (June 1947), 199–204.

Ricoeur, Paul, 'Universal Civilisation and National Cultures' (1961), repr. in Paul Ricoeur, *History and Truth*, trans. by Charles A. Kelbley (Evanston, IL: Northwestern University Press, 1965), pp. 271–84.

Roberts, Jennifer T., *Athens on Trial: The Antidemocratic Tradition in Western Thought* (Princeton: Princeton University Press, 1994)

Roberts, John, 'Towards an Arriere-Garde, Or, How to Be Modern and Return to Sources', *Art Monthly*, 69 (September 1983), 28–30.

Rogers, Ernesto, 'Continuità o Crisi?', *Casabella Continuità*, 215 (1957), 3–4.

Rorty, Richard, 'Postmodernist Bourgeois Liberalism', *Journal of Philosophy*, 80.10 (1983), 583–9.

Rorty, Richard, 'Habermas and Lyotard on Postmodernity', in *Habermas and Modernity*, ed. by Richard J. Bernstein (Cambridge, MA: MIT Press, 1985), pp. 161–75.

Rorty, Richard, *Contingency, Irony, and Solidarity* (Cambridge: Cambridge University Press, 1989).

Rosanvallon, Pierre, *Notre histoire intellectuelle et politique 1968–2018* (Paris: Seuil, 2018).

Rossi, Aldo, *The Architecture of the City*, trans. by Diane Ghirardo and Joan Ockman (Cambridge, MA: MIT Press, 1982).

Rowan, Jan Christopher, 'Editorial', *Progressive Architecture* (January 1964), 99.

Rowe, Colin, *The Mathematics of the Ideal Villa and Other Essays* (Cambridge, MA: MIT Press, 1987).

Roy, Tirthankar, *India in the World Economy: From Antiquity to the Present* (Cambridge: Cambridge University Press, 2012).

Rykwert, Joseph, 'How Great is the Debate?', *RIBA Transactions*, 4.2:2 (1983), 18–31.

Said, Edward W., *Orientalism* (London: Routledge; Kegan Paul, 1978).

Said, Edward W., 'Opponents, Audiences, Constituencies and Community', *Critical Inquiry*, 9.1 (1982), 1–26.

Sakellaropoulos, Christoforos, *Μοντέρνα αρχιτεκτονική και πολιτική της αστικής ανοικοδόμησης: Αθήνα 1945–1960* (Athens: Papazisis, 2003).

Saliga, Pauline and Robert V. Sharp, 'From the Hand of Mies: Architectural Sketches from the Collection of A. James Speyer', *Art Institute of Chicago Museum Studies*, 21.1 (1995), 56–69, 77–8.

Salmas, Anastasios A., 'Παραποίηση και προσβολή του αρχιτεκτονικού χώρου', *Αρχιτεκτονική*, 9 (1958), 7–9.

Salvataggio, Nantas, 'Quando la libertà odora di eresia', *Il Tempo*, 1 August 1980, 3.

Sarfatti-Larson, Magali, *Behind the Postmodern Façade: Architectural Change in Late Twentieth-Century America* (Berkeley: University of California, 1993).

Sartoris, Alberto, *Gli elementi dell'architettura funzionale: Sintesi panoramica dell'architettura moderna*, 2nd edn (Milan: Hoepli, 1935).

Saunders, Frances Stonor, *The Cultural Cold War: The CIA and the World of Arts and Letters* (New York: New Press, 1999).

Schwenkel, Christina, *Building Socialism: The Afterlife of East German Architecture in Urban Vietnam* (Durham, NC: Duke University Press, 2020).

Scoffier, Richard, 'Approaches to a New Spatiality: Modern Architecture in Post-War Greece down to the Dictatorship', *Tefchos*, 10 (1992), 63–72.

Scott, Felicity D., *Architecture or Techno-utopia: Politics after Modernism* (Cambridge, MA: MIT Press, 2007).

Scully, Vincent, *The Shingle Style: Architectural Theory and Design from Richardson to the Origins of Wright* (New Haven, CT: Yale University Press, 1955).

Scully, Vincent, 'Doldrums in the Suburbs', *Journal of the Society of Architectural Historians*, 24.1 (March 1965), 36–47.

Scully, Vincent, 'Introduction', in Robert Venturi, *Complexity and Contradiction in Architecture* (New York: Museum of Modern Art, 1966), pp. 9–11.

Scully, Vincent, *The Shingle Style Today: Or, The Historian's Revenge* (New York: Braziller, 1974).

Scully, Vincent, *The Earth, the Temple, and the Gods: Greek Sacred Architecture*, 3rd edn (New Haven, CT: Yale University Press, 1979).

Scully, Vincent, 'The Star in Stern: Sightings and Orientation', in Robert Stern and Vincent Scully, *Robert Stern* (London: Academy, 1981), pp. 8–19.

Semper, Gottfried, *Anwendung der Farben in der Architektur und Plastik des Alterthums und des Mittelalters* (Dresden, 1836).

Serraller, F. Callo, 'La presencia del pasado: La arquitectura postmoderna', *El Pais*, 20 September 1980, 3.

Sharr, Adam, 'Leslie Martin and the Science of Architectural Form', in *Quality Out of Control: Standards for Measuring Architecture*, ed. by Allison Dutoit, Juliet Odgers and Adam Sharr (London: Routledge, 2010), pp. 67–78.

Simeoforidis, Yorgos, 'Αρχιτεκτονική γλώσσα της δεκαετίας 1980–90: Επιστημονικό συμπόσιο αρχιτεκτονικής στην Ύδρα', *Journal of the Association of Greek Architects*, 7 (1981), 27.

Simeoforidis, Yorgos, 'Σύγχρονη ελληνική αρχιτεκτονική στην Ολλανδία', *Journal of the Association of Greek Architects*, 9 (1981), 24–6.

Simeoforidis, Yorgos, 'Foreword', *Design + Art in Greece*, 14 (1983), 16–18.

Simeoforidis, Yorgos, 'Regionalism as a Cultural Tendency in Architecture', *Design + Art in Greece*, 14 (1983), 19–26.

Simeoforidis. Yorgos, 'ΥΔΡΑ 83 ή Τι συνέβη σε ένα Διεθνές Αρχιτεκτονικό Συνέδριο', *Journal of the Association of Greek Architects*, 19.5/6 (1983), 13–15.

Simeoforidis, Yorgos, 'Foreword', *Design + Art in Greece*, 16 (1985), 14–15.

Sioutis, Theodore, 'Ο δάσκαλος, Δημήτρης Αντωνακάκης'. Unpublished undergraduate essay, National Technical University of Athens, 2017.

Sisci, Francesco, 'Under the Same Sky: A New World-view from China', *Diogenes*, 221 (2009), 74–82.

Skopetea, Eleni, *Το 'Πρότυπο Βασίλειο' και η Μεγάλη Ιδέα: Όψεις του εθνικού προβλήματος στην Ελλάδα 1830–1880* (Athens: Polytypo, 1988).

Skoutelis, Nikos, ed., *Συν-ηχήσεις με τον Δημήτρη Πικιώνη* (Athens: Plethron, 2018).

Slessor, Catherine, *Concrete Regionalism* (London: Thames & Hudson, 2000).

Slessor, Catherine, 'Editorial View: Reframing Critical Regionalism for the Current Age', *Architectural Review*, 25 July 2013. Online. www.architectural-review.com/essays/editorial-view-reframing-critical-regionalism-for-the-current-age/8651301.article (accessed 30 June 2021).

Sloterdijk, Peter, *In the World Interior of Capital: Towards a Philosophical Theory of Globalization*, trans. by Wieland Hoban (Cambridge: Polity, 2013).

Sloterdijk, Peter, *What Happened in the Twentieth Century? Towards a Critique of Extremist Reason*, trans. by Christopher Turner (Cambridge: Polity, 2018).

Smith, Maria, 'Ethics have a Sell-by Date', *RIBA Journal* (September 2018), 75.

Smithson, Alison, 'Aldo van Eyck at Bridgwater CIAM 6, 1948', *Architectural Design*, 30.5 (1960), 178.

Spanos, William Vaios, 'The Detective and the Boundary: Some Notes on the Postmodern Literary Imagination', *boundary 2*, 1.1 (1972), 147–68.

Speaks, Michael, 'Architectural Ideologies: Modern, Postmodern, and Deconstructive'. Unpublished doctoral thesis, Duke University, 1993.

Spencer, Douglas, *The Architecture of Neoliberalism: How Contemporary Architecture Became an Instrument of Control and Compliance* (London: Bloomsbury, 2016).

Speyer, A. James, 'Όταν οι δάσκαλοι γερνούν', *Ζυγός*, 36–7 (1958), 33–6.

Speyer, A. James, 'Ludwig Mies van der Rohe: Εντυπώσεις του κορυφαίου αμερικανού αρχιτέκτονος απο το ταξίδι του στην Ελλάδα', *Αρχιτεκτονική*, 15–16 (1959), 42.

Speyer, A. James, ed., *Mies van der Rohe* (Chicago: Art Institute of Chicago, 1968).

Speyer, A. James, 'Mies van der Rohe', *Architecture in Greece*, 4 (1970), 95–9.

Speyer, A. James, 'Oral History of A. James Speyer', in *The Chicago Architects Oral History Project*, ed. by Pauline A. Saliga (Chicago: Department of Architecture, the Art Institute of Chicago, interviews June 1986), pp. 1–135. Online. artic.contentdm.oclc.org/digital/collection/caohp/id/10267/rec/1 (accessed 15 July 2021).

Spivak, Gayatri Chakravorty, *Other Asias* (Malden, MA: Blackwell, 2008).

Spon, Jacob and George Wheler, *Voyage d'Italie, de Dalmatie, de Grèce, et du Levant fait aux années 1675 et 1676* (Lyons, 1678).

Stanek, Łukasz, *Architecture in Global Socialism: Eastern Europe, West Africa, and the Middle East in the Cold War* (Princeton: Princeton University Press, 2020).

Steen, Andrew P., 'Radical Eclecticism and Post-Modern Architecture', *Fabrications*, 25.1 (2015), 130–45.

Steiner, Michael and Clarence Mondale, *Region and Regionalism in the United States: A Source Book for the Humanities and Social Sciences* (New York: Garland, 1988).

Steinmann, Martin, 'Reality as History: Notes for a Discussion of Realism in Architecture', *Architecture and Urbanism A+U*, 69 (1976), 25–35.

Steinmann, Martin and Thomas Boga, eds, *Tendenzen: Neuere Architektur im Tessin. Dokumentation zur Ausstellung an der ETH Zürich vom 20. Nov.–13. Dez. 1975* (Zurich: ETHZ Organisationsstelle für Ausstellungen des Institutes gta, 1975).

Stephen, Douglas, Kenneth Frampton and Michael Carapetian, *British Buildings 1960–1964* (London: Adam & Charles Black, 1965).

Stern, Robert A.M., *New Directions in American Architecture* (London: Studio Vista, 1969).

Stern, Robert A.M., 'Post-Modern Architecture' (1975), repr. in *Architecture on the Edge of Postmodernism: Collected Essays, 1964–1988*, ed. by Robert Stern and Cynthia Davidson (New Haven, CT: Yale University Press, 2009), pp. 33–7.

Stern, Robert A.M., 'Gray Architecture as Postmodernism, or, Up and Down from Orthodoxy' (1976), repr. in *Architecture on the Edge of Postmodernism: Collected Essays, 1964–1988*, ed. by Robert Stern and Cynthia Davidson (New Haven, CT: Yale University Press, 2009), pp. 38–42.

Stern, Robert A.M., 'The Doubles of Post-Modern' (1980), repr. in *Architecture on the Edge of Postmodernism: Collected Essays, 1964–1988*, ed. by Robert Stern and Cynthia Davidson (New Haven, CT: Yale University Press, 2009), pp. 128–46.

Stern, Robert A.M., 'Giedion's Ghost: A Review of Frampton's *Modern Architecture: A Critical History*', *Skyline* (October 1981), 22–5.

Stern, Robert A.M., 'Regionalism and the Continuity of Tradition', *Center*, 3 (1987), 58–63.

Stern, Robert A.M., 'From the Past: Strada Novissima', *Log*, 20 (2010), 35–8.

Strauven, Francis, *Aldo van Eyck: The Shape of Relativity* (Amsterdam: Architectura & Natura, 1998).

Stuart, James and Nicolas Revett, *The Antiquities of Athens Measured and Delineated*, 3 vols (London, 1762–94).

Stylianou, Aris, 'Το Εργαστήρι-66', *Αρχιτέκτων: Ενημερωτικό Δελτίο Συλλόγου Αρχιτεκτόνων Κύπρου*, 10 (March–April 1990), 62–9.

Svoronos, Nicolas, *Histoire de la Grèce moderne* (Paris: Presses Universitaires de France, 1953).

Szacka, Léa-Catherine, 'Exhibiting the Postmodern: Three Narratives for a History of the 1980 Venice Architecture Biennale'. Doctoral thesis, University College London, 2011.

Szacka, Léa-Catherine, *Exhibiting the Postmodern: The 1980 Venice Architecture Biennale* (Venice: Marsilio, 2016).

Tabb, Philip James and A. Senem Deviren, *The Greening of Architecture: A Critical History and Survey of Contemporary Sustainable Architecture and Urban Design* (London: Routledge, 2014).

Tafuri, Manfredo, *History of Italian Architecture, 1944–1985*, trans. by Jessica Levine (Cambridge, MA: MIT Press, 1989).

Takeyama, Kiyoshi, 'Tadao Ando: Heir to a Tradition', *Perspecta*, 20 (1983), 163–80.

Taki, Koji, 'Minimalism or Monotonality? A Contextual Analysis of Tadao Ando's Method', in *Tadao Ando: Buildings, Projects, Writings*, ed. by Kenneth Frampton (New York: Rizzoli, 1984), pp. 11–23.

Theocharopoulou, Ioanna, *Builders, Housewives and the Construction of Modern Athens* (London: Black Dog, 2017).

Thucydides, *History of the Peloponnesian War*, Loeb Classical Library (Cambridge, MA: Harvard University Press, 1919).

Tournikiotis, Panayotis, 'Greek Architecture at the Unclear Confines between Theory and Tradition', *Architecture in Greece*, 23 (1989), 70–7.

Tournikiotis, Panayotis, 'Κριτική της σύγχρονης ελληνικής αρχιτεκτονικής: Επιμύθιο', *Architecture in Greece*, 24 (1990), 22–4.

Tournikiotis, Panayotis, ed., *The Parthenon and its Impact in Modern Times* (Athens: Melissa, 1994).

Tournikiotis, Panayotis, 'The Rationale of the Modern and Locus: A View of Greek Architecture from the Seventies to the Nineties', in *20th Century Architecture: Greece*, ed. by Savas Condaratos and Wilfried Wang (Munich: Prestel, 2000), pp. 53–62.

Tournikiotis, Panayotis, 'Barriers and Jumps in Greek Urban Culture of the 70s', in *Great Unrest: 5 Utopias in the 1970s, a bit before – a bit after*, ed. by Thanasis Moutsopoulos (Athens: Voreiodytiko Sima, 2006), pp. 288–93, 367–8.

Tournikiotis, Panayotis, ed., *Atelier 66: The Architecture of Dimitris and Suzana Antonakakis* (Athens: futura, 2007).

Tournikiotis, Panayotis, 'Quoting the Parthenon: History and the Building of Ideas', *Perspecta*, 49 (2016), 153–66.

Towner, John, *An Historical Geography of Recreation and Tourism in the Western World, 1540–1940* (Chichester: Wiley, 1996).

Trachtenberg, Stanley, ed., *The Postmodern Moment: A Handbook of Contemporary Innovation in the Arts* (Westport, CT: Greenwood Press, 1985).

Tracy, Maria, 'Exhibitions and the Public: Venice Biennale', *Crit.: The Architectural Student Journal*, 11 (Spring 1981), 17–19.

Tsakopoulos, Panos, *Reflections on Greek Postwar Architecture* (Athens: Kaleidoscopio, 2014).

Tsiambaos, Kostas, *From Doxiadis' Theory to Pikionis' Work: Reflections of Antiquity in Modern Architecture* (London: Routledge, 2017).

Tsirkas, Stratis, *Η χαμένη άνοιξη* (Athens: Kedros, 1976).

Turan, Neyran, *Architecture as Measure* (Barcelona: Actar, 2020).

Turner, Frank M., *The Greek Heritage in Victorian Britain* (New Haven, CT: Yale University Press, 1981).

Turpin, Etienne, ed., *Architecture in the Anthropocene: Encounters Among Design, Deep Time, Science and Philosophy* (London: Open Humanities, 2013).

Tziovas, Dimitris, *Ο μύθος της Γενιάς του Τριάντα: Νεωτερικότητα, ελληνικότητα και πολιτισμική ιδεολογία* (Athens: Polis, 2011).

Tzirtzilakis, Yorgos, 'Toward a Point Marked X: Some Thoughts about Post-War Architecture in Greece and Some Hypotheses about its Near Future', *Tefchos*, 1 (1989), 21–31.

Tzirtzilakis, Yorgos, 'Αρχιτεκτονική και μελαγχολία: Πολιτισμικές πρακτικές στο έργο του Δημήτρη Πικιώνη', *Εν Βόλω*, 31 (2008), 26–35.

Tzonis, Alexander, 'Commentary', *Le carré bleu*, 3 (1970), 3.

Tzonis, Alexander, *Towards a Non-Oppressive Environment: An Essay* (Boston: I Press, 1972).

Tzonis, Alexander, *Das verbaute Leben: Vorbereitung zu einem Ausbruchsversuch* (Düsseldorf: Bertelsmann, 1973).

Tzonis, Alexander, 'The Predicaments of Architecture: Narcissism and Humanism in Contemporary Architecture', *Harvard Graduate School of Design Publication Series in Architecture*, A-7906 (1980), 1–17.

Tzonis, Alexander and Liane Lefaivre, 'In the Name of the People: The Development of the Contemporary Populist Movement in Architecture' (1976), repr. in *What People Want: Populism in Architecture and Design*, ed. by Michael Shamiyeh (Basel: Birkhäuser, 2005), pp. 288–305.

Tzonis, Alexander and Liane Lefaivre, 'Narcissisme et humanisme dans l'architecture contemporaine', *Le carré bleu*, 4 (1980), 1–17.

Tzonis, Alexander and Liane Lefaivre, 'The Narcissist Phase in Architecture', *Harvard Architecture Review*, 1 (Spring 1980), 53–61.

Tzonis, Alexander and Liane Lefaivre, 'The Grid and the Pathway: An Introduction to the Work of Dimitris and Suzana Antonakakis, with Prolegomena to a History of the Culture of Modern Greek Architecture', *Architecture in Greece*, 15 (1981), 164–78.

Tzonis, Alexander and Liane Lefaivre, 'Het Raster en het Pad', *Wonen-TA/BK*, 20–1 (1981), 31–42.

Tzonis, Alexander and Liane Lefaivre, 'Expression régionale et architecture contemporaine: "de la trame au cheminement"; l'œuvre de Dimitri et de Suzanne Antonakakis', *Le carré bleu*, 2 (1982), pp. 1–20.

Tzonis, Alexander and Liane Lefaivre, 'De terugkeer van regionalisme', *Bouw*, 9 (April 1983), 9–11.

Tzonis, Alexander and Liane Lefaivre, 'Lewis Mumford en de gevaren van regressief regionalisme', *Bouw*, 10 (May 1983), 15–18.

Tzonis, Alexander and Liane Lefaivre, 'Het naoorlogse regionalism en de toekomst van kritisch regionalisme', *Bouw*, 11 (June 1983), 16–18.

Tzonis, Alexander and Liane Lefaivre, 'A Critical Introduction to Greek Architecture since the Second World War', in *Post-War Architecture in Greece, 1945–1983*, ed. by Orestis Doumanis (Athens: Architecture in Greece Press, 1984), 16–23.

Tzonis, Alexander and Liane Lefaivre, 'Het onvoltooide project van de moderniteit', *Bouw*, 18 (September 1984), 23–4.

Tzonis, Alexander and Liane Lefaivre, '"The Anti-Aesthetic. Essays on Postmodern Culture": Μια βιβλιοκρισία', *Design + Art in Greece*, 16 (1985), 64.

Tzonis, Alexander and Liane Lefaivre, 'El regionalismo critico y la arquitectura española actual', *Arquitectura y Vivienda*, 3 (1985), 4–19.

Tzonis, Alexander and Liane Lefaivre, *Classical Architecture: The Poetics of Order* (Cambridge, MA: MIT Press, 1986).

Tzonis, Alexander and Liane Lefaivre, 'Why Critical Regionalism Today?' (1990), repr. in *Theorizing a New Agenda for Architecture: An Anthology of Architectural Theory 1965–1995*, ed. by Kate Nesbitt (New York: Princeton Architectural Press, 1996), pp. 484–92.

Tzonis, Alexander and Liane Lefaivre, 'Human Life Remains the Central Issue', in *Context and Modernity: A Post-Seminar Reading*, ed. by Gerard Bergers (Delft: Stylos, 1991), pp. 110–11.

Tzonis, Alexander and Liane Lefaivre, 'Lewis Mumford's Regionalism', *Design Book Review*, 19 (Winter 1991), 20–5.

Tzonis, Alexander and Liane Lefaivre, *Times of Creative Destruction: Shaping Buildings and Cities in the Late C20th* (London: Routledge, 2017).

Tzonis, Alexander, Liane Lefaivre and Anthony Alofsin, 'Die Frage des Regionalismus', in *Für eine andere Architektur: Bauen mit der Natur und in der Region*, ed. by Michael Andritzky, Lucius Burckhardt and Ot Hoffmann (Frankfurt am Main: Fischer, 1981), pp. 121–34.

Tzonis, Alexander and Alcestis Rodi, *Greece: Modern Architectures in History* (London: Reaktion, 2013).

Ungers, Oswald Matthias, 'Planning Criteria', *Lotus*, 11 (1976), 13–41.

Urban, Florian, *Postmodern Architecture in Socialist Poland: Transformation, Symbolic Form and National Identity* (London: Routledge, 2021).

Utzon, Jørn, 'Platforms and Plateaus: Ideas of a Danish Architect', *Zodiac*, 10 (1962), 112–40.

Vamvakas, Vassilis and Panayis Panagiotopoulos, eds, *Η Ελλάδα στη δεκαετία του '80: Κοινωνικό, πολιτικό και πολιτισμικό λεξικό* (Athens: Perasma, 2010).

Vamvakas, Vassilis and Panayis Panagiotopoulos, eds, *GR80s. Η Ελλάδα του Ογδόντα στην Τεχνόπολη: Συλλογισμός, περιεχόμενο και μεθοδολογία για μια έκθεση* (Athens: Melissa, 2017).

Van Dijk, Hans, 'The Banner Critical Regionalism Hauled Down', in *Context and Modernity: A Post-Seminar Reading*, ed. by Gerard Bergers (Delft: Stylos, 1991), pp. 16–20.

Van Eyck, Aldo, 'The Interior of Time', in *Meaning in Architecture*, ed. by Charles Jencks and George Baird (London: Barrie & Jenkins, 1969), pp. 171–2.

Van Eyck, Aldo, 'R.P.P. (Rats, Posts and Other Pests)', *Architectural Design News Supplement*, 51.7 (1981), 15–16.

Vassiliadis, Dimitris, 'Μια δημιουργία υψηλού αισθητικού ήθους: Η διαμόρφωση των λόφων γύρω από την Ακρόπολη', *Αρχιτεκτονική*, 36 (1962), 31–41.

Venturi, Robert, *Complexity and Contradiction in Architecture* (New York: Museum of Modern Art, 1966).

Venturi, Robert, Denise Scott-Brown and Steven Izenour, *Learning from Las Vegas* (Cambridge, MA: MIT Press, 1972).

Vidler, Anthony, 'The Idea of Type: The Transformation of the Academic Ideal, 1750–1830', *Oppositions*, 8 (1977), 94–115.

Vinegar, Aron, *I AM A MONUMENT: On Learning from Las Vegas* (Cambridge, MA: MIT Press, 2008).

Viollet-le-Duc, Eugène, *Entretiens sur l'Architecture* (Paris, 1863).

Voulgaris, Yannis, *Η Ελλάδα από τη μεταπολίτευση στην παγκοσμιοποίηση* (Athens: Polis, 2008).

Vrieslander, Klaus and Julio Kaimi, *Το σπίτι του Ροδάκη στην Αίγινα* (Athens: Akritas, 1997).

Vujicic, Lejla, 'Architecture of the Longue Durée: Vittorio Gregotti's Reading of the Territory of Architecture', *Architectural Research Quarterly*, 19.2 (2015), 161–74.

Wainwright, Oliver, 'Revealed: How Developers Exploit Flawed Planning System to Minimise Affordable Housing', *The Guardian*, 25 June 2015. Online. www.theguardian.com/cities/2015/jun/25/london-developers-viability-planning-affordable-social-housing-regeneration-oliver-wainwright (accessed 19 July 2021).

Wallerstein, Immanuel Maurice, *The Modern World System: Capitalist Agriculture and the Origins of the European World-Economy in the Sixteenth Century* (New York: Academic Press, 1974).

Watkin, David, *A History of Western Architecture* (London: Barrie & Jenkins, 1986).

Welsch, Wolfgang, *Unsere postmoderne Moderne* (Weinheim: Acta Humaniora, 1987).

Weston, Richard, 'Oriental Star: Tadao Ando: The Yale Studio and Current Works', *Architects' Journal*, 190.12 (20 September 1989), 91.

Weston, Richard, 'Corrective Studies in the Art of Construction', *Architects' Journal*, 203 (7 March 1996), 54.

Winckelmann, Johann Joachim, *Geschichte der Kunst des Alterthums*, 2 vols (Dresden, 1764).

Woditsch, Richard, ed., *The Public Private House: Modern Athens and its Polykatoikia* (Zurich: Park Books, 2018).

Xanthopoulos, Konstantinos, *Alvar Aalto and Greece: Trailing Ariadne's Thread* (Athens: Melissa, 2019).

Xydis, Alexandros, 'Ο Μετα-μοντερνισμός εισβάλλει στη Σίφνο', *Αντί*, 328 (1986), 50.

Yakovaki, Nassia, *Ευρώπη μέσω Ελλάδας: Μια καμπή στην ευρωπαϊκή αυτοσυνείδηση, 17ος–18ος αιώνας* (Athens: Estia, 2006).

Yingle, Zhang, 'Pikionis, Lewerentz, Venezia and Siza: The Narrative Experience in Eight Itineraries'. Unpublished doctoral thesis, Escuela Técnica Superior de Arquitectura de Madrid, 2019.

Zakaria, Fareed, *Ten Lessons for a Post-Pandemic World* (New York: Norton, 2020).

Zervos, Christian, ed., *L'art en Grèce, des temps préhistoriques aux débuts du XVIIe s.* (Paris: Cahiers d'Art, 1934).

Zumthor, Peter and Mari Lending, *A Feeling of History* (Zurich: Scheidegger & Spiess, 2018).

Index

9H 139

Aalto, Alvar and Elissa Mäkiniemi 20, 74, 133, 153, 158, 163–5, 170, 176, 241, 254, 362
  Säynätsalo Town Hall 149, 150, 151, 163

abstraction 36, 64, 67, 74, 75, 79, 80, 101, 167, 175, 176, 189, 201, 212, 278, 350, 365

Academy of Athens 102

Acropolis, Athens 103, 105, 106, 112, 149, 152, 157, 196, 197, 204, 207, 223–4, 226–7, 257–61, 273, 278
  Erechteion 193
  Parthenon 189, 191, 192, 194–8, 224

activism 61

Adamson, Glenn 8

adaptation 3, 4, 43, 50, 66, 77, 200, 255, 262, 270, 280–1, 284, 288, 343, 362, 365

adhocism 56 (n17)

advocacy planning 56 (n17)

Aegean Sea 262

aesthetics 35, 51, 53, 76, 93, 95, 100, 193, 197, 232, 264–5, 268, 289, 297–9, 323, 327, 353, 357

Africa 157, 341, 362
  sub-Saharan 355
  West 359

Agarez, Ricardo 360

agora 157, 309

Aidonopoulos, Gabriel 55 (n8), 234, 235

air conditioning 98, 154, 364

Akcan, Esra 9

Algarve 360

alleys 36

Alofsin, Anthony 16, 19, 20, 54, 60, 63, 65–72, 74–7, 81–4, 90, 348, 360

Althusser, Louis 174

ambiguity 36, 117, 132, 304–5, 327, 333, 342, 366

America 66–7, 69, 75, 81, 84, 130, 138–9, 235, 325, 349, 355, 365
  Latin 356
  North 1–3, 9–12, 14, 16, 18, 19, 32, 39, 40, 42, 44–6, 49, 50–3, 55, 59, 60, 69, 72, 74–6, 78, 81–3, 92, 106, 116, 123–4, 130, 132, 180, 189, 191, 194, 199–203, 212–3, 215, 225–6, 250, 331, 341, 345, 351, 360, 365
  South 138

American Institute of Architects 325, 349
  Architecture 325
  Gold Medal 349

Amourgis, Spyros 14

analysis 6, 15, 16, 22, 61–3, 72, 98, 100, 112, 135, 150, 167, 171, 175, 182, 203, 211–12, 218 (n34), 223, 230, 263, 265, 267, 347, 351–2, 358, 365, 367 (n30)

Anderson, Perry 10

Ando, Tadao 21, 119 (n36), 121 (n83), 136, 154, 156, 175, 178–9, 181, 249, 349

Andriolas, Dimitris 315

Andritzky, Michael 76

Angelidi, Antouanetta 331

anglophone 3, 5, 100, 123, 345, 347–8

anonymity 1, 197, 235, 241, 261, 268, 278, 295–7, 304, 360

Anthropocene 180, 357

anthropology 6, 38, 63, 94

Ἄνθρωπος + Χώρος [*Human + Space*] 329

antiparochi 289–90

antiquity 4, 67, 157, 190–1, 193–4, 198–9, 258

Antonakaki, Suzana 137, 229, 239, 241, 249, 255, 257, 261–2, 264–6, 268–9, 270–2, 284, 288, 295, 303, 314, 316–17, 330, 361
  Apartment building at 44 Doxapatri Street, Athens 303

Antonakakis, Dimitris 33–7, 100, 109, 112–15, 229–30, 232, 237, 239, 241, 243, 245, 250, 255–9, 261, 265, 267–8, 273–4, 291, 295–7, 312–15, 325, 328, 330, 349

Antonakakis, Dimitris and Suzana 1, 10, 12, 18, 20, 22–4, 32–8, 55, 59, 85, 90, 97, 99–102, 106–18, 136, 154, 156, 169, 170–1, 179, 201–4, 206–8, 211, 214, 216, 222, 225, 228–50, 254–75, 278–306, 309–30, 332–3, 338, 349, 354, 359, 365
  Apartment building at 118 Benaki Street, Athens 23–4, 97, 109, 112, 116, 202, 207, 238, 241, 247, 249, 274, 278–80, 283–303, 305–6, 310, 312–13, 318–20, 322, 333
  Apartment building at Argolidos Street, Athens 313, 324
  Archaeological Museum on Chios 108, 110, 112, 229–31, 236
  furniture design of the Theotokos Foundation 229

National Technical University 23, 35, 100, 109, 229, 235, 237, 241, 254, 264, 266, 270–3, 315
Atlantic 14, 18, 20, 44, 46, 51–2, 54, 91, 93, 97, 130, 132, 343–4, 365
Attica 195
Australia 172, 341
    Brisbane 134
Austria 348
authenticity 11, 14, 43, 95, 100, 140, 299, 318, 358
authoritarianism 102, 192, 230, 235, 240, 353, 355
authorship 10, 12, 16, 19–20, 25, 59–65, 71–2, 75–6, 80, 84, 89–90, 101, 106, 109, 115, 118, 129–30, 141, 150, 155, 190–1, 194, 213, 215, 221, 228, 235, 240, 298, 337, 340, 343–4, 350, 359–62, 365–6
autonomy 6, 71–2, 79, 94, 152, 164, 172, 230, 238, 301, 305, 313, 328, 338
avant-garde 6, 20, 93, 98, 127, 131, 134, 136, 138, 153, 164–5, 197, 199, 342–3, 353–4
aura 15, 222, 317

Babalou-Noukaki, Boukie 13, 234, 240, 324
Baird, George 156
Bakhtin, Mikhail 348
balconies 36, 112, 157, 204, 280–2, 284, 304, 316, 320
Balkans 17, 195
Baltics 158
Bangladesh 356
Banham, Reyner 189, 323
Barcelona 41, 173, 348
Baroque 36, 44, 80, 242
Barragán, Luis 49, 52, 119 (n36), 124, 154, 175
Bateson, Gregory 153, 180
battlefield 50
Bauhaus 19
Bay Area, San Francisco 67, 69
bazaar 157
Beaux Arts 67, 74
belonging 5–6, 207
Berlin 139, 165, 195, 258
    Wall 337–42, 345
Berman, Marshall 338–9
Bernini, Gian Lorenzo 162
    Sant' Andrea al Quirinale in Rome 162
Bescós, Ramon 166
Biennale of Architecture exhibition, Venice 6–9, 12, 14–15, 18–20, 31–5, 38–9, 43–55, 72, 75, 89–94, 97–9, 101, 116–18, 125–7, 129, 131–2, 136–7, 165, 174–6, 225–6, 306, 309, 325, 328, 339, 344–6, 356
bipolarity 341–2
Biris, Kostas 218 (n38)
Blade Runner 341
Blake, Peter 200
Blouet, Abel 195
Blundell Jones, Peter 129
body, human 54, 90, 150, 159, 206, 211, 268–9, 352

Bofill, Renato (Taller de Arquitectura) 49, 126
    Walden 7 126
Bohigas, Oriol 52, 95, 119 (n36), 137, 172–3, 333
Böhm, Gottfried 49
Bolsonaro, Jair 2
border 2, 13, 203, 221, 228, 250, 254, 334, 339, 364
Botta, Mario 52, 95, 119 (n36), 125–6, 137, 152, 154, 156, 165, 170, 249
boundary 52, 112, 114, 118, 126, 142, 230, 239–40, 288, 338, 354, 359
Boyarsky, Alvin 132, 135, 138
Brazil 2, 100, 351–2
Brexit 2
brief, architectural 116, 236, 238, 243, 270, 302
Brinckerhoff Jackson, John 65
Britain 133, 181, 190
British Empire 17, 352
Broch, Hermann 348
Brolin, Brent C. 200
Bru, Eduard 154, 339
Brutalism (New) 100, 166, 182, 279, 353
Buffington, LeRoy S. 69
Burckhardt, Lucius 19, 60, 63–5, 69, 77–82, 357
bureaucracy 62, 133, 203, 304, 344, 353–4, 367 (n30)
Byzantine art and architecture 157, 161, 167, 264–5, 273, 309

Cadaqués 200
California 68–9, 73
Canada 1, 181
Canadian Centre for Architecture 348
Candilis, Georges 203, 225
Canizaro, Vincent B. 16
canon 9, 18, 21, 31–2, 40–1, 50, 84, 123, 133, 149, 165, 179, 181, 189, 196–7, 202, 206, 215, 218 (n34), 226, 229, 348–9, 365
capitalism 3–4, 14, 39, 74, 95, 127, 140, 174, 289–90, 342–4, 347, 353–5, 357–8
Carloni, Tita 119 (n36), 154
Le carré bleu 123
Carrilho da Graça, João Luís 154
Casabella Continuità 139
Casanova, Pascale 350
catalogue (exhibition) 43, 48, 50, 90, 93–4, 232, 309, 332
Catalonia 95, 126, 172–3, 348, 356
catharsis 202
Celsing, Peter 119 (n36)
Center for the Study of American Architecture at Austin, TX 130
'centres' 1, 10, 12, 15, 17–22, 33, 38, 55, 90, 97–8, 100, 125, 134, 136, 139, 141, 190–1, 193, 195–202, 212–13, 216, 250, 341, 343–4, 348, 350, 355, 360
ceramics 157, 322
Chareau, Pierre 95
    Maison de Verre 95
charrette 238
chauvinism 339, 363
Chermayeff, Serge 60, 80
Chile 100, 138

critics 16, 18–19, 32, 35, 38–9, 42, 45–6, 48, 74, 89, 91, 116–18, 122, 124–6, 128, 131, 155, 191, 203, 252 (n31), 279, 306, 323, 325, 330–1, 338, 345, 356, 365
critical theory 43, 67, 92, 115
criticality 5, 15, 63, 91, 130
cross-cultural exchange 2–5, 10, 16–21, 23, 25, 59–60, 67, 84, 89–90, 96, 115, 118, 134, 142, 148, 150, 155–62, 164–6, 173–82, 190, 203–4, 207, 211, 216, 254, 273–5, 334, 345, 348, 352, 358–9, 362, 364
  East meets West 174–6, 178, 181, 352
Cuba 125
Cubism 200
Cullen, Gordon 112
culture 2, 13–17, 19–20, 22–3, 33, 42–5, 49, 53–5, 63, 66, 81, 93–6, 98–9, 105–6, 113, 116, 122, 126–8, 130–2, 135, 138, 140–2, 148–9, 151–3, 156–61, 169–71, 173–6, 178–82, 190–2, 201, 207, 212, 214, 221–2, 238, 251 (n9), 261, 263, 274–5, 299, 305, 332–3, 338, 342–3, 348–50, 356, 358–9, 363–6
curator 8, 31, 39, 45–7, 51–3, 112
Curtis, William J.R. 33, 51, 189, 192, 226
cybernetics 4, 6
Cyclades, Greece 114, 195, 200, 204, 268
Cyprus 120 (n50), 205

D'Ancona, Hedy 338
Da Silva, Minnette 351
Dada 94
Daedalus 139
Dardi, Constantino 49
Daskalakis, Konstantinos 234, 242
Davey, Peter 134
Davies, Colin 190
Davis, Alexander Jackson 194
  United States Custom House, New York 194
De La Sota, Alejandro 154
De Melo, Duarte Cabral 156
De Oiza, Francisco Javier Sáenz 154
De Sola-Morales, Ignasi 91
death 43, 134, 224, 235, 269, 325
decentralisation 77, 138, 172–3
decolonisation 363, 366
deconstruction 96, 130, 342
Deconstructivism 5, 148, 339
defamiliarisation 5, 84
Dekavallas, Konstantinos 282
Delft, Technical University 71, 124, 137
  Antonakakis–Pikionis exhibition at the Greek Festival 109, 225, 230–3
  'Context and Modernity' seminar on critical regionalism 14, 337–40, 354
democracy 11, 102, 135, 191–2, 195, 236, 347, 354–5
Denmark 77, 159–61, 181, 344
dependency theory 343
Derrida, Jacques 342
Descombes, Georges 137

desertification 357
design 2, 5–6, 19–20, 22–5, 36, 39, 47–8, 60, 62, 64, 67, 71–2, 76–7, 79–81, 90, 100–6, 110, 112, 117–18, 131, 134, 136, 138–9, 142, 149, 157–9, 166, 175, 190, 200, 205–8, 211–13, 221, 223, 229, 234–6, 253 (n52), 256–61, 268–72, 278, 281–3, 287–306, 307 (n11), 310–22, 325–9, 333, 337, 348, 354, 356–62, 364–5
  collaborative (non-hierarchical) 22–3, 236–48, 295–303
despotism 74, 101–2, 192
Despotopoulos, Ioannis (Jan Despo) 197
Desylla, Eleni 55 (n8), 108, 234–5
detailing 36–7, 117, 142, 157, 160, 167, 173, 175, 204, 242, 246–8, 265, 267, 280, 302, 316–8, 321–4, 340, 353, 360
determinism 192–3
developers 24, 281, 290, 304, 306–7 (n11), 358
Dias, Adalberto 154
dictatorship (military junta) 10–11, 13, 32, 114, 205, 222, 228, 235–6, 279, 299, 315, 332, 354
dimensioning 142, 245–6, 265, 268, 302, 357
discourse 3, 8, 10, 12, 14–19, 21–2, 24, 31, 33, 39, 45, 48, 52–4, 59–60, 71, 79–81, 84, 89–93, 95–7, 99, 113–18, 119 (n25), 122–32, 135, 138–9, 149–52, 155, 162, 163, 165, 171, 173, 177, 180–2, 190, 201–3, 207, 210, 212–16, 221–4, 226, 228, 232–3, 250, 256, 268, 275, 305–6, 312, 327, 329, 331–3, 338, 340, 347, 350–3, 356–60, 362–5
disjunction 84, 98, 177, 365
display 91, 150
diversity 6, 8, 18, 21, 32, 45, 47–8, 52, 62, 67, 69, 80, 83, 117, 126, 139, 150, 156–7, 180, 182, 212, 214, 257, 263, 270, 273, 279, 295, 313, 328, 339, 347, 357, 365
'documento Stern' 45, 47–8, 57 (nn52–3)
Dolka, Maria 258
Dolka, Pattie 290, 298
Dolkas, Lampis 290, 298
Doshi, Balkrishna Vithaldas 121 (n83), 156, 181
Doumanis, Orestis 84, 99–100, 109–10, 206, 223–4, 257, 269, 329
Doxiadis, Constantinos A. 203, 257–8, 276 (n15)
draftsmanship 167
drawing 23, 47, 110, 113–14, 142, 167, 175, 179, 231, 240–2, 255, 258, 263–5, 272, 281, 285, 288, 291, 293–5, 302, 310, 313, 317–19, 321–2, 324
Drew, Jane 351
Dublin 348
Duterte, Rodrigo 2
dwelling 92, 269, 273, 283, 297, 299
dystopia 341

earth 262, 291, 364
earthwork 152

East 150, 157–62, 165, 174–8, 181, 339, 341–2, 347, 352
    Middle 17, 157, 342
eclecticism 8, 31, 35–6, 39–42, 44, 46, 48, 50–1, 55, 56 (n17), 125, 155, 327, 330
economy 2, 4, 19, 44, 60, 62–4, 71, 79, 101, 118, 131, 164, 235, 250, 280, 290, 298, 303, 341, 343, 347, 355, 357–8, 364
ecumenism 105–6, 162
editorship 39, 42, 50–2, 61, 76, 99–100, 126, 132–6, 138–42, 148, 184 (n60), 204–6, 209, 234, 325, 353
Eggener, Keith L. 15–16, 131, 201, 216, 350
Egypt 154, 191
Eisenman, Peter 6, 75, 132, 135, 140, 179
Eisenstein, Sergei 276 (n15)
elitism 24, 71, 140, 303, 306
emancipation 8, 11, 67, 98, 102, 106, 108, 130, 195, 331, 345
empire 4, 17, 76, 81–3, 175, 191–2, 341, 345, 352
Encyclopedia Brittanica 153
end of history 338, 345
England 69, 72, 85, 112, 122, 132–3, 166, 203–4, 207–9, 216, 276 (n36), 350
Engonopoulos, Nikos 255
environment 44, 61–2, 64–5, 67, 72, 77, 79–80, 92, 95, 114, 153, 175, 205, 284, 288, 364
    built 1, 6, 11, 34, 141, 213–14, 235, 269, 278, 280–1, 290, 295, 304, 310, 315, 325, 364
Erskine, Ralph 39–40, 48, 52
    Byker Wall estate in Newcastle upon Tyne 40
Erten, Erdem 122, 133
essentialism 43, 175, 181, 213, 312, 348, 363–4
ETH Zurich 170, 325–6
    'Tendenzen: Neuere Architektur im Tessin' exhibition 170
    'Wander through a Greek Architectural Reality' exhibition 325–6
ethics 64, 347, 357
ethnography 224
Europe 1, 11, 17–18, 22, 44, 47, 51, 55, 60, 63, 81, 84, 101–2, 105, 116, 138, 140, 159, 163–4, 166, 169, 174, 179, 191–5, 197, 199–200, 215, 263–4, 337–8, 343, 348, 355, 364–5
    Central 76, 348
    continental 123, 130, 138, 181
    Eastern 164–5, 339, 341, 347–8
    European Charter of Cultural Heritage 315
    European Community 11, 337
    European Union 345
    Northern 181, 190
    Western 1–2, 6, 9–12, 18, 32–3, 38–40, 45, 50–3, 55, 59, 77–8, 106, 121 (n83), 123–4, 132, 136, 138, 154, 163, 165, 174, 180–1, 189–90, 194, 197, 199–203, 210, 213, 215, 225–6, 250, 331, 341, 344, 352, 354, 360, 365
everyday 23, 36–8, 44, 64–5, 77, 94, 106, 170, 205, 215, 241, 250, 265, 274, 280–1, 289, 296, 299, 304, 306
evolutionary tree 125

exhibitions 6–7, 10, 18, 31–5, 38–9, 43–54, 90–1, 93–4, 109, 122, 124–5, 135, 140, 169–170, 204, 208–11, 225–6, 230, 232–3, 309, 325–6, 332, 345
experimentation 125, 248, 282, 289, 295, 304, 306, 309, 322, 327
expertise 39, 61–3, 181, 290, 297
extraction 4, 343
fabric, urban 38, 44, 170
façade 47, 55, 72, 74–5, 280–4, 312–13, 318–20, 322, 328
Farrell, Terry 8
fascism 74
Fathy, Hassan 154, 346
Fatouros, Dimitris 12, 100, 116, 199–201, 232, 240, 255, 268, 279, 282
    Apartment building at 109 Patission Avenue, Athens 282
    National Gallery, Athens 232
Fehn, Sverre 156, 164, 170–1, 174–6
    Nordic Pavilion at the Giardini Biennale, Venice 176
feminism 9, 130
Ferlenga, Alberto 227
Festschrifts 25, 356
fetishisation 25, 169, 173, 357
fiction 53, 341
figuration 365
films 2, 34, 283, 341
Finland 344, 362
Finley, Moses I. 191
First World 1, 4, 341–7, 351–5, 359, 365–6
flat world (flattening of differences) 81, 346–7
flooding 357
floor 18, 32, 52, 128, 159, 167, 232, 238–9, 241, 246, 249, 278, 280–1, 283–5, 287–8, 291, 293, 295, 298–300, 314, 316–18, 322, 352
folk 69, 80, 95, 251 (n9), 261–3, 265, 299
formal(ism) 36, 38, 46, 51–2, 71, 77, 101–2, 114, 199, 212–13, 254, 261, 270, 284, 301, 305–6, 309–10, 312–13, 320, 360
Foster, Hal 122, 129, 148
Foster, Norman 116, 125, 156
Fotiou, Theano 13, 234, 324
fragment 62, 105, 142, 157, 165, 213–14, 258
Frampton, Kenneth 1, 12–17, 19–22, 24–5, 33, 39, 42–3, 45, 48, 51–5, 59–61, 76–7, 79, 81–2, 84, 89–100, 106–8, 113, 115–18, 119 (mote 36), 122–42, 148–57, 159, 161–82, 190, 202–16, 222, 224–8, 232–4, 248–50, 255, 279, 305, 309–10, 312, 314, 325–7, 332–3, 337–40, 342–4, 347–8, 350–60, 362–4
France 63, 96, 122, 138, 164, 181, 190–1, 195, 199, 250, 253 (n54), 276 (n36), 348
Frank, Andre Gunder 343
Frankfurt School 54, 344
Franklin, Geraint 8
Fraser, Murray 16
Freud, Sigmund 179
frontier 172

Fry, Maxwell 351
Fujii, Hiromi 178–9
Fukuyama, Francis 338–9, 355
function 6, 80, 114, 135, 175, 197, 247, 301,
 310, 314, 327, 330, 334, 358, 360
functionalism 6, 8, 43, 45–6, 49, 67, 89, 99,
 117, 164, 176, 179, 197, 202–3, 232, 235

Galfetti, Aurelio 119 (n36), 154, 170
Gallaratese 164
Galleano, Luis Fernandez 139
galleries 36, 165
Gartzos, Kostis 55 (n8)
Gaudí, Antoni 40–1
 Casa Batlló in Barcelona 41
Gehry, Frank 57 (n52)
genealogy 23, 93, 161, 203, 211, 223, 229,
 254, 275, 305–6
General Building Code, Greece 235, 280–1,
 290–4, 315
Generation of the 1930s 255, 262, 267
genius loci 43, 226
geography 16, 18, 83, 130, 139, 149, 192,
 334, 344–5, 350, 352, 355
geology 357
geometry 257–60, 269
geopolitics 14, 190–3
Germany 19, 60, 63–4, 69, 76, 84, 101–2,
 138, 181, 190, 194, 250
 West 164–5
 East 164–5, 341
Getty Museum 348
Getty Research Institute for Architecture 348
ghetto 172
Ghika (see Hadjikyriakos-Ghika, Nikos)
Giacumacatos, Andreas 11, 325, 327
Giddens, Anthony 342
Giedion, Sigfried 41–2, 133, 140, 164,
 196–7
Gisel, Ernst 119 (n36)
Giurgola, Aldo 39, 42
Glaser, Ludwig 156
glass 46, 282, 316
globalisation 2–5, 15–18, 21, 31, 81, 84, 134,
 148, 173, 180–2, 337, 340–1, 345–9,
 352, 354–5, 358–9, 363–4
Glotz, Gustave 191
Goethe, Johann Wolfgang von 102, 105,
 347–50
golden section 257–8, 263
Gothic 177
 Revival 160
governance 4, 140, 191, 195, 236, 341
gradient 95, 230, 284
Grafton Architects 356
Grand Tour 192
Grand Turc 192
Graves, Michael 39, 57 (n52)
Greece 1, 10, 21, 161, 167–9, 192, 195, 198,
 344, 363
 ancient 18, 21–2, 106, 157, 177, 189–95,
 197–9, 202, 258
 modern 10–13, 16–19, 20, 21–4, 32–8,
 55, 60, 84, 89–90, 97, 99–110, 113–18,
 122–3, 157, 170, 182, 190, 192, 195–7,
 199–216, 221–37, 240–2, 248–50,

 254–75, 281–4, 289–91, 296, 298–301,
 303, 305–6, 312–14, 325–34, 354, 356,
 364–5
 War of Independence 195
 Civil War 10, 267, 287, 332, 364
Greek Revival 102, 194
Greenberg, Allan 57 (n52)
Greenberg, Clement 179
Gregotti, Vittorio 99, 139, 152, 156, 177
grid 22–3, 101–2, 106, 110, 112, 114, 179,
 207–8, 211, 213, 215, 227, 230–2,
 245–6, 254, 256–60, 271–2, 281, 295,
 302, 312–15, 328, 330, 358–9
 'The Grid and the Pathway' essay 1, 5, 12,
 19–20, 22, 84, 89–90, 97, 100–6,
 110–11, 113–14, 122, 177, 201, 204,
 206–8, 211, 222–5, 227–30, 232, 254,
 269, 314
Gropius, Walter 76, 81, 195
 US Embassy building, Athens 195
gross domestic product (GDP) 352
ground 167, 258, 287
growth 4, 17, 41, 233, 235, 237, 287, 345,
 355
Grumbach, Antoine 49

Habermas, Jürgen 130, 339
Habsburg Empire 76, 81
Hadjikyriakos-Ghika, Nikos 23, 255–6, 262–4,
 268
Hadjimichali, Angeliki 224, 251 (n9)
Hadjimichalis, Costis 234, 240, 242, 291
Hadjimichalis, Nikos 322
Hamdi, Nabeel 134
Hanseatic 160
Hansen, Christian and Theophil 102
Harvard Architecture Review 78
Harvard Design Magazine 139
Harvard University (Graduate School of
 Design) 19, 60–1, 63–5, 67, 78
Harvey, David 354
Harwood, Elain 8
Hatherley, Owen 10
Hays, K. Michael 8
Heidegger, Martin 43, 92, 179, 291, 339,
 358
Hellenistic period 157, 309
Herder, Johann Gottfried 192
heritage 167, 255, 315
Hertzberger, Herman 37–8, 125, 137, 154,
 156, 170, 173, 325, 360–1
 Centraal Beheer offices, Apeldoorn 173,
 360–1
heterogeneity 8, 16, 167
hierarchy 2, 20, 22–4, 59, 62, 64, 67, 98, 134,
 157, 232, 234–5, 246, 248–9, 260, 272,
 290, 299–302, 306, 313, 341–4, 350,
 352, 354, 365–6
Hirayama, Akiyoshi 156
historicism 8, 31–3, 35, 38, 47–8, 50–4,
 89–90, 97–8, 102, 105, 116, 125, 127,
 131, 155, 201–2, 227, 274, 323, 327,
 330, 337
historiography 5, 10–12, 19–21, 25, 33, 39,
 41, 50–3, 60, 76, 78, 81, 98, 127, 133,
 164, 174, 182, 189–90, 196–7, 199–201,

Kizis, Yannis 224
Kleihues, Josef Paul 57 (n53)
Jensen-Klint, Peder Vilhelm 160
   Grundtvig Church 160
Klotz, Heinrich 52–3, 156
Knight III, Carleton 325
Kokkinou, Maria 210
Kolb, David 131
Konstantinidis, Aris 22–3, 99, 101–4, 106,
     108, 110–11, 119 (n36), 120 (n50),
     123, 138–9, 154, 203, 205–9, 211,
     214–15, 222–4, 226, 229–32, 254–6,
     258, 312, 314–15, 329, 331–2
   Archaeological Museum in Ioannina,
     Greece 108, 110, 230
   Garden exhibition, Kifissia, Athens 208
   Hotel Triton, Andros 104
   Hotel Xenia, Mykonos 104
   House in Elefsina, Greece 208
   Weekend House in Anavyssos, Greece 104,
     110
   Xenia Motel, Meteora 111
Konstantinidis, Dimitris 208–9
   House on Patmos, Greece 209
Konstantinidis, Nikos 304
Koolhaas, Rem (OMA) 57 (n53), 137, 226–7
Kostis, Kostas 17
Kostoulakis, Stelios 253 (n52)
Kotionis, Zissis 314–15
Koukis, Sotiris 311, 315, 317, 321
   Athenaeum Intercontinental Hotel,
     Athens 315
   Office building, Rhodes 311, 315, 317, 321
Koulermos, Panos 120 (n50), 205, 208, 327
Koumarianou, Efi 249
Kourkoulas, Andreas 210, 332
Krier, Lèon 49
Kroll, Lucien 39
Kruft, Hanno-Walter 8, 33, 51, 53
Ktenas, Nikos 210
Kundera, Milan 348
Kunneman, Harry 338–9
Kurokawa, Kisho 39, 223

labels (stylistic) 46, 50, 52, 93, 261, 312, 328,
     331, 333–4
labour 43, 64, 92, 290
labyrinth 12, 157, 207, 244
Lampugnani, Vittorio Magnano 125
land 102, 192–3, 214, 289–90
Landau, Roy 116
landings 36, 112–13, 267
landscape 19, 60, 64–5, 69, 71, 76–7, 80–2,
     102–4, 105–6, 112, 122, 149, 152, 157,
     169, 199, 213, 223, 226–7, 257–9, 262,
     278, 327, 356, 358
Lasithiotakis, Stelios 253 (n52)
Latin 192
Lefaivre, Liane 1, 5, 12–15, 19–20, 22–3, 25,
     59–65, 69, 71–85, 89–90, 97, 99–108,
     110–14, 117–18, 122–4, 130, 133–4,
     137, 148, 150, 177, 182, 190, 201–4,
     206–8, 211–13, 215–16, 222–5, 227–32,
     250, 254, 256–8, 269, 274, 314, 337–9,
     342, 344, 348–52, 354, 358–9,
     361–5

Left 51, 61, 80, 127, 133, 170, 207, 236, 327,
     342, 347
legislation 355
legitimisation 5, 35, 38, 55, 63, 102, 110,
     192–3, 197, 200, 268, 353
Legoretta, Ricardo 154
Lending, Mari 227
Leo, Ludwig 119 (n36)
Levant 192
Levinson, Nancy 139
Liakos, Antonis 17
liberal 142, 195, 330, 347, 355, 366
lifeworld 92
light 36, 98, 154, 159–60, 213, 265, 280, 284,
     288, 299, 364
Lim, William S.W. 351
limit 71, 92, 141, 162, 180, 216, 248, 279,
     284, 291, 313–14, 338, 345, 362
Linazasoro, José Ignacio 156, 181
linguistics 6
literature 63, 255, 347–50, 352
Llorens, Tomás 156
local 1–2, 11–13, 15–18, 22–3, 25, 32, 69–70,
     72, 76–7, 80–3, 96, 102, 133, 138,
     140–1, 153–4, 161, 163, 171, 174, 177,
     179–80, 182, 190, 199–201, 204,
     207–8, 210–16, 221–3, 226–7, 235,
     250, 254–6, 275, 307 (n11), 320–2,
     328–9, 331, 343, 348, 350, 354, 356–7,
     359, 362–4
locale/location/locus 15, 22, 67, 69, 101,
     182, 204, 212, 215, 221, 257, 296,
     353
lockdown 355
London 50, 61, 124, 131–2, 205–6, 208, 216,
     225–6, 329
Loos, Adolf 175, 254
Lotus 139
Loyer, François 199, 253 (n48), 256–7
Luchinger, Arnulf 156
Lukacs, Georg 153, 180
Lyndon, Donlyn 73
Lyotard, Jean-François 8, 339

Maastricht Treaty 337
Mackay, David 172, 333
Madrid 154, 166
magazines (architectural) 46, 59, 78, 99–100,
     120 (n50), 132–5, 138–42, 206
Makrinitsa, Greece 265–6
Makris, Georgios 210
manifestos 44, 62–4, 81, 95, 98, 170, 216,
     256, 362–6
manufacturing 64, 74
Marcuse, Herbert 92, 153
marginal 15, 17, 20, 22, 61, 76, 96, 98, 125,
     141, 152, 190, 196–8, 201–2, 204, 215,
     225, 342–4, 350, 353, 362
market 14, 20, 44, 62, 64, 132, 257, 278, 280,
     289–90, 303, 307 (n11), 337, 339, 347,
     358
Martin, Reinhold 8
Martorell, Josep 172–3, 333
Marxism 141, 343–4, 347, 351, 353, 355
mass (building) 278, 281–2, 291
mass culture 342

Massachusetts Institute of Technology (MIT) 349
Mateo, José Luis 154, 339
material 2–3, 18, 21–2, 25, 34, 36, 38, 45, 47, 51, 54, 64, 70, 79, 93, 102, 110, 112, 142, 150, 152, 154, 157, 160, 171, 175, 180, 210, 244, 255, 265, 280, 287, 295, 298, 302–3, 316, 322, 325–6, 330, 353, 356–8, 360–1, 364–5
Matsui, Hiromichi 177
Maya civilisation 157
Maybeck, Bernard 67–9, 83
  Chick House 68
Mazower, Mark 17
McGill University 63
McKean, John 128–9
McLeod, Mary 171, 353
meaning (in architecture) 6, 8, 43, 49, 52, 69, 112, 128, 149–50, 175, 200–1, 279–80, 290, 309
measure 11, 47, 51, 101, 113, 193, 198, 212, 244, 265, 280, 295, 302
media 3, 9, 20, 23, 85, 96, 98, 118, 122–3, 125, 132, 135–42, 172, 328, 349
mediation 15, 22, 31, 63, 114, 152, 177, 182, 190, 203–4, 208, 210, 214, 267, 290
Mediterranean 17, 36, 79, 117, 157, 166, 175, 200–1, 227, 356, 358, 364
megalopolis 14, 98, 165, 344
Megas, Georgios 265
memory 46, 54, 127, 189, 236, 257, 261, 265, 284, 314, 328, 330
meritocracy 355
metastatements 5
methodologies 61, 267
methods 67, 157, 167, 235, 268, 270–1, 299, 328
Mexico 80, 100, 124–5, 154, 159, 180, 201
  New 65–7
Meyers, Barton 121 (n83), 156, 181
Michelangelo 42
Michelis, Panayotis 23, 255–6, 264–8, 272–3, 276 (n36)
Mies van der Rohe, Ludwig 23, 35, 46, 102, 179, 195, 211, 228–9, 241, 254–5, 268–73, 274
  New National Gallery, Berlin 195
migration 4, 161, 355, 358
Migge, Leberecht [Spartakus in Grün] 64
Milanovic, Branko 355
militant 10, 343
military 10, 13, 32, 114, 195, 222, 228, 315, 332
millennium 81, 106, 157, 191, 340
minimalism 281
mining 66, 245
models 11, 16–17, 41, 43, 47–8, 62, 76–7, 111, 132, 134, 139, 191–5, 213, 224, 238, 241, 246, 255, 267, 270–1, 281, 289, 302–3, 310, 318–20, 344, 345, 354–5
modern movement 34–5, 41–3, 45–6, 48, 51, 69, 74, 100, 120 (n50), 127, 133, 197, 261, 263, 273, 290
modernism 1, 6, 8, 12–13, 16, 19–20, 22–4, 35, 38–9, 41–6, 49, 52–3, 55, 69, 72, 76, 81, 84, 89–92, 94–6, 98, 101–2, 106, 108, 116–17, 125–8, 130–1, 133, 135–6, 140, 157, 163–5, 170, 173, 177, 189–90, 196–7, 200–3, 207, 213, 215, 218 (n34), 221–3, 225–9, 235, 240–1, 255–7, 259–65, 267–75, 278, 281, 297–9, 309–10, 312–15, 323–5, 328–34, 338–9, 343, 347, 352, 353–4, 359–60, 365
modernity 14, 24, 67, 108, 130, 164, 191, 305, 312, 337, 339, 343, 362, 365–6
modularity 102, 177, 181, 245–7, 268–9, 361
Mondi, Narendra 2
mondialisation 347
Monemvasitou, Aleka 13, 234, 291, 324
Moneo, Rafael 49, 154, 156, 165–6, 176
  Bankinter Building, Madrid 166
montage 167, 276 (n15)
Montesquieu 192
monumentality 6, 93, 95, 164, 193–4, 236
Moore, Charles W. 39, 42, 44, 57 (n52), 72–3
  Sea Ranch, California 73
  Piazza d'Italia, New Orleans 73
Moraitis, Kostas 331
moralism 329, 331
Morocco 157
morphotypology 337
movement 4, 9, 39, 41, 48, 61–2, 64, 71, 80, 83, 95, 101, 112, 117–18, 130, 133, 140, 148, 172, 191, 195, 230, 257, 262, 269, 289, 291, 317, 328, 340, 357
multivalence 52, 155, 166
Mumford, Lewis 19–20, 60, 69–70, 72–7, 82–3, 90, 127, 256, 351
Murcutt, Glenn 123, 172
  Fredericks/White House, Jamberoo, New South Wales, Australia 172
Museum of Modern Art (MoMA), New York 46, 124
Mylonas, Pavlos 232
  National Gallery, Athens 232
myth 83, 156, 162, 189, 201, 204, 207, 262, 299, 331, 333

'The Narcissist Phase in Architecture' 19, 71, 75, 79
narrative 3, 32, 71, 79, 112, 126–7, 157, 341, 343, 345, 366
nationalism 2, 4, 74, 82–3, 96, 108, 173, 177, 200–1, 299, 339, 363, 366
nature 14, 34, 40, 64, 81, 92, 189, 193, 213, 259, 284, 288, 292, 299, 357–8, 364
needs 1, 6, 62, 64, 70, 74–5, 77, 92, 94–6, 175, 236, 240, 267–8, 275, 278, 280–1, 295–7, 299, 301, 358
neoliberalism 345–7, 349
Neo-Rationalism 32, 51, 94–5, 164, 339
Netherlands 38, 95, 117, 122–3, 170–1, 179, 181, 230, 337–40
Neutra, Richard 153, 351
New Empiricism 74
New World 192
New York 15, 46, 91, 124, 131–2, 140, 194, 208, 340
New York Five 51

New Zealand 341
Nezis family 290, 298
Nicolin, Pier Luigi 139
Niemeyer, Oscar 351
Nigeria 351
nihilism 164
Nikoloudakis, Yannis 253 (n52)
Nobel Prize in Literature 255
non finito 265
Norberg-Schulz, Christian 39, 42–3, 45, 48–9,
    54, 99, 156
normalisation 17, 240
Norway 43, 181, 227, 348
nostalgia 19, 22, 33, 76, 105–6, 165, 224,
    274, 296, 353–4
Noukakis, Antonis 13, 234, 324

Old World 192
Olumuyiwa, Oluwole 351
Olympia 238
openings 18, 36, 98, 246, 265, 267, 299
operative 21, 24, 41, 50, 150, 212, 306
Oppositions 61, 93, 124, 131, 138,
    140, 212
oppression 10, 61, 67, 195
optimisation 92, 94, 98, 160, 206, 213,
    342
oral history 221
Orbán, Viktor 2
order 2–3, 16, 34, 61, 102, 106, 157, 257,
    313, 331, 341, 343
organic 158, 166, 170, 179, 262, 314
Orient 102, 161, 174–5, 189
Orientalism 175, 192, 352
orientation 43, 80–1, 132, 257, 275, 284,
    288, 314, 334, 347, 356
ornament 251 (n9), 323
Ottoman Empire 102, 175, 192
outdoor spaces 111, 167, 245, 283–4, 316
outsider 15, 22, 132, 177, 180, 182, 190,
    203–4, 206–8, 212, 214, 226, 348
outsourcing 4, 355

Paestum 195
pagoda 159–60, 177, 181, 352
painter 224, 255
painting 23, 255, 365
palimpsest 167
Palladio, Andrea 33, 36
    Villa Foscari 'La Malcontenta' in Mira 33,
        37
Panou, Stavros 253 (n52)
Papadaki, Stamo 196–7
    Villa Fakidis in Glyfada, Athens 196
Papadakis, Andreas 50, 126, 132, 135–6, 138
Papadolampakis, Manolis 331
Papageorgiou, Alexandra 209
Papageorgiou, Alexandros 105
Papageorgiou, Elena 249
Paris 125, 164, 227
Parnell, Stephen 132, 135, 138, 140
Paros, Greece 268
participation 8–9, 18, 20, 39, 44, 48, 52, 64,
    77, 90, 94, 101, 106, 117–18, 119
    (n36), 205, 236–7, 261, 289–90,
    334, 348, 354

past 2–4, 6–7, 12, 15, 17–18, 31, 35–6, 38,
    53–5, 67, 75, 96, 99, 101, 106, 123, 125,
    171, 173, 189–90, 195, 197, 199, 207,
    218 (n34), 275, 299, 309, 330, 332,
    334, 340–1, 353, 356, 362–3
pastiche 8, 95, 135
Patelaros, Michalis 253 (n52)
pathway 22–3, 101, 103, 105–6, 110–14, 121
    (n76), 157–8, 168–9, 204, 207, 211–13,
    215, 224, 227, 229–30, 232, 254,
    256–60, 312, 314, 328
patriarchy 74
Patteeuw, Véronique 135
pattern 83, 101–2, 106, 112, 114, 117, 121
    (n76), 207, 278, 312
Pavitt, Jane 8
Pearce, Mick 351
Peloponnese, Greece 195
penthouses 280
performance 355
Pericles 190–1
'peripheries' 1, 3, 10, 15–18, 20, 90, 97–8,
    125, 134, 138–9, 141, 197, 199–202,
    212, 216, 222, 257, 334, 341–4, 349,
    350, 352, 360
Perspecta 42, 125
Peru 138, 181
Pesce, Gaetano 34–5
Pevsner, Nikolaus 40–1
phenomenology 15, 32, 43, 90, 92, 96, 99,
    117, 152, 173, 180, 211, 213, 358, 364
philhellenism 192
Philippidis, Dimitris 11–12, 199, 215, 228–9,
    282, 327–8
Philippines 2
Philopappou Hill, Athens 105, 278
philosophy 2, 6, 8, 96, 131, 153, 155, 175,
    177, 180, 190, 215, 224, 264, 292, 302,
    339, 352, 364
photogeny 142, 150, 152, 206, 357
photography 47, 102, 110, 112, 133, 142,
    149, 195–6, 206–7, 210, 327
Piano, Renzo 137, 156, 349
Picturesque 72, 76, 112, 133, 276 (n15)
Pidgeon, Monica 138
Pietilä, Reima 49, 52
Pikioni, Agni 225–6
Pikionis, Dimitris 101, 105–6, 116, 154, 157–8,
    163, 167–9, 200, 203–4, 206–8, 209–11,
    214–15, 222–7, 229–33, 254–63,
    269–70, 272–3, 287, 295, 309, 315, 332
    Experimental School in Thessaloniki
        261, 263
    Landscaping project around the
        Acropolis 103–6, 112, 149, 152, 157,
        204, 207, 223–4, 257–61
    St Dimitrios Loumbardiaris 158
    Potamianos House, Filothei 269
    School at Pefkakia, Lycabettus,
        Athens 261–2
    syneresis 259
piloti 189
Piñón, Helio 154
place 1–2, 19, 43, 45, 79, 81–3, 92, 95, 98–9,
    101–2, 106, 114, 117, 124, 140, 152–3,
    165, 168, 170, 174, 177, 192, 208, 213,

reconstruction 1, 6, 21, 43, 60, 84, 142, 148,
150, 173, 191–2, 195, 276 (n15), 364
reductivism 8–9, 18, 43, 48, 52, 91, 94, 127,
131, 150, 152, 164, 176, 206, 215, 250,
333
reformism 74, 108
refugees 282, 358
regionalism 2–3, 5, 12, 14–24, 38–9, 44, 46,
50, 54–5, 59–60, 63–7, 69, 71–84,
89–90, 94–6, 98–108, 112, 115, 117–18,
122–4, 126–7, 129–36, 141, 149, 155,
157, 164, 171, 174, 176–7, 179–80,
182, 190, 200–3, 206–7, 210–15,
221, 223, 226, 229–30, 249–50, 254–6,
261–2, 268, 273–5, 280, 284, 297,
299, 312–13, 329–30, 332–3, 338–40,
343, 349, 350, 356–8, 360–6
bioregionalism 16, 153
critical 1–5, 10, 12–25, 31, 52–3, 59–60,
62, 65, 75–82, 84, 89–91, 93, 95–101,
103–9, 115–18, 122–35, 137–9, 141–2,
148–57, 162, 163, 165, 167–82, 190,
200, 201–4, 206–8, 210–16, 221–3,
225–33, 249–50, 254–6, 261, 275,
305–6, 309–10, 312, 327–8, 330, 332–4,
337–66
constructive 19, 65–71, 74–7
'Context and Modernity' seminar at TU
Delft 14, 337–40
historicist (Neo-Classical) 102, 201
International Working Seminar at
Pomona 14
points 76, 98, 363–6
populist 105
Romantic (Nationalist) 72, 83, 96, 108,
173, 177
unsentimental 19, 21, 33, 116, 136, 148,
151
Renaissance 36, 192
resident(ial) 44, 106, 110, 157, 169, 204,
210, 240, 245, 280–1, 284, 289–90,
295–9, 301, 303, 306, 358
resistance 1, 3, 5, 10–12, 14–15, 17–20, 24,
32–3, 52, 75, 80–1, 91, 93–6, 98, 126–8,
130–1, 134, 141–2, 148, 152, 165, 206,
227, 236, 249, 274, 278–80, 284, 289,
295, 297, 299, 304–6, 312, 327, 329–30,
333, 339, 343–4, 347, 349, 353–4, 361,
365
retreat 2, 280, 358
'returns of the 1960s' 23–5, 101, 222, 275,
312, 353–4, 357
Revett, Nicolas 193, 197–8
revisionism 8–10, 14, 24, 40, 51, 96, 98, 117,
130, 202, 204, 210, 226, 228, 232,
261–2, 295, 312, 362–3, 365
revival 42, 44, 50, 102, 133, 160, 194, 228,
299
revolution 94, 127, 191, 195, 323, 342–3,
347, 353
Rewal, Raj 154
rhetoric 4–5, 12, 41, 50, 128, 191, 207,
228–9, 302, 331, 339, 343
rhizome 359
Rhodes, Greece 24, 214, 306, 310–28, 332–3
Richards, James M. 133

Richardson, Henry Hobson 69
Ricoeur, Paul 96, 151, 153, 156, 174, 207,
352, 354
right-wing 236
alt-right 363
Rizos, Dimitris 234
Rizos, Iason 315
Athenaeum Intercontinental Hotel,
Athens 315
Rizzoli 116, 136, 141–2, 148, 153, 155–6,
184 (n60), 204, 206–7, 211, 234, 327,
332, 349
Robbins, Edward 134
Roberts, John 130
Rodakis, Alexandros 204
House on Aegina, Greece 204–5
Rodi, Alcestis 279, 332
Rogers, Ernesto 139
Roman period 191–3
Romania 276 (n36)
Romanos, Aristidis 206
Romanticism 42, 46, 72, 74, 101–2, 133, 164,
166
Rome 80, 162, 192
roof 36, 157–60, 261, 273, 284, 352
Root, John 69
roots 17–21, 43, 49, 59–62, 65, 72, 84, 93–6,
101, 106, 112–13, 118, 148, 163, 170,
174, 180, 182, 189–90, 200–1, 204, 222,
227, 233, 302, 352, 357–8, 366
Rossi, Aldo 34, 44, 49, 51, 75, 164, 240, 328,
337
portal to 'The Presence of the Past'
exhibition 34
Teatro del Mondo 34, 328
Rowe, Colin 218 (n34)
Royal Institute of British Architects (RIBA) 97,
128, 135
Annual Discourse 96–7
Gold Medal 349
'The Great Debate' lecture series 122,
127–8, 329
RIBA Transactions 128
Ruchat-Roncati, Flora 169, 362
Rudolph, Paul 351
ruins 102, 195, 224, 260
rules 10, 102, 196–7, 215, 256, 260, 264,
272, 295, 328, 337
Ruskin, John 106
Russia 165, 195, 345, 348
Rykwert, Joseph 15, 128–9, 156

Said, Edward W. 130, 352
Salmas, Anastasios A. 223–4
Salmona, Rogelio 154
San Francisco 67, 69, 74
Santa Fe 66
Sartoris, Alberto 99, 197, 202–3
Sartre, Jean-Paul 179
Saudi Arabia 134
scale 1, 4, 6, 17, 36, 46–7, 64, 77, 79, 93,
110, 117, 122, 133, 137, 141, 164, 170,
195, 207, 212, 214, 235–6, 240, 242–3,
246–8, 260–1, 265, 289–90, 303–4,
306, 317, 320, 333, 340, 348, 354,
357, 363, 365

Scandinavia 69, 74, 134
Scarpa, Carlo 52, 119 (n36), 154, 161–3, 167–71, 327
    Brion Cemetery in San Vito d'Altivole 167
    Fondazione Querini Stampalia, Venice 161–2, 167
    Museo de Castelvecchio, Verona 168–9
scenography 1, 19, 33, 53, 89–90, 98, 126, 142, 152, 165, 215, 224, 330, 342, 353
Scharoun, Hans 158
Schinkel, Karl Friedrich 101
Schnebli, Dolf 119 (n36), 154
Schumacher, Thomas L. 61
science 6, 61–2, 67, 90, 92, 170, 193, 207, 342
Scott, Ridley 341
Scott-Brown, Denise 39, 42, 44, 57 (n52), 94
Scully, Vincent 39, 42, 44–5, 48, 50, 199
sculptor 65, 206, 291
sculptural 153, 204, 206, 284, 318, 320, 327
sea-level change 358
Second World 4, 341–5, 347–8
Seferis, Giorgos 255–6, 274
self-building 62, 77–8
Selva, Giovanni Antonio 194
    Mausoleum of Antonio Caneva in Possagno, Italy 194
semiology 6
Semper, Gottfried 195
senses 6, 54, 90, 128, 150, 157, 164, 197, 205, 207, 212–13, 218 (n34), 232, 238, 248–9, 265, 278, 302–4, 306, 322, 358
sensibilities/sensitivities 23, 34, 38, 44, 48, 60, 95, 106, 114, 171–2, 174–5, 180, 190, 202, 206, 211, 216, 226, 236, 254, 257, 264, 340, 353, 356, 362, 365
setbacks 280
Shaker 160
Shaw, George Bernard 348
shingle style 44
Shinohara, Kazuo 121 (n83), 156, 180,
Shinto 160, 175
Shu, Wang 123
Sifnos, Greece 287, 298–9, 322, 327
sight 34, 90, 150, 197
Simeoforidis, Yorgos 206, 208, 331–2
Singapore 201, 351
Singaporean Design Partnership 351
sites 1, 10, 17–18, 22, 32, 98–9, 152–3, 155, 165, 175, 177, 180, 195, 213, 223, 230, 235–6, 242, 257, 280, 287–8, 290, 295, 322, 332, 356, 364–5
Siza, Alvaro 15, 119 (n36), 123, 154, 156, 165, 172, 175, 338
sketches 129, 142, 159–60, 204–5, 246–7, 259, 270, 283, 287–8, 292, 295, 310, 321
Skolimowski, Henryk 153, 180
Skyline 140
Sloterdijk, Peter 364
smell 150
Smith, Thomas Gordon 57 (n53)
Snozzi, Luigi 154, 170
socialism 61, 127, 174, 339–40, 342–4, 347, 351, 353
sociology 19, 27 (n30), 60, 63, 67, 153, 175, 342

Socorro 66–7
Soleri, Paolo 119 (n36)
Soon, Tay Kheng 351
South, Global 347
Souto de Moura, Eduardo 154
Soviet Union (USSR)/Soviet Bloc 4, 94, 127, 165, 337, 340–1, 344, 345, 347–8, 355, 367 (n30)
space 15, 25, 36–7, 42, 44–5, 47, 69, 89, 101, 105–6, 110–14, 117–18, 142, 150, 155, 157, 160, 162, 167–8, 170, 178, 191, 206, 224, 230, 236, 238, 257, 260, 264–5, 269, 273, 282–4, 287–92, 295–7, 302, 307 (n11), 312, 314–18, 329–31, 341, 359–60, 363–5
    of appearance 92, 358
    interior 36, 284, 288, 297–8, 300, 312, 316–18
    intermediate 36, 114, 283
    outdoor 111, 167, 245, 283, 316
    private 110, 113–14
    public 33, 36–8, 62, 106, 110, 112–14, 243, 245, 267, 284, 291, 312, 314, 316–17, 322, 357
    postmodern 78
    semi-enclosed 36, 292
    transatlantic 130, 132, 343
    transitional 112, 287
Spain 66, 91, 95, 123, 125, 138, 166, 173–4, 181, 339, 344
Speyer, A. James 23, 35, 254–6, 269–73
spirit 102, 106, 150, 157, 189, 196, 233, 255, 261, 328, 330
Spivak, Gayatri Chakravorty 352
Spon, Jacob 192
Sri Lanka 134, 351
stage 54, 287, 291, 312, 360
staircases 36, 247, 265, 273, 281, 284, 288, 291–3, 295, 317–18, 320
standardisation 74, 102, 104, 149, 152, 160, 177, 181, 259, 267–8, 280–1, 302
Stanek, Łukasz 347
star system 15, 23, 99, 137, 141, 249, 349
Steinmann, Martin 54–5, 156
Stephen, Douglas 120 (n50), 128, 205
Stern, Robert A.M. 18–20, 31–3, 39, 42, 45–54, 57 (n52), 59, 91, 116, 122, 126–7, 130–1, 344
Stevens, Thomas 120 (n50)
stigma 24, 312, 331–2, 334
Stirling, James 49, 69, 74, 166
    Leicester University Engineering Laboratory 166
stone 102, 204–5, 284, 287, 298–9, 322
Strada Novissima 7, 32, 35, 38, 47–50, 52, 55, 72, 91, 97, 116, 313, 328
'strangemaking' 76
Strefi Hill, Athens 278
strollology 19, 81–2
Structuralism, Dutch 94–5, 117, 170, 179
Stuart, James 193, 197–8
style 1, 3, 8–10, 12, 14, 18, 31–2, 38, 41–2, 44, 46, 48–53, 62, 66–7, 69–71, 74, 76–7, 80–3, 92–3, 96, 127–9, 131, 133, 140, 178, 194, 200, 203, 227, 241, 270, 298–9, 301, 327, 334, 357–8

subversion 23, 178, 212, 272, 281, 289–90, 301, 329, 331, 342, 344, 355
Sukiya teahouse 178
Sullivan, Louis 69
Super-8 (video camera) 33–4, 37, 283
supply chains 2, 62, 355, 357, 363
surfaces 36, 150, 246, 258, 289, 316, 320, 360
Svoronos, Nicolas 17
Switzerland 19, 60, 77, 95, 134, 138, 181, 192, 227, 236, 344
symbolic form 47, 53, 83, 93–4, 160–2, 177–8, 200–1, 279, 291, 304, 334
symmetry 258, 263, 281–2, 284
syntax 95, 157, 330
systems theory 4, 80
Szacka, Léa-Catherine 31, 89, 91, 93, 135

Tabassum, Marina 356
taboo 24, 312, 334
tabula rasa 43
tactility 54, 95, 98, 142, 150, 152, 167, 173, 174, 180, 360
Tafuri, Manfredo 51
Takeyama, Kiyoshi 177–8
Tami, Rino 154
taste 133, 140, 297–9
Taut, Bruno 177
Tavora, Fernando 154, 182
taxonomy 94, 125–6, 129
teahouse 177
Team 10 20, 34, 38, 43, 48, 90, 117, 138, 255, 354
Technical Chamber of Greece 232
technology 1, 6, 14–15, 49, 67, 71, 76, 79, 92, 94, 102, 130–1, 149, 152, 154, 206–7, 250, 350, 357
techno-science 6, 61, 67, 90, 92, 342
tectonics 14, 20, 90, 98, 126, 131, 149–52, 157, 165, 173, 180, 232, 338
Tefchos 139
temples 159, 177, 189, 195, 197, 199
La Tendenza 152
terraces 36, 267, 314
territory 66, 98, 100, 152, 181, 191–2, 363
Terry, Quinlan 15
textures 150
Thames & Hudson 123, 140
theatre 54, 284
Theocharopoulou, Ioanna 209, 214, 304
Theodoros 206
theory 1–6, 8–9, 11–12, 14–25, 31–3, 42–3, 45, 47–8, 51–2, 55, 59, 61, 63, 65, 67, 74–6, 79–80, 89–94, 96, 98, 100–1, 108–10, 114–15, 117–18, 122, 129, 131, 133, 142, 149–51, 153–7, 164, 171, 175, 180, 182, 190, 192, 195, 200–1, 207, 211–16, 221–2, 230, 239, 243–4, 249–50, 255, 257–8, 263–5, 304–6, 312, 314, 328–31, 333–4, 338, 342–5, 347, 348–50, 353–9, 361–3, 365
Third Reich 13, 69, 74, 80, 338
third way 127, 342, 344
Third World 134, 341, 343, 345–7
threshold 36, 95, 112, 265, 284, 289, 299, 360

Thucydides 191
Ticino 124, 154, 169–72, 344, 362
Tigerman, Stanley 57 (n52)
timber 157–9, 299
time 2, 15, 42, 67, 71, 99, 105–6, 114, 129, 149, 153, 157, 170, 189, 196–7, 200–1, 214, 230, 234–6, 239–40, 243, 248, 259–60, 280, 284, 288–9, 295, 309, 338, 348, 360–1
Time 46, 135
tokenism 363
Tonnies, Ferdinand 153, 180
topography 1–2, 23, 77, 106, 149, 192, 209, 211, 213, 226, 254, 257, 259, 338, 364
topos 331
Toulouse-Le-Mirail 203
tourism 14, 110, 235, 304
Tournikiotis, Panayotis 11, 328
Town, Ithiel 194
   United States Custom House in New
   York 194
Townscape 112
trabeation 189
traditions 5, 13, 18–19, 22–4, 31–3, 35, 39, 41–3, 46–8, 54, 56 (n17), 65, 69–72, 76–7, 95, 105–6, 117, 125, 127–8, 130–1, 134–5, 152, 157, 161–5, 172, 174, 182, 200, 202, 215, 221–4, 228–9, 237, 255, 261, 262–9, 273–5, 280, 284, 296–7, 299–302, 304, 312–13, 330, 332–3, 352
tragedy 106, 192, 202
translation 70, 80, 121 (n71), 138, 199, 204, 206, 209, 242, 253 (n54), 276 (n36), 350
transnational 12, 14, 17–18, 226, 338–9, 348, 363
travel 32, 34, 36, 38, 67, 99, 116, 181–2, 192, 200, 204–5, 268, 321
Triantafyllou, Lucy 249, 296
Tritsis, Antonis 55 (n8)
triumphalism 4, 91, 347, 353–5, 363
Trump, Donald 2
Tsalapatis, Yannis 253 (n52)
Tsarmakli-Vrontisi, Efi 55 (n8), 234–5
Tsioni, Xenia 249
Turkey 192–3
Turnbull, William 73
Tusquets, Óscar 49
typology 23–4, 36, 38, 46, 65, 71, 75, 94, 113, 117, 134, 157, 159, 165, 189, 245, 258, 261–2, 265–7, 269, 278–81, 283, 288, 291, 295, 297, 301, 305, 310–11, 313–16, 320, 330, 337, 342, 352
Tzanakakis, Charalambos 253 (n52)
Tzirtzilakis, Yorgos 279
Tzonis, Alexander 1, 5, 12–15, 19–20, 22–3, 25, 59–65, 67–9, 71–81, 84–5, 89–90, 97, 99–114, 116–18, 122–4, 130, 133–4, 137, 148, 150, 156, 177, 182, 190, 201–4, 206–8, 210–13, 215–16, 222–5, 227–32, 250, 254, 256–8, 269, 274, 279, 314, 332, 337–40, 342, 344, 348–52, 354, 358–9, 361–5

CPSIA information can be obtained
at www.ICGtesting.com
Printed in the USA
BVHW020805240822
645320BV00011B/121

9 781800 081345